The Buried Astrolabe

Canadian Dramatic Imagination and Western Tradition

CRAIG STEWART WALKER

McGill-Queen's University Press

Montreal & Kingston · London · Ithaca

© McGill-Queen's University Press 2001
ISBN 0-7735-2074-0 (cloth)
ISBN 0-7735-2075-9 (paper)

Legal deposit first quarter 2001
Bibliothèque nationale du Québec

Printed in Canada on acid-free paper

This book has been published with the help of a grant
from the Humanities and Social Sciences Federation of
Canada, using funds provided by the Social Sciences
and Humanities Research Council of Canada. Funding
has also been received from the Faculty of Arts and
Science, Department of Drama, and Office of Research,
Queen's University.

McGill-Queen's University Press acknowledges the
financial support of the Government of Canada through
the Book Publishing Industry Development Program
(BPIDP) for our activities. We also acknowledge the
support of the Canada Council for the Arts for our
publishing program.

Canadian Calatoguing in Publication Data

Walker, Craig Stewart, 1960–
    The buried astrolabe : Canadian dramatic imagination
    and western tradition
    Includes bibliographical references and index.
    ISBN 0-7735-2074-0 (bound) – ISBN 0-7735-2075-9 (pbk.)
    1. Canadian drama—20th century—History and criticism.
    I. Title.
    PS8177.W35 2001   C812'.5409   C00-901038-6
    PR9191.5.W34 2001

This book was typeset by True to Type in 10/12 Sabon.

Contents

Preface

> But now
> That the forests are cut down, the rivers charted,
> Where can you turn, where can you travel? Unless
> Through the desperate wilderness behind your eyes,
> So full of falls and glooms and desolations,
> Disasters I have glimpsed but few would dream of,
> You seek new Easts.
>
> Douglas LePan, "Coureurs de Bois"

This book offers a critical introduction to Canadian drama by way of six of the country's most important contemporary playwrights. Each chapter constitutes a study of the poetics particular to one of the playwrights, showing how a personal vision – a "desperate wilderness" – has been explored and dramatized over the course of the writer's career to date.

What unifies the book is a set of ideas about the circumstances that Canadian playwrights have had to absorb or surmount to achieve the mature poetics found in the work discussed here. The most difficult part of that struggle, and the most significant achievement of the playwrights, has been to establish a mythopoeic context within which a dramatic imagination could reconfigure Canadian experience in its own image rather than a conspicuously borrowed disguise. The very idea of a national drama implies work that is in some essential respects original to the country in question and not wholly derivative; but in Canada's colonial culture, to transume established European conventions imaginatively was not easy. Although "transume" (or "transumption") is not a common word, I use it regularly here because it captures (better than, say, "adopt" or "assume") the important imaginative notion of taking over, of transferring or translating a concept or a convention that originated elsewhere so decisively as to make it one's own. A sketch of the stages by which a Canadian transumption of European conventions was achieved is the principal matter of the prologue, which uses as stepping-stones three poems by Douglas LePan.

Each of the subsequent chapters has been made as self-sufficient as possible, so that a reader who has a particular interest in, say, George F. Walker (who, by the way, is no known relation) can turn directly to that chapter with no real loss of coherence. Reading only the analysis of a single play, however, would prove less satisfactory in that each chapter argues towards a perspective on that playwright's work as a whole. Hence, while the plays are generally treated in chronological order, the discussion of any individual play depends heavily on the larger context for its full significance.

Still, the reader who follows the book from beginning to end will find a number of comparative insights quietly developed from one discussion to another. The playwrights appear here in the chronological order of their births: Reaney was born in 1926, Cook in 1933, Pollock in 1936, Tremblay in 1942, Walker in 1947, and Thompson in 1954. This looks somewhat arbitrary, but it happens to support a subtle impression that the significant changes in sensibility from one playwright to the next were in some part made possible by the changes in Canadian culture from one generation to the next. It is difficult to imagine someone of Reaney's generation writing Thompson's plays, or vice versa; but as soon as we see no more than seven years' difference between the playwrights' ages, the feeling that there is some area of shared aesthetic sensibility immediately increases. Nevertheless, the order is meant to facilitate, not to insist upon, inferences about the development of Canadian dramaturgy as a whole.

My primary criteria in choosing these particular playwrights were simply that each should have a substantial body of work to discuss and that the work should be of an excellence that would reward extensive analysis. Simply put, I believe the six playwrights discussed here are among the very best and most important Canada has produced. However, by no means do I believe these are the only playwrights who belong in the top rank; other considerations influenced my selection, not the least of which was whether I felt I had anything of importance to say about the writer's work.

Inevitably, my inclusion of Michel Tremblay will be questioned by some, both because it has become customary to treat the French and English literatures of Canada separately and because he is the sole francophone playwright among the six. Yet, aside from my reluctance to think of Canadian drama as cleanly split into two unrelated traditions, I have several reasons for believing that Tremblay belongs in this group. Tremblay is among the internationally best-known Canadian playwrights, and having been so extensively translated and staged, he is just as well known in English-language theatre as any of the other five. Indeed, nearly all of Tremblay's plays – and certainly all of the most important ones – have now been published in translation. Hence, even though this book is restricted to readers of English, it just seemed perverse to exclude Tremblay.

Finally, I should add that while the selection of playwrights happens to be drawn from across much of the country, no attempt has been made to represent any of the geographic or political regions of Canada proportionally. I hope the reader finds a suggestive, if not exactly representative variety of "regions of mind" here; but as far as any politically based categories go, the chips must fall where they may.

Acknowledgments

My heartfelt thanks go out to the following people, who read and made invaluable comments on various sections of this book: David Blostein, Ronald Bryden, Alvin A. Lee, Robert Nunn, Richard Plant, Ann Saddlemyer, Wanda Romer Taylor, and especially Susan Kent Davidson, the copy-editor. As a first-time author I could not have wished for a better source of guidance and encouragement than Roger Martin at McGill-Queen's University Press. Naturally, any faults that remain despite their kind assistance are entirely my own responsibility. I would also like to express my gratitude to the late Douglas LePan for his gracious generosity in permitting me not only to quote from his poetry but to put it to uses far removed from the contexts and meanings he intended. If the excerpts I have included from these powerful, haunting poems prompt any reader to discover the originals for the first time, I will feel honoured indeed to have made the introduction.

Parts of the discussion of James Reaney's *The Donnellys* previously appeared in *Australasian Drama Studies*; much of the discussion of Michael Cook's *Colour the Flesh the Colour of Dust* and *Tiller* first appeared in a different form in two linked articles for *Theatre Research in Canada*; and two paragraphs of the discussion of George F. Walker's *The Prince of Naples* have been extracted from an article published in *Modern Drama*.

Some portions of the research for this project received generous financial support from Canadian taxpayers through the Social Sciences and Humanities Research Council of Canada.

The Buried Astrolabe

Prologue: Desperate Wilderness

What is essential at the beginning is the resolve to reach the saturation point. Ideally, the trip should end only when the members are making no further progress within themselves.

Pierre Elliott Trudeau, "The Ascetic in a Canoe"

In August 1867, just over a month after the confederation of Canada, a fourteen-year-old boy named Edward Lee was helping his father to clear a farm lot abutting the Green Lake marshes near Renfrew, Ontario, when he turned up a piece of moss to reveal a circular metal object about six inches across. Upon investigation, the object turned out to be an astrolabe, an instrument used to navigate by the stars, stamped with the date 1603. The lot was located amidst a series of small streams and lakes connected to the Ottawa River, so historians surmised that this was an astrolabe Samuel de Champlain had lost in 1613, more than 250 years earlier, during a long portage between the lakes now known as Olmsted and Muskrat (Macnamara, "Champlain's Astrolabe"). We can only imagine how the loss was received at the time by Champlain, who was using the astrolabe to map the land roughly as he explored it. It was certainly inconvenient, forcing him to guess at all subsequent latitudes; to the non-natives in his party it well may have seemed catastrophic. In a vast land almost entirely unknown as yet to any European, every instrument that helped to tell where they were, and so how they might return home to France, must have seemed precious indeed.

Douglas LePan imagines a different possibility, however, in his 1982 poem "Astrolabe." There Champlain's explorations are evoked metaphorically to describe a lover's at first anxious and awkward encounter of a new love, "a new world, where anything might happen."[1] The explorer-lover grows bolder as his love becomes more familiar, until

> At last the moment came when
> he searched no longer for the stars, throwing away
> his astrolabe to rust beneath a pine-tree,
> and moved at last at ease in a world he never dreamed,
> this new world, ours, where savagery and sweetness melt as one.   (173)

It is a beautiful thought, this romantic gesture of casting aside the established guidelines and referents of an earlier life and older world to embrace the new experience boldly, in all its dangers and delights. Yet if we turn the metaphor in another, and what may seem an equally natural, direction – towards culture – a contradiction arises. For what may be in some situations a necessity for a lover, and a conceivable if highly romantic gesture for an explorer, is a flat impossibility for an artist. There is simply no real possibility of art's throwing away its astrolabe and losing its bearings to embrace nature anew.

Through art we encounter, amidst the indifferent natural universe, a world corresponding to the human imagination. There desire and concern, anxiety and fantasy, enjoy absolute dictatorship. Where nature enters, it is according to their indulgence, for art subordinates nature to its own ends. To be sure, art never represents nature with anything like perfect assurance. But whatever villainous or mawkish use nature finds itself put to, it must confine its contradictions to its own domain. Art informs itself chiefly with reference to itself and cultural tradition; as they say, every writer is a reader first and every painter a viewer. Furthermore, the human encounter with nature is itself directed by artistic conventions: as E.H. Gombrich has demonstrated, art provides a "grid of perception" through which we view the world. Any given work of art is formed in relation to existing works of art, and the meaning of the work is mainly determined by its perceived relation to other human creations – the culture into which it enters.

What is true of art as a whole is especially obvious in the case of theatre. Theatre depends upon a clear relation to its cultural context perhaps more urgently than any other art form because, being live and public, it makes its meanings immediately within a living social group. Establishing significance in the theatre cannot be deferred so easily as in, say, a novel or a painting; a misunderstood production of a play seldom has the chance to abide quietly until the time arrives for it to enter into a culture that has established the social mind-set and the conventions needed to comprehend it. Hence, the most auspicious eras for theatre have been those in which history and location have yielded a strong and relatively unified sense of social self-consciousness and, accordingly, a widely recognized lexicon of dramatic conventions. In such circumstances the virtues of theatre emerge with a convincing efficacy.

But to say that a play or any other work of art takes its primary meaning from the world created by the art preceding it leaves us with a dissatisfying sort of chicken-and-egg formulation. We know that somewhere back in time there must have been life before art; so at least one human imagination must have created something – even if the initial impulse was not what we would recognize as an "artistic" one – in response to the natural world rather than the world of art. However immemorial its origins may be, any given culture at some point *began*. Of course, it is equally clear that the development of a broad cultural context from which individual works of art take their meaning is not a sudden event. Culture, in E.B. Tylor's classic definition, is "that complex whole which includes knowledge, belief, art, morals, law, custom, and any other capabilities and habits acquired by man as a member of society." To this we may add that, generally speaking, these elements of the "complex whole" will all be found in some way to bear the configuration of the geographical circumstances in which they have arisen. They depend on highly developed ideas of what is "natural" in all senses of the word, from knowledge of the local flora and fauna to sophisticated philosophical concepts.

The process by which nature is subordinated to a culture involves a slow accrual of meaning to human perceptions of the natural world that takes place over many centuries. At last, from this slowly accrued meaning comes a profound sense of place and community. This, at least, could serve as a normative model. But it is clearly a poor fit for Canada, a nation where the nagging cultural question for many years was, as Northrop Frye famously put it: "Where is here?"[2] In other words, for most of Canada's history as a nation, its citizens have been unable to articulate a clear sense of place through their culture. There has been no shortage of nationalist sentiment about the matter; but, as Frye implied, the country is too vast and differentiated to lend itself to the sort of clear and ready formulations that those of a nationalistic bent have often sought.

Still, notwithstanding the longevity of the problem, we can see that it has not always presented itself in such a way.

Several years ago I drove west across Canada on a holiday, hoping to see as much of the country as possible in a single trip. After several days of travelling I was struck by the peculiarity that, while the natural features of the landscape varied tremendously from region to region, the commercial, mainstream culture I casually encountered was oddly undifferentiated in any way that corresponded to the pronounced geographical distinctions. It was curiously alienating, despite its being – or rather, *because* of its being – all so very familiar. Upon reaching Vancouver, however, I visited the Museum of Anthropology at the University of British Columbia, where I saw their magnificent exhibition of artifacts gathered from aboriginal tribes right across the country. With the shock that comes from recognizing what undoubtedly has long been obvious to others, I suddenly realized that here, laid out in a neat sequence, one could see the soul of each of the various regions seemingly captured in the style of that region's artifacts. It was not that the natural features of each distinctive landscape were directly represented; but the inner feeling evoked by that landscape and the communal experience of those who had lived and educated their imaginations in that region were clearly inherent in the distinctive styles of each of the respective tribes.

Alas, as we well know, the cultural traditions that produced these artifacts were irreparably ruptured by European colonization. Now, we need not indulge in any simplistic, ritual sneering at European imperialism here. Given the vast complexity of the history of civilization, blameful revisionism is not only fruitless but ultimately senseless. Nevertheless, to assess the problematic cultural legacy left to Canadians clearly, we must consider the effects that European settlement had upon the indigenous people. Apart from the material devastation that colonization entailed for the natives, the arrival of European settlers precipitated an abrupt shift from a civilization dominated by a group of oral, regional cultures to one dominated by a massive, foreign, multinational written culture. The indigenous sensibility rooted in an ancient history of mythopoeic identifications of social psyche with place – the mythological inheritance and the capacity to go on confidently making new myths – was almost totally destroyed. In that mythopoeically created native sensibility had inhered the sense of cultural continuity and unified higher consciousness for the people of this country, their social, ethical, and spiritual ideas, their metaphysical aspirations, their sense of collective destiny. But the cultural disruption wrought by colonization left most of that in chaos.

As for the European cultural paradigms that began to supplant (and seldom assimilate) native mythic and cultural traditions, it would be many years before the best of European culture would establish any secure footing. At first the relation of the Europeans to the country was chiefly dictated by commercial and political interests. The explorers proceeded on instructions to seek out and provide an account of the exploitable resources of the "new land," and the occasions on which there was any enduring transcendence of the mandated mercantilist objectives were rare. Where the natives' complex, pantheistic, mythic understanding of the land had prevailed, the Europeans used scientific instruments such as the astrolabe to locate each outstanding natural site and assign it a place with respect to global geographic knowledge. Then each new landmark was given a place in what was effectively the grand inventory they were preparing of the stock of natural resources.

We can see several consequences of this mercantile foundation for the culture of Canadian theatre. On the one hand, in a society preoccupied with mercantilism, a new mythopoeicization of the country remained, unsurprisingly, a low priority – a fact that gave rise to complaints about Canadian philistinism that persisted into the latter half of the twentieth century. On the other, the focus on the administration of the "new world" resulted in the fairly early erection of the kind of cultural framework necessary for politically based drama. Hence, by the nineteenth century there had already arisen the beginnings of a rich tradition of politically based satirical comedy; yet those more poetic dramas that were based in the imagination remained rather stilted.

To be sure, we must acknowledge that the nineteenth-century *weltanschauung* of industrialism and individualism seems not to have been particularly auspicious for poetic drama in Europe either. The sense of mythic social destiny against which the aspirations of individuals could be tested had been in decay almost everywhere since the seventeenth century (Germany offering the most significant exceptions), and the paradigms for depicting the transformed world in poetic drama were narrowly confined within the lines of melodrama. In any case, the important point for our purposes is that, in the nineteenth century, Canada faced a peculiar paradox concerning its drama. If Canadians enjoyed a number of decent satiric dramas that effectively critiqued the administration of Canadian society, they lacked the kind of indigenous tradition of poetic drama that might have helped to define their society's underlying sense of place and direction by probing and dramatizing the more profound sources of the social self-image within the Canadian environment.

It is rightly remarked that the amount of scholarly attention devoted to Canadian poetic drama has been at times wholly disproportionate to both its quality and quantity. Certainly, in studying the history of theatre, we must always beware of using the accident of publication as a guide to significance, for the fact that a closet verse drama is extant is almost meaningless in itself. But my purposes are a little unusual. I intend to focus more extensively on poetic drama here than I would were I engaged in an objective historical survey of Canadian drama because I want to argue the cultural significance of the very weaknesses and paucity of the tradition of Canadian poetic drama. To secure a fair hearing for such a curious project, I need to ask readers to set aside some of the more negative associations we often make between "poetic drama" and stale, academic verse plays. Instead I ask them to try to conceive of poetic drama in the idealized classical forms that many unfortunate verse dramatists were struggling to recapture. I further suggest that, when we use the term "poetic," we accommodate the many contemporary forms of drama that may be legitimately labelled so, even though they discard those awkward verse-drama conventions by which many playwrights felt bound even two centuries after they had exhausted their utility.

In its best examples, poetic drama examines how the higher ideals and practical contradictions of a society have found conflict or resolution by setting these within an alternative reality, or an imaginative world, that provides a figurative relation to quotidian experience. The tropes by which we instinctively identify a drama or any other piece of writing as poetic – the metaphors, metonyms, synecdoches, ironies, the rhythmic structures, the fantastic constructions, and so on – combine to create an *isotopy*, a conceptual place in which self-reflexiveness may be resolved into a coherent vision.[3] In the early stages of a culture it is clear that the creation of such isotopies in their various forms is mythopoeic, in that they help to construct the characteristic patterns in which a society imagines itself. But even in later stages of a culture, poetic drama at its most powerful retains something of this mythopoeic function because it continues to posit and probe new possible realities for a society and presents these explorations (conceptually, if not always actually) in an ensemble art form before an immediately present community of spectators – the social microcosm offered by the theatre.

The question of whether a drama is in verse or not is irrelevant to most such functions. What is essential is that the playwright be able to construct an imaginative isotopy with some modicum of conviction, which, in turn, may compel the imaginations of an audience. It is precisely this difficulty that frustrated the efforts of many early Canadian playwrights and, indeed, artists of all kinds. Now, it is unlikely that their personal thought was slavishly mercantilist-centred; indeed, they often earnestly wished to reimagine and culturally enrich the country in which they found themselves. But, with no possibility of establishing a wholly fresh cultural relation – because these artists already belonged to European tradition – most efforts to mythopoeicize the Canadian landscape and experience consisted of a series of attempts to affix recognizable European conventions to the "new land" and its people.

A case in point is Marc Lescarbot's *Le Théâtre de Neptune en la Nouvelle-France*, the short *réception* (a masque-like drama written to celebrate the occasion of a special visit) that was created for the safe return of the Founders of New France to Port Royal, providing the earliest recorded theatrical performance in what would become Canada, on 14 November 1606.[4] Lescarbot sets the tone for the mythopoeic endeavours of dramatists for many years to come when he has the Third Indian declare to the returning Founders:

> It is not only in France
> That Cupid reigns
> But also in New France.   (Lescarbot, 42)

No doubt this seemed a pretty sentiment in the fleeting moment of performance. But the inappropriateness of the image and the awkward wishful thinking are manifest upon any closer examination; and of course this assertion of the relevance of classical myth is only made more obviously false for being placed in an aboriginal mouth. I don't mean to reproach Lescarbot, who was merely writing within the European conventions then fashionable – and in some ways using them quite ingeniously. The point is that these and related conventions were forced into play because they were integral to the formal structure and mythology within which the European mind thought artistically.

Similar are those poetic conventions that many of the early verse plays deploy to raise some aspect of Canadian experience to the level of mythology. Frequently, these direct attempts to mythologize take the form of a revisionist patriotic celebration of a historical event in conventions drawn from the European heroic verse-drama tradition. George Cocking's *The Conquest of Canada; or, The Siege of Quebec* (1766), for example, cleaves closely to its model, John Dryden's *Conquest of Granada*, in order to set in a heroic light the decisive (albeit, in truth, rather sordid) battle on the Plains of Abraham; Antoine Gérin-Lajoie certainly has Corneille in mind in his lionization of *Le Jeune Latour* (1844); and Sarah Anne Curzon's *Laura Secord, the Heroine of 1812* (1887) follows Edward Bulwer-Lytton's dramaturgical example (and therefore, indirectly, Victor Hugo's) in ennobling a historical subject with a blend of romantic verse and melodrama.

As Malcolm Ross has remarked, during the high modernist period of Canadian literature there was a tendency to dismiss many such earlier Canadian works out of hand, as colonial in mentality and derivative in form (Ross, 166–7). That attitude now looks not merely excessively harsh but wholly unproductive in its romantic premise about originality. By the same token, of course, the insidious indulgence of patriotically exaggerating the merits of early Canadian work must be avoided. If those nineteenth-century plays seem stiff and unconvincing to us today, to lay the blame on their use of European tradition is still too facile a conclusion. European tradition was their ineluctable heritage;

there was no evident alternative. Furthermore, we must appreciate that those early playwrights were attempting to establish a preferred historical account. In doing so they inevitably drew very heavily on that "historical sense" that, according to T.S. Eliot, would compel the poet of European heritage to write with a sense that the work partakes of the order composed by European literature as a whole (Eliot, *Selected Essays*, 13–22). In short, European cultural tradition was already as embedded in the Canadian psyche as Champlain's astrolabe was embedded in Edward Lee's father's field. However much other circumstances changed, European tradition remained an ineradicable influence through successive generations. Indeed, it still pervades the culture into which we Canadians are born, and it infuses just about every area of our imaginations.

Yet what of those elements in the Canadian experience that initially proved elusive to European conventions? To this point our argument may seem to imply a dismal closed circle in which European conventions dictated how the "New World" would be experienced and represented, thus begetting a series of imitative works that awkwardly included Canadian content without ever doing anything to release Canadian drama from its culturally indentured service to Old World perceptions. However, as many of the mature and compelling plays studied in the following chapters show, the difficulty of rendering the New World mythopoeically did not finally prove insurmountable. Paradoxically, the path towards a solution began with the sharp awareness among many artists, including playwrights, that to be Canadian was indeed to belong to a "belated" culture, to a culture that was one of the last out of the gate.

The frustrating and even disheartening feeling engendered by that sense of belatedness is summed up beautifully in one of Douglas LePan's early poems, "A Country without a Mythology" (1948). The title itself has been quoted frequently over the years but, like Hugh MacLennan's "two solitudes," has probably more often been carelessly and despairingly misapplied than used according to the author's intentions.[5] Simply put, LePan's poem proves to be an ironic commentary on its title. The "stranger" of the poem moves through an overwhelming natural landscape that evinces, he feels, an almost malevolent indifference to the human scale. Then, in the sixth stanza, a new perception is described, which, alas, proves fleeting:

Sometimes – perhaps at the tentative fall of twilight –
A belief will settle that waiting around the bend
Are sanctities of childhood, that melting birds
Will sing him into a limpid gracious Presence.

The hills will fall in folds, the wilderness
Will be a garment innocent and lustrous
To wear upon a birthday, under a light
That curls and smiles, a golden-haired Archangel.

And now the channel opens. But nothing alters.
Mile after mile of tangled struggling roots,
Wild-rice, stumps, weeds, that clutch at the canoe,
Wild birds hysterical in tangled trees.

And not a sign, no emblem in the sky
Or boughs to friend him as he goes; for who
Will stop where, clumsily constructed, daubed
With war-paint, teeters some lust-red manitou?   (LePan, 75–6)

The last stanza suggests the sad irony of the stranger's blindness to the mythic tradition the natives have implanted in the land. He is thereby doomed to go on occasionally sensing that there is in his experience of this landscape some kind of epiphany that is fated to remain forever just out of reach.

Still, the stranger's belief, which arose "sometimes – perhaps at the tentative fall of twilight," persisted in raising itself within the imaginations of many early Canadian artists and writers. In their quest for a truly Canadian art it held out a sort of elusive grail: a transcendent experience in the Canadian environment that would be sufficient to empower the poetic creation of a mythology. Such attempts to figure forth poetically experiences of a kind or magnitude that seem incommensurate with ordinary tools of expression fall into the category of the sublime – Thomas Weiskel defines it in *The Romantic Sublime*, "that moment when the relation between the signifier and signified breaks down and is replaced by an indeterminate relation" (xiii). Weiskel goes on to say that: "The essential claim of the sublime is that man can, in feeling and in speech, transcend the human. What, if anything, lies beyond the human – God or the gods, the daemon or Nature – is a matter for disagreement. What, if anything, defines the range of the human is scarcely less sure" (3).

In short, he argues, "a humanistic sublime is an oxymoron." Yet Weiskel does not therefore simply assume that the sublime is the inevitable response to a possibly divine transcendent experience. Rather, he argues that it is a central element in a deliberate effort to empower the self by "joining with the great"; and he claims that "the true function of the sublime is to legitimate the necessary discontinuities in the classical scheme of signification and to justify the specific affective experience which these discontinuities entailed" (17). Weiskel suggests that the need for this function is a consequence of the modern mind's "incurable ambivalence about authority"(8). Furthermore, he also connects these "discontinuities" to the struggle against a sense of "belatedness" that, according to Harold Bloom's thesis of the "anxiety of influence,", all poets suffer with respect to their precursors.[6]

In other words, the sublime disrupts the control of the status quo – whether that entails the burden of a precursor, of history, of traditional culture, of prevailing political forces, or of the pressure applied by some other conventional mode of thought – in order to allow an influx of power from some alternative, higher, noumenal authority. In effect, then, the claim of the sublime to invoke a transcendent experience should be regarded as an essential strategy of poetic creation.

The relevance of this theory of the sublime to our discussion of the development of Canadian dramatic imagination is easily demonstrated. In the poetic dramas of nineteenth-century Canada we repeatedly see an attempt to discover an indigenous romantic sublime. Once captured, this "Canadian sublime" may become the linchpin of a mythopoeic scheme, thus bestowing a transcendent authority upon a whole poetic structure and thereby overcoming the disempowering sense of belatedness inherent in the idea of Canadian culture.

A good example of that strategy is found in Charles Mair's *Tecumseh* (1876). Alan Filewod incisively exposes the political agenda of this play when he calls it an attempt "to give dramatic form to the pro-Empire, anti-American, and anti-francophone nationalism of the Canada First movement, of which [Mair] was a co-founder" (321). That is certainly true enough; however, if we can resist being baited into a political quarrel, we see that what lifts *Tecumseh* beyond the merely contemptible and, indeed, makes it rather interesting is Mair's earnest attempt to ennoble and promote his view of the Canadian experience to a transcendent poetic level. In this enterprise, Mair's use of the sublime in several key tropes is indispensable. For instance, here is Tecumseh, Homerically soliloquizing on the battlefield:

> This is our summer – when the painted wilds,
> Like pictures in a dream, enchant the sight.
> The forest bursts in glory like a flame!
> Its leaves are sparks; its mystic breath the haze
> Which blends in purple incense with the air.
> The Spirit of the Woods has decked his home
> And put his wonders like a garment on,
> To flash, and glow, and dull, and fade, and die.
> Oh, let not manhood fade within my soul!   (Mair, 120)

The stakes of the battle are placed on a spiritual footing, with Tecumseh's mystic reading of the land invoking a pastoral ideal that hangs precariously in the balance of a contest between "nobility" (i.e., benevolent British imperialism) and "ignobility" (i.e., wicked American expansionism).

We find a kind of emblem of what Mair is himself attempting to do in Lefroy, the young Caucasian hero of *Tecumseh*, who is in love with Iena, a (what else?) beautiful Indian maiden who is the personification of the exotic charms of the Canadian wilderness. Lefroy speaks poetry directly to the forest as if, Orlando-like, to attach his imaginative creation to the landscape, and thus compel it to conform to his mythopoeic encoding:

> There was a time on this fair continent
> When all things throve in spacious peacefulness.
> The prosperous forests unmolested stood,
> For where the stalwart oak grew there it lived
> Long ages, and then died among its kind.
> The hoary pines – those ancients of the earth –
> Brimful of legends of the early world,
> Stood thick on their own mountains unsubdued.
> And all things else illumined by the sun,
> Inland or by the lifted wave, had rest.
> The passionate or calm pageants of the skies
> No artist drew; but in the auburn west
> Innumerable faces of fair cloud
> Vanished in silent darkness with the day ...   (21)

The resonance of this passage with, on the one hand, Wordsworth's "Intimations Ode" and, on the other, "the green dark forest too silent to be real" of Gordon Lightfoot's "Canadian Railroad Trilogy" suggests the provenance and the continuing usefulness of invoking the romantic sublime in the Canadian landscape.

This passage also offers a convincing example of the empowering function of the sublime. For here the "civilized" and "ordered" European world from which Lefroy hails is suspended for a moment, together with denotative discourse, and the paean to the noumenal history of this landscape invokes an alternative and "infinite" authority, investing it in the Canadian environment. Mair's poetic rendering is meant to offer a kind of salvation, a mythologization, to a landscape that would otherwise remain commonplace and unanimated to the European mind – a "country without a mythology" because, as Lefroy suggests, it was in their view a land that "no artist [had drawn]." By means of this process the cultural negatives "unsettled" and "uncivilized" are transformed into positives: "uncompromised" and "sublime."

Naturally, the different attitudes towards heritage in English and French Canada beget somewhat different poetic emphases. English Canadian poets and dramatists found themselves burdened by the very continuity of their European heritage, and therefore used the romantic sublime to establish discontinuities and opportunities to reassess the Canadian experience creatively. The result was effectively an extremely subtle aesthetic revolt within the tradition to establish a new voice – a Canadian literary tradition of revolt, so to speak. In contrast, French Canada was faced very early with a discontinuity of heritage in the form of the conquest of New France. That threat of discontinuity was met by French Canadian authorities with much more repressive control of social discourse through government and the church than was felt in English Canada. Alongside these circumstances, at the national level French Canada suffered for many years from an acute sense of political marginalization. These two forces meant that French Canadian culture was marked by a sense of repression and disenfranchisement. Consequently – though, to be sure, the distinction cannot be maintained absolutely – we find a stronger emphasis on romantic revolt in French Canadian drama than on a poetic sublime. In terms of the struggle to create a mythopoeic field of resistance to the colonial hegemony, it is evident that plays about heroes such as Latour, Papineau, and Riel dramatize a sense of revolt within tradition more trenchantly than an aesthetic emphasis upon the sublime ever could.

Yet, while the French Canadian emphasis on a romantic depiction of political resistance results in a mythological foundation that is distinct in many respects from the English Canadian emphasis on an aesthetic rendering of the sublime, the parallels between the two traditions of depicting revolt – the political and the poetic – should not therefore be discounted. The themes have a common origin in European romantic poetry, where they are more usually partnered than not. In their Canadian usage these two traditions are driven by a comparable need to transcend the inherited colonial culture in order to forge an authentic, indigenous imaginative space. In short, in the context of dramatic conventions the romantic revolutionary may properly be considered an explicitly politicized counterpart to the romantic sublime.

At this point we come to a passage from the third and last LePan poem I will draw upon, "*Coureurs de bois*" (1948):

<blockquote>
But now
That the forests are cut down, the rivers charted,
Where can you turn, where can you travel? Unless
</blockquote>

Through the desperate wilderness behind your eyes,
So full of falls and glooms and desolations,
Disasters I have glimpsed but few would dream of,
You seek new Easts ...
You hesitate. The trees are entangled with menace.
The voyage is perilous into the dark interior.
But then your hands go to the thwarts. You smile. And so
I watch you vanish in a wood of heroes,
Wild Hamlet with the features of Horatio.   (73)

The attempt to attach a poetic sense of Canadian identity to outward circumstances, particularly to the natural landscape, could only go so far. To achieve a satisfactorily rooted indigenous drama, Canadian playwrights still needed to transform their external experience of Canada into a personal imaginative cosmos that could then be explored dramatically. Hence we find that in the twentieth century both traditions of Canadian poetic drama begin to take a decisive inward turn. An excellent transitional example of the political revolutionary tradition taking an inward path is Alexandre Huot's *Le Songe du conscrit* (1918), in which François Bigot (the putatively corrupt intendant of New France) and Samuel de Champlain appear as phantoms, projections of two sides of a young conscript's mind as he determines whether to resist compulsory military service. But perhaps the most intriguing modernist example of the development of the romantic sublime to adumbrate an interior landscape is found in Herman Voaden's plays, such as *Northern Song* (1930), *Rocks* (1932), *Earth Song* (1932), *Hill-Land* (1934), and *Ascend as the Sun* (1942).

Voaden combined music, sound, light, dance, and poetic language into a whole he called "symphonic expressionism," which he gradually developed in an effort to capture theatrically a mystic union between nature and human spiritual aspiration. Voaden's dramatic innovations were inspired in part by the advances in Canadian painting made by his friends in the Group of Seven. There is even a parallel in the manner of their artistic breakthroughs. We know that J.E.H. MacDonald and Lawren Harris had found a stylistic model for their efforts to capture the Canadian sublime on canvas in the 1913 exhibition of Scandinavian landscape painters (such as Gustav Fjaestad and Harald Sohlberg) at the Albright Museum in Buffalo. Similarly, Voaden found a means of theatrically rendering his interior response to Canadian nature by combining elements of German expressionism, which he had studied in university, with aspects of Wagner's music-drama. In both cases an artistic breakthrough in representing Canadian experience was found by drawing on a set of conventions lying just outside the main colonial traditions; the discontinuity of convention was embraced as coinciding with the kind of psychic discontinuity with ordinary experience that is inherent in the sublime.

Certainly, in Voaden's case, his intensely mystic rendering of a Canadian sublime was part of much larger project to transcend the limitations he saw in Canadian culture – a project that, as Anton Wagner has shown, amounted to a religious faith (Wagner, 187–201). Within that faith the mystic encounters with the Canadian sublime were effectively religious experiences, moments of ineffable insight that, according to William James's description in *The Varieties of Religious Experience*, begin with "a sense that there is something wrong about us as we naturally stand" and move to "a sense that we are saved from the wrongness by making proper connection with the higher powers." This latter sense, James tells us, results in the subject's consciousness "that this higher part is coterminous and continuous with a MORE of the same quality, which is operative in the universe outside of him, and which he can keep in working touch with, and in a fashion get on board of and save himself when all his lower being has gone to pieces in the wreck" 507–8). Certainly the encounter with the romantic sublime in Voaden's plays provides a central epiphany that is essential to the progression of his heroes from despair, self-doubt, and a rejection of conventional faith to a transcendent state of new faith – a pattern closely correspondent to Voaden's own passage from a profound dissatisfaction with Canadian culture through to his passionate espousal of "symphonic expressionism." In other words, in both the spiritual themes of the plays and the aesthetic transformation of dramatic convention, the sublime provides the essential source of discontinuity with tradition and the introduction of a new authority.

Now, Voaden is admittedly an unusually extreme example of a playwright using the sublime as the cornerstone of a new poetics and philosophy. But Voaden's promotion of this phenomenon to the level of a religion is, in my view, simply a more intense version of a pattern seen among other playwrights. The difference has to do with the divine character that Voaden attributed to his insights. But in this matter we can refer again to William James, who points out lucidly of religious experience that "whatever it may be on its *farther* side, the 'more' with which in religious experience we feel ourselves connected is on its *hither* side the subconscious continuation of our conscious life" (512). My own attitude to the whole question of the sublime is similarly agnostic (as it is to any of the religious or quasi-religious elements in the poetics of the playwrights I discuss in the subsequent chapters). For me, the essential point of interest is the role such insights play in the dramatic imaginations of these playwrights.

The concept of the sublime, then, implies that a particular kind of experience of nature can pierce through surface appearances to make contact with the noumenal forces latent in nature. But that image may easily be turned around to emphasize that the sublime experience pierces through ordinary knowledge and habitual thought to some unconscious level of the imagination, providing an extraordinary sense of access to the inner mind. Here begins the exploration of the desperate wilderness mentioned in LePan's poem. Whereas the rational, mercantilist colonial tradition had made difficult any extended mythopoeicization of the natural landscape, there was still rich promise in the sense of discovering an inner wilderness. The phenomenon is similar to that discussed by Northrop Frye in his theory of the "garrison mentality" in Canadian literature. Frye suggests that the initial stage of the garrison mentality involves people huddling together against a threatening external wilderness to create a feeling of community. But at a later stage that feeling of community has become repressive to the individual imagination, and there is a consequent figurative identification of the outward wilderness with the wilderness of the inner self. That inner wilderness is "desperate" because of its hunger for some kind of transcendence of constraining cultural circumstances, for an identification of a more meaningful and satisfactory way to bridge individual aspirations and communal values.

Thus, the romantic sublime initiates a tentative identification of some elements of an outward wilderness with an inward wilderness that can thereafter be more extensively explored. In the words of Earl Wassermann, we are looking at an example of "the special integrative, or constructive, act of poetry," whereby the "lyric" functions of poetry achieve the "constitution of a self-sustaining reality," a "special cosmos," leaving the "dramatic" functions to "make the further discoveries this reality has made potential" (10). The idea has special significance in Canadian culture in that, having imaginatively claimed a feral space in which an untamed poetic activity could be domiciled or centred, and from which it could venture forth to explore other areas, there was a greater possibility of an effective transumption of European conventions. To put the point in terms of our astrolabe metaphor: locating the sublime in the Canadian experience was akin to discovering new stars to add to the constellations by which the poetic explorer navigated. While the European-made astrolabe remained, the meaning of finding one's way home had changed because home itself had been located in a different manner; the problem of where "here" was had begun to resolve itself.

The big surprise, however, was that when the most convincing answers to "where is here" began to emerge in the twentieth century, they entered into a world rapidly becoming more and more "postnational." Hence, while for some years there was a fervent determination to articulate "here" in a nationalist sense – a determination that reached its peak in the period around the Centennial celebrations in 1967 – from our vantage-point at the end of the century we must recognize that the answer is considerably more complex than any monolithic concept of nationalism will allow. An adjusted form of the nationalist argument breaks up the monolith to suggest instead that the Canadian national identity is merely the sum of its geographic or political regions; but even there it is difficult not to be impressed by the heterogeneity among the individual artists working within such regions. More recently, the critical impulse to understand Canadian art in nationalist terms has reticulated into the idea that it is better understood as comprising a series of socio-political "regions," which are to some degree independent of geographic location and instead partake of sets of transnational, materialist categories: race, ethnicity, gender, sexuality, social class, etc. Personally, I can't see how that solution is a whit more promising than the discredited monolithic constructions of national identity. To identify oneself electively in terms of such materialist categories is one thing; but to universally ascribe identity to others wholly in terms of "standpoint politics" is not only illiberal and dehumanizing but demonstrably inaccurate. The reality remains much more subtle and complex than any such construction will allow.

Hence, the context into which I place Canadian drama is much more personalist. While it is certainly true that at various times various playwrights have striven mightily to articulate a nationalist or political or regional or sexual or ethnic identity through their work, there is no one framework that can be consistently and usefully applied across the board. Moreover, the most usual circumstance has been that any given playwright has a whole complex of concerns based in these and other themes of identity, and it is through the effort to grapple with these particular concerns that much of the playwright's originality emerges. The objection might very well be raised that such an argument gives very little legitimate basis to this book, which is, after all, focused on a selection of one nation's playwrights. But I hope to clarify this paradox with the last part of my historical argument.

I argued earlier that the act of locating a poetic sublime could be seen as one of the most effective means of invoking the authority necessary to transcend a sense of belatedness. The idea that Canadian playwrights began in the mid-twentieth century to devise an alternative authority on which to base their poetics happens to be consonant with a kind of anti-authoritarianism that is evident in the European poetic dramas of that time. Whereas the modernist poetic drama of Yeats, Eliot, Cocteau, Fry, and so on was a defiant reaction to what its authors saw as the prevailing technocratic and positivistic aspects of mass consciousness, the mid-century Canadian drama was tilting at different, albeit similar, windmills. The neatest way of labelling the authorities that were being resisted in Canada is to call them philistines and pharisees, for in different measures some combination of these two categories appears repeatedly in the role of nemesis. By contrast, the role of protagonist is filled by a fledgling, creative cultural dignity that hopes to transcend the colonial status perpetuated by the forces of philistinism and pharisaism.

The pattern is easily seen in the work of two of Canada's most historically important playwrights, Gratien Gelinas and Robertson Davies, both of whom emerged with highly significant plays in 1948 – respectively, *Tit-Coq* and *Fortune, My Foe*. Because both Gelinas and Davies later became such icons of the Canadian theatre establishment, it is easy to efface the fact that their early plays were expressions of anti-authoritarian protest. In *Tit-Coq* the *devoir* of social etiquette that forms the basis of most classical French tragedies re-emerged in terms of the struggle of an illegitimate Quebecois to find dignity and a sense of belonging in the face of a sexually repressive, church-dominated society. Gelinas's close depiction of the details of life among lower-class Quebeckers prompted a hugely enthusiastic response, which only served to support the underlying implication of the play: that a potentially rich Quebec culture was being stifled by a pharisaic colonial legacy. Similarly, Davies's *Fortune, My Foe* depicts the stifling of a creative impulse when the attempt of a young professor to get a puppet show about Don Quixote off the ground meets with the uncomprehending negativity of local philistine officials.

In the works of both playwrights we can see a fusion of the tradition of political satire, which had maintained a healthy persistence throughout the history of Canadian theatre, with the imaginative revolution that had been fomenting in the more poetic dramas. In both there is the strong sense that what hinders the development of Canadian culture is not merely inept or corrupt administration, nor a lack of "the noumenal" in the Canadian environment, but a narrow, atrophied colonial mind-set. In short, these playwrights were attempting to foster a revolt within the Canadian imagination, and in this respect their plays sounded a clarion for other playwrights to follow.

Naturally this does not mean that all at once there was an indigenous tradition established within which all subsequent work would proceed. On the contrary, in the following chapters the indebtedness of Canadian playwrights to international cultural traditions will be evident far more often than any influence of their Canadian forebears can be discerned. But with the post-war plays of Davies, Gelinas, and several others, the possibility that Canadian playwrights could achieve a transumption of the established conventions with an original vision, and could thereby compel a shift in the imaginations of their audiences, had been conclusively established.

1 James Reaney: Metamorphic Masques

If the doors of perception were cleansed
Everything would appear to man as it is ... infinite
For man has closed himself up
Till he sees all things through narrow chinks of his cavern.

William Blake

RECOVERING "THE CEREMONY OF INNOCENCE"

What surely strikes most of us first about James Reaney's work is its paradoxical combination of sophistication and naïveté. Among Canadian writers Reaney is one of the most self-conscious craftsmen, bringing a staggering level of erudition to his work, though always insisting on childlike simplicity in its theatrical execution. Gerald Parker's 1991 study of Reaney's theatre is aptly named *How To Play*. Juxtaposition of complexity and triviality is one of the hallmarks of modernism, yet there are some who find Reaney's particular variant off-putting rather than engaging. Louis Dudek, for example, complained in 1974 that in contrast to the moderns, Reaney follows William Blake's bad example in the *Songs of Innocence*, becoming at times "childish or stylistically insipid." This, Dudek speculates, is because, "faced with an audience of mindless biddies and croquet intellects, such as we may have in Canada in the outlands, the poet has taken drastic means to simplify. His philosophical outlook and his audience relationship have combined to create a childish theatre" (21–2).

For any serious attempt to come to terms with Reaney's place in Canadian culture, Dudek's essay stands obstinately in the path like a Great Bojg. Dudek articulately expresses reservations others may share, so it is well to mention his criticisms plainly at the outset of our discussion, and then see how they hold up. The basic question is this: what is at stake for Reaney in writing the kind of drama that he does?

Why should so learned a writer assume the childlike stance of which Dudek complains? The answer lies in Reaney's struggle to find a personal poetics through which he could achieve a transumption of his cultural heritage. It is worthwhile digressing a little to give a theoretical account of this imaginative struggle, not only for its value in understanding Reaney's drama but as a crucial example of the kind of process Canadian dramatic imagination has had to undertake to achieve maturity.

Two of Reaney's remarks about the context in which he became a writer offer an illuminating inroad. In 1978, in response to a question about which playwrights he had read and been influenced by in his youth, Reaney mentioned the Greeks, Shakespeare and his contemporaries, Wilder, O'Neill, Eliot, Cocteau, Beckett, etc., including no Canadians (Anthony, 143–50). But Reaney's sketch of the literary context of his dramatic imagination needs to be juxtaposed with a second remark, about the external circumstances of his Canadian boyhood. In 1977 he described the prevailing sensibility of the cultural milieu of mid-century Canada, the environment in which he began to write:

Thirty years ago, a young person drawn to the life of metaphors and vision in *this* country perhaps found the puzzling situation that while European poets had long been reacting in the manner described above [i.e. composing the "mad songs" of modernism] to what Blake calls "single vision and Newton's sleep," while Rimbaud had been chartering "drunken boats," Isabella Crawford and our nineteenth century poets had been writing about canoes in forest ponds filled with lily pads, central symbols in long narrative, not lyric poems. For a long time for us the collision most interesting to watch has been that between human society and primeval wilderness, not man and the so-called benefits of progress.   (*Real Foundation*, 5)

In other words, Canadian culture had not as yet transcended its colonial habit of regarding the natural environment with eyes informed by a sentimental Victorian aesthetic.

Reaney is not alone in holding such a view. Ann Douglas has argued that Victorian sentimentality exerted a more powerful and sustained influence in North America than in Britain (5). Douglas, a feminist social historian, suggests this was the effect of a movement by middle-class women, made idle by the Industrial Revolution, "to gain power through the exploitation of their feminine identity as their society defined it" (55). A sort of alliance between church ministers and "ladies' groups" in the mid-nineteenth century became a major cultural force. Reaney portrays just this phenomenon in his first play, *The Sun and the Moon*, where the ladies of the Millbrook Women's Institute share an uneasy alliance with Reverend Kingbird. Unfortunately, says Douglas of these groups, "their efforts intensified sentimental rather than matriarchal values," a culture of sentimentalism that continued well into the twentieth century (11).[1] The influence of this kind of aesthetic is particularly evident in the environment of Reaney's youth: rural, small-town Ontario, where there were no professional artists to speak of.

Hence, while Reaney's reading had familiarized him with international literature, he lived in a world still innocent of modernist sensibility. His solution to the conundrum was to collapse a century of literary revolution into a single approach that may be called "romantic modernism." This term may seem redundant, given that modernism is the clear heir of romanticism, but modernism met romantic themes and myths with a great deal of irony and scepticism, qualities less evident in Reaney's work. Whereas there are strong romantic affinities in Reaney's themes and philosophy (and therefore in his central myth), in symbolic technique and in form he is more clearly modernist.

Reaney's central myth is founded on the recovery of what Yeats called "the ceremony of innocence."[2] In essence this is the same story Shelley told with *Prometheus Unbound* or Blake with his prophecies. Northrop Frye (a close friend of Reaney's, and whose theories have an essential relation to the plays[3]) offers perhaps the clearest explication of a specific version of this myth in *Fearful Symmetry* (124ff). The myth begins with the sense that the natural spirit of humanity is being stifled, that humans are psychologically repressed or politically oppressed – which boils down to pretty much the same literary essence. At one time these factors were united in the attitude of Romantic poets towards the French Revolution, which they saw as much in terms of psychological as social liberation. Hence, the celebration of personality and individuality in the face of conformist pressures resulted in a sort of institution of the imagination as a political force.

Reaney is the Romantics' heir in this regard, for he often conflates the threat to the individual personality with social oppression of a political sort. To cite an obvious example, in *Sticks and Stones* Reaney explicitly identifies the literal narrowness of the Donnellys' farm-lot (a result of the callous surveying policies of the authorities) with the Donnellys' subjection to pressures to conform to socially acceptable notions of personal character. This identification is accomplished by means of theatrical metaphor: we see and hear the Donnellys systematically hemmed in by, alternately, their neighbours' opinions and their own property boundaries (15–28).

One typical Romantic response to this sense of oppression is an idealization of childhood as a pre-anxiety paradise. Reaney once wrote of Edith Sitwell's poetry that her "childhood seems not just a period of her life but another country where she once lived" ("Edith Sitwell," 29). As much could be said of Reaney's own work, which, like Sitwell's, indulges in a pastoral idealization of childhood. In this tradition, childhood becomes a symbol of spiritual perspicacity; the child is a sort of demi-Christian prophet, sacrificed to age in order that adulthood may be redeemed by memory. The most famous poetic statement of the idea is Wordsworth's Immortality Ode: "There was a time when meadow, grove and stream [...] did seem / Apparelled in celestial light ..." In *Afternoon Moon*, Reaney's early and only partially published novel, the Wordsworth poem finds a revealing echo in a passage that begins: "There was a time when I could work myself up into quite a poetical frenzy over the tastes and smells I had experienced as a child" (41). In a brief poetic prolegomenon, Reaney declares:

> I am an exile from the paradise of childhood
> Each year as I grow older, I weep because I am older
> My heart is a red watch, a time-bomb set within my breast to blow
> me up. (38)

Apparently, the completed novel would have been a sort of *Prelude* in prose, an extended semi-autobiographical disquisition on the adventures of the author's poetic soul, centring on memories of poetic revelation – a myriad of swirling, sensual recollections working together in a Proustian manner to evoke a particular state of mind. The premise submits that the adult has been bullied and compromised into a fallen state of passivity; hence, the value of the memories lies not so much in themselves "but that the soul," as Wordsworth puts it in *The Prelude*,

> Remembering how she felt, but, what she felt
> Remembering not, retains an obscure sense
> Of possible sublimity, to which
> With faculties still growing, feeling still
> That whatsoever point they gain they still
> Have something to pursue. (II.315–22)

Thus, a personal sort of redemption takes place; the imagination is prompted to revolt against its state of passive materialism and recover the creative energies of the childhood spirit.

This, then, is the "ceremony of innocence," but there are significant differences between Wordsworth's ceremony and Reaney's. For whereas Wordsworth saw these uplifting qualities as deriving from an interrelation with Nature, Reaney follows Blake in attributing these qualities strictly to the spirit or imagination. He states his position explicitly in a poem that forms a sort of keystone in his oeuvre, "To Bishop Berkeley," the theme of which is repudiation of materialism:

Oh Wordsworth and nature-walkers
    Thy nature barnyard is;
Her trees are plaster, wainscot hills,
    Handy vale and miry mess.
Wherever walks your lantern self
    The crop of wonder then sprouts up;
        Five kinds of music,
The spear of time, the spatial cup. (*Selected Shorter Poems*, 70)[4]

According to the immaterialist philosophy of George Berkeley, "*esse* is *percepi*," but individual human perceptions are said to partake of the universal perception belonging to God.[5] For Berkeley man and God were two very different things, whereas Reaney's work suggests something of the Romantic's creeping indifference towards the distinction. Still, in "your lantern self" there is a nod towards Christianity we were best to heed, for it marks an important transition in Reaney's central myth. The phrase recalls Jesus' metaphor of the individual spirit as a light not to be kept under a bushel but allowed to "shine before men" (Matt. 5:14–16), and so hints at what Brian Parker has called the "evangelical" aspect of Reaney's work ("Reaney and the Mask of Childhood," 279–89).[6]

It appears that Reaney considerably refined his thought on this matter in the course of writing his doctoral thesis, "The Influence of Spenser on Yeats" (1958). Particularly relevant is his discussion of Yeats's recurrent use of a tower as a symbol representing the stages through which the spirit must ascend to reach purity – the journey upwards being a variation, it would seem, of "the ceremony of innocence." At the top of one such tower, in "Blood and the Moon," stands "God-appointed Berkeley that proved all things a dream." Here we find "everything that is not God consumed with intellectual fire" (*Yeats's Poems*, 351–3). Yeats's explanation of this fire has an important relevance to Reaney's work. As described in *A Vision*, the "intellectual fire" is produced by two states of consciousness: the primary, or objective state, in which environment dominates mind, is sometimes called the Terrestrial Condition; and the antithetical, or subjective, in which mind dominates environment, is called the Condition of Air. The state of equilibrium – that of wisdom – is called the Condition of Fire,[7] and it is this level of perception that is associated with the top of the tower. In his thesis Reaney emphasizes that it is difficult to know when exactly one has reached the top of Yeats's towers. Sometimes, he tells us, "people reach the apparent top [of Yeats's towers] only to find that if they really want to get to the real top [...], they must start climbing down right away into an acceptance of the fallen cyclical world as a potentially redeemable place." Reaney describes this idea as a "need for the true marriage of heaven and the fallen world, not just an escape from the fallen world," and he compares it to a tenet of Buddhism, wherein "it is claimed that we must take the whole of creation with us to enlightenment, that we cannot just abandon it to its fate, as all human beings are as near to us as our relatives are."[8] In short, this evangelical romantic faith demands not only that one should revolt against the passive materialism of the quotidian world to recover "the ceremony of innocence" for oneself, but also that one should show the way back up the tower to as many people as possible. It was this imperative that motivated Reaney's change in emphasis from what he called the "inner-faced" gaze or the "reticent mask" of the lyric poet to the outward-projecting attitude of the theatrical practitioner.[9]

Reaney's Promethean aspirations with regard to theatre did not emerge overnight but were developed through a dialectic between form and process developed over a number of years. His playwriting may be broken into two major periods and a transitional phase, a pattern he concedes, once describing his career as a dramatist in these terms: "I started off writing the verse plays T.S. Eliot said you should be writing and I ended up writing plays with actors' bodies and voices rather than a pen; but I ended up this way only after taking a detour through the world of plays for children" (Real Foundation, 11). The first period, then, is, as Reaney indicates, characterized by a more traditional "poetic drama" resembling that of T.S. Eliot. Most of these plays are collected in The Killdeer and Other Plays and Masks of Childhood. The second and still current period begins with Listen to the Wind; these plays demand the broader rubric "poetic theatre," and may be broken into a series of subsections. In between are a number of children's plays in which Reaney's style may be seen in transition, particularly those collected in Apple Butter and Other Plays.

Naturally, the children's plays show Reaney most clearly in a teaching, or evangelical, capacity, although this aspect is important throughout his work, virtually all of which is either hortative or heuristic. He has said that "choosing to be a university teacher involves one in the first step I myself had to take out of the private world of lyric poetry, a step into the world of public action" (*Real Foundation*, 7). It is a step he takes again and again in his plays. I've called this inclination Promethean, and to extend the analogy, the fire that Reaney steals to empower his followers (here we should remember Yeats's "intellectual fire") is the transfiguring power of metaphor.[10] In Reaney's vision a properly trained talent for metaphoric thought is a sort of alchemy through which the dross of the material, quotidian world is transformed into the precious spiritual element necessary to our redemption.

This vision is embodied in a theme that begins early in Reaney's work and is remarkably persistent: the ascent of a repressed mind from the narrow horizons of parochial, small-town life into a liberated, boundless world of imagination and goodness. Whereas in most coming-of-age stories the attainment of identity involves a change of setting (consider *The Three Musketeers* or *Great Expectations*, for example), Reaney resists the idea that spiritual liberation is in any way an attribute of place. In part this has to do with the anti-Wordsworthian aspects of his brand of romanticism; but it may also have roots in his antipathy to any suggestion that Canada or any Canadian region is necessarily second-rate. In any event, Reaney's protagonists never leave Canada to find their true selves elsewhere, and seldom even budge from their home counties. The better part of Reaney's work is based in rural southwestern Ontario, which, following the late artist Greg Curnoe, he calls "Souwesto" (Bowering, 13). Souwesto is Reaney's Wessex, Yoknapatawpha County, or Manawaka – even, in that it is also his workshop, his Giverny.[11] In sticking to this setting he has effectively applied himself to a regional answer to Frye's great Canadian riddle "Where is here?"

In the short stories he wrote in the 1940s Reaney's answer was most often a bleak one. "Dear Metronome," "Clay Hole," "The Box Social," and "The Bully" all in one way or another depict the futile hopes of sensitive young people (usually women) for a more meaningful life. In these stories "here" is the place where the aspiring soul struggles against a grim, irremediably philistine society and is eventually stifled into submission or even death (not that Reaney suggests that there is much to choose between the two, spiritually speaking). "Elevator" varies the theme in that Roberta, an elevator operator, ascends through the third floor of the Ontario Department Store into the heavens. Too rarefied for one element, she simply disappears into another, like the angelic daughter in *One Hundred Years of Solitude*. "Mr Whur: A Metamorphosis" and "The Book in the Tree" are variations on the Fall myth. Mr Whur aspires to become as tiny as his toy miniatures and finally succeeds (a metaphor for the parochial mind-set, the opposite of the hubris of Adam and Eve or Faust). "The Young Necrophiles" is not particularly bleak in tone, but its subject is a group of children whose favourite pastime is the upkeep of a toy cemetery, a notion that perhaps speaks for itself.[12] Only "The Book in the Tree" ends on a truly positive note: a young woman is tempted by a forbidden book hanging in an orchard; having read it, she is enlightened, abandons her dim-witted companion, and leaves her fool's paradise.[13]

In the poetry of that period it seems that, approaching the same theme (sensitive soul versus philistine society) lyrically, as in "Play-box," "The Dead Rainbow," "The Canadian," and "The Upper Cana-dian," Reaney's inclination is elegiac.[14] There are elegiac overtones to some of the short stories as well, but even in the darker stories one detects an inclination towards satire. That is perhaps not surprising since, by and large, satire finds narrative form more hospitable than it does lyric.

But the two tendencies meet in *A Suit of Nettles* (1958), where Reaney takes up "Punch's stick [to] beat fertility into a sterile land" (xxi). This is probably Reaney's most important work of poetry, and certainly among the most accomplished extended poetic works ever written in Canada. Its importance to the present study is threefold: it constitutes the first complete statement of Reaney's central myth; it shows Reaney in full command of the style of symbolic language and authorial tone that brands all his subsequent work; and, perhaps most important, it is here that Reaney's dramatic skill decisively emerges.[15] Inspired by Spenser's *The Shepheardes Calendar*, Reaney's *A Suit of Nettles* comprises twelve eclogues (one for each month), covering the journey from birth to death. Silly geese represent various elements of a philistine society. From this society, Mopsus attains a sort of spiritual illumination as coached by Effie, who has returned from her own per-sonal transcendence to attempt to bring the other geese of the barnyard to enlightenment, to a sort of Nirvana where the "cramped stupid goosehouse world" may be left behind and the chopping block approached with relief.

There are two eclogues I want to single out: March and September. The March eclogue features Effie's parable of the doorknob and the door, a kind of reworking of Jesus' parable of the door to the sheep-fold (John 10). In this version the utility of the door is nothing without the metaphoric imagination of the knob, for the latter proves to have been a "necessary angel" when it is removed and the door inevitably smashed into splinters.[16] The knob, however, is left a "toy to children dear, / Still thinking, dreaming, showing them / How to be Ham, Japhet and Shem / And drunken Noah as all men must / Who for the height of being lust" (16). The important points here are, first, the connection Reaney makes between the metaphoric imagination and spirituality; and second, the essential homeliness of the image that Reaney has given so onerous a duty. By encouraging the broadest possible interpretation, he effectively makes the simple doorknob into what Northrop Frye calls a "monad": a symbol that, viewed from an anagogic perspective, becomes the centre of one's total literary experience (*Anatomy*, 121).

The September eclogue features the apocalyptic Mome Fair, a sort of Coney Island of Reaney's mind. This is the kind of poetry usually associated with the anagogic perspective, for the traditional images of circles, cycles, and journeys are provided by ferris wheels, merry-go-rounds, and fun-houses. There is also a sideshow and a sermon. Through all this Reaney achieves an encyclopaedic figurative effect that identifies the overwhelming appeal to the senses made by a county fair with the imagination as a whole: history, philosophy, religion, literature, and science are all piled together upon these symbolic vehicles.

Two related points require special notice here. The first is that while Reaney freely draws on international ideas in the form of the philosophers he mentions, he is aggressively local in his history and geography. That distinction may seem obvious enough, but the reasons for it bear some reflection. Evidently Reaney places deliberate boundaries around his conceptions of intellectual property. Philosophy is general property because it is primarily literary; geography and history are only secondarily so. So, in the one case he seems to say: "look how easily these ideas can belong to you"; in the other: "look how interesting what belongs to you is." The second point has to do with two impulses that at first appear to make uneasy bedfellows: to teach history and to mythologize. Continually cropping up in Reaney's work is the revelation of certain little-known facts on the one hand, coupled with an appeal to fantasy on the other.

Reaney is by no means the only writer to demand this double response, but few have so deliberately made a poetics out of it. In 1960 Reaney founded a literary journal called *Alphabet*, outlining its theme in the introductory editorial: "Let us make a form out of this: documentary on one side and myth on the other: Life and Art. Into this form we can put anything and the magnet we have set up will arrange it for us (2). These ingredients combine to create the Berkeleyean vision, the "lantern self." Through the juxtaposition of myth and document Reaney strives to unite imagination and environment; the ensuing vision is the same fire we see resulting from Yeats's dialectic of the objective and subjective states of consciousness, the Terrestrial Condition and the Condition of Air.

When reference is made to the strong currents of dramatic effects running through *A Suit of Nettles*, what is most often referred to is Reaney's evident talent for representing voice. These poems certainly make a strong appeal to the inner ear, as it were, and one of Reaney's earliest encouragements as a dramatist came from the director Pamela Terry after she had heard portions of *A Suit of Nettles* read on radio (Lee, 118). But the dramatic qualities of the work are also evident in the three character groups here, which are sustained through almost all Reaney's plays: the heroes and their allies, usually sensitive souls; the villains, generally philistines in possession of raw material power; and the potential proselytes, who add a dimension of suspense to the contest between the first two parties.

Another important proto-dramatic aspect of *A Suit of Nettles* is its *opsis*, or its capacity to excite the visual imagination of the reader. There is a terrific liberality of imagery here, which emerged to a degree in the symbolism of the early plays but would be fully unharnessed only in the second period. For the time being, however, there were inhibiting factors; so Reaney began by writing, as he called them, "the verse plays T.S. Eliot said you should be writing" (*Real Foundation*, 11).

WHAT THE POSSUM SAID: THE EARLY PLAYS

In recent years Reaney has been rather dismissive of his early plays, saying on one occasion, "I was trying to write like Christopher Fry or someone. Who cares about verse drama in Canada? Not Nathan Cohen, anyway" (OISE Seminar).[17] Reaney's disdain for the early work does an injustice to his younger self, for while it is true that Reaney's greater accomplishment as a playwright lies with his later work, when his theatrical technique was fully developed, the early plays are tremendously inventive and need only some imaginative direction to show their theatrical viability. In terms of their significance to this study they are similar enough to one another in their poetic form – with the important exception of *One-Man Masque* – to be treated as a unit, and thus provide a first view of the schematic arrangement of Reaney's poetic theatre as a whole.

In his study of his father's work for the stage James Stewart Reaney identifies two principles of narrative structure, the linear and the cyclical. The linear narratives lead up to a "revelation" that changes everything, while the cyclical works set forth "one circular vision, encompassing all the previous changes" (31). The dramas employing a linear narrative are *Night-blooming Cereus* (1952), an opera libretto about a group of people who gather at the home of Mrs Brown to watch the centenarial blooming of an enormous flower;[18] *The Sun and the Moon* (1958), which depicts the struggle for the spirit of a small community between the Reverend Kingbird and the "abortionist of the body and mind," Mrs Shade; *The Killdeer* (1960),[19] about the efforts of Harry and Rebecca to rescue the backward Eli from Madam Fay; *The Easter Egg* (1962), about another struggle for a spirit, this time between Polly and Bethel over the backward Kenneth; and *Three Desks* (1967), in which Edward, a new teacher, is caught between the struggle of two older teachers, Niles and Jacob.

Clearly, these plays are closer to Eliot's verse drama than are the cyclical narratives. However, in contrast to Eliot's urban settings, each of Reaney's early plays has a rural or small-town setting – with the possible exception of *Three Desks*, the last of this group, which takes place at "a small liberal arts college somewhere in Canada" (95).[20] Accordingly, Reaney's plays seem generally less urbane than Eliot's, but this difference is contingent not merely on the settings. To look at it another way, both Eliot's and Reaney's poetic dramas offer versions of the comedy of spiritual order, but with an important difference. Eliot used ancient Greek models such as *Oedipus at Colonus*, *Eumenides*, or *Alcestis*; consequently, each of his plays follows a pattern whereby a central adult character undergoes a spiritual transformation as a consequence of increased sophistication and maturity; this in turn results in the character's detachment from his and our world. By contrast, Reaney's verse plays are closer to the romance genre. As Brian Parker explains, they "usually involve a situation in which a sensitive child, or child-like man, has his maturity threatened on the one hand by a stifling provincialism and on the other by perversions of his own creativity, both sexual and imaginative" (*Masks*, 280). The spiritual transformation, in approaching true, not perverse maturity, demands a recovery of something from the pre-corrupted state; it needs "the ceremony of innocence." Naturally, an urban setting, with its inherent sophistication, is more appropriate to the first pattern than the second, and this difference in ethos results in substantial differences in the manner whereby revelation is presented in the respective plays.

The schematic arrangement of Reaney's early plays also shares with Eliot's work the use of groups of characters to articulate specific moral forces. We may say of Reaney what Frye said of William Blake; he is "so conscious of the shape of his central myth that his characters become almost diagrammatic" (*Fearful Symmetry*, 143). The struggle between good and evil forces in Reaney's plays is plain, as even the brief descriptions above show. Nevertheless, those critics who have only perceived that "all the characters symbolize either the good or the evil" (Barr, 78) have been reading or attending the plays rather narrowly.[21] At even a superficial level the observation is incorrect in that it omits the all-important third group, the potential proselytes who may be won over to one side or the other. As J. Stewart Reaney points out, "tension in [Reaney's] drama arises not so much in the conflict between the two camps – which is frequently left unresolved – but rather in the doubts and confusions of the characters in the middle" (90).

In any case, our reading should not be limited to moral exegesis but should include at least three perspectives. There is the obvious perspective in which the drama is seen as a battle for social power between two camps with some characters left in the middle; there is the symbolic perpective, in which this battle is seen as a manifestation of an apocalyptic struggle; and then there is the psychological perspective, concentrated on the the potential proselytes, and in which the battle is seen as an inner struggle. We see the analogy with Blake here, in that the literal action of Blake's Prophecies operates with almost comic-booklike simplicity, yet their significance lies in the conduit suggested between the anagogic and the individual imagination.

To be sure, Reaney's work is not so explicitly allegorical as Blake's. Rather, Reaney follows Eliot in attempting to telescope an entire moral cosmos into a narrow quotidian domain. In Frye's terminology, the myth is "displaced" (*Anatomy*, 136–8) so that the demands of apocalyptic imagination are kept more or less tethered to the limits of plausibility. When less tethered, this can result in a certain amount of confusion; the suggestion in *The Easter Egg*, for example, that George feels obliged to marry Bethel because he has killed a bat (62) is exasperating if one is trying to understand the play in terms of ordinary, realistic motivation. Stranger things have happened, but this surreal event is presented with a seemingly blithe air of normality that is discomfiting to an unsuspecting audience.

With regard to this mixture of reality and fantasy, J. Stewart Reaney argues that his father "strives to unite his Gothic vision of life *and* his optimism into the mood of the Romance," adding that "the nature of Romance permits a story like *The Killdeer*, composed of tempests and calms, separation and escape, magic and spectacle, to patiently find its own form" (17). It may be that the younger Reaney overestimates the indulgence of romance. Indeed, one of the perennial problems with romance is its tendency towards entropy when transferred from its prose prototypes to its stage versions.[22] That particular difficulty has not been overcome in Reaney's early plays, however successful they are in other respects. An exception is the opera, *Night-blooming Cereus*, which is one of the most successful of Reaney's early works, perhaps because it shares with that short masterpiece, Gian Carlo Menotti's *The Medium*, an appealingly compact plot revolving around a central event of discrete yet vital significance to each member of the dramatis personae. Unfortunately, *Night-blooming Cereus* is alone in its remarkable cohesion. One complaint levelled at the early plays is that they begin promisingly with a strong satirical bent but veer sharply into mystical romance, thereby confusing, or losing, the audience (Dudek, 19).[23] Another criticism has it that they forfeit a sense of epiphany because "the fragments of the action fly irretrievably apart and the playwright, having lost control, takes refuge in a kind of coy whimsy" (Tait, 135).

The difficulty of making the romance cohere in Reaney's plays has something to do with the problem of reconciling the earnestness of his lofty moral aspirations with an ironic, even cynical awareness of the mind-set of the modern age. In his poetry Reaney's personal means of reconciliation is through the imaginative cosmos Alvin Lee calls "Reaneyland" (124). Having switched to drama, however, Reaney needed to find a way of persuasively conveying the precepts of Reaney-land within a mimesis of a particular situation. The task of his poetic theatre was that "special integrative, or constructive, act of poetry" whereby, according to Earl Wassermann, the "dramatic" follows the "lyric" – "not only [to] realize a special cosmos but also [to open] the opportunity for further conceptual discoveries in that cosmos" (10). Reaney's specific solution in the early plays is to satirize a social mind-set he views as perverse, then to introduce special loci, containing embryonic insights that can in time inspire the redemption of the society with a general revelation based in the creative innocence of his central myth. Indeed, the narrative structure usually follows just that order.

Yet, while romance often takes a critical stance towards one society by comparing it with another (e.g., *The Winter's Tale*, where oppressive Sicilia is left for liberal Bohemia, then vice versa), Reaney, as we said, declines to dislocate his characters in order to facilitate their romantic passage. The perverted world satirized by Reaney is therefore not materially any different from the idyllic world he exalts. The small-town southwestern Ontario society is never dismissed out of hand; rather, the plays promote a change of attitude towards what is valuable within that society. Hence, the central myth is usually depicted as a passage of the potential proselytes from one relationship (or alliance) to another among the schematically arranged groups of characters. The allegorical function of these groups is like a set of poetic vectors, suggesting imaginative forces rather than representing individual entities.

The most potent means of conveying poetic meaning in these early plays, as the verse leads us to expect, is language, Reaney drawing heavily on the skills he acquired as a poet. Indeed, in *One-Man Masque* he has a foot in each camp; more staged poem than poetic drama, it is the play most dependent on verse. Yet it is atypical of Reaney's dramatic language of this period. Usually Reaney eschewed the more sophisticated prosody that characterized his poetry, preferring to write dramatic verse in the classic English metre: the simple four-stress line that compromises between the rhythms of ordinary speech and metrical regularity, permitting fluid transitions from conversational to heightened language. The regular four-stress rhythm controls the tempo, maintaining a discreet musical quality in the speech, from which sudden poetic effects are launched. A fine example is Ira's recollection, in *The Easter Egg*, of a childhood epiphany – his glimpse of the clouds of glory Kenneth trails, so to speak:

When my brother was still alive, we as students
Went with butterfly nets to the woods
Around the Big Pond. Kenneth, Kenneth,
I looked up to see what my brother saw;
It was you. At five years old. Stark naked.
Out of a silk scarf of your mother's you'd
Made a turban. That was all your dress.
While your parents had their afternoon nap
You escaped from this house, ran naked,
Through the sleeping village, the meadow,
Naked through the forest – just for fun.
You saw us. You stopped. A naked child
With all green light and sun streams about you.
You turned and vanished. I'll take that.
So far as I see that's what it all means.
And that naked innocent who gave me God
Is still lost in the forest and I shall bring him
Back to the friends who love him.   (16)

The power of this passage depends to no small degree on its rhythms. The delightful shock of Kenneth's uninhibited ecstasy is thrice emphasized with a late caesura setting off the double-stressed "stark naked," "ran naked," and "naked child." In "Out of a silk scarf of your mother's you'd / Made a turban," enjambment defers the surprise. In "Through the sleeping village, the meadow, / Naked through the forest – just for fun"; or in "With all green light and sun streams about you.

/ You turned and vanished. I'll take that" the more regular rhythms work together with the disruptions to create an ebb and flow that imitate Ira's own alternate recollection of rapture and present effort to capture the wonder in a few words.

So Reaney's dramatic verse builds anticipation through rhythm in order to disrupt it creatively; but it sometimes has another function, which we might call incantatory. In these cases the verse rhythms detach a scene from the ordinary world in order to evoke a supernatural significance. In the first scene of *The Killdeer*, for example, this makes the difference between an Avon Lady calling upon a housewife merely because she wants to sell her some make-up, and Evil calling upon Complacency in order to court her into an alliance with the Forces of Darkness. To be sure, the effect created by the verse is not quite so obvious as that; it suggests rather than declares, merely nudging the audience's imagination in the direction of allegory.

A similar function is apparent in Reaney's use of devices such as stichomythia. A good, extended example of this is the scene (II.3) between Mrs Soper, the jailer's wife, and Harry in the 1960 version of *The Killdeer*. At times the mesmerizing to-and-fro evokes the ritualistic aura of a catechism:

MRS S: You know what I am thinking. How?
HARRY: It's the important thing. You – the jailer's wife.
MRS S: The jailer's wife is the jailer when the jailer's away.
HARRY: The important thing is what are you like?
MRS S: The jailer's wife is like this. Wife to a bunch of keys.
HARRY: Wife to a bunch of keys. What's that one for?
MRS S: Her cell on the second floor. And this one –
HARRY: That looks like the father of the other keys.
MRS S: It's the key to the great gates of the courtyard.
HARRY: Still – what *is* the jailer's wife like?
MRS S: She hates the bunch of keys. Hates shutting up people.
HARRY: Hates the bunch of keys. Hates shutting up people.
MRS S: Hates the lust that locks a soul in a jail of mud.
HARRY: Hates the key that locks us in a life.
MRS S: And still she's a jailer's wife and has his children.

(*The Killdeer and Other Plays*, 38–9)

Here the dialogue drifts somewhat from the usual four-stress metre, for that is less important at the moment than the rhythms of word repetition – appearing here in the devices formally known as anaphora, anadiplosis, and ploce.[24] The repetitions imply an almost mantra-like insistence, as if drilling through to an unconscious layer of thought more personally honest and more spiritually truthful than the so-called "rationality" that has put Mrs Soper in her unnatural and unhappy occupation.

A variation of this incantatory function is found in the dithyrambic speech that occasionally emerges. One of the most interesting examples of this (perhaps because it is one of the weirdest) occurs in the scene between Mrs Budge and Mrs Delta at the top of act 2 in *The Killdeer*. The scene opens with Mrs Budge in a peculiar state of passionate inspiration:

> MRS BUDGE: Oh the river of time, the river of time.
> The clouds of moments, the clouds of moments,
> Clouds of escaping birds from the dark barn:
> I grab here, I grab there, birds you escape me.
> The wind of the hours, the wind of the hours,
> The snow of the minutes, the snow of the minutes,
> It all falls into the river of time and is swept away.
> MRS DELTA: Oh the river of time, the river of time.
> MRS BUDGE: What am I to dust now?

In the original version the women are cleaning the courthouse, but Reaney later revised this to have them cleaning Mrs Gardner's cottage (*Killdeer*, 30; *Masks*, 233). In this respect, at least, the original version has a slight edge; it seems somehow more appropriate and certainly more meaningful that Mrs Budge should suddenly find herself bursting into inspired lyricism in an empty place of institutional authority than in an ordinary living room.

In any case, it is not clear from the text what exactly is going on here. There is a dithyrambic outburst from Mrs Budge, which Mrs Delta attempts to join before finding herself rebuffed (so it would seem). There is no indication of a naturalistic context that would justify this fairly wild use of poetic imagery. Mrs Budge has found herself dislodged from her ordinary attitude to life by the drama unfolding around her. In this speech she glimpses, fleetingly, a fuller spirituality, a life of imagination and creativity rather than narrowness and conformity. Nevertheless, she is unwilling to share this insight with Mrs Delta, so what is needed theatrically is for Mrs Budge to be swept up in a dervishlike ecstasy, only to plummet again self-consciously to reality.

There is little indication of how this scene should be staged. One might decide to do it with Mrs Budge launching from quiet humming into a full-scale song-and-dance routine – a flamboyant theatrical trope commensurate with the extravagantly imagistic language – but there are no such directions. Here we see one of the chief differences between Reaney's early and his late work. In the later plays he would likely have come up with a theatrical trope first, then found the appropriate dramatic language. In the early plays, however, the action seldom generates the same level of excitement as the language. It may be that the structural disunity some complain of in the early plays is a sign that Reaney's imagination was struggling to accommodate itself to too restrictive a theatrical form.

Yet the seeds of the form that Reaney eventually developed are evident in these early plays. The imagery of the poetry becomes the opsis of the stage through an actual physicalization of the "objective correlative." In the later plays, this technique assumes a more extravagant shape, but in the early plays it is generally used to create a theatrical "epiphany" (of the Joycean variety) at the point that Reaney Jr called the "revelation" in the linear structure. Earlier, I mentioned that the differences in ethos between Eliot's plays and Reaney's result in a difference in the presentation of this "revelation." In Eliot's work the central moment of his protagonist's spiritual awakening is dramatically presented as a suspension of time (a point that will be revisited in the chapter on Michael Cook). But in Reaney's verse plays the revelation usually becomes centred on a particular object in which the history of the characters is symbolically inherent. The point of thematic "revelation" is therefore often presented as the revelation of this object, which in turn becomes catalyst for a sudden metamorphosis in one or more of the characters.

This technique of concentrating symbolic value in a central prop may be called "talismanic symbolism," a term reflecting the quasi-mythological powers with which Reaney has endued these objects. The talisman is often eponymous, as in *The Killdeer*, *The Easter Egg*, or *Night-blooming Cereus*. For example, a killdeer elicits a sudden confession from Madam Fay at the climactic trial; a glass Easter egg suddenly releases Kenneth from the mute state he has been in since childhood. In both cases the talisman is a repository of a particular childhood memory, analogous to what psychologists call an "eidetic image" – that is, a memory from childhood that is of central importance to the individual's personality and so is unusually vivid (see Haber, 36–44).

The egg and the killdeer, as well as Reverend Kingbird's diary in *The Sun and the Moon* and Jacob Waterman's son's exam paper in *Three Desks*, are also analogous to the voodoo talisman discussed by Frazer in *The Golden Bough*. Each is a personal item through which the possessor holds power over the owner; the latter two objects clearly have a practical application for a blackmailer (like Poe's purloined letter), but all four items serve a similar function. In the theories of Jacques Lacan they would be identified with the "lost phallus," that is, "a copula [...], even, one might say, the hyphen in the evanescence of its erection [...], the signifier par excellence of the impossible identity" (cited in Lemaire, 86, 145).

The night-blooming cereus functions rather differently as a symbol in that it is not a private item (though technically it belongs to Mrs Brown) and each character has his or her own connection with it. In this respect the flower is an icon in the pre-Piercean sense: a material thing that both represents and serves as the locus of religious experience. It also has its *own* process of transformation, and it is with this *process* that the metamorphoses of the characters (and implicitly their community) are associated. It is as if the myth of the Phoenix merged with the story of *Brigadoon*, so that the miraculous reawakening of the latter depended on the transformation of the former. Thus, the night-blooming cereus has the opposite function of a scapegoat in that, rather than fixing all their blame on a symbol that is driven out of their society, the characters fix all their hopes on a symbol that is integrated into their society.

Of course, the eponymous symbol of *Night-blooming Cereus* must be set apart from the symbols of the other early plays by simple virtue of its enormous size and consequent theatricality. Nowhere else (except, perhaps, *One-Man Masque*) is a visual trope foregrounded to this extent. The essential difference is that the opening of the cereus is inherently an instance of the sublime, whereas the other objects are carefully integrated into the context of ordinary life, sharing the magnitude and ontology of other objects in the play. Kenneth's glass Easter egg, for example, exists on the same level and is presumably about the same size as the cutlery he plays with. Similarly, the diary could have been just another book on the shelf, the exam any paper in the desk; the killdeer (to stretch a point) might have lain dead among the debris Mrs Budge and Mrs Delta sweep up. These symbols are all made extraordinary by what the characters *say* about them; their centrality is determined solely through verbal syntax.

I am conscious of the redundancy of the phrase "verbal syntax," but I use it in order to introduce the notion of another sort of syntax. Poetic concepts such as syntax and diction are not made obsolete when the "poetic" is amplified to that plastic expression of poetry that Jean Cocteau found in theatrical symbolism; such verbal concepts may also be expanded to apply to other media, and thus to embrace a fuller theatrical context of meaning for the individual symbol. As it happened, Reaney's realization of the advantages of expanding his symbolism in this way took place in his home town, at the Stratford Festival:

Cocteau is right when he says that theatrical metaphor is like lace; when the big reading image of Richard III came up – bluebottle, spider in a bottle, or whatever – it just whizzed by in a second, hardly noticed. On the page I used to linger over it. In the Alec Guiness–Tyrone Guthrie production, what one was thrilled by was the larger design around all the scores of metaphors – a malignant shape in the centre of a circle eventually and suddenly banished after bending the circle for a long time in whatever way it pleased.   (Anthony, 144)

The analogy may be slightly muddled (what Cocteau actually said was that whereas ordinary written poetry was like lace, poetry of the theatre should be like the rigging of a ship),[25] but Reaney accurately captures the spirit of Cocteau's argument. And he began gradually to integrate this approach to poetic theatre with his own Romantic Modernism.

An early version of this approach may be seen in the one "cyclical" work for the stage from this period, One-Man Masque (1960), which is a sort of ur-Colours in the Dark. Here the author is almost literally inside a playbox: alone with his toys, his words, and his imagination. Theatrically, the play is almost purely a succession of talismanic symbols, for it is a staged series of epiphanic poems, with the focal images of the poems transferred from the verbal realm to a series of props on stage. In this sense One-Man Masque belongs with Beckett's Act without Words and Cocteau's Les Mariés de la Tour Eiffel, which were also based on the interaction between the protagonists and a symbolic sequence of props. However, whereas those earlier plays centred on a series of images presented externally to the character for his response, the poet/performer of One-Man Masque makes his own choices, and thus seems to have some comprehensive grasp of, if not control over, his own destiny.

Jay Macpherson's analysis of the symbolic structure of this play cannot be surpassed, so I will ride on her coattails. She demonstrates that the "circular vision" J. Stewart Reaney pointed out in One-Man Masque (as well as Colours in the Dark and A Suit of Nettles – to which ranks the Performance Poems must now be joined), is in part derived from the mandalas Frye used to describe the shape of literature as a whole. MacPherson suggests of One-Man Masque that "in imaginatively exploiting Frye's two grammars of poetic myth [i.e., Fearful Symmetry and Anatomy of Criticism] it also bridges them" (96). In other words, the wheel of Blake's central myth, the revolution that moves from one world to another (i.e., Luvah, Tharmas, Urizen and Los), is axled to Anatomy's wheel of generic cycles (i.e., romance, tragedy, irony, and comedy). In the context of this elaborate mandala the protagonist makes a personal journey from innocence, to experience, to enlightenment.

Of immediate interest to our discussion is the theatrical execution of this idea, which consists in a sort of counterpoint between the cycle of eight lyrics forming the textual core of *One-Man Masque* and the circle of props among which the poet/performer moves over the course of the play. These props include such traditionally allusive items as a ladder and a spinning-wheel – "items with which one can construct perhaps the most basic Fryekit do-it-yourself can-opener," says MacPherson, as well as less conventionally portentous items such as a cardboard box. (That, however, placed opposite a coffin on the circle and making the link to a cradle, morbidly recalls Reaney's short story "The Box Social.") The poetic ordering of words that creates the mythic cycle is complemented by the poetic ordering of props that creates the circle on the stage. Through an interplay between verbal and plastic symbols Reaney's vision is gradually revealed, with the physical cycle of props and the narrative cycle of lyrics meshing in a clockwork of epiphanies.

In the centre of the circle of props are two mannequins, a male and a female. In part they represent sexuality, the yin and yang necessary to set the whole system of various cycles in motion. But a further significance emerges in a stage direction at the close of the play: "The speaker lifts the tray of lighted candles up and puts them on his head. The two mannequins float up and disappear" (193). Reaney confirms this indicates that they have been enlightened (see "An Evening with Babble and Doodle"). Indeed, without the image, the evangelical section of his central myth would have been left unrepresented. The image essentially bespeaks Reaney's optimism about the effect he might have on his audience. With his children's plays he necessarily began to confront that interest much more directly, for, as anyone who has ever performed for children can attest, the question of whether one is having one's desired effect on the audience is answered immediately, unmistakably and volubly.

THE CHILDREN'S PLAYS

Reaney's first play for children was *Names and Nicknames* (1963), commissioned for the Manitoba Theatre Centre by the late John Hirsch. Hirsch was a fortunate director *cum* midwife for Reaney in that he shared so many of the playwright's preoccupations with myths and archetypes, as well as an interest in children's entertainment and a related belief in the power of theatre to educate and transform.[26] One of Hirsch's favourite rehearsal techniques was to encourage (well ... *demand*) improvisation around a central image or theme, building the action up to a ritual-like precision. Often he would start with a simple game or series of gestures that would gradually be integrated into the scene at hand. This approach was based on a conviction of the indivisibility of plays and play, a conviction evident in *Names and Nicknames*. As the names Farmer and Mrs Dell suggest, the play is a theatrical elaboration of the children's game "The Farmer in the Dell." That naming game is integrated with choruses built out of an 1890s speller belonging to Reaney's father (*Names and Nicknames,* 5). The *dramatis personae* are rounded out with an alazon (a deceiving or self-deceived character who attempts to block the life-force in a comedy: see Frye, *Anatomy,* 365), Grandpa Thorntree, who tries to pervert the socially integrating process of naming.

As Reaney has acknowledged, Hirsch's workshop of *Names and Nicknames* deeply influenced his playwriting technique ("Ten Years at Play," 77). Where the Cocteauvian inference Reaney drew from the Stratford Festival encouraged an expansion of the symbolism of his poetry to the stage, the experience of workshopping a children's play with Hirsch suggested that the dramaturgical device of talismanic symbolism could be integrated into the play-making process itself. Moreover, that process could be expanded from Reaney *qua* playwright to include the cast and director and even the audience. In short, Reaney was developing nothing less than a complete philosophy of theatre.[27]

Looking back, one sees the roots of this philosophy in his theory of the imagination: making "intellectual fire" out of the Yeatsian dialectic between subjective and objective, imagination and environment, myth and document. This understanding of the poetic process is implicit in what I have been calling his central myth. The end of the myth is essentially the recovery of this process for himself and others, for the evangelical aspect of the myth demands that others should be coached through the creative journey in order that they may recover and rejuvenate their own poetic imaginations. As such, Reaney's goal is to include the widest possible group of people in the poetic process. In somewhat grandiloquent terms, Reaney wants to take the German Romantic concept of the *poeta-magus* – the intuitive interpreter of all finite things as if they were hieroglyphs and symbols representing the infinite – and democratize it to the point where everyone becomes an apprentice magus and the sleeping giant of humanity's imaginative powers awakes.[28]

Reaney's experience with Hirsch and children's theatre convinced him that making theatre was an inborn skill that could be recovered if only people would recollect childhood play. Promoting that idea became a part-time crusade for Reaney. In 1976, inaugurating an occasional theatre newsletter, *Halloween,* he explained that the title was inspired by "the one theatrical event put on in this country which doesn't seem to need directors brought in from foreign lands; it is put on by thousands who are really into their parts [...]; the audience for Halloween numbers in the millions, understands the script thoroughly even when it involves the most esoteric matter of Light's yearly fight with Darkness [...] Halloween stands for direct, sentimental, sensational primitive theatre." There is a Rousseauvian flavour to this notion that, unbound by conventions, people naturally come up with essential poetic and cultural ideas on their own. It runs in the face of a notion with equal claim to ancient provenance: the poet as shaman. Joseph Campbell argues for the latter point of view: "the ideas and poetry of the traditional cultures [...] come out of an elite experience, the experience of people particularly gifted, whose ears are open to the song of the universe [...] There is an answer from the folk, which is then received as an interaction. But the first impulse in the shaping of a folk tradition comes from above, not from below" (Campbell with Moyers, 85).[29]

Indeed, much as Reaney likes the idea of folk-driven theatre, it appears that he is not prepared to do away with the shaman. In a 1983 interview he agreed with the shaman analogy, arguing that a collective creation built without a playwright's guidance produced something more like a raft than a canoe. So, while the initial impetus for a play might come from a group of people, Reaney explained, "What you do then is try and guide things around to something that you really want to do" (MacKay, 138). Still, Reaney's accounts of various workshops he has conducted leave little doubt that, once in full swing, there emerges from most groups a considerable creative energy.[30]

This paradoxical attitude towards the creative freedom of groups is not as contradictory as it may seem, for Reaney endorses Northrop Frye's notion of "the educated imagination," the idea that a free mind requires discipline and education. (In Frye's favourite analogy, one is not free to play the piano until one has learned the keyboard; one is not free to think until one has learned to reason.) The concept shows up in some of the plays, most notably *Ignoramus* (1967), a children's play about a contest between two educational theorists, one "traditional" – Dr Hilda History (based on educational theorist Hilda Neatby: *Ignoramus,* 5), – the other "progressive" – Dr Progessaurus. Doctors Progressaurus and History each take a group of ten homeless orphans off to remote locations to be educated for a seventeen-year period, at the end of which the respective success of their methods is to be judged by the Governor General of Canada.

Reaney had already declared his attachment to pedagogical discipline years before in the July eclogue in *A Suit of Nettles,* so *Ignora-*

mus holds no surprises there: the children who are systematically educated have well-disciplined yet creative imaginations. What is interesting, however, is that Reaney has the "progressively" educated children, though starved of any real ideas or important information, inexorably and instinctively drift towards a spiritual and imaginative life through their worship of the little bird that appears on a Bon Ami can and through secret study. They are led in this by Beatrice, a young girl with a precocious intellect and ravenous curiosity, who purloins texts in order to put together a substantive curriculum subversively. Thus, even while the traditional method is demonstrated to be more effective, Reaney's refusal to abandon romantic optimism leads him, at the risk of eroding the propaganda, to provide the benighted "progressive" students with a miracle: Beatrice, a guiding spirit to lead all these little might-be Dantes to enlightenment. In short, Reaney has his cake and eats it too; shamanism and grassroots creativity work in concert to imitate the traditional pedagogical relationship he favours.

Geography Match, written later in the Centennial year,[31] also features a contest between two groups of students led by feuding educators. However, whereas *Ignoramus* was concerned with the development of the imagination according to general theories, *Geography Match* demonstrates the integration of the imagination with the Canadian environment. For example, the Iceberg Lady introduces the children to what, paradoxically, is one of the most fertile images in Canadian art and literature;[32] and Nanabozho, the Sleeping Giant of Indian mythology, makes an appearance to acquaint the children with Canada's own Finn MacCool (the Irish hero who sleeps beneath Dublin).

The children's plays initiated a change in Reaney's technique that moved him in the opposite direction from that taken by Eliot. Whereas Eliot abandoned the (London) Group Theatre's imagistic style for the *terra firma* of text-based poetic drama (see Sidnell, *Dances of Death*, chap. 4), Reaney moved from symbolic events made of language to ones made of concrete objects and action. From the early poetry on, the poetic tropes shift progressively further into the foreground, moving from verbal image to talismanic symbol to a collectively created theatrical trope, until the epiphany that was experienced by the characters in *Night-blooming Cereus* is, in the later plays, virtually placed in the laps of the audience.

This shift in symbolic technique is central to Reaney's poetics. In her 1983 interview with Reaney, Jean McKay mentions the effect of the theatrical symbolism: "A very kaleidoscopic pattern [...] pops up all over the place in your work [...] Things move in and out from regional to universal, from private to public, from personal protestant to group liturgical, and in all kinds of other ways. The thing that makes it possible for me to slow that down and grab it, is to be able to stop on the objects for a while and pant before I have to go charging off again. The objects seem to be little buoys in the sea." Reaney's reply – "The plays are probably masques, you know, masques are like that" (144) – apparently refers to the emphasis on spectacle in his later plays. But the plays resemble masques in other respects as well. In *Anatomy of Criticism* Frye writes that the masque "is usually a compliment to the audience, or an important member of it, and leads up to an idealization of the society represented by that audience [...] It thus differs from comedy in its more intimate attitude to the audience: there is more insistence on the connection between the audience and the community on stage" (287–8).

After the children's plays, such an attitude is typical of Reaney's theatre. It is apparent in the growing regionalism, aimed at educating a community about its history and its present character, which reaches its epitome in the "urban community plays." It is also apparent where the emphasis on audience participation in the children's plays begets a stronger implicit invitation to participate in the poetic creation. Audience enlightenment was merely suggested through imitation in *One-Man Masque*; in the later work it is practically demanded, for a constantly shifting symbolic context insists upon a corresponding adjustment in the imaginations of the audience. That adjustment involves a suspension of ordinary descriptive reference that Paul Ricoeur has called *epoché*, the imaginative function that allows "the projection of new possibilities of redescribing the world" and so complements and completes logic by creating "positive insight into the potentialities of our being in the world" (152–3).[33] Without such a mental shift, the concrete symbols of the later plays are simply inanimate objects and jejune nonsense. But a simple one-time suspension of disbelief will not suffice; rather, a continual metamorphic flow of meaning among the actors and the objects on the stage ensures that theatrical poesis is an ongoing and joint effort. The children's plays provided a decisive shift towards Reaney's fully developed version of poetic theatre: the "metamorphic masque."

THEATRE OF REJUVENATION

In Reaney's production notes to *Listen to the Wind* (1966), his first play for adults after *Names and Nicknames*, he writes of how the workshop process with Hirsch had drawn his attention to the connection between children's play and theatrical creation, arguing that this concept deserved a place among the major theories of the modern stage: "We've had theatre of cruelty (the rebirth of tragedy – the imitation of our death wish); we've had theatre of the absurd (the rebirth of comedy – the imitation of our bitter laughter); we've had the theatre of detachment (the rebirth of the miracle play – Mother Courage drags her cross). The one thing we never imitate enough is games, play ... imitation itself, the instinct just to 'have fun'" ... (141–2).

The three types of theatre named here correspond to three genres: Reaney names both tragedy and comedy, and (though the point is a little cloudy because all these "rebirths" belong to the ironic age), the "theatre of detachment" is apparently irony. (Had Reaney continued his rhetorical rhythm, he might have said that the "rebirth of the miracle play" was the "imitation" of cynicism or lack of faith). If this is correct, Reaney is saying that heretofore three of Frye's four genres have been reworked in the twentieth century, the fourth being romance. It comes as no surprise that Reaney places his work in that genre, but if his remarks indeed constitute a logical set, the associated parameters may be extended to create a label and a definition for Reaney's theatre – say, "Theatre of rejuvenation (the rebirth of romance – the imitation of our playfulness)." At any rate, such a label is very obviously appropriate to *Listen to the Wind* and *Colours in the Dark*.

Listen to the Wind comprises a frame story and an inner story. Owen, a sick boy whose parents are in the process of breaking up, enlists the help of three girls and some friendly adults to dramatize a favourite novel, "The Saga of Caresfoot Court." The real source of this invented novel is Rider Haggard's *Dawn*, which Reaney calls a melodrama *(Listen,* 142).[34] Reaney's enthusiasm for melodrama is unusual in our age, and may prove an obstacle for those used to thinking of melodrama as an essentially neurotic art form, one that obsessively conventionalizes "dangerous" desires rather than coming to terms with them. For example, Louis Dudek has complained that while "the parent-son relationship in the play is charged with deep feeling," he sees "a comic-parodistic effect in the counterpoint of the Victorian novel and actual life – unless Reaney is more sentimental and melodramatic in earnest than we are able to be" (23). Dudek is half right, in that earnestness is an important key to the play. But part of the problem lies in the word "melodrama" itself, which in the twentieth century has become such a casual pejorative that it requires some qualification.

Melodramas generally evoke horror and sentimentality, cousins to fear and pity, the difference being that only the latter pair lead to Aristotle's catharsis. In melodrama the conflict remains largely external rather than psychological, so melodrama is not generally regarded as spiritually restorative in the way that tragedy or romance is. Now it is undoubtedly true that *Dawn* shares many of the characteristics of stage melodrama, various dire incidents, villains and heroines. However, Reaney is careful to stress that *Dawn* "affects [him] very powerfully" in that "it guides you out of the abyss we live in"; furthermore, he emphasizes, "Owen does not find the story laughable" (142). In fact, when Owen's friend Harriet describes an incident in the story as "Terribly melodramatic," Owen replies, "What's melodramatic?" (15) So Reaney is indeed being "sentimental and melodramatic in earnest" because he is recreating melodrama from a child's reading, which moves it closer to the realm of myth. From this perspective it is evident that, however melodramatic *Dawn* may be, the recontextualization of the story in *Listen to the Wind* means that it is more properly regarded as a romance.

In her introduction to *Listen to the Wind* Jay Macpherson mentions that the play began as a treatment of the Brontë family (3), and she quotes from one of Branwell Brontë's letters in which he complains of loneliness: "Nothing to listen to except the wind" (7). While much of the Brontë inspiration remains in the play, if the imperative of Reaney's title hasn't quite that Branwellian tone of despair, it is because it comes more directly from a passage in Haggard's *Dawn*. Here the heroine, Angela, sits as a child at her mother's gravesite – quite cheerfully if pensively – and explains her yearning for spiritual contact to Reverend Fraser:

If one listens in the quiet, I always think one may hear something that other people do not hear [...] I hear things, but I cannot understand them. Listen to the wind in the branches of that tree, the chestnut, off which the leaf is falling now. It says something, if only I could catch it.   (95)

Angela's ear for the spiritual world proves to be the ruling humour of her character, and as Haggard shows – particularly through contrast with her rival, Mildred Carr – it is this that enables her to live an emotionally rewarding and psychologically complete existence.

The tension that *Listen to the Wind* maintains between the frame story and the story enacted by the children corresponds to the two different allusions invoked by the title. Whereas Angela is drawn by her spiritual yearning into a happy, hopeful ending, true love prevailing over malevolence as if guided by the angels, Branwell Brontë remains lonely and despondent, never turning his spirituality to any productive end. The contrasting fates throw their shadows across Reaney's play in that, while the imaginary story under the control of Owen and his friends ends as Angela's does, in the material world of Owen's home life the tragedy of cheated hopes wins out – because of all those who cannot hear the wind. Owen's mother leaves after all, unable to see or unwilling to be moved by what has enraptured her son in "The Saga of Caresfoot Court."[35]

In this way a new poetic schema is created. The theme of Angela's spirituality, so intricately developed in Haggard's novel, is brushed over lightly in the play-within-a-play and instead thrown forward on to the frame story, refocusing the theme on Owen and those who are helping him to "dream it out" (27). "Once there were four children who listened to the wind" the chorus says (17), and later, "Once there were four grownups who helped the children listen to the wind" (25). This split of the story into four central characters and four mentors is complemented by the imagery of the four winds. The North Wind brings evil in the form of Geraldine Eldred and her doll (17); the South Wind brings Devil Caresfoot, Spring and Summer (43–4); the East Wind brings darkness, foreboding, and Owen's sickness (108); and the West Wind brings Arthur back to his love Angela and also brings the Evening Star (137). There is also a Night Wind, which is associated with imagination, childhood memories, and eternity (84). As the four points of the compass have already been spoken for, this Night Wind evidently blows from straight above. That sounds bizarre, but help is offered in something Reaney had said a few years earlier: "there is a rule in literature which says that to any tea party, or gathering of any sort, the Four Living Creatures of Ezekiel's vision attend" ("An Evening With Babble and Doodle," 39). Those four creatures Ezekiel sees (*Ezek. 1*) are really the sedan-bearers to Jehovah himself. So when, in the short scene called "The Night Wind Speaks," Owen tells us that "Four chairs can be anything. They can be the pigkeeper's hut by a stream in the forest whose leaves are beloved by the night wind" (84), he echoes Reaney's evangelistic idea that correct understanding belongs to the imagination, which reveals through metaphor that all things are one in God.[36]

In other words, the process of imagining and creating seen in Reaney/Owen's theatrical technique is a form of religious experience, as the following passage hints:

JENNY: Doesn't it sometimes frighten you ... How much we know about Caresfoot Court and no one else does.
OWEN: Last night I dreamt I was at Caresfoot Court. I was Arthur ... I'd got locked in the yards at the back where the dogs are kept and I couldn't get out. I woke up thinking why couldn't I have been a normal person instead of always dreaming it out. Always listening to the wind.
ANN: I worship the world we make up stories about. I can never stop

thinking about new things for Geraldine to say and do. It's idolatry ... And yet I can't live without it ... Without dreaming it out.

HARRIET: I don't feel guilty. The wind we listen to blows white sails to ...

CHORUS: Eternity ...   (88)

Evidently Owen's unhappy state is, at least in part, a condition of being in a world indifferent to matters spiritual. This becomes a kind of test of the audience, who are offered the loaded choice of being sympathetic to the workings of Owen/Reaney's imagination or being insensitive clods allied with Mrs Taylor/Lady Eldred's cold indifference. Needless to say, this is not the sort of test that appeals universally. Dudek's comments show that, faced with the ultimatum of either "going-along-with-the-spirit-of-the-thing" or being a soulless party-pooper, some simply choose to poop that much more truculently.

In any case, the important point here is Reaney's attempt to provide the audience with an experience that is commensurate with Owen's. With the spirituality theme displaced on to the frame story, the children's approach to "The Saga of Caresfoot Court" becomes a sort of model for the audience's own relationship to Reaney's play, so the four children and the four mentors play a role much like that of the four Evangelists of the New Testament. On a more concrete level, the children actually demonstrate Reaney's symbolic ideas in their use of theatrical tropes. This works on at least three levels, each less explicit than the last. The first level shows, in a "nothing-up-my-sleeve" sort of way, how the simple objects on the stage, together with the actor's bodies and voices, become the material of the story, as in Owen's declaration that the four chairs can represent anything, including "the pigkeeper's hut by a stream in the forest." Reaney identifies this approach to theatrical tropes with the Peking Opera, where "Art is made by subtracting from reality and letting the viewer imagine or 'dream it out'" (141). The second level is the use of tropes by the characters within the story. Good examples are the maple keys that Arthur and Angela throw when running away from Douglas (82) or the candle-boats they float down the stream (85), which leave the audience to make their own connections between the maple keys, fertility, freedom, the wind, and spirit in the one case and candles, individual spirits, the river current, and the leap of faith in the other. While these symbols are not accompanied by any explicit interpretation, they are placed in an explicitly theatrical context, which tacitly invites the audience to interpret the tropes. However, the third level requires the audience to take the initiative by standing back from the story to see it from Reaney's point of view. An example is Reaney's stage direction for the last scene: as the children enter with their chairs, "Huge shadows are cast behind them. They are free in Eternity. They will never taste death again" (138). Obviously, an audience member does not have the reader's benefit of this note. Nevertheless, it is evidently Reaney's hope that the imaginations of his audience will have been sufficiently trained over the course of his play to recognize and at least intuitively understand such a trope.

All these tropes are varieties of what Charles Pierce described as "translucently iconic signs." In other words, the correspondence between signifier and signified, while neither transparent nor conventionalized, is one that may be recognized and understood under certain conditions, within a certain context. Four chairs resemble the four corners of a hut once we are told that is what they are meant to represent; similarly, maple keys and candles have a spiritual significance so long as one is looking for it; and children casting shadows may be seen as epiphanal where a pattern of tropes developed over the course of a play has prepared the audience to read the image as such. In short, these tropes are legible to the educated imagination.

Still, there are occasions where Reaney's tropes suppose an imagination educated and focused to an improbably meticulous degree. Such is the case now and then in *Colours in the Dark* (1967), where the mandalas of *One-Man Masque* are developed with a Byzantine elaborateness that undoubtedly leaves the audience, as Reaney suggests, with "that all-things-happening-at-the-same-time-galaxy-higgledy-piggledy feeling" (*Colours in the Dark*, 7). The earlier play had stitched together eight lyrics with transitional monologues to form a cycle; *Colours in the Dark* similarly draws on earlier poems, such as "The Sundogs," "The Royal Visit," "Antichrist as a Child" (all three 1949), "Granny Crack" (1959), "A Message to Winnipeg v: A Crowd" (1960), "Letters to a Small Town: Eighth Letter" (1962), and "The Dance of Death at London, Ontario" (1963) – some of which already pose a considerable challenge to the reader. These are joined by fragmented versions of the 1965 poem "Gifts" (itself a reworking of 1959's "The Yellow-Bellied Sapsucker"), which provides a sort of lyric refrain for the play, a poetic meditation on the themes of faith, imagination, and interpenetration – Blake's "world in a grain of sand" expounded.

As in *Listen to the Wind*, the story of a sick boy with an active imagination provides the frame tale for *Colours in the Dark*. This premise has the advantage of linking the agility of the childlike imagination with an urgent demand for its exercise. Ostensibly it is the child's need to "dream it out" that is the justification for all the play-making; so the conviction that brought Wallace Stevens to call metaphor "the necessary angel" emerges in the rationalized guise of poetic therapy. The story is presented as a series of flashbacks, with the sick child of the central story played by his son from the frame story – a neat way of illustrating that "the Child is father of the Man."

The plot consists, generally, of a journey from innocence to experience, marked by the numerous versions of the "ceremony of innocence" necessary to attain the mature vision that synthesizes the two states. These experiences are organized into eight sections, each labelled by colour, so that the entire light spectrum (including white and black) is covered, purple doing customary double duty for violet and indigo. (See chart.)

Each of the colour sections has a thematic subtitle (with the exception of purple, though "Dance of Death" is the principal theme there). A glance across these reveals a pattern loosely based on a child's evolving awareness of his heritage and environment. The idea of one's self as a divine creation is followed by a sense of one's self as a genealogical product; as product of social and political heritage; as product of a psychological heritage; as the product of a number of existential choices; as a product of geography; as a mortal product of time; and as a whole, living thing. There is also something of phylogeny recapitulating ontogeny in the horizontal progression of this chart, for at one point Reaney offers the stage direction: "Dimly we realize that not only are we going through the hero's life and the stories he has heard as a child, we also are going through Canada's life – glacier and forest – and the story of the world" (30).

Looking down through the columns, we notice that the connections among the various items on the list are usually, although not invariably, apparent.[37] In the first column, for example, which comprises the clearest group of symbols, white is pure light, from which all colours proceed; hence it represents Holy light and eternity; Bible Sal represents the life pervaded by religiosity; Sunday is the first day of the week and the Christian Sabbath, set aside for worship of the Creator; Alpha is the beginning of the Greek alphabet, associated with the beginning of all things; the White Trillium is the flower of Ontario, Reaney's home province, his personal place of origin; the significance of the harmonium is slightly less clear, but it contains the melodic spectrum, is associated with churches, and is also an antique instrument; the Sun is the source of all light and life; "Shall We Gather at the River" refers to the rite of baptism, the beginning of religious life; and "Big Rock Candy Mountain" is an anagogic folksong imagining a kind of paradise.

Glancing across the "harmonium" row, we find that not every column has an item in that row and that those items that do appear are incommensurable. Possibly these items have an idiosyncratic significance outside the schema, but in any case, while the scheme is

Colours in the Dark: Motif Chart

Colour	Subtitle	Day	Letter	Flower	Special symbol	Astral body	Religious song	Secular song
White	Bible Sal	Sunday	Alpha	White Trillium	Harmonium	Sun	Shall We Gather at the River	Big Rock Candy Mountain
Red	Ancestral	Monday	BCDE	Red Zinnia	Ancestors	Moon	Psalm	Won't You Buy My Pretty Flowers
Orange	Parade & Visit	Tuesday	FGHI	Orange Lily		Mercury	Beulah Land	Lillibullero
Yellow	Antichrist Child	Wednesday	JKLM	Sunflower	Swallowtail Butterfly	Venus	Beckwith's "Hymn"	Mendelssohn's "On the Wings of Song"
Green	Various Fragments	Thursday	NOPQ	Jack-in-the-Pulpit		Mars	Willson's hymns	Japanese Sandman
Blue	Winnipeg Sketches	Friday	RSTU	Chicory		Saturn	Doukhobor hymn	Pierre Falcon's "Chanson"
Purple	[Dance of Death]	Saturday	VWXY	Wild Aster	Halloween	Jupiter		
Black	Recovery	Some day	Omega	Indian Pipes	Z	Earth		

Reaney's, the chart is not, so its lack of tidiness is no rebuke to him. It gives some idea, however, of the difficulties inherent in making sense of the elaborate patterns in *Colours in the Dark*. Such an encyclopaedic array of themes and symbols could not be comprehended by any one person's viewing of a single performance – which raises the question of exactly how (and if) all these poetic architectonics are functioning. One answer lies in a remark made by Branwell, the central character in *A Suit of Nettles*, in reply to Effie's parable of the door and knob in the March eclogue:

> The meaning's felt often before it's seen
> My heart knows what my rusted mind does not.
> Thank you, Effie. Such moments have I sought
> When I might smile or pick at such a knot
> As logic fingers could not ravel out at once.   (16)[38]

Colours in the Dark presents organized experience, then, with the idea that an opportunity to sense and discover truths is valuable even where the process itself is not fully comprehensible.

Whether or not this supposition is justified remains an open question. Reaney often uses the stage direction "dimly we are aware ..." to draw attention to an idea in his text that is important but that he would like to be subordinated to the dominant motif of the moment. It may be helpful to think of this as essentially a variation of the "isotopy" concept – Gerard Manley Hopkins's separation of poetic meaning into "overthought" and "underthought." "Overthought" is the surface pattern that is apparent to everybody; "underthought" is the location of the more important meaning that may not be lucidly understood by even the poet himself, but is revealed through the interplay of tropes. Reaney has created a surface that initially appeals to "overthought" but leads the audience to discover the "underthought" on their own. Again, this process harks back to the dialectic of primary and antithetical states of consciousness that Reaney shares with Yeats. Reaney is attempting to recreate for the stage a sensation occasionally found in life, one he described in "To the Secret City: From a Winnipeg Sketchbook":

Every once in a while you catch ordinary experience turning into artistic experience. At just the right moment so far as meaning is concerned there is a low mutter of thunder [...] As the images flew thick and fast of birth, dying, rebirth, the bridge, heaven, hell, the three old women, the two rocking chairs, one became aware of some other world behind this world of appearances, a world that if you asked it enough questions sometimes revealed for a few moments its possible golden order to you as it had to me [...] Beneath [this city's] *mask* of disorder and disconnection there lay somewhere a poetic city, a possible New Jerusalem, sometimes breaking through to whatever part of one's mind catches such messages. (175-7)

Colours in the Dark captures this sense and thereby turns the stage into a place of layered symbolism, images spread across it in a pattern that may be glimpsed only in parts, flashes of significance and interconnectedness encouraging the individual to search and discover meaning for himself. In effect it is a representation of Reaney's imagination within which the viewer is invited to play.

THE DONNELLYS TRILOGY

The reconceptualization of the theatre in Reaney's work reached a new plateau with his next major work for the stage, *The Donnellys* trilogy (1973-75), which undoubtedly stands as one of the greatest accomplishments in Canadian drama. Audiences arriving for the première of *Sticks and Stones* by the NDWT company at Toronto's Tarragon Theatre found the dark walls surrounding them covered with chalked inscriptions in Reaney's own handwriting – phrases and key words from the script, it gradually emerged.[39] These effectively created a collective memory for the audience, substituting theatrical environment for cultural tradition, so that as the play unfolded there was experienced a kind of *déjà vu* (or perhaps *déjà entendu*). Reaney may have borrowed the idea from one of his own early plays, *The Easter Egg* (1962), where Polly, in her attempt to penetrate Kenneth's hysterical semi-autistic state, is said to have "made a list of all the words / He uses and taught him to write them / In chalk all over the walls of his room" (12). In both versions the chalked words act as touchstones for liminal experience, helping to maintain a connection between two worlds by functioning in both. For Kenneth, however, they reinforce his grip on the real world; for the spectator of *Sticks and Stones* they intensify a connection with the world of Reaney's imagination.

The technique was further amplified over the course of the three years during which the trilogy was premièred, for in the second and third plays, key events, gestures, and words were repeated from the preceding instalments. At one point in *Handcuffs* a full scene from *Sticks and Stones* is repeated verbatim, and Reaney writes: "The audience should now begin to grasp the structure of the play and experience a 'double' feeling about the next events. The sewing machine should help us transfer our mind back to the earlier shebeen scenes" (241). Apparently the technique was effective, for the critic Urjo

Kareda reported that such repetitions sent "a ripple of recall through the audience" ("Donnellys," 181).

The story of the Donnelly family is a vehicle well suited to achieving such effects because of the recurring pattern of moral struggle inherent in their history. Jim Donnelly and his family had been labelled "Blackfeet" in Ireland in the mid-nineteenth century because they refused to co-operate with the "Whitefeet" terrorists who were burning Protestant landowners and their families alive in their beds. When they moved to Biddulph Township in Ontario, the "black and white" feud was revived among their neighbours and sustained over the next thirty-three years until, finally, the Donnelly family met with the very fate they had refused to inflict on others.

In rough outline the story resembles the Icelandic tale *Njal's Saga*, also about a long, complicated feud with broad cultural implications, culminating in a family's being burnt to death in their own home. *Njal's Saga* is probably Iceland's most important work of literature because it identifies the national character in a powerful manner, linking the emergence of a stable social and political structure with a sort of Christian Passion. The similar potential of the Donnelly story was bound to be noticed sooner or later, and in the heady days of the fervent nationalism sweeping the Canadian artistic community in the late sixties and early seventies, it suddenly attracted a remarkable amount of interest. Denis Johnston, in his history of Toronto theatre in this period, mentions no fewer than four dramatic versions of the Donnelly story in 1973–74 alone: Reaney's *Sticks and Stones*; Theatre Passe Muraille's collective *Them Donnellys*; Peter Colley's *The Donnellys* at Theatre London; and an unnamed production at Trent University (*Up the Mainstream*, 126–7).

For Reaney the Donnellys' story was an auspicious subject for several reasons: first, the story was set in his beloved home turf of Souwesto; second, the Donnellys were identifiable (on a larger scale) with the romantic anti-heroes of his earlier work who fight against an unjust and philistine society; and third, the story was set far enough back in time to be, in terms of the comparatively short span of the history of Canada, part of the primordium of the nation's social development (like *Njal's Saga*) while still recent enough to compel identification with the Souwesto of today. In short, this was a subject that would allow all the most characteristic elements of Reaney's poetics – the romantic central myth, the militant regionalism, the juxtaposition of myth and document, the invocation of a larger moral cosmos – to work to optimum effect. What had been so personal and apparently idiosyncratic in his earlier work could assume, in this context, the shape of a mythically resonant, socially defining, major historical epic.

Reaney found opportunities to expand the story's mythic dimensions in the folk culture that the Donnellys would have known. The trilogy begins with a version of the folk ballad "John Barleycorn Must Die," a song about making whiskey that fastens on the cyclical process of life, death and reconstitution (metaphorically a resurrection) undergone by the barley grain. The ballad resembles the Adonis myth as discussed by James Frazer, wherein the vegetative cycle on which life depends is echoed in the story of a beloved god who grows to maturity only to be sacrificed for the good of society, then rises again in a different incarnation to repeat the cycle (*The Golden Bough*, chaps. 29–50). The ballad becomes a refrain in the play, laying the groundwork for the principal poetic argument of the whole trilogy: the spirit of the Donnellys is virtually a force of nature, Promethean in its persistence and its power of revolution. As Reaney says in his forward to *Handcuffs*, "it's hard to handcuff wheat" (187). Will Donnelly's lameness, called "a badge of [God's] favour" (37), is also integrated into this theme, suggesting something of the earthbound role of the god of a vegetative-based cult (see Graves, *The White Goddess*, chap.18).

The theme of a resilient spiritual cycle is further expanded with allusions to the best-known version of the Adonis cult: Christianity. The Roman Catholic catechism is revised to suit the heterodox religion into which the Donnellys have been thrust. Beset with repressive social forces, family becomes the venerated institution: for the Donnellys, mother, father, and brothers are "the sacraments that can only be received once" (84).

Even more significant, albeit less explicit, is the imagery of a speech near the end of *Sticks and Stones* that responds to the choral question "Why was I a Donnelly?" The speech is nominally assigned to Jennie, but its importance extends far beyond any personal utterance. Its rhetorical power, its distribution among the chorus, its dramatic function (it ends the first part with a clear choice of destiny), and its ambivalent time-setting – simultaneously, the time when Jennie's parents were still alive, her remembrance of them after their deaths, and the present theatrical time – all this establishes the speech as the credo not just of the Donnelly family but of Reaney's trilogy itself, of the Donnellys as the spirit of defiant assertion of right in the face of wrong, however powerful:

Because from the courts of Heaven when you're there you will see that however the ladders and sticks and stones caught you and bruised you and smashed you, and the bakers and brewers forced you to work for them for nothing, from the eye of God in which you will someday walk you will see [...] that once, long before you were born, *sometimes together, sometimes solo* you chose to be a Donnelly and laughed at what it would mean, the proud woman put to milking cows, the genius trotting around with a stallion, the old sword rusted into a turnip knife. You laughed and lay down with your fate like a bride, even the miserable fire of it. So that I am proud to be a Donnelly against all the contempt of the world. I am proud that my mother confirmed my brother in the forest with the fiddle, long before the bishop and the friar could get hold of him, and I wish now I had shared my mother's fate beside her. *solo* But oh, still would it have [had?] been different. I loved my mother and I nearly saved her even three days before they burnt her with their coal oil.

Because you were tall; you were different / and you weren't afraid, that is why they burnt you first with their tongues / then with their kerosene.   (93)

Here the John Barleycorn imagery ("bruised and smashed," "bakers and brewers") is integrated with biblical imagery, particularly the psalmic reference to walking in "the eye of God"; and the image of the Donnellys' earthly fate as a "bride" recalls the metaphor of Christ as the bridegroom divinely chosen for the symbolically female city of men (e.g., Rev. 21:3). There is also the parodic confirmation of Will with a fiddle, a symbol of the Donnellys' commitment to the expressive soul; and, in the final elegiac paragraph, a recollection of the revilement and crucifixion stages of the Passion.

True to Reaney's poetics, the mythic elements of *The Donnellys* resonate with the historical. Where the mythical figures are caught between the oppositions of heaven and earth, immortality and death, the material world provides support with a whole series of opposing forces that, within the overall poetic pattern, are shown to "rhyme" (so to speak). So, for example, the Blackfeet-Whitefeet, Grit-Tory, and Protestant-Catholic oppositions find echoes in concession roads segregated by faith and in the images of the narrow farmland and the rows of corn. In Reaney's romantic ethic these various historical delineations create a kind of vise of conformity that threatens to crush the spirit of the Donnellys.

As I mentioned earlier, *Sticks and Stones* identifies the literal narrowness of the Donnellys' farm-lot with the pressure on them to conform to socially acceptable norms. The most innovative aspect of this conceit is the manner in which Reaney gradually impresses the identification of historical and imaginative forces on the audience by means of theatrical tropes. In each of the three dramas, those tropes depend upon a complex of poetic imagery drawn from children's play, and thus invite the audience to give free "play" to its own unfettered, childlike imagination.

In the first play there are the eponymous sticks and stones. The obvious reference is to the child's defensive taunt, but Reaney makes it clear that name-calling *does* do a great deal of damage, a theme he treated earlier in *Names and Nicknames*. The sticks and stones introduce the theme of the dualities, the array of various opposing forces that are united in their efforts to crush the Donnellys. These images are given a physical presence in the ladders (sticks) and barrels (stones) of the play's set and props as well as in the conceptualized staging, which has the chorus continually breaking into "sticks" and "stones" factions – sometimes as armed Protestants and Catholics, sometimes as a simple gauntlet of enemies. The actors deliberately, relentlessly define the theatrical space: they dance in a reel that turns into a gauntlet; ladders are used to map out Biddulph (23–4) and to pin a Negro settler to the ground while his house is burnt (26); barrels filled with thorns and nails, in which social dissenters are rolled, come precariously close to steam-rolling members of the Donnelly family (15–28); rope is used to create an enormous cat's cradle – a plastic expression of the complex tensions between opposing ideological forces. Gradually, systematically, we see and hear the Donnellys threatened and hemmed in by, alternately, their neighbours' opinions and their own property boundaries.

Wheels and tops dominate the stage imagery in the next play, *St Nicholas Hotel*. At a basic level these are used synecdochally to represent the competing stage-coaches at the centre of the struggle between the Donnellys and their neighbours. However, they are also associated metaphorically at one point with the four Living Creatures of Ezekiel's vision (113), another hint of the religious dimensions of Reaney's poetics.

While *Handcuffs* reprises much of the imagery of the previous two plays, it also employs a curtain drawn across the middle of the stage, which is used for shadow play (e.g., 265) but is also finally identified, in the central epiphany of *Handcuffs* and perhaps the whole trilogy, as a liminal symbol separating present and past, natural and supernatural, life and death (254). In an ironic confrontation between some youths from the present and the ghosts of Mr and Mrs Donnelly (standing for our own encounter with the Donnellys legend), Reaney has the Donnellys speak of drawing aside the curtain "like a foreskin from the thigh of demon lover Christ himself ... like the mighty eyelid of God the Father's eye ... like the wind from the mouth of the Holy Ghost that flutters her veil as she speaks" (254).

Around these central images coalesce innumerable other tropes. Some tropes are ironic, such as the bishop's washing of his hands (226), evoking Pontius Pilate and the persecution of Jesus. There are also staged synecdoches, such as the shirts hanging on Mrs Donnelly's washing-line to represent her sons (11); and metaphors, such as the image of the Donnellys as bowls and their enemies as nine-pins (21). In one of the most effective tropes, a block of ice, having been used to freeze a customer's feet and bring him in to the St Nicholas Hotel, sits in a tub on stage throughout the evening until it is used to scrub up Mike Donnelly's blood, a scene set more than twenty years earlier (106), metonymically hinting at the magical ability of the imagination to subvert laws of nature.

Still, the most obvious and most important metamorphoses take place among the company of eleven actors who play a huge cast of characters as well as objects. Here the process of identification is most fluid and the main poetic rule is most evident: while the story will be successively identified with everything on the stage, the identity of any one thing on stage will never be fixed. So, while a given character is usually played by one actor, that actor performs many parts; there are even some cases, as in Jennie's speech quoted earlier, where a single character is played by more than one performer.

Clearly, a good number of Reaney's theatrical tropes are the product not just of his private imagination but of the process of collective creation and play-making he inaugurated with *Listen to the Wind*. Watching *The Donnellys*, one easily surmises some of the games Reaney asked the actors to play, an experience begetting something analogous to Brecht's *Verfremdungseffekt*; alongside the primary experience of each theatrical effect arises a secondary critical curiosity about how and why this effect was created. As with Brecht, Reaney's enthusiasm for this aspect of his theatre, which disengages emotional involvement in favour of speculation, lies in its educational potential, its value as goad to the minds of the audience. But Reaney is less interested in activating the capacity of his spectators for political analysis than in awakening their creative imaginations.

Reminded continually of the various "rhymes" established for the key concepts of the Donnelly story (e.g., the recurring use of "sticks and stones" imagery), the audience may themselves rediscover the vitality of these tropes. Their imaginations are thereby enabled more actively to discover identifications between discrete entities, to see metaphorically, or spiritually, as it were – to comprehend the unity of a philosophically and spiritually focused outlook. Metamorphosis is here to be considered an act of faith; in an endeavour to know the mind of God, the individual identifies with the Creator's power to change things, to transfigure. Ideally, having been repeatedly taken on a journey of creative epiphany, the audience will become familiar enough with the path to find their own way.

One effect of the recognition of these complexes of tropes and images is to provide a vital coherence for the sprawling trilogy. The conventional narrative aspect is somewhat muted in favour of elaborate imagery, and this is related to the effect of modernist poetry, where discontinuous structure is given coherence through the repetition of certain poetic motifs. In fact, it is precisely this foregrounding of poetry, of the metamorphoses of theatrical tropes, that demonstrates that *The Donnellys* is much less a historical epic than an epic of a sensibility, and the various members of the family less important as historical entities than as representative elements of this sensibility. There are various hints at such an interpretation – for instance, Reaney's description of Mr Donnelly as "a small square chunk of will" (18). Yet in the end, most telling is the impression that the play leaves on the spectator's imagination, for while at times certain characters – especially Mr and Mrs Donnelly or Will – make a definite impact, the much more powerful impression is less of any individual than of the rebellious, romantic, religious spirit of the family as it is embodied in the production as a whole.

THE SOUWESTO HISTORY CYCLE

With *The Donnellys*, all the major elements of Reaney's poetics were in place and his playwriting techniques had reached a fully refined state. No single work among the later plays brings together such magnitude of subject, seriousness of tone, poetic intensity, and sophistication of dramaturgy. Yet this does not mean that the later plays represent a decline, for after *The Donnellys* Reaney's work reticulates into various explorations and disseminations of his poetics; hence, it is arguably necessary to apply a different standard to the work of this later period.

No sooner had the militant regional evangelist of the imagination discovered and perfected his approach to theatre-making than he began generously to encourage others to explore the techniques on their own. In *Fourteen Barrels from Sea to Sea*, his journal of the national tour of *The Donnellys*, he describes some of the workshops he and members of NDWT conducted in schools to demonstrate how accessible the creation of a piece of theatre could be, and in essays such as "Ten Years at Play" and more recently in *Performance Poems*, he actually provides recipes and instructions for such creations. As for his own plays, Reaney began to expand the work he had done on the Donnellys story by writing a cycle of history plays set in Souwesto for the NDWT company, often collaborating with the communities in which the plays were set.

Baldoon (1976) was one of the "two Ontario stories" Reaney felt "needed doing" after *The Donnellys* (*Wacousta!* 7). The play is based on a historically documented event in a settlement near Wallaceburg, Ontario, from 1829 to 1830, wherein a man and his family were tormented by a series of terrifying "spiritual manifestations." At last the man visited a doctor whose daughter was said to be "gifted with second sight and the mystical power of stone reading," and, after following the girl's advice, the family was relieved of its torment (Gervais and Reaney, 105–9).

Baldoon was written in collaboration with another playwright, C.H. Gervais, yet many of Reaney's characteristic themes are evident. Here, once again, a minority society of visionaries is set against a conventional and oppressive society. In this case the distinction between visionary and repressive influences is suggested through the use of contrasting music:

As the company enters [...] they should be singing Tunkard, Mennonite and Shaker hymns; there should be a great feeling of bells, wind instruments – joy in God, the easy attainment of His light and His creation. This should be contrasted with the more austere, bleak music of the Presbyterian Psalm-book which we'll use at the beginning of Act Two. (1)

This contrast is also emphasized in the respective speech patterns of the characters – "lilting" as opposed to "direct" – and in their costumes, the "soft richness" of one side contrasting with the "dark, practical clothing" of the other (114).

There is, however, a major difference in *Baldoon*'s presentation of the struggle between the visionary and the repressed communities. Whereas Reaney's previous work had shown the visionary groups at a distinct power disadvantage, and found them prevailing only through an effort of faith (if at all), in *Baldoon* the visionaries, Dr Troyer and his family, are in the privileged position of being sought after for their special spirituality. Troyer is a traditional "magus" figure of literary romance, as in the John Fowles novel of that name or in Shakespeare's *Tempest*, or (in a different guise) as David Willson in Reaney's later work *Serinette*. In all these stories the poetic argument between opposing imaginative forces develops by means of a sort of conversion of the protagonists (respectively, John McTavish, Nicholas Urfe, Ferdinand and the court figures, Colin Jarvis), who find themselves isolated in an unfamiliar, magical setting in which they are forcibly detached from the habits and security of their usual social environment by a mysterious, charismatic figure.

This brings us round once again to the notion of shamanism and its role in the dissemination of poetic sensibility. Joseph Campbell has compared the role of the shaman who visited Black Elk as a boy to a psychoanalyst, in that "instead of relieving the boy of the deities, the shaman is adapting him to the deities and the deities to himself" (Campbell with Moyers, 89). There is a parallel to this notion in *Baldoon*, and indeed, in Reaney's whole central myth, in that malevolent forces are invariably shown to be linked with some kind of personal repression. John McTavish is freed from the tormenting poltergeists by an act of confession (he has fathered an illegitimate daughter), by relinquishing his ego and asking forgiveness, by embracing with love what he has previously denied. This theme is set forth in a short poem amidst the final choral passage, as a sort of moral:

Confession is a story
that troubles us all
it is something in words
about the way we can fall
Something that draws us
away from the mirror
to pull us from ourselves
or the truth that we fear
[...]
For the story of Baldoon
is made for us all to see
to focus on the other
who must be set free.   (104)

As it turned out, *Baldoon* was not one of Reaney's more successful plays. NDWT's annual report for 1976–77 declared that their production of *Baldoon* had "suffered from lack of sufficient preparation" (cited in Johnston, *Up the Mainstream*, 247). The play may also have demanded from toronto audiences a suspension of disbelief that they were simply unwilling to make. Patricia Ludwick, a prominent member of the NDWT company, complained later of "urbanites who refuse to be carried away into romance" (83–5; cited in Johnston, *Up the Mainstream*, 248). Reaney himself remained defiant of any incredulousness towards the work. In the notes to the published play he declares that he chooses to believe in witches and poltergeists "principally because it's a great deal more interesting to, than not" (118).

This question of the relationship between history and imagination was explicitly raised in Reaney's next NDWT play, *The Dismissal* (1977), commissioned by Reaney's alma mater, University College in the University of Toronto, for its sesquicentennial. The college administrators may have got more than they bargained for. Reaney decided to portray a time when "sacred cows and stuffed shirts dominated this campus" (*The Dismissal*, 4). A rebellion against these had been led in 1895 by a young professor, William Dale, and some prominent students, an idealist named James Tucker and the young and already very politically minded prime-minister-to-be William Lyon Mackenzie King. In a characteristically Canadian manner, the rebellion itself fizzled out, even while the changes demanded by the students gradually took hold – albeit in a muted way far short of the decisive event they cherished. Dale was dismissed, Tucker expelled, and King, equivocating and protecting his personal interests, was co-opted by the establishment.

As we might expect, in lashing out at the pharisees of 1895 Toronto, Reaney gets in a few licks at the narrow-minded spirits of 1977. Historical fiction always tempts an author to infiltrate the past at least partly in order to leave time-bombs for the present. Here, that temptation is not resisted. At one point Dale asks his class how many believe that Romulus and Remus were suckled by a wolf, and how many by a prostitute named Lupa. Only Tucker holds the former (i.e., for Reaney, the correct) opinion. Dale responds: "It may be a part of our history one day, the history of Ontario, that we believed only those things that could so obviously have really happened" (17). Knowing of NDWT's difficulties finding a sympathetic audience for *Baldoon*, the cryptic resonance of Dale's statement is unmistakable.

In *The Dismissal* the poetic treatments of history rather than bare facts once again generate dramatic tension. Dale demands an explanation for his dismissal early in the play (12); as with the murder of the Donnellys, this injustice provides a refrain that contextualizes all the other events in the story. The play presents a certain "point of view," then, a point that is underscored by some *Verfremdungseffekt* techniques. For example, the actors playing the Premier and the Minister of Education bear placards depicting "their nineteenth-century selves" (14), and the audience is often addressed directly with historical information (e.g., 9, 54).

While some of these techniques foreground the poetic argument of the play – domestic, liberal thought must rebel against imported, pharisaic thought – it occasionally seems that Reaney is merely attempting to "jazz up" some of the drier stuff. This impression occurs, for instance, in one of the most extravagant scenes in the play, where Tucker's editorials are staged as a series of goals for a hockey team (32–3). The justification for this trope lies in the fact that "as editor of the Varsity [Tucker] was captain of the student team" (32): in effect, Reaney builds a staged metonym out of the contiguity of Tucker's two roles. While this has the advantage of using a very Canadian sport in the presentation of an essentially nationalist argument, it also obfuscates any dramatic qualities inherent in Tucker's editorial arguments. And it must be conceded that the real hockey games are irrelevant to the plot. Hence, though the actual verbal sallies are spoken by Tucker, the specific emotional context of the comments is momentarily lost.

The presence of the hockey game in *The Dismissal* probably has something to do with the workshops Reaney and NDWT were conducting at that time, based on Major John Richardson's *Wacousta*: a novel in which lacrosse is essential to the plot. *Wacousta*, was the second of the two "Ontario stories" Reaney had declared "needed doing" after *The Donnellys*. But his use of the novel had been prophesied (after a manner) even earlier by Dudek, who, scoffing at *Listen to the Wind*, declared that if Reaney was so absurd as to adapt Rider Haggard's *Dawn*, which was "no better than some of our own Canadian Anglophonies of the nineteenth century, as a good nationalist [he] might just as well have taken one of those – *The Golden Dog*, or *Wacousta*" (24). Unperturbed, or provoked, by Dudek's sarcasm, Reaney happily obliged.

Richardson's *Wacousta* tells the tale of Colonel De Haldimar, commander of Fort Detroit, and his children, during the Pontiac uprising of 1763. The local Indians are led by a gigantic warrior, Wacousta, who is actually Reginald Morton, an erstwhile friend whom De Haldimar had betrayed in youth, stealing through trickery his fiancée, Clara. Wacousta avenges himself by destroying the whole De Haldimar family except one son, Frederick. Frederick's progeny (the Grantham brothers) go on to meet Wacousta's progeny (the Desboroughs) and mutual destruction in Richardson's sequel, *The Canadian Brothers*, which is set during the War of 1812.

The appeal of Richardson's *Wacousta* for Reaney is obvious. This nineteenth-century Canadian romance is set in the border region of "Souwesto" and Michigan, and blends elements of myth with historical fact. Though it is not a novel that naturally suggests theatrical adaptation, so large is its scope, it had been adapted for the theatre once before, in 1856, and that fact inspired Reaney to push ahead with his project (7).

NDWT produced *Wacousta!* in 1978, after two years of workshops in various locations around the province. Five years later, after NDWT had disbanded, Keith Turnbull directed Reaney's adaptation of *The Canadian Brothers* at the University of Calgary. Aside from what is directly attributable to the novels, the most obvious difference between the structures of the two plays has to do with the treatment of time. In *Wacousta!* Reaney amplifies Richardson's tendency to jump about in time (perhaps the added exclamation mark represents intensification),but he makes *The Canadian Brothers* more linear, even though

Richardson's second novel is the more erratic in time-scheme, peppered with numerous flashbacks. Reaney takes all the background material that is only gradually revealed in *The Canadian Brothers*, expands upon it, and places it in his first act. His second act then begins where the novel does, and the whole play is framed as a flashback within a scene taken from the end of the novel.

As a consequence, Reaney's *Canadian Brothers* has a more stream-lined shape than *Wacousta!* The content of the sequel may be less excit-ing, but its structure makes it the more effective play. This undoubtedly also has something to do with the more fantastic nature of the first novel, which offered more themes for improvisation during the two-year workshop preceding the production. Clearly, innumerable innov-ative ideas were generated, and many found their way into the final script. Richardson's *The Canadian Brothers* is less fanciful, and Reaney's less extravagant narrative interpolations reflect this tone.

Both plays show their romantic sources (like *Listen to the Wind*), being extraordinarily crowded with incident. However, the audience is not led to expect the kind of intricate psychological description that accompanies these incidents in the novels. Instead, attention is drawn to performative aspects, to the intricate theatrical conceptualization. In other words, Reaney once again throws the focus forward from the characters on to the theatrical poetry. Take, for example, the back-ground story in Richardson's *Wacousta*, the story of De Haldimar and Morton (later Wacousta) in Scotland during their youth. This story of the struggle between two young men who share a brotherly love and a competitive enmity is an archetype traceable back through *Two Noble Kinsmen*, Esau and Jacob, and even *Gilgamesh*. Furthermore, Morton's personal story – while lost on a hunt, he encounters a beau-tiful woman in a mysterious place, and this precipitates a fall from innocence – resonates with Pwyll's story in *The Mabinogion* or Alain-Fournier's *Le Grand Meaulnes*. Richardson alludes to none of those works explicitly, yet these parallels suggest something of the evocative control of tone and imagery in the novel – of "its appeal," as Carl Klinck put it, "to the poetically minded as a gigantic symbol for some-thing in the frontier places of every mind" (xiii).

Few of the subtle narrative techniques used to achieve this resonance in a novel are open to the playwright. Instead, Reaney picks up the stray resonances of the novel with a system of staged symbols. Morton is first seen as a young man painting a miniature of the twins Castor and Pollux with the faces of De Haldimar and himself (pre-betrayal) – their presence in that tiny oval itself a gesture towards Leda's egg (78). The smooth and hairy contrast between the men is amplified by making De Haldimar a spit-and-polish philistine, while Morton is unkempt and bohemian (79-80). The stag Morton pursues, leading him to Clara Beverley, is given a collar and named "Fidelity." Moreover, the stag is played by actors wearing antlers and frolicking about; pastoral and play thereby become identical.[40]

In *The Canadian Brothers* Reaney similarly conveys the menacing aura surrounding Matilda in the novel by expanding a theme only hinted at there: an episode in which Matilda cures Gerald of a snakebite is developed into full-blown ophiolatry. Under instructions from her dead grandparents, Ellen and Wacousta, she tames a rattlesnake, naming it Ophian (after the Titanic serpent of Greek myth). The inauspicious "Temple" at which Matilda lives in the novel thus becomes a place of snake-worship in the play (Reaney, *The Canadian Brothers*, 670, 681). Reaney uses this technique – explaining reams about his characters with a simple symbol bearing a powerful mythological resonance – again in the contrast of two letter seals. Julia de Gaspé, the warm and moral yet unrequited lover of Gerald, sends him a love note sealed with the image of Hector being disarmed by his wife Andromache; cold and evil Matilda's letter, by contrast, is sealed with the image of Achilles dragging Hector's body behind his chariot. The most tender relationship in *The Iliad* is contrasted with the most horrific. Every major poetic facet of Richardson's story has a counterpart in Reaney's drama, although Reaney's tropes tend less to be implicitly within the world of the characters (as the letter seals are) than explicitly in the possession of the audience (as are the model forts and the effigies).

The expansion of symbolism is not, however, limited to amplifying the latent themes in Richardson's novels. Many of Reaney's innovations simply make the stories more fantastic; they "turn up the volume" of the romance, so to speak, and push the plays towards Reaney's own literary predilections. The most striking alteration is the change in sex of one of Richardson's characters. Colonel De Haldimar's son Charles becomes Charlotte. Richardson's character had many "feminine" qualities, but it is more than a happy accident that the feminization of the name Charles nods towards Reaney's favourite family of writers, and introduces a whole new sub-plot. One new moment has Frederick, Madeleine, Clara, and Charlotte alone on an island, daydreaming: "If we could stay here forever – just the four of us" (20) – like the Brontë children with their Angria and Gondal fantasies. Charlotte is labelled mad by her father and tethered to a log, an image evoking Rochester's attic-locked wife in *Jane Eyre* and the fear of unsanctioned, unfettered female behaviour that feminist criticism has observed in much Victorian literature. "You've not only tethered my feet, father, but you've tied up my mind as well" says Charlotte (67). Indeed, he seems also to have divided her mind neurotically into opposites: inside versus outside the fort, her father versus Wacousta, deception versus rage, repression versus wildness. In short, her "madness" might be diagnosed as an advanced case of "garrison mentality."

But the divisions are also another version of Yeats's division of primary and antithetical states of consciousness, so this is a disease for which we would expect Dr Reaney to possess homeopathic remedies. Accordingly, Charlotte's prospect for unifying these split worlds arrives in the person of Le Subtil, a young Indian warrior she meets on the green pastoral island and with whom she falls in love (21). The "miscegenation" theme (to use a now happily defunct expression) is emphasized on stage by two symbols that represent the divided systems of thought: "stage right a heraldic lion; stage left a shaman pictograph" (10). Le Subtil teaches Charlotte his language, to free her from the mentality in which "The so-called wise prefer gazing at the cruel stars that teach them to invent new machines of destruction and at the same time trample tiny flowers whose fragrance might teach you the way back to Eden" (22). The imagery harks back to a passage in Colours in the Dark, ("a flower is a star" 99), just as the images for which Le Subtil teaches Charlotte the Cree words constitute another sort of "Existence Poem" (Colours, 29): the crystal flood, the chequered shade, tree bole, a birch tree, earth, and radiance or light (22).

Of Richardson's two novels, Wacousta is certainly the more effective. The romantic themes are stronger there than in The Canadian Brothers, which relies more on "character humour" (much of which is, frankly, embarrassingly racist – e.g., the black servant, Sambo – and the rest not notably amusing). Reaney not only extirpates the dull and objectionable aspects of The Canadian Brothers (Sambo becomes Samuel, for one thing); he also creates a more unified tone for the duology by having certain images and themes repeat themselves over the two plays, as he had done in The Donnelly Trilogy. In Richardson's Wacousta, for example, Colonel De Haldimar dies banally, bloodlessly fading away after Wacousta destroys his family. In Reaney's Wacousta! the two men die locked together in a death grip (103), an ending borrowed from The Canadian Brothers, where Desborough and Henry Grantham grapple their way over the precipice at Queenston Heights, thus creating resonance between the end of the first play and that of the second. Similarly, in The Canadian Brothers Reaney borrows from Wacousta (and, incidentally, Haggard's Dawn) by rooting the enmity between the Granthams and the Desboroughs in an acquaintance in youth, rather than attributing it merely to family heritage as Richardson had. He also echoes *Wacousta* by having Phil Desborough, as a boy, secure entry to the Grantham's house by following a stray ball (669), a mimicry of the lacrosse ruse by which Pontiac and his warriors took eight of nine British forts (all save Detroit) in 1763.

However, the most powerful echo of *Wacousta* added by Reaney to *The Canadian Brothers* is in the effigies of Wacousta and "Mad" Ellen that preside over the play to ensure that their vengeance is satisfied. The subtitle of *The Canadian Brothers*, "A Prophecy Fulfilled," which had been somewhat obscure in Richardson's novel, is thereby made the dominant narrative motif.

BISHOP BERKELEY MEETS BUSBY BERKLEY

After *Wacousta!* Reaney was commissioned by his high school, Stratford Central Collegiate, to write a play. This became the first in a series of three commissioned "urban community plays" (Reaney, letter 2) that treat the history of three Souwesto cities: *King Whistle!* (1979), about the Stratford General Strike of 1933; *Antler River* (1980), a celebration of life in London, Ontario, on the occasion of its sesquicentennial; and *I, the Parade* (1981), about Waterloo's Professor C.F. Thiele, a "local whiz bandmaster" of the twenties (letters 1 and 2). The through-line from Reaney's earlier work is easily seen in these plays; in his mind they are: "part of a playwright's manifesto and movement which are rooted in Summer Theatre '65, '66, '67 at Western here [...] When NDWT's plays are put on in conjunction with those originated by Theatre Passe Muraille, we have together written and shown a theatrical history of our province ("The Story Behind," 50). Moreover, the "urban community plays" were all created with amateur groups in the respective communities, using the methods perfected with NDWT. Reaney regards *Antler River* and *I, the Parade* as mediocre and has therefore published only *King Whistle!* (Reaney, OISE seminar). Accordingly, I concentrate on that play.

Reaney witnessed the Stratford General Strike of 1933 as a child of seven, and it made as indelible an impression on his mind as it did on the usually sedate town of Stratford. Indeed, Reaney claims, half-jokingly, that the strike was "the reason Tom Patterson started the Stratford Festival – to get rid of the shame" (OISE seminar). The confrontation began when six hundred grossly exploited furniture workers were organized into a union by some Marxist representatives of the Workers' Unity League from Toronto. The strike they began escalated until, at its height, more than two thousand workers were out in support and the mayor persuaded the federal government to send in the army with tanks to crush the revolt. The workers, however, responded with a huge parade and rally; management finally gave in (more or less); and the local leader of the workers, Oliver Kerr, was elected mayor of Stratford the next year.

Reaney decided that the form best suited to accommodate the talents and energies of the students and non-professional community volunteers was musical comedy. Inevitably, the idea of marrying the Depression era to musical comedy led him to Busby Berkley's classic film, *Gold Diggers of 1933*. In Berkley's sensibility he recognized much of what he had been trying to achieve in his own work:

That film was a turning point for me; it handles grim material both frivolously and deeply; it rings the changes on a collapsing society which nevertheless is still laughing, still scrunching each other's knees under tables, still has dreams, still refuses to believe that poverty is the answer. What we were going to do was take the reality of 1933 and, like this film, pour all that sadness and economic puzzle into a form that has tap dances, ballets, songs. ("The Story Behind," 51)

In other words, Reaney had found an aesthetic in which his vision from Yeats's tower, of the juxtaposition of myth and document, as well as his ensemble-based creative process, could be married to his romantic optimism and love of dazzling, energetic spectacle: Bishop Berkeley had met Busby Berkley.

Reaney's research for the *King Whistle!* story involved a series of interviews – effectively an oral history of the Depression-era Stratford in the manner of Studs Terkel or Barry Broadfoot. Much of this factual content turns up in the finished script of *King Whistle!* although it appears in the context of Reaney's poetic and philosophic preoccupations. "Fact is always a sort of dragon which Art has to lick into shape without quite killing," he declares in "The Story behind *King Whistle!*" (55). Thus, social forces are personified in the poetic tradition of William Blake (for example, the power of money is seen, Reaney explains, like Blake's Spectre of Urthona, as "the personification of our will to control the environment which often gets away from us and starts controlling us"); and the philosophical context is "Kenneth Galbraith's no doubt heretical version of Marxism" (52). All that sounds rather abstruse until one remembers that these ideas were presented within the parameters of the Busby Berkley musical-comedy aesthetic.

Reaney emphasized that his play was not a literal history of the General Strike by changing some of the key names: Oliver Kerr, for example, became Ollie Kay, and, as in *Wacousta!*, he even changed the sex of one character – Izzy Minster became Leslie Scarlett. Predictably, there were many who were bewildered by this approach, who complained that "this isn't real, this isn't life; you don't have a woman do a male part." Reaney responded: "In a play you obey the anatomy of the play's body, not the anatomical laws of so-called real life" (58). In *King Whistle!* this meant that to Reaney, Izzy Minster's most important characteristics are that he was, first, a member of an oppressed minority – an Odessa Jew – who startled the staid Stratford residents with his preparedness to buck the system; second, a visionary whose hope for a class revolution was ahead of his time (or out of its place); and third, a misunderstood, underappreciated, and unfairly reviled scapegoat.

Izzy's transformation into Leslie Scarlett, "a young woman dressed in a man's suit" (*King Whistle!* 22), probably generates a more immediate and clear-cut sympathy for someone who may have been ahead of her time. For in this age following the feminist revolution, a feisty woman of fifty years ago, with parochial sexism as well as parochial anti-Red paranoia stacked up against her, is pretty much a surefire retrospective sympathy generator. By contrast, the precise significance of Izzy Minster's situation would not be so clear. Stratford of the 1930s was undoubtedly at least cryptically anti-Semitic, like most WASP-dominated societies of the time; but in the post–Third Reich world the spectre of 1930s anti-Semitism carries a great deal of baggage that has little to do with the social evolution of Stratford into its present form. The social relevance of sexism, however, especially given that female workers were a crucial part of the General Strike, is indubitable.

Leslie Scarlett becomes less of a political cypher as we see her wrestle with dilemmas based on her dual feminist and socialist sympathies, as when she is asked for her advice by Jessie, the leader of the "girls" at Swifts, about how to respond to the plant management, which has shut the workers out in favour of strike-breakers. Leslie thinks (in soliloquy) of telling Jessie and her women to smash their way through the gates and allow themselves to be crushed by the tanks in order to let "the Earth rise in new foundations," so to speak. But she finds herself wondering "if it isn't all a male trick to use you – give you this chance to lead and then, if you don't die – never, never let you use that power ever again" (33).

There are also poignant moments when it seems that the reflexive aggressiveness born of Leslie's frustrated determination to change things on both the labour and the gender politics fronts has interfered with her effectiveness in winning the people's trust. At one point Reaney sets up a contrast between the townspeople's reception of Leslie and of Collins:

LESLIE: Yes, they all liked you – you were the tough hair on the chest leader of men. But whenever I walked down the street they called their kids into the house.

COLLINS: The women and kids loved you, Leslie – once they got over the man's suit – stop being so –

LESLIE: Subjective. Subjective. Yes – now where would you say I made my biggest mistake?   (42)

The answer to Leslie's question draws out one of the chief philosophical themes of Reaney's work, though it is offered somewhat indirectly. Leslie had tried to strong-arm Ollie Kay and two other strike leaders who were ready to compromise by threatening to denounce them as "enemies of the people"; the threat failed when Kay and the rest of the townspeople boycotted the meeting (42–3). But Collins adds, "I don't think it's calling him 'Class Enemy Number One' that did it – it's something else," and at that moment two children from Kay's Sunday school walk by, carrying boxes. The reference is to a earlier scene in which Leslie asks children which of two boxes they will pray to: the God box, which is empty, or the Lenin box, which contains an ice-cream cone (38).[41]

In other words, the failure of Leslie Scarlett and Fred Collins to win Stratford over to Communism is the result of a choice the people were forced to make between two sorts of power: spiritual versus material. The tension implicit in this choice is not only maintained throughout the play – Kay argues Christian forbearance even as he leads the worker's revolt – but is an idea mentioned by Reaney elsewhere. In the obituary he wrote for Northrop Frye, Reaney praised *Words with Power* as,

among other things, a direct answer to Chairman Mao's infamous statement that the only power worth having comes from the end of a rifle [...] Chairman Mao turns out to be just another prophet in a hurry and it is the crazies such as Ezekiel or Isaiah who weld the stories and metaphors that eventually produce a young man, Jesus, who by his words alone, destroyed an empire and renewed it [...] – renewed it not with violence but with "words with power": Love Thy Neighbour.   ("Northrop Frye," A22).

For Reaney, the real revolution in Stratford would have to take place, as in *The Sun and the Moon*, in the minds of the people rather than the streets of this small and rather backward town.

Reaney's criticism of "prophets in a hurry" reaches even beyond the ideological questions raised in the Frye obituary and the plot of *King Whistle!* His position is related to his philosophy of poetic theatre, which stresses the patient, organic, imaginative revelation and self-transformation over the direct, positivist quick fix. In his memoir of the *King Whistle!* project he mentions that some people argued they should not have to attend the workshops of the play in order to participate in the final rehearsals and presentation. Where one might expect a retort along the lines of "If you want to dance you've got to pay the piper," Reaney instead responded by saying "No, no – you can't climb into a Temple down its chimney; you have to proceed through the series of graded enclosures the laws of artistic development set up" (58).

Clearly, Reaney continues to see theatrical creation as a form of religious experience. The "series of graded enclosures" and the figurative "Temple" of Reaney's response on this occasion recall Yeats's tower and its serried levels approaching enlightenment; and we should also recall Reaney's remark about the Buddhist idea that we should take "the whole of creation with us to enlightenment, that we cannot just abandon it to its fate, as all human beings are as near to us as our relatives are" ("The Influence of Spenser," 127–8). In short, the people of Stratford who took part in the workshops of *King Whistle!* were being offered an opportunity to rediscover and recreate (by "welding" stories and metaphors together) the same realization of Christian enlightenment that Reaney found implicit in the outcome of the General Strike of 1933.

In this sense, the "urban community plays" represent the quintessence of Reaney's art quite independently of what he has set down on the page for posterity to read. In Reaney's attempt to impel the individual to recreate imaginatively his local environment (particularly Souwesto), his most powerful strategy is to lead them directly through the process himself. Here the traditional division between audience and performer is unimportant, even intrusive. The paradigm for the workshop process of the "urban community plays," the "Listeners' Workshops," as Reaney called them, did not consist of a group of people listening to Reaney but of a group led by Reaney to help one another "listen to the wind," to the still small voice of inspiration and spirituality.

THE CHAMBER PLAYS

Gyroscope (1981) explores the idea of making poetry out of life in another way. Reaney's protagonist, Gregory La Selva, is married to a poet, Hilda, who uses his character as material for her work, which she refuses to let him read.[42] Gregory responds by turning poet himself and infiltrating his wife's "women only" poetry club, the Harp Poetry Guild, in drag, prompting a contest that leaves the guild in shambles but rejuvenates his marriage. Lest nosy academics should wonder if Reaney is alluding to his wife, the poet Colleen Thibaudeau, he introduces Mattie, a doctoral student writing on the interrelationship of Hilda's biography and work, whose meddling implicates her in the La Selvas' quarrel, leaving her dissertation unfinishable and herself nearly destroyed.

I have called *Gyroscope* and the other plays of this section "chamber plays" after Strindberg's late, small-scale works, which, he said, would "seek the intimate in the form; the little motif, thoroughly developed; few characters; broad points of view; free play of the imagination but based on observation, experience, carefully studied, simply but not too simply, no large apparatus" (Strindberg, 93). Reaney's chamber plays have none of the brooding austerity of Strindberg's, of course, but they share their reduced scale, intimate settings, and (with the exception of *Gyroscope*), their brevity.

Perhaps because Reaney's involvement with NDWT was winding down, the "chamber plays" recall his earlier, primarily verbal version of poetic theatre. In particular, the premise of *Gyroscope* provided Reaney with an opportunity to indulge his facility for poetic language with an intensity unheard of since *Colours in the Dark*. Consider, for example:

Why Orpheus? Because descends
A Plowman looking for lost gardens –
Trochaic serpent tethered to six foot post
Suddenly rockets guest ghost.   (*Gyroscope*, 12)

Yet *Gyroscope* by no means completely resurrects the dramaturgy of the early plays. Indeed, Reaney continues to foreground poetic elements in a manner similar to that of the more imagistic plays of the second period; the difference is that here the characters share the foreground with all these tropes. The difficult balance is achieved by means of a metapoetic, metatheatrical ethos in which the characters are fully conscious of the poetic devices in use and regularly draw attention to these.

As for the metatheatricality, where in *The Donnellys* the metamorphosis of an actor from one character to the next carried an implicit poetic message, in *Gyroscope* the line between actor and character is sometimes deliberately blurred:

MATTIE: Henry is taking off his apron.
GREG: Well, he's becoming Nicholas.
NICHOLAS: I'm Professor Puzzle too. Did you think all this was real life? Oh no, Gregory, it's a dream.   (58)

The moment highlights the principal theme of the play – metamorphosis and its relationship to poetic identification – and is reinforced by the numerous references to the myth that *Gyroscope* "displaces": Orpheus and Eurydice. Frye's concept of displacement is directly discussed in the play, Mattie defining it as "the graded adaptation of the unbelievable to the almost believable to the all-too-believable" (60–1). The story of Orpheus is the most tragic failure of poetic identification in Ovid's *Metamorphoses* (itself fundamentally an anthology of tales of failed imagination and will) and for a time the Harpers of Hilda's Guild threaten to turn into vengeful Maenads.

The theme of "metamorphosis and poetic identification" is dramatized in an argument over whether one of Hilda's poems is "about" Gregory or not. Hilda's denial is an ingenious piece of sophistry. She tells Gregory that he is: "undergoing the difficulty the Sumerians underwent when they first started labelling their shipments of tallow with symbols of sheep – tallow comes from sheep, doesn't it? [...] You are a shipment of tallow who has confused himself with his bill of lading – this poem" (14). Hilda's example is a translucently iconic sign, so Gregory can easily identify himself with the sign if only he has a point of reference to fix the context in which meaning is endowed. There lies the rub. As Reaney writes in his prologue, "in this play personality and place are forever spinning out of one phase and into another" (i). At various points man becomes woman; woman becomes man; life becomes poetry; poetry becomes life; study becomes subject; etc. This boundless mutability leads Agnes to utter one of the more blatantly metatheatrical lines: "Sometimes I feel there's NO RELATIVITY between Time and Space at all. Gyroscopes and magnets are big right now re symbols to use. The confessional poets have become concrete" (58). Yet, bewildering as these metamorphoses are at times, they can also be a blessing.

In his introduction Reaney speaks of "personalities spinning into other personalities, sometimes as the only way of preserving their own freshness, their own individuality." This amounts to a rebuttal of arguments against "appropriation of voice," a point made clear when Hilda and Gregory have borrowed from one another's dreams to make poems, with the result that "for the first time with the help of a poet each of them glimpses the deep well of his or her self" (64). In the end, what makes the difference between existential despair and exhilaration over this facility is the presence of love. When Hilda and Gregory are playing "muse in the manger," as Gregory puts it (50), when they are refusing to partake of and contribute to one another's imaginative lives, they find their selves disintegrating; but when they come together to create in love – the sexual act becomes "pen" and "foolscap" in Reaney's metaphor (66) – they find peace and contentment in the harmonious metamorphoses of mutual poetic identification.

The other chamber plays spring from a commission Reaney received from TNT (The Nostalgic Thespians), a group of retired actors based in London, Ontario. The first play written for this group was *Cloud Shadows* (1980), though it was rejected in a vote by the group. Four of the twelve Nostalgic Thespians had voted for *Cloud Shadows*, and Reaney felt these people "deserved a play." Accordingly he set to work on a "three old, two young play that contained two opposing stories – one about young people defeating older people, one about them leading them to a new life" (letter 2). This two-story play has been split into two shorter plays: *The Perfect Essay* (1985) and *Stereoscope* (1983).

Stereoscope is set in "a town not unlike Stratford, Ontario, but in pre-festival days" (175). In Reaney's early plays that setting would have meant a controlling philistine power of some kind; here the greater danger is that the older characters are becoming pharisees. Cyril Simpson, a retired Anglican clergyman, lives with his sisters Una and Britomart[43] and their young "servant girl," Hetty. That the lives of the older three have become stale and devoid of passion, that they are moralizing in the absence of any lively spiritual conviction, is illustrated by their recital of "a poem by a poet in our fold and of our faith" (176): T.S. Eliot's "Gerontion," which points out the inadequacy of "the thoughts of a dry brain in a dry season" to meet the demands of "Christ the tiger" (177). Hetty, by contrast, is innocent of religious dogma, though she maintains an innate spiritual connection. An idiot-savant of sorts, she is said to have "a limited ability to distinguish language from the things it denotes" (176). This sensibility identifies her with the first Viconian phase of language described by Frye in *The Great Code* (1982), in which "there is relatively little emphasis on a clear separation of subject and object: the emphasis falls rather on the feeling that subject and object are linked by a common power or energy" (6). In other words, her habitual mode of thought is metaphorical or spiritual.

Into this group comes Roland, nephew to the Simpsons and a student at the local Bible college. He is their "chance to get saved" (184), to be raised "up out of the ashes" (186). Roland's allegorical affinities to Christ are emphasized when he disrupts the Simpsons' lives, forcing them to re-examine preconceptions; he is described as "a tiger who'd eat grass with a sheep just to put it at ease" (190). The salvation Roland brings to them is, as the title hints, a means of restoring their flat lives to a full three dimensions. When Roland first arrives, the Simpsons bear the "bird mask faces" (187) of stereo-scopes, but after his influence takes effect, Una declares, "I'll never look through a stereoscope again. Who needs to see pirates in Foochow, when you can see the third dimension in your own front parlour" (195). Una and Britomart are converted fairly quickly, but Cyril is resistant: "We've fallen in love with the father and the son. Don't make us lose our chance again," the sisters plead (198). The scales do not fall from Cyril's eyes until the tablecloth is torn from their table to bandage an injured girl outside, and Cyril sees himself in the table's varnished surface (198). By this point Roland's unorthodox (read: earnestly Christian) tactics have upset much of the town, and Cyril, facing an ultimatum, chooses to join his nephew and the women to face down the ugly mob gathered outside to demand Roland's expulsion.

Roland says that he has read both his father's and his mother's diaries, which has enabled him to know the Simpsons "stereophoni-cally" (188). When we recall who the Father and Mother of Roland's allegorical counterpart are (i.e., the Godhead and the exemplar of pure humanity), it is clear that the three-dimensionality Roland brings to these lives is a form of the Blakean "double vision" from which Frye's posthumous book takes its title, the concept of seeing both the tempo-ral and the spiritual world at once. Roland's double vision also brings to the fore something that lurks throughout Reaney's work: the Chris-tian tie-in to the dialectic between the primary and antithetical states of consciousness, the juxtaposition of myth and document. The Son of Man is, in the ecclesiastical metaphor arrived at in Lambeth, both fully divine and fully human; to this holy alloy Reaney's poetic alchemy aspires.

In *The Perfect Essay* the Christ allegory is inverted. The young man is a correspondence student registered with Starevall College, and the dusty old academics marking his papers are destroyed when, with the help of a Beatrice-like Instructress, he repeatedly rewrites a paper until it is a Perfect Essay that consumes them in a Pentecostal flame. This time the young man is allegorically an Anti-Christ who repeatedly shouts "Evil!" as the "frail tattered reply" of "No. Good. Always good" fades gradually away (96ff). The chief attraction of *The Perfect Essay* is the dazzling wordplay with which Reaney wittily satirizes the characters' pedantry. Yet the poetically rich dialogue and the allegori-cal context still convey Reaney's conviction about the benefits of poetic thought. Garcon evidently speaks for Reaney himself when she says: "I often feel a good metaphor or simile might be a child's small stocking, down which a kind unthinking father or mother stuffs, on Christmas Eve – a grapefruit, and then a toy Noah's Ark" (105).

RECENT METAMORPHIC MASQUES

Since *Gyroscope* and the short works for The Nostalgic Thespians, only one of Reaney's works for the theatre is a play *per se* – his dramatic adaptation of Lewis Carroll's *Alice through the Looking Glass*, which premiered at the Stratford Festival in 1994 and was revived two years later. The play was immensely successful (indeed, I would crassly suggest that it is the most lucrative thing Reaney has written), though it is a quite straightforward dramatization of Carroll's original. Still, the simplicity of the theatricalization may be deceptive, for this task appears to have eluded many a previous dramatist.

Whereas many thousands saw Reaney's *Alice* at Stratford, no more than a few hundred could have seen his short masque *"In the Middle of Ordinary Noise ..."*: *An Auditory Masque*, created with his long-time collaborator, the composer John Beckwith, for a single performance at "The Legacy of Northrop Frye" conference in 1992. The masque is called "auditory" because it builds a collage of musical and literary quotations, sound effects, ideas about music, and personal snippets from Frye's life, and arranges all these into the mandala patterns of his *Anatomy of Criticism*, one notion or sound blending fluidly into the next just as literary conventions do in Frye's scheme. Though it is all done quite brilliantly, it is difficult to imagine the masque reaching any larger audience than the small (but enthusiastically receptive) group for whom it was created.

But Reaney's chief preoccupation during this time has been a number of opera librettos, performance poems, and the ongoing theatrical workshops. *Performance Poems* is not only an anthology of the poems Reaney has written for performance since *One-Man Masque* and *Colours in the Dark*; it is also a sort of recipe-book that shows how to make mythopoeic theatre out of far-flung sources – the theme of Reaney's workshops. For example, he shows how he based scripts on "a weather diary [he] once kept for four months in 1939, and a journal kept by a local farmer in 1846" (67). Following the cyclical principles of *One-Man Masque* and *Colours in the Dark*, Reaney organizes the pieces in *Performance Poems* into a calendric pattern, attaching a theme to each month. Inevitably, he finds a model for this cyclical organization of insights in the traditional memory systems detailed by Frances Yates in *The Art of Memory* and *Theatre of the World*, systems designed to provide frameworks for associated ideas and the fluid metamorphoses from one abstract entity to the next (71–8).

In the opera librettos the most prevalent dramaturgical trend is Reaney's continuing effort to expand his tropes to include the audience in the intimate, self-reflexive manner associated with masques, each opera making figurative use of the performance itself. For example, an invitation to play "make-believe" is inherent in his unfinished opera *The House by the Churchyard*, which tells the story of the Brontë children and their imaginary world. In choosing his title Reaney may have had in mind the unfinished story told by Mamillius, the little boy in *The Winter's Tale* – "There was a man ... dwelt by a churchyard ..." (II.I.29–30) – for Mamillius's line is misquoted by Reaney during *In the Middle of Ordinary Noise* as "Once there was a man who had a house by a churchyard" (270). Mamillius's story, invented at a time of distress, and with its juxtaposition of a life and a cemetery, has a connection with the Brontës' skill at creatively spinning fanciful stories in the face of morbidity.

The theatrical space in which *The House by the Churchyard* unfolds represents both the Brontës' playroom and the world of collective imagination to which children retreat from the outer world. "With a burst of music," Reaney writes, "the cast of the entire story pours out from beneath the stage. [This] develops into a ballet with children naming and plot-shaping on the side" (15). Once again we have a metatheatrical play about the making of both play and a play. The projected opera is essentially an elaboration and revision of the frame-story from *Listen to the Wind*; again we see "huge shadows of the four children on the backdrop," but now the characters are aware of the gigantic minds of their creators, so the tension between the outer and inner plays is increased. The most extreme example of this tension is in Branwell's development of a Napoleonic character for one of his toy soldiers, about which Reaney writes: "he becomes Branwell's alter ego and eventually destroys his creator" (14).

A similar metatheatricality supports *The Shivaree* (1978), a previous opera by Reaney and Beckwith. Here Reaney displaces the Persephone myth, resetting the story in 1900 rural Ontario. Mr Quartz, a rich miser, has married young, beautiful Daisy and brought her to his sepulchral house, where he and his sister spend their days counting their wealth. In the role of Ceres or Demeter is Miss Beech, the local schoolteacher. However, by adding Jonathan, a young suitor whose catastrophic hesitation drove Daisy to accept Quartz's proposal, Reaney effectively moves the story towards the Orpheus myth. Orphic Jonathan does indeed sing in his effort to rescue Daisy from the clutches of Quartz; but more instrumental (the pun is unavoidable) to his strategy is the assistance of a group of "shivareers" who show up to harass Quartz and his bride.

There is a sort of brinkmanship inherent in the Persephone and Orpheus myths: the stories suggest a race against time where the symbolic consummation of the bride's marriage to death will make any subsequent return to life impossible. Reaney evidently saw an echo of that desperate need to delay the consummation of a marriage in the idea of a shivaree, the old custom whereby a group of male noise-and-music-makers pester a newlywed couple on their wedding night until given money or alcohol to send them on their way. The notion of shivareers' antics forestalling death-like consummation stands at the centre of the opera, then, and also provides a figure to understand the performance itself. The opera is performed as a musical act of faith in vitality; it uses joyful noise to distract moribund philistinism until providential imagination is able to redeem young life. Jonathan indeed creates a diversion long enough for a *deus ex machina* to arrive in the person of Miss Beech, who reveals that Quartz has filled in the marriage certificate with not Daisy's name but that of his first wife. And, as we would expect of Reaney's affinities with romance by now, he contrives to redeem even Quartz from misery at the end of the play by providing him with an alternate wife, the tomboy Annie, from among the male shivareers.

Crazy to Kill (1989), yet another collaboration with John Beckwith, takes *The House by the Churchyard*'s metatheatrical concept of a play made with a cast of dolls and pushes it that much further. In the 1941 detective novel by Stratford author Ann Cardwell on which Reaney and Beckwith based their opera, the narrator, Agatha Lawson, is a patient in a psychiatric hospital in which a series of murders is taking place. The most interesting aspect of Cardwell's novel is the "whodunit" surprise ending – which I regret I must now spoil, though Reaney himself does not much rely upon the surprise. The novel boasts one of the more extreme examples of an unreliable narrator in literature, for Agatha, unrevealed to the reader and partially unknown to herself, is herself the murderer. In Reaney's libretto the revelation of this fact is not as surprising, for the simple reason that, by making the opera a creation of Agatha's mind and by using dolls to represent certain characters, he has given the whole production a slightly demented air: the narrator's unreliability is palpable from the beginning.

However, what Reaney's libretto forfeits in surprise, it gains in sense of absurdity bestowed by a powerful encompassing trope. Like Coulmier in *Marat/Sade*, when Detective Fry enters, "he treats the whole audience chamber as the private asylum" (5). That the theatre is a place of madness is not only emphasized by the set, which Reaney describes as "like Bluebeard's closet – filled with many unpleasant surprises. Above, there hangs a screen for back projection of images in the murderer's soul" (7–8). The expressionistically conceived staging foments ambiguity: the devices may be dramaturgical attempts to tell what took place earlier, or to represent the workings of Agatha's distorted mind in the present, or even to represent the hallucinations of the audience. That nothing in this theatre has a fixed ontology is demonstrated near the end of the opera when Agatha shoves the pianist off the bench to accompany herself (44).

Serinette (1990), a collaboration with composer Harry Somers, is an appropriate work with which to end this chapter, for it represents the epitome of Reaney's efforts to include the audience in a central trope, its most impressive and meaningful talismanic symbol of the opera being the theatre itself. *Serinette* mixes fiction and fact, myth and document, to tell a story beginning in 1812 of two boys in the Jarvis family of Toronto (then York), one of whom leaves home for Sharon, Ontario, to join the Children of Peace, a visionary community that broke from Quaker roots to follow the charismatic David Willson. Willson was a polymath who not only wrote all the beautiful hymns sung by his congregation but designed a magnificent three-storey temple embodying a unique symbolic architecture. To inimitably compelling effect, it was inside this temple and upon the grounds outside that the production of *Serinette* took place. The night-blooming cereus that Reaney, wishing to envelop the audience in epiphany, suggested should ideally expand to fill the whole sky found a perfect physical counterpart in Willson's awesome temple.

The Children of Peace community also provides particularly fertile ground for Reaney's central myth. In *Serinette* they are the embodiment of the Romantic ideal of community – a sort of Romantic utopia. The "Davidites," as they were called, maintained the Quaker emphasis on charitable works, but David Willson added a non-Quaker emphasis on the use of music in worship (see Reaney, "David Willson"). In Reaney's hands, belief in the spiritual value of music becomes a kind of synecdoche of the group's larger social significance, the chief means of contrasting spiritually revolutionary Sharon and pharisaic Toronto: the hymns of David Willson (or Somers's version thereof) on one side and the serinette on the other. That contrast finds its central symbol in the serinette, a tiny pipe organ used in the eighteenth century to train wild birds to sing classical arias. Thus, native Canadian music and culture is set against what Reaney calls the "Family Compact rigidity, [the] birdbox imitation of European culture and politics" (letter 2). A further dimension to this symbol emerges through its use in the poem called "Serinette," which appears in Reaney's *Performance Poems*, where he complains of the serinettes of top-forty radio stations that relentlessly grind out American hit songs (31–2).

In short, the Children of Peace serve Reaney's vision in two ways: first, as a nationalist embodiment of organic culture opposed to imported pretension; second, as a romantic embodiment of the forces and energies of poetic thought, the sacred creativity of the human spirit struggling to emerge from beneath the dead weight of repressive convention. In the Davidites' attempt to imitate the harmonious "music of the spheres" in their community we glimpse an impulse corresponding to Reaney's own career movement towards an increasingly formal synthesis of spirituality, beauty, and play. We may even see in *Serinette*'s fanciful romance and infatuation with musical order a hint of the themes that preoccupied Shakespeare in his late romances.

Indeed, in some respects Reaney seems hardly less visionary than David Willson himself. The difference is that Reaney's community is really one composed of many theatres rather than contained within a small village like Sharon. He once suggested that, because he had himself been inspired by the theatres he had been in, he was trying to "help build a society where this fact keeps repeating itself over and over again until our whole nation loses its stiffness and becomes itself a sort of theatre. Not the sort of theatre it is now where Technology [...] creates ever more horrifying and sinister spectacles; no, but a place where we ourselves, with just our bodies and the simplest of props (albeit in abundance) available to everyone, create a civilization where it finally seems true that to be wise is to know how to play" (160). The problem is that not everyone wants to play – not, at least, the game Reaney is offering. So we return to Dudek's criticisms.

To someone acclimatized to the ironic sensibility that dominates modern literature, not to mention one as pessimistic in sensibility as Dudek's poetry suggests, the indefatigable optimism of Reaney's work must at times seem nearly Panglossian. Surely we see a hint of that irritation in Dudek's assertion that Reaney condescends to his audience by taking the Gospel teaching "Except ye become as little children" too literally. Moreover, Dudek declares, any attempt to bring "the divine" back to the theatre is hopelessly naïve in that "today we are not quite sure of what we mean by the divine" (29). He goes so far as to suggest that we live in an age (the nadir of a Spenglerian decline?) when the very concept of drama itself is obsolete.

Alas, there is little hope of cultivating enthusiasm for Reaney's work in anyone who wants to relinquish drama itself as a useless archaism – too dismal a line of thought to pursue. But I hope I have demonstrated that Reaney's symbolism is always schematically arranged according to a highly sophisticated poetics, a complex framework that integrates a philosophy of the imagination, a poetic grammar, and a theory of theatrical creation. The heuristic, experimental, and mythopoeic aspects of Reaney's theatre continuously rediscover and redefine "the divine" through the exploration of the actual, identifiable effects of faith on human behaviour. In Reaney's work the divine seldom appears as a familiar, fixed, denoted entity, rather as an inference drawn from and defined by specific circumstances. Any conception of the divine, no less than any given work of art, is no more or less valid than the interaction it provokes.

Finally, the childlike quality in Reaney's plays will always be subject to personal taste, but clearly, Reaney's intent is anything but condescending. Indeed, the implicit demand of Reaney's metamorphic masques – that each spectator should recover a personal ceremony of innocence by participating in the theatrical interaction – is every bit as profoundly challenging as the apparently simple Gospel passage that instructs us to become as little children (Matt. 18:3).

2 Michael Cook: Elegy, Allegory, and Eschatology

> We are dying, we are dying, so all we can do
> is now to be willing to die, and to build the ship
> of death to carry the soul on the longest journey.
>
> D.H. Lawrence, "The Ship of Death"

COOK AND ANGLO-IRISH TRADITION

In Paris during the autumn of 1896 William Butler Yeats was introduced to a young Irishman, John Millington Synge. Yeats seldom missed an opportunity to promote Irish nationalism, and he quickly seized on this one, as he relates: "He told me he had learned Irish at Trinity College, so I urged him to go to the Aran Islands and find a life that had never been expressed in literature, instead of a life where all had been expressed. I did not divine his genius, but I felt he needed something to take him out of his morbidity and melancholy" (*Autobiographies*, 343). The suggestion proved an inspired one, for Synge followed Yeats's advice in 1898 and found in the Aran Islands the catalyst for his finest work. Something rare and dignified in this remote culture struck a romantic chord in Synge's imagination. Indeed, his attempts to articulate the peculiar allure of these islands are often redolent of the Preface to the *Lyrical Ballads*: "Their way of life has never been acted on by anything much more artificial than the nests and burrows of the creatures that live round them, and they seem, in a certain sense, to approach more nearly to the finer types of our aristocracies – who are bred artificially to a natural ideal – than to the labourer or citizen, as the wild horse resembles the thoroughbred rather than the hack or cart-horse (25).

The similarity to Wordsworth's fascination with the Lake District is underscored by Synge's remarks on the speech of the Aran islanders, who spoke English as their second language: "A few of the men have a curiously full vocabulary, others know only the commonest words in English, and are driven to ingenious devices to express their meaning" (16). From the seeds of these "ingenious devices" grew the poetic dialect employed in *Playboy of the Western World*. To be sure, Synge's dramatic treatment of the Aran islanders' speech is not strictly realistic, but his acquaintance with these people prompted him to discover his own distinctive poetic voice. Yeats himself made such an observation when, after Synge's death, he described his friend as "a drifting silent man full of hidden passion, [who] loved wild islands, because there, set out in the light of day, he saw what lay hidden in himself" (*Essays*, 330).

On the evidence of his work for the stage, the geography of the late Michael Cook's imagination was as closely identified with Newfoundland as John Millington Synge's was with the Aran Islands. The relation was also of a similarly indirect character – that is, Cook's interest in Newfoundland was less the straightforward mimetic interest of the realistic playwright he was often carelessly supposed to have been than the mythopoeic interest of a poetic dramatist. Cook's version of Newfoundland indeed includes many elements of realistic observation, but these have been integrated with elements of literary convention, religious allusion, and social analysis to suggest an imaginary world that parallels and comments upon, and sometimes even overlaps with the real Newfoundland. In short, Cook's Newfoundland always exists in a state of poetic tension: a "fallen" world haunted by its noble promise; a harsh and often brutal place that, notwithstanding, still bears traces of an alternative, idealized cosmos against which the deficiencies of ordinary experience may be measured.

The comparison between Synge's relationship to the Aran Islands and Michael Cook's to Newfoundland may be found without reaching, for Cook drew the analogy himself in a 1982 interview:

Newfoundland had a growing language when I hit it. The people were always seeking to make connections. Language was used as a stabilizing force between themselves, experience and the universe ... I'll never forget driving my neighbour – an old schooner and logging man – one night for a doctor's appointment ... He was getting fidgety in my little car; finally he turned to me and said, "for the love of God, Michael, will you stop, I need to capsize me cock ..." Another time, up towards St. Anthony, I saw the remains of an elm tree ... An old fellow comes up and looks at me looking at it and says, "Oh, I remember when she lifted her skirts to the wind." That's what Synge got out of the Aran Islands! It's a language that reflects the metaphor of being there, of being alive in that place. Now it's been eroded by what is laughably passed off as the "North Atlantic" dialect – you know, every CBC radio announcer desperately tries to sound like everyone else. It's a great tragedy. (*The Work*, 161–2).

The "great tragedy" was not, in Cook's view, a simple matter of the reformation of dialect to conform to standards set by mass communication. Rather, he regarded the normalization of language as symptomatic of the inexorable loss of an entire culture and of a corresponding something in the human spirit. In an article arguing the importance of theatre to Newfoundland, Cook warns of

the threat to a language and culture which, if it is denied expression may succumb entirely to the assault of the media and the perpetuation of the myth that the cheapest and tawdriest elements of the American Dream are preferable to the realities of the Newfoundland experience. First the Beothuks, then resettlement. Finally, the people themselves. When the soul is gone, who rides the water? ("Under Assault," 138)

There is, then, an elegiac cast to Cook's vision of modern Newfoundland that parallels Synge's response to the Aran Islands. Yet, significantly, both these men were actually outsiders to the cultures they admired: Anglo-Irish residents of modern, techno-materialist societies who wistfully identified the lost elements of their Irish heritage with the strange-and-yet-familiar rural island cultures. Synge felt he had glimpsed in the Aran islanders the life of his Irish forefathers prior to British influence; Cook saw in Newfoundland what he called "the recreation of a Celtic culture in North America" (*The Work*, 164).

It may be that Anglo-Irish culture is inherently predisposed to elegiac expression. The very term bespeaks a loss – the alien conqueror permanently prefixing the remains of the traditional indigenous culture. Indeed, one may trace through Anglo-Irish literature what has been called a "continuity in loss," a persistent suggestion that there was a power, dignity, and spiritual integrity left behind in the earlier culture, now apprehensible only through an effort of poetic recollection (O'Driscoll, 143). The notion is closely related to the central myth of pastoral poetry, where the demise of a simpler rural life is regularly depicted as a recent tragedy and the blame pinned on historical events such as the Industrial Revolution. Yet there is a little projection inherent in such ideas, for the pastoral tendency is nearly as old as literature itself; the paradise of rural simplicity has *always* been conceived as a recent loss. Accordingly, pastoral elegy is more productively read as a figurative rendering of the self than as a mimetic rendering of some real place.

However, the particular Anglo-Irish elegiac tradition in question differs from the general run of pastoral elegy in that the lost or disappearing Celtic culture is not necessarily – and indeed is seldom presented as – wholly paradisal. The searing of Christy Mahon's leg in

Synge's *Playboy of the Western World* leaves an indelible scar on any simply idyllic picture of this society, and that savagely ironic view of the Irish heritage continues with writers like Flann O'Brien, James Joyce, and Samuel Beckett. To be sure, there is also a more sentimental elegiac Anglo-Irish tradition, one easily found in Newfoundland, but Cook has argued that this is not the vein in which he writes: "my work is still viewed with suspicion, because as an outsider I have not followed the current trend – the Irish trend, actually – of romanticizing and mythologizing the glories of the past. It was a very dark and soul-destroying past in many ways, a survival culture" (*The Work*, 157). Assuming that Cook is using "romanticizing" and "mythologizing" in a casual, pejorative sense – to mean "sentimentalizing" and "falsifying" – this assessment of his own work (regardless of what we think of his assessment of the prevalent Newfoundland culture) is accurate. Yet if we use those verbs "romanticizing" and "mythologizing" more formally, we find that, on the contrary, this is exactly what Cook does with the past of Newfoundland.

While the Newfoundland that Cook portrays is often harsh and unforgiving, his presentation of the role of humanity in this environment relies heavily on both mythology and romanticism. Not only does he follow Synge in ascribing an unusually vivid presence of something like a "poetic soul" to a culture on the periphery of the modern techno-materialist world, but his descriptions of the relation between Newfoundlanders and the Newfoundland landscape regularly evoke the romantic sublime:

By the time this gets into print, the ice will still be holding us in the womb of the North Atlantic, the reason for our existence. From the air, it's hard to distinguish land from the ice pack. Landsmen after seals walk out sometimes five, 10, 15 miles. The landscape is terrifyingly beautiful, a moon landscape of clumpers, bergs, growlers. From a distance, the sealers look like characters from a Noh play. Their movements are refined, stylized yet full of force and purpose. The world moves beneath their feet. It is an environment of immense menace and fluidity, subject at any moment to explosive and deadly change. Though the seals rarely come close to land now in vast numbers, men still go out. Because the ice is there. Children walk across harbours or practise jumping from pan to pan. The black water waits patiently, as it always has. ("Trapped," 117)

There is certainly a Yeatsian touch in the phrase "terrifyingly beautiful," and accompanied as it is by the mention of Noh, it may lead us to recall Yeats's use of techniques derived from Japanese theatre to articulate the moments of passage between the quotidian world and what he sometimes called Faeryland (which, as James Reaney said in his dissertation, should be regarded as "a state within human consciousness rather than without it" – 115). Cook has called Newfoundland "the edge of the world," ("Introduction," 74), and in terms of poetic liminality, it serves just that function in his work – a representation of the outer reaches of the civilized, quotidian world where it verges on the unknown or noumenal.[1]

THE HISTORY PLAYS

At the centre of nearly all Cook's work is the death struggle of humanity caught between two mighty opposites, nature and civilization. This struggle leads to a deeply ambivalent portrait of human nature, for the scope of human action in the plays corresponds to the desperate amorality that we would expect of creatures in their death throes. Admittedly, there is some courage to be found in the drama, but there is more rage, brutality, stubbornness, cruelty, and pusillanimity. This has been the source of some confusion and even open hostility, for Cook has often been perceived to be savaging Newfoundlanders, the very people he was expected to support. *Colour the Flesh the Colour of Dust* (1972) demonstrates how Cook's conflation of a bewildering array of social, political, and intensely poetic perspectives arouses and confounds audience expectations.

The play is set in St John's during the winter of 1762, when the French captured and held the city for several months before losing it once more to the English. The political and social ramifications of this national flip-flop generate part of the dramatic interest; another part has to do with the personal development of three characters: Gross, Captain of the defeated English battalion; Mannon, his Lieutenant; and a Woman (called Marie in one scene) with whom Lieutenant Mannon has an affair. The separateness of these areas of interest is, in some respects, compounded rather than mitigated by the diffuse dramaturgy. Brian Parker has written that Cook's work "can be thematically confusing because it combines an almost reflex sympathy for the underdog with a more existentialist concern with the strain isolation imposes on human relationships" ("On the Edge," 22). These two themes elicit somewhat conflicting expectations. The former suggests a leftist political slant, and Cook's ample use of Brechtian dramaturgy certainly encourages this expectation. The latter suggests an individualistic struggle for authenticity which is largely indifferent to political ideology. To be sure, this is the combination of themes that Jean-Paul Sartre brought to his literature, managing to integrate these with varying degrees of success, but there is always a bedrock of philosophical and ideological certainty beneath Sartre's work that leaves the reader in little doubt about the author's intentions. In Cook's work there is no such doctrinal certainty, and in this respect *Colour the Flesh the Colour of Dust* follows its most important stylistic prototype, Georg Büchner's *Danton's Death*. Hence, dramaturgical elements that, in certain contexts, might evoke Brecht or John Arden and Margaretta D'Arcy – such as the violent confrontations between soldiers and citizens, the use of ironic protest ballads, and the parable-like characterizations of authority figures like the Merchant and Magistrate – do not signify a correspondingly focused political position. The representation of the crowd as, alternately, victims of economic oppression and perpetrators of senseless violence is simply inconsistent with any such ideological intent; yet the political element remains a strong enough presence that the plot line that focuses on the "more existentialist concern," the affair between the Lieutenant and the Woman, has been "condemned as a misleading cliché."[2]

While there is no question that the dramaturgy of *Colour the Flesh the Colour of Dust* is diffuse, and it may even be that, as Brian Parker argues, "the overall effect is incoherent because [Cook] has tried to cram too much into it without a clear sense of priorities" (24), it is also true that a great many of the immediate difficulties with thematic focus would recede were the play presented to an audience as primarily a poetic work. In other words, many of the elements in this play that seem to be at cross-purposes philosophically and politically may nevertheless be easily united in a structure that is conceived as articulating an imaginative rather than a rationalized social vision. A sense of that structure would begin with its mythic shape, an overview of which is introduced to the audience in the heavily symbolic theatrical trope of the first scene.

A corpse is hanging from gallows and being watched over by two drunken soldiers. On the instructions of Lieutenant Mannon, the body is cut down and given to the dead man's former lover, Marie. She cradles it, creating the image of a pièta; then, after the soldiers exit, she sings a ballad:

... I sold my body
rich and warm
to poor fishy creatures
fleeing the storm
But to you I gave
As give I must
to colour the flesh
the colour of dust

[...]
Swing by the neck,
hang by the toes
from birth to death
the swinging goes
But it's a fool
Who doesn't trust
to give himself
because he must ...   (7)

Life persists in the face of death and death persists in the face of life; they are locked into a cycle and are the ineluctable fate of human beings. The theme, in other words, is the first and most basic mythic concern: to relate the interconnectedness of life and death. Set against this stark background of fatalistic mortality, other concerns become more obviously secondary, so that the political allegory suggested by the Brechtian stylistic affinity remains marginal. In the same scene one of the soldiers, speaking to the Lieutenant about the hierarchy that assigns them such apparently different stations in life, observes:

> I mean – we know that our lives and yours run on two different levels
> so to speak – but when it comes to loving and hating and owing, and
> breeding bastards while you're away, well – there's not much to separate
> us, is there? (6)

Indeed, faced with the overwhelming concern for bare survival imposed by the harsh Newfoundland environment, political concerns seem absurd except in so far as they immediately affect the individual's welfare.

The type of community built in an environment like this is, of course, a garrison, and if the play's setting in an actual garrison were not enough to remind us of Northrop Frye's "garrison mentality," the ambivalence expressed by the characters with respect to their society would surely do so. Attempting to build a civilization on the survival of individual families feels futile in the face of such seemingly inimical natural forces. Captain Gross despairingly summarizes:

> I've watched year after year. People build. Then fire. Or drowning. Or
> famine. Or disease. Or just – failure of the spirit – Somebody else comes
> and carts the house away – for timber or firewood. The thin scrub
> marches back across the cleared land – The flake rots into the sea – I have
> seen places (Pause) I have seen places – where people once lived, where
> even the land no longer bears the scar – It makes me frightened. (36)

So, fearfully, the Crowd (the masses are represented as a kind of unified force) huddle together within the walls of a garrison, attempting to maintain collectively a bulwark against both human enemies and the harsh wilderness. Yet a union of this kind, while it may assist biological survival, does little to mitigate the threat to the human spirit. Any such garrison community must maintain a high degree of civic order; the consequent intolerance for expression of unrest or dissent of any kind is demonstrated by the spectacle of the hanged man at the opening. Crushed in this way between the exigencies of survival and an overbearing social order, the Crowd quickly become cynical about traditional humane values such as honour (17) or honesty (15).

Yet the effect runs deeper than this somewhat obvious sociological observation suggests, for the fearfulness of the power of nature, combined with a consistent dissatisfaction with the ruling order, creates in the Crowd a primitive tribal relation to power and hope. The Magistrate sneers cynically:

> The people. They'd cheer a flag a week. They need emotion to brighten their lives. Need causes. But when one is done, the old order re-establishes itself – They'll follow a saviour one day and hang him the next – Cheer the French for freeing them from British oppression and cheer the British for freeing them from French corruption.   (35)

Here lies the essence of Cook's mythic representation of history in this play. The cycle of life and death introduced in the first scene is specifically related to the flip-flop of power, and lest this sense of eternal recurrence should not resonate strongly enough, the story is further connected to the change of seasons. That the actual history took place from the fall of one year to the spring of the next is true enough, but Cook is careful to evoke a Frazerian vegetative myth for context. As the British order falls to the French, a crowd of people dance and sing a macabre song of bloody victory. When the song stops:

> *suddenly the Spokesman snatches a grappling hook from one of the crowd – as the first [British] soldier, breathless, falls to his knees – he stands in front of him – the crowd fall silent – [...] Magistrate and Merchant and Officer watch as the Spokesman pushes the point of the spike against the soldier's groin. He says one word.*
> SOLDIER 1: No. (*The Spokesman presses harder – the soldier's voice rises to a scream*) [...] I have a wife and children. (*His hands clutch the spike*)
> SPOKESMAN: And this is for mine. (*He impales him – the soldier falls*) [...] *The crowd – as if after a communal orgasm – turn and drift slowly out.*
> (27)

The incident, while gruesome, is not gratuitous; it is, rather, another theatrical trope providing the audience with a central exposition of the mythical structure of the play.[3] Readers of Frazer's *The Golden Bough* (430, 619) or Robert Graves's *The Greek Myths* (70, 75) will remember that in one version of the Adonis myth the fertility demi-god is gored to death by a boar's tusk, which catches him in the groin. The powerful sexual overtones to this death emphasize its ritual status – an allusion to a myth about fertility, death, and regeneration. A phallic tusk (or grappling hook) emasculates the young male figurehead of the outgoing social order or season in order that the sexual potency of the incoming order may be shown clearly to have superseded the Adonis-figure's potency, which, until replaced, had been so important to the survival of the community. The penetration of the soldier's groin, then, does indeed lead to something like a "communal orgasm," a not-so-*petite mort*, in which one world is lost and another begins.

The event provides a kind of mythological centrepiece for the play that may be interpreted in two interrelated directions, as a representation of cosmic order and as a representation of human nature. As a myth about cosmic order it recalls the theme introduced in the first scene of the play, where the cruel but ineluctable cycle of life and death was starkly set forth. In that first scene the woman's name, Marie, together with her pietà-like cradling of the hanged man, encourages a Christian allegorical interpretation, but this notion is made explicit and derided by Soldier 2, who snarls sarcastically: "Is he Jesus Christ? Are we the Romans? Is she Mary?" (7) The woman's subsequent song offers a more brutal, atavistic interpretation of what life and death mean in this play, and the Adonis-like murder of Soldier 1 seems to reaffirm this view. Still, his comrade's proleptic dismissal notwithstanding, once mentioned, the Christian mythic vision thereafter hangs in the air like the irrational hope of humanity – that a better world may lie ahead. What renders this hope unlikely is the view of human nature the murder reveals: the inherent blindness of the Crowd to the real source of their misery, and the relish with which they vent their outrage in the ritualistic slaughter of an innocent man. For the present, humanity is crushed between the political alternatives of tyranny on the one hand and terror (i.e., post-revolutionary proletarian violence) on the other, able to rest with neither but merely to cry out in anguish.

The veneer of civilization having been torn away and the underlying social order revealed as so cruelly correspondent to the cosmic cycle, the nihilistic inclination is to identify the human spirit with the feral natural world outside the garrison rather than the oppressive human world within. A figurative pattern emerges linking inward despair with the harsh elements outside the garrison. Humanity, according to

Captain Gross, is adrift at sea without a rudder (38). Of their fate under these conditions, he confesses at another time: "I see icebergs in my sleep. All the time" (23). His dream suggests a kind of morbid sublime, the Freudian death-wish attached to a primal force capable of obliterating civilization. Canadian literature has a long and ambivalent relationship with icebergs and similar awesome wintry threats. The monstrous, beckoning iceberg of E.J. Pratt's *The Titanic* or the mystic-sublime icebergs of Lawren Harris are only two of the most famous precursors of Captain Gross's terrifying and seductive extra-garrison companion. As Margaret Atwood points out, Canadian folklore "established early that the North was uncanny, awe-inspiring in an almost religious way, hostile to white men, but alluring; that it would lead you on and do you in; that it would drive you crazy, and, finally, would claim you for its own" (22). Yet while the Captain may yearn after such absolute oblivion, he lacks the resolve to seek it actively, and instead shrouds himself in the temporary oblivion of the fog, which "makes life more bearable" (36). Cook's use of this image recalls Eugene O'Neill's *Long Day's Journey into Night*, where Edmund, attempting to explain the source of his instinct for poetic expression to his father, speaks of a veil lifting for a momentary glimpse of meaning followed by the fall of the veil, "and you are alone, lost in the fog again, and you stumble on towards nowhere, for no good reason" (153–4). Having lost or betrayed his faith in civilization as the source of meaning, Captain Gross finds himself, like O'Neill's "fog people," groping through his shroud for some meaning on the other side of daily life and society, in an almost wistful relationship with the sublime.

The predicament of Captain Gross, it seems, is only partly under-stood by Lieutenant Mannon and not at all by the other characters. As a monomaniacal materialist, the Merchant is entirely uncomprehend-ing of Captain Gross, and the two simply speak at cross-purposes (e.g., 38); while the Crowd understand only that, as a defeated authority-figure, the Captain is now impotent and therefore contemptible (e.g., 35). For his part, the Lieutenant is a bourgeois liberal humanist who is unwilling to renounce his faith in civilization as the Captain has done. He is the central figure of the play, and presumably represents the point of view held by the majority of the audience: neither wholly militaris-tic nor wholly cynical, for the most part sceptical of ideology, but ulti-mately loyal to the ideal of supporting a range of humane values with a moderately ordered social structure. The ideal has certainly not been realized yet, he concedes; but to the Captain's despair at the evident ephemerality of any attempt to build a civilization, he responds: "There isn't enough of a hold yet. That's all. Children and children's children" (36).

Lieutenant Mannon's liberal-humanist outlook proves to be an essential factor in the dramaturgical structure of the play. It enables him to move freely among these three sectors – Captain, Merchant, people – fluidly and with some understanding of, if not sympathy for, their perspectives. There is also a fourth sector, his relationship with the Woman. Each of these sectors is presented in an appropriate dramaturgical form, so the play is structured in a pattern of linguistic and theatrical blocks; and while the divisions between these blocks are not strictly delineated, it is at least possible to see how they are roughly defined. The scenes involving the Crowd make use of a number of devices we associate with Brecht or Arden. These include not only the obvious features such as the explicitly political ballads but the device Brecht called *social gestus*. The impaling of the soldier is one example of this device; another is the episode in which the Merchant forces a Boy to add sawdust to the flour – a concrete symbol of the sordid economic dimensions of the interpenetration of life and death (11). As for language, aside from the songs, we notice that the language of the Crowd is relatively non-figurative. It shares this quality with the language of the group we may call the power-brokers, which includes the Merchant and Magistrate (as well as the Captain before he is stripped of his authority). Their dialogue establishes their interests and methods by revealing them in terms of their investment in the power structure of the play and by showing that, accordingly, their sole mode of understanding is instrumental reason. Their single-mindedness in this regard accounts for their status as virtually two-dimensional cardboard figures.

From this point of view the marked contrast between the power-brokers and the other two sectors is obvious: they have little in common with either the defeated Captain's realm of nihilistic despair or the realm of the Woman's relationship to the Lieutenant, which for the moment we may characterize loosely as humanistic. We have already seen some examples of Captain Gross's mode of expression: his bleak ironic gloom and his figurative identification with violent and inanimate nature. The Woman also uses figurative speech in conversation with Lieutenant Mannon, but in contrast to the Captain's speech, her imagery – at least in so far as it pertains to herself or the Lieutenant – is much more animate, earthy and organic:

Oh yes. Wash yourself in the blood of the lamb. It's alright for Jesus – but fer Chrissake – you can't fill the world with crucifixes to justify pain. And nobody wants a virgin. And even you – even you, with your dignity ruffled like a sparrow's in the gale – even you – you're not a Roman. [Here she speaks of the relentless cycle of war. (ed.)] It isn't even any good having

children anymore because they grow away from the breast ... [...] Once
upon a time I had a man who was a trapper. We lived in the cold woods
but there was meat and fire – and the world seemed to be in my stomach
every day – and one morning, on the lake – some lake – there are so many
– we met an Indian. It was early morning, and he was paddling in a canoe.
And the water was still. And the sky, a soft pink – soft – like a child's
neck. And the ripples from the paddle seemed to stretch into the sky. [...]
He seemed to be at one with the water and the sky and the movement of
water and the sky.

The mood of the speech is broken when the Lieutenant asks, "Did he
just stay there?" and the Woman responds:

No. My man shot him. He didn't stop to think. I didn't stop to think to
stop him. He raised his gun and shot him. And the Indian half rose in his
canoe and spread out his arms and fell into the lake. And the canoe went
floating onwards – on and on and the ripples stream out behind it – and
the water was tinged with blood – and it seemed as if nothing had happened. I didn't think anything of it at the time – But often since.   (29–30)

Despite the contrast the abrupt and brutal ending provides to its idyllic
imagery, the Woman's speech suggests that her role within the mythological structure of the play is to represent a conventionally female life-
force. This accounts for the fact that she is almost always referred to
as "Woman" or "Girl" rather than Marie. In any case, the formal
effect of these defined sections is somewhat analogous to the segments
in *Playboy of the Western World* that Synge in his manuscript labelled
"Comic" or "Poetic." Here we might label the sections "Political,"
"Poetic: Nihilistic," or "Poetic: Humanistic." They create the impression not merely that different characters have taken the stage but that
the whole play has adjusted its bearings and is moving in a particular
direction.

These different means of expression, and implied differences in performance style, signify different kinds of understanding. Thus, the play
uses formal fragmentation to present a struggle between (and, to a
degree, an uneasy confluence of) different modes of consciousness. In
a sense it is a struggle between two ways of understanding history. The
political struggle between the authorities and the people conveys a
material understanding accessible to instrumental reason: a vision of
the world as a field in which various social interests vie for power and
civilization, as a pattern of successive and overlapping hegemonies.
Essentially, that struggle evinces what today might be called a Fou-
cauldian outlook. Working against it is the notion of the Romantic

soul, the notion that there is some kind of "depth" to a human being, that there are realms of experience not susceptible of purely rational analysis. This latter notion, which we might associate with Schopenhauer, is antithetical to the concept of a human being as an environmentally determined tissue of various power-interested discourses. Whereas the first kind of historical understanding focuses on social relationships, the latter focuses on individual experience. I include the Captain's poetry of nihilistic despair with the latter because it is presented very much in terms of sublime imagery that encourages the notion of depth – to cite the most obvious example, "I see icebergs in my sleep" (23). Related to this is the Woman's natural imagery, suggesting an ideal of spiritual wholeness that, though it has been squandered and so has now receded out of immediate reach, remains an experience in which meaning resides and which is at least potentially recoverable. In effect these two types of poetic expression are two sides of a single coin: not quite Experience and Innocence, because both are elegiac, but, say, Shelleyan despair (e.g., *Alastor*) and Wordsworthian regret (e.g., *The Prelude*).

Given that the main theme of *Colour the Flesh the Colour of Dust* is the paradox of death as an integral part of life, the varieties of survival and death presented in the play assume a certain significance. The Crowd live on, of course, because they are an embodiment of the natural cycle, as we hear in the philippic against the status quo that is directed at the audience by the Spokesman: "We are the nature you try to subvert, divert, convert; and in general, screw up in a lot of ways," he says, "But one day, we'll kill you all" (42–3). What was implicit in the impalement scene is here made explicit: nature will inevitably rise, however malevolently, to defend itself; and the oppression of humanity for political advantage begets a physically violent people. Lieutenant Mannon, having refused to surrender his faith in the notion of social order, decides to soldier on (literally) and "win peace in some bloody parody of heroics" (42). Bloody parody it is too, for he dies absurdly, torn to pieces by "friendly fire" just as the battle has been won. The Captain, having lost his grip on the instrumental reason appropriate to the authorities, considers offering the fact of the Woman's existence (i.e., *qua* life force) as justification for his refusal to defend the garrison.

The possibilities of salvation for this society then, are bleak. But there is a stubborn will to survive. The final image is of the Woman, pregnant and singing a refrain of the ballad from the beginning of the play, the song of the cycle of life and death. This turns the salvation question back to the theme of procreation and the regeneration myth, leaving the question of the meaning of this cycle – that is, whether it is a static repetition leading nowhere but despair, or an eternal recurrence that, affirmed, leads to progress – open for interpretation.

Still, despite the unity that the poetic framework of *Colour the Flesh the Colour of Dust* provides for its dialectic of Romantic and Existentialist outlooks, it must be admitted that there remains, finally, a confusion of mood in the play. By the same token, however, we need to acknowledge that such confusion may be inherent in Cook's attempt to achieve a compelling vision of the fragmentary nature of modern experience, as many outstanding modernist works suggest. Consider, for example, the formal flux that Joyce's *Ulysses* or Eliot's *The Wasteland* use to capture the confusion of modern experience. In any case the array of styles and attitudes embraced by *Colour the Flesh the Colour of Dust* evidently had a common source in Cook himself, for the play explores many of the themes that would re-emerge in his subsequent work.[4]

For instance, the theme introduced in the Woman's story about the Indian who was at one with his world until murdered by a "civilized" man becomes the centre of Cook's next history play, *On the Rim of the Curve* (1977). The play deals with the genocide of the Beothuks, who (with the Micmacs) were the original people of Newfoundland, the last of whom, as far as we know, died in captivity in the early nineteenth century.[5] *On the Rim of the Curve* is written in a style we might call "historical displacement dramaturgy." The actual historical basis of the drama cannot be properly located, for the simple reason that the main subjects of the history as well as their descendants are all extinct. Hence, an *alternative* history, a displacement of the true history, is presented in its stead.

Now, obviously, the mere fact of a dead historical subject is not so very unusual. Indeed, the invention of the parts of a history one doesn't know is a vital feature of historical fictions; as John Dryden observed, "Where the event of a great action is left doubtful, there the Poet is left Master" (Preface to *Don Sebastian*, 287). Here, however, the incompleteness of the historical evidence is made thematic rather than merely incidental. In effect, the drama is the story of why any attempts to reconstitute history truthfully – or, in terms of poetic structure, to recover the still point at the centre (represented in the Woman's story by the Indian in his canoe) – must always be frustrated.

Now this suggestion is essentially a complaint about interference with, or obstacles to, poetic expression. In order to make such a comment effectively, a piece of literature must at least imply the presence of the poet's personality – as we find, for example, in lyric. In drama the case is similar. Peter Szondi has written about the "epic I" implicit in much of modern drama, the sense of a controlling consciousness that surveys and directs the action, selecting scenes and deciding when and where they will be set, conspicuously foregrounding the sense of the drama as an interpretation of events. It is precisely this "epic I" that is necessary to convey directly the *attempt* at poetic expression in a drama. To this end, the "epic I" in *On the Rim of the Curve* is baldly represented as an onstage character, "the Author." At the beginning of the play the Author steps forward to claim what follows as a personal quest:

I started to write a play, colours and contours filling the stage of the mind until they overflowed and fought like scavengers for their particular images, before falling and folding into dreams made ghostly by the sun [...] Even those who made contact with them, the Beothuks, [...] struggled for expression, wrestled with vanishing images as a man lifted from sleep reaches for the tail end of dreams and clutches at air, going on down to breakfast with nothing save a vague nausea troubling the stomach.   (9–10)

In effect, the monologue identifies the struggle to present this particular history with the poetic process as it was understood by the Romantics – that is, as a reaching after some abstruse and elusive experience or vision. This is the sensation of fleeting poetic inspiration that Shelley described as being like a "dying ember," in which any contact made with the subject, historical or noumenal, is essentially ineffable; the poet can only gesture back vaguely in the direction he has come.

In this case, the trail is marked with archeological detritus that the Author pursues like a paleontologist:

How d'you write of a vanished people? Out of a bone? A book? A lock of hair? A litany of lies? Or simply honest confusion? [...] help me piece the skeleton together, match bone to bone, let the dark flesh it out.   (10).

To look at this in another way, the poetics suggested here are a variation of those expounded by Ludovico Castelvetro, the Italian Renaissance theorist who conceived of poetry as an augmentation to history. The difference is that this attempt to represent history is not to be evaluated in terms of verisimilitude, for the whole point of the Author's monologue is that the audience should be sensible of the loss or the absence at the core of the drama. The focus of the drama is displaced from the history itself on to the subjectivity and fragmentedness of the available evidence of that history, some of which is manifestly false.

The disparate notions of historical displacement and romantic intimation are brought into a single focus by the myth of the lost society on which the play is premised. Cook suggests that the genocide of the

Beothuks is tragic not merely for humanitarian reasons but because these people were possessed of a unified sensibility that is now extinct. Whereas *Colour the Flesh the Colour of Dust* only hinted at this loss of a unified sensibility in the story about the Indian in the canoe, *On the Rim of the Curve* makes the point more explicit. The Europeans gossip mindlessly and make unimaginative and bigoted suppositions about the natives they encounter. The Beothuks, by contrast, speak in a pantheistic poetry:

> I sing a song of the salmon flicking the dark sea aside with his tail. He comes from beyond the place where the birds are. How far have you come to me, leaping into the sun to make rainbows? What God sent you to fatten the child in my belly? (12)

This representation of the Beothuks as naturally thinking in poetry is clearly of a piece with the pastoral elegiac view discussed earlier. The concomitant notion is that among the European invaders there exists a "dissociation of sensibility" such as T.S. Eliot saw manifest in Western culture from sometime in the seventeenth century (*Selected*, 287–8). The world inherited from the Europeans, then, is a fallen one. This is a further reason that the dramaturgy of *On the Rim of the Curve* is such a motley patchwork of perspectives. The problem is not merely that the central figures left no living descendants to bear witness but that, from a mythical standpoint, we have been dispossessed of the sensibility necessary to reimagine the story properly. Thus, in mythological terms the play is written from a post-lapsarian perspective.

That the mythical argument is not fully consistent with certain features of the play – specifically, the playwright's apparently undiminished ability to represent Beothuk thought – is not a serious obstacle to this interpretation, for the mythical element of the play appeals more to the imagination than to reason. In any case this inconsistency is related to a paradox inherent to elegy: the poet asserts the inconsolability and inexpressibility of his grief; yet the elegy is in itself an attempt to capture and represent precisely what was lost, to transmute the living relationship with the beloved into the medium of poetry. What Northrop Frye said of the New Testament might equally be applied to elegy: "The critical principle involved is that the text is not the absence of a former presence but the place of the resurrection of the presence" (*Myth*, 26). So, while elegy is *concerned* with an absence at its core, it is itself an occasion to bring forth a presence, in much the same way that a seance is meant to work.

One must keep in mind, however, that in the case of the Beothuks we – meaning Cook's implied audience, the participants and beneficiaries of modern North American culture – are not simply bereaved bystanders but, at some level, parties to the murder. Further, what we chiefly know about the Beothuks is that whatever they might have been able to teach us died with them, and for dramatic purposes it is richer to suppose the Beothuks to have had an active rather than a passive relation to this fact. For these two reasons, then, it is appropriate that the dissociated sensibility with which we are supposed to approach the subject be made a deliberate consequence of our (implied) ancestors' actions. In other words, the post-lapsarian theme is consolidated with the suggestion that our condition of mind is, in its mythical function, a punishment akin to the concept of original sin. It is as if, to revert to the elegy paradigm, the Author lacks adequate means to describe our collective loss because the departed had a value far beyond the range of ordinary life experience, being possessed of a life-force that, drained from this world, took with it the force commensurate to describing the loss.[6] This concept is conveyed dramatically in the Beothuks' decision to refuse to allow that story to be told. Shanadithit, the last survivor, resolves this in conversation with the ghosts of her family:

> SHANADITHIT: I, Shanadithit
> was chosen to be
> the book of my people
> was asked to render up
> the mysteries of word and faith
> to chant, in a strange tongue
> our mythologies ...
> NONOSABUSUT: Do not trust them, Shanadithit.
> The wind has heard our singing
> and the land folds about us.
> Only the water must mirror our passing,
> then no harm may befall us.   (47)

Thus, the difficulty in telling the story has been displaced on to the story itself, has become a function of the plot.

So while the Beothuks are, indeed, partially represented, the manner of their depiction insists upon their mystery. As Erich Auerbach remarks of the literary style of the Bible, the lives of the Beothuks are conveyed with "the externalization of only so much of the phenomena as is necessary for the purpose of the narrative[;] all else is left in obscurity; [...] thoughts and feelings remain unexpressed, are only suggested by the silence and the fragmentary speeches; the whole [...] remains mysterious and 'fraught with background' (11–12). In lieu of attempting to engage directly and fully with the Beothuks, to "appropriate their voices," as it were, the drama remains disengaged, using either indirect representations such as the journals of European invaders or a formal, distanced style, as in the dialogue between Shanadithit and the ghosts. In effect, the "epic I" retreats to an ironic viewpoint that, while not engaged with the Beothuks, purports disengagement from the Europeans as well: a "perspective of perspectives."[7]

The most obvious of these devices for representing the separateness of the two modes of consciousness in *On the Rim of the Curve* is the set, which contains separate playing areas for Beothuks and Europeans, with a centre platform serving as neutral ground on which the two races meet for joint scenes. These platforms are supported by "thick palings reminiscent of the type used by the Beothuk Indians to trap the caribou as they crossed the Exploits River in the Spring" (9) and are placed diagonally, so that the last "ends, literally, on the rim of a curve" (9). Presumably the rim of this curve marks the edge of the known world as it verges on the noumenal. The set thereby unites historical allusion and symbolism, though, significantly, these functions are never explicitly mentioned. The Europeans remain unaware of the symbolic value of the space in which they find themselves. To be sure, there is a problem attached to this symbol, which Cook perhaps did not anticipate; while the European characters rightly remain ignorant, neither would this historical allusion have any significance for the audience, with the rare exceptions of those familiar with Beothuk hunting practices.

Another device Cook uses to establish the perspectives is theatrical pastiche. The Beothuks having been characterized as archetypical sensitive romantic souls, there could scarcely be a theatrical form more antithetical to this spirit than the brash cacophony of a three-ring circus. Accordingly, Cook creates a kind of second-tier "epic I": a Ringmaster who appears as the Author exits from his opening monologue, and who acts as host for the evening. The device not only allows for a broad spectrum of theatrical effects (by analogy with a three-ring circus) but enables Cook to suggest the smothering vulgarity of tone beneath which the spirit of the Beothuks struggles, and thereby to convey a sense of the interference any attempt to understand that spirit must encounter.[8]

The effect of the Ringmaster is reinforced by a distinction between different kinds of theatrical speech. In contrast to the poetic dialogue spoken by the Beothuks, we find the Europeans speaking a pastiche of arch drawing-room comedy style:

1ST LADY: I heard that Lady Mary has been seen several times of an evening with one of the Red Men. She claims ... to be educating him in the courtly skills.

2ND LADY: She always did have a lust for the rude and the ignorant.

1ST LADY: True. But setting one's cap low can often bring pleasure with some measure of safety.

2ND LADY: That's possible. But I think I'd rather risk my head than the pox, or some disgusting Indian disease. What satisfaction does she get from him? Have you heard?

1ST LADY: Who should say. He cannot speak. And she does not choose to. But it can hardly be less than the silly Genovese got for bringing them back in the first place.

[*Both laugh. The music fades into one faint bird cry ...*]

INDIAN MAN: I sing a song of her who lay long with me in the liquid days. We cast one shadow sleeping. When she sang, the caribou lifted their heads in the high places and were still. Moon. Throw my shadow to her across the big water.   (12–13)

Ostensibly, "artificial" speech is contrasted with "natural" speech; in fact the forms of speech are equally artificial, for the Indian's style is one developed by North American romantic writers, fitting in somewhere between James Fenimore Cooper and Walt Whitman. The two forms – arch dialogue on the one hand, lyric monologue on the other – function through the distinct associations they evoke. Both are derived from European forms of verbal expression, but one belongs to an extroverted popular theatre and, taken along with the influence of the Ringmaster, suggests crassness when juxtaposed with the introverted and sublime romantic poetry spoken by the Indian. The poetic form in which the Indians speak marks them as Noble Savages, natural aristocrats like Synge's Aran islanders.

While it was not unknown to earlier cultures, the idea of the Noble Savage became most prominent in the literature of the late eighteenth century, a development that, Hayden White argues, was related to the political interests of a rising middle class (183–96). It is easy enough to see the parallels between the idea of exalting the essential dignity of a down-trodden and despised race, and the concept of social revolution, where the lowly rise in the social hierarchy by dint of their essential virtue to overtake the degenerate aristocracy. But White's argument presses further than this, and he introduces a note of scepticism (even cynicism) into the debate about the Noble Savage tradition that leads us in the direction of Cook's next play. White argues that in the Romantic period

the idea of the Noble Savage is used, not to dignify the native, but rather to undermine the idea of nobility itself [...] Given the theory of the classes prevailing at the time, Noble Savage is an anomaly, since the idea of nobility (or aristocracy) stands opposed to the presumed wildness and savagery of other social orders as "civility" stands to "barbarism." As thus envisaged, the Noble Savage idea represents not so much an elevation of the idea of native as a demotion of the idea of nobility [...] It appears everywhere that nobility is under attack; it has no effect whatsoever on the treatment of the natives or on the way the natives are viewed by their oppressors [...] The principal aim of the social radicals of the times was to undermine the very concept of nobility – or at least the idea of nobility tied to the notion of genetic inheritance. (191–2)

White's argument, while important to our discussion, should be taken with a grain of salt, for, illuminating as it may be, there is no reason to allow this cynical view to prevail utterly over our understanding of Cook's use of the theme of the Noble Savage. The more important idea in the present context is perhaps best expressed by the anthropologist Claude Lévi-Strauss. In *The Savage Mind* Lévi-Strauss argues that there exists in primitive cultures a condition of mind, an uncorrupted engagement with the cosmos, which we are in peril of eliminating utterly from our lives. The concept is closely related to Giambattista Vico's "poetic wisdom" (II:374–7, 400) and the mode of consciousness Owen Barfield calls "original participation" (Barfield, chap. 7; cf White, 150–82). This is consonant with the idea that the Beothuks possessed a sensibility that had not yet become "dissociated" in the fashion Eliot describes. Nevertheless, to understand how the Noble Savage myth works at one level is not to preclude its relevance to another. Hence, White's observations about the political dimensions of the myth may serve as a gloss on the relationship of *On the Rim of the Curve* to *The Gayden Chronicles* (1978).

The political questions are especially relevant to *The Gayden Chronicles* because the play is set in the early nineteenth century, just after the social radicals to whom White refers were writing and when the Romantic movement was imminent. The political concerns of these people are very much present in *The Gayden Chronicles*. The French and American Revolutions are discussed; Tom Paine is quoted at length; William Blake appears; and the whole play is structured with an eye to the intellectual framework of Romanticism. In no other play of Cook's are the politics and poetics of the Romantic movement foregrounded to quite this extent. Still, there are important differences between Romanticism and Cook's work; indeed, it would be peculiar if there were not.

In his comparative study of the English Romantic poets Harold Bloom sketches out the intellectual context of the movement in several bold strokes, arguing that "the most important political event in early-nineteenth-century England was one that failed to take place: the repetition among Londoners of the revolution carried through by Parisians" (*Visionary Company*, xiii). Accordingly, Bloom declares that "the French Revolution [...] is the single most important external factor that conditions Romantic poetry" (xiv). He also points out that "the poetry of the English Romantics is a kind of religious poetry and the religion is in the Protestant line, [... which has been] astonishingly transformed by different kinds of humanism or naturalism" (xvii). These factors are brought together in the Promethean myth upon which *The Gayden Chronicles* is constructed.

William Gayden was the last man to be whipped through the fleet in the British Navy, a particularly gruesome form of execution.[9] In Cook's hands the story becomes a good example of the form of historical drama Herbert Lindenberger has called the "martyr play." The protagonists of martyr plays, says Lindenberger, "are usually unsuccessful conspirators or the victims of conspiracy, or something in between" (39). The last is Gayden's story. He is martyred for his unsuccessful attempt to lead the sailors against the oppressive naval command and the society it represents, mutiny being preliminary to full-scale revolution; but he is thwarted by the machinations of Admiral Duckworth and his Lieutenant, who spy on Gayden and gather evidence of his mutinous thoughts from his diary.

Yet a martyr must represent something that transcends his own simple desires. To those who follow Gayden it is clear that he represents a life-force beyond their ordinary experience. The cooper's daughter with whom he has a disastrous sexual liaison describes her first impression of Gayden when he arrived as an indentured servant: "Ye was so angry I thought ye was on fire, and yet – afeared. I could smell the fear in ye. I wanted to touch yer, to see if ye burned. I wanted to burn with ye." Gayden's reply suggests a Christian (or perhaps Marxist) outlook: "the world's full of us and we're all afire and we're all angry. And ye must learn to love us all" (11). Like Christ, Gayden redirects love for himself to a universal love for mankind. Even Douell,[10] Gayden's companion and reluctant ally, finds himself, despite his misgivings, sensing such a force in Gayden:

> William, they's times when I've looked at ye sleeping. Ye sleeps with yer eyes open. And sometimes. I've seen spring grass behind yer eyes ... I seen me self on the grass, and the hills folding up into the sky like a raisin' o' white bread, and I sees meself running up into them hills ... and I fight it, d'ye hear ... fight it. Fer I knows I'm not looking at anything that's green but the bloody eyes of a man who'd kill fer a whore or a bottle and it makes no damned sense to me. None at all. [*he pauses in tears*] Christ ... but I love you, William. (47)

But as Douell's fear attests, the promise of a pastoral idyll, of unfettered passion and spiritual freedom that Gayden represents, comes at a terrible cost of blood, even death.

Gayden is to his society as Prometheus was to the Olympians or Christ to the Romans: an anti-hero. Here we see how, as White argued, the championing of a figure set apart from the upper echelons of social power is related to the theme of the Noble Savage; for the pastoral greenery behind Gayden's eyes will only be reached when the fire in his spirit has burned away the entire hierarchy that assigns social roles according to birth.

The mythical overtones of Gayden's story are supported by a strong pattern of symbolism and imagery. Northrop Frye has argued that in literature the Romantic revolution was essentially an inversion of poetic imagery, the way in which the sense of reality was projected spatially. Where the pre-Romantic world had used "upward and outward" imagery to represent social unity and spiritual authenticity, the Romantics defied the traditional hierarchy and depicted spiritual authenticity as something downward and inward. Consequently, upward and outward came to be associated with social oppression and alienation (see Frye, *A Study*). In *The Gayden Chronicles* this arrangement of imagery is represented physically in the structure of the ship that supplies the play's main set. On the upper deck stand the officers, overseeing the operations of the ship as a whole, meting out punishment to those who fail to conform; on the mid-deck live and work the ordinary seamen, who, though they experience social alienation, find a rough companionship in one another; below decks, William Gayden is shackled, and it is from down there, within his mind, that the play is projected. In this context Gayden recalls Demogorgon in Shelley's *Prometheus Unbound*: he embodies a powerful life-force lurking far below the quotidian surface, hidden from the light of day, which must be unleashed if a day of universal emancipation is ever to come.

However, the very fact that the play is mostly a projection from Gayden's mind distinguishes it from Romanticism proper, linking it instead with one of Romanticism's descendants, Expressionism. What renders Cook's vision unsuitable for a purer form of Romantic dramaturgy is the intensity of its anxiety and alienation, which one would not expect from a *bona fide* Romantic work. We see this in the violence of Gayden's anger and also in the absoluteness of his solitude. His attachments to others such as Rowena and Douell are only fleeting; his agony is all his own. The anxiety and alienation stem from the same extirpation of faith that lay behind Romanticism, yet its progress has advanced to a point where faith, not only in a conventional cosmic order but in the essential goodness of humanity and even in the motives of the self, is in question. Now the only tenable faith is in that savage combination of heuristic self-revelation and violent social revolution that are the stock in trade of Expressionism.

This Expressionist incursion into a Romantic framework accounts in part for the dramatic structure of *The Gayden Chronicles*, but a closer look at the theatrical figuration will help to refine this concept a little further. We notice that the projection from Gayden's mind takes the shape of a series of anachronic (i.e., non-chronological) reflections recalling later quasi-Expressionist works like *Death of a Salesman* (which Miller first titled *The Inside of His Head*). This reordering of time is parallelled by a spatial displacement. Gayden's mind and body are often seen in separate contexts: for example, in the recurring image of him being whipped through the fleet we see Gayden singing his eponymous ballad below decks while "the presence of Gayden is simulated on the upper deck," the mainmast being lashed "as if Gayden were present" (18–19). These devices are the equivalent of the process through which the "epic I" in *On the Rim of the Curve* was able to create a metahistory from which it distanced itself. Here the "epic I" is located in Gayden himself, who is poetically remaking his personal experience as an object for reflection and thus forging a new sort of existential awareness that, ideally, would provide a paradigm for a revolution in human consciousness at large.

Indeed, this process of self-discovery comes to resemble a kind of religious passion, presented as it is in the context of a Promethean *cum* Christian martyrdom myth. While there are allusions to this myth throughout the play, it is not until late in the third act that Gayden makes a kind of declaration of his version of religious belief, saying to Douell:

> A man does what he has to do, what's in him. Must vomit out his soul and carry it before him ... on the point of a knife till the time comes fer him to swallow it agin, ugly and rotten though it might be. (66)

While one would hardly mistake such Grand Guignol imagery for Paul Tillich, Gayden is nevertheless promulgating a recognizably existential theology here. His concept of self-actualization is a transcendental ideal that abjures the disguises and compromises necessary to earthly success, and he deems this higher principle sufficient for which to suffer martyrdom.

Lindenberger declares that "the typical internal action of a martyr play is a movement 'upward' as the martyr rids himself of earthly things and readjusts his desires toward more spiritual endeavours" (45). However, most accounts of martyrdom are by no means so smooth as Lindenberger's brief comment may imply. I suggest there are at least six stages apparent in the typical martyrdom story. These do not always occur in the same order, or even successively, but they all seem necessary to the concept of martyrdom. They are: (1) the establishment of the martyr as an individual of special promise and integrity; (2) the growth of a schism between the martyr and the prevailing ideology and power structure of his society; (3) the association of the martyr with a group of followers; (4) the temptation to refuse martyrdom and live a peaceful albeit compromised life, and the refusal of this temptation; (5) the passion; (6) an elegiac response.

All six stages are easily identified in *The Gayden Chronicles*. The establishment of Gayden as an individual of special promise and integrity is based on three factors: first, the associations made by other characters between Gayden and a life-force, which have already been cited; second, his literacy (unusual in a common sailor) and acute intelligence; and third, the notion of Gayden as a natural poet, which is established stylistically. This latter notion is essential to *The Gayden Chronicles* in so far as the drama itself is poetic – that is, because the parameters by which the ethos of the drama is understood are poetic, the measurement of the hero must be plumbed in terms of the poetry of his soul.

One finds a parallel in the "natural" poetry of Christy Mahon in *Playboy of the Western World*. For whatever factors are involved in making Christy a false hero to the village people, his poetic facility makes him a genuine hero to the audience because it bespeaks a profound soul. Similarly, in *The Gayden Chronicles* it is not Gayden's pugnaciousness that settles the audience in his favour but the poetic expression of his soul. In part this emerges through Gayden's dialogue, as when he makes love to the cooper's daughter – "Ride me down the night like the moon riding the clouds, for I'm off to London this night ..." (11) – or confides in Douell:

> Ye know Douell, when it's done, that's all ye remembers. A bit o' light on the water. Sunlight, moonlight, streaking the water. A woman asleep, breasts moving like corn in the wind as she breathes, the light streaking her hair. (45)

These passages are important because within the mythical framework they bind Gayden closely to the deep, inner, life-giving, natural, creative force implicit in the Promethean struggle. They convey the Romantic notion that social rejuvenation begins with a primitive, poetic remaking of the cosmos in the face of instrumental reason.

The growth of the schism between Gayden and the prevailing power structures is obvious enough that it requires little exposition, but it is worth noticing the manner in which the contrasts are set up. Gayden does not simply fall upon the works of Tom Paine on his own; they are given to him by William Blake, so that political radicalism is explicitly attached to poetic creativity. Again, this is important because it sets up the notion of one side of an essentially political quarrel being inherently more soulful. The idea is consolidated when we turn to the other side of the argument and find that soullessness is the inevitable end of this form of reasoning. The Admiral alludes to Plato's idea "that the aggressor is more to be pitied than the victim" (15; also cited in *On the Rim of the Curve*, 11) because he sees how they drift towards a Machiavellian inhumanity (15). At one point, horrified at his Lieutenant's mechanical, soulless destruction of Gayden, he explodes: "My God, man ... are you my inheritor?" and the Lieutenant replies: "Your ... successor, sir. Perhaps" (44). That it is a military inferior who augurs the dystopia is not incidental, for like Yeats, notwithstanding revolutionary sympathies Cook sees this lack of spirit as a kind of vulgarity that threatens to swamp a frail and dwindling aristocratic soul.[11] Spiritual sensitivity is given to the upper-class Admiral in order that the awful philistine vulgarity of his middle-class Lieutenant may be revealed. Here again is a paradox such as White argued with respect to the Noble Savage: nobility as a concept of human excellence is celebrated in order to condemn nobility as a birthright.

Gayden's association with a group of followers is also established poetically, not only through the individual encounters in which he speaks in richly imagistic language but in a scene in which he whips a group of sailors into a mutinous frenzy with a rhythmic recital of the respective means of their fellows' deaths that segues into a savage group rendition of "Johnny I Hardly Knew Ye." When the song reaches a crescendo, Gayden "explodes out of the group," spouting the ideas of Tom Paine (54–6). The use of rhythm in this scene is analogous to its role in ritual, where repetition serves as incantation, evoking the transcendent object. Here the transcendent object is the idea of universal emancipation, and its invocation leads directly to mutiny and the murder of the ship's Captain.

The mutineers are eventually caught, except for Gayden, who escapes to France. Here the temptation to avoid his martyrdom is strongest; post-revolutionary France is Gayden's Gethsemane, a peaceful, pastoral idyll in which he rests away from the awful fray. However, he recognizes that he is "not a child of contentment" and resolves to return to the battle and suffer martyrdom for his beliefs (59–65). The distance between this decision and Gayden's "passion" is only the length of two short dialogues: a restatement of his principles, leading to the establishment of Douell as a reluctant disciple; and a final,

Pilate-like interview with the Admiral. Gayden's passion is presented indirectly, as a rhythmic arrangement of drums, laughter, and mime that reaches a crescendo as the lash is about to fall, the flogging itself being left in darkness. Then, when the lights come up on the Admiral and the Lieutenant, Gayden is absent from the stage for the first time, which seems to suggest a kind of apotheosis – like a stone rolled away to reveal an absence. The Admiral provides an elegy, singing a phrase from Gayden's ballad, then asking rhetorically: "to whom can I say that I feel as if I have lost a relative ... too little known. Death always interrupts our most important dialogues" (77).

The answer to his question is, of course, the modern, democratic, post-Romantic audience. Still, if the audience is left flattering itself for being on the side of progress, the Admiral's reference to unfinished dialogue hints that while the events comprised by *The Gayden Chronicles* are past, its central themes grapple with human conundrums not confined to any one age. In the next group of plays, Cook examined these problems from another point of view: imagining forwards rather than backwards.

THE PARABLES

We have seen that, thematically, Cook's history plays depend upon a dialectic between (and sometimes convergence of) Romantic and Existentialist outlooks on variations of the life-death struggle of humanity. That broad theme is sustained by the other plays, but there are substantial differences in emphasis and corresponding differences in form. For example, in certain plays the elegiac elements of the histories recede to shift the focus to eschatological concerns – that is, ideas about the end of the known world, with particular focus on the "four last things": death, judgment, heaven, and hell. Now this leap from elegy to eschatology is by no means an erratic one. Hints that the world might or should cease together with a loved one are commonplace in elegiac poetry, and there are cases in which a personal calamity is so overwhelming that it seems to strip the world of all sense of meaning or order.[12]

Leaving aside the psychological connection, the first thing we notice when moving from elegy to eschatology is that focus shifts from a sense of what has been lost to a sense of what the meaning and consequences of that loss will be. In other words, the orientation shifts from past to future. Complementing this shift is an important change in the ethos of the works; for while a *loss* of some transcendent object or ideal may be presented as a rupture with the noumenal (thus leaving the noumenal indirectly represented, a palpable absence, as it were), the presentation of *arrival* at some point of transcendent meaning requires a more direct representation of the noumenal, in that it must be made dramatically present in some way.

Eschatology suggests the timing of the dramatic arrival of this noumenal presence – the end of quotidian time. But it also entails the notion of an eternal truth that stands at the end and gives meaning to quotidian time. In religious terms, this is the revelation of the rational order that God has prescribed for the universe and human existence. Biblical scholars describe eschatological thought as "centred on a divine revelation concerning God's coming intervention to do justice upon the wicked and reward the good in a new aeon. The backdrop to this conviction [...] was a deterministic view of universal history seen as culminating in the triple drama of crisis-judgement-vindication" (McGinn, 526). A shift from elegiac to eschatological thought, then, entails a displacement of narrative authority from a despairing self or "epic I" to an implied divine intelligence, for effectively the author assumes the stance of a prophet whose message is not merely personal but a revealed truth.

For this reason, I would call *Tiln* (1971) and *Quiller* (1975) "parables," following J. Hillis Miller's use of the term:

Though the distinction cannot be held too rigorously, if allegory tends to be oriented toward the past, toward first things, and toward the repetition of first things across the gap of a temporal division, parable tends to be oriented toward the future, toward last things, toward the mysteries of the kingdom of heaven and how to get there. Parable tends to express what Paul [...] calls "the revelation of the mystery, which was kept secret since the world began, but now is made manifest" (Rom. 16:25–6; Miller, 181).

Thus, parable depends upon apocalypse, in that the former derives meaning from a sense of the imminence or immanence of the latter (see Kermode, *Sense,* 6ff). Put another way, a parable is a local example that refers to the universal context of apocalypse.

Apart from religious overtones, the term "parable" is also relevant to Cook's work where it describes the distinct modern literary genre practised, for example, by Kafka and Borges; and, of course, the distanced, ironic ethos that characterizes those works crops ups again in certain works of Beckett (*Watt,* for instance). The characters in such literary parables, because of the degree to which they are subordinated to the work's *dianoia*, made mere functions of the theme, tend to become delimited in intelligence: "flat" rather than "round," in Forster's terms (73–80). The formal effect is related to a common thematic current in such parables: the idea that the characters are subject to external forces beyond their ken. Together these two elements, the formally delimited characterizations and the theme of subjection to obscure sources of power, provide much of the distinctive ethos of the modern literary parable. In combination they convey that sardonic vision of comic yet nauseous haplessness which has been called "Vomedic irony."[13]

Looking from this vision back to the religious analogues, we can see why apocalypse has assumed the "immanence" in much of modern literature that Frank Kermode has noticed. The anxious experience of the proud modern mortal who dwells in an absurd and apparently inimical world finds an eminently suitable framework in the idea of apocalypse, where obfuscation and revelation work together to demonstrate, first, that beyond any doubt, human understanding is too impoverished for mortals to be truly efficient as the custodians of their own souls; and second, that the matter is and always has been in the hands of a superior intelligence under no obligation to reveal the master plan until good and ready.[14] Plainly, it is fitting that this experience be presented in the tones of "Vomedic irony," comprising as it does both a sense of nausea and a sense of purgative reconciliation.

Tiln and *Quiller* are parables, in both senses of the word, that consider the apocalypse myth in an ocean-side setting similar to that of Cook's other work. Accordingly, the metonymic identification of life on the edge of the ocean with life on "the edge of the world" is compounded with an eschatological framework. *Tiln* is set in a barren post-apocalyptic world in which Tiln lives on a lighthouse island, reluctantly keeping company with Fern, a ship-wrecked refugee in frail health. Eventually Fern's health so declines that Tiln plunges him into a pickle-barrel to preserve the body from rotting.[15] Cook describes the setting of *Tiln* as "the ultimate wasteland – in which the keepers of the light become the only outpost, the only outcasts, left in a world destroyed by nuclear holocaust. Fern drifts in from that world to the world of Tiln, Lord of the Tilting Universe, Master of the Wasteland, which he alone surveys" ("On Tiln," 245). Naturally, the titles Cook gives Tiln are ironic. What Tiln discovers is precisely that he has power over nothing and that this fact is a kind of judgment on his soul.

I have argued that the idea of external judgment requires the dramatic presence of a noumenal force, and since Tiln and Fern are the only two characters in this play, it is not surprising that the sense of this presence is conveyed through production elements, a theatrical equivalent of the literary figure prosopopoeia.[16] Both lighting and sound work together to create the effect. The lighthouse is established by means of "an arc light suspended directly over the playing area, the edges trimmed to give the illusion of an expanding cylindrical shape" (*Tiln*,

7). Yet this image also works negatively; that is, if we look at ground rather than figure, we are confronted by the suggestion of the "nothingness" outside the cone. Thus *Tiln*'s light also conveys how limited his understanding is: while he can be lord of all he surveys, his ability to survey is, cosmologically speaking, sharply delimited. The darkness remains an inscrutable mystery, or at least an intractable one. Now, if the darkness were left as complete nothingness, there would be little sense of something missed, but Cook has made it prosopopoeically animate, giving it the voice of seagulls, wind, and waves. Moreover, these are not heard randomly, but are scripted to respond "mockingly" and "derisively" at times, though with apparent sympathy at others (e.g., 10–11). In short, these sound effects work together with the light to suggest an independent intelligence, an entity that is not itself bound by the cosmological parameters by which Tiln's existence is measured.

Samuel Beckett has been an important influence on Cook from the beginning, as a glance at Cook's early, unpublished novel, *Maurice O'Leary: A Document*, will attest. The similarities in its tone of humourously bleak rumination to Beckett's *Murphy*, *Watt*, or *Molloy* are unmistakable. In *Tiln* we see Beckett's influence in the premise of two characters vainly playing out a drama of domination, in a claustrophobic shelter, set within a post-apocalyptic wasteland, all of which recalls *Endgame*. Furthermore, Tiln's megalomaniacal story about his mastery over his environment (32–6) recalls Hamm's similar tale in *Endgame* (116–18). Tiln's obsession with picayune detail such as the number of stairs up to the lighthouse beacon is also reminiscent of certain Beckett characters, such as Watt, who attempt to compensate for the patent meaninglessness of their lives by minutely documenting their daily routines. Cook acknowledges the importance of Beckett's influence on his work, though with a qualification: "I fight against his existential view. Once you've been raised a Jesuit Catholic, you never excape [sic] it. The pain that my characters share results from their trying to make sense of an absurdist, ridiculous world. They all ask Why? Like Job" (*The Work*, 165). This Catholic residue accounts then, for the prosopopoeic representation of an inimical noumenal environment in *Tiln*, which one would not expect to find in Beckett's work (Protestants tending on the whole to lapse less problematically), and it helps to focus the significance of other elements in the parable.

For example, Tiln appears seriously to entertain the idea that, by embracing the destruction that has left him all but the last mortal alive, he somehow renders himself omnipotent:

What a world! Spread with ... Laid on ... The cold handkerchief of the Lord. Rock and waste. Desolation and water [...] It's beautiful. Holy. [The

sea and wind sounds rise rhythmically, steadily ...] In the beginning was
the water ... Gospel according to Saint Tiln. Then storm. Then cloud.
Then the splitting. Then the upheaving. The boiling rock cascading. Then
God. And after ... Tiln. [...] ME. Tiln. (10–11)

This tortured creation-apocalypse myth condenses much of the work's
questioning, troubled religious stance. The ambiguously mixed reference to both the separation of the heavens from the earth as described
in Genesis and to the breaking up of a ship is evidently a disguised
description of a nuclear holocaust. It seems that the crisis of apocalypse
has prompted Tiln to forge his own new myths, which will reconcile the
cataclysm he has experienced with the models he knows best: biblical
and nautical. Moreover, in the extremity of his alienation he has begun
to fancy himself the Supreme Being. Yet he cannot comfortably maintain this solipsistic stance. As the sounds of sea and winds fade, Tiln
"looks about, as if expecting to see someone, as if he has been over-
heard. He then chuckles, hugs himself and laughs out loud" (11). Tiln
retains enough of the old piety to be made nervous by his own hubris.

Fern's function is to remind Tiln periodically, naggingly, of traditional Christian faith, of the importance of maintaining such a faith
even – perhaps especially – now. He repeatedly plays a worn-out record
of "Eternal Father Strong To Save," a hymn that uses nautical imagery
to express God's trustworthiness. Yet the symbol is double-edged, for
the corniness of the hymn, together with the archaic format of the
recording, only serves to emphasize the absurdity of maintaining piety
under these demoralizing circumstances. Tiln mocks pious sentiment,
telling Fern as he debates whether or not to light the beacon that "if
God had meant lamps to be lit, he'd have hung them in the Garden of
Eden" (15). The lighting of the beacon becomes the symbol of enduring Christian faith – seemingly derived from Jesus' injunction to "Let
your light so shine before men, that they may see your good works,
and glorify your Father which is in heaven" (Matt. 5:16) – and the
central issue of the drama becomes the question of whether Tiln will
continue to demonstrate his faith by keeping the beacon lit, this standing allegorically for the situation of mankind. Tiln is caught between
his lingering, faint sense of piety and his new-found megalomania,
which is his insurance against despair. He alternates between whining
and breast-beating, savagely telling Fern in frustration, "There's none
left to light the lamp for," then complaining, "No one ever lit the lamp
for me. I survived" (14), and finally declaring despotically, "I am Tiln
come to his inheritance. A rock. A light that I may not light" (15).

This assurance of his own *de facto* divinity is bolstered by the bold-
ness of his language, a poetry made of tyrannical ranting and apotheg-

mic figures, rife with nautical imagery and biblical cadences. Cook has subsequently regretted the extent to which he used poetic language in *Tiln*, arguing that this "spoilt" the play (*The Work*, 165). That point is arguable, for as they stand, *Tiln*'s poetic outbursts, while admittedly grandiose, are not simply gratuitous colouring. On the contrary, they play an important thematic role, for – following the implications of the etymology of the word "poet" – Tiln has set himself up as a rival "maker" to God. Thus, his pompous use of figurative speech is of a piece with his self-idolatrous masquerade, as if he believed that his *own* "words were with power" (cf Luke 4:32 AV).

Tiln is not simply a parable of hubris punished, for in the end, with Fern's death, Tiln is left to rule the universe on his own, which is precisely what he has openly wished for throughout the play. Yet Fern has brought Christian piety to the lighthouse with him; at one point his arrival is discussed:

TILN: It was never my light. It was your light. I had lived happily with its blind eye. Cyclops.
FERN: But you lit it.
TILN: Because you cried out of the darkness.   (22)

As Cook's statement about his upbringing implies, once a believer, it is difficult ever to fully abandon faith. Accordingly, Tiln's act of pity has dislodged him from his carefully cultivated role of pitiless monster and bound him to a resurgent sense of hope and faith, a fact that only emerges at the end of the play.

Tiln desperately claims that he has retrieved his cherished pitilessness when he shoves Fern's body into the barrel of pickle-brine, saying at one point, "You plagued me with your Christian conscience. Ringing like an alarm clock" (39). But even then he wavers, remembering the pity he once felt for Fern and the warmth they shared. Finally he succumbs to his renascent conscience. He lights and rotates the beacon, ironically calling himself "Jonah's hangman" (42) – a reference to the sailors who were afraid to throw Jehovah's anointed into the sea, yet finally did so, only so that Jonah could be swallowed by a whale and cast up ashore to continue to do his divinely prescribed duty. When Tiln returns, however, he realizes that Fern is dead; so he has been left adhering to Christian faith in what is, to all rational thought, an entirely hopeless situation. This is Tiln's awful fate: that he cannot despair absolutely and cannot convince himself that he is his own God.

In contrast to the weirdness of *Tiln*, *Quiller* seems at first glance a relatively straightforward, realistic play. Brian Parker, for example, suggests that *Quiller* is a "mainly realistic monologue [...] without any of the symbolic excitement of *Tiln*" (34–5). Yet while it is undoubtedly true that *Quiller* is more realistic than *Tiln*, there are symbolic levels at work below (which later erupt upon) the play's realistic surface. In this it stands in contrast to another monologue by Cook written in an otherwise similar vein, *Therese's Creed* (1976). Both plays make use of a single working-class outport character who rambles on without apparent aim, offering simple folk-wisdom in a Newfoundland dialect; but the latter play is strictly realistic, a Maritime character-study in the vein of Antonine Maillet's *La Sagouine*. Therese's monologue contains hints of the religious dimensions that an outport culture inevitably attaches to human survival, but her references all remain pretty much earthbound. If anything, Therese is haunted by her sense that she lives in a cosmos void of meaning. Therese's "creed," such as it is, seems to be to acknowledge the worst and yet buoyantly to prevail.

By contrast, *Quiller* evinces a symbolic pattern that corresponds both to J. Hillis Miller's definition of parable and to the characteristics of literary parable (though in its puzzling shift from a light-hearted surface to questions of deeper perception *Quiller* is slightly more Borgesian than the Beckettian *Tiln*). Once again, the first trope to strike the audience's imagination is the set, which serves as a synecdoche for the ethos of the play as a whole: the bridge of an outport house. Cook adds: "The total effect is of perfect balance, harmony. There is, however, a surrealistic effect to this perfection. The clapboard exterior is white, even, immaculate. The windows are identical. The day bed, with its curved headboard, matches the remainder. The woodwork gleams. The blankets are without wrinkles. It has the sombre and unnatural look of a coffin's interior" (*Quiller*, 46).

Such imagery unmistakably evokes the paintings of Cook's fellow Newfoundlander, Christopher Pratt. Like *Quiller*, Pratt's paintings have also been described simply as "realistic"[17] – which is to ignore the better part of the experience evoked by the actual canvases (the reproductions are admittedly less impressive). Cook himself has argued against this view of Pratt's work in a brief article written for a Canadian art magazine not long after *Quiller* was first produced. He writes that "it is nonsense to equate Pratt with schools Realistic and Magic for [this] negates the impression and influence of place" ("Christopher," 89). Yet Cook is ready enough to place Pratt in a different context: "What are the lineaments of his vision? Isolation. Dignity. Perfection. Detachment. Fury. Examine any of his exteriors ... *Cottage, Coley's Point, Shop on an Island*. Pristine, isolated, vested with immense dignity, it is easy at first to see them casually as obvious and familiar artifacts lovingly recreated until brought to a state of grace.

But that is to ignore the exterior environment, the sea and, in *Coley's Point*, the sky also, reflected in the door" (89).

Cook then quotes the first few lines of the Bible to give a sense of the metaphysical context in which he sees Pratt's work: "The creation myth from Genesis is at once moving and yet terrifying in its abstraction, but the artist is drawn, as in a dream or nightmare, to respond to it, either to will the creation of a new and private universe or to despair at that which has been created" (89).

That remark recalls Tiln's tortured reworking of the creation myth to incorporate a nuclear holocaust (10–11). Certainly, it seems to be linked in Cook's mind with one of *Tiln's* prototypes, Beckett's *Endgame*, which he goes on to cite as an instance of the artist's response to biblical abstraction and which leads him to his most illuminating observation:

in Beckett more than any other artist, in any form, one can find at times a parallel vision in [sic] the work of Christopher Pratt [...] But [...] whereas in the theatre Beckett's characters, having articulated their bleak vision, leave us with nothing save the muddy stirrings of alternatives that themselves would be doom-laden, Pratt's work brings us, by the nature of the form itself, to a terrible beauty. The possibilities of a longed-for perfection stand before us as artifacts of immense strength and moulding, tangible things to hold up against the implacably destructive will of fate. Or God. (90)

This then, is the setting in which Quiller lives and from which he speaks to his God: an apparently realistic outport house that is yet endowed with an obscure, mystical perfection.

Apart from the vague suggestion of its "surrealistic" effect, the hint that noumenal powers inhere in its architecture, Cook specifies that Quiller's outport house should evoke two ideas. Like the set of *Endgame*, it suggests a face; the two windows are "the eyes to the nose of the house" and the blinds "are drawn to three inches above the sill," like sleepy eyelids. Cook also points out that the house should resemble a ship – like the house in *Jacob's Wake* or Shaw's *Heartbreak House* – adding: "This is not mere fancy. The association between ships and houses in Newfoundland is very strong, and thus, in the outports, most houses have a 'bridge.' [...] But the analogy doesn't stop there. Many still speak of 'going to bunk' at bedtime" (82). In its resemblance of a face the house seems to personify a silent, watching personality: perhaps the God to whom Quiller speaks, or some other Being, to whom he does not. As ship, the house conveys a sense of detachment from the physical world beyond its walls; one feels that it is (or might soon be) under sail rather than firmly lodged in its environment. Both associations underscore the drama of Quiller's own condition. He is uncertainly poised between the quotidian and the noumenal worlds, unsure of the status of either.

That central dramatic theme is revealed by a number of devices that gather force through the play. Most immediately, the division of Quiller's consciousness between two realms is established through his own speech patterns. By far the greater part of his monologue is addressed to God. He speaks to God with great familiarity – respectfully, and with humility, but without obsequiousness or self-consciousness. He makes no serious attempt to alter his diction or dialect to suit religious convention but speaks in much the same way that he does to his neighbours. This is something of a blind, because Quiller's humility and folksy piety invite the audience's condescension – that is, to some (perhaps slightly arrogant) minds, the very naïveté of Quiller's religiosity may be the strongest evidence against its making any kind of authentic contact. Hence, however strongly a God-like presence may be suggested by other elements, such as the quasi-animate set or the three cock-crows as the play begins, it seems that Quiller's chatter will never achieve authentically divine colloquy. In short, Quiller's manner and dialect point in the direction of the realistic, folksy sensibility that permeates the kind of character-study play mentioned earlier, while at the same time a transcendent idea is consistently evoked even within this humble guise.

Quiller's divided consciousness is also apparent in his virtually total alienation. Again, it may seem that the least significant form of alienation here is his apparent estrangement from God; for while it is true that Quiller at first receives no certain response to his stream of questions and anecdotes, this is hardly less than we would expect, common experience suggesting that conversations with God are almost invariably one-sided. Such alienation, then, is only remarkable in that, given the society in which he lives, Quiller's persistence in keeping up this chatter seems pathetic, as Quiller himself acknowledges, after a fashion: "Onced was, I weren't the only one who talked to ye? Everone talked to ye at one time or another" (51).

More remarkable, however, is Quiller's alienation from humans: the apparent indifference and disregard of his neighbours. Again, the situation is deceptive, for the audience may reasonably suppose that Quiller is simply a sad, slightly dotty old man whom his neighbours ignore because of his tiresome peculiarities. Yet enough is made of this alienation to throw that interpretation into question. After several attempts to contact those he sees from the bridge of his house, Quiller reveals his "inner agony" in a lyric plea to the luscious Mrs Ivany: "Let me in. Let me in to all the t'oughts of men rooted in ye, bloomin' like flowers" (60). Plainly, this alienation is more acute than mere loneliness, a notion supported by Quiller's observation: "Onced was when I was a part of 'em. And they was a part of me. [Puzzled] I'm still here. And they is still there, but it ain't the same. I could ... I could go amongst them" (62). Yet he cannot bring himself to do so. Apparently, Quiller has been cut off from humanity in some inscrutable way, and his only primary relation now is his uncertain connection to God.

The division of quotidian and noumenal consciousness is also reflected in the uncertain symbolic significance of everyday objects. At the outset of the play Quiller's determination to find portents all around him seems the pathetic attempt of a lonely man to find meaning in his life – a slightly less advanced case of the disease described in Nabokov's short story "Signs and Symbols."[18] The details to which Quiller ascribes meaning seem insignificant enough in themselves: a door is found closed that he believes he left open (47); he forgets to wash the shaving lather off his brush before dumping the water (49); swinging on an old rope, he breaks it (61–2); he is suddenly reminded of a long forgotten punt, the heel of which he had carved from a tree years ago (and which, in Quiller's mind, was symbolically phallic, a sort of personal Golden Bough – 67–8). Yet, as in Nabokov's story, authorial control is felt strongly enough that we gradually begin to wonder if these minor events might be omens after all.

If *Quiller* is indeed a parable pointing to apocalypse, the most important representation of divided consciousness is the uncertain representation of time. In *The Sense of an Ending* Frank Kermode explains the difference between *chronos* and *kairos*. The former is quotidian time, one thing after another without any sense of it all leading somewhere; the latter is "a point in time filled with significance, charged with a meaning derived from its relation to the End" (47), when the ultimate divine purpose and the destiny of mankind will be revealed. In *Quiller* the distinction between *chronos* and *kairos* is ambiguous, for Quiller has drifted into a state of mind in which all events are *kairoi*. Even ordinary acts such as shaving assume a ritual significance. Hence, any disturbance of routine, however slight, holds an apocalyptic meaning for him (49, 69). Naturally, this tendency further arouses our scepticism because, as Kermode argues: "Normally we associate 'reality' with *chronos*, and a fiction which entirely ignored this association we might think unserious or silly or mad; only the unconscious is intemporal, and the illusion that the world can be made to satisfy the unconscious is an illusion without a future" (50). As these comments would suggest, our initial inclination is to dismiss Quiller's mystical perspective. Yet despite our scepticism there is something real in these dubious *kairoi*; indeed, we find *Quiller*'s apocalypse upon us before we are entirely ready for it, not having seen its imminence in these moments as Quiller (more or less) has. In effect, what is revealed by this unexpected ending is that there are two ways of reading or viewing the same phenomenon, and some combination of the two is necessary to a full understanding of this play. Kermode compares this dualism to the "principle of complementarity" in physics: just as experiments with light can be set up to produce results in either waves or particles, "we might imagine a constant value for the irreconcilable observations of the reason and the imagination, the one immersed in *chronos*, the other in *kairos*; but the proportions vary indeterminately" (63). Analogously, in *Quiller*, what was interpreted in the context of "reality" on first acquaintance may in hindsight be fully consistent with a mystic or surrealistic interpretation.

Where ideas of time corresponding to "reason" and "reality" are thrown into doubt to the degree that they are in *Quiller*, however, it follows that there may be some difficulty placing the ontology of the character, in deciding where the fictional cosmos is ultimately located, so to speak. One possibility is that Quiller himself is already dead and that the ordinary human activity he perceives (and which we occasionally overhear but never see) is a kind of residue of worldly life, like the after-impression left on the retina by a bright image. In this aspect *Quiller* is a fiction like Ambrose Bierce's story "An Occurrence at Owl Creek Bridge," William Golding's novel *Pincher Martin*, or Bruce Joel Rubin's screenplay *Jacob's Ladder* – that is, a story about a character gradually and confusedly divesting his soul of worldly attachments in preparation for his ultimate destiny.[19] This reading is encouraged by Quiller's mesmerized carving with his razor of his own tombstone in the door of his house while speaking to the – physically, at any rate – absent Amos (70-1). Then, having suddenly recognized what he has done, the aghast Quiller says, "Lord, I've sailed wid ye all me life, even when I weren't sure where ye was leading me. And now I'm confused, Lord. T'ings is different. But they is the same" (72). The confusion is not Quiller's alone, for there are other elements in the play that steer interpretation as much towards general apocalypse as towards private eschatological vision.

What makes the transition to a less personal theme possible is the play's parabolic nature, particularly the "negative capability" of the character Quiller as an ironic, diminutive, everyman figure of the "flat" type typical of Vomedic comedy. In other words, because he is more caricature or clown than fully fleshed-out human being, the ethical centre of *Quiller* is placed rather more in *dianoiac* revelation than in personal exploration. The latter, of course, is the province of the character-study plays such as *Therese's Creed*, *La Sagouine*, or

Lucien, and in this rests the most important distinction between *Quiller* and those plays. There is in *Quiller* enough of the folk realism of the character-study plays to encourage reference to a precise external reality, but there is also enough contrary information to ensure that interpretation will not rest comfortably there. In essence, this is to argue that the same "principle of complementarity" between realism and surrealism that Cook saw in Christopher Pratt's work is present in our response to Quiller; that the ironic simplicity of the character prompts us to look at least as much without as within for the source of the surrealist effects.

There is, moreover, an amply established external context to account for this surrealistic contribution: religious allusion. This is not evident only in Quiller's addresses to God but in Cook's careful use of the nautical imagery incidental to his Newfoundland setting, which indigenous poetic tradition has infused with religious symbolism. The centrepiece of this effort is the old Methodist hymn "Will Your Anchor Hold in the Storms of Life," of which Cook says: "The ability to translate the metaphors of daily life into a sung Christian vocabulary was one of the energizing forces of the early Methodist movement, a vocabulary vigorously sustained by many Quillers on the east coat of Newfoundland" (82). In this context the resemblance of outport houses to ships assumes a whole new significance, and even Quiller's casual, barnacled dialect marks him as a Christian pilgrim.

As a result, when Quiller witnesses the spectacle of Amos's boat exploding on the water (an event that, he tells us, actually occurred twenty years before – 74), the imagery powerfully evokes apocalypse:

> The bridge is bathed in the reflected glow of flames. Quiller leaps to his feet. "What in the name of? ..." He runs to the right of the bridge and looks out. He shouts. "Amos ... Amos ..." A cacophony of sounds filter through space, flames crackle. Wind, cries of lamentation, a church organ resolve into a congregation singing slowly, painfully ... "Will your anchor hold in the sea of life ..." (72–3)

It may be that in this context the name Amos alludes to the biblical Book of Amos, in which the prophet inveighs against the Hebrews who have turned away from God and taken up newer materialist interests. The biblical Amos is ignored and expelled by these people, upon whom Jehovah's wrath then falls. He promises to "make the sun go down at noon, and darken the earth in broad daylight" (Amos 8:9) – which is what happens in *Quiller* – and proceeds to lay city after city to waste with fire. A further parallel between *Quiller* and this story is the character of the biblical Amos: a rustic who prophesies to more urbane people.

Yet the ultimate significance of this prophetic and apocalyptic imagery does not seem to lie merely in the idea that Quiller is an ignored prophet, and it is this lack of direct and consistent correspondence that keeps the story from being a pure allegory. Instead the play is a parable, the significance of which devolves upon the individual's correct relation to his world, to his own spirit, and to God. In this reading Quiller is an everyman figure who lives in a fallen world and has consequently been blind to higher spirituality (instead projecting on to this world a false pantheistic significance). The apocalyptic vision of Amos's immolation affords Quiller a glimpse of his own death and, by implication, the death of the world. Thus, ordinary perception is burned away, allowing Quiller a sense of the deeper significance of human existence:

> We ain't dust, Lord. That's what it is. I've bin foolish. [...] I s'pose, Lord, I let ye down after all. Made ye a figure of fun t'rough me. [...] Dat's a powerful piece of knowledge ye give me, Lord, even though I don't deserve it after the way I treated ye [...] We ain't dust. We's all fire and water.   (79–80)

Both *Tiln* and *Quiller* have been called parables; however, the plays are not merely the sum of their parabolic meanings. Indeed, there is a certain amount of self-contradiction inherent in these plays if one attempts to reduce their significance to a single clear-cut meaning. *Tiln* remains suspended between an existential repudiation of God and the despairing existential leap of faith that affirms God, the poetic structure of the play supporting both or neither of these interpretations. Similarly, from one point of view, following the apocalyptic imagery, *Quiller* resumes in a sort of anti-climactic afterlife, with Quiller's ramblings not very different from what they had been before. Yet there is also a suggestion of a reawakening of spiritual vision from a sleep of dullness and foolishness, summed up by Quiller's "We ain't dust. We's all fire and water." Quiller's anagnorisis reconciles him to death in some way, but there is no unequivocal sign that his revised relationship to God and the world is correct. It is certain only that he is closer to death than when the play began – is, perhaps, already dead.

Both parables use apocalypse as an organizing principle for their structure, then, without allowing the religious context to impart a readily educible meaning. In this light we see how *Tiln* and *Quiller* are fundamentally different from parables that have an immediate religious (i.e., doctrinal) function. Whereas Cook's parables are aimed at exploring confusion to embrace the full complexity of truth's uncertainties, religious parables are intended to dispel confusion, offering certainty in its stead.

THE ALLEGORIES

In distinguishing between parable and allegory, J. Hillis Miller declares that the latter "tends to be oriented toward the past, toward first things, and toward the repetition of first things across the gap of a temporal division." We might add that allegory also implies two parallel narratives: the apparent or actual course of events, and a substrate narrative, the conceptual relation that lies behind the surface. As Miller observes, however, "the distinction [between parable and allegory] cannot be held too rigorously." His caveat is important here, for while the labels conveniently distinguish two styles of Cook's play-writing, there is considerable overlap between the two approaches. Indeed, the overlap is central to *Jacob's Wake* (1975), which is a sort of fusion of allegory and parable, its narrative extending from first to last things.

Similarly, the principal characters of *The Head, Guts and Soundbone Dance* (1973) are backward-looking, so in that way the play corresponds to Miller's description of allegory as "oriented toward the past." Yet the play's subtitle is: "a controversial play that deals with Newfoundland's future." This paradox of looking forward and backward at once is complemented by the theme of order and disorder that runs through the play. While *The Head, Guts and Soundbone Dance* concerns the efforts of the principal characters to impose the order of the past on the present, it demonstrates the absurdity of clinging to an order that has become inappropriate to the present.

The theme of order and disorder is introduced in the set itself, a fisherman's splitting room, of which Cook notes: "The whole effect must be one of apparent mess and confusion, an immense variety of gear representing man, fish and the sea in a tottering, near derelict place, and yet also reveal, as we become accustomed to it, an almost fanatical sense of order" (450). The splitting shed belongs to Skipper Pete, and the order hidden within its squalour is an ancient moral and social order of which Skipper Pete is the declining patriarch. The plot concerns the day's activities of Skipper Pete, his son-in-law and partner, Uncle John, and the Skipper's mentally backward son of sixty, Absalom. The three men go through the motions of their old fishing routine, which, on this day, brings in a catch of six fish, to be duly cleaned and cooked. They have three sets of visitors: the Woman (the Skipper's daughter and John's wife, called Rachel in the cast list), who comes to summon them unsuccessfully to a funeral; a child who comes to tell them that Jimmy Fogarty, a small boy, is drowning in their heedless presence; and Lew and Aiden, men from the town, who come to investigate Jimmy's drowning, only to be met with the Skipper's steadfast unresponsiveness. There are, then, three summonses, each of which goes unheeded, and these three events provide the principal narrative framework for the allegory.

Before investigating the significance of each of these events, we need to clarify our understanding of the order that Skipper Pete is attempting to uphold. In his introduction to the first publication of this play Cook wrote of Newfoundland: "in the small places, the elements of a great Civilization survive, a civilization whose life experience is essentially Greek, profoundly tragic [...] The experience of such people teeters between private suffering and defiant joy. Their expression is essentially artistic, a satanic struggle to impose order upon experience rendered frequently chaotic by a blind and savage nature" (74). Thus, Skipper Pete's sense of order is rooted in that uncorrupted culture of the past to which Cook attributes an unalienated, "poetic" sensibility. In particular, the Skipper's sensibility is founded on the sector of the community that most directly confronts the ocean: the society of fishermen.

Interpolated into the middle of Cook's only published play for children, *The Fisherman's Revenge* (1976), is a long choral passage in verse in which this society of fishermen is presented in its most romantic aspect:

... the schooner men who sailed out
in the springs of the years
to the Labrador Coast, leaving
the safe places nestled amongst rocks
in Green Bay, White Bay, Trinity,
Notre Dame, Conception, Bonavista,
braving the dark water, the sudden gales,
the cathedrals of ice tumbling about them
in the long bright nights.
    Though strangers, they knew each other,
knew all the distant places, the names
that ring like a bell at the harbour mouth,
and times, when the wind was fierce
or the fish run slow
they would gather together in play,
and speak of dead men, drowned men, and lovers,
and sing of heroic deeds
and laugh at averted disaster,
and shed secret tears for the faraway girls
waiting on the wide strand of the world.   (47–8).

Skipper Pete's toughness of spirit was begotten of the harshness of such a life; accordingly, a strong sense of dignity and integrity inheres in his obdurate attachment to his ideals.

Yet the notion that a sensibility that prevails in the face of adversity is *ipso facto* admirable is extremely problematic, as *The Head, Guts and Soundbone Dance* demonstrates. However much Skipper Pete's unflinching assurance and pride elicit our understanding and sympathy, over the course of the play his stubborn mind-set gradually becomes nightmarish. In this respect the play resembles a Greek tragedy. As an old-order patriarch, Skipper Pete is the ethical equivalent of Agamemnon in the *Oresteia* or Creon in *Antigone*: the tyrannical personification of a conservative social order so self-assured and absolute as to foster a delusion that human nature has been transcended decisively, therein causing what proves to be a fatal blindness to ordinary humane values. However, *The Head, Guts and Soundbone Dance* differs from these two tragedies in that the drama is not based on the conflict between two clearly defined positions of *devoir*, or duty, but on a monomaniacal allegiance to tradition that verges on insanity. The Skipper rules his diminishing principality with a single-mindedness and a horrifying disregard for human life that, in the end, is revealed as effectively psychopathic. Accordingly, Uncle John's awakening to the full dimensions of his part in the tragedy recalls Agave's gradual recognition of the corpse of Pentheus in *The Bacchae*. In short, the tragedy is more Dionysian than Apollonian, based not on the necessary misfortune inherent in a community that recognizes two conflicting imperatives but on the unnecessary madness of a community that recognizes only one.

Plainly, it would be possible to see Skipper Pete as merely an old fisherman who misses the life of the sea and has acquired the obsession with time's attritions that is common among the elderly. In that case, the dimensions of the tragedy would be confined to the realm of *faits divers*. To read the play in this way, however, is to ignore its allegorical function, through which the story transcends tabloid luridness and achieves a religious dimension. A number of symbols evoke this substrate narrative, although they are somewhat scattered and do not permit anything as straightforward as a parallel biblical reading.

The first clue encountered by the audience is a concrete symbol embedded in the set: "The left wall has a ragged window – once a church window, saved from an abandoned church window and put to use by a crude insertion into the room" (450). However, during performance, attention is not explicitly drawn to this window until the end of the play, when, following the departure of the other characters, the Skipper returns to his routine and the stage lights dim until only a single shaft of light is seen coming through the church window (477). This one symbol suggests the interpretation that should be given to much of the action that falls between the two stage directions; the splitting shed is not simply a place of work habits but a place where a kind of ritual is observed. The nature of the ritual is described in the title of the play; the head, guts, and soundbone are those parts of the fish that are thrown away when it is cleaned, so a dance that celebrates these things is like obsequies honouring the detritus of a dead past.

Perhaps the most obvious allegorical symbols are the names of the characters; two fishermen named Peter and John cannot help but evoke the Apostles. The allusion provides a standard against which these characters may be measured. Plainly, there is something wrong, for these Apostles are not fishers of men except on the tragically ironic occasion of Absalom's retrieval of the drowned body of Jimmy Fogarty. Absalom's name, of course, alludes to another biblical story altogether; but if one keeps in mind that David's great hopes for the future of his nation rested in his son, for whose death he was ultimately responsible, then the responsibility the Skipper bears for his son's mental ruin becomes more significant. Similarly, Rachel (the Woman) has semi-barrenness in common with her biblical namesake, which suggests that God's blessing has somehow become forfeit. Complementing their respective theological emphases, the Old Testament allusions provide a strong sense of the status of the community as a whole in the eyes of God, while the New Testament allusions convey a sense of the moral expectations these particular characters are failing to realize.

The structure of the plot is also of symbolic value. The three sets of outside visitors are, in effect, three summonses. The Skipper heeds none of these; John is brought around on the third. The Skipper's refusal of the three summonses recalls the Apostle Peter's threefold denial of Jesus, but there are also internal symbols that expand on the simple overall pattern. When Rachel arrives, she asks the men if they intend to come to Aunt Alice's funeral (apparently the sister of the Skipper's late wife) at the Pentecostal church. Skipper Pete refuses, saying, "Never been to a Pentecostal service in me life and I'm too old to start that foolishness now [...] I'll not be going to any arm-raising mumbo jumbo like that. [As an afterthought] Not while I'm alive, anyhow" (460). Aside from the obvious point that this shows the Skipper's bigotry, it introduces the idea of Pentecost, the day on which the Holy Spirit descended upon the Apostles, and the modern charismatics' testimony to a similar experience. The Skipper's refusal thus assumes the symbolic overtone of a refusal of the Holy Spirit (i.e. divine revelation), and his afterthought suggests the concomitant idea that eventually, in the afterlife, he will be asked to testify before the risen Christ and found wanting.

The second summons, from the child who is directly attempting to alert them to Jimmy Fogarty's drowning, carries a similar symbolic relevance, although in this case it is very much subordinate to the immediate fact of their refusal to help the drowning child. While they ignore the child, they occupy themselves with the grim recollection of a horrible death of a companion who fell overboard many years before, the son of a fisherman named Amos. One naturally feels diffident about tracing any implied theological comment in such a case, but it may be that the name Amos, together with the other biblical allusions, is meant to emphasize that Peter and John, whose identities are allegorically attached to the gospels, remain occupied by ideas associated with the old-time prophets at the cost of ignoring the new divine reality that has come upon them in the immediate present. To the extent this point applies, of course, it has nothing to do with the relative validity of Judaism and Christianity, and everything to do with the proper destinies of these characters as implied by the allegorical references.

Finally, there is the episode in which the body of Jimmy is brought forth by Absalom, when Rachel and the men from the town demand that Skipper Pete and Uncle John account for their behaviour. The dredging up of the dead boy by the idiot son of the patriarch recalls the similar moment in Shepard's *Buried Child*, when Tilden brings the tiny muddied corpse in from the (allegedly) barren field behind the house – the fruit of the family's labour. The image serves a similar function here, for in Absalom's hands the dead child seems to represent the death of hope, the catch that Skipper Pete and Uncle John deserve. The symbolic reference is somewhat complex, for there seem to be two allusions to the risen Jesus here. There is the episode in which the risen Jesus comes upon Peter and John with empty nets and, following his instructions, haul in a full catch of fish (John 21:4–8); and there is the episode in which Peter and John hear from Mary that the body of Jesus is missing from the tomb: John seems immediately to understand the significance of this, whereas Peter fails to grasp the meaning at first, "for as yet they knew not the scripture, that he must rise again from the dead" (John 20:1–10).[20] With respect to these allusions, the symbolism suggests that, because they have ignored the will of Jesus, John and Peter haul in not sustenance for life but death itself; and, rather than being confronted with the signs of a risen body that Peter is slow and John quick to comprehend, they are confronted with a dead body, the significance of which John painfully recognizes while the Skipper obdurately continues to resist comprehension.

To look at this in another light, we may ask ourselves what exactly the "head, guts and soundbone dance" is. Does the title merely refer to the macabre and bizarre dance that the Skipper, John, and Absalom perform to celebrate the day's catch, singing a song of survival amid death, "The Sea Will Drag You Down"? The more powerful assumption is that this dance is a synecdoche for the activity of the whole play. Every occurrence is subsumed into the ritual of the splitting shed: the summonses, the denials, the death of the boy (a sacrifice), the pitiful catch, the macabre celebration, and the Skipper's return to the stasis of a fixed routine. Moreover, the deity this macabre ritual invokes is as terrible as the ritual itself: a savage and pitiless god of death.

Ultimately, the extremity of the tragedy enables Uncle John to tear himself free of the ritual at the end, and so to see the present more realistically. Having done so, he attaches to his leg the killick he has been making, to bear "in Memoriam," as the Ancient Mariner bears the albatross about his neck (477). Skipper Pete allows only a flicker of such recognition – in which "the hand that touched the dead child's face [is lifted] to his throat, as if it is a weight that will choke him" (476) – before retreating in silence to the world of ritual once again. Here we may recall Kermode's point that an unrelieved adherence to *kairos* seems unrealistic and deranged. In effect, that is the state of consciousness the Skipper has chosen. It is the fundamentalist mode of thought, where the particular, ritual invocation of divine reality begins to pervade all of life, so that there are no profane, only sacred moments. The danger is, of course, that no other reality becomes admissible, and anything less than thoroughly ritualized thought (that is, any thought not repetitive of a sacred idea based in the inscribed primordial order) is regarded as contemptibly weak and egregiously false.

To be sure, the allegorical and religious dimensions of *The Head, Guts and Soundbone Dance* are not, perhaps, the most obvious features of the play to a casual reading or viewing. Rather more striking is the wealth of closely observed, naturalistic detail of which the ethos of the drama is composed – naturalistic, in that a profound connection exists between the behaviour of the characters and their environment. This connection is evident, for example, in the concrete elements of the play: the detail of the splitting shed; the real props (fish and stove, etc.); the physical activity (making nets and killicks); and the costumes all evoke a particular setting. This effect is furthered by the dialogue, which is spoken in a Newfoundland outport dialect that St John's audiences adjudged accurately represented (see Conolly, ed., 118). Even the more explicit religious symbols are carefully chosen indigenous phenomena: the salvaged old church window (450); the discussion of the discontinued custom of building arches to celebrate the arrival of the Bishop (452); the Pentecostal funeral (460); the biblical names; and, of course, the fishing imagery associated with early Christianity. All this belongs to the specific time and location of the society upon which the play draws (demonstrating that the demotic and the poetic are not *sui generis* but draw on the same sources).

Unfortunately, it appears that the abundance of naturalistic detail in *The Head, Guts and Soundbone Dance* has encouraged the view that, as Cook suggested, has been the bane of Christopher Pratt's career: the perception that his work consists of "obvious and familiar artifacts lovingly recreated until brought to a state of grace" ("Christopher," 89). The misunderstanding has engendered much confusion and a certain amount of hostility. The reviews are a case in point: the first production met with a deeply mixed critical response that evinced little understanding of the work. One St John's critic cocked a sceptical eyebrow at Cook's presumption "that he has something to say about Newfoundland that Newfoundlanders have not said for themselves" (presumably Cook was still a "come-from-awayer" in this critic's eyes), but admitted that it was "one of the most perceptive things I have ever seen" (Conolly, ed., 118). In Montreal a critic called the play "a folksy exercise which no experienced theatregoer is likely to confuse with legitimate drama" (121). In Fredericton a critic expressed some admiration for the play but wrote that it was "unpleasant," "pessimistic," and "full of disagreeableness." She was especially displeased with the episode in which the Skipper and John ignore the drowning boy, complaining that "the lack of response by the men is extremely difficult to accept as realistic drama" (121–2). Indeed, this latter complaint was shared by all the reviewers, none of whom seemingly ever paused to consider that Cook might be attempting something beyond simple realism.

Jacob's Wake met with the same problem a few years later. "Cook finds himself backed into the corner by all the overcharged 'realistic' melodrama which obviously has gotten completely out of hand" was the way one critic, Myron Galloway, put it, as if the label "realistic" had been nailed to the stage by Cook himself (Conolly, ed., 188). The critic for the *Ottawa Citizen* described the play's climax as "one of the most ludicrous cop-outs in the annals of Canadian theatre. After all the purple melodrama, cheap sentiment, ringing phrases and dragging of skeletons out of cupboards, the playwright finally extricates himself from his play by having the legless Skipper come striding downstairs" (190). This is breathtaking superciliousness, to see a legless character walk and attribute it to the playwright's ineptitude.

Yet however shocking and depressing such arrogance and obtuseness may be, they are not unprecedented. In fact the critical reception of these two plays closely parallels that faced by John Whiting's *Saint's Day*.[21] The comparison is instructive in that all three plays are complex allegories, a full understanding of which depends on an audience with, on the one hand, an extensive acquaintance with the Bible and, on the other, the critical acumen and willingness to invert these symbols ironically in order to comprehend an apocalyptic vision – a combination of qualities that is possibly in short supply. Moreover, in fairness we should acknowledge that the very point that these plays are allegories may not be immediately apparent even to a sophisticated theatregoer. Indeed, at a superficial glance they can seem fairly realistic, although they quickly become perplexing unless one's imagination is prompted – e.g., by the recognition of one or more of the symbolic allusions or some other poetic element in the theatrical apparatus – to look elsewhere for meaning. The difficulty is one that faces virtually all contemporary poetic theatre: to make workable a marriage of close social observation and poetic figuration.

Judging from the introductory notes to *Jacob's Wake*, it seems that Cook had given some new thought to the problem of balancing realism and symbolism. He writes that "the play can be staged in a variety of ways. The most obvious [...] is total realism" (7). He goes on to describe the set in great detail, remarking that "it is in fact, minute attention to realistic detail that heightens the progression towards symbolism and abstraction in the action of the play" (9). But he adds: "An acceptable alternative would be a stark, skeletonized set [...] A structure as white as bone, stripped of formality, the house equivalent of a stranded hulk of a schooner, only the ribs poking towards an empty sky would serve the play's purpose, and free the director for an existential interpretation of the play" (9).

The première production of *Jacob's Wake* took the realistic route and received the reviews cited above. But a revival directed by Neil Munro and designed by John Ferguson at the National Arts Centre in 1986 took Cook's idea even further than the stage direction suggests, doing away with the house entirely and setting the family in "an open wilderness of painted ocean and floating masses of ice." The actors' faces were caked with grey make-up, and they moved in a zombie-like fashion; from the waist down they were covered in white as if they were struggling through snow drifts. Only certain pieces of furniture, such as the stove, the kitchen table and chairs, and so on, were realistic. Judging from the reviews, this production met with better success than the first. Ray Conlogue (who is, admittedly, also a rather more perceptive and sympathetic critic than those who reviewed the première production) wrote: "The metaphor that has captivated Munro is the idea that the living 'are also a servant of the forces of the dead.' In Newfoundland, the bodies of lost sailors wash up months or even years after their deaths, and in the hearts of their families there exists a cult of the dead, and an awareness of imminent death for the living. To carry this metaphor he has taken the drastic step of presenting the entire play as a dance of death. *Everything* is black, white and grey"

("A Chilling," CI). Yet, according to Conlogue, this approach was not entirely unproblematic either. "Munro," he writes, "who perhaps intended to heighten the underlying metaphor of the play – death in life – has raised it up so high and dark that it overwhelms the living texture of the piece." The question of optimum balance between the play's mimetic and its poetic functions therefore remains open – although it seems that Munro's production at least had the considerable advantage of not confusing the audience by raising and then cheating expectations of thorough-going verisimilitude.

The play concerns three generations of the Blackburn family: the ancient Skipper Eli Blackburn, a legless former sealing captain; Eli's son Winston, a rather crude unemployed alcoholic; Winston's wife Rosie; his sister Mary, a schoolteacher; and Winston's and Rosie's three sons: Wayne, a provincial politician; Alonzo, a tavern-keeper, and Brad, a priest. Like David Storey's *In Celebration*, or Shepard's *Buried Child*, the drama is premised on the return of the younger generation to the family home, where submerged emotions and concealed facts are revealed in stormy circumstances. In this case the storm is literal, and it serves not only as a force containing the drama (as in murder mystery tradition); it also comes to have a larger symbolic significance through a prosopopoeia similar to that seen in *Tiln*. The date of the setting is important as well as the location: the evening of Maundy Thursday and the full day on Good Friday. Like the storm, the holiday not only provides the occasion for the family reunion but a symbolic religious context for the action.

Aside from the storm, *Jacob's Wake* repeats a number of other devices Cook had used in his earlier work. Of course the Newfoundland dialect is once again used, probably to its greatest effect yet. The dialect is altered according to character and circumstance to achieve a broad range of speech patterns with which to control the dramatic ethos, and indigenous features of speech are employed for particular effects. For example, when we hear at one point, "Ye're not dressed fer the Divil wettin' his mudder an' it blowin' a livin' starm out dere" (93), the local term for a sunshower lends resonance to the symbolic use of the storm as a supernatural force. Once again too, the analogy between the standard outport house and a ship is turned into a central metaphor. The figure is established subtly at first, simply through the physical resemblance of the house to a ship (or an abandoned hull, in the case of the "existential" design) and through the ravings of the old Skipper, who periodically imagines that he is back at sea among the ice-floes. Later, the Skipper establishes the metaphor more directly, telling Winston: "A house is a ship. Lights agin the night ... Some adrift ... Some foundered, some rotting old hulks full of the memories of men ...

They's no difference" (119). By the end of the play the metaphoric transformation is complete, for the Skipper has taken charge and Winston and his sons serve as the old man's crew as they steer into the storm.

Jacob's Wake also returns to several of the themes explored in the earlier plays. The problem of social order, past and present, which was allegorized in *The Head, Guts and Soundbone Dance*, is revived here, although the allegory is somewhat more complex. As Brian Parker has observed, the three generations of the Blackburn family "represent successive stages of alienation from nature" (36). At the junior level we see that the occupations of the three sons reflect the three principal estates of modern social order: politics, commerce, and the church. At the next level, Rosie, the only member of the household who does not share the Blackburn bloodline, seems to have no clear allegorical function. It is evident, however, that Rosie is used by all the members of the Blackburn family for their own purposes. Even Mary, who criticizes the men for treating Rosie like a servant, is just as guilty of assuming that Rosie will wait on her (62, 44).

To understand the allegory of this middle generation, it is important to figure Jacob, Mary, and Winston's dead brother into the equation. Once again, there are strong religious sources for the allegory at this level. Mary is, like her namesake, supposedly a pious Christian and a virgin; but Winston insists she is a fraud, that her piety is simply prudery and her virginity the effect of frigidity, citing her sadistic beating of a child as evidence (46–8). While Winston is not the most reliably objective source, what we see of her character subsequently seems to bear him out in this opinion. In any case, the importance of her personality to the drama is inseparable from her allegoric function. The Skipper says of Mary: "Can't believe she ever sprung from these loins. Mustn't have known what I was about then, mother. A poor substitute for Jacob, so she was" (41). Whereas Mary's name is associated with Christianity, Jacob's is associated with Judaism. In the Bible, Jacob is the ultimately favoured son of Isaac; he robs his brother, Esau, of his birthright and goes on to father the Israelites, the chosen people. In that the Jacob of *Jacob's Wake* has been killed long ago, he seems to represent the path of destiny that has been lost – the old covenant for which the new was substituted. This leaves Winston somewhere in the middle, for his name invokes neither religious tradition.[22] Neither is he of his sons' modern world of opportunistic careerism, nor of his father's world of the savage struggle with nature. He is an Esau figure in that he has no clear birthright, but he is, at least nominally, the head of the household, and if anyone is to take direction, it must be him.

Skipper Eli's proper name, as we find out from the log, is Elijah (85). The connection with the prophet is cemented in the passage in which the Skipper has Winston look out across the sea with a telescope to check the state of things. Winston is asked to do this twice, but it is called a "ritual" and is evidently something that he has often done before. The allusion is to the biblical passage in which Elijah has won a decisive battle with the priests of Baal and sends his servant seven times to check the horizon for the apocalyptic storm that will wreak Jehovah's vengeance on the world for failing to obey his edicts. In the biblical story, eventually "there ariseth a little cloud, out of the sea like a man's hand" (1 Kings 18:42–6), a sign that the storm is about to begin, like that finally seen by the Skipper and Winston (119–20).[23]

Yet the identification of the Skipper with the prophet is not straightforward, for while the Skipper's name was originally Elijah (i.e., "My Lord is Jehovah," because Eli = Lord; jah = Jehovah), he is now simply called Eli: "the Lord." This, of course, is the name by which Jesus addressed God while on the cross: "Eli, Eli lama sabachthani?" (Matt. 27:46; cf Psalm 22). Moreover, the significance of Eli's name is still further complicated. In the Bible, Samuel, addressed by God, mistakes His voice for that of the biblical Eli; but God clarifies the matter, telling Samuel that He is going to ruin Eli and his sons, "For I have told him that I will judge his house for ever for the iniquity which he knoweth; because his sons made themselves vile and he restrained them not" (1 Sam. 3:13). Hence, the single character of Skipper Eli comprises several symbolic functions: he is implicitly a prophesier of apocalypse; he is tentatively identified with God, and in particular the God who leaves His son to deal with the world; but he may be also – perhaps even foremost – a progenitor of wickedness who is no God at all but a doomed hubristic mortal.

Because of the anti-rational, mythical nature of Cook's sort of poetic theatre, these various functions need not cancel one another out but may be woven into the fabric of a single allegorical narrative. Still, to avoid confusion, it is necessary to keep in mind that the religious symbols do not portend specific religious doctrine; rather, they indicate a mythological framework within which the allegory may be interpreted. Indeed, there are several indications that the Blackburns, despite appearances, have left any conventional religion far behind them. I have already spoken of Mary's fraudulent piety; Brad is a similar case. Shortly after he first enters, his Aunt Mary asks him, "What made you think you could use God as a crutch for your fantasies?" (16) Her question is not without point: Brad's fantasies include a paranoid delusion of his own martyrdom, yet he took up religion only after impregnating Mildred Tobin, who later died with her baby in the snow (66; 111–12). Cook writes of him: "His is not true insanity, but the glorification of a mutilated ego as narrow as it is intense" (109). Brad's flight to religion was not a true calling, then, but an astringent that removed Brad from life's complexity to monomaniacal obsession. Winston says to Brad, of Mildred Tobin, "It's time ye kept that picture in front of ye son. Instead of a God ye've invented to please yerself and a book ye don't understand" (113). In the most negative view, Winston's opinion of the self-serving nature of Brad's God may be taken to indict the entire estate Brad represents. Just as Alonzo represents the pimping merchant class and Wayne all whoring politicians, Brad represents a hypocritical, dispirited church that has betrayed its own faith. The death of Mildred Tobin and the sins of the others seem to crave a final judgment, and much of the force of the drama comes from this sense, which hangs over the stage like the spectre of the dead girl in J.B. Priestley's *An Inspector Calls*.

Yet the distance between the Blackburns and conventional religion is measured not only in terms of fraudulence but also in terms of defiance. The Skipper, being told it is Good Friday, simply responds: "They's places in the world where 'tis jest a normal day" (55) – an indication not of simple secularism but, it emerges, a kind of devout apostasy. That oxymoron is the best description of what has become a kind of alternative religion for the Skipper, forged in repeated contact with the cruel sea, of which he has made himself Eli, the Lord. He describes his first outing as Skipper at the age of eleven in terms that themselves make a kind of allegory of apostasy: "I took me own schooner out of Trinity, conning through the gut, the church rising and falling behind, the bells ringin' ... Women prayin' to God to send we back ... But not too soon" (56). Again, indigenous symbols are conveniently suited to Cook's purpose, for the ubiquity of religious imagery in Newfoundland – a bay named Trinity, a colloquialism that draws an analogy between a narrow strait and a whale's intestine, the predominance of church spires in coastal skylines – easily lends the environment to allegory.

This image of leaving conventional religion behind on the shore to sail forth into the unknown and make one's own destiny is integrated with the metaphor of house as ship. As the Skipper has said, this house is "adrift" (119), a reference to the family's lack of moral direction. Seaworthiness, in this figure, is the soundness of one's spiritual system, the degree to which it is worthy of faith. Like the characters in Shaw's *Heartbreak House*, this shiplike household is approaching a moment of crisis where the soundness of their vessel will be tested. The question is: how will it fare? Will it come through the storm safely? Or will it sink, leaving not a wrack behind? At any rate, whatever happens to it is largely up to Winston, for while the Skipper's ravings and memory may have provided much of the context for the problem, it is Winston who is in control of its direction. In an interview Cook supported this view:

Yes, there is a spiritual dimension to the play. When the poor old mother is talking about the loss of Sarah which is the one thing that is unbearable to Winston – a daughter, the feminine symbol of life, died – she says, "well, it's God's will." God had nothing to do with it! There's madness and there's death; there's nothing in between. It's a totally existential vision of humanity. And it's Winston's. It's Winston's vision that colours that play, not Elijah's. (*The Work* 167–8)

Perhaps it seems difficult to reconcile this idea with the identification of the Skipper as a God unto himself, but let us recall that the Skipper's time has passed. He has abdicated control of the household, and his chosen inheritor, Jacob, is dead. There is the "substitute" represented by Mary, but her values seem inadequate to the circumstances. Winston is left in an absolute, existential position of ineluctable free will, to forge a new direction for the household. In this light, and considering that he is the son of the previous God-figure and must assume control on Good Friday, the allegory is brought into focus. Winston is not being identified *as* Christ, because that would confuse the criticism of the predominant church through Mary and Brad. Rather, he is in the Christ-like position of taking control of the future of the myth of this drama into his own hands.

Like Reaney's libretto *Night-blooming Cereus*, or, more similarly, Whiting's *Saint's Day* or Eliot's *The Family Reunion*, *Jacob's Wake* requires a point of theatrical epiphany, a moment when the action of the play turns decisively and the noumenal realm that has hovered just above the action is embraced and fully integrated. In terms of apocalypse, it is the moment when *chronos* gives over entirely to *kairos*, the equivalent of the opening of the seven seals, when the final action is portentously announced. In *The Family Reunion* Agatha provides the message with her speech "The eye is upon this house" (Eliot, *Complete*, 316). In *Saint's Day* it is Stella's "Careful! We are approaching the point of deviation" (Whiting, 132). In *Jacob's Wake*, despite exposing Brad as a self-serving phony who doesn't even understand the Bible that is his ubiquitous prop, Cook evidently still has the cake he has eaten. Brad, false prophet or not, becomes the harbinger of Truth: "It is today, mother. Today. Listen. Listen to the Voice of the Angels." The stage directions make explicit the significance of Brad's speech:

Clothed in the richness of his fantasy, in the words of revelation, he becomes at this instant, radiant, superior, his words imbued with an impact beyond his own fragile identity. He is The Messenger and even Winston and Alonzo are spellbound by this immolation of spirit.   (109)

Shortly thereafter the moment of reckoning arrives, appropriately announced from outside the house, by the radio, which is playing "Amazing Grace" with "the cadences and the implication of a dirge for the fallen." The lights go out and "into the blackness a rather panicky announcer" declares a state of emergency. As the lights return at half power, the storm begins to shake the whole house and the Skipper announces that they are "adrift." From this point on, the power of the storm and the drama inside the house mount together until the final destruction.

As we have noted, the storm revives the prosopopoeia of *Tiln*. Cook writes in his production notes: "It is essential if we are to believe and participate in the tragedy of the Blackburn family [...] that the storm becomes a living thing, a character whose presence is always felt, if not actually heard, on the stage" (139). Hence, such stage directions as: "the storm howls. It is very eerie ... Like a voice out of an elemental past" (117) and "there is the quality of an inhuman voice in the sound, an intense and savage fury" (120). These climax in "the sound of a cosmic disaster, a ripping and a smashing, the final release of the insensate fury of nature that has been building during the play" (138). The voice in the storm is related to, if not identical with, the voice of the Lord that "answered Job out of the whirlwind" (Job 38:1) and the "still small voice" Elijah hears after a storm, an earthquake, and a fire (1 Kings 19:11–12). But plainly, Cook's representation of the environment is not only biblical but part of the tradition Atwood observed in Canadian literature. Cook acknowledges as much when, having cited supporting accounts, he writes that he has

extended the known reality to encompass the possibility of an environment no longer responsive to the timeless bonding between itself and man which makes communion upon this earth possible, an environment with the will for destruction to match our own and a greater capacity to ensure that destruction, an environment which bred E.J. Pratt's Titanic-sinking iceberg, a vast neolithic structure created for just such a time when man's hubris had made him blind to nature, his own matching nature and that harmony which alone makes survival possible. The storm then has a voice and a presence complementary to the voices and presences on the stage, but one which ultimately outstrips them, engulfs them, destroys them.   (139-40)

Here we have the romantic sublime at its furthest extreme. In the face of continuing human intransigence – hubris, selfishness, and the idolatry of ratiocination – the sublime has been made vengeful and homicidal. It is a figurative extension of that delicate invocation of the lost noumenal in *Colour the Flesh the Colour of Dust* found in the Woman's story about the Indian. Paradoxically, the wholesale destruction by elemental nature of civilization (as represented by the Blackburns) is fully consistent with the valorization of unreason and integration with nature seen in the peaceful vision recalled by the Woman. The violence and the quiescence share one source.

Taken as a whole, Cook's plays echo the Judaeo-Christian mythical framework of the Fall, the immanence of Grace and the ultimate revelation of Apocalypse with a sequence of elegy, allegory, and eschatology. That Cook employs the imagery associated with the Newfoundlanders' relationship to the ocean to give symbolic shape to this pattern prompted the epigraph to this chapter, taken from D.H. Lawrence's "The Ship of Death." The poem is a vivid and eloquent poetic version of "memento mori," an exhortation to prepare the soul for death as if one were building a ship in preparation for a sea voyage. It seems peculiarly apposite to Cook's work when we consider not only the settings of *Quiller*, *The Gayden Chronicles*, and *Jacob's Wake*, which seem to be "ships of death" like that imagined by Lawrence, but also how many of Cook's plays end with one or more deaths, deaths with which the plays are concerned from the outset. And, of course, nearly all the plays depend on a mental relation between the characters and the sea. The sea has always been one of the most bounteous sources of the sublime in literature – embodiment of the most mysterious and frightening aspects of our natural environment. Hence, it is perhaps inevitable that a romantic-existentialist playwright like Michael Cook, finding himself in a community that finds in the sea its greatest source of both life and death, would begin building poetic ships to venture forth into the greatest of unknowns.

3 Sharon Pollock: Besieged Memory

The struggle against power is the struggle of memory against forgetting.

Milan Kundera, *The Book of Laughter and Forgetting*

THE QUESTION OF AUTHORITY

Speaking at a 1991 conference, "Voices of Authority," Sharon Pollock declared, "I have trouble with the word 'authority.'" Indeed, she added, "I have trouble with authority" (cited in Zimmerman, *Playwriting*, 93). The uneasy relation of the author to authority is by no means a recent phenomenon. Perhaps the most notorious early case is that of Geoffrey Chaucer, who, in an attempt to establish "auctoritee" for *Troilus and Criseyde*, fabricated an imaginary classical source called Lollius (Chaucer, 810–12). Of course, Chaucer had to deal with an age that maintained an all but adamantine faith in authority; so, having no adequate historical source for his poem (his real source was Boccaccio, too near a contemporary for comfort), he decided to allay his readers' doubts by providing a fictitious one. Pollock, by contrast, lives in an age in which claims to authority are increasingly held in suspicion, so her disclaimer may in fact be the closest a contemporary author can come to assuring her readers of her commitment to truth.

Still, where there is an author, there is a kind of tacit claim to authority of some sort, as the etymology implies. And it is in the struggle to represent this apparent contradiction truthfully that the poetics of Sharon Pollock's drama take root. She has criticized an authorial assumption she claims is "often typical of the white male artist: the belief that centrality and universality is manifested in his person; that anything he happens to write about belongs to him, emanates from him. To be authentic I think one needs to tell the story in such a way that it acknowledges structurally the position of the originator, the mechanism whereby that story has been absorbed and is now emerging" ("Towards," 35). Notwithstanding the uncharacteristic whiff of chauvinism, this statement is an important key to Pollock's work because of her explicit equation of authenticity with acknowledgment of subjectivity.[1] Whereas Chaucer sought to claim authenticity by disguising the ostensibly corrupting role of his subjective imagination with an invocation of the objective authority of Lollius, Pollock invokes the corrupt legacy of putatively objective authors in order to claim authenticity for her subjective imagination. Paradoxically, in both cases the claim to authenticity involves a gesture of humility, a disavowal of personal authority.

Now, were Pollock simply taking refuge in a bald espousal of relativism, her claim to authenticity would be defensible, but shallow. For where an authorial vision has no validity beyond the author's own experience, nor any power to compel the imaginations of readers, there is little reason for giving the work our attention. But as did Chaucer, having addressed the anxieties about sources up front, Pollock quietly settles the real issues of authority on terms negotiated by the work itself, through its encounter with our imaginations. In the end, we admire Pollock's writing as we admire Chaucer's: because it answers all the most important questions about authority by appealing to our common personal experience and social ethics, and to our willingness to project ourselves into the circumstances of the plays.

Yet it is one thing to speak about the authority of the imaginative truths against which we measure ourselves and our material world, and quite another to establish the authority for those alleged truths that actually govern this world. It was into this disparity that Pollock's first full-length play, *A Compulsory Option* (1972), entered. The play has a strong absurdist bent quite unlike the tone of her later work. At the centre of the story is Pete Chalmers, one of three new male college teachers who have been assigned shared living quarters. The first roommate he meets is Bob Enns, a paranoiac who arrives with a substantial arsenal of weaponry and the conviction that an isolated, picayune act of rebellion from years before (he protested when his college cafeteria served blancmange five days in a row) has brought him under surveillance by sinister, covert representatives of "the big money boys ... the establishment" (12). Pete at first attempts to persuade Bob of the irrationality of his fears, but gradually he is seduced into sharing much of Bob's obsession. The third roommate is Leslie Lawrence, who becomes the main focus for the others' paranoia, partly because he happens to be in the bathroom while they first meet, but also because he happens to be gay. In the end Pete realizes that Leslie is innocent of any subterfuge and manages to pull Bob back from imminent violence by persuading him to "play it cool" for the time being, with the idea of making a fresh start when their work in this town is done (53).

There are reasons why this play remained unpublished despite Pollock's subsequent renown. It will seem rather slight to those familiar with Pollock's later work, and it evinces little of her typical skill at characterization and thematic development – probably because it relies too much on stereotypes and hackneyed comic conventions. (The attempt to build Leslie's effeminate mannerisms into a farcical motif is particularly embarrassing.)

Notwithstanding such weaknesses, however, *A Compulsory Option* is interesting for the early glimpse it provides of some of the main concerns and themes revisited in the more mature work. To be sure, there is some gentle, topical satire of the New Left in the play, as Robert Nunn remarks ("Sharon," 73), but some of the more trenchant criticisms implicit in *A Compulsory Option* anticipate a number of Pollock's later themes in that they target certain vile aspects of human behaviour that appear to be endemic to civilization itself. In this aspect the play functions as a minimalist existential sketch of society, taking the bleak but all too plausible view that in any group of three people, two are likely to form an alliance against the third – a premise shared by Sartre's *Huis clos* and Pinter's *The Dwarfs*. Considered within Pollock's oeuvre, however, any purely existential exploration of the dynamics of aggression and alliance in *A Compulsory Option* is less important than Pollock's interest in the instruments used to support such dynamics.

To judge by her work thus far, Pollock's chief ongoing concern has to do with the difficulty of establishing truth, and hence an integrated self, in circumstances where personal agency is badly corrupted by the insidious and ubiquitous systems of social power and by self-serving distortions of reality. For example, the paradoxical title *A Compulsory Option* suggests the ambivalent status of personal agency; where individual judgment is deprived of a reliably objective source of knowledge, the skewed context in which choices are made is likely to have a deterministic effect. While Pete is clearly the best candidate in the play to provide a proxy for the perspective of the audience, the chief source informing his decisions is Bob. In practice it is easy enough for us to decide that Bob's persecution anxieties are paranoid delusions merely by comparing his ideas to norms drawn from ordinary experience. But within the play there is no independent source to refute (or verify) Bob's interpretations of key events; it is precisely this lack of an objective source that threatens the rationality of Pete's own perspective. As a basic theme, this is promising dramatic material. Essentially, it is a version of Hamlet's dilemma: how does one act with personal integrity in disintegrating circumstances that include, externally, an environment rotten with corruption and, within, an incoherent self?

Pollock's dramaturgical framing of this question throughout her work returns again and again to two particular elements: the condition of siege and the struggle to authenticate memory. This is not to suggest that the notion of siege always finds a literal presence in her plays. But considered loosely, as a metaphor by which experience may be structured, siege provides one of the most important motifs in Pollock's oeuvre. As for *what* is besieged, most frequently it is our power to remember correctly. I say *our* power because Pollock always takes care to implicate her audience, whether through treating crucial issues in Canadian history, raising ethical questions endemic to contemporary society, or simply by providing a dramaturgical framework in which our perceptions are held up to scrutiny.

The trope of besieged memory makes plain the connection between the relatively straightforward personal dilemma in *A Compulsory Option*, where there is a deprivation of reliable sources of fact to correct false memory, and Pollock's concern in subsequent plays with the susceptibility of the imagination to mythological or culturally biased suggestion. If what is at stake in the one case is the sense of individual agency rooted in personal memory, in the other it is the notion of collective agency rooted in cultural memory. The difficulty of guaranteeing free agency in either case is that memory is always interpretive. Appropriately, memory is more often called an art than a science, for within memory itself there is no way of ever fully separating the realm of objective perception and reason from the realm of concern and desire. Indeed, it would seem that memories are fundamentally an integration of those two realms.

One of the more literal examples of the siege motif is found in *And Out Goes You* (1975), Pollock's third play (after *Walsh*, which I will discuss in the next section) and the second of two early full-length scripts that remain officially unpublished.[2] The play anticipates George F. Walker's *Love and Anger* (1989) to a remarkable extent. But the similarities are probably due less to any direct influence than to devices that naturally suggest themselves in approaching this kind of political subject. In *And Out Goes You* a motley family of eccentrics face imminent eviction from their home so that the commercial development of their neighbourhood can proceed. The play begins with a formal procession, a bizarre domestic memorial service commemorating the 1935 Dominion Day Riot in Regina, when the grandmother, "Goose," an old-style radical, was shot in the head and sent into a coma. The ceremony is interrupted by the arrival of Bob Handal, an ineffectual clerk serving final notification of expropriation. Close behind Bob are two powerful establishment figures, the Premier and the Chairman (scathing caricatures of Dave Barrett, then premier of British Columbia, and Bill Bennett, leader of the opposition),[3] who pass out campaign buttons reading "Know Your Place."

Seemingly powerless to stand up for themselves, the family are about to succumb to the machinations of the establishment when Goose is awakened from her forty-year coma by a bump on the head. She rallies the family, berating them for their apathy, indolence, and uselessness. Even the best of the lot, her granddaughter Elizabeth, who keeps the household going, is culpable in Goose's eyes, being the very type of the quiet liberal whose passivity allows injustice to be perpetuated. George, Goose's son, insists that he may have been defeated but he never forgot the ideas of political activism Goose had instilled in him. "You remembered what," she snaps back; "You forgot why!" (46)

The distinction Goose insists upon has to do with different attitudes towards memory. The memorial ceremony with which the play begins manifests memory of a sentimental kind, a nostalgic attitude towards history that is incapable of resolving itself into the kind of personal integrity necessary to form a coherent political response to the exigencies of the present. The sort of memory Goose embodies, however, is a memory of driving principles and concerted action. Like Pollock herself, she is less interested in ritualizing the past than in mining it for inspiration with which to confront the present.

So Goose, true to her name, gooses the whole household into shape, raising their morale and directing a scheme that involves kidnapping the Premier and the Chairman in order to perform for them a piece of guerrilla theatre along the lines of the satiric agit-prop skits mounted by SDS (Students for a Democratic Society) at Berkeley in the sixties. This play-within-a-play becomes a sort of kangaroo court wherein the Premier and the Chairman are charged with "arrogance, hypocrisy, and possession of an india-rubber conscience" (87). However, the police surround the house, and in the ensuing stand-off Goose is again shot. The family return her to the stretcher while the Premier and Chairman go out to address the media unctuously.

It may sound a rather ponderous theme to attach to such a humorous piece, but *And Out Goes You* essentially depicts the moral struggle of personal humanist conviction against impersonal political bureaucracy, a recurrent concern in Pollock's work. It also shows, in the radical past of Goose, something of the technique Pollock pursues in her treatments of cultural history and mythology. Generally speaking, Pollock's efforts to compensate for distortions of mythologies based on prevailing power interests devolve upon the development of alternative mythologies. Sometimes she actually constructs a corrective, countervailing distortion, though more usually she favours a personalist-based mythology involving the slow integration of an honourable self at the core of the dramatic setting, measuring the degree to which the environment is a balanced one. This latter technique emerges most vividly in the history plays.

THE HISTORY PLAYS

In the introduction to *Bury My Heart at Wounded Knee*, the classic history of the American West from the point of view of the Indians, Dee Brown writes: "Americans who have always looked westward when reading about this period should read this book facing eastward" (xii). Sharon Pollock's *Walsh* (1973) is a play about the Canadian West that faces eastward, telling the story of the brief sojourn of Chief Sitting Bull and his tribe in our country from a perspective in which the tribulations of these people seem real and immediate while the actions of the Eastern politicians, who made fatuous jokes about the man's name, seem strange and remote from reality.[4]

At the centre of the play is Major James A. Walsh himself, superintendent in the late 1870s of the North West Mounted Police at Fort Walsh, which had been designated headquarters for the supervision of Sitting Bull and his people. The play begins in the year 1898, seventeen years after Sitting Bull was forced, by the starvation and disease resulting from the Canadian government's policies, to return to treachery, captivity, and, eventually, assassination in the United States.[5] Walsh is now commissioner of the Yukon but also a drunk, his imagination haunted by the memory of the role he played in the disgraceful episode. "The scene," writes Pollock, "is from Walsh's point of view [...] The impression given is similar to that experienced when one is drunk or under great mental stress" (*Walsh*, 7).

This is the first use of the quasi-expressionist distortions of perception that introduce nearly all of Pollock's subsequent work. In this case the effect evokes something of the deranged understanding of history presumed to have been bequeathed to us, the audience, through the legacy of prevarication and chicanery constituting the official propaganda. Whether or not, as Margaret Atwood once suggested, there is an "archeological tendency" in Canadian literature as a whole, it is certainly true that Pollock has devoted a great deal of energy to unearthing truths in the past in order to see the present more clearly; and indeed, she has spoken explicitly about her efforts to correct what she sees as the received version of Canada's history: "Canadians have this view of themselves as nice civilized people who have never participated in historical crimes and atrocities. But that view is false. Our history is dull only because it has been dishonestly expurgated" (Hofsess, "Pollock," 103). Nowadays, there may be considerably less whitewashing of Canadian history, yet this expansion of truth might never have occurred had it not been prompted in the late nineteen-sixties and early seventies by those who (like Pollock) sought to debunk the popular mythology that had settled around the cherished Canadian notion of innate decency. As an ideal to live up to that notion is irreproachable and has been the source of much goodness; but as a gloss upon our national history it bespeaks a contemptible evasion of self-knowledge. Hence, even in her light-hearted musical allegory about Canadian nationalism for children, *The Wreck of the National Line* (1977), Pollock has one character claim of the history of Adanac (Canada spelled backwards):

> We got along together,
> I think,
> At least that's what they say
> In history books

She then has another character respond mockingly: "I think you think they say" (7–8). To be sure, the history book that would actually make such a claim would be rare indeed, but it seems that since *The Wreck of the National Line* is ultimately aimed at instilling a patriotic sense of good-will and understanding in its young audiences, Pollock feels obliged to debunk at least a few sentimental notions about Canadian history up front.

The subject of *Walsh* – the Canadian government's method of dealing with the politically inconvenient presence of Sitting Bull and his people – is a good example of how Canada's historical reliance on remote communication has allowed certain ethical conundrums to remain concealed in plain sight, appearing in the public mind only as dull bureaucratic contingencies. In essence, the pattern by which such information about Canada's past has been conveyed is a result of the largely mercantilist and bureaucracy-based growth of Canadian political culture, as distinct from the frontier-based culture of the United States. Where the United States expanded through a succession of frontier battles followed by settlement, Canada expanded more as a system of trading and government outposts, depending less on an advancing armed border than on gradual bureaucratic consolidation of a communications network among all the mercantile franchises spread over the enormous territory. Thus, our geopolitical circumstances have meant that the Canadian experience of power struggle has almost always been felt less in the vulgar terms of lawless confrontation than in the much subtler form of lawful repression. Or, put another way: the "peace, order and good government" provision of the Canadian constitution, in contrast with the American "right to bear arms," characterizes what is typical in our history, that the most familiar use of force has been imposed from the top down, rather than face to face.

Admittedly, this emphasis on repression over confrontation has rendered many advantages to Canadian civic culture, not the least of which is the relatively low homicide rate. Yet it is too easy to become complacent about the relative absence of overt violence in our national history while remaining blind to the more insidious effects of our preference for repression. It is primarily a determination to rectify such blindness, and to contemplate the guilt that is part of the Canadian patrimony, that motivates all of Pollock's history plays, including *Walsh*.

So, in the drunken Prologue to *Walsh* we find Pollock reaching through the figurative stupor in which our collective memory languishes to restore neglected ethical dimensions of our past to our present consciousness. In the case of James Walsh the ethical quandry Pollock sees has to do with the impossibility of maintaining personal honour when one's only personal authority is bound to the service of a bureaucratic system, the chief concern of which is political expediency. Thus, the ethical framework here rests on the familiar tragic opposition between personal integrity and duty to the state – like that seen in *Antigone*, say, or *Philoctetes*. However, Pollock sees the dilemma less in Sophoclean terms – of a catastrophic necessity to choose between two ethical imperatives, each of which has a profound claim upon humanity – than as an opposition between humane integrity and self-interested bureaucracy.

Accordingly, the shift from the ethos of Walsh's tortured conscience in 1898 to the documentation of his part in the slow destruction of Sitting Bull's people about twenty years earlier is not presided over by Walsh himself but by the cynical Harry. Harry's ironic detachment from any kind of moral conscience allows his character to set the tone for what follows with a narrative that, rustic dialect aside, is of the grotesquely Machiavellian sort one associates with the monstrous villains of Jacobean tragedy. (However, his character perhaps owes more to Eugene O'Neill's Smithers in *The Emperor Jones*, whose despicable blend of racism, coarseness, stupidity, and racism are similarly juxtaposed with a "noble savage" type to demolish any assumptions about the inherent dignity of the white race.) In using this mask of cynicism, Pollock invites, near the outset of the play, the audience's revulsion at the means by which the past is conveyed to our imaginations. By extension, this revulsion towards our ostensible conduit into the past presumably fosters our critical scepticism towards the whole historical ethos that allowed an event of the kind depicted to take place.

In fact, it is the progressive awakening of Walsh to the ethos he has blindly functioned in that forms the main action of the play, rather than the awful suffering of Sitting Bull and his people (the inherent passivity of which probably makes it unpromising material for dramatization). Accordingly, we see much less of the effects of the material siege of Sitting Bull and his followers by the Canadian government than of the effects of the bureaucratic siege inflicted upon Walsh's personal dignity. As he finds his attempts to behave honourably and humanely stonewalled by the intransigent forces of political expediency, Walsh gradually recognizes that he is the principal agent of a government deliberately conniving at genocide in order to preserve genial relations with the American authorities.

When Walsh's moment of anagnorisis comes, it appears as a sudden, overwhelming, desperate sense of futility:

> I've always been a man of principles, Harry. I've always thought of myself
> as a man of principle ... Honour, truth, the lot ... They're just words,
> Harry. They don't exist. I gave my life to them and they don't exist.   (91)

That this confession is made to the cynical Harry, who is never troubled by any pangs of conscience, only serves to emphasize the isolation Walsh experiences, like all tragic protagonists. The ethical dilemma that has alienated him from his society must remain incomprehensible to those for whom experience is interpreted exclusively in terms of instrumental reason.

Just prior to that passage, another aspect of Walsh's psychological reaction to this moral catastrophe is revealed that eloquently bespeaks the weakness Pollock finds at his core. While sharing a flask of liquor with Harry (in itself a kind of indictment), Walsh asks if he is familiar with Brockville (a small town in eastern Ontario), briefly becoming eclogic:

> WALSH: Pretty town ... trees. Shade in the summertime ... cool and green.
> HARRY: Hell of a change from this place I reckon.
> WALSH: My wife lives in Brockville ... and my two girls.
> HARRY: Ain't got a son?
> WALSH: No. No son ... just as well ... no son. Pretty place though.   (90–1)

Walsh is presumably grateful that he has no son to follow in his foot-steps, to whom he would have to pass on a tainted paternity consisting of either (hypocritically) his prior belief in or (candidly) his present dis-illusionment with the traditional manly virtues: honour, forthrightness, bravery, compassion – the virtues that he has now so utterly degraded. Walsh perhaps hopes his wife and daughters will be spared such disil-lusionment, being female and living a sheltered existence in Brockville, which has assumed a sort of pastoral value in his imagination: the tidy, comfortable, domestic place where traditional values seemed real and supportable.

The scene reveals a sad kind of infantilism; when neither the gov-ernment nor the forces will support him in what he believes to be the honourable course, Walsh retreats into drunkenness and self-pitying wistfulness. Harry's later song sums up Walsh's attitude accurately: "This country's a bleeding fraud / And I want to go home to my Maw!" (109) And, because he suffers rage and humiliation at his impotence to do his own will, Walsh inflicts the same upon Sitting Bull, insulting the physically depleted but still proud chief and then sending him sprawling on the floor with a kick to the backside (101). Too weak to stand alone for what he knows is right, Walsh childishly tries to exculpate himself by degrading the source of his bad conscience, thereby further compounding the wrong.

In terms of the mythology of westerns, then, Walsh is certainly no Will Kane, the stalwart hero of *High Noon*.[6] Yet there is something in *Walsh* reminiscent of the style of the most famous director of westerns, John Ford. Ford's films often dabble with something akin to Blakean innocence and experience by juxtaposing true and false versions of cowboy heroes.[7] The dramatic structure of *Walsh* recalls that pattern. Walsh's lamentable progress into cynicism is contrasted with the genuine maturation of a young recruit to the Mounted Police, Clarence. Asked how he came to join the force, Clarence explains:

> I got to thinkin', out here in the Territories, that was where everything was happenin', the Indian Wars and Openin' the West and Wild Bill Hickock sittin' on the biggest, blackest horse you ever saw! [...] I wanted to do what was right, and excitin', and ... and make me mum proud of me. (72)

Initially inspired by this naïve boyish fascination with frontier mythol-ogy, Clarence eventually moves on to the more difficult adult stance of actually striving to embody the virtues suggested by the mythology (though seldom present in the sordid reality). Whereas Walsh chooses to become party to the disgraceful betrayal of Sitting Bull rather than jeopardize his career, Clarence openly flouts his orders and the unjust law to smuggle what provisions he can to Sitting Bull's people. Another discovery Clarence makes has to do with the order bestowed upon the world by Indian mythology, which stands in contrast to the popular frontier mythology that had captured his imagination. In Sitting Bull's short lecture on native cosmology (60–1) Clarence glimpses a system conceived in terms of balance and moral order rather than the dynamic process extolled in the "Openin' the West" model with its cynical materialist expediency. Clarence's solitary stance is ultimately insufficient to offset the prevailing direction of the tragedy, but his determination to resist the brutal and seemingly omnipotent bureaucratic forces speaks to the future, encouraging the audience to say: "Never again."

And Out Goes You, the play written after *Walsh*, was, because of its use of old popular songs and its setting in a slum house peopled by eccentric characters, not to mention the hostage-taking, compared by Malcolm Page to Brendan Behan's *The Hostage*, a dark political satire with music that is set in a Dublin brothel and was developed under Joan Littlewood's tutelage at Theatre Workshop in 1958 (Page, 106). Yet the comparison seems at least as appropriate for Pollock's next play, *The Komagata Maru Incident* (1976), which uses a brothel setting to comment on a political situation unfolding beyond its walls and which, while not using songs, employs a Master of Ceremonies to achieve a grotesque alienation effect. Of course, the use of a brothel setting for political commentary had not previously been unique to *The Hostage*; the device appears in such plays as John Gay's *Beggar's Opera* (and so Brecht's *Threepenny Opera*), as well as Jean Genet's *Le Balcon*.

As in its predecessors, it seems that the chief use of the brothel setting in *The Komagata Maru Incident* is to underscore the disparity between public posture and the closeted truth. If there is little offered to appeal to the prurient interests of either the voyeur or the prude, it is because the sexual element of this brothel is primarily intended as a sort of index to the moral candour of the scenes unfolding therein – that is, in this setting social bigotry and political interest have been stripped as bare of any guise of principled morality as we would expect sexuality to be denuded of civil etiquette.

The principal character of *The Komagata Maru Incident* is William Hopkinson, the head of intelligence for the Department of Immigration. His circumstances are similar to those that besieged Walsh; he has been given the task of surreptitiously implementing a hostile government policy towards a group of refugees who have arrived in Canada looking for haven. Again, the story has a historical basis. In this case the refugees are a group of Sikhs who came into Vancouver harbour in 1914 aboard the ship from which the play takes its title. East Indians have replaced Plains Indians, and now it is essentially pure racism that makes them unwelcome in Canada. According to Pollock's preface, "the Canadian government believed it had devised an airtight method to virtually exclude immigration from Asia" (iii). The embarrassing judicial difficulty facing the Canadian government in 1914 was not merely that many of the Sikhs aboard the *Komagata Maru* were British subjects but that the men were mostly veterans of the British Army and so were legally entitled to a privileged immigrant status. However, T.S., the Master of Ceremonies, describes two orders-in-council that are used to prevent access to this privileged immigrant status:

> If an immigrant wishes to enter the country through a western port, he must make a continuous voyage from his own country to here [...] There's not a steamship line in existence with a direct India-to-Canada route and for our second ace-in-the-hole – a tax, two hundred dollars per head, to be paid before entry [...] In the land of his birth, the average Indian's wage is nine dollars a year. There – you see how we operate, Hopkinson? Never a mention of race, colour, or creed – and yet – we allow British subjects to enter; they are British subjects; we don't allow them to enter.   (10–11)

The spanner in these nefarious works is that a group of local Sikhs have raised enough funds to pay the head tax and intend to covertly pass the money on to those on the Komagata Maru (11). Hence the government has sufficient warrant only to keep the refugees aboard ship in the harbour temporarily; meanwhile, they seek a more conclusive pretext for denying the Sikhs entry. The stand-off lasts two months. In the end, having coerced the captain of the *Komagata Maru* to allege mutiny, they force the ship from the harbour with an armed navy cruiser.

So in this play as in *Walsh* a very literal siege is enforced against the refugees, who suffer serious deprivation of food, of medical provisions, of liberty, and of dignity. Yet this siege is even less present to *The Komagata Maru Incident* than the siege of Sitting Bull and his people was to *Walsh*. Indeed, the only representative of the refugees we see is the nameless Woman with her infant child, who is positioned behind a "grill-like frame" (v) at the upper rear of the stage – like a nagging thought at the back of a mind. Initially this may appear to be a strange choice, for Pollock informs us that the great majority of the refugees were men. Why, then, would a woman be chosen to represent all those on the boat?

The choice becomes less puzzling when we recognize that, once again, the siege that Pollock has made the central dramatic focus of the play is not the literal siege of the refugees but the metaphoric siege of her protagonist's mind. From this perspective it seems likely that a Woman with a baby represents the Sikhs to Hopkinson's stricken conscience because the figure looming largest in his guilty conscience is also a mother: his own. About two-thirds of the way through the play we discover that Hopkinson is the child of a "miscegenous" marriage, his mother East Indian and his father English. He fiercely represses this fact about himself (e.g., 14) and is enraged when Evy, his favourite at the brothel, taunts him with it (48–51). The implication seems to be that Hopkinson's zealousness in ridding Vancouver of the Sikh refugees is commensurate with the desperation with which he denies his racial origins. In this way Pollock integrates the social and personal dimensions of her play so that racial prejudice emerges as a kind of self-hatred. That is undoubtedly one of the fundamental paradoxes underlying all xenophobia; viciousness towards other races is almost invariably engendered by a pitiable weakness and anxious self-doubt in the bigot's own character.

But another element also lends power to the choice of the Woman and her child as the representatives of the Sikhs. In the Western world the notion of a mother and child being cruelly denied refuge inevitably, even if only subconsciously, evokes the Christian Nativity. By means of this double allusion to two non-historical contexts – the psychological and the theological – Pollock is able to extend the culpability for a historical incident much further into the private consciences of her audience. Thus, guilt for the wrong done in this play escapes from the shameful episode in the national past where it had been more or less comfortably confined, to become part of a parable about the way humans perennially seek to rationalize the betrayal of their moral convictions.

Pollock further sketches the moral context for the story in a subplot involving Georg Braun, a German expatriate who works as a spy and adviser to Hopkinson. Were there any doubt about the historical associations Georg is intended to evoke, it would be dispelled by the brief, pseudo-scientific, "Aryan" analysis of racial politics he offers to the sympathetic ears of Hopkinson:

> The laws of evolution that have shaped the energy, enterprise, and efficiency of the race northwards have left less richly endowed the peoples inhabiting the southern regions [...] This process is no passing accident, but part of the cosmic order of things which we have no power to alter. The European races must administrate; all that's needed to assure their success is a clearly defined conception of moral necessity.   (17)

This complacent arrogance about racial superiority provides the keynote for the ethos framing the whole play. Pollock has taken the superciliousness inherent in the conception and execution of the government's immigration policy and translated it into theatrical convention.

The main theatrical expression of the supercilious ethos is T.S., a sort of grotesque authority figure who maintains an unremitting attitude of savage irony. In an interview Pollock related the genesis of this character:

How on earth could I communicate all that information in a way that might be vaguely entertaining? When I read the newspaper accounts of the day I discovered the wonderful circus or carnival atmosphere of the dock area with the marching bands and popcorn, the apples and balloons. That is the image that began to dominate my mind. Then I thought, if this is a carnival, or circus, I could have a Master of Ceremonies. Then who would be the wild animal? Who's the savage beast? Well, of course, the savage beast is the person sitting out on the *Komagata Maru* and the town people are the "civilized" ones (*Work*, 119–20).

The effect is similar to that achieved by Michael Cook through the use of the Ringmaster in *On the Rim of the Curve*, which, notably, shares not only a mediating figure who embodies a whole society's callousness but the peculiar remoteness of the characters who are the victims of that callousness.[8] From a dramaturgical point of view the combination of the grotesque mediators and the flat victim characters throws the emphasis forward upon the theatrical frame, thus intensifying the alienation effect. But from a humanist point of view the ironic mediator provides a mask, a crude disguise for the relation between ethical failures and the limits of imagination. It is true that in Pollock's play, as in Cook's, the historical victims are insufficiently vivid from the standpoint of humanist ethics; they barely appear to be any more than what their persecutors regard them as – "savage beasts," in Pollock's phrase. If Terence's maxim is our touchstone, something human remains alien to us here, bespeaking a failure of some sort. But whose failure is it? The failure could be laid at Pollock's own feet, as more than one critic has, complaining, for example, that "the decision to portray [the Woman] as a type-character robs her of much of her humanity and makes the painful experience on shipboard seem distant rather than immediate" (Salter, xviii). But the failure can as easily be read as a kind of deliberate ploy, a means of structurally representing an imaginative failure in Canadian society, from which the inhumanity arose in the first place.

To my mind the latter reading results in a more satisfying and useful understanding of the play, yet the dramaturgical technique is not altogether unproblematic, for there is a risk of the irony becoming too heavy-handed. Pollock has not been able to avoid this weakness altogether. T.S.'s bigoted sneers about the Japanese origin of the ship (1), the colour of the refugees (5), and their religion (26), for example; or his speech to the ship's captain, which includes an acrostic on "mutiny" (52–3); or his final soft-shoe dance (72) – all this lays the irony on with a trowel. The attitude of this coarsely inhumane, obscenely cheerful exploiter of misery is so very invidious that it encourages little subtlety or thoughtfulness in our response. It seems all but inevitable that we will shrink from and deplore the unfathomable, inexhaustible nefariousness of the bigoted Canadian authorities.

Where it is too easy for us to condemn racism, we are too easily made righteous; we indulge in a kind of *pro forma mea culpa* that does not really examine the conflicting desires that gave rise to the vileness in the first place.[9] To be sure, there is a good deal of effort put into making the motivation of Hopkinson himself plausible and dramatically accessible. But, as Diane Bessai neatly puts it, "Hopkinson is a special case rather than a typically motivated example of racist thinking" (129). Thus, the specific personal element is not wholly fused with the play's political message. Expounding the latter aspect remains chiefly the job of T.S., resulting in a true but rather unengaging polemic.

For all its sophistication and theatricality, *The Komagata Maru Incident* is less successful on the whole than *Walsh*. Still, in the complexity of Hopkinson's character and in his ambiguous relationships with others, the play makes significant advances. It is in this area – the exploration of ambiguous character – that Pollock's next several plays would be rooted, resulting in some of her strongest writing to date.

Because *One Tiger to a Hill* dramatizes a historical, political event, like *Walsh* and *The Komagata Maru Incident*, it seems sensible and convenient to lump the work in with the history plays. However, a word of caution is in order. It is true that, in separating the groups of plays in this way, I am following a well-trodden path. Several critics have descried a shift in Pollock's dramatic themes from a "political" (or public) focus in the seventies to a "domestic" focus in the eighties. Robert Nunn describes it as "a gradual shift from big issues to the characters on whom (and within whom) these issues have their impact" ("Sharon," 81). Others, such as Diane Bessai, describe slightly more abrupt versions of such a shift, in which *Blood Relations* (1980) is a "turning point" into a more "personal" focus (127) or, as Cynthia Zimmerman sees it, a shift in the sense of authority to focus on "the paternalistic, dictatorial structure of the family" (*Playwriting*, 73).

In these accounts of her development *One Tiger to a Hill* (1980) is cited as the last of the overtly political plays. However, as each of the above critics acknowledges to a degree, the theory of a schism between the early and the later works can be exaggerated. From the most literal point of view it should be noted that *Blood Relations* is also based on a historical incident that, however private originally, finally had broad political implications. Furthermore, even its place in the order of the plays is not a clear-cut matter. The earliest version of *Blood Relations*, called *My Name Is Lisbeth*, was staged in March 1976, only two months after the première of *The Komagata Maru Incident* and four full years before the first production of *One Tiger to a Hill*.[10] Chronology alone therefore discourages the ascription any shifts in topic to an abrupt transformation in Pollock's imagination.

Moreover, working from the premise that the historical settings of the plays are largely incidental to dramatic and thematic content (given that any two playwrights will derive quite different plays from the same historical events),[11] we may see a continuous development in Pollock's dramaturgical articulation of a focused group of concerns and principles. At least as significant as the change in material from historical-political subjects to the realm of domestic concern is the shift in dramatic technique from the ironic epic style to the more character-based dramaturgy of the three plays that premièred in their finished versions within the same year, 1980: *One Tiger to a Hill* in January, *Blood Relations* in March, and *Generations* in October.

In *One Tiger to a Hill* the alienation devices that create the theatrical frames for *Walsh* and *The Komagata Maru Incident* – the use of the despicable Harry as a historical narrator, and the offensive T.S. as the master of ceremonies – are replaced by a character who fosters a sense of close familiarity and identity with the audience. Everett Chalmers (named after Pollock's father), whose soliloquy begins the play, is a genial, decent, middle-class, middle-aged suburban type, the sort with whom an audience at a mainstream regional theatre is likely to identify with easily and cheerfully. The connection is facilitated by the first words out of Chalmers's mouth – a well-mannered introduction of himself using the diminutive of his given name, followed by an immediate appeal to a base of common experience:

> My name is Ev Chalmers, Everett Chalmers ... No one calls their kids that any more. It's all Robyn and Jason today. My kids, Robyn and Jason – and Anne with an e, that's my wife. (76)

The point of cultivating this intimacy between character and audience quickly becomes evident when Chalmers speaks of his troubled conscience vis-à-vis the Canadian prison system:

What if the things you hear, the things you don't want to hear, the things
they won't let you hear, what if those things really happen inside? Would I
be any different in essence from all those good Germans who passed
Dachau and Buchenwald and never asked questions?   (76)

While the starkness of the moral analogy drawn by Chalmers may be
slightly hyperbolic (there is as yet no evidence suggesting that Correc-
tions Canada has committed itself to the systematic genocide of an
innocent people), the point that any injustices within the penal system
are in part made possible by the conniving of the average citizen is
carried home strongly and inescapably – all the more so because the
messenger is an exemplar of that privileged, old-fashioned decency
with which most of the audience is likely to be familiar.

One Tiger to a Hill differs from Pollock's other historical plays in
that the occurrence on which the story is based was taken from very
recent history. In 1975 at a penitentiary in New Westminster, British
Columbia, there was a hostage-taking incident in which a rehabilitation worker was shot (8). That event provides a literal siege around
which the events of the play unfold. As with so many sieges, for a time
both parties were entrapped: the prisoners by the armed guard outside;
the authorities by the threat to the hostages within.

In Pollock's version of the story the representatives of the prison
establishment are the warden, Wallace; his head of security, McGowan;
and a guard, Hanzuk. The prisoners are represented by Tommy Paul,
a Métis in his late twenties, and his younger, mentally disturbed sidekick, MacDermott. The other five characters are all intermediaries of
one kind or another: Chalmers, the outsider called in to mediate once
the crisis has begun; Lina Benz, an older, leftist spokesperson for prisoners' rights; Stocker, a teacher in the literacy program who is acci-
dentally caught up in the affair; Soholuk, a rehabilitation officer; and
finally his colleague, Dede Walker, the idealistic and naïve young social
worker who is shot.

At first glance Walker may seem the embodiment of virtue confronted by corruption, a martyr to social injustice. However, Pollock
has no such simple equation in mind, as she discussed in her 1982
interview: "I see Walker as the ultimate villain in the piece. And there's
this terrible tendency for people to want to make her a heroine, to see
her as this wonderful individual in love, no matter what it is I have her
say. She's that well-meaning person who causes the shit to hit the fan.
I don't know that she should have been killed for what she did. Well,
in fact she isn't. It's [Hansuk] who shoots her, and he sees her actions
as betrayal" (*Work*, 121). It would appear that the discrepancy
between the view of Walker that Pollock repudiates and the one she

advocates has to do with whether the play is read as melodrama or as existential parable. To be sure, we may see, if we wish, the stock characters of melodrama: the powerful and socially invulnerable villains in those who run the prison; the simple, downtrodden and misguided but earnest poor in the prisoners; and the bewildered but courageous and charitable middle-class protagonists in the group of intermediaries; and finally, in Walker, the virginal, innocent, ingenuously virtuous heroine who provides the moral centre of the melodrama.

However, it would be difficult to remain comfortable for long with the melodramatic interpretation. Above all else, what makes such a reading incongruous is that opening speech by Chalmers. For it is only possible to retreat into melodrama's reassuringly stark delineations of good and evil if we ignore the questions Chalmers poses at the outset of the play. What happens when we are removed by ignorance and apathy from responsibility for actions taken on our behalf? What is the existential effect upon us? With these as our parameters, the culpability of Walker becomes more apprehensible. She sees the prisoners through a screen of sentimentality that is closely related to the melodramatic perspective, and she thereby effectively abrogates her own responsibility for their circumstances.

Her relationship to Tommy Paul in particular is built on a dishonest foundation. While he takes Walker's affection for him at face value, she eventually admits: "I love you as ... as a person who's been ... fucked up, and screwed around but – that's as far as it goes" (134). In short, she has pity and compassion for him in the abstract, but no real interest in him for himself. So the main accusation against the penal system, that it is dehumanizing, may be turned against Walker herself.

Now, if all this seems unduly harsh towards Walker, dilating a minor and, after all, rather common character flaw for the sake of façile scapegoating, I should hasten to add that the point here is by no means to lay righteous blame. As Pollock suggests with Chalmers's opening speech, the point is that we should ruthlessly scrutinize our own complicity in the injustice rather than moralizing sanctimoniously. Hence, while it is Chalmers who stands as the mentally besieged protagonist equivalent to Walsh and Hopkinson (though his active role is not nearly so central as theirs), the ultimate target is undoubtedly us in the audience. Pollock's comments in her 1982 interview support this reading: "It's a memory play and Chalmers has now taken a positive stance in terms of what has happened to him. Even though the play ends with him asking is everything lies, his speech at the beginning asks more, asks if we are the same as the Nazis. I want the audience to be able to make that speech he has at the beginning after they leave the play" (Work, 121). In short, Pollock's ultimate intent is to sow seeds of doubt in any complacent righteousness that is the result of ignorance.

The root of the problem may be that professionalization of the penal system in the modern age has effectively removed it from public consciousness, its activities now entirely outside the average person's ambit. As Michel Foucault argues in *Discipline and Punish*, in the modern judicial system, punishment "leaves the domain of more or less everyday perception and enters that of abstract consciousness; its effectiveness is seen as arising from its inevitability, not from its visible intensity ... As a result, justice no longer takes public responsibility for the violence that is bound up with its practice" (9). Yet physical coercion, restraint, and, inevitably, actual violence, all continue to play an integral role in the system. *One Tiger to a Hill* forces us to look past the realm of abstract consciousness to witness the system at its point of impact upon real human beings, and it does so in much the same way that Walker's abstract "love" is forcibly confronted with the reality of Tommy Paul's emotional life: we are confined among the prisoners themselves, our ignorance besieged with knowledge of these characters.

Now, in itself, that may be a somewhat extravagant way of describing the effect of the play, making it sound more like the theatrical terrorism of something like the Living Theatre's production of *The Brig*, where, following Artaud's theory, the sensory overload of the production inflicts a cruelty upon the audience supposedly similar to what the prisoners endure. Yet the description is not very far wrong, for an analogous confrontation, albeit less shocking and more contemplative, is forcibly encountered by the audience as soon as they begin to reason their way ethically out of the narrative of Pollock's play to return to their own familiar world. Here the siege motif has its greatest effect. It is unlikely that the violent ending of the play will correspond with anyone's inner desires, but the question of how the siege might have been more satisfactorily lifted returns us again and again to the central dilemma – and, hence, to something of the guilty perplexity seen in Chalmers. Many in the audience will be left in a mentally besieged condition in which they find themselves questioning the relationship between a liberal and a liberated conscience.

BRINGING IT ALL BACK HOME: THE FAMILY PLAYS

Pollock's most produced play, *Blood Relations* (March 1980), again draws her audience into a besieged state, although in this case the sense of familiarity used to engage us depends not upon class identification, as it did with Ev Chalmers, but a personal identification with her heroine. Needless to say, this task would be made difficult by Lizzie Borden's preceding reputation; Pollock confronts the point directly. Not far into the play the Actress character refers to the skipping rhyme that is the first (and often the last) thing that most of us ever knew about Lizzie Borden:

> Lizzie Borden took an axe
> Gave her mother forty whacks.
> When the job was nicely done
> She gave her father forty-one.

As we hear these words, we may recall the delicious morbidity of the scandal as we first learned the chant. But at this point in the play the year is 1902, a decade after the murders and Lizzie's acquittal. Miss Lizzie is sanguine and ironic about the matter, not at all the crazed fiend we might have expected. Indeed, we feel fairly comfortable in her company; she seems reasonable, confident, and congenial. The chanting of the children in the street might speak for the suspicions on their elders' minds, but as sieges go, this does not seem a very distressing one. Windows can be shut against the irritating taunts outside; within, Miss Lizzie seems to be very much the mistress of her own household. Life had been far less endurable, it seems, when her father and stepmother were still alive and she was in thrall to their rule of the family home.

The recovery of those circumstances, the circumstances in which the murders took place, is the subject of *Blood Relations*. But the memories of Miss Lizzie herself prove to be only an elliptical, tentative guide. Instead it is the Actress, a surrogate for us in the audience, who attempts to recover the past, to conjure a memory that is not her own but that gradually assumes the vividness of a lived history. The punning title refers not merely to biological relatedness and to those interactions among people that result in the spilling of blood, but to the *telling* of how that blood was spilt, to the act of relating the history of an event. The play demonstrates the creation of cultural memory by inviting us to place our modern selves in historical roles through a combination of cultural and psychological assumptions. It is the latter sort of "blood relation" that gives rise to what Pollock calls the "dream thesis" of 1892 (13).

The Actress claims that her inquiries of Miss Lizzie are driven by "a compulsion to know the truth" (19). But we should be careful about taking this at face value. There is a prurient sort of craving after answers that seeks no further than an answer to "Did she or didn't

she?" and Pollock makes it clear that the truth's complexity in this case
is unlikely to be crammed into quite so simple a polarity. When Miss
Lizzie asks the Actress what she thinks, the Actress's response could
well serve for the audience were it speaking to Pollock about the story:
"I think ... that you're aware there is a certain fascination in the ambiguity ... You always paint the background but leave the rest to my
imagination" (20). Leaving the details to the Actress's – or the audience's – imagination is a sort of invitation to step into Lizzie's shoes,
and this is precisely what the Actress does, becoming Lizzie in 1892,
while Miss Lizzie takes on the role of Bridget, the maid.

Having an actress portray an Actress who, in turn, offers a representation of Lizzie provides *Blood Relations* with a metatheatrical
dimension that is the source of much of its complexity and appeal.
Lionel Abel suggests that metatheatre has taken the place of tragedy in
the modern age because moral order is no longer generally conceived
as existing independently of our lives – that is, as a structure against
which a tragic protagonist exerts resistance – but is rather improvised
from within ourselves. *Blood Relations* appears to support this notion,
for it is implied in the play that what, in a more straightforward rendering, would have been Lizzie's "tragic dilemma" springs from her
refusal to accept the ordering of her life by others. But instead of a pure
tragedy – desperate actions chosen within the absolute confines of
mortality – we have Actress/Lizzie provisionally improvise Lizzie's
destiny. It is as if Hamlet had asked the Player not merely to perform
the speech about Pyrhhus's murder of Priam and the "Murder of
Gonzago" but to step into his own shoes to improvise possible narratives for the play. Indeed, Hamlet's story is, in one aspect, the tragedy
of the very impossibility of such a transference of character and
destiny, the burden of making definitive choices where there is only one
life to live, whereas *Blood Relations* is about what can happen when
such a transference is indeed possible – even *essential*, if history is to
be recovered from the domain of casual myth and rumour. To wit: we
must imaginatively don the lives of others in order to begin to understand life in general.

However, the difficulty of stepping into another's role – particularly
a historical role – is demonstrated at the opening of the play. The lights
rise on the Actress performing the courtroom speech of Hermione from
The Winter's Tale. It is likely that the audience will wonder how
Hermione's words apply to Lizzie Borden; but any parallel drawn
between the falsely accused, saintly Hermione and Lizzie (whose guilt
remained an open question, at the very least) is bound to have an ironic
edge, no matter how earnest the plea for compassion. Part of the irony
here falls back upon the Actress herself, who proceeds smoothly until

she reaches the line "I doubt not then but innocence shall make / False accusation blush and tyranny / Tremble at patience" (III.ii.30–3), at which point she stumbles, unable to remember the word "patience." It is a well-established principle of acting that difficulty remembering any particular phrase usually indicates a failure to assume the process of thought from which the phrase arises. The Actress has trouble with the word "patience" because it is precisely that quality she lacks. Too modern and self-possessed a woman to be fully comfortable in the long-suffering Hermione's shoes, she will find that taking on the role of Lizzie, though the setting is a bare decade earlier, is similarly difficult. The life led by Lizzie in 1892 seemingly belongs to a whole other world from that known by the Actress, a woman of the twentieth century who enjoys an independent career.

The constraints upon Lizzie's character are established fairly quickly as Miss Lizzie/Bridget paints in the background. Sometimes she does this obliquely: for instance, through playing a scene with and reminiscing about Harry Wingate, brother to Mrs Borden and a stupid, coarse-minded, chauvinistic type who wields a regrettable influence upon Lizzie's life. At other times the coaching is more direct, as in the mild rebukes to Lizzie for her use of coarse language (24–5). But most direct of all are the occasions when Miss Lizzie/Bridget actually explains aspects of her own life, such as her scandalous tomboy childhood and her persistence in daydreaming, at thirty-four, of living in a "corner house on a hill" where she could hold "grand parties" at which "everyone [would] be witty" (28–9).

There is something of the stifled spirit of Hedda Gabler in this, but if Lizzie seems rather less pathetic than her precursor, it is partly due to her friendship with Doctor Patrick, a handsome Irishman who is no Judge Brack. The doctor frequently visits, as Miss Lizzy/Bridget explains, because:

he's hoping to see someone [...] who's yanking up her skirt and showing her ankle – so she can take a decent-sized step – and forgetting everything she was ever taught in Miss Cornelia's School for Girls, and talking to the Irish as if she never heard of the Pope!   (31)

Playing the role of the local defier of sexist and bigoted social protocols can seem like something of an adventure to the secure modern mind that is impatient with the hidebound attitudes of the past – especially when one has an appreciative audience. At this point the playful spirit in which the role-playing began is still alive, and Lizzie is easily the most attractive character – the one whom a spectator would most like to play.

But the first fly in the ointment is revealed here, in that Doctor Patrick is not only a prudent Irishman living in a bigoted WASP society: he is married. Consequently, his admiration for Lizzie must remain somewhat muted, and certainly unconsummated. It appears, after all, that she really is rather isolated in this life. That is by no means the only factor that makes the role of social rebel more tedious than it seemed at first. Miss Lizzie/Bridget begins to heap on other conditions as if she were a scientist adding variables to an experiment. "They're sayin' it's time you were married," she tells Actress/Lizzie, "... though I don't know what man would put up with your moods!" "What about me putting up with his!" is Lizzie's glib and confident response. "Oh Lizzie," sighs Miss Lizzie/Bridget, knowing that such confidence will be sorely tried by events to come (34).

What the Actress is not yet reckoning with is shown in the scene immediately following, where Mrs and Mr Borden and Harry discuss what is to be done about the "problem" posed by Lizzie's wilful character. Afterwards, Miss Lizzie/Bridget asks:

Do you suppose there's a formula, a magic formula for being "a woman"? Do you suppose every girl baby receives it at birth, it's the last thing that happens just before birth, the magic formula is stamped indelibly on the brain – Ka Thud!! *Her mood of amusement changes* ... and ... through some terrible oversight ... perhaps the death of my mother ... I didn't get that Ka Thud!! I was born defective ... *She looks at the Actress.*
LIZZIE: *Low.* No.
MISS LIZZIE/BRIDGET: Not defective?
LIZZIE: Just ... born. (36)

It may be that in reality Lizzie is struggling against *environmental* determinacy; but the notion of *biological* determinacy is so universally assumed in this environment that it comes to have the force of an ineluctable truth, one inevitably accepted to some degree even by Lizzie herself. It is no accident that the "Ka Thud" Miss Lizzie uses to describe the imprint of biological determinacy is such a near homonym for the repetitive "ka thunk" that the children's ball makes against the wall as they chant "Lizzie Borden took an axe ..." Any idea socially repeated often enough begins to assume in the individual mind the deterministic status of established fact.

However, there is another aspect to this siege of Lizzie's will by deterministic social perceptions. What keeps Lizzie in the home of her father and stepmother, where her will is so regularly frustrated, is her expectation of her patrimony. Indeed, as the play depicts her life, it is primarily the prospect of being denied an independent share of the inheritance, of being bereft of the privileged material position she expects as compensation for her dull life, that motivates her to commit murder. Her home is a prison precisely because of her inability to imagine a life in conditions other than the luxurious environment to which birth entitled her. The idea of going out and working for a living (which, however unpleasant, in the late nineteenth century would have been the lot of the vast majority of Americans, women or men, who did not belong to the monied classes) is literally inconceivable to her. The point is made forcefully in an exchange between Bridget and Lizzie near the end of act 1, when Lizzie is beginning to despair:

BRIDGET: ... You should try bein' more like cook, Lizzie. Smile and get round them. You can do it.
LIZZIE: It's not ... *fair* that I have to.
BRIDGET: There ain't nothin' fair in this world.
LIZZIE: Well then ... well then, I don't want to!
BRIDGET: You dream, Lizzie ... you dream dreams ... Work. Be sensible. What could you do?
LIZZIE: I could
MISS LIZZIE/BRIDGET: No.
LIZZIE: I could
MISS LIZZIE/BRIDGET: No.
LIZZIE: I could
MISS LIZZIE/BRIDGET: No!   (43)

It is not in Lizzie's – nor the Actress's – character to passively accept the unfairness of life (as the working-class Cook must); and yet when the Actress, in her role of improvisor, begins to consider the idea of making other circumstances for herself, Miss Lizzie/Bridget, as the "director" of the role-playing, refuses to allow the conception utterance. Instead the Actress is permitted to conceive of only one alternative to the impending violence: a carousel dream that depicts the effacement of her identity and the ultimate annihilation of her soul.

In her introduction to the volume that includes *Blood Relations* Diane Bessai writes: "The playwright is still concerned with character in its social role; in this there is a general similarity to the portrait of Walsh, as a man who is personally devastated by the public role imposed upon him from the higher authority of the system he serves. Lizzie, of course, does not literally 'serve' a system, but she is the product and victim of the materialistic bourgeois social conventionality of her day that gives no breathing space to individuality or eccentricity" (9). We undoubtedly recognize the accuracy of this description of Lizzie's relation to her society. Still, it would seem perverse to allow the label of "victim" to remain attached to Lizzie in the final analysis. Just as we would find it peculiar to consider Walsh the principal victim of a play in which (to take a harsh view) he chooses to become the instrument of so many casualties rather than risking the loss of his comfortable station in life, so it seems odd to consider Lizzie a victim when, in 1902, she is the comfortable mistress of her own household while her father and stepmother lie in their graves, brutally murdered. The ambivalent status of Lizzie as murderer or victim is precisely what generates so much of the interest in this play. To what extent are Lizzie's actions to be considered fully volitional, the play asks, and to what extent does murder seem merely a natural response to her circumstances?

The symbol Pollock uses to suggest the stakes of Lizzie's situation within her father's home is a familiar one in dramatic literature: at the close of the first act, Mr Borden kills Lizzie's pet birds. He does so in a spasm of ruthlessness that is nominally intended to dissuade local children from trespassing on his property to see the birds but that plainly arises more immediately from his frustrations with Lizzie. Probably the most famous prior example of the device is in *Miss Julie* (1888), where Jean kills Miss Julie's bird supposedly in order that they may flee the estate unencumbered. In Strindberg's play it is a brutal demonstration of the sort of expedient soul-murder that is forced by the rise of a new classless order. Another likely influence on Pollock is Susan Glaspell's suspenseful one-act play of 1920, *Trifles*. There, while the male authorities investigate the murder of a farmer named Wright, two women quietly discover from various domestic clues that Mrs Wright strangled her husband after he had capped a long history of brutality towards her by wringing the neck of her canary.

A particular link between *Trifles* and *Blood Relations*, apart from the vengeful murders that follow the killing of the birds, is the close association of the birds with the inner lives of the wronged women. Mrs Wright had, we are told, been a bright and cheerful singer herself before the grim years of social isolation and marriage to a brute took their toll. "If there'd been years and years of nothing," remarks one of the women, "then a bird to sing to you, it would be awful ... still, after the bird was still" (Glaspell, 428). Lizzie's birds are on several occasions in *Blood Relations* similarly identified with her stifled spirit. They are first mentioned when Miss Lizzie speaks of them as an alternative to her daydream about the house on the hill (29); then they are brought up again, when the neighbouring children attempt to get into the shed to see them during Dr Patrick's visit – the implication being, on that occasion, that Dr Patrick's visits to

Lizzie constitute a similar act of trespass upon her father's property (33). Finally, just before Mr Borden kills the birds, Lizzie is attempting to assert her rights to the farm. Her father erupts, shouting, "You and those god damn birds! [...] There'll be no more of your god damn birds in this yard!!" (46). His slaughter of the birds, then, seems effectively to kill Lizzie's place within the farm. It is a declaration that there is no room for her spirit in this home, just as Wright's killing of his wife's bird was his attempt to strangle her residual maiden spirit.

Another symbol familiar from previous literature that is used to express Lizzie's situation is the image of the bell jar. At one point Lizzie is described as feeling

> *caught in a dimension other than the one in which the people around her are operating. For Lizzie, a bell jar effect. Simple acts seem filled with significance. Lizzie is trying to fulfil other people's expectations of "normal."* (55)

Then, two pages later, "*Lizzie and Mr Borden look at one another. The bell jar effect is lessened.*" Although the image is only used in Pollock's stage directions, it none the less indicates a probable context for some of her thinking about Lizzie. The most famous use of the bell jar symbol is, of course, Sylvia Plath's brilliant autobiographical novel, in which the protagonist loses her sense of reality as a result of her efforts to play the role she infers from the expectations of those around her. The novel has had a tremendous impact upon feminist thought because its depicts what unfortunately seems to have been a common syndrome: the tendency of the violent resentment born of the protagonist's gradual self-effacement to be turned inward, where it erodes the core of her identity[12] and thereby destroys from within any possibility of establishing genuine relations with other human beings. Hence, the "bell jar effect." The trope describes the sense of living a life that is sealed off from the lives of others, of living in an existential vacuum, one effect of which is, naturally, that the individual is detached from the ethical implications of her actions because she lacks any sense of a basic experience of life sympathetically shared with other human beings.

The problems attaching to such a situation are far-reaching in their existential implications, and while there are no clear and unequivocal solutions, Pollock does not shy from posing the problems. What I mean in this case by that often elusive word "existential" is the philosophical principle that a person is assumed to be, in the first place, a free agent, but must also exist within a community of others. The individual educes the meaning of her own person within that double context and so, despite having to contend with the defining context of her society, must ultimately be held responsible for her own behaviour and specific actions. In *Blood Relations*, however, Pollock appears to be interested in presenting the case for special circumstances in such way that not only are Lizzie's actions seen more sympathetically than such crimes might ordinarily be (compare, for example, the general revulsion that met reports of Lyle and Erik Menendez's murder of their parents for their property in the mid-1990s), but the matter of responsibility is hedged in such a way that it refuses to rest on Lizzie's own shoulders.

It is certainly not the case that Lizzie has no sense of responsibility for her own acts, or that the "bell jar effect" makes consciousness of others totally inaccessible to her. She plans to murder her stepmother from behind so that she will "retain no image of me on [her] eye" (64), and she decides to murder her father because she cannot bear his hatred (67). Yet in the end the question of responsibility is confused not only by the mitigating circumstances in which Lizzie makes the putative decision to murder but by the fact that "Lizzie" is not Lizzie at all, but the Actress. As a viewer's attempts to see the subject of a cubist painting always return to the paint upon the canvas, all questions of guilt and innocence in *Blood Relations* fall back upon the surface of the role playing. "Lizzie, you did [murder]," says the Actress to Miss Lizzie at the very end of the play. "I didn't. You did," she replies.

The doubling of Lizzie's identity bears an interesting relation to Bergman's film *Persona*, where Alma, the younger woman played by Bibi Andersson, finds herself swept into a sort of mental vortex caused by the refusal of Elizabeth, the older woman played by Liv Ullmann, to speak for herself. Alma takes on a surrogate function in the film wherein the reality of events and the identity of the players becomes confused, bewildering. As it happens, the elements of *Blood Relations* that resemble *Persona* were brought to the fore in what is perhaps the most successful production of the play to date, that directed by Martha Henry at the Grand Theatre in London, Ontario, in 1989. The two leading women maintained an eerie sort of shadow relation throughout the production, so that Miss Lizzie's influence always remained palpable, and the actress playing Miss Lizzie/Bridget herself remained a constant presence. When Diana Leblanc as Lizzie/Actress at last mounted the stairs to accomplish the murders, on the stage below Frances Hyland as Miss Lizzie/Bridget performed a macabre dance with a bucket, kicking it in a way that evoked the falling of the axe.

But Pollock moves the conceit of *Persona* into a slightly different place by implying that the Actress is also the surrogate for us in the audience. The notion is brought home when the Actress turns to face the audience as the last two accusatory words are spoken. The gesture ought to nip in the bud any tendencies towards glib sentimentalization of Lizzie's victimhood because we are no longer enjoying the comfort of the jury box: we are now in the dock. The accusation, I think, goes beyond the somewhat façile idea that, as members of society, we are somehow culpable for all crimes because of our contributions to various social pressures. Rather, it suggests something about the kind of emotional engagement the play invites in its best productions, moving us in the audience beyond simple voyeurism into an active wish that Lizzie committed those murders – not merely to satisfy a prurient interest in the lurid but because we have felt something of her repressed passion and hatred, and are at some level persuaded that vengeful murder is the inevitable consequence. It is that sense of *inevitability* that makes us culpable, for if the improvised narrative indeed seems to have only one satisfactory ending, then in our minds we have not so much exonerated "Lizzie" from an objective standpoint as we have subjectively shared in the guilt.

In certain respects *Generations* (October 1980) can be read as a thematic inversion of *Blood Relations*. First, there is the similarity in the titles of the two plays, both of which are puns alluding to family. However, whereas the title *Blood Relations* anticipates a violent issue of such relationships, the punning of *Generations* is more optimistic, suggesting that history and productivity are related. Family has always provided some of the richest dramatic material, primarily because it has been the main unit of organization mediating between the individual and formal social structures. Consequently, it is often used as a dramatic receptacle for all the tensions arising from the difficulty of reconciling individual wills and collective interests.

By implication, one's attitude towards the institution of family *per se* is to some degree indicative of one's faith in the prospects of success in any larger social groupings. Where the family is firmly believed to be an inherently, inevitably, and viciously repressive institution, the prospects for a successful surrender of autonomy to an even larger community usually look dim (though, needless to say, that is not necessarily the case where any alternatives to family are mooted). Naturally, this is not an either/or situation, for as a practical matter most people are willing to commit themselves to a limited sphere of compromise between their own wishes and social demands. Hence, ambivalence about families is probably best addressed on a case-by-case basis, there being very few incessantly happy families outside of old television sitcoms, while each unhappy family, as Tolstoy remarks, is unhappy in its own way.

Notwithstanding the limitations of general pronouncements on the viability of families, we inevitably look sometimes, as Pollock does in *Blood Relations*, for political and philosophical implications of dysfunctional examples. Larger questions about human sociability refuse to detach themselves from dramatic treatments of the family. And it may be that Pollock, mother at this time to a rather large family herself,[13] having spent several years exploring the untenable family situation she found in the Borden household, quite naturally began to ask herself why some families happen to survive and even flourish despite their adverse conditions, and what this implies for civilization.

Generations addresses this other side of the issue. As we would expect, Pollock's framing of the questions is at least as sceptical as it is sentimental; but the answers implied here allow for a far more optimistic perspective on family prospects than that offered by *Blood Relations*. This may be because, unlike the Bordens, the Nurlin family is beset by at least as many external as internal forces. There is certainly a good deal of strife within the family itself, but in the struggle against the siege without they have a sense of some common purpose to bind them together, however tentatively. The sources of the siege are several – social and technological progress, political forces, natural elements – a sort of brief catalogue of the various factors that make farming such a notoriously difficult occupation. Specifically, the local Indians, who have a contract with the federal government to irrigate the area, have dammed the river in protest against what they feel is government exploitation. But it is the local farmers, whose crops are threatened by drought, who are suffering the effects of this siege most acutely.

There are three generations of farmers in the Nurlin family. Old Eddy, now in his late seventies, founded the farm fifty years ago as a young newlywed. Alfred, his son, dutifully took up the burden with the assistance of his wife, Margaret. Now there is David, Alfred's son, who vacillates between a determination to continue the family tradition and doubt that it is worth the trouble. David's doubts are fostered by his brother, Young Eddy, who has moved to the city and become a prosperous lawyer. But Young Eddy has his own reasons for encouraging misgivings in his brother; he hopes to persuade the family to sell the farm so that he can purchase a founding partnership in a new law firm. More influential still is David's fiancée, Bonnie, who is devoted to David but impatient with his passive acceptance of the destiny that has been handed to him. The final character is Charlie Running Dog, an old Amerindian who is senior even to Old

Eddy and who functions as a sort of extension of the presence of nature in the play. Pollock describes him as looking "like some outcropping of arid land" (141), an association encouraged by his philosophic placidity.

At the heart of the play is David's dilemma of whether to remain on the land or leave to invent a new life. Behind that question stands another: the uncertainty about whether David has ever truly consulted his own wishes in allowing himself to be tied so closely to the land. Bonnie believes he has not:

> It's like all your choices have been made for you and ... sometimes you rant about this or that, but you keep right on going! You never ask why am I doing this, do I really want to do this! You ask how to do it, when to do it, where to do it, you never ask why! (169)

The question of whether David has ever actively chosen his life echoes the doubt that Lizzie could have free agency when her environment had so severely restricted her thinking. Both characters have a sense of besieged constriction, of having been environmentally overdetermined to the point of coercion.

But there is a rather different ethical construction placed upon the dilemma in the later play, which is rooted in the attitude to the land. Whereas in *Blood Relations* the farm was seen solely in terms of material value – Mr Borden's concerns are limited to the commercial value of deeds and the effrontery of the trespassing children; Lizzie's interest has to do with the financial independence that comes with inheriting her father's property – in *Generations* the farm is given a metaphysical value that resists any reduction to real estate. The Nurlins' relation to their land is the heart of the family itself, the greatest constant in their lives, though naturally that relationship is itself extremely volatile. Explaining the point, Pollock comes as close as any contemporary playwright has to reviving the mysticism Herman Voaden attached to the Canadian landscape. "In a sense," she writes, "THE LAND [Pollock's emphasis] is a character revealed by the light and shadow it throws on the Nurlins' lives [...] There should be some sense of the omniscient presence and mythic proportion of THE LAND in the design" (141). Thus, there is profound significance in David's attachment to the farm – this farm – as there was not in Lizzie's case.

Yet, for David, the question of what exactly that meaning is remains open for most of the play. His unconscious sense of belonging has thus far gone unexamined. Now, falling under scrutiny for the first time, it threatens to lose any force of conviction. Finally, a kind of understanding does emerge. Early in the play a context of sorts is provided for David's dilemma. Young Eddy describes a debate between the two old men about the true nature of the land. Old Eddy argues that the land is "like some kind of monster a man [has] to wrestle and fight," while Charlie believes that it is "like a woman, you gotta woo her and win her" (165). These might be two positions in an old quarrel over the nature of a god, the sense of supernatural power over life interpretable as either a violent challenge or a difficult love. In either case the intensity of this relation to The Land transcends the human. The passion of each old man indicates the purposefulness each attaches to this aspect of his life. In short, their relation to The Land constitutes a kind of shared faith (though each conceives this faith in his own distinctive way). But, as is often the case, their faith remains inscrutable to those who do not share it.

So much is not wholly evident in the first part of the play. Indeed, not until the last scene does the difference in perception lying at the heart of this matter begin to emerge with clarity. Still frustrated at what she sees as the unthinking surrender of personal autonomy to mere family habit, Bonnie begins to speak her mind to David's mother, Margaret:

BONNIE: I marvel at ... how you can submerge yourself in all this. Be nothing but ... an extension of this ... I would not want that to happen to me.
MARGARET: I don't feel *submerged* – I am *tired* on occasion.
BONNIE: I'm afraid of that happening to me.
MARGARET: Why?
BONNIE: Why? Because ... I don't want ... to lose *myself*.
MARGARET: Lose *yourself*? Lose yourself ... And what would you know about loss? ... It's true I might not have a mind, but I do have a memory, and I remember the thirties. I remember us all huddled round the radio hopin' for somethin' to get us through the next day, and what did we get? Bennett babblin' about managin' money, when none of us had any money to manage. Oh yes, the Nurlins were lucky, they hung on to this place but some of us, we weren't so lucky ... My father, first he lost his livestock, then his faith, and in the end, the bank took what was left, so we moved to the Hat and lived hand-to-mouth, god knows how ... When I met Alfred Nurlin, and he asked me to marry him, I knew I had a chance to be part of something again ... And you talk about losin' yourself? Are you so special, so fine, so wonderful, there's nothin' bigger worth bein' part of? ... Good ... You be whole then, be complete, be self-sufficient. And you'll be alone. And in the end, you'll be lonely.
BONNIE: There's worse things than lonely.
MARGARET: Are there?

BONNIE: Yes.

MARGARET: I don't know what *they* are.   (188–9)

The dispute remains unsettled, and indeed, Pollock stresses her own sense of ambivalence about this matter: "I don't know [...] whose side I'm on in that play. Part of me relates to Margaret and part of me is with Bonnie. I don't know whether there's worse things than being lonely or not. I have a real interest in people who are willing sacrifices. On the other hand, it can't be a sacrifice to the person who does it. That's what I'm trying to deal with in that play: when a society no longer has those kinds of people who realize what it is they're doing and still do it willingly, that society is doomed" *(Work*, 117). Pollock's conception of the issue in terms of whether or not to make a "sacrifice" is an important key. Essentially she is saying that, regardless of whether it is sympathetic, Margaret's position constitutes an actual faith that commands respect. Indeed, the purposefulness Margaret finds in life on the Nurlin farm (the identification of her essential self with what she calls something "bigger worth bein' a part of") approaches the level associated with religious vocation. Her response to Bonnie is not very different from that which religious officials usually give when asked to explain their perseverance in an ostensibly thankless occupation.

In light of Pollock's work as a whole, it is significant that Margaret's expression of the matter is set almost wholly in the context of memory. Memory provides the egress from an immediate state of besiegement to that larger purposefulness through which personal integrity is maintained. To be sure, in this specific case the siege is quite minor, namely Bonnie's challenge to Margaret's integrity. But the point of Margaret's reply is surely that, despite various adversities, she maintains commitment to her humble role on the farm by recollecting the emergence into purposefulness she felt upon joining the family.

In this regard, then, The Land and memory are intertwined. Those characters with the longest memories, Old Eddy and Charlie, are also those with the strongest connections to the land. Temporal and spatial dimensions are virtually interchangeable in so far as both represent a body of ideals that transcend immediate, individual concerns, ideals for which the farming Nurlins find it worthwhile to surrender their personal autonomy. So, on the one hand, David's setting fire to the fields at the end of the play is a flat defiance of these values. But on the other (just as those who desecrate a flag reinforce its significance as an icon in the very act of publicly refusing obeisance), by directly attacking the land rather than simply abandoning it or commodifying it as his brother does, David is acknowledging its power. He admits as much to Bonnie when the immediate crisis of the fire is over:

> I can rail and I can fight against all kinda things, but I know *one thing*, alright? Out *there* ... is ... something – I know it. Out there ... is a feelin' ... you don't get other places. Other places it's hidden in all the dinky scenery, but on the *prairies* it's just *there*. A *power*.   (196)

David derives his identity from his relationship to this mystic power. Bonnie, however, cannot comprehend David's state of mind; it is more than coincidental that she is also unable to define herself. Hence, David and Bonnie's outlooks remain not only divided but perhaps irreconcilable.

By contrast, Old Eddy, despite his brief scuffle with David, seems to understand his grandson's actions fully. In the final section Old Eddy describes to Charlie his defiant confrontation of the sun as he stood in the fields the morning after his wife's death. "Look at me, yuh Old Bitch," he recalls shouting; "I'm still here!" (198). This is one siege that can never be victoriously lifted, so the paramount objective lies simply in endurance of the struggle.

While Pollock takes care that these last points are well established, the play nevertheless seems to end abruptly. Noting but discounting this impression, Richard Perkyns argues that Pollock "reaches a resolution of the situation with a neatness and economy" in that "the fire says it all" (608). Notwithstanding the truth of Perkyns's observations about the completeness of plot, the sense of abruptness in question is probably rooted more in the emotional cadence of the play's ending, which seems to leave something undramatized, than in rational coherence. Perhaps the abruptness of the dénouement in *Generations* is a reflection of the difficulty of finding words to express the experience inherent in the land. Herman Voaden's attempts to bring a coherent dramatic shape to a supra-humanist mystical experience of the landscape were never more than equivocally successful, perhaps because drama is fundamentally a human medium. The task cannot have grown easier since then.

The opening stage directions for *Whiskey Six Cadenza* (1983), Pollock's most complex play, set us within a very different type of landscape.[14] Or at least we find ourselves within a very different *attitude* towards the physical environment. The setting is historical (1919–20, during Prohibition), and the first image of "the town that might have been, Blairmore," is a sort of idyllic pastoral vision: "All is as if seen through a soft rain" (141). But that image quickly fades, exposed "as no more than a gray, dusty, cob-webby affair much as a spider might spin in the entrance to an abandoned mine shaft" (139). So the first image suggests nostalgia and the second, disillusionment.

Whiskey Six Cadenza is a memory play, and these shifting images serve as expressionistic guides to the audience. Now and then Pollock's poetic stage directions sound much like Reaney's: "The landscape extends into the infinite, giving an impression of viewing eternity through a glass, a telescope, a microscope, a kaleidoscope." A little later, a similarly poetic conception of sound design is specified: "Voice-overs are heard, they sound like the wind, blowing softly, stirring tumbleweeds, increasing and dying" (141). To be sure, Pollock emphasizes that the dance sequences, the voice-overs, the "gossamer depiction of Crowsnest Pass" are optional, being drawn from the 1983 première at Theatre Calgary. But she declares that these devices are all "strong indicators of the play's ambience" (139). The story is seen, then, through a lens of memory tinged with nostalgia, regret, and disillusionment.

The subject who generates the memory here is Johnny Farley. Johnny sets the plot in motion with his return to his home town from an absence less prodigal than prudent: a failed attempt to better himself. Unlike the prodigal son's return, Johnny's is cause for dismay, not rejoicing; his family thought he'd escaped Blairmore for a better life. Johnny is no happier about the situation himself. Desperation, not homesickness brought him back, and despite his love for his family he is fully conscious of the deadly aspects of his hometown. As a son returned to view his patrimony through newly objective eyes, Johnny is comparable to Serge, the returned son of Tremblay's *Bonjour la, Bonjour*, or Arkady in Walker's *Nothing Sacred*. More immediately, though, he joins Pollock's several narrating "epic-I" characters who have been transformed, even wounded by the events recalled: Walsh, Chalmers, and, in her own way, the Actress in *Blood Relations*.

Johnny's older brother, Will, and his father, Cec, both work in the local coal mine. His mother, whom we know only as Mrs Farley, is something of a religious zealot – prohibition activist, hymn singer, and overbearing moralizer. Yet she is also a warm-hearted and sensitive woman. Her fanatically puritanical stance has been assumed as practically the only means at her disposal to resist the despair and spiritual degeneracy that are seemingly endemic to Blairmore and the primary source of the sense of besiegement in this play. "She needs a cause to keep goin,'" says Cec Farley of his wife (152). Merely enjoying life is not a viable vocation in an place as bleak as Blairmore.

Mrs Farley's attitude seems excessively rigid and neurotic at first, but it gradually becomes more comprehensible. We see why she feels that her husband and her eldest son have already been lost to her through their employment in the coal mine. Of Cec, she says to Johnny: "That's not a man, Johnny, that's a thing, a utensil belonging to Dominion Colliery" (146). The comment has a vaguely political tone that is surprising in such a character; but later, as when she turns her back on the brutalization of her husband by the authorities (232), it becomes evident that she indeed views her husband as a sort of thing, as if he had already so far forfeited his dignity and selfhood to the mine that she could no longer bear to think of him as a human being. Pollock reinforces the point in less explicitly political ways. For example, the virtually impossible task Cec and Will have of cleaning the black from their faces (146–7, 149) is a figure for the inextricable social forces in their characters. Cec is resigned to the situation, but Will continues in vain to struggle, scrubbing himself with lye for the sake of his fiancée, Dolly. Alas, by the end of the second act he is dead, killed by a falling beam in the mine – or, says Mrs Farley, by the slow reflexes caused by his drinking. In any case, the circumstances of his life have inexorably come together to kill him.

As a personification of spiritual resistance, however, Mrs Farley represents only one polar alternative. At the other pole is one of Pollock's most dynamic and compelling creations: Mr Big, bootlegger, local hero, and proprietor of the Alberta Hotel and "speakeasy," where he is assisted by his wife, Mama George, and his adopted daughter, Leah. Johnny is drawn to the Alberta Hotel principally by the lovely Leah. But he is also fascinated by Mr Big himself, a big man in seemingly every respect: in stature, in social power, in wealth, in charisma, and in his personal magnanimity. He is capable of brazenly outfacing the police over the prohibition laws, yet he cannot, it is said, so much as "pass a mewling cat" – and there are seventeen cats in his house to prove the truth of that assertion (157). A stark contrast is created between the enormity and vitality of Mr Big and his household and the cramped mental conditions that characterize the Farley home.

Pollock flirted with romantic pastoral in *Generations*, where the prairies were a sublime sanctuary from the corruption of the city. With Mr Big she dallies with another romantic trope: the cult of personality. The idea is strongly associated with, for example, Lord Byron, who was so much more vital than his peers that he appeared to be infused with a sort of divine afflatus, and so to have acquired privileges beyond those of ordinary mortals. This is the notion of a man seen as unusually inspired, heroic, grandiose in his individuality, which the poet Jules Laforgue captured with his ironic phrase "Moi-le-Magnifique." Mr Big thus seems to transcend the sense of besiegement from which the Farleys suffer, remaining untouched by the degradation infecting the souls of so many in this town.

Ethically speaking, Mr Big's transcendent state is ambiguous. Like most comic heroes, he is on the side of vitality rather than morality. Yet the morality of prohibition itself is dubious. As Johnny declares, if drinking is truly criminal, "the whole bleedin' country's criminal" (197). Mr Big asks rhetorically, "Can you keep a man sober thro' coercion a law? Can a man be made moral by threatnin' punishment" (194)? Given the pharisaism of those who support the law (particularly the petty-minded prohibition officer, William "Bill the Brit" Windsor), it is not difficult for the charming, large-hearted, defiant Mr Big to win our sympathy.

While there is more than a little of Foghorn Leghorn about Mr Big, in other respects he is heir to the outlaw heroes of Romantic drama such as Goethe's Goetz von Berlichingen or Egmont, or Schiller's robber baron, Karl Moor. Mr Big shares not only their outlaw status but a fetching aristocratic disposition that revolts as much at the inferior character of those representing the establishment as at any actual injustices they perpetrate.[15] Hence, a key scene in establishing the character of Mr Big is his baiting of Bill Windsor over the tortured contradictions and absurdities inherent in the officer's thinking, a combination of jingoistic loyalty to the British Empire, proto-fascist notions of racial purity, and puritanical commitment to prohibition (162–4). We see what Mr Big means when he says that Bill Windsor is "a void. A vacuum. The man has no character" (159). Windsor's mind is so full of shop-soiled, unexamined prejudices that he can hardly be said to have a mind of his own.[16] As Johnny suggests, it is Windsor's indignation at the spectacle of independent thought rather than any question of criminality that makes Windsor hate Mr Big. "A moral man," declares Windsor, "don't need to think" (231).

By contrast, then, Mr Big seems altogether visionary in his originality. We see him in action, inspiring the imaginations of others and generating a sense of vitality and excitement rare to Blairmore, when he casts the habitueés of his bar in a re-creation of the episode in which he met Johnny on the train (174). Using a metatheatrical episode such as that to establish a character's creativity and spiritual magnanimity touches directly upon the mode in which the audience is imagining, and places the character at the heart of the creative process underway. But Pollock seems further interested in placing Mr Big's particular kind of creativity in a specifically romantic context. "Why," he asks Johnny, borrowing Cassius's sarcastic description of Caesar, "do I bestride the world like a colossus"?

> I've mastered the art a seein' the multiple realities a the universe, and more than that. I have embraced them, though they be almost always conflicting, but equally true. (203)

"Do I contradict myself?" asks Walt Whitman in "Song of Myself." "Very well then, I contradict myself. (I am large. I embrace multitudes.)" (90). The language is not identical, but the sentiment is not far from Whitman's romantic outlook.

Mr Big echoes another romantic poet in describing his first vision of Leah:

> MR BIG: Here's this scrawny little girl-child walkin' along without castin' a shadow.
> LEAH: It was rainin', Mr Big.
> MR BIG: For you! For me there was a radiance all around you, and it was comin' from you. From you, Leah. And I didn't stop for more than a ... it coulda been a hundred years, or a second, or no time at all! Like an instantaneous gatherin' up, like God descendin' to take his Chosen up into heaven in a fiery chariot!
> LEAH: Are you God, Mr Big?
> MR BIG: At that moment I was. Invincible, Leah.   (157)

Mr. Big's insistence on the certain truth of his subjective visions of divine radiance (hallucinations, they might be called by less sympathetic listeners), together with his simile drawn from Ezekiel's apotheosis, both speak very strongly of an affinity to William Blake. Now, in noting such affinities, we cannot ignore that they are delivered with an amusing display of extravagance on Mr Big's part that is half-teasing, half-serious. Nevertheless, the allusions indicate something of the scale of Mr Big's ego, which by Blairmore standards assumes breathtaking romantic proportions.

To be sure, there remains something a little false about Mr. Big's grandiose visions, however appealing and (like his MacLaughlin "whiskey six" car) "seductive" they may be at moments. But they seem less suspect than the alternative "vision" we are offered: that of St John the Divine, whom Mrs Farley quotes (from Rev. 1:13–18) just as Johnny is cementing his attachment to Mr Big. John's mystical vision of the Second Coming is a powerful piece of poetry in itself, but Mrs Farley's use of the passage loses something when, moments later, trying to dissuade Johnny from entering Mr Big's employ as a bootlegger, she blurts out desperately: "You'll make me a laughin' stock, you know that!" (196) Then, as she proceeds to denigrate Mr Big, among her list of his faults is her despicable citation that his "only friend [is] a Jew" (199). As for her profession of love for Johnny, he declares to her: "You are crushin' me with your love as sure as Will was caught and crushed by a timber" (199). The self-interest, bigotry, and general fearfulness of life that lie at the bottom of Mrs Farley's religiosity all undermine any righteousness attached to her position. So the vitality of Mr Big's visionary heterodoxy becomes all the more appealing by comparison with Mrs Farley's puritanical orthodoxy.

Eventually, however, the appeal of Mr Big's romantic outlook is itself undermined. The centrepiece of his claim to spiritual magnanimity is his adoration of his adopted daughter, Leah, whose "radiance" makes her the source of spiritual energy in his personal cosmos. "You know, if I could choose one image to carry with me through all of eternity," says Mr Big, "it would be that of Leah, as she stands there today, at this moment" (203). But by this point Mrs Farley has planted a seed of doubt in Johnny's mind: Leah, she insists, is Mr Big's mistress, so Johnny's response to Mr Big's image of Leah as frozen ideal is to compare it to the work of a taxidermist (204). This idealization of her is a kind of transfixion, parallelling Mrs Farley's suffocating, rather Jocastan love for him.

Johnny's disillusioned discovery that the woman he admires is a willing (?) partner to an incestuous (or at least quasi-incestuous) relationship recalls the situation in *Pericles* where the hero discovers the relationship of Antiochus and his daughter. Here, however, Leah is not regarded automatically as irremediably corrupted by her incestuous contact. Indeed, a crucial context is invoked by her name. The biblical Leah is the first wife of Jacob, who, having agreed to work for Leah's father, Laban, for seven years in order to win the hand of Leah's sister, Rachel, is beguiled by Laban, who substitutes Leah for Rachel, then forces Jacob to work seven more years before he can have Rachel as a second wife (Gen. 29). Johnny is in the position of Jacob, taking the job with Mr Big so thathe can woo his daughter; but Leah is not the potential bride she appears to be. In a way the Leah of Pollock's play is the equivalent of both of Laban's daughters – the adored and idealized bride as well as the substitute. The question the biblical reference opens is whether something happy and productive will come of Johnny's attachment to this woman with two aspects, as it comes of Jacob's marriage to Laban's two daughters. And despite the tragic situation the question remains open until almost the end of the play.

The virtually insurmountable obstacle to a non-tragic ending is, of course, the incest. Mr Big's monumental ego has embodied the chief alternative to the slow death of soul and body inherent in the Dominion Colliery. But where bootlegging is a defiance of conventional morality that seems only to add to his stature, there seems little hope of his magnificent individualism sustaining the divulgation of something so unequivocally immoral as his exploitation of Leah. To be sure, it is not *technically* a case of incest, but M. Big's anti-pharisaical ethics would never permit him to take refuge in a cheap equivocation of that kind.

Sure enough, in the last scenes Mr Big begins to crumble in a crisis of self doubt. The event initiating this crisis is a conversation between Leah and Dolly, the fiancée of Johnny's late brother, Will. "You gotta start fresh," Leah tells Dolly. "I couldn't," Dolly replies; "nobody can [...] You're who you are and who you were and who you met and what you did and ..." (224). Eventually Leah tears up Dolly's photograph of Will and leaves the stage. The meaning of the exchange to Leah gradually becomes more apparent, both to us and to Mr Big, who has sat silently watching this scene. It is time for Leah to move on, but she sees she will never entirely outgrow her relationship to Mr Big because that is an integral part of who she is. Hence there is nothing that Mr Big can do to make amends for his transgression of her trust; Leah is marked for life. Brooding on this point, he begins to contemplate his own memories, to look back on the crucible in which his own character was formed:

> MAMA GEORGE: Is your great and glorious construction a the universe based on nothin' more than the frail embrace of a child?
> MR BIG: ... Would it be ... any less valid were that to be so?
> MAMA GEORGE: Children grow up.
> MR BIG: Do they? ... I remember – a little boy ... not so unlike Leah when I found her ... but this male child, an unattractive child, an ugly child who found no Mr Big ... so he created one.   (234)

It seems that the same little boy's anxieties are the source of both Mr Big's magnanimity, his sense of having an ego bigger than all of life's travails, and of his weak need for approval, his feeling of being insufficient without receiving the affection and devotion of a child. The first allowed him to generously extend his protection towards Leah; the second caused him to selfishly exploit her.

In earlier plays Pollock explored the complicated links between memory, integrity of character, personal autonomy, and environmental determinism. The closing scenes of *Whiskey Six Cadenza* contain some of the most complex and painful examination of these interrelated factors in her work. Desperate to restore Mr. Big's self-confidence, Mama George reminds him of his proud declarations on the subject of autonomy and free will. Prompted by her, he recovers much of a speech he once gave on the topic:

> Men are most like animals and least like gods when they relinquish choice! Heaven is freely choosing with respect for the choice of others ... [Which]

means the one thing that keeps us from achievin' Holy Grace is government! For governments remove choice. It's only when individuals choose and suffer the consequences of their actions that humanity can progress! (235–6)

The problem is that, in taking advantage of her vulnerable situation while she was still a child, Mr Big has allowed Leah little or no choice in her actions. As Dolly points out to Leah, we are not free to choose our *pasts*; they are *already* part of us.

Mr Big fears that he has developed his fantastic, romantic vision as a means of concealing the truth of his weaker self, which includes his abuse of Leah's innocence. But he defensively argues to Johnny that it is the other way around, that it is actually his imagination and personality that have created the conditions under which Leah has become herself:

> I'm hearin' it said that my ... fantastical comprehension a comic design does not spring from revelation or wisdom, intuition or insight ... It is, rather, mere invention and lies – which serve ... to legitimize ... an on-going affair ... with a child [...] Look at her! She's the product of my vision, not the inspiration of it! Could falsehood and contrivance bring forth such perfection? I ask you. Look at her ... of course I love her. Who would not love her? ... She is proof that my grasp of all worlds, real and imagined, is sound – and that soundness is proof that she's sound. I swear to you Johnny, Leah is without flaw or injury. She is founded on truth. *He appears spent.* And my love ... for her ... which I do not deny ... is as ... my love ... for you ... whom she loves.   (242)

The stammering conclusion to Mr Big's speech belies his bluff. Even if Johnny could be convinced by the awkward lie, no amount of self-aggrandizement will be sufficient for Mr Big to absolve *himself* of his wrong. That wrong is not merely a matter of some violation of social protocol, for, while he is no slave to moral convention, Mr Big's recollection of his existential belief in the paramount importance of self-determination is proof that he has betrayed what he most deeply believes is right. True memory implacably insists upon integrity of character, and the attempt to obfuscate principles with romantic boasting about self-contradictions is a futile defence against self-knowledge. Independence of spirit is what Mr Big has instilled in his protégé, Johnny. Now, faced with the indisputable fact of Leah's autonomy in the form of her love for Johnny, Mr Big must recognize that his control and use of her, his constriction of the circumstances under which she has grown, is a terrible violation of his own ethics.

These realizations are never actually uttered in their full dimensions because suddenly news comes of a blockade that Windsor has set up down the street. The external social forces have combined into one emblematic siege. Johnny rushes out to burst through the blockade with the "whiskey six," thus escaping with the conclusive evidence of the bootlegging operation and making, perhaps, a conclusive demonstration of his own independence of will (though again, the influence of Mr Big on Johnny raises the question of whose will is truly being served). For Leah, however, there seems to be no possibility of ever escaping the past and hence no real sense of autonomy. So, at her request, while she runs for the door, Mr Big shoots and kills her. The action returns to a confusing collage of sounds and images as at the play's opening, and Johnny, older and worn, says:

> I was caught in his kaleidoscope worlds cartwheelin' through space. I believed in his crystal-shard people radiatin' light like a rainbow. She was livin' proof of transcendence [...] Mr Big once asked me – what do you suppose an oyster thinks of a pearl? ... What *does* an oyster think of a pearl? I didn't know. He didn't tell me [...] It may all have been lies, but that still doesn't mean it weren't true. (247).

A pearl is made when a grain of sand enters an oyster shell, irritating the creature so much that it forms a pearl around it as a protection against the pain. Mr Big's vision – and indeed Leah, as the embodiment, the "proof" of that vision – may have been created with a great deal of inner pain (for Mr Big, for Leah, even for Mama George). Nevertheless, there was real beauty there. Evidently, the glimpse that Johnny had in his innocence of romantic transcendence is not something he is willing to relinquish altogether because of the bitter lessons of experience that followed.

One of the most interesting ways of thinking about *Whiskey Six Cadenza* is as a dramatic version of the genre of fiction called "elegiac romance." According to Kenneth Bruffee, who identified the genre (including works such as *Heart of Darkness*, *The Good Soldier*, *The Great Gatsby*, *Moby Dick*, and *Humboldt's Gift*), the main characteristics of elegiac romance are as follows: a narrator, a self-effacing and usually male character, reminisces about his relationship with a heroic, usually older man, now deceased, for whom the narrator still feels a kind of residual admiration. "The narrator's hero in elegiac romance," writes Bruffee (in a description that fits Mr Big like a glove), "combines traits of both the traditional and the Byronic hero. In most cases he is drawn "bigger than life," above the level of common everyday life in every virtue and every flaw, and he is drawn apparently profound in sensibility and apparently Satanic in arrogant resistance to the needs, virtues and possibilities of everyday life" (55). The romance aspect of the story has a twofold application, for where the narrator's hero is "involved in a quest on a grand scale," the narrator himself "is launched on a more modest, but ultimately more interesting, inner or metaphysical quest of his own" (48). In other words, the narrator is involved in an act of self-recovery that is accomplished by telling the tale of his erstwhile hero. "Elegiac romance implies, therefore, an important contrast between the true symbolic act the narrator accomplishes in the fictional present in telling the tale, and the flawed symbolic act he indulged himself in during the fictional past when he encountered an impressive-seeming fellow and transformed him into a personal hero" (52). Essentially, the genre is a revisionist exploration of the very idea of heroism as an aspect of the self. Accordingly, "the exemplary nature of the elegiac romance narrator is based on careful, conscious, voluntary disillusionment" (57). Bruffee does not extend his analysis of elegiac romance to drama, but it is clear that Pollock has absorbed the conventions into *Whiskey Six Cadenza*. Because the story is set within the expressionistic frame of Johnny's memory, the psychological impact on him becomes the foreground of the play as effectively as, say, Ishmael's narration of Ahab's story sets the whole tone of *Moby Dick*.

Thinking of *Whiskey Six Cadenza* in terms of its relation to elegiac romance provides a compelling link to Pollock's next play, which is, by her own admission, the most autobiographical of her works – *Doc* (1984). Here the heroic figure is, as the heroes of elegiac romances so often are, eponymous. As is also often the case (as with, for example, *The Great Gatsby*, *The Good Soldier*, *Lord Jim*), the title makes a partly ironic comment upon the hero. Ev is the "Doc" of the title. The nickname stems from his profession, but he is also the father to Catherine, whose return home sets off the series of memories that are counterpointed to her conversations with her father in the present. The irony lies in Catherine's feeling that while, as Doc, her father is a hero to the public because of his extraordinary devotion, at home, as Ev, he failed as a father, a husband, and a friend. The discrepancy between Ev in his heroic and flawed aspects provides the main dramatic tension of the play.

The convention associated with elegiac romance, of a contrast between the narrator's attitude towards the heroic figure in the past and the one she has assumed in the present, is made immediately apprehensible in *Doc* by having an adult Catherine in the present-day scenes who also remains to look on while a younger version of herself, Katie, plays out the childhood memories. The daughter-father rela-

tionship is atypical of elegiac romance, however, as is Ev's living presence in the fictional present of the play. Catherine's mother Bob (a
nickname from Eloise Roberts) and "Uncle" Oscar, Ev's closest, lifelong friend, are both dead. Oscar died only very recently. Indeed,
Catherine only discovers the fact during her first conversation with Ev
(29). Bob's death took place much earlier: she committed suicide when
Catherine was a girl (that is, when she was Katie), and the unresolved
anger, guilt, and grief left in the wake of that suicide cause much of the
present turbulence in Ev and Catherine's painful relations.

Whiskey Six Cadenza had audiences enter into the world of the play
through a montage of the fragments recollected by a single consciousness in what Pollock called a "kaleidoscope" effect (141). Doc also
employs "the kaleidoscope of memory" [vii]. But it is combined with a
stereoscope, so to speak, the truth emerging from the fragmented recollections of two equally haunted minds. As Pollock puts it in her
introduction: "Much of the play consists of the sometimes shared,
sometimes singular memories of the past, as relived by EV and CATHER-
INE, interacting with figures from the past. Structurally, shifts in time
do not occur in a linear, chronological fashion, but in an unconscious
and intuitive patterning of the past by EV and CATHERINE" [vii]. This
choice of a double narrative source probably has something to do
again with Pollock's reluctance to represent herself as an authority and
her determination to rectify the tendency for "truth" to be merely the
preferred account of the controlling interests in any given case.
Knowing of the extent to which the play is autobiographical, it is difficult to read Doc without admiring Pollock's integrity in representing
the truth in its complexity rather than succumbing to the temptation to
present a self-serving version of her life with her father. One review of
Doc used the headline "Daddy Dearest" (Knelman), alluding to the
vengeful portrait of Joan Crawford written by her daughter. But, apart
from the coincidence of a daughter writing about a parent, any comparison of Pollock's play to Crawford fille's memoir is misleading and
inappropriate. The latter, irrespective of its accuracy, is little more than
a self-serving lament aimed at prurient readers, while Pollock's play is
not only a very considerable work of literature but devoutly even-
handed.[17]

Pollock's own life informs Doc in several publicly well-documented
respects (see Zimmerman, Playwriting, 84, 97). Her father was, like
Ev, a family doctor much lionized by his community, after whom the
Everett Chalmers Hospital in New Brunswick was named. Both
Pollock's grandmother and her mother (as in the play, an alcoholic
former nurse named Eloise Roberts), indeed committed suicide,
although the deaths occurred later in Pollock's life than they do in

Catherine's. And, of course, Pollock is, like Catherine, a successful writer, formerly married to an actor (Michael Ball). All this is less important in itself than as a gauge of how much truth Pollock deliberately confronted with this play. That is, if *Whiskey Six Cadenza* is a *fictional* rendering of Johnny's process of self-recovery, *Doc* serves something like that function for Pollock in *reality*.

This matter of self-recovery may be brought further into focus by putting it in terms borrowed from Martin Heidegger. By doing so we can also better see how the concerns pertinent to *Doc* are consonant with what we have seen of the rest of Pollock's work so far.[18] In *Being and Time* Heidegger argues that living only in the present, accepting the "on-handedness" of the world, as it were, constitutes a degraded state, a lack of integrity and authenticity. Integrity is achieved only when we apprehend ourselves in our temporal movements, as having arrived in the present from a past and as moving into a future to become that which we determine, always mindful that our lives are finite. Whereas "clock time" consists of an infinite succession of "nows," thus according the present the paramount reality, in "existential time" the past and the future have as great a reality as – and indeed, give meaning to – the present. Hence, the authentic human self requires a bridge from present to past in order that future possibilities may be considered. The barrier to authenticating the self is the tempting ease with which we can merely repeat conventional platitudes, or distract ourselves with a pointless absorption in novelty, to avoid the struggle that living with reference to past and future entails.

To translate this idea into the figurative terms I have been using throughout this chapter, these temptations are equivalent to the state of siege that besets the self in Pollock's work: the external determinants to which the authentic, integrated self might easily succumb. The work of memory is thus the essential means of combating the state of siege; hence, any evasion of difficult historical truths is a kind of tactical failure, a loss of authenticity to the forces of inauthenticity, resulting in a reduced, fragmented, unchosen self.

The relevance of the Heideggerian model of self-recovery to *Doc* is not difficult to see. The very structuring of time in the play, as described by Pollock, is a dramaturgical rendering of the temporal phenomenon outlined by Heidegger. Catherine's efforts at self-recovery have to do principally with developing a balanced perspective on her father, so that both her resentment and her admiration will find a basis in an integrated human being. In other words, in piecing together an understanding of her father out of fragmented impressions, she is also piecing together a more integrated concept of herself. At the same time, the audience pieces together a coherent family out of the kaleidoscopic fragments of Ev and Catherine's memories, and consequently also pieces together an understanding of their personal relation to the play.

Now, attaining a valid understanding of our parents as independent, fully rounded human beings presents a struggle of sorts to most of us at some point in our lives. But the difficulty would certainly be compounded in Pollock/Catherine's case by, on the one hand, the heroic reputation her father had attained within the community, and, on the other, her sense that he was in some degree responsible for her mother's suicide. Likewise, Ev's self-righteous defence of his good works (which have been so compulsive in nature that the motive of charity is open to question) seems only thinly to mask those painful doubts about the familial responsibilities he is reluctant to face. The paralysis inherent in these suspended judgments, paralysis not merely in the matter of the evaluation of Ev's character but in the arrested development of father-daughter relations, is the main element corresponding to the "siege" condition found in Pollock's other work. In other words, the principal obstacle in this play is the siegelike stalemate in the family's relations with one another, the deceased as well as the two survivors. The principal means of lifting this siege is, once again, the use of memory to develop a true and coherent rendering of the past. "Remember more," says Katie to her Uncle Oscar at one point (40), a phrase that could be Pollock's motto.

The reason Katie is so anxious to learn more about the past is to ensure her own autonomy. Any act of free will must have a context in which its meaning is ascertained if it is to be free in any real sense. For Katie, as for the adult Catherine, the construction of such a context involves not only an understanding of the actions of those closest to her but some sense of how far prior determinants might actually affect her present and future behaviour. She frets over the extent to which her own actions lie beyond her control, wondering, in light of her mother's suicide (and, she suspects, her grandmother's), if such self-destructiveness is in some way hereditary. So Oscar's answer to her demand to "remember more" is upsetting:

> OSCAR: I think your father got his drive from your Gramma and you get yours from him.
> KATIE: Are you saying I'm like her?
> OSCAR: In some ways, perhaps.
> KATIE: I would never walk across a train bridge at midnight!   (42)

Later, Katie asks: "Do you think if you get an ugly name you start to look like your name?" To which Catherine adds: "Or be like who you were named after" (54)? Strictly speaking, this may be more a fearful superstition than a reasonable concern about determinism, but it underscores the larger theme.

The concern is present throughout the play, partly because Ev seems such a monumentally independent and self-determined personality that those around him pale by comparison. Oscar, describing the contrast between himself and Ev, says:

> I don't have ambitions and desires and goals in my life. I don't need 'em.
> My old man has my whole life mapped out for me and I know what I'm
> supposed to do. I'm supposed to read and follow the map. That's it.   (40)

Oscar's sense of powerlessness is pathetic in itself, and we may be inclined to agree somewhat with Ev, who, pointing out that Oscar never makes house-calls, calls him a "lazy son of a bitch. If it weren't for the remnants of your old man's practice you'd starve to death" (68). However, Pollock is careful to offset such impressions. When Katie's wrist is injured, it is treated not by her brilliant father, who is "never home," but by reliable (however mediocre) Uncle Oscar (58–9). On balance, Oscar's alleged sloth becomes rather refreshing in comparison to Ev's "damn the torpedoes" approach to practising medicine.

Indeed it seems to be as much for a consoling sense of fellow, mortal dimensions as affection that Bob ends up in Oscar's arms (77). Early in the play she complains that Ev: "doesn't care. He doesn't care about anything except his 'prac-tice' and his 'off-fice' and his 'off-fice nurse' and all those stupid, stupid people who think he's God" (6). Juvenile as such carping sounds, the validity of Bob's sense of abandonment cannot be gainsaid. While Bob shares Oscar's weak fatalism to an extent, Pollock is again careful to balance our understanding by presenting Bob's plight in a sympathetic light. For example, we discover that her career as a nurse was curtailed because Ev argued that his renown made it impossible for any local doctor to treat his wife with equanimity (55–7). Privately, however, he admits: "I just don't want her there" (58).

Bob's problem, then, is twofold. On the one hand, she lives in a sexist society that deems it fully appropriate that she should surrender her career to devote herself instead to supporting her husband domestically and emotionally (despite his lack of interest in any domestic life). On the other, there is also a difficulty based in character; Bob is no match for Ev's willfulness (few could be), and her efforts to assert herself collapse into self-destructive alcoholic binges. Katie and Catherine describe the cycle:

KATIE: What she does is, she starts doing something. Something *big*. That's how I can tell. She's all right for awhile – and then she decides she's gonna paint all of the downstairs – or we're gonna put in new cupboards – or knock out a wall! ... We got so many walls knocked out, the house started to fall down in the middle! Can you believe that? – And we had to get a big steel beam to put through in the basement!
CATHERINE: It's true.
KATIE: And before she gets finished one of those big jobs – she starts.
CATHERINE: And she never finishes. Someone else comes in and they finish. (91)

Furthermore, once Bob is into one of her alcoholic binges, she suffers another humiliation: the local stores refuse to sell liquor to the wife of "Doc." So she sends her maids instead, firing each maid once the storekeepers discover who her employer is (103–4). Virtually the whole of Bob's environment is an extension of her husband's will, so her sense of powerlessness has some real basis. "When I was little," she tells Katie, "I would sit on our front porch, and I would look up, look up at the sky, and the sky, the sky went on forever. That was me" (115). Now she lives in a severely restricted world not very different from Lizzie Borden's.

Judging by Bob's desperation, Ev's neglectful treatment of his wife seems callous if not cruel in some respects, and Oscar becomes our mouthpiece for such accusations. But Ev has his answers: Bob merely uses the circumstances of her life as an excuse for her drinking; her behaviour is totally irrational and out of control; and, in the matter of neglect, "she'd let the kids starve to death if it weren't for the maid" (106). When at last Bob kills herself, Oscar is blunt: "She asked for goddamn little and you couldn't even give her that," he says. Then, making Ev sound like Agamemnon, he adds: "You got your eye fixed on the horizon, and while you're striding towards that, you trample on every goddamn thing around you!" (122) But even to these accusations Ev has answers, and he finally demands:

Supposin' it were, her death my fault, put a figure on it, eh? Her death my fault on one side – and the other any old figure, thousand lives the figure – was that worth it? (123)

The question goes unanswered, for what answer can there be?

Moreover, the play demonstrates that we seldom have any real opportunity to choose the paths of our lives in terms of questions like those, or indeed any clear-cut alternatives. Ev is driven to some extent by the memory of watching his own father physically shrink as he was overcome by poverty and indignity (79). So his crusade against the poverty, ill health, ignorance, and squalour in the region are part of a crusade against the spectres of his own past. For her part, when, near the end of the play, Katie asks for her father's permission to leave home, she declares: "I'm like you, Daddy. I just gotta win – and you just gotta win – and if you say no – you'll have lost" (124). As the play ends, Catherine and Ev together burn the letter from his mother that she had left behind at her death. The gesture is ambiguous. Is this a pact between the wilful father and daughter not to succumb to self-loathing? Or do they merely intend, having done their best to reconcile themselves to the past, to put it to rest? Perhaps it is a little of each. They can only strive, in imperfect circumstances with uncertain strength, to stay what they believe to be their rightful course.

Looking back over Pollock's series of family plays, we may consider whether, as a whole, they exemplify some sort of coherent attitude towards the family as an institution. Earlier I alluded to Cynthia Zimmerman's comment about Pollock's shift from looking at public sources of authority to focus instead on "the paternalistic, dictatorial structure of the family" (*Playwriting*, 73). In some respects that is an apt enough description, but I believe there is still something more subtle in Pollock's work than the use of such a pat phrase will admit. In support of her comment Zimmerman cites her own interview with Pollock: "Within the family I see the same dominant and submissive positions that are acted against or reinforced as people try to preserve power or seize power. People try to choose and things block their choices. Basically I don't see any difference in the outside [public] plays and the inside [private] plays. In essence they're all about the same things" (*Playwriting*, 93; "Towards," 36). The difference between what Pollock is saying and what is implied in Zimmerman's summary has to do with the ambiguous status of individual agency. This is not to suggest that there are *not* "paternalistic, dictatorial" elements that emerge from the various families in Pollock's plays, but rather that it is essential to each play that the personal and social dilemmas be understood to be as much internal as external *or systemic* matters. When Pollock curtly sums up the power problem by saying that "People try to choose and things block their choices," she is thinking also of mental obstacles that are every bit as problematic as the externally imposed or systemic ones.

Part of the problem in characterizing this situation is that Pollock's plays admit no easy isolation of individual will from social context. It is by now widely acknowledged that social structures often establish their most trenchant effects by being "internalized" (assimilated to become a integral part of the individual's personality). We often see this observation at work in these plays. But this still does not entail a full surrender to the notion of social determinism. Pollock's work continues to insist upon a concept of individual autonomy, albeit one with a divided existence, both engaged in and standing apart from external structures. Her most profound character portraits show us individuals examining their own motivations and their sense of inner authority in more complex ways than could arise were she satisfied with blaming dictatorial circumstances.

If we turn, for example, to the most notoriously repressive family situation in these plays, in *Blood Relations*, we indeed find paternalistic and dictatorial forces with which Lizzie must contend. But to suggest that the murder of the Bordens arises *because* of these forces is to disregard the entire dramaturgical apparatus Pollock uses to blur the culpability. It could hardly be suggested that Pollock wants to condone parricide in general on the basis of the repressive nature of the family. And, had she aimed merely to exonerate Lizzie, then the manipulation of the actress, as well as Lizzie's suggestion that Emma shares the guilt, and the implication of the audience in the outcome of the play – all these would have been unnecessary. Taken as a whole, the thrust of the play is rather to examine the complicated question of individual responsibility in light not only of social conditions but of self-deceptions, personal manipulations, half-understood motives, and complicated ethical questions treading the border between personal dignity and pure selfishness. In short, it is in the ambiguity of the whole notion of authority rather than the ascription of a single pernicious source that the play finds its dramatic force.

In that respect, the question of Lizzie's personal authority and responsibility with respect to her family is at least as complicated as the question in *One Tiger to a Hill* of the personal responsibility and authority of Chalmers (and the rest of us) with respect to the penal system. There, too, Pollock reveals authority and oppression to be forces that partly stem from within ourselves. Similarly, in *Generations* David discovers that much of his oppression is self-generated. The external circumstances that make farming so difficult are undoubtedly a force to be reckoned with, but the main way he becomes capable of combating his sense of siege is by knowing his own mind, taking responsibility for his own actions. Then, in *Whiskey Six Cadenza* the most paternalistic figure, Mr Big, is hero, villain, and victim all rolled together. If there is a common problem among the characters, it is personal weakness more than paternalistic oppression. Finally and most explicitly, in *Doc* the question of the degree to which the paternalism of the family is the main problem is kept open, again by posing questions about individual will and personal responsibility, as well as the nature of courage, emotional histories, and ethical imperatives. What emerges for Catherine is precisely the futility of blaming an "oppressor" for her painful family history. It is not that paternalism played no role in the problems her family experienced, nor that it is impossible to ascribe social responsibility for any injuries sustained, but that to arrive only at such answers entails a false exculpation of the self – which inhibits personal growth. Instead Catherine tries to create peace within herself and with Ev by seeing the truth clearly and by overcoming the blame and guilt with which they have been living.

SANITY AND SOCIAL DISORDER

If the most recent decade of Sharon Pollock's writing career looks less fruitful than the period from the mid-seventies to the mid-eighties, it is due at least in part to her absorption in other aspects of theatrical work, such as the artistic directorships of Theatre Calgary (1984) and Theatre New Brunswick (1988–90), and, more recently, the Garry Theatre, a co-operative which she founded in 1992.[19] As for her playwriting, however, there was no new stage play by Pollock produced between the premières of *Doc* in 1984 and *Getting It Straight* in 1989.

The period may well have been a kind of retrenchment for her. Pollock's 1984 tenure at Theatre Calgary was difficult and controversial (as would be her later appointment at Theatre New Brunswick), and she had also gone through a divorce shortly before, so it would be unsurprising to see evidence of mental exhaustion. As it happens, however, Pollock was at work on a new play, called *Egg*, which in the end was never produced – or rather, it was never produced in that form, for from the large-cast *Egg* was eventually hatched the one-woman *Getting It Straight*.

In her 1982 interview Pollock speculated on the direction of her work to come, declaring: "I think that the plays that I'll write in the future will be more about women. I know there's a play that follows *Blood Relations* about what happens to a woman who is unable to kill either her father or her mother or, indeed, even herself. Obviously it's about women and madness" (*Work*, 118). Pollock's two subsequent plays vaguely answer this description. Leah feels trapped by her perverse relations with her foster parents (including Mama George's conniving at the situation) and ends up having Mr Big kill her. In Catherine we see a daughter haunted by the spectre of her mother's and grandmother's self-destruction and by the overwhelming figure of her father, though in the end the play embraces the possibility of positively reconciling parental-daughter tensions. But Pollock was to enter upon the theme of "women and madness" far more directly in *Egg*.

The tone of *Egg* is quite unlike the work for which Pollock is best known. In some ways it resembles the kind of grotesque irony associated with George F. Walker. Among Pollock's works it is closer to the absurdist satire characterizing her two early unpublished plays than any of the more subtle, psychologically based drama she had been writing in the intervening years. However, *Egg* is far more complex and grotesque than either of those early plays. There are three interrelated spheres of action in *Egg*, arising from an attempt to show how multinational corporations, military syndicates, and ordinary human beings affect one another. The central character is Martha, an escaped mental patient who is the forerunner of Eme in *Getting It Straight*. It becomes apparent that Martha's "mental illness" is a result of her inability to live in the nuclear-bomb-threatened world created by patriarchal, corporate, and militaristic interests. Her husband, George, is a general engaged in a promotional campaign intended, as he explains, "to get people round the world behind the concept of war as a means to peace. There are worse things than turning the globe into a cinder falling through space, but it isn't an easy proposition to sell" (24). Consequently, when Martha escapes, the doctors decide not to "impose on the General at this time a lot of hullabaloo concerning a looney tunes wife he was basically warehousing at our institution" (24). Instead they announce that she has been infected with a "deadly, eighteen-hour" virus.

Meanwhile, at the offices of Universal Inc., the military's partner in the "Whole Earth Nuclear" campaign, we see two contrasting groups. In one room three women – a television producer, a financial officer, and a secretary – unpack eggs from a carton and calmly discuss the problems of sexism in their homes. In another the male CEO of the company, R.D. Farkerson, rants erratically and paranoically to a male subordinate about his distrust of the women who seem to be infesting his company:

> We are surrounded by women. Have you noticed that? They're every-where. It's frightening. Everyplace you look. Women. I'm starting to notice their faces. I catch myself, every once in a while, looking right into their faces ... We need some statistics on their numbers. Because I think there's more of them. And I'll tell you something else. There's got to be a reason the Chinese kept leaving them out on river banks because the Chinese are a very smart people. (42)

As it turns out, Farkerson's fearful misogyny has some basis in the emergent circumstances, for, led by Martha, a massive international coalition of women (and Beggs, the General's male assistant, who renounces his manhood and dons drag so that he can join – 51) decides to overthrow the absurdly violent patriarchy and set up a peaceable matriarchal civilization in its place.

The approaching showdown between the male and female forces appears at times almost apocalyptic, though at others a much smaller, localized revolt. Meanwhile, Martha rallies her followers with a series of strange inspirational speeches augmented by poetic passages from a disembodied "voice":

MARTHA: We are living inside an egg, sisters, and the egg is blue, and if you screench up your eyes just a little, open your mind just a little, and try to listen a little ...
VOICE: ... The unseen world is no longer a dream
It's floating just within grasp
A shimmering radiant heavenly orb
I know the way
To move, yes move towards that.
MARTHA: ... We can stop the spread of war, we can give the word to the women of the world, that word's Unite. No more war. It's started, sisters. Listen. *(She holds the hand containing eggshells up. There is a murmuring of women's voices in a number of languages.)* All you have to do is believe, sisters [...]
We take control. We talk to the world of women. We deliver a culture shock to the world of men via satellite link-up!
We blast their dislocated minds into meaning.
We tell them loud and clear
We do not believe your promises!
We will not follow your commands!   (50–2)

The women capture Farkerson and force-feed him a giant boiled egg, including the shell. Farkerson regresses to a childlike mind-set and tells the story of how, at his birth, he was mistakenly named "R.D." by a nurse who did not understand that his mother was calling him "Artie" (60).

It appears Pollock had not quite decided how to end the play when she abandoned it. The other men are still determined to fight, as they declare by singing:

For fatherland, motherland, homeland
We have the right to die
We love our land, we'll make a stand
Nation is all
The state will not fall

Let women wail
Men will prevail.   (79)

But, as the forces outside besiege them, Martha speaks to Farkerson:

Did you know, Arthur, that we are living inside an egg? And the egg is
blue. It's a royal blue that's been lightened up with buttermilk ... the egg
opens up, like ... a thousand suns ... and the egg ... says... stare ugliness in
the face, don't ... don't turn away from the pain and suffering ... no
...maybe you can just do a little bit ... but if a great many do a little bit ...
then a lot will get done ...   (95)

And here the play ends, with a hint of personal responsibility, but with
the plot largely unresolved.

Because *Egg* was never finished to a production-ready state (a note
to director Guy Sprung written on the typescript makes it evident that
this is an early draft), there are a number of outstanding questions that
make it difficult to interpret the play with any great confidence. For
example, it is tempting, with the hindsight bestowed by *Getting It
Straight*, to consider the action as a projection from Martha's mind – a
"psychomachia" drama. However, apart from the play's beginning
and ending with Martha's monologues and a few non-realistic elements, there is not enough to support such a reading in the draft as it
stands.

The non-realistic elements in the play would be at least equally com-
patible with the sort of fabulist, satiric propaganda that is found in,
say, Brecht's *Good Woman of Setzuan*. The puppets and songs and the
montages of advertising and radio announcements that punctuate the
action would neatly support an ongoing ironic commentary were that
Pollock's intention, though as it stands the propaganda is rather under-
developed.

The political implications are better integrated in *Getting It Straight*
(1989), the main difference being that everything is set unequivocally
within the frame of a genuinely mentally distressed woman who is
attempting to work out a sane understanding of an irrational world.
Where, in *Egg*, the grotesque distortions sometimes detract from the
political criticism, here the seamless transitions from legitimate fear
and anger into paranoid terror and hostility not only make for a persuasive psychological portrait but create a compelling, passionate argument for a sane and coherent world-view.

In *Getting It Straight*, as Eme says at one point, "real and unreal
[are] shuffled like a deck of cards" (89). That puts heavy demands on
the spectator or reader; but the difficulty of discriminating between

sane analysis and insane distortion supports a main theme of the play, that sometimes insanity is the most rational response to a disordered world. Or, as Eme herself puts it, "they say I'm mad / I say enola gay little boy fat man!" (89). She is referring to the bomber plane, *Enola Gay*, and the two atomic bombs that it dropped on Hiroshima and Nagasaki in 1945; "little boy" and "fat man" were the respective code names for the smaller and larger prototypes developed through the Manhattan Project.

The plot of *Getting It Straight* is fairly straightforward, though it takes some close attention to pick it out of the text. Eme (short for Emily), a mentally disturbed middle-aged woman, has been taken on a group outing to a rodeo, has left the group on the pretext of going to the washroom, and is hiding beneath the grandstand. Less clear is the background story to which Eme continually but elliptically alludes throughout her monologue. Most of Eme's allusions are in the nature of personal memories of her immediate family. We hear, for example, of her affection for her grandfather, and also of minor, seemingly arbitrary details about her father and brother.

One passage, lifted almost verbatim from *Egg*, concerns Eme's father's name, transcribed by a nurse at his birth as "R.D." though his mother had been calling him "Artie." The joke is not a rich one, so at first glance this seems an odd detail to preserve for transference from *Egg* into the new script. But in a play dealing with mental illness it is likely that Pollock is nudging our attention in the direction of history's most famous "R.D.," R.D. Laing. The idea is supported by Eme's mention of a "layman's guide to schizophrenia" (89), a reasonably accurate description of R.D. Laing's controversial bestselling 1960 study of schizophrenia *The Divided Self*. There Laing tried to invert established preconceptions about insanity by arguing that labelling some individuals "crazy" is merely expedient mutual agreement used in dysfunctional circumstances where one person does not fit what has been determined to be the norm. Applied to Eme's situation, the theory implicitly asks whether it is not the social norm (which, in the Cold War, included the terrifying logic of maintaining nuclear-overkill capacity to deter war) that should be regarded as insane. Thus, buried in the homonym "R.D./Artie" is the question: who is mad?

Another seemingly insignificant detail is Eme's recollection that, in childhood, the "only way bubu [her brother, now a wealthy and powerful man of forty-two] could win a board game was by divine intervention." Her parents told her "games aren't that important let bubu win tonight" (101). This is a common parental request of an older sibling, but in the context of Eme's anxieties about global power it may be a microcosm for passive acceptance of the geopolitical "boys'

game" of nuclear deterrence. More recent among Eme's scattered ruminations are her references to Myrna, apparently a fellow patient, and
Freida, a patient who apparently jumped or fell to a concrete surface
(107). It is difficult to tell whether this latter image is a fantasy or actually occurred at the rodeo Eme has just fled, repelled by the violence
inherent in the sport.

However, most striking among these ambiguous images are Eme's
references to her husband's briefcase. To the extent that these allusions
can be made coherent, it seems she once secretly opened it, finding documents pertaining to nuclear warfare. She fears that, in a state of
horror, she then murdered her husband (125). But this notion is
dubious even to Eme:

> maybe I dreamt it
> myrna says they say I dreamt it
> I say no
> no
> I say strike out strike down this is a lesser
> crime I am guilty of that I accept that I hope I
> have killed him, to have known and done
> nothing? that is the crime of that I am not guilty
> not guilty of that   (125–6)

Much as Laing questioned the validity of judgments about the madness
of some people living in alienating and destructive circumstances, Eme
questions the immorality of murder in a situation where to be peaceful
is to connive at plans involving the possible obliteration of the human
race.

Set against these "memories" is Eme's vision for the future, which is
chiefly drawn from *Egg*. Indeed, Eme often uses egg imagery in passages taken almost verbatim from the earlier play:

> we are living
> inside an egg and I
> I see that it's blue
> and the egg opens up
> and a bright light
> like a thousand suns and if I can open my eyes
> just a little open my mind just a little try to
> listen a little [...]
> the visible world   is no longer real
> it's shattered   and turned into glass
> a mirror   of ugliness   agony   shame

you know the way   you know the way to change
to change all of that the unseen word
is no longer a dream   it's   floating   just within
grasp a   shimmering radiant   heavenly   orb you   know the
way to   move yes move ... (123–4)

The egg image is appropriate in several ways: an egg encloses potential
for future life, yet is sealed off from the outside world, and the life
within cannot emerge without effort; the fragility of an egg suggests the
vulnerability of the earth, which can be destroyed through recklessness; the egg's surface is continuous, without beginning or end, like the
vast unity Eme dreams of; the egg is associated with nurturing by
females. As did Martha, Eme ends the play with a "call for action" to
"all members a the female sex" (126). She envisages them spinning

> a gossamer net of women's hand's and rapunzel's hair and that net will
> encircle the globe and if a person stood on the far left star of the utmost
> edge of cassiopeia's chair that net would twinkle in the inky cosmos like
> fairy lights on a christmas tree – and what would it spell?   (126)

Earlier, when she gave the same speech to Myrna, Eme's answer was
"love." Myrna had laughed, so Eme furiously tried to smash Myrna's
face into the floor (122). The irony of Eme's violent response perhaps
indicates Pollock's scepticism, her awareness of the difficulties of realizing such a transfiguration of the world into a place of universal
co-operation.

Still, Eme's interweaving of mythical figures and cosmic imagery to
create a vision of universal harmony is undoubtedly pleasing. Her allusions to Cassiopeia (who aroused the wrath of the patriarchal
Olympian, Poseidon, by boasting of her daughter's beauty), and to
Rapunzel (locked away because of her beauty), raise again the question
of whether it might not be that she has incurred entrapment because
her thinking is too beautiful and good for the world, rather than too
flawed. As usual, Pollock prefers the ambiguity of the open question to
definite answers. Perhaps the biggest open question is inherent in the
grandstand shadows cast across the space that Eme occupies, suggesting, says Pollock in her opening stage directions, "what may be bars
[or] ribs." Is Eme's condition necessarily one of imprisonment behind
the bars of insanity? Or is she, like Jonah within the ribs of the whale,
trapped only temporarily in her despair, her entrapment a stage in a
journey whose ultimate objective is universal enlightenment?

Pollock has turned again to historical subjects for her most recent
plays. *The Making of Warriors* is a 1991 radio play that interweaves

the stories of Sarah Moore Grimke, a nineteenth-century American abolitionist, and Anna Maria Pictou Aquash, whose unsolved murder occurred during the confrontation between the FBI and the American Indian Movement in the mid-seventies. In 1993 *Fair Liberty's Call* premiered at the Stratford Festival, and *Saucy Jack* was produced by Pollock's own company, the Garry Theatre. In 1994 Pollock published *"It's all make believe, isn't it?" – Marilyn Monroe*, a short play set in the last moments of Monroe's life. This latter play is loosely related to *Getting It Straight* as well as *Fair Liberty's Call* and *Saucy Jack* in that it depicts Monroe (referred to only as "She") losing her grip on her sanity as an alliance of criminal and political forces (the Mob, the Kennedys, and the CIA) converge upon her.

Several aspects of *Fair Liberty's Call* recall Pollock's earlier work. As well as returning to a historical setting comparable to the early history plays (in this case a 1785 Loyalist community in New Brunswick), *Fair Liberty's Call* also returns to the family-based themes Pollock explored in the eighties. However, there are significant differences in the treatment of these circumstances in *Fair Liberty's Call*, which arise from the concerns Pollock had been addressing in the intervening years.

For example, Joan, the matriarch of the Roberts family, is thematically related to Martha from *Egg* and Eme from *Getting It Straight*: a middle-aged woman who, through grief and despair, has become mentally disordered, unable to reason and often uncertain of her location or the identity of others. As we might expect from Pollock's previous work, Joan's mental state stands as a touchstone for the disordered world of the play as a whole. Her mental crisis indicates a dysfunctional environment as surely as Hamlet's malaise signals that something is rotten in the state of Denmark. And, as we also may have expected, the environmental dysfunction here has something to do with unreconciled relations with the past. In this case, however, the dramatic issue is not focused upon one individual cultivating a healthy perspective on history; rather, it is the concern of a whole community. So Joan's predicament is much what we would see if we were to discover Eme, not secluded with her own thoughts beneath a grandstand but among a fractious and confused family who had not yet foresworn the violent outlook that caused her mental breakdown in the first place.

If something of the circumstances and force of personality of Clytemnestra were combined with the helpless distress of Cassandra, there would result a character much like Joan Roberts. Her husband, George, is a former Bostonian loyalist who fought against the American Rebels, a violent-minded man who remains angry at the Rebels and embittered at being beholden in his adopted country to the plutocratic Committee of Fifty-five Families. Joan and George lost both sons, Richard and Edward, to the War of Independence, but they still have two daughters, Annie and Eddie. The latter was born Emily but has been dressing and living as a man since she took her dead brother's name and place as a soldier at sixteen. An honorary member of the Roberts family is Daniel Wilson, Annie's fiancé and an ex-corporal in the loyalist Legion. The other two loyalist characters are Major Abijah Williams, representative of the local establishment, and Black Wullie, an ex-slave and scout for the Legion and Eddie's loyal companion. Finally, there is Major John Anderson, who eventually reveals himself to be a vengeful Rebel.

While the characters are all highly conscious of the need to establish correct relations with the past, they are by no means in agreement about how these are to be constituted. The play begins with the Roberts family directing a series of interlaced speeches about the past towards the audience and one another. Pollock says of this scene: "They have a compelling need to tell; to tell before someone else tells; to correct a former mistelling; to tell before they're unable to tell, or prevented from telling" [17]. Despite this competition to establish their own narratives, the Roberts are sensible of the need to arrive at some kind of joint account of the past. To this end, the loyalists of the household have devised a "Remembrance Ritual" (not unlike the ceremony Pollock had devised twenty years earlier for *And Out Goes You*, in which Goose's family commemorate the Dominion Day riot of 1935). "Totems, souvenirs and trophies of war" (36) are dragged out to serve as properties invoking the honourable struggles that gave the Roberts family its essential identity. "Gotta fill the place up with things that speak of the past," says Daniel. To which the Major responds: "Else how's a man to know who he is" (37).

The impulse to affirm identity in this way appears to stem from a demand tacitly made by the land. The choral, shared first line of the play is "You want to know where to put your eye so you can hear the heartbeat of the country comin' into bein'" (19–20). But by then Pollock has already introduced the idea in her description of the initial setting:

A bare stage, the floor of which radiates in a dark-hued swirl of colour, represents the "virgin" land. Although this space appears empty and uncorrupted, it projects an aura of foreboding, a sense of the unseen. A subtle sound fills the space as if the air itself is vibrating just below the level of conscious hearing. (19)

This sense of place is related to that described by Douglas LePan in "A Country without a Mythology." The difficulty, as in LePan's poem, is not that there is no history but rather that its true nature is not disclosed to the observer. The sense of incipient power effectively demands that its past be divulged truthfully, that the menacing emptiness of place be dispelled by proper attention to the collective history.

As with all tribal recollections of primordial struggles, there is a selective bias at work in the memories of the participants; their several notions of which elements of the past should be remembered are not always in concert. An exchange between Annie and Anderson sums it up: "I notice you've got a powerful recollection of some things, and none at all for others." "An accident of war" (43). Even among supposed allies there is no guarantee of agreement. While the ritual is underway, the exasperated Major yells at Daniel, "You're not rememberin' right!" (53): that is, through the appropriate haze of veneration.

But the paramount source of dissent in the Remembrance Ritual arrives in the person of Major Anderson, the former Rebel who brings into this house his indictment of the Loyalists. Late in the play Anderson recalls the battle of Waxhaws. While Eddie is prepared to acknowledge the disgrace of this bloody Loyalist victory (albeit weighing it against the subsequent slaughter of Loyalist troops at the hands of the Rebels in the battle of King's Mountain), Major Williams refuses to see in it anything but a glorious conquest, and Daniel refuses to hear about it at all. Anderson, however, is relentless:

> when it was over, well over, some of you went from one pile of bodies to another, pullin' off the dead and killin' the wounded and the livin'. And one of the livin' was a fourteen-year-old boy who had time to cry "quarter" 'fore the sabre came down. Do you remember that boy? ...
> None of you remembers that boy?
> DANIEL: We don't want to remember. We spend time forgettin'.
> ANDERSON: Well I can't forget, nor do I want to.   (62)

The boy, it turns out, was Anderson's brother. So Anderson's plan is to hold the others hostage until the murderer of his brother is surrendered for execution.

In some respects Anderson's function in *Sweet Liberty's Call* is similar to that of the Inspector in J.B. Priestley's *An Inspector Calls*, or even the ghostly gunfighter in the Clint Eastwood western *High Plains Drifter*. He is a stranger who, like an avenging angel heralding Judgment Day, arrives in an arrogant, corrupt, and hypocritical environment to forcibly polarize differences and galvanize the search for truth among the inhabitants. Anderson's siege of the Roberts home quickly shows that the pieties regularly invoked by the Loyalists throughout the play are hollow shams. The vaunted commitment to courage and honour crumbles into craven self-preservation as each man tries, by turns, to shift the blame on to the shoulders of another or to offer reasons why his personal value suggests that his life particularly should be spared. Or, more precisely: each of the white men reveals such despicable weakness. Pollock is careful to preserve the dignity of the one black man, Wullie, and Eddie, whose transvestism keeps her among the men (indeed, she proves the most "manful" of the lot).

Pollock's effort to discriminate between the behaviour of those who are white men and those who are not is, I suggest, less a matter of insisting upon essentialist differences in race or sex than of her being interested in finding fresh ground upon which less violent and adversarial cultural alternatives might take root. Surely a new world is conceivable in which people would see the incongruity in the very idea of a "due process" in condemning a man to death? And since those dominant in the established culture are male and white, the founders of Pollock's alternative culture are not.

In pursuing this optimistic notion of a new society, *Fair Liberty's Call* at times drifts closer to the conventions of romance than those associated with the history play. Reconciling these two genres poses no little difficulty. For where the ethic of the history play (at least in Pollock's hands) is founded upon the paramount value of truthful remembrance, the ethic of romance is based in the hope of redemption, optimistic values having more to do with faith than with a ruthless scrutiny driving the search for historical truth. Where, after all, in examining the past, *does* one put one's "eye to hear the heartbeat of the country coming into being?" One is looking for "the substance of things hoped for, the evidence of things not seen" (cf Heb. 11:1).

Pollock's solution is to juggle her depiction of the known facts of history delicately so as to place them within conventions of romance that can accommodate real moral concerns. For example, taking her cue from the reciprocal moral transgression attached to both sides of the War of Independence, Pollock uses a version of the mirror-plotting common to many romances in order to lift the siege in this play. Anderson's single-minded determination to avenge his brother's death is dissolved when he finds himself faced with Annie's admission that she betrayed a Loyalist spy into the hands of the Rebels to avenge her own brother's death. Realistically, the idea that this would suddenly end the hostility is no more "natural" than that the "natural perspective" embodied by Viola and Sebastian at the end of *Twelfth Night* should bring that play to a happy conclusion. Both devices are sleights of hand, using fortune's symmetries to distract our attention from the past and turn it to new beginnings. Thus, Major Williams is a sort of vanquished *alazon* figure, leaving the Roberts home with a final threatening speech like Malvolio's, thereby clearing the way for the inauguration of a new world. Joan, in a moment reminiscent of Hermione's resurrection and her reunion with her lost daughter at the end of *The Winter's Tale*, begins to recover her life in the present, to see that Eddie is indeed her daughter, Emily. "It's a new world, Mama," says Eddie, "you gotta look up close" (78).

Finally, pursuing the hope for a better world Pollock hinted at when she preserved Eddie and Wullie from degradation, the freed slave and emancipated woman declare they will remain together to start a new family. Meanwhile, Joan envisages a blessing from another alternative to patriarchal authority:

I feel my feet pressin' flat 'gainst the surface of the soil now. I kneel readin' the contours of the skull and listenin' to the words spoke by the man with the missin' jawbone, and the caps of my knees make a small indentation in the dirt [...] And the red woman with the baby on her back steps out from under the glade of trees and she holds out a bowl, she offers a bowl of earth [...] Eat, she says, swallow. And I do. (79–80)

It is as though the canoeist of "A Country without a Mythology" had at last recognized and received benediction from the Manitou hidden among the trees. The new world being made here is meant to transcend the antinomies and violence of the old, to begin new lives, having acknowledged and atoned for the errors of history.

Admittedly, Pollock could be charged with indulging in a biased mythologizing of the past not much different from the one she condemns the Loyalists for perpetuating. One might argue that she has given way to the temptation to revise the past according to her own wishes by putting something as improbable as Eddie's transvestism and union with Wullie into her play. But in defence we might reply that, improbable as such events may be, they are not *impossible*, and are thus within the bounds of poetic licence. Yet the whole argument seems somewhat beside the point, for by this stage Pollock had grown less interested in precisely reconstructing history than in exploring ways of reconciling her sense of the mistakes of the past with her project of encouraging ethical constructions for the future.

Pollock's *Saucy Jack* (1993) was certainly approached in such a frame of mind. *Saucy Jack* treats a subject that has fascinated many writers, the mystery of the most famous serial killer in history, Jack the Ripper. Yet where most treatments of the Ripper focus on the questions of who he was and why he committed the murders, Pollock argues that such questions are irrelevant. For her, the nub of the issue is that "the women are killed because they can be killed with relative or complete impunity. It is done because it can be done. That reason is sufficient for those who undertake such actions" (*Saucy*, 5). That may be a thin theory of human nature, and it disregards the obvious fact that Jack the Ripper differed from the vast majority of the population living in London in 1888, who, notwithstanding the opportunity, did *not* choose to become serial murderers and indeed were horrified by the crimes. After all, that is precisely why Jack the Ripper became so notorious. Still, the comment is a focused declaration of the political premises underlying this play. The character Kate might speak for Pollock when she sings, ostensibly as a warning to Montague:

There's no time to tell you how
He came to be a killer
But you should know as time will tell
That he's society's pillar
For he is not a butcher
Nor yet a foreign skipper
He is your own light-hearted friend
Yours truly, Jack the Ripper.   (28)

In short, social implications, not the personal details of the man known as Jack the Ripper, are the issue here. Accordingly, while there are a number of similarities between *Saucy Jack* and Pollock's treatment of the late nineteenth century's next most legendary murderer in *Blood Relations*, there are significant differences in the approach to characterization and conflict in these two plays.

For instance, in *Saucy Jack* Pollock's political thesis demands that Jack should not be a lone, monstrous figure but someone who operates with the assistance, or at least the connivance of others. The whole point is that the murders should not be seen as social transgressions but, on the contrary, as acts that enjoy social support. Hence, it is left unclear just who was responsible for the actual murders, Eddy (Prince Albert Victor, grandson to Queen Victoria and heir to the throne) or Jem (James Stephen, friend and former tutor to the prince, and the more forceful personality). The responsibility is thus immediately spread, and a further blurring of the guilt will follow. Jem's plan is to displace suspicion for the murders on to their mutual acquaintance, Montague, by murdering him and planting evidence upon the body. The only other character in the play is Kate, a "music hall entertainer and actor" whom Jem has hired to enact each of the murdered prostitutes.

Jem's motive for having the murders re-enacted is also left unclear, despite a comment of Pollock's that I will come to in a moment. In part the uncertainty arises because Jem has received a head injury sometime in the past that makes him frequently speak and behave in very peculiar ways. The play begins with his delivering a long, frighteningly irrational monologue in the presence of Kate. Apart from its creation of a sense of anxiety in the audience for Kate's safety, the effect of the speech is to discourage us from expecting Jem's subsequent behaviour to have logical reasons attached to it. So, although Jem says that his object in having the murders re-enacted is to "save Eddy," it is not at first apparent how this could be, especially given that Jem is at least equally suspect. The element of sadistic nostalgia that reportedly prompts psychopaths to preserve souvenirs of their murders perhaps also figures to some extent, yet neither does this satisfy as a final explanation of Jem's motivation, because there is no sign of the salacious glee we would expect in such a case.

Pollock raises the issue in her introductory note, saying: "The end or objective or motivation for the re-enactment of the women's deaths in the play is not to achieve the death of the women, but to achieve some other end or objective that relates to the relationship between the men. Love, loyalty and friendship are words the men use, but the actions through which such noble sentiments manifest themselves are the ones of betrayal, duplicity and murder" (5). To be sure, they could hardly be out to "achieve the death of the women" because the women are already dead. Yet Pollock's point about the "objective that relates to the relationship between the men" remains somewhat cryptic. The men are indeed utterly despicable, regardless of what they say, but this is little help. In what sense does their discreditable partnership motivate the re-enactment? A little further on, however, Pollock declares:

I am less interested in whether Jem, or Eddy, or some combination of them and possibly others, are indeed guilty of the murders than I am interested in the whys and ways Jem attempts to bind Eddy to him as well as to confirm or negate his fearful suspicions regarding his own role in the Ripper events. He's caught in a terrible dilemma. If he is indeed guilty of the crimes, he is "sane" for his clouded recall is founded on reality. If he is innocent of the crimes, his memory and mind are serving up false data and he's "insane". (5–6)

Thus, the key to sanity, in Pollock's formulation here, is not whether one's *behaviour* is rational or psychotic but whether one *remembers* accurately or not. This would be a remarkable assertion were it not that we have been prepared for it by the decisive role played by memory in virtually all of Pollock's previous plays. Where Ibsen's plays showed how the past could determine a character's destiny, Pollock shows how the retelling of the past determines one's destiny and, hence, sanity. Jem wants the murders re-enacted because he seeks validation for a certain version of the past. At one level he hopes that Eddy can tell him who was actually responsible for these murders; but the main question is whether Jem and Eddy (and, in his own way, poor foolish Montague) will remain partners in the act of recollection.

Further light is shed on this matter by the style in which the re-enactments are written. It is quickly apparent that the vignettes are not meant to be realistic, either in the sense of capturing what the murdered women might actually have said in the street or in the sense of being likely versions of what might be devised by two murderous aristocrats and a music-hall performer. For one thing, the writing is too poetical to be commensurate with either such project. For example, here is Kate as Polly:

> Call me Polly. Can I help you? Is there anything I might have you might want? I was a good girl once but me old man ran off with me best friend who acted as a midwife when Sarah was born – Oh he come back. They always come back. I wish to God he'd stay away.
> [*sings*] Oh hear me cry Almighty Host
> > I quite forgot the quail on toast
> > Let your kindly heart be stirred
> > And stuff some oysters in that bird.
>
> So he comes back and I have another one – the little boy who lives with me father now – and the old man kicks me out because a me drunken habits [...]
> > Up and out and in, with the cry a slaughtered horses ringin' in me ears, and the press a Buck Row bricks markin' me back – But hold – look – look at the sky, it's glowin', yes it's ... there's a wonderful fire down on the docks and it's lightin' up the heavens, oh I wish I could be there, see the flames feedin' on the wood, reachin' up over the water, the water and fire and wood, wish I could be up close, right in the middle, surrounded by flames burnin' in hell and floatin' to heaven on a spire a golden smoke.   (26)

The speech offers a stylized, poetic condensation of Polly's whole character, the combination of stream-of-consciousness, catch phrases, fragments of autobiography, and mental imagery quickly, deftly adumbrating a whole life, a soul. The contrast between this and the coroner-like forensic inventory initiated by Jem that immediately follows could not be more starke.

In Kate's speeches the important level of meaning lies not with mimetic but with symbolic and thematic concerns. Plainly, the re-enactments in *Saucy Jack* have quite a different function from the re-enactment in *Blood Relations*. In the earlier play the Actress enters into the terms of a reality prescribed by Miss Lizzie so as to work through the sense of Lizzie's situation, to speculate sympathetically on the motives for Lizzie's real or imagined behaviour. Miss Lizzie already knows what happened in the past; the re-enactment is intended to achieve understanding in the Actress (and of course, the audience).

The actress in *Saucy Jack* is far more autonomous. Because Jem does not himself know the extent of his and Eddy's role in the murders, he cannot be much of a coach to Kate; and at any rate, he certainly has nothing of Lizzie's interest in teaching his actress. Indeed, it is pointedly established that the prior contact between Jem and Kate has been minimal (one is reminded of a magician's introduction of a "volunteer"). She is never called Kate by the others; it may be that Kate's name and occupation is known only to us. Except when performing, she remains a silent, anonymous figure, seeming to occupy a different level of reality from that of the men.

The significance of maintaining Kate's dramatic autonomy and providing her with such evocative, stylized renderings of the murdered women seems to be this: Kate is engaged in a sort of mortal competition with the men for the control of the past. The contest is mortal not in the sense that anyone's actual life is at stake (though Montague's is certainly endangered, and Kate's may be). What is most potently at stake is the inner lives of the murdered women and, by inference, the inner lives of all women, their possession of their own souls. The matter is related to Pollock's recurrent theme of the role of memory in protecting individual integrity against deterministic forces. Jem seeks validation for his dubious memories even at the risk of conclusively establishing his own and Eddy's guilt. In Pollock's dramatic world the power of recollection bestows not only sanity but validity, so those whose memories prevail set the terms of sanity, deciding (here again we recall R.D. Laing) who shall be determined sane or insane, who will be deemed valid or invalid.

Hence, Jem passionately wants to "re...member," as he frequently puts it, to re-establish the validity of his (and his class's) vision of the world by reassembling, or re-membering, the dismembered fragments. It is as if the dismemberment of the women's bodies had caused a fundamental disintegration of objective truth itself. But Pollock intends that Jem should find no such validation. Accordingly, far from reestablishing themselves as arbiters of truth, the men are made pathetic and impotent by their imperfect attempt to remember. In contrast, Kate grows stronger and more powerful through her vivid re-enactments of the souls of these murdered women.

Pollock writes that through her performances Kate evolves "from a silent, unknown, nameless figure [...] to the only vital or potent figure or force in the play when the final blackout occurs. Her exploitation has not victimized her; it has empowered her. She is larger than herself at the end [...] She lives. They die" (6). It is irrelevant to the case to object that, realistically, Kate would not be allowed to escape with her life were the men really the ruthless murderers they are meant to be. The point is that Pollock creates a confrontation between two versions of the past and poses the question of which is more valid. And, because this trial takes place within the dramatic imagination, the authority that determines the outcome of the confrontation is not that of social class, or brute force, or even political office, but an authority of the imagination, which answers this appeal: which is more convincing, which more compelling, which more truly vital? There is little doubt that, in such terms of the spirit, Jem and his cohorts – and all those like them – are quite, quite dead.

4 Michel Tremblay: Existential Mythopoeia

Guru books – the Bible
Only a reminder
That you're just not good enough
You need to believe in something...

Joni Mitchell

SEXUALITY, RELIGION, AND ALIENATION: FOUNDING A MYTHOLOGY

In *Thérèse et Pierrette à l'école des Saints-Anges* (1980), the second novel of Michel Tremblay's Chroniques du plateau Mont-Royal series, there is a passage in which Dr Sanregret, the attending physician of the rue Fabre, is watching the annual Saints-Anges pageant with Ti-Lou, an infamous, retired Ottawa courtesan. Held on the school's front staircase, this *"reposoir"* features a huge cast of schoolgirls, boy scouts, and others, lavishly costumed and arranged in various tableaux and processions, with one lucky little girl starring as the Blessed Virgin. All this is intended to demonstrate publicly the parish's piety and unabashed love of God, but Dr Sanregret remarks:

> Cette mascarade a quelque chose de sexuel qui m'ébahit chaque année. Voyez ces enfants offerts, immobiles, qu'on oblige à poser et qu'on admire pendant des heures au bord des transes. L'inconscience est vraiment la mère de toutes les cérémonies religieuses.

> This masquerade has something sexual about it that amazes me every year. Look at those children offering themselves, immobile, forced to pose and be admired for hours, on the verge of a trance. The unconscious is truly the mother of all religious ceremonies.

Ti-Lou replies:

> Chez nous, à Ottawa, dans ma maison de la rue Roberts, c'était le
> reposoir à l'année longue. (57)

> At my place on the rue Roberts in Ottawa, it was a repository all year
> long.[1]

Dr Sanregret has put his finger on an idea that lies close to the heart of
Tremblay's poetic theatre: that religion and sexuality often spring from
a common source in the unconscious. Indeed, it is interesting to turn
Dr Sanregret's remark inside out as Ti-Lou does and observe that there
is always something religious about Tremblay's treatment of sexuality.

This fusion of religion and sexuality reaches its epitome in *Damnée
Manon, Sacrée Sandra* (1977), where pious Manon fixes her religious
passion upon an enormous rosary with a sensuality that matches the
religious intensity the transvestite Sandra fixes upon a green lipstick.
Tremblay is by no means the first to remark the similarities between
religious and sexual ecstasy. The analogy informs some of the most
important metaphors of Christianity, such as Christ the Bridegroom or
Nun as bride, and lies behind the otherwise incongruous inclusion of
the Song of Solomon in the canon. More locally, Tremblay's fellow
Montrealer, Leonard Cohen, has practically made a career out of
metaphors bridging sexuality and religion.[2]

The sexuality-religion analogy holds particular interest to a study of
Tremblay because it stands at the psychological centre of an elaborate,
idiosyncratic mythology extending through his work. All poetic theatre
is to some degree mythopoeic and hence indirectly concerned with religion, but Tremblay goes further than many playwrights. Indeed, he has
referred to himself as a "mystic" (Usmiani, 22), and his plays so consistently build and illuminate a mythology as to constitute a kind of
religious drama, though that would be a misleading label in so far as it
implies the service of religious orthodoxy. Tremblay's work is pointedly
heterodox, often deliberately written in the face of Roman Catholicism
even as it uses the religion as a source of poetic grammar. Wherever
there has been a single dominant mythology, as in Quebec, there is a
shared legacy of allusion; but inevitably there is also for some a sense
of alienation from spiritual fulfilment and belonging. Thus, a paradox:
Tremblay's responses to the church and other elements of Quebec
society are often adversarial, but they are so comprehensive as to form
a kind of alternative mythology – an anti-mythology.

Indeed, the mythopoeic element in literature is usually most apparent where an author feels compelled to address his or her noumenal

interests in an idiosyncratic manner because of a sense of alienation from prevailing orthodox mythologies. Such writers commonly evince a divided consciousness based on a dual sense of mythology. On the one hand, mythology is understood as a social complex of deceptions that serve to alienate and repress certain groups; on the other, it is the means by which these writers overcome a sense of alienation to create a healthy, whole self-image. In his early work Tremblay addressed his sense of alienation through rather abstract mythopoeic fantasies, but as time has passed his treatments of the theme have become increasingly more concrete and direct.

Over the last two decades the stunning Chroniques du plateau Mont-Royal series – beginning with *La Grosse Femme d'à côté est enceinte* (1978) – has made Tremblay nearly as well known as a novelist as he is as a playwright.[3] These novels are not only rewarding in themselves; they also provide an invaluable enrichment of the world and characters of the plays. When the novels first began to appear, they filled in the background of Tremblay's existing drama while still seeming fully independent; but as the characters have reappeared in new plays, his dramatic and fictional conceptions have become profoundly integrated. Indeed, for certain plays, such as *Marcel poursuivi par les chiens* (1992), a knowledge of the fiction – in this particular case, *Le Premier Quartier de la lune* (1989) – is indispensable to a full appreciation of the play's nuances.

Because the success of the Chroniques du plateau Mont-Royal followed Tremblay's great success as a playwright, some incorrectly assume that Tremblay began writing fiction only relatively late in his career. In fact, he has been writing both fiction and drama from the beginning. His earliest available work consists of two pieces of juvenilia written when he was just sixteen, a short story, "Les Loups se mangent entre eux" (The wolves eat one another), and a remarkably strong short play called *Le Train* (written in early 1959 but broadcast on radio only in 1964, after winning Radio-Canada's young authors prize). Reminiscent of Edward Albee's *The Zoo Story* (which was written about the same time), *Le Train* features two men, X and Z, who meet on a train and have a discussion about their radically different lives, ending with one murdering the other.

From that point on, however, Tremblay's plays assumed the tone he has maintained throughout most of his mature work. The case of his fiction is somewhat different. Whereas the style of the recent novels – a combination of realistic characterizations and poetic descriptions of inner thoughts – is fully consistent with that of the plays, the style of the earliest fiction is much more fantastic in conception. In the collection of short stories *Contes pour buveurs attardés* (1966; published in

English as *Stories for Late Night Drinkers*) and the novel *La Cité dans l'oeuf* (1969; The City in the Egg) Tremblay creates imaginary worlds in which he gives free rein to fantastic creatures such as sorceresses, vampires, and monsters, as well as all manner of supernatural events, regularly contrasting this fictional cosmos with the banality of the quotidian world.

Most of the short stories are brooding Poe-like or Kafkaesque nightmares, but occasionally there are allusions to the prospect of a better fate. In one of the best stories, "La Dernière Sortie de Lady Barbara" (The Last Outing of Lady Barbara), the narrator seeks admission into a secret brotherhood like Balzac's "Treize" (an influence Tremblay acknowledges more explicitly in his later work) and is assigned the task of assassinating the tyrannical Lady Barbara during one of her wheelchair promenades in order to bring about a better world:

> A plusieurs reprises, le courage me manqua et je faillis laisser Lady Barbara au milieu de la route et prendre mes jambes à mon cou; courir, courir vers Londres, vers ma maison, vers la liberté ... Une tasse de café le matin et le cinéma deux fois la semaine ... Mais je ne suis pas né pour mener une vie de bourgeois. Je suis né pour parcourir le temps et l'espace, pour remonter le fleuve de la vie vers sa source et revêtir la robe blanche des Confréries du Cosmos. Je suis né pour planer au-dessus de mes semblables! [...] Je me devais de défier le monde de Lady Barbara et je le fis. (58–9)

> At several points my courage faltered and I nearly left Lady Barbara in the middle of the road and took to my heels; to run, to run towards London, towards my house, towards freedom ... A cup of coffee in the morning and the movies twice a week ... But I wasn't born to live the life of a bourgeois. I was born to soar across time and space, to swim up the stream of life towards its source, and to don the white robe of the Brotherhoods of the Cosmos. I was born to soar above my peers! [...] I had to defy Lady Barbara's world and so I did.

This story of an underdog who attempts the dangerous act of willing a better world into existence is expanded in *La Cité dans l'oeuf*. There François Laplante, an ordinary Montrealer, is dissatisfied with his life and disgusted by the idea of living in an empty self-made world:

> Je réalisai alors toute l'horreur de l'Univers, de cette création infinie dont on ne sait rien et dont on ne saura jamais rien. J'avais fait de moi le monde et le monde n'était rien! Et j'ai senti [...] les autres mondes, tous les autres mondes eloignés et perdus eux aussi, avec des êtres différents de

moi, monstrueux pour moi qui étais un monstre pour eux! [...] Soudain je
me mis à trembler à la pensée qu'il n'y avait peut-être pas d'autres mondes
... Non! Il fallait absolument qu'il y eut d'autres mondes! Je ne voulais pas
être seul dans l'Univers!   (53-4)

Then I realized all the horror of the universe, of this infinite creation of
which we know nothing and never will know anything. I had made the
world of myself, and the world was nothing! And I felt [...] the other
worlds, all the other worlds, far away and also lost, with their beings different from me, monstrous to me who was a monster to them! [...] Suddenly I started to tremble at the thought that there might not be any other
worlds ... No! There must be other worlds! I did not want to be alone in
the universe!

Later François travels by means of a magical egg to the fantastic city of
the title, where he is acclaimed as a saviour, then enlisted in the attempt
to overcome a regime of evil deities and recover a lost world ruled by
love. The important point here is that in both cases the narrator moves
from a sense of disenchantment and alienation with the world in which
he lives to a determined faith in a world better suited to his existential
requirements. In these early prose fantasies the imagined worlds are
blatantly fanciful and abstract. When we move to the major plays we
encounter a more realistic environment, but there persists the combination of alienation alongside the suggestion of an alternative means of
achieving a relation with what Martin Buber would call an Eternal
Thou – the authentic sense of the divine experienced with the whole
soul.

As I have suggested, Tremblay belongs to an underclass in more than
one sense. In the first place he is very much one of that generation of
Québécois artists who argued that the identity of their whole culture
was historically that of a socially repressed underclass, and whose
rebellion against this condition gave rise to the Quiet Revolution. The
document that comes nearest to standing as a manifesto for the Quiet
Revolutionaries is Paul-Émile Borduas's polemical essay *Refus global*
(1948).[4] When it was first published Borduas received little public
support, but by the sixties his essay seemed an extraordinarily pre-
scient clarion for the cultural uprising then underway, a milestone of
which was the production of Tremblay's *Les Belles Soeurs* in 1968. The
stark terms in which *Refus global* lays out battle grounds provide a
clear context for Tremblay's own myths. Borduas castigates the church
and the state for their complicity in creating a submissive, convention-
bound, spiritually barren people. He declares that the Québécois have
been

Un petit peuple serré de près aux soutanes restées les seuls dépositaires de la foi, du savoir, de la vérité et de la richesse nationale. Tenu à l'écart de l'évolution universelle de la pensée pleine de risques et de dangers, éduqué sans mauvaise volonté, mais sans contrôle, dans le faux jugement des grands faits de l'histoire quand l'ignorance complète est impracticable.

A little people, clinging to the cassocks seen as sole repositories of faith, knowledge, truth and national wealth. [They have been] shielded from the universal evolution of thought [seen as] so risky and dangerous, educated without malicious intent, but without discretion, in false interpretations of historical events when complete ignorance was impracticable.

He urges his readers to cast off their conventional identities: "Au diable le goupillon et la tuque! Mille fois ils extorquèrent ce qu'ils donnèrent jadis" (To hell with the aspergill [a device used to sprinkle holy water] and the tuque! They have extorted a thousand times what they have given us). And he condemns the "peur d'être seul sans Dieu et la société qui isolent très infailliblement" (fear of being alone without God and the society which are both inevitably isolating – 45–7). Finally, Borduas argues, the duty of the Québécois is clear: to break with all of society's conventions and to refuse to co-operate with "the system" any longer; to refuse to be what American Blacks call "Uncle Toms" (that is, those who court favour from those in power by a show of non-threatening simplicity and subservience). In other words, the myth of the meek, rural, simple, devout Roman Catholic French Canadian, which certain members of the Church and the Duplessis government have collectively promoted for so long, must be rejected and an alternative society created to supplant the conventional authoritative structure. "Place à la magie! Place aux mystères objectifs! Place à l'amour!" (Make way for magic! Make way for objective mysteries! Make way for love!), he writes (51). In effect, Borduas envisions a moral inversion similar to that embraced by Romantics like Blake, who insisted that evil and negativity proceeded in the form of oppression from above – that is, from both religious and secular authority figures – while goodness and creativity proceeded from below – that is, from the dispossessed subculture figures.

Tremblay subscribes to Borduas's model of the Québécois culture repressed by authority figures, but expands his celebration of the subculture to include – indeed, to be most often embodied by – women and gay men. In *La Grosse Femme d'à côté est enceinte* (1978) Tremblay, writing of the sense of shame and embarrassment experienced by pregnant women in Montréal, speaks eloquently of the role played by women in general in his society. For its vituperation of the Church and its representatives, as well as its tone, it is a passage that easily might be appended to *Refus global*:

Écrasées par cette religion monstreuse qui défendait toute sorte de moyen de contraception, cette religion fondée sur l'égoïsme des hommes, pour servir l'égoïsme des hommes, qui méprisait les femmes et en avait peur au point de faire de l'image de la Mère, la Vierge Marie, Mère de Dieu, une vierge intacte et pure, inhumaine créature sans volonté et surtout sans autonomie qui s'était retrouvée un jour enceinte sans l'avoir désiré, par l'opération de l'Esprit-Saint (qu'on osait représenter sous la forme d'un oiseau! enceinte d'un oiseau, la Mère de Dieu!) et qui avait enfanté sans avoir besoin de mettre au monde, insulte ultime faite au corps des femmes; gayées par les prêtres de phrases creuses autant que cruelles où les mots "devoir" et "obligations" et "obéissance" prédominaient, ronflants, insultants, condescendants, les femmes canadiennes-françaises surtout celles des villes, avaient fini par ressentir une honte maladive d'être enceintes, elles qui n'étaient pas dignes, comme l'autre, de mettre un enfant au monde sans qu'un homme, leur propriétaire et maître, leur passe dessus et qui, surtout, n'avaient pas le droit de se dérober à leur "devoir", à leurs "obligations" parce qu'elles devaient "obéissance" à ce merveilleux outil du destin que leur avait fourni directement la Volonté de Dieu: leur mari. La religion catholique, en un mot, niait la beauté de l'enfantement et condamnait les femmes à n'être *jamais* dignes puisque la mère de leur Dieu, l'image consacrée de la Maternité, n'avait été qu'un entrepôt temporaire d'où l'Enfant n'était ni entré ni sorti. (258–60).

Crushed by this monstrous religion that prohibited any kind of contraception, this religion founded on the egoism of men to serve the egoism of men, who despised women and were so afraid of them that they created the image of the Mother, the Virgin Mary, Mother of God, a virgin, intact and pure, an inhuman creature without volition and, above all, without autonomy, who discovered one day that she was pregnant without having wished it, by the operation of the Holy Spirit (whom they dared to represent in the form of a bird! Impregnated by a bird, the Mother of God!), and who had a child without having to give birth, the ultimate insult to women's bodies; crammed by priests with phrases as hollow as cruel, in which pompous, insulting, condescending words like "duty" and "obligation" and "obeisance" predominated, French Canadian women, particularly those who lived in the cities, felt in the end an unhealthy shame at being pregnant, they who were not worthy, as was the Other, of bringing a child into the world without having a man, their owner and master, on top of them; women who, above all, had no right to refuse their "duty," their "obligation," because they owed "obeisance" to the marvellous instrument of fate that came directly to them through the Will of God: their husbands. The Catholic religion, in a word, denied the beauty of child-bearing and condemned women to *never* be worthy, because the mother of their God, the consecrated image of Motherhood, had been only a temporary depository which the Child neither entered nor left.

A similar anger is seen when Tremblay writes of the shame and embarrassment homosexuals are made to feel in this culture. In *Hosanna* (1973), when Cuirette discovers during a midnight jaunt that his old haven for sexual rendezvous, the Parc Lafontaine, has been harshly exposed by floodlights, he explodes with a tirade:

> Gang d'hosties, d'écoeurants, vous avez toute changé, hein, vous avez toute changé! Maudits chiens sales! Vous avez peur qui reste des coins noirs, hein, vous mettez des lumières partout! Ben, sacrement, on va vous faire ça dans'face! [...] On va vous faire ça dans'face, hostie! Y'a autant de tapettes dans'police qu'y'en a ailleurs! Pis y'a autant de tapettes dans gars de bicycle qu'y'en a ailleurs, j'ai l'honneur de vous l'apprendre! Ça fait qu'on va toutes faire ça ensemble, en pleine lumière, les culottes baissées, au beau milieu du terrain de baseball, sacrement! (68–9).

> You bunch of bastards, you pricks, you've gone and changed it all, eh, you've changed everything! Goddamn filthy pigs! You're scared they'll be a few dark corners left, eh, so you put your lights up all over the place! Well fuck you, 'cause now we're gonna do it right in your faces! [...] Right in your faces, goddamn it! There's just as many fags in the police as anywhere else! And there's as many fags riding bikes as anywhwere else, let me tell you! So let's get it on, our pants 'round our ankles, in full light, right in the middle of the baseball field, goddammit!

Cuirette's shock and disappointment may be a secondary theme in the play, but it reinforces the humiliation of Hosanna "herself," who finally acknowledges the inadequacy of her masquerade to disguise the primary fact of her identity – that she is really Claude, a man.

That Tremblay represents the repression of both women and gay men in terms of an unjust sense of shame is a vital consideration in any attempt to contextualize his work. Here the work of Jean-Paul Sartre, especially where it concerns the writer Jean Genet, is illuminating. Shame and embarrassment play an important role in Sartre's philosophical system, for they are the emotions attendant on the experience he uses to explain the crucial concept of "being-for-others": being caught in the act of looking through a keyhole, finding one's status as an observer suddenly overwhelmed by the awareness that one is observed and judged by another. One of Sartre's most important explorations of this concept is his study of Genet's life and work, *Saint Genet: Comédien et Martyr* (1952). To a degree Genet's life is merely an opportunity for Sartre to expound his own system, but the common ground between Tremblay and Genet – such as their interest in the theme of gay subcultures and the philosophical implications of transvestism – especially recommends some of Sartre's ideas to our attention.

Among Sartre's several provocative suggestions, two are of particular interest. He argues that women and gay men (together with criminals and other "relative beings") have a special problem with self-consciousness; there is a paralysing schism in their "being-for-itself" because of the disproportionate pressure of their "being-for-others." What this means, briefly, is that their essence is caught up in their consciousness of the perceptions of others rather than in self-defining actions – the latter, according to Sartre, being the case for most men. This point of view was shared by Sartre's partner, Simone de Beauvoir, who based her argument in *Le Deuxième Sexe* (1949) on the idea that women are socially identified as "the Other" – as a deviation from the male norm (see especially the introduction and second chapter). Sartre explains the point using the example of a mirror (his favourite existential symbol). Heterosexual men check a mirror, he says, in order to show what is perceived by others to their real (i.e., inner) selves; women, gay men, and criminals, because they are defined by others, check a mirror in order to show their real selves (i.e., their appearances) to their perceptions (the inner self being uncertainly defined) (89–90). All this is arguable, but the accuracy of Sartre's example on the level of individual psychology is less important here than its deft delineation of a social complex.

We can clearly see an opposition between an establishment perspective on the one hand – which, so far as Tremblay is concerned, is anglophone, male, heterosexual, elitist, morally prohibitive, and socially conventional – and, on the other, the dispossessed or disenfranchised perspective, which is, in Tremblay's work, francophone, female, homosexual, proletarian, licentious (in a non-pejorative sense), and bohemian. Tremblay consistently inverts the establishment perspective in his authorial point of view: anglophones almost never appear in his work (which is significant, considering that Montreal was, until recently, nearly half anglophone), and most of the heterosexual males are either marginal and negative characters or aligned with the disenfranchised through a handicap of some sort (e.g., deafness, incestuousness, lunacy). Thus, the usual sense of "on et l'autre," of "us and them," is quite deliberately reversed in Tremblay's work.

Nevertheless, the consciousness that this point of view has been created as a subversion of the prevailing social point of view remains a powerful force in the mythopoeic process. The myths created by Tremblay must always convey something of the impact made by the world to which these myths are a response. This brings us to another of Sartre's suggestions about Genet, and will also take us full-circle to where this chapter began.

The title of Sartre's study, *Saint Genet*, indicates the paradox that Sartre sees at the heart of Genet's work: the aura of religiosity surrounding Genet's treatment of certain criminal or homosexual acts. To explain this phenomenon, Sartre marries his existentialism to the theory Mircea Eliade had expounded in *Le Myth de l'éternel retour: archétypes et répétition* (1949).[5] There Eliade explains the difference between sacred and profane acts as a distinction between those that have primordial archetypes and those that don't. He argues that human beings find a sense of regeneration in rituals that imitate primordial events and that, in doing so, recreate the original connection humans believe they had with eternity. The quotidian world moves linearly from one profane, meaningless moment to another, but the sacred world is immutable, consisting of a few sempiternal events that are continually re-enacted in holy rituals. Sartre sees an equivalent to Eliade's view of mythic primordiality in the events that existentially created Genet's sense of self. Specifically, he suggests that Genet's first realizations that he was perceived as a criminal or a homosexual became his definitive myths, and his subsequent work recreates this experience with a sense of sacred ritual because it isolates his identity from the profane succession of acts that he is disinclined to treat as existentially defining (see book 1 of *Saint Genet)*.

We have already remarked a similar paradoxical religious element in Tremblay's work, but there is an important difference between Genet's and Tremblay's primordial myths. In Sartre's view Genet remained essentially isolationist, a self-proclaimed *poète maudit* who set himself against the world. Tremblay, by contrast, is a fundamentally social writer: as the early prose fantasies demonstrate, he has always been interested in offering salvation to the socially damned through the depiction of alternative societies. The sense of having himself and his own community damned by the powers that be is always an important part of the myth; but the ultimate goal is always to wrest these judgments away from the established authorities, to reclaim for his community the power of self-identification, to refuse to let the disdain of others create self-destructive neuroses. To apply Sartre's adaptation of Eliade to Tremblay, we might say that in his mythology the sacred moment is that in which the will to identify oneself and one's community subjectively is recovered.

BUILDING THE GARRISON: RUE FABRE AND LA MAIN

Tremblay's first great success came with the 1968 production of *Les Belles-Soeurs*. A great deal of controversy was aroused by his use of what was then called *joual*, a literary rendering of the Québécois dialect. So much has been already written on this element of Tremblay's writing[6] that there seems little point – especially for an anglophone – in dwelling on the matter, except to notice how it contributes to the mythopoeic aspect of the play. Tremblay's adoption of an argot specific to the lower-class Québécois community was not only more realistic than the elegant literary dialogue used by his predecessors, such as Marcel Dubé; it was also a blatantly political act inasmuch as it represented a reclamation of a community's discourse about itself. The dialect is imbued with a particular world-view that is absent from standard French, the cultural history of Quebec inhering in *joual*, just as the history of the Israelites may be traced in the etymology of the Hebrew language.[7] The diction and idioms that distinguish *joual* from standard French are like scars or footprints recording the various social pressures felt by the community over the years. The two most salient elements of *joual* are the many anglicisms and the nature of the profanities, or *sacres*, that pepper Québécois speech. The anglicisms, of course, reflect the situation of the Québécois as a French-speaking minority on an English-speaking continent; the *sacres* reflect the omnipresence and repressive influence of the Roman Catholic church in Quebec society. Profanities initially derive their power from their subversion of social taboos. So, where modern English generally favours profanity of scatological or sexual nature, *joual* uses the names of sacred articles (*câlice, hostie, tabernacle, ciboire*, etc.) as well as more familiar curses such as Christ's name.[8] These blasphemies are frequently compounded with a *maudit* (damned), which brings home the main point about the *sacres*: they draw their power from a defiance of religious authority.

In *Les Belles-Soeurs* the women speak *joual* and thus express all the discomfort of a culture in thrall to repressive moral authoritarianism, yet they are still highly conventional and parochial. The main exception is Pierrette, the youngest Guérin sister; the younger women who sympathize with her also show some small promise of breaking from convention. Significantly, however, Pierrette is an outsider to the main group of women. She is paying a rare visit to her sister's house on the Rue Fabre, ordinarily being an habituée of La Main.[9]

Nearly all Tremblay's characters are associated with one or both of these two settings, the rue Fabre and La Main, which are ultimately ways of distinguishing between two competing inclinations or states of mind, as we see in *En pièces détachées*, which straddles both settings, or when a character like Pierrette brings the sensibility of one world into another. Tremblay may seem an unlikely candidate for Frye's "garrison mentality," but the rue Fabre, which typifies the sort of repressive conventionality of which Borduas complained, indeed resembles the inside of a garrison, where there is no escape from the eyes of others. As for the other part of the framework, however, the hostile nature that is kept at bay by the garrison is not a literal wilderness but the wilderness of human nature – what Camille Paglia calls "chthonian nature," contrasting it with Apollonian thought (*Sexual Personae*, 5–6). It was precisely this nature from which, according to Borduas, the Church and the schools attempted to shield Quebeckers throughout much of their history. Characters living on the rue Fabre struggle to keep the fearful dangers of unfettered chthonian nature out of sight, but forfeit a part of themselves to the security of communal solidarity. By contrast, characters associated with La Main may indulge their desires with moral impunity but pay a price in both lost security and an amplified sense of social alienation.

In *Les Belles-Soeurs* Pierrette has returned home to the rue Fabre from La Main to attend her sister Germaine's stamp-pasting party. Germaine has won one million trading stamps in a contest and invited over a group of female relatives and friends to spend the night pasting stamps in booklets. When the play was first produced, there was a good deal of discussion about the accuracy of Tremblay's rich satire of the lives and manners of these women; but in the end, any criticism about realistic accuracy is probably too nice in light of the play's stylized theatricality – principally evident in the arrangements of speech inspired by classical dramatic form. Tremblay steeped himself in classical literature from an early age, and while the classical influence on his work is not always superficially apparent, its effect is invariably felt in his skilful constructions and adroit use of rhetorical and dramatic conventions.

The choral speeches, isolated colloquies, and soliloquies in *Les Belles-Soeurs* evoke ancient Greek and classical French dramatic conventions, and in doing so serve a double function. In so far as they

lend a highly formal means of expression to these women, their lives
– or at least the articulations of their predicament – are ennobled, and
the play moves beyond the domain of simple satire to suggest a tragic
dimension. At the same time there is an ironic overtone in these formal
speeches, but the sardonic commentary is directed not only at the
women themselves but at the expectations implicitly raised by the convention. The lives of these women fall considerably short of the ethos
of the classical theatre, and in this ironic distance lies a palpable
rebuke to their society.[10] The most obvious instance of Tremblay's
ironic use of conventional form is the "maudite vie plate" (goddamn
lousy life) chorus, which begins with a pastiche of an idyllic pastoral
opening derived from classical literature or idealistic dramas such as
Rostand's:

> Dès que le soleil a commencé à caresser de ses rayons les petites fleurs
> dans les champs et que les petits oiseaux ont ouvert leurs petits becs pour
> lancer vers le ciel leurs petits cris ...   (23)

> When the sun starts to caress with its rays the little flowers in the fields
> and when the little birds open their little beaks to pierce the heavens with
> their little cries ...

As the "petits" suggest, there is a sneering overtone here. The lofty
opening gives way to a suffering more banal than noble:

> Là, là j'travaille comme une enragée, jusqu'à midi. J'lave. Les robes, les
> jupes, les bas, les chandails, les pantalons, les canneçons, les brassières,
> tout y passe! Pis frotte, pis tord, pis refrotte, pis rince ... C't'écoeurant, j'ai
> les mains rouges, j't'écoeurée. J'sacre. A midi, les enfants reviennent. Ça
> mange comme des cochons, ça revire la maison à l'envers, pis ça repart!
> L'après-midi, j'étends. Ça, c'est mortel! J'hais ça comme une bonne! Après,
> j'prépare le souper. Le monde reviennent, y'ont l'air bête, on se chicane!
> Pis le soir, on regarde la télévision.   (23)

> So, then I work like a madwoman until noon. I wash. Dresses, shirts,
> stockings, sweaters, pants, underpants, bras, everything. And scrub and
> wring and re-scrub and rinse ... It's sickening, my hands are chapped, I'm
> sick to death. I curse. At noon, the children come home – eat like pigs,
> turn the house upside-down and leave. In the afternoon, I hang out the
> wash. That's the killer. I loathe that more than anything! Afterwards, I fix
> the supper. They all straggle in like beasts and start squabbling. Then in
> the evening we watch television.

Sarcasm of that kind is not to be found in plays such as Euripides' *Trojan Women*, yet it is a measure of how well Tremblay has integrated the pathetic with the risible that the dramatic tensions of *Les Belles-Soeurs* bear comparison to those of such a classic tragedy.

Of course, the two plays are superficially similar in that they both centre on large female casts, but a much more important point of comparison is the similarity of political ethos. *Trojan Women* poses an alternative to Homer's perspective on the Trojan War, one written not from among the warriors but over the shoulders of those who suffered the war without ever waging it. While *Les Belles-Soeurs* is not about war victims as such (though by heritage they are a conquered people), it does convey a related sense of frustration and impotence, for as autonomous and self-contained as the relationships among the women seem, they bear the configuration of the pressures of the outside world as surely as the Trojan women, even in the absence of the Greeks, have been redefined by defeat.

In effect, the stamp-pasting party is like a pressure-cooker through which the effects of external social forces work upon the women in Germaine Lauzon's kitchen. The catalyst and continuing heat source for the whole process is the prize of a million trading stamps – an invitation to greed and envy that amplifies the effects of the society in which they live. At the outset of the play Germaine actually expects the trading stamps to bring social justice to her household:

> J't'avertis, Linda, j'commence à en avoir plein le casque de vous servir, toé pis les autres! Chus pas une sarvante, moé, icitte! J'ai un million de timbres à coller pis chus pas pour les coller tu-seule! Après toute, ces timbres-là, y vont servir à tout le monde! Faudrait que tout le monde fasse sa part, dans'maison. (17)

> I'm warning you, Linda, I'm getting sick to death of always being at your service, you and all the others. I'm not a slave, you know! I've got a million stamps to paste and I'm not about to paste them all on my own! After all, those stamps are going to benefit everybody. So that means everybody in this house has gotta do their share.

A naïve capitalist, Germaine assumes that where wealth is accrued by any one member of the community, the prospect of a trickle-down effect will automatically ensure an equitable division of labour: the stamps will be a great leveller, setting Germaine and her family on an equal footing inside the house and bringing the family as a whole into the middle class at one blow.

Were there any question of her hopes being realistic, it would be dispelled by the litany of junk Germaine dreams of accumulating with all her trading stamps (20–1). Practically speaking, Germaine's aspirations may be circumscribed by the trading-stamp catalogue, but the other women, whose dreams are limited only by their imaginations, are no better off. Like the women in Tomson Highway's *The Rez Sisters*, they are obsessed with bingo; its prizes – the ashtray floorlamps and Chinese dogs (86–7) – are the grails of their imaginations. Time and again they effuse over various contests they have entered, only to be deflated by Yvette's inevitable response: "Pis, avez-vous gagné quequ'-chose, toujours?" (But have you ever won anything? – 44 and passim). They all cling to improbable, commercially devised, grossly material dreams and, in the unlikely event that one of their companions wins, they are consumed with envy of her good fortune and with rage at the injustice of one of their own breaking away from the common fate of their group.

The stifling combination of disgust for their community, intolerance towards the least hint of unconventionality, and contemptuous xenophobia (the one exception to this rule, the insufferably parvenue Lisette, is herself despised for her europhile tastes), is the principal effect of their social position, the consequence of the habitual narrowness of spirit brought on by frustrated desire, petty thought, and enforced humility. Thérèse Dubuc, who loathes her mother-in-law yet is enraged to hear her criticized by anyone else (70), is an example in miniature of the community's hothouse complex. Yet the ugliest characteristic of this social attitude is their pitilessness towards others. As feminist historian Ann Douglas remarks: "The cruelest aspect of the process of oppression is the logic by which it forces its objects to be oppressive in turn, to do the dirty work of their society in several senses" (11). The intolerance of the women of the Rue Fabre falls most heavily upon anyone who dares to act on the desires they share; one reason cited for their hatred of French movies is the compassion with which the films treat extramarital pregnancy (101). Thus, their most heartfelt censure is reserved for those of their own community who have transgressed their repressed standards.

Here we find another parallel with *Trojan Women*. Pierrette's treatment at the hands of her (literal and figurative) sisters is a slightly lesser version of the attitude of the Trojan women towards Helen. Much of the hatred for both of these characters is rooted in the simple fact that they have not kept solidarity with the other women; they are ostracized because their experience outside the rigid codes of sanctioned behaviour is viewed as an unforgivable transgression. On the rue Fabre lust is seen as the principal threat to social order, and the clubs of La Main are the worst dens of iniquity. In this petty moral cosmos a club is "un vrai endroit de perdition" (the fastest road to hell – 77). Hence, Pierrette, a club employee, is shunned and openly despised.

Ironically, Pierrette is in no way reaping benefits from her bold defiance of the rue Fabre's social prohibitions. Although she laughs off the narrow-mindedness of the other women, saying "Si l'enfer ressemble au club ousque j'travaille, ça m'fait rien pantoute d'aller passer mon éternité là, moé!" (If hell is anything like the club where I work, it'd be no skin off my nose to spend my eternity there – 78), this is mere bluff, for she later confesses to the audience that she has been abandoned without prospects by Johnny, the club owner who lured her away from home and persuaded her to work for him for the past ten years. Tremblay extends the dramatic irony by juxtaposing Pierrette's soliloquy of disillusionment and despair with her niece Lise's soliloquy, in which Lise expresses anxiety for her present situation (pregnant and determined to abort) and envy of Pierrette's presumed freedom and happiness (94–5).

Evidently, Lise follows in her aunt's footsteps somewhat, for when she reappears in *En pièces détachées* (1969)[11] she is unhappily working in a cafeteria and supporting her callous, lazy boyfriend. Plainly, she will soon be as hardened as her co-worker Thérèse, an ex-habituée of La Main and the main character of *En pièces détachées* (as well as, in *Thérèse et Pierrette à l'école des Saints-Anges*, the bosom childhood companion of Pierrette). At the Coconut Inn, a club on La Main, Thérèse hears Les Aurores Sisters singing a country and western ballad that warns of the fate of women like her:

Quand Hélène est partie de chez elle
Quand elle a ouvert les ailes
Quand Hélène a ouvert les ailes
Est tombée en bas du nid, pauv'elle!
Méfiez-vous, petites filles
De la grande ville vile
Restez avec votre mère
Vos frères, vos soeurs et votre père! (40–41)

When Hélène left her home
When she spread her wings
When Hélène spread her wings
She fell out of the nest, poor thing!
Beware, little girls
Of the big evil city

Stay home with your mother
Your brothers, your sisters and father!

Corny though the song may be, it does suggest the miserable fate of Thérèse and Pierrette and, incipiently, of Lise once they leave the rue Fabre.

The Hélène of the song is most directly identified with Thérèse; in the 1969 version of *En pièces détachées* Thérèse is actually called Hélène.[12] Interestingly, Tremblay dedicates his novel *La Grosse Femme d'à côté est enceinte* "à Hélène qui s'est révoltée vingt ans avant tout le monde et qui en a subi les conséquences" (to Hélène, who rebelled twenty years before everyone else and who had to suffer the consequences – 7). Possibly Tremblay's Thérèse/Hélène is based on some historical Hélène, but the precise biographical content is less important than what this recurring figure represents to Tremblay. The point is worth dwelling upon because the system of cross-references among Tremblay's various works is such an important aspect of his oeuvre. It is a cardinal principle of comparative mythology that the *names* of mythic figures are a less important means of identification than their *function* within the mythology. The same principle applies to Tremblay's work, for his characters are often essentially recurring manifestations of particular imaginative forces. Thérèse/Hélène, for example, wherever she appears in Tremblay's work, embodies a spirit of rebellion. Her sense of independence and vitality is always set against the repressed and embittered conventionality of her mother Albertine (originally called Robertine in *En pièces détachées*), an outlook consonant with the general attitudes of the Rue Fabre. In the person of Thérèse the ethos of Tremblay's two worlds, the rue Fabre and La Main, are brought into passionate conflict.

In *En pièces détachées*, however, Thérèse is a failed rebel. She retains her fighting spirit, but it has turned into a spiteful, inward battle, not very different from the constant, destructive rage at the world seen in her mother at her worst (i.e., Albertine in her forties and sixties, as seen in *Albertine en cinq temps*, *La Grosse Femme ...*, or *La Maison suspendue*). The play does, however, offer some sense of how Thérèse arrived at this point. While the action of *En pièces détachées* covers only two days, the seven scenes depict several situations in which Thérèse has lived, thereby sketching the shape of her biography as well as touching on several of Tremblay's recurring themes.

The play opens on the rue Fabre. A group of women gossip about Thérèse and her family – their regular screaming matches, Thérèse's scandalous history, and so on. The second part shows Thérèse at Nick's Café, where she works as a waitress. Bitter disillusionment shows at every seam, not least in her intolerance of her innocent younger colleague, Lise. The third scene is set at the Coconut Inn, the club on La Main where Thérèse had been employed until she suddenly found herself on the outs with the criminal element of La Main. Futilely, she schemes for reinstatement. Her best avenue for escaping her life has been closed off. Scenes 4 and 6 return to the comments of the chorus of neighbours. In 5 and 7, Thérèse is among her family. Gérard, her husband, is a hapless weakling. Thérèse is clearly the strongest-willed person in the household, but is nearly mad with rage and despair. Only her mother, who has lived on disapproval rather than hope, can stand up to her properly.

In the last scene Marcel, Thérèse's brother, returns home unexpectedly from a mental asylum. The compassion each member of the family eventually, grudgingly, extends to Marcel, temporarily indulging his craving for a pristine home in which everyone wears white, is the most humanizing force in the play. As the play ends one member of the family after another repeats chorically "Chus pus capable de rien faire!" (I just can't do anything anymore – 90–2), except for Marcel, who has the last word:

> Moé, j'peux toute faire! J'ai toutes les pouvoirs! Parce que j'ai mes lunettes! Chus tu-seul … à avoir les lunettes. (92)

> Me, I can do anything! I've got all the powers! Because I have my sunglasses! I'm the only one … that's got sunglasses!

Madness is, then, an escape of a sort; but the price of that freedom is the ultimate sense of isolation.

Taken as a whole, *En pièces détachées* is perhaps less satisfying than many of Tremblay's plays. The chief problem is referred to by the punning title: the lack of unity. While the fragmented structure accommodates a wide array of themes, it also dissipates any strong overall impression. Tremblay usually keeps an eye to the neoclassical unities, unfolding one main theme continuously in a single setting, yet the scenes in *En pièces détachées* have no real causal relation. The reason for this diffuseness is the play's origin in a set of short plays called *Cinq* (1966). Tremblay took three of these and added new material to make *En pièces détachées*. The two remaining plays, *Berthe* and *Johnny Mangano and His Astonishing Dogs*, along with a new sketch, *Gloria Star*, ended up on television as *Trois petits tours* (1969).

LIFE ON LA MAIN

All three of the *Trois petits tours* are set at the Coconut Inn on La Main. *Berthe* and *Johnny Mangano* are bleak, to say the least, and it may be that *Gloria Star*, which hints at a weird magic, was added to countervail the despondent impression a little and to suggest something of the mysterious siren appeal La Main holds for so many of Tremblay's characters. These plays are the first to be confined wholly within the world of La Main, and as such introduce the performance theme to Tremblay's work, La Main being primarily a huge venue for performances of various sorts. Each play uses the theme of performance to offer a kind of existential parable, to explore the relationship between image and reality on the premise that any conspicuous disguise reveals something about its wearer. The existential reading of the performances in each play is open not only to psychological but to political interpretation. For, as in virtually all of his work, Tremblay, a long-standing Quebec nationalist, puts his characters into situations in which they can be (and often are) read allegorically, as personifying a vision of Quebec as a society ambivalently aspiring to become a sovereign nation but suffering the inner conflicts of self-doubt.

Berthe is an eponymous monologue from the Coconut Inn's box-office attendant, who sits "enthroned" in her glass booth wearing cat's-eye glasses and reading movie magazines while the doorman shouts "Showtime! Showtime!" with idiotic regularity. Berthe is tormented by dreams of stardom that contrast cruelly with her actual station; instead of displaying her grandeur to the world on the silver screen, Berthe displays her very banality in a glass booth before a seedy nightclub. She is trapped in an existential prison: "Si j'rêve pas, j'vas étouffer" (If I don't dream I'm gonna suffocate), she declares (18). But, tethered by her limited imagination and by the doorman's ironic refrain, her mind can never stray far from the dismal truth of her situation.

Johnny Mangano and His Astonishing Dogs is the title not only of the play but also of a cabaret act. Conspicuously absent from the billing is Carlotta, Johnny's lover and partner, who is ostensibly in the act only to pose behind the dogs, showing off her legs. Yet we discover that the dogs – or rather, dog, for among the dogs there is only one very old poodle named Kiki who has any talent to speak of – will obey only Carlotta, who has been the real trainer all along. Johnny is in fact a untalented mediocrity, and though he bullies and humiliates Carlotta, when she threatens to leave he is terrified of going on stage without her, for he will simply have no act. If that were all, the story would be only rather coarsely ironic and not particularly interesting. What turns the play from the farcical to the macabre is Carlotta's intelligent complicity in all this. Carlotta knows full well that the act is pathetic and that Johnny is a charlatan, yet she goes on playing his sidekick. At the outset she declares herself determined to leave this ghastly situation and seems to gather resolve throughout the action. However, when Johnny finally breaks down and begs her to stay, Carlotta is moved to relent – not by love or pity but by her feeling of triumph when she hears his words "Chus pas capable, tu seul!" (I can't do it alone) and sees the image of Johnny on his knees before her reflected in the mirror (57).

The sudden insight in which one's own situation is seen in a mirror, as though through another's eyes, is a classic existentialist gestus.[13] In this moment Carlotta sees the objective confirmation of her secret role, of her power within the relationship. She is the chief agent in Johnny's delusion of power and self-sufficiency, and so long as this is acknowledged by both of them she will go on masochistically playing her role in the private psychological routine, regardless of her contempt for the tawdriness of the public act.

The dramatic action of *Gloria Star* is mainly a dialogue between the Coconut Inn's stage manager and Gloria Star's agent, called La Femme. La Femme boasts at first that Gloria Star represents the "apotheosis" of the strip act to date (76), but makes a direct appeal to the stage manager:

Il est une partie du public que j'ai toujours négligée, une partie du public qui est en train de devenir majorité: la partie du public qui demande quelque chose de neuf! Les femmes aussi veulent être provoquées, transportées, jeune homme!   (81)

There is a part of the public I've always neglected, a part of the public who are about to come of age: the part of the public who demand something new! Women also want to be provoked and transported, young man!

La Femme's idea is to invert the traditional direction of the objective existential gaze by having a man display his body for the delectation of women.[14] The play ends as Gloria Star's act begins. She makes Carlotta and Berthe disappear and lures the stage manager out to dance with her while La Femme laughs wildly. Evidently a turnabout in the process of objectification of the Other has begun; women who attempt to escape the gaze of others through a fantasy life (e.g., Berthe) and women who connive at their own humiliation (e.g., Carlotta) are obsolete where men have become objects for the gaze of women.

The idea that Berthe and others live in an existential prison may appear to contradict the argument that La Main represents a wilderness outside the garrison, but two points should be considered. First, Tremblay's characters are all seen as part of an oppressed society of the type that Borduas described; therefore, escape from the garrison is only an escape from a particular community's stifling response to external oppression to take up the battle on one's own. Second, in freeing oneself of repressive social conventions, one necessarily also leaves behind an identification with that community to reforge one's own identity. Thus, to escape from the confining garrison of the rue Fabre to the wilderness of La Main is to be not only *existentially free* to perform a new role, but *ineluctably obliged* to assume a more revealing disguise. Accordingly, a recurrent theme of the La Main plays is the paradox that the very means of self-discovery may be one's disguise,and Tremblay's existential performers *par excellence* are his transvestites, who embrace irony so thoroughly.

About ten years ago, in a book intended to guide aspiring actresses to contemporary plays with interesting roles for women, Tremblay's monodrama *La Duchesse de Langeais* (1969) was featured (Heys, 24, 124, 150). What is remarkable about this is that La Duchesse is indubitably a man: Albertine's brother Edouard, as we discover in the novel *La Duchesse et le roturier*. As Heys is otherwise always careful to note when she is suggesting cross-gender playing, we are left to guess whether she believed a gay transvestite's perspective was so wholly interchangeable with a woman's that the fact of La Duchesse's sex needn't even be mentioned, had merely been careless, or is unusually naïve. To be sure, others have not found the idea of casting a woman as La Duchesse bizarre: the role was first played by Doris Saint-Pierre, and Renate Usmiani has argued that the sex of La Duchesse is of little significance:

In terms of human interest, the play deals with the problems of aging; in particular, the humiliation of a "woman" who has been deserted for a much younger partner. In this respect, the fact that the Duchesse is a male transvestite appears merely incidental; any woman of sixty, abandoned after a brief affair with a nineteen-year-old, would react in the same manner. For the Duchesse, the case is somewhat more complicated because it involves her professional pride. As a prostitute of international repute and forty years' standing, she considers it shameful to have allowed herself the unprofessional weakness of falling in love   (97)

In my view, such an interpretation suggests a serious misreading of the play. On the contrary, it is highly unlikely that a woman of any age would behave in exactly this way, and the complicating factor is hardly La Duchesse's "profession" so much as "her" sex. Of course, etiquette demands that transvestites be referred to as "she," and La Duchesse may even manage to think of herself without those constant quotation marks around the feminine pronoun; but if the audience slips permanently into that illusion, they will miss much of the meaning of the play.

Indeed, the question of La Duchesse's sex provides *La Duchess de Langeais*'s presiding poetic device; for the theatrical effect depends heavily upon the irony derived from our continual recognition that, however much indication there may be to the contrary, La Duchesse is *not* a woman: or, more precisely, *is* a "not-woman." The exaggeratedly effeminate parody of "womanliness" is a kind of counter-litotes (i.e., "hyperbole which tends to deflate an idea," in Dupriez's definition – 116). It does not point so much *positively* to the idea of "man" as *negatively* in the direction of "woman," suggesting something "woman-like" perhaps, but ultimately and essentially "not-woman." The effect resembles one implicit in Genet's *Les Bonnes* or *The Maids* (1947), where Genet intended that his two maids should be played by boys. Commenting on *Les Bonnes*, Jean-Paul Sartre picks up on an idea raised by Genet in *Notre Dame des fleurs* (1944), suggesting that a sign should be posted beside the stage announcing that the women were being played by men. Sartre explains:

De cette pâte féminine elle-même, Genet veut faire une apparence et le résultat d'une comédie. Ce n'est pas Solange qui doit être une illusion de théâtre, c'est *la femme Solange*. [...] Ce qui paraît aux feux de la rampe, c'est donc moins une femme que Genet lui-même vivant l'impossibilité d'être femme. On donne à voir d'abord le travail parfois admirable et parfois grotesque d'un jeune corps mâle en lutte contre sa propre nature et, de peur que le spectateur ne se laisse prendre à son jeu, on l'avertit en permanence – au mépris de toutes les lois de "l'optique" théâtrale – que des comédiens tentent de le tromper sur leur sexe. Bref, on empêche l'illusion de "prendre" par une contradiction maintenue entre l'effort de l'acteur qui mesure son talent à sa capacité de tromper et l'avertissement de la pancarte.   (676)

It is this feminine stuff itself Genet wishes to make appear the result of a performance. It is not Solange who is to be a theatrical illusion; it is *the woman Solange*. [...] Thus, what appears on stage is not so much a woman as Genet himself living out the impossibility of being a woman. One sees the effort, at times admirable and at times grotesque, of a youthful male body in a struggle with its own nature, and, lest the spectator be caught up in the game, he would be warned throughout – despite all the laws of stage perspective – that the actors are attempting to disguise their sex. In short, the illusion is prevented from "taking" by a sustained contradiction between the effort of the actor, who measures his talent by his ability to deceive, and the warning of the placard.

To be sure, there are significant differences between this situation and Tremblay's play. The most important is that in *Les Bonnes* Genet and Sartre place the schism between *actor* and theatrical illusion, whereas in *La Duchesse de Langeais* the actor-role relationship is the conventional one, and the schism exists instead between *character* and theatrical illusion – that is, between the man we might as well now call Edouard and the character he plays, La Duchesse. The difference is one of theatrical framing; the real sex of the actor is ironic at a metatheatrical level in Genet's play but an internal theatrical level in Tremblay's. Or, to put it another way: *Les Bonnes* uses literal transvestism only as a theatrical device, whereas *La Duchesse de Langeais* is, to a degree, about transvestism itself. Accordingly, Tremblay's theme differs from Genet's in that the social issue of the feminine image (which Sartre saw in *Les Bonnes*) is less central to the drama of *La Duchesse de Langeais* than are the implications of La Duchesse's personal failure to meet her self-imposed ideal.

Hence, there is a cryptic dialectic between the persona of La Duchesse and the man beneath the façade. This provides a kind of dramatic irony, but it is an unusual kind, because the dialectic is available to both the audience and the character. However, there is still a sense of irony based on concealed and revealed information, for the drama is expressly based on La Duchesse's reluctance to face the recent consequences of this dialectic. The irony of being "not-woman" has been very much at the heart of La Duchesse's personal allure in the past. The elaborately effeminate character coupled with male anatomy has proved intoxicating to men whose sexual desires spring from a divided consciousness, who are aroused precisely by the "perversity" of the experience of heterosexual male behaviour laid across a homosexual act. The word "perversity" is not used here to express any moralistic or pejorative judgment, of course, but in cognizance of a point Michel Foucault argues in his *Histoire de la sexualité*; in the modern age all sexuality comes in a precisely labelled category. "Perversity" names the psychological concomitant of this particular kind of irony, the sensation attendant on appropriating the framework of a conventional form of sexual behaviour to convey a contrary act, where erotic pleasure consists in subversion, in deliberately disguising the "deviant" as the "normal."

Evidently, La Duchesse has been extraordinarily adept at manipulating this complex appeal. She has subtly, precariously played upon the theme of "camp," or "pornokitsch,"[15] there being always modicum of self-parody in self-consciously assuming "feminine" clichés. However, La Duchesse has apparently just crossed the fine line between an alluring self-contradiction and a grotesque masquerade; she is simply too old now to play the *femme fatale*. As she rapidly becomes a sort of "drag queen" Miss Havisham, her ironic performance is no longer amusingly erotic but a pathetic and somewhat repellent joke:

> *Sur un ton neutre. Sans conviction*: Dans un bal costumé, chez la Choquette, l'année passée, j'ai faite la belle au bois dormant. J'ai jamais vu du monde rire comme ça! *Elle s'asseoit. Silence.*   (89)

> *In a neutral tone. Without conviction*: At the costume ball, at La Choquette's place last year, I went as Sleeping Beauty. I've never seen people laugh like that! *She sits down. Silence.*

This is what La Duchesse now finds so distressing in the dialectic: the balance between eroticism and comedy has been upset. Susan Sontag, in her "Notes on Camp," suggests that "to name a sensibility, to draw its contours and to recount its history, requires a deep sympathy modified by revulsion" (276). That seems to describe not only Tremblay's perspective in creating the character but the way in which La Duchesse now regards herself.

When self-deprecation and self-parody begin to cut too close to the bone, La Duchesse seeks refuge in relativism, retreating from the ironic dialectic between image and truth and dwelling only on the image, casting reality aside and making a spectacular show of frivolity and rhapsodic reminiscence, with more than a little fantasy interspersed:

> Quand j'ai commencé a faire la duchesse, on venait de loin pour me voir! Tous les hommes, les vrai, les mâles, les beus, se traînaient à terre devant moi dans l'espoir que je daigne jeter un regard sur eux! J'les poussais, comme ça, du bout du pied ... Ça, c'est à l'époque où j'ai été vedette ... J'étais une grande artiste, dans mon genre ... [...] *Très "actrice"*: Il fallait me voir en Edwige Feuillère dans la scène finale de "La dame aux camélias"! *Elle renverse la tête par en arrière. Tousse un peu.* J'étais sublime! Ça, j'faisais ça pour mon vendeur de glace ... Y bráillait, le pauv' cheri, que c'en était déchirant! Pis après, y me donnait vingt-cinq piastres! (89-90)

> When I started doing la Duchesse, they came from miles to see me! All the men, the real ones, the males, the bulls, would crawl before me hoping that I'd shoot them a glance. I'd push them, like this, with the tip of my foot ... This was in the days when my fame was at its height ... I was a

great artist in my own genre ... [...] *Very "grand actress":* You should have
seen me as Edwidge Feullière in the final scene from "La Dame aux
Camèlias!" *She throws her head way back. A little cough.* I was sublime! I
used to do that for my ice salesman ... He sobbed, poor dear, enough to
break your heart! And afterwards he'd hand me twenty-five bucks!

Alas, it is a performance doomed to failure, for in the absence of
madness, self-delusion will eventually expose itself. When La
Duchesse's performance runs out of steam, she relies on scotch, but
even that will not hold reality at bay indefinitely. At last disillusionment overtakes both pretence and intoxication:

Tout s'est envolé! Même ton faux goût pour un marin Péruvian se sauve
cul par-dessus tête! Ben souffre, ma sacrement. C'est de ta faute! Paye, ma
câlice, paye! Tu le savais que ça finirait comme ça! Tu le savais! Tu te
vantes partout d'avoir auarante ans d'expérience, ben pourquoi t'as pas
faite c'que ton expérience te disait de faire! Ben crève, astheur! Essaie pas
de lutter, ça set à rien! [...] Ben non, ma chérie on meurt pus d'amour par
les temps qui courent pis tu le sais ben! Tu mourras pas, c'est ben ça
qu'y'est effrayant! Ben oui, c'est correct, t'as d'la peine, là, mais ça va se
passer ... T'as déjà vu pire! Fini, l'amour, astheur, c'est ben correct ...
Braille un bon coup, roule un peu sous la table, là, pis après, fais comme
toujours: dis-toi que t'es la plus belle pis la plus fine, pis que le monde est
rempli d'hommes qui t'attendent! *Elle se lève péniblement.* Les hommes
sont à tes pieds, duchesse! *Elle retombe lourdement sur la table.* [...] On
m'appelle "La Duchesse de Langeais" parce que j'ai toujours rêvé de
mourir soeur, Carmélite ... En buvant du thé! (105–6)

It's all flown away! Even your phony crush on the Peruvian sailors has
taken off ass-end over teacups. So suffer, you bitch! It's your own fault.
Pay, you cunt, pay! You knew that it would finish like this! You knew!
You're always bragging about your forty years experience, so why didn't
you do what your experience taught you to do? So, die, right now! Don't
try to fight it anymore! [...] But no, my dear, no one dies of love nowadays, as you know very well! You're not dying and that's what's so horrible. Sure, that's right, you're in pain, but it will pass. You've seen worse.
Love is dead from this moment; that's right ... Have a good cry, roll
around under the table there, and then, do the same as always: tell yourself that you're the most beautiful, the most refined, and that the world is
replete with men all waiting for you. *She struggles to her feet.* The men are
at your feet, duchesse! *She falls heavily on to the table.* [...] They call me
"la Duchesse de Langeais" because I've always dreamed that I'd die a
Carmelite nun ... sipping tea!

Only here, in the last line of the play, does La Duchesse allude to the source of her "stage name," one of three linked tales in Honoré de Balzac's *Histoire de les Treize*. In Balzac's story the Duchesse is a high-society coquette who, having toyed with an ardent lover's affections for too long, is emotionally devastated when, in bitterness, he apparently closes his heart to her. She becomes a Carmelite nun, having chosen to spend her last days among women who, as Balzac puts it, "soupirai[en]t après ce long suicide accompli dans le sein de Dieu" (sigh after this long suicide accomplished in the breast of God – 194). Her lover finally arrives to rescue her, only to hear she has died an hour or so earlier. The contrast between the dignified romantic tragedy Balzac allows his Duchesse and the pathetic degeneracy in which Tremblay's declines is clear enough. Such coquetry, however misguided, had its place in Balzac's romantic world; reset in Tremblay's ironic ethos, the tragic consequences become sordid, a sad attempt to conceal reality behind a worn-out mask.

La Duchesse de Langeais returns in a supporting role in *Demain matin, Montréal m'attend* (1972), a musical comedy that is far more light-hearted than any other La Main play. Louise Tétrault, a small-town girl, wins a trophy in a local singing contest and goes to Montreal, where her sister, Lola Lee, is established as a professional singer on La Main. In an attempt to discourage Louise, Lola Lee takes her on a tour of La Main that includes the "Meat Rack," a "bar spécialisé de Montréal," frequented by La Duchesse and other transvestites and prostitutes (including Hosanna and "her" companion Cuirette, the cast of Tremblay's next play). Louise is somewhat dismayed by what she encounters but nevertheless decides to stay in Montréal, declaring: "J'finirai peut-être icitte [i.e., the brothel] un jour, mais j'vas commencer ailleurs! Ailleurs! Plus haut!" (I may finish up here one day, but I'll start higher, much higher! – 79–80). Tremblay pulls no punches in depicting the seediness of La Main, but on balance *Demain matin, Montréal m'attend* is still fairly uplifting, as most musicals are. Louise is the most optimistic version of characters like Pierrette, Thérèse, Lise, and Carmen: young women drawn to the glamour of La Main in search of freedom from their dull and repressive lives. Thus, *Demain matin, Montréal m'attend* fills an important position in Tremblay's overall mythology in that it provides the clearest expression of the ambiguity of La Main's allure; its at once glamorous and tawdry promise is symbolized by Louise's huge, hideous trophy, which occupies the stage at the top of the show.

As in *La Duchesse de Langeais*, dramatic tension is stretched between the poles of disguise and disillusionment in *Hosanna* (1973). Hosanna is a young transvestite who is obsessed with the image of

Elizabeth Taylor as Cleopatra. The action of the play is set in Hosanna's apartment on the night she has returned home from a humiliating ordeal at a La Main club belonging to an older transvestite, Sandra. Sandra had plotted with others, including Hosanna's companion, Cuirette, to ridicule Hosanna by filling the club with transvestites dressed as Cleopatra on the night she intended for her grand entrance. The affinities between La Duchesse's drama and Hosanna's are symbolically acknowledged at one point. Hosanna relates that La Duchesse was leaving Sandra's club, uncharacteristically dressed as a man, just as she, Hosanna, was arriving (68). Apparently La Duchesse had dressed as a man to protest the deliberate humiliation of Hosanna, but then drank so furiously while waiting that she was too drunk to warn Hosanna comprehensibly when they passed in the street.

In that moment it is as if a baton of both humiliation and self-recognition has been passed. The chief thematic difference between *La Duchesse de Langeais* and *Hosanna* is that La Duchesse is at the end of her long career, Hosanna just setting out. Hence, La Duchesse looks back on her sexual conquests and social triumphs with a bitterly nostalgic eye, accepting that her days of being La Duchesse have come to an end. Hosanna, however, has only recently become a transvestite (at least one of any notoriety), so she is looking back on a spectacular failure in the final stage of her metamorphosis: a disastrous emergence from the cocoon, as it were. The traces of the life that Hosanna lived as Claude Lemieux before she assumed this quasi-female character have not yet been completely erased. Consequently there remains for Hosanna the possibility of retrieving from behind her disguise a former identity that has some future, whereas La Duchesse has little left behind her worn-out, now faintly ludicrous persona, and hence little future to speak of.

Still, the question of Hosanna's identity is not easily resolved. As we saw earlier, the escape from the repressive conventions of the home community to La Main usually entails assuming a new identity by means of a disguise. What the identity of someone who refused community definitions and stood *independently* might be is an open question, but one that *Hosanna* begins to answer. A crucial aspect of Hosanna's struggle has to do with her relationship to her – or rather Claude's – mother. Claude has never told his mother he is gay, let alone about "Hosanna." Hosanna expresses fervent hatred of Claude's mother, although the woman's only fault seems to be the common and forgivable one of excessive motherliness. The hatred appears to be rooted in an existential dilemma: the existence of Claude's mother is proof of Hosanna's fictitiousness.

Cuirette reinforces the existential dilemma by observing that although Hosanna tries to maintain her female disguise even at home, problems arise when she tries to speak earnestly:

> quand on s'enguele oubedonc qu'on a quequ'chose de sérieux à se dire, tu sais pus comment parler de toé, hein? Tu le sais pus si t'es un gars ou ben si t'es une fille, hein? Tu sais que c'est ridicule de continuer à parler de toé au féminin parce que j'peux te r'mettre ça tu-suite sous le nez, comme j'le fais là; pis tu sais que c'est encore plus ridicule de parler de toé au masculin rapport à c'que t'as dans'face, pis des guénilles que tu portes ... Que c'est que t'es, Hosanna, hein, que c'est que t'es quand t'es t'amanché de même? (45–6)

> When we start fighting, or try to talk serious, you don't know how to act, eh? You don't know if you're a man or you're a woman, eh? You know it's ridiculous to go on talking like a woman, because I'm gonna throw it right back in your face like I'm doing now; but you know its even more ridiculous to start acting like a man with that shit on your face and wearing that stuff ... What are you anyway, Hosanna, eh, just what are you exactly?

Hosanna clarifies this question of identity and disguise when she reveals a glimpse of her own psychology:

> Y'a du monde, comme ça, qui méritent pas de vivre parce que leurs noms sont trop laids! C'est pour ça que les travestis pis les acteurs changent de noms: par-ce-qu'y-mé-ri-tent-pas-de-vi-vre! Cha-cha-cha! (56)

> There are some people, like these, who don't deserve to live, their names are too ugly. That's why actors and transvestites change their names: be-cause-they-don't-de-serve-to-live! Cha-cha-cha!

As is so often the case, the flippancy masks real pain: Hosanna is suggesting her transvestism was prompted by self-hatred. To put it bluntly: Hosanna was created in order to kill Claude.

The self-hatred is also manifest in Hosanna's masochism, something that Cuirette points out when (sounding like Carmen speaking to Manon, in *A toi, pour toujours, ta Marie-Lou*) he says "Que t'aimes donc ça, souffir, Hosanna, que t'aimes donc ça" (You just love suffering like this, Hosanna, you really love it – 21). The habit of martyrdom is especially evident in Hosanna's choice of fantasy role and scene: Elizabeth Taylor as Cleopatra making her entrance into Rome. Though never directly mentioned, a crucial aspect of Hosanna's fetish is that

Cleopatra enters Rome as the main attraction in a parade of conquered people, as a sublime sex object: a queen enslaved. Hosanna's apocalyptic fantasy of self-realization lies in the very apotheosis of the subjugated, fully possessed sexual object that is most glorious in its furthest degradation. From an existentialist point of view, Hosanna has embraced and nurtured Claude's overwhelming sense of being-for-others to the point of fantasizing the ultimate consummation of "Claude" in a sort of *auto da fé* of objectification. The allegorical applications of the idea to Québécois nationalism need hardly be stressed.

Ultimately Hosanna realizes that humiliation, however sublime, is still humiliation; real pride must always begin with the honest acceptance of oneself. Accordingly, at the end Claude steps forward to reveal his (literally) naked self and declare himself a man. Cuirette experiences a parallel realization: he must accept himself for what he is, gay; and, for the sake of his own dignity, must be unafraid of being so recognized by others. This parallel self-realization is staged with Hosanna/Claude and Cuirette speaking simultaneously, while facing the audience (70). Like an operatic duet, the specific words each character utters are finally subordinate to the harmonious effect of two voices as one complex sound. This theatrical metaphor shows two persons approaching a new sort of unity, two voices independently declaring themselves and intertwining to make the uncanny poetry of a meeting between two newly discovered spirits.

AN ORATORIO ON FORBIDDEN LOVE

"Musical" arrangement of speech is the dominant theatrical trope of *Bonjour, là, Bonjour* (1974). Its theme also recalls *Hosanna* in that again a young man comes to terms with his identity through the courage to embrace a "love that dare not speak its name" – in this case, sibling incest. Serge, a sort of prodigal son, has returned home to Canada from Paris, having taken several months to rethink his life, especially his sexual relationship with his sister Nicole. Serge's trip to Paris sets him apart from the rest of his family in an important symbolic way. Paris, the *cité d'illumination*, the city redesigned by Haussmann to open up long, uninterrupted vistas radiating from a central focal point, represents cosmopolitan enlightenment, sophistication, and ordered perspectives; the idea is reinforced by the contrast between the parochiality shown by Serge's family as they question him and Serge's own poise and self-assurance.

Traditionally, a "Grand Tour" of Europe has been a kind of a coming-of-age ritual for the scions of the privileged classes in Britain and North America. But a trip to France by a family's fair-haired boy assumes a particular resonance among the Québécois. In *Refus global*, Borduas inveighs against the perpetual subjugation of Québécois culture from generation to generation, which he complains is perversely abetted by these pilgrimages to the heart of French civilization:

> Notre destin sembla durement fixé. [...] Lentement la brèche s'élargit, se rétrécit, s'élargit encore. Les voyages à l'étranger se multiplient. Paris exerce toute l'attraction. Trop étendu dans le temps et dans l'espace, trop mobile pour nos âmes timorées, il n'est souvent que l'occasion d'une vacance employée à parfaire une éducation sexuelle retardataire et à acquérir, du fait d'un séjour en France, l'autorité façile en vue de l'exploitation améliorée de la foule au retour.   (46)

> Our destiny seems harshly fixed [...] The breach widens, shrinks, then widens further. Travel abroad increases. Paris is all the rage. But, too far in time and space, too volatile for our timorous souls, it is often the occasion for time off to complete a retarded sexual education and to acquire, on the basis of a stay in France, façile authority for improved exploitation of the crowd on return.

Serge's return from Paris is more the kind Borduas would like to see; he has come home not to exploit others but, having taken the time and distance to recognize himself, to reclaim his identity.

Serge's reclamation of his identity is the central dramatic action of *Bonjour, là, bonjour*, as Hosanna's was in her play, but the story is told in a very different manner. Serge's sisters, aunts, and father each suggest various aspects of Serge's own biography – elements of his heritage, as it were – and the narrative is stitched together out of scraps from his relations with these various family members. The establishment of his identity involves choosing which aspects to embrace and which to reject. One needn't reach far to see an allegory with the social concerns articulated by Borduas: Serge is a young Québécois returning to consolidate what is best in his culture and discard the rest rather than compound the errors of his forebears.

From that point of view, Armand provides a standard against which Serge himself may be measured.[16] In Armand's pride and enraptured interest in Serge's trip one hears all the tragedy of thwarted passion and missed opportunity:

> Aie pas peur de me parler de Paris, t'sais! J'y ai jamais été, mais j'ai ben lu! Chus renseigné pareil! La carte géographique de Paris, je l'ai là, dans'-caboche! Aie, c'pas un fou, ton père!   (30)

Hey, don't be afraid to tell me about Paris, y'know! I may've never been there, but I've read loads! I know it all anyway! I've got the whole map of Paris right here in my head! Hey, he's no fool, your old man!

The symbolic aspirations of Haussman's design – making Paris the city of enlightenment – continue to resonate within Armand, underscoring the pathos of his unfulfilled dreams. Furthermore, in the current state of Armand's life (a sort of internal exile circumscribed by the wearisome carping of his sisters and by the deafness that isolates him from the rest of the world) we find an image of Serge's possible fate. Should Serge, after his taste of cosmopolitan enlightenment, submit to conventionality and succumb to the social pressures personified by his stridently demanding sisters, he may end his days in spiritual mediocrity, his passions compromised into petty eccentricities.

The sense of possible destiny embodied in Armand works together with the various possible lives suggested by Serge's sisters to create the play's dramatic tension. The actual plot line is scant examined in linear form: Serge returns home from Paris; he visits his father and aunts, then each of his sisters in turn, ending with Nicole; then he returns to his father's house and invites the old man to live with Nicole and himself. However, rather than building dramatic action by moving Serge *through* a series of events that develop his character, Tremblay intersperses vignettes showing Serge *among* the various forces impinging on the development of his character. The basic concept behind this dramatic structure is again not far from the basic premise of existentialist psychology: that the make-up of an individual's character is best understood as a figure adapted to the configuration provided by his or her family (see Laing and Esterson). Personal history is always inextricably bound up with the familial pressures that moulded one's character in the first place, and much of individual behaviour consists of responses to that pattern of stimuli. Accordingly, in *Bonjour, la, bonjour* the members of Serge's family are all simultaneously present, despite their separate geographic locations; the characters become parts of a visually unified whole, the contraction of space indicating psychological proximity.

However, the principal trope in this play is musical arrangement of speech, a feature Tremblay emphasizes by entitling the scenes "Trio," "Duo," etc. In effect, a series of polyphonic variations stands for Serge's personal experience of the various influences that he must somehow reconcile. Each character contributes a leitmotif featuring one or two recurring themes. Among Serge's three oldest sisters and aunts these themes are particular expressions of their general discontent. In the case of Denise the themes are gluttony and lechery; for

Monique, drug-addiction and emotional dependency; for Lucienne, conspicuous consumption and self-justification; for Gilberte and Charlotte, each other, cooking, and Armand's hopelessness. By contrast, Nicole contributes a fairly simple but beautiful motif consisting of love and affirmation; and Armand's motif is based in the spiritual affinity with Serge described earlier. When the voices of these latter characters break through the others – for instance, when Armand's powerful speech to his son pierces the chatter of his sisters in No. 20 Trio, or when Nicole's speech prevails over Lucienne's harangue in No. 25 Duo – the musical effect is akin to a heterogeneous polyphony (the voices of many crowding in on Serge) giving way to counterpoint (Serge a silent but emotionally engaged partner with Armand or Nicole). The emotional appeal inherent in the dialogue spoken by these two is so strong that they provide the equivalent of an autonomous melody suddenly dominating an arrangement of subordinate voices, a major aria bursting through the leitmotifs. The musical form most analogous to this complex arrangement of characters' voices is the oratorio, for while a story lies amidst the polyphonic interplay, it is subordinate to the themes represented by each character.

Noting the similarities between *Hosanna* and *Bonjour, là, bonjour* is important for a recognition of the unity of Tremblay's mythopoeic interests, but before moving on we should examine more closely the differences between the two plays. Of course, one is set on La Main and the other comprises various domestic settings related to the Rue Fabre, but the difference between the settings of the two plays also provides the two distinct dominant tropes. In *Hosanna* the dominant trope is the irony inherent in transvestism and its attendant play upon the theme of illusion; the mirror on the vanity, the costumes, and the neon light from outside all amplify the ironic figure. In *Bonjour, là, bonjour* the domestic settings provide the dominant trope: the metaphor of musical arrangement, representing an individual amidst his various familial influences as a sort of melody and variations.

These very different tropes are well calculated to convey the specific existential dilemmas of the central characters. Claude is primarily defined negatively, by his illusory Hosanna persona; hence, his shedding of this persona at the end of the play is the resolution of a dialectic between the fact of his body and the fiction of his behaviour. However complex the irony, it plays upon what is at base a simple opposition: illusion versus reality. Serge is set within a number of influences that do not invite so simple a dialectical construction. Even if all the women in the play (with the exception of Nicole) were crowded into one force that was to be rejected, the action by which Armand is integrated into the union of Serge and Nicole argues a more complicated sort of equation.

Whereas *Hosanna* ends with Claude poised on the brink of a new definition of self, and so demands only a simple rejection of the false self, *Bonjour, là, bonjour* ends with the birth of a small society in which some elements of Serge's heritage have been rejected but others reaffirmed and consecrated with love. Clearly, there is more at stake here than just Serge's personal fate. Tremblay universalizes Serge's particular circumstances by departing from a literalistic representation of a family conflict and reconfiguring the elements of the drama into a poetic complex that encourages broader interpretation. Thus, the musical arrangements of speech and the abstract blocking work together not only to establish a psychological matrix for Serge's personality – in so far as the other characters extend or embody Serge's inner ruminations – but to represent the more universal field of conflicting values in which Serge's existential, and ultimately spiritual imperative must be apprehended.

LA TRILOGIE DES BRASSARD

A toi, pour toujours, ta Marie-Lou (1971) predates both *Hosanna* and *Bonjour, là, bonjour*, but the play is properly considered in tandem with *Sainte Carmen de la Main* (1976) and *Damnée Manon, Sacrée Sandra* (1977), which together form a trilogy. Indeed, the three plays were remounted in fall 1991 as La Trilogie des Brassard, so named for the surname of the family, though only in his novels does Tremblay use the name.[17] Not only are characters and themes shared and developed from one play to the next in La Trilogie des Brassard, but each uses some kind of musical arrangement of speech for comparable effects.

A toi, pour toujours, ta Marie-Lou, for example, is written in a polyphonic arrangement of four voices, grouped in two conversations that oscillate between concurrent and discrete time-settings. While all four voices are given approximately equal amounts of dialogue, the conversation between Carmen and her sister Manon predominates because it exists in the present, ten years after their parents' double suicide, and also because it presents a conflict still in hope of reconciliation. By contrast, the conversation between their parents, Léopold and Marie-Louise, is spoken by ghost voices. Their dialogue typifies the perennial conflict that was the essence of the marriage: a weary tension between two implacable opposites that threatens to become the paradigm for all relationships stemming from this family. Léopold and Marie-Louise provide a synecdoche of the general past to which Carmen and Manon continually refer, the echoes of the parents' conversation in the daughters' suggesting the profound effect this past has had in configuring the present.

These two parallel time-settings – the present and a sort of distillation of the past – encourage a further analogy to Mircea Eliade's distinction between the orders of sempiternal and quotidian, or sacred and profane time. Eliade's theory about ritual re-enactment of a primordial event and its recovery of meaning for the present may easily be applied to those moments in *Marie-Lou* in which Carmen and Manon transcend their own time-setting to rejoin their parents in the past. But the analogy points up the distinction between Carmen's and Manon's response to their past. Manon comes much closer to making a genuinely religious experience out of the battle between her parents; in her extremely partisan view, her parents' marriage was a simple struggle between good and evil. Seduced by the self-righteous piety with which her mother justified her aversion to sex, Manon forges an intense identification with what she regards as her mother's martyrdom, as Carmen bluntly points out:

> T'aimerais trop ça qu'y t'arrache ton chapelet en se moquant de toé comme y faisait avec elle [...] Pauvre innocente! Tu t'es jamais rendue compte que maman se servait de la religion exactement comme toé tu t'en sers? [...] Maman, est-tait pas plus religieuse que moé, Manon! A se servait de la religion comme paravent! A se cachait en arrière de son paravent pour faire plus pitié! (76–7)

> You'd love it if he yanked that rosary right out of your hands and threw it in your face, like he did with her [...] You poor fool! Are you never going to realize that she used religion, just like you do? [...] Mom was no more religious than me, Manon! She used her religion as a blind! And behind that blind she was just trying to get more pity!

For Carmen, however, reflection on the past essentially serves as a liberating exorcism of its influence. She rejects the moral simplicity of her sister's myth, instead seeing merely a mutually destructive struggle between two iniquitous adversaries:

> C'est correct, not'père y'avait des côtés écoeurants, mais y'était pas si pire que ça! Arrête de le noircir même! A t'entendre parler, c'était une sainte, elle [...] T'es complètement folle! Notre mère, c'était pas ine martyre, pis not'père c'tait pas le yable, bonyeu! (61)

Okay, our father was a bastard, but he wasn't as bad as that! Stop painting him so black! To hear you talk, mother was a saint [...] You're completely insane! Our mom was not a martyr and our Dad was not the devil!

And later she adds:

J'savais qu'y continueraient à se mettre les torts sur le dos l'un de l'autre jusqu'à la fin de leu'vie! Pis sans jamais découvrir que c'était de leu' faute à tous des deux! Pas rien qu'à popa, Manon. (87)

I knew they'd go on blaming each other to the end of their lives. And never actually discovering that it was both their faults. Not just Dad's, Manon.

Whereas Manon is stuck obsessively refighting the parental battle within herself, because Carmen sees the faults inherent in each parent's intransigent position, she steers her own course between those shoals of self-destruction to achieve personal equilibrium, and thus discover a new life beyond the paradigm of her parents' marriage. This distinction carries through to their respective sequels, for while Carmen looks outward to extend the recreation of her self to her community, Manon looks for ever more intensive means of dramatizing her martyrdom.

The most abstractly musical use of speech in *Marie-Lou* occurs in the opening, where each character in turn speaks the first word, then a phrase, then the whole of their first lines:

MARIE-LOUISE: Demain ...
CARMEN: Aie ...
LEOPOLD: Ouais ...
MANON: Pis .. .
    Silence.
MARIE-LOUISE: Demain ...
CARMEN: Aie ...
LEOPOLD: Ouais ...
MANON: Pis ...
    Silence.
MARIE-LOUISE: Demain, faudrait ...
CARMEN: Aie, ça fait déjà ...
LEOPOLD: Oui, je sais ...
MANON: Pis on dirait ...
    Silence.

MARIE-LOUISE: Demain, faudrait aller manger sus ma mère ...
CARMEN: Aie, ça fait déjà dix ans ...
LEOPOLD: Oui, je sais... pis ça m'écœure
MANON: Pis on dirait que ça s'est passé hier ...   (37)

MARIE-LOUISE: Tomorrow we gotta go eat at mother's ...
CARMEN: Wow, it's already ten years ...
LEOPOLD: Yeah, I know ... Makes me sick
MANON: Still, it feels like yesterday ...

This repetition suggests an old song or poem, tentatively begun thrice in succession as the singer or reciter gains confidence, feeling the rhythm return as the words break the air. There is even a circular effect in the first four words alone, which form a kind of cycle both in the inflection of voices (presumably rising from first to second and descending from third to fourth), and in the meaning: tentative hope in the mention of the future; enthusiastic exclamation conveying a love of life; reconciled and cynical acknowledgement; resigned and atrophied morale. Considered as such, the cycle even echoes Borduas's description of the cyclical history of Québécois morale and dignity: an abyss of submissive despair that seems to close for a while but then opens up once again. To be sure, it would be absurd to declare the presence of political allegory in these short phrases; the point is, rather, that the cycle in which Tremblay roots this family drama is ultimately of a piece with his mythopoeic representation of the various historical patterns – both personal and social – that must be escaped.

Escape (at least *attempted* escape) from such patterns is precisely what *Sainte Carmen de la Main* is about. Carmen's friend Bec-de-Lièvre – Harelip – tells the audience that when Carmen heard of her parents' death in a car crash,

> Y parait qu'au lieu de fondre en larmes, Carmen avait pris Manon dans ses bras en criant: "C'est un signe, Manon, c'est un signe que le ciel nous envoye! Manon, aujourd'hui est notre jour de déliverance!"   (74)

> They say that instead of dissolving into tears, Carmen took Manon in her arms and cried: "It's a sign, Manon. It's a sign that heaven has sent to us! Today is our day of deliverance!"

– to which the chorus responds with an echo: "Aujourd'hui est notre jour de déliverance!"

In this play Carmen has recently returned from Nashville, where she has been plying her considerable talent as a country and western singer.

Affirming the perpetual paradox of the artist in exile, while she was away Carmen began to feel the impulse to write songs about her life on La Main, and in doing so discovered the power inherent in self-expression rather than merely parroting popular clichés. Now, like Serge, she has come home to extend her personal emancipation, her discovery of self-assertion through art, to the entire community. As she becomes a sort of visionary leader to the dispossessed figures inhabiting La Main, the exploitative mediocrities who control La Main begin to feel threatened. The solar imagery dominating the first half of the play gives way to thunder and lighting and in the end the loathsome Toothpick, whom Carmen once ridiculed, murders her and quashes the threat of any posthumous power by declaring that Carmen was secretly contemptuous of those whom she championed in her songs.

The most striking point about Tremblay's use of musically arranged speech here is that the central trope of this kind in the play, Carmen's performance celebrating her friends on La Main, remains unheard. In this Tremblay has followed Sophocles' *Antigone*, the closest prototype of *Sainte Carmen de la Main*, where Antigone's burial of Polyneices is the central event around which the entire drama unfolds, even though it is never seen by the audience. (Naturally, the analogy is imperfect, because Carmen's talent as a singer is an important factor, whereas the question of the effectiveness of Antigone's burying skills is, to say the least, inconsequential; still, there is a comparison to be made in terms of plotting devices.) The advantage offered by an indirect representation of the central event is that a simple act of defiance – singing some songs, throwing dirt on a cadaver – can be made to seem sublime by way of the social response. In effect, the audience itself is implicated in the act of defiance because of its efforts to supply a nexus from effect back to cause. In the case of Carmen's singing, moreover, to attempt any more direct representation of the crucial performance would be finally futile, however well done. The sympathetic response to Carmen's message springs from the characters' personal revelation; it is a mystical experience, which is by definition ineffable. One doubts that any performance of country and western songs, however fine, could be expected to elicit a parallel response from the audience.[18]

Similarities to *Antigone* by no means exhaust the classical resonances of *Sainte Carmen de la Main*. With the arguable exception of *Les Héros de mon enfance* (1976), his musical reworking of classic fairy-tales, *Sainte Carmen de la Main* is the most distinctly mythical of all Tremblay's plays; it is written in what Frye would call the "high mimetic" mode, and it carries Dionysiac overtones.[19] Furthermore, a plot that tells of an extraordinary singer's descent into an underworld, bringing redemption and salvation through the sheer power of song, inevitably evokes the myth of Orpheus and Eurydice. There are subtle echoes of that myth throughout; for example, we are told that the thuggish boss, Maurice (perhaps named to evoke the autocratic premier of Quebec in the fifties, Maurice Duplessis), was brought to tears by Carmen's songs (14–15), just as Orpheus's songs caused Hades himself to weep. Naturally one wonders, once Carmen is identified with Orpheus, if there is a character who could be associated with Eurydice. Bec-de-Lièvre fits the bill to a degree, but it is more convincing see La Main itself as the beloved one unkindly condemned to an underworld existence. In Carmen's passionate plea to Maurice, she suddenly breaks into a personification of La Main that supports this reading:

> C'est pas parce que La Main se traîne dans' crasse depuis que tu la connais qu'y faut continuer à la laisser faire! D'un coup qu'au fond a l'arait ... a l'arait envie d'changer! [...] D'un coup qu'a l'arait envie de crier au monde: "R'gardez, chus là, me v'là!" au lieu de chuchoter: "Oubliez-moé, chus laide!" D'un coup qu'a l'arait envie d'être quelqu'un qu'on écoute pis qu'on respecte au lieu d'être une traînée qu'on viole pour vingt piasses la nuit pis qu'on ignore le jour sauf de temps en temps pour dire d'elle qu'on n'a honte pis qu'a mérite pas de vivre! La Main mérite de vivre mais y faut l'aider à s'en rendre compte!   (64)

> Just because La Main has been crawling in filth ever since you've known her doesn't mean she should be left like that! There's a chance that deep down she would like ... she would like to change! [...] There's a chance that she would like to shout to the world: "Look, here I am, over here!" instead of whispering: "Forget about me, I'm ugly!" There's a chance that she would like to be someone who's listened to and respected instead of being a tramp who gets raped for twenty bucks at night and ignored during the day except from time to time when it's said that she's a disgrace and that she doesn't deserve to live. La Main does deserve to live, but she needs some help to figure that out!

Thus, Carmen is not merely attempting to resurrect a lover from the dead, but a whole community of loved ones. Accordingly, the effect of her efforts is seen not through the aborted escape of these characters from a deadly environment but rather in their incipient ability to end their subordination to an existential hell – or, put more plainly, in their emergent self-confidence.

The incipient emancipation of La Main is conveyed in the responses of a three-level group: Bec-de-Lièvre, Sandra and Rose Beef, and the chorus. Bec-de-Lièvre represents the kind of individual downtrodden personality Carmen attempts to save. Her gain in self-confidence brings a specific personal dimension to the general effect Carmen has on the residents of La Main:

> Carmen a parlé de moé! Carmen a dit des affaires dans ses chansons qui venaient de ma vie, à moé! A l'a conté mon histoire avec Hélène... pis a l'a dit que c'était pas laid! A l'a même dit que c'était beau! Carmen a chanté que mon histoire était belle pis que moé, Bec-de-Lièvre ... comment c'qu'a l'a dit ça ... que j'étais une chanson d'amour endormie dans une taverne! Pis Carmen a chanté que je pourrais ben me réveiller, un jour!   (49)

> Carmen talked about me! Carmen spoke of things in her songs that come from my life, mine! She told the story of me and Hélène ... and she said that it wasn't ugly. She even said that it was beautiful! Carmen sang that my life is beautiful and that I, Bec-de-Lièvre ... how was it she said this ... that I'm a love song asleep in a tavern! And Carmen sang that I might just wake up someday!

Sandra and Rose Beef, as the chorus leaders, represent an intermediate stage between the individual level and the more general public. As such, they play an emblematic role, speaking short, compact, lyric phrases aimed at controlling imagery and atmosphere, but revealing little character.

The control of atmosphere is further advanced by the speeches of the chorus itself. From the outset of the play these set a ritualistic tone that becomes the overriding means of controlling what Suzanne Langer called the "virtual future" of the drama, the sense of architectonic destination (306–25). The sheer formality of choral speech in itself sets up an elegant self-consciousness that stands in stark contrast to the view of La Main as a lost cause. The latter is the "realistic" view in both the pessimistic and the aesthetic sense: the more realistic the tenor of a scene, the more likely it is that we will hear La Main's detractors vividly describing her drawbacks. For example, Carmen's predecessor as resident star of the Rodeo nightclub, Gloria, says that everything on La Main stinks of fried grease (29); and in the speech that prompts Carmen's passionate apology, Maurice describes the regulars of La Main as

> une gang de sans-dessein, pis sans-coeur, pis de soûlons, pis de dopés qui savent pas la moitié du temps c'qu'y font ni c'qu'y disent pis qui se câlis-sent au fond des chansons que tu peux leur chanter!   (61)

a bunch of losers, cowards, drunks and junkies who half the time don't
know where they are, let alone what they're saying, and who couldn't give
a shit what songs you sing to them!

But the chorus belies Maurice's description, expressing their rapt interest in Carmen's progress with coruscating polyphony.

The choral speeches tend to cluster around a succession of particular images or phrases. This appears to be a formal complement to
Tremblay's mythopoeic theme in that Carmen's new-found confidence
is envisaged as ideally having a ripple effect; that is, were Carmen's
efforts to continue as successfully as they began, her influence would
continue to act indirectly on a large number of independent people
until the community as a whole became emancipated. Or, to choose a
more precise metaphor than ripples, we could say that Carmen hopes
to catalyse a process of crystallization by "slowly producing local areas
of coherence which spread and enlarge; in the end the myriad small
events will have performed a complete structural revamping of their
medium from the bottom up, changing it from a chaotic assembly of
independent elements into one large, coherent, fully linked structure"
(Hofstadter, 347). Such a process is manifest in the choral speeches,
which respond to certain events by drawing on a particular image and
phrase, and expanding rhapsodically from this seed. Specific examples
are the opening speeches of the play, which centre on the rising of a
magnificent new sun; the response to the arrival of Gloria, "une vraie
reine déchue" (a real fallen monarch – 27–8); and the excitement when
the crowd arrives at "le Rodeo" to hear Carmen (36–43). But the
process is most evident in the response to Carmen's songs; as the
formal expression of her emancipation, these are the seeds most deliberately calculated to initiate "crystallization."

In the initial response to Carmen's performance the chorus fixes on
Carmen's exhortation: "Réveille-toé!" (Wake up!) Hardly breathtakingly original in itself, this message nevertheless accrues a good deal of
power when it is part of a complex chant recited by the excited chorus.
Other phrases from Carmen's songs are recalled – again, none of them
particularly captivating in itself (with the exception of Bec-de-Lièvre as
"une chanson d'amour endormie dans une taverne"), but through repetition the words begin to symbolize a consolidation of their collective
will. Later on (67–70) there are accounts of an epidemic of emotional
release, the singing spreading through all of La Main as even the least
likely of characters, Greta-la-Vieille and "même les beus" (even the
cops – 69–70), give way to sudden outbursts. Because all this was initiated by Carmen's performance, the suggestion of quasi-miraculous
intervention, in keeping with the effect of the missing central trope,

redounds to our sense of the nature of Carmen's performance. Because our conceptualization of the principal trope of the story has been thrown forward on to the choral response, the degree to which the choral speeches approximate ritual forms determines the sense of religious experience we accord to Carmen's unheard performance.

Repetition plays an important role in both poetry and ritual, so we need not belabour the resemblance the choral passages bear to incantation on that score. However, what makes the fact of particular relevance in *Sainte Carmen de la Main* is the context in which this repetition (of phrases, images, outbursts of singing) appears. Mainly, it is the social use of this poetry that nudges it towards ritual incantation: the varieties of repetition are located in, and entail a gathering of resolve within a particular sector of the community. Furthermore, the choral speeches are isolated dramatically from what would normally be called (misleadingly) "the main action" of the play, the conflict between Carmen and her adversaries. To be sure, they draw their impetus from this conflict, but they do not directly take part in its action, their own activities being directed towards abstract rather than physical ends – or towards the spiritual rather than the temporal. Yet this "alternative" action constituted through the chorus is, thematically, the *central* action of the play. For the play's main theme is the gradual creation of a quasi-religious community built on articles of faith Carmen salvages from their fallen world, and the tragic failure of this community to emancipate itself owing to the sudden removal of their visionary leader.

The discovery and nurture of sacred elements within a profane world occur on another level in *Damnée Manon, Sacrée Sandra*, which is, in a sense, an introvert version of the extrovert mythopoeia of *Sainte Carmen de la Main*. The earlier play showed the development of a quasi-religious faith through a social response to a particular interpretation of the community. In *Damnée Manon, Sacrée Sandra* quasi-religious faith is developed through the personal responses of two individuals, Manon and Sandra, to their own existential needs. Their needs involve attaching a specific identity to a complex of psychological, sensual, and noumenal desires and anxieties; and their responses approach a faith similar to that which Sartre observed in Genet.

The best word for the quasi-religious faith of both Manon and Sandra may be "fetishism," a word that has fallen from fashion as a legitimate anthropological term in inverse correspondence to its rise as a psychological term. The anthropological use of the word "fetish" was derived from the resistance of Europeans to recognizing legitimate religious activity in what they regarded as a primitive use of pseudo-icons by African savages. With late twentieth-century hindsight we can see that any differences between a plaster Madonna and a wooden fertility symbol have more to do with cultural accident than theological validity, but the colonial idea and its psychiatric analogy have left us a term defining the grey area where prevenient grace, existential predilection, and psychotic compulsion all meet in a profound, perhaps even pre-conscious identification with certain special items.

Superficially, of course, Manon's fixation on her giant rosary resembles conventional religiosity, while Sandra's erotic fixation on the green lipstick looks like sexual fetishism as it is commonly understood today. But, as the variations of the two kinds of fetishism are obsessively played out, the initial distinction becomes as blurred as that between the European and the African use of icons. Tremblay explores what is complementary in these apparently antithetical personalities, and where their noumenal interests meet he finds the basis for a rapprochement between the two halves of his imaginative garrison separating rue Fabre and La Main. Here we see the orderly, almost mathematical sense of artistic form that provides the structure for the humane warmth of Tremblay's writing, for he manages to articulate this rapprochement of personalities on at least three different theatrical levels: physical imagery, the arrangement of speech, and spoken imagery. The broadest means of representing the rapprochement of Sandra and Manon is the conceptualization of the space to represent two complementary inner worlds. The setting is described as follows:

> Dans sa cuisine complètement blanche, Manon, une dévote toute vêtue de noir, se berce. Dans sa loge complètement noire, Sandra, un travesti tout vêtu de blanc, se fait les ongles. (27)

> In her completely white kitchen, the devout Manon is dressed in black, and rocking. In her completely black dressing room, Sandra, a transvestite dressed in white, is doing her nails.

If this were a photograph, we could almost say we were looking at a black and white image and its negative; although which is the positive image is a relative judgment. Or, one may be reminded of a chess set, with its matching pieces in opposite shades. In any case, we are plainly looking at two halves of a whole idea, a yin and yang in counterpoint, each ineluctably bound to derive her identity through contrast with the other.

According to conventional Western symbolism, of course, white is associated with holiness and black with damnation. In these terms the initial theatrical image – especially in conjunction with the play's title – makes a simple, direct statement. On one side is a damned figure within a sacred world; on the other is a sacred figure within a damned world. In effect, the image is a version of what Douglas Hofstadter calls a "recursive figure" – that is, "one whose ground can be seen as a figure in its own right" (67). This point is underscored by the resemblance that the black and white design of *Damnée Manon, Sacrée Sandra* bears to those M.C. Escher lithographs that Hofstadter uses to illustrate the concept of recursive figures, in which the black space among a flock of white birds becomes a school of black fish and so on. Just where Sandra locates the sacred in her own sexual activities – "J'vas écrire un livre pornographique sur son corps. Ma Bible à moé" (I'm going to write a pornographic book on his body. My very own Bible – 46) – Manon finds exactly what is most profane to her prudish outlook and commitment to pristine self-denial. Correspondingly, that external world, ordered and pervaded by God, in which Manon places her faith – "Si tout le monde comprenait ce qui se passe dans le monde comme moé j'le comprends ... Mais y'en n'a pas gros qui savent comment déchiffrer les messages" (If only everyone could understand what's going on in the world like I do. But there aren't many who know how to decipher the messages] –44) – is contiguous with the profane world of convention Sandra has abjured in favour of her mystic experience of the sacred.

Tremblay's balancing act between the perspectives of Manon and Sandra extends to the arrangement of the two characters' speeches. While there is no actual dialogue in the play until its closing moments, reciprocity is carefully maintained by having the characters follow parallel courses of thought and speak in passages of roughly equivalent length and tenor. The play begins with thirteen alternate lines from each character; then there is a long pause, "comme si les deux personnages préparaient leurs confessions" (31) (as if the two characters were preparing their confessions –31). Each of the two confessions is broken into four large segments, spoken alternately, to make four central movements, together with the twenty-six-line introduction and a concluding apotheosis movement.

In the first of the four central movements the characters speak of their respective acquisitions of a new item – Manon of her enormous rosary (31–6), Sandra of her green lipstick (36– 41). In the next each speaks of a kind of passion: Manon relates the story of encountering a divine sign (a missal in a garbage can), which she understands to mean that she must throw her precious new rosary away (41–4). Eventually, she tells us (after she has reneged on her commitment to obey the divine will), she realized that the divine message was actually only intended to test her devotion, just as Abraham was tested by the demand that he sacrifice Isaac, "dans l'histoire du buisson ardent" (in the story of the burning bush – 44).

Manon's reading of the Bible is evidently a trifle spotty because the burning bush is, of course, a sign offered to Moses, not Abraham (cf Gen. 22 and Ex. 3): a hint, lest Manon's rationalizations should in themselves prove insufficiently transparent, that we should not accept her piety at face value. For her part, Sandra relates a sexual fantasy about Christian, her black lover, in which the green lipstick features as the central image (45–8). Like Manon's story, this is more a projection of Sandra's personal desires than a fantasy Christian is likely to share. The meaning of the resonance between Sandra's erotic objectification of Christian's body and Manon's sensual pleasure in caressing the black wooden body of Christ on her enormous rosary hardly needs explication.

There is an important shift in the third movement: the rapprochement assumes a different form as each character inclines towards something in the world of the other. Manon speaks wistfully of her childhood friendship with Michel, and of the terrifying (to her) Hélène, a renegade spirit who lived with them on the rue Fabre, and in whose footsteps Michel eventually followed (48–53). Sandra speaks of costuming herself as the Virgin Mary, so that when she is sodomized by Christian, she can play "le rôle de notre Mère à tous dans les bras de la Race montante" (the role of our Holy Mother in the arms of the ascendant Race – 55)! Clearly, this fantasy does not stem simply from a desire to outrage and blaspheme (whom could she outrage with an entirely private fantasy?), but is part of Sandra's attempt to reconcile her sexuality with her mysticism and the prevalent religious framework of her society.

The fourth movement (56–64) expands on the hint of inadequacy that had been revealed by the mutual inclinations discovered in the third. Here the sense of alienation troubling each character creeps into the foreground. Manon's prayer complains of her feeling of abandonment by her God. She speaks like a bewildered, jilted spouse: she has been constant in her devotion; why has He become cool towards her?

On demande pas comme ça à une pauvre fille de sacrifier pendant quinze ans pour la laisser tomber ensuite! Chus t'obligée d'acheter des chapelets gros comme des montagnes, astheur, pour vous amadouer, pis de passer par Votre Sainte Mère pour vous rejoindre!   (58)

One doesn't ask a poor girl to sacrifice herself for fifteen years like this only to suddenly dump her! I'm forced to use rosaries big as mountains to sweet-talk You, and go through Your Holy Mother to contact You.

This is more or less alienation in the original meaning of the word, describing estrangement from God as a sort of punishment. The only difference rests in the (somewhat fine) theological distinction that Manon's alienation is rooted in her personal, not to say sensual religious experience rather than any doctrinal sense of what her relationship to God should be.

The sort of alienation experienced by Sandra, however, is closer to the modern social-psychological meaning it has acquired under the tutelage of Karl Marx, Erich Fromm, and others (see Schacht). Sandra keenly feels the vacancy of a sophisticated faith in her life; earlier, she had confessed that

> des fois en se réveillant, hein, on a beau se trouver potable on sent comme un creux dans l'estomac ... Y'a comme ... de l'insatisfaction dans l'air (37).

> there are times, waking up, eh, when as much as you want to feel okay, there's something like an emptiness in your gut ... It's like ... there's dissatisfaction in the air.

In the fourth movement this dissatisfaction is associated with her awareness that she became ever more isolated from the world of her childhood as she developed her transvestite persona. Hers is alienation from a sense of belonging to a particular community (rue Fabre), and it is this rootedness she envies in Manon.

Finally, there is an apotheosis movement, beginning with Manon's monologue relating her ecstatic reunion with her God. Significantly, it is Manon who leads the apotheosis, with Sandra riding on her coattails, so to speak; this indicates an important difference between the respective fetishisms of the two characters. Manon's religiosity, however idiosyncratic, is ultimately fixed on a transcendent object: Christ. Sandra's religiosity, by contrast, finds its ultimate destination in her own body. It must therefore be Manon who leads their escape from their earthly fates. Nevertheless, she can't do it alone. At one point, as her mounting ecstasy falters, Manon says:

> V'nez vite me chercher, j'ai l'impression d'exister juste dans la tête de quelqu'un d'autre! Laissez moé pas retomber, c'est pas mon corps à moé que j'vas retrouver! Si vous me laissez tomber mes lèvres pis mes ongles vont être verts! Aidez-moé! Aidez-moé à renier mon corps!   (65)

> Come get me quickly, I have the feeling that I only exist in the head of someone else! Don't let me fall, it's not my own body that I'll find! If you let me fall, my lips and nails are going to be green. Help me! Help me to renounce my body!

There is just a hint of B-grade horror movie here. The near madness and the fastidious horror at aspects of human nature evokes the failed experiments of Wells's Doctor Moreau or of the mad scientist in *The Fly*, where, as here, the cost of a failure to transcend the material conditions of life is a nightmarish entrapment in a far less palatable state of corporeality.

Manon's transcendence requires the help of Sandra, who adds her will to Manon's at the crucial moment. Only after Sandra calls out "Vas-y, Manon ... monte!" (Go on, Manon ... mount! – 65), unifying sexual and religious ecstasy in a pun, is Manon able to take flight spiritually. Manon and Sandra are two extensions of a single personality – each "inventée par Michel" (65) – and accordingly it is only through recombination that they can achieve the spiritual wholeness necessary to transcend their immediate situations. In other words, only by embracing human nature in its totality can the apotheosis that Manon and Sandra seek take place. Only by resolving themselves into a whole "I," by acknowledging that they are two parts of "Michel," can they become adequate to meet the Eternal Thou.

TREMBLAY AMONG THE PHILISTINES

An important shift in Tremblay's mythopoeic perspective occurred at about this point. That the apotheosis of Manon and Sandra incorporates an acknowledgment of their inventor, Michel, implies that he is somehow included in that apotheosis; and indeed, Tremblay's subsequent plays suggest a release from the garrison-like tension between rue Fabre and La Main that had previously dominated his work. With *Damnée Manon, Sacrée Sandra*, Tremblay had reached behind the surface of cultural differences to reveal a common humanity, evinced in a shared yearning for the noumenal. The fusion of Manon and Sandra's minds represented a personal dimension in that broad mythopoeic movement towards a new community of inclusion and mutual understanding that had been increasingly implicit in Tremblay's work; he was exploring the human element that makes rapprochement between communities possible. That this was the effect of a broadening humanist sympathy was made clear with *L'Impromptu d'Outremont* (1980).

Tremblay's first play of the eighties found him working in the home territory of his erstwhile adversaries. The four Beaugrand sisters, scions of an upper-middle-class French-speaking family, gather to celebrate the fortieth birthday of the youngest sister, Lucille. In the course of the play they drift from squabbling to hilarity to grief as they compare and contrast their own moral and cultural values. The title evokes Molière's

L'Impromptu de Versailles, in which the playwright placed himself on stage in the midst of his detractors (mainly Montfleury and his company) in order to respond to their criticisms. Outremont is one of the wealthiest and most upwardly mobile of the French-speaking neighbourhoods in Montreal, and it was from this sector of Quebec society that Tremblay found the most trenchant criticisms of his work had emerged. Yet the drama itself belies the expectations raised by such a bald description of its origins. The values of the Beaugrand sisters are indeed called into question, and there is a great deal of wry wit at the expense of the Outremont community; but the scathing indictment one might have anticipated never emerges. Indeed, the satiric content of this play is ultimately less corrosive than that of *Les Belles-Soeurs*, which, in contrast to *L'Impromptu d'Outremont*, portrays a community to whom Tremblay is deeply sympathetic.

There are two reasons for this paradox. In the first place, if it is correct to see *Damnée Manon, Sacrée Sandra* as Tremblay's casting-off of the garrison mentality of his earlier work, had he now simply picked up a new black-and-white opposition, the mythopoeic accomplishments of his work thus far would be irremediably diminished. The second reason has to do with the ethos of Tremblay's literary imagination. In Tremblay's work anglophones and heterosexual men seldom appear anywhere but the margins unless there are major extenuating factors (madness, incest, etc.). In short, Tremblay makes the "establishment" perspective into "the Other." Suddenly and utterly to switch the locus of his imagination, and so invert the ethos of his work, could be no easy matter. Hence, once again Tremblay's characters are francophone women, and he is perhaps more disposed to sympathize with the Beaugrand sisters than he would have been had he confined himself to characters more purely representative of an "establishment" perspective. In effect, Tremblay's response to his Outremont detractors was not to place himself in their midst in order to say "Look how ridiculous you are!" as Molière had done, but rather to transplant his imagination to their territory and, in rendering their perspective, to say "I understand you all too well."

As it happened, Tremblay's new ethos of inclusion did not find universal approbation. The first production of *L'Impromptu d'Outremont*, a fairly straightforward, realistic staging, was received with dissatisfaction by many, including the director himself, Tremblay's long-time collaborator André Brassard. Brassard could not reconcile himself to Tremblay's sympathetic portrayal of the middle-class characters. Accordingly, he mounted a second production in a manner flatly ridiculing the Beaugrand sisters rather than admitting any understanding whatsoever for them: the women were played by men in drag

248 The Buried Astrolabe

and by puppets, and generally made as grotesque as possible. Brassard defended his choice in this way: "If you want to say a certain class of people are wrong, you should not start to understand [...] because then you make no statement" (cited in King, 45).

Morally dubious though Brassard's outlook is, that he used anti-realistic theatrical devices to realize it, and thus ran against the grain of the drama as written, usefully points up the question of the implied poetics of the play. *L'Impromptu d'Outremont* is, in its original form, one of the most realistic plays Tremblay has written, despite the many elements that are continuous with Tremblay's usual poetic approach. Formally the play is a kind of quartet for women's voices, each of which has a theme that eventually blossoms into an aria.

The drama stresses the isolation of the sisters. External events have virtually no impact on their conversation, which centres instead upon their internal conflicts and shared history. The varying degrees of isolationism among the sisters are related to each one's perceptions of her respective status. Fernande, the oldest, adheres most conservatively to their mother's parvenu snobbery and isolation from other social groups. Yvette, the second eldest, is a compulsive sufferer who is bitterly aware of her own mediocrity and desperate to be convinced that her suffering is somehow ennobling; she embraces the ennui that Tremblay suggests is the curse of the Outremont class. Lorraine, the second youngest, has married outside the Outremont social class and accordingly suffers the low-caste status so many societies attach to "miscegenation." The youngest sister, Lucille, is disdainful of snobbish social distinctions and acutely aware of the misery her family's isolationism entails; the world is passing them by. She is the only one of the four who does not deliver a long, despairing soliloquy; instead she harangues her sisters for their repression and stagnation:

> Ce que pensent les étrangers est tellement plus important pour nous que tout ce qui se fait dans notre propre pays, hein? C'est tellement plus facile de se mettre en dessous de la culture de quelqu'un d'autre plutôt que de s'en créer une! Mais ce que je comprends mal, c'est pourquoi notre sainte élite ne réagit pas plus énergiquement! Où est sa belle prestance d'antan? Où est son bagout? Au lieu de nous réfugier dans notre coin et de nous gratter le bobo, pourquoi est-ce que nous n'en produirons pas des créateurs qui vont répondre aux autres et lutter pour nous? (102)

> What foreigners think is so much more important to us than anything that's going on in our own country, eh? It's so much easier to just tap into someone else's culture than it is to create one. But what's hard for me to understand is why our sainted élite doesn't react with more vitality! Where

is the great profile of yesteryear? Where has all the big talk led? Instead of hiding in the corner and licking our wounds, why aren't we producing creative people who will answer those others and speak on our behalf?

Lucille provides the dramatic tension that keeps the play from drifting into a self-contained, circular bickering match. Hers is the weight that imbalances, for although the women close off the external world so that the four themes must develop in response to one another in a hothouse atmosphere, Lucille tips the circular argument off its centre by alluding to the idea of creative progress. This factor should have obviated the need for any of the extreme theatrical measures Brassard used to prove the futility of the Beaugrand sisters' cultural stance.

To his figuratively musical quartet of voices Tremblay adds two actual musical pieces, that serve to fix the situation of the sisters within a larger social context. The first is Dido's lament from Purcell's *Dido and Aeneas*, a recording of which the suffering Yvette is playing for the sixth or seventh time as the action of the play begins. Already we see that Tremblay is of two minds about his characters. Yvette's obsession with the aria tends to undercut the seriousness of its effect somewhat; yet at the same time Dido's lament conveys emotions of real pain and loss, so it brings at least a hint of tragedy to the fate of the Beaugrand sisters, who are like the abandoned Dido in that their values are being left behind by a society marching forth to a more important destiny. That Tremblay wishes to convey the painful sense of abandonment felt by the sisters cannot be doubted. Some of the sisters' remarks approach a naked grief at which it would be difficult to sneer. Consider, for example, Fernande's question: "Tu veux absolument me voir avec les mêmes yeux que mes enfants qui meurent de honte chaque fois que j'ouvre la bouche?" (You find it absolutely necessary to see me with the same eyes as my children, who die of shame every time I open my mouth? –89). Even the most patriotic Roman must have felt pity hearing Virgil's description of Dido's grief. It seems likely that Tremblay expected a similar response from his Québécois audiences.

The other song is "Jeune fillettes, profitez du temps," which is sung by the sisters at the end of the play. Here, once again, Tremblay's intent is presumably ironic, but as before this irony is not the sort meant to prompt jeering; rather, the irony is (to begin with, at least) bitter-sweet because it is self-conscious on the part of the characters. The sisters are returning to the simple optimism of their childhood, which stands in stark contrast to the unhappy state of their adult lives, and in plumbing the depths of their mutual past they remember the lesson their mother associated with the song: "Il faut toujours se réconcilier, dans vie, les enfants, c'est moins dangereux! Et le plus intelligent cède toujours le premier!" (You must always reconcile yourselves, in life, children, it's the least dangerous way! And the most intelligent always gives in first! – 113). Such advice they would do well to heed in their present situation. Yet Lucille, more keenly ironic than the others, remarks "Quelle farce!" and the song is suddenly interrupted by a burst of machine-gun fire, which closes the play.

Perhaps that ending represents Tremblay's final attitude towards the women and their society, but it seems more likely that it represents the inevitable intrusion of the passionate and exasperated Québécois society outside Outremont, which they have effectively excluded from any of their discussions. Like the characters in Genet's *Le Balcon*, whose compulsive masquerading is interrupted by the outbreak of revolution, so the social enclave in Outremont finds their navel-gazing rudely disrupted by a sudden surge of indignation: anger of the sort that precipitated the October Crisis of 1970, and a wake-up call of the kind that in 1980 many sovereigntists were hoping would be delivered by the Quebec referendum on independence.

Les Anciennes Odeurs (1981), Tremblay's first play after that referendum had been held and secession rejected, also portrays members of Montreal's middle class. However, the differences between the Beaugrand sisters and Jean-Marc and Luc, the two former lovers of *Les Anciennes Odeurs*, are significant. Luc is the younger man; at thirty-two he has suddenly found commercial success as an actor, playing a ridiculous lisping character in a Quebec sitcom. Jean-Marc is a thirty-eight-year-old French teacher, and a long-aspiring novelist. The play begins when, unannounced, Luc enters the house he shared with Jean-Marc until abandoning the relationship. The two men reminisce about the emotional turmoil of their former partnership and express their doubts about their current lives: Luc wants to break free of his character and make his sexuality publicly known; Jean-Marc is beginning to fear that he is only a mediocre novelist, that his real vocation is the less glamorous profession of teaching. The title alludes to the nostalgia invoked by familiar smells, and the play brings into focus the melancholy idea that one can never really return to the passions of one's past life; one must instead press on into the future for better or for worse.

Although Jean-Marc is a *failed* creative writer, it is difficult to resist seeing Tremblay in Jean-Marc because the character is closer to Tremblay's own person, in terms of age, social class, occupation, and personality, than any previous character in Tremblay's work. Furthermore, the play is also the most realistic in all Tremblay's oeuvre, even more so than *L'Impromptu d'Outremont*. Even the usual possibility of finding political allegory in Tremblay's work seems just a little inappropriate here, although without excessive stretching one might descry a melancholy acceptance of what, right after the 1980 referendum, seemed to be the end of the sovereigntist dream. For the most part, however, there is an utterly straightforward and direct psychological nakedness in this play, which appears to pick up on the sort of honest self-knowledge invoked by the literal nudity at the end of *Hosanna*. *Les Anciennes Odeurs* is a less exotic but perhaps even more searingly honest variation on that earlier play. Both *Les Anciennes Odeurs* and the gentle romantic novels featuring Jean-Marc, *Le Coeur découvert* (1986) and *Le Coeur éclaté* (1993), follow the period of mythopoeic reconciliation; it seems that, having liberated himself from the La Main–rue Fabre tension, Tremblay felt he could reveal himself more directly than he had been able to heretofore.

DECONSTRUCTING THE OEUVRE

In his most recent work for the theatre Tremblay has been returning to the scene of the crime, as it were, by revisiting characters and situations taken from his earlier work. Each of five more recent major plays is in some sense a revision of the dialectic between the opposing forces (most often apparent in the tension between the characters of the rue Fabre and those of La Main) that had characterized his work until the period of rapprochement in the seventies. *Albertine en cinq temps* (1984) reconsiders a sworn adversary of La Main, and deconstructs the idea of the single-minded adherent to conservative values; in *Le Vrai Monde?* (1987) the playwright puts his own reliability and integrity to the question in so far as he is in a subjective relation to his own community; *La maison suspendue* (1990) resurrects three generations of characters and discovers a kind of harmony among them; *Marcel poursuivi par les chiens* (1992) looks sympathetically at how the greatest dreamer of rue Fabre was finally unable to face up to the dangers of La Main; and *Encore une fois, si vouz permettez* (1998) turns a loving eye exclusively upon Nana, *la grosse femme*, the very heart and soul of rue Fabre, whom Tremblay modelled upon his own mother.

In all five plays the resolution that Tremblay had reached at the end of the Trilogie Brassard is in some way implicit. There is a certain emotional detachment or wisdom that suggests he is writing from a new moral high ground, from which he is able to bestow compassion upon characters who seemed rather unsympathetic in earlier works and even guide them towards a kind of redemption. What particularly facilitates this change is that the garrison mentality that had riven the communities in his earlier work has come to be wholly regarded as a dichotomy inherent in human nature.

That perspective had informed *L'Impromptu d'Outremont*, but it emerges more definitely in *Albertine en cinq temps*. The trope on which this play is founded is best understood as a kind of prism that, instead of refracting light into the component colours of the spectrum, refracts a character, Albertine, into the component personalities of her lifetime. Formally, this is a metonym, physical distinction (i.e., a group of five different women) standing for the associated idea of temporal change. That breakdown of identity would drift into theatrical chaos, however, were there no static point of reference from which to measure these transformations. Hence, the ageless Madeleine serves as the confidante of the five Albertines and the still point in this non-linear theatrical cosmos.

Over the course of the play the five Albertines quarrel amongst themselves and look to Madeleine for guidance and interpretation. There are affinities between the thirty-year-old and the seventy-year-old Albertine, also extending tentatively to the fifty-year-old Albertine, all three characters possessing an outlook that is, on the whole, rather positive. At forty and sixty, however, Albertine is a hard, cynical woman. At forty she evinces merely a petty intolerance bred of disappointment; but at sixty her mood has grown much darker and she is full of venom, spite, and regretfulness.

As is the case in most of Tremblay's dramas, there is not much plot in the conventional sense; instead, a "back story" lying behind this fragmented personality is gradually revealed through the dialogue. At the age of thirty Albertine found that she was disappointed with marriage and family life; through her forties she grew progressively more frustrated with the thankless job of being mother and wife in a household rife with various discontents. At fifty she rebelled and left her home and family behind, abdicating all responsibility for her troubled children, Marcel and Thérèse. However, this illicitly procured (as she felt in retrospect) optimism was utterly crushed by the sudden, violent death of Thérèse. Consequently, at sixty she became increasingly dependent on drugs to keep her anxiety and depression at bay. That abuse eventually led to a dangerous overdose; at seventy she has just recovered after a long internment in the hospital where she was brought back, literally, from death.

In allowing his character a second lease on life at so advanced an age, Tremblay has extended a clemency entirely consonant with his new, magnanimous spiritual outlook. Elderly and reflective, the seventy-year-old Albertine looks back across the other incarnations of her adult self to choose a particular moment in which to ground her reverie. At thirty Albertine sits on the veranda of the old family house at Duhamel with her sister and confidante, Madeleine, talking leisurely about life while they await Madeleine's husband, Alex. Madeleine enters into the world of the play through this moment and setting, but her character becomes timeless and the companionship she provided to the thirty-year-old Albertine is extended through all the other Albertines to the present-day seventy-year-old.

With time collapsed into a sempiternal setting in the cosmos of this play, this one moment serves a double poetic function. Within the story we know has already occurred, the thirty-year-old Albertine stands at the threshold of middle age, with most of the mistakes and tragedies of her life, the fluctuations of bitterness, retreat, and regret still ahead of her. These facts are part of a fixed destiny that the Albertines, like the six characters of Pirandello's play, *must* live through. Yet the moment is liminal in another sense: the seventy-year-old Albertine is at the end of her life, sitting among these ghosts and at the same time waiting with Madeleine for Alex's headlights to swing into the driveway, shine up on the old house, and end the moment of reverie. This sense of waiting for the next moment, for the escape from the fixed life, finds a resolution befitting its paradoxical dual temporality, for the play ends with the moon, enormous and blood red, rising above the six (or two) women. The answer to the poetic riddle Tremblay poses has been deflected on to the celestial timepiece, immortal yet ephemeral, eternal yet cyclical, the traditional symbol of femininity and of the elusive promise of other worlds.

Madeleine reappears, together with Alex, in *Le Vrai Monde?* Bred of the moral humility endemic to the spiritual high ground, this is Tremblay's theatrical *mea culpa*, in which he implicitly challenges his own right to use the world as the model for his art. As the title suggests, a questioning of reality lies at the heart of this play, which examines the role subjectivity plays in determining how reality is perceived and represented. This issue was, of course, addressed to an extent in *Albertine en cinq temps* as well. Albertine's view of reality fluctuates with her circumstances. Her belief at fifty that her life was something she could walk away from proves illusory at sixty, and the cynicism she has acquired at sixty is roughly shaken by her revivified perspective at seventy. In *Le Vrai Monde?* the issue is built around the contrast between the simplistic certainties of a particular vision and the more ambiguous reality. Claude is plainly a semi-autobiographical character, a young playwright whose first play is based on his own experience, featuring characters based on members of his family. Tremblay confirmed this in an interview:

Ma tante, la modèle d'Albertine, est morte. Dès ce moment, la culpabilité – j'haïs tellement ce mot –, la culpabilité judéo-chrétienne est apparue. "Elle est morte maintenant. Avais-je le droit? ... Avais-je le droit, pendant tous ce temps, non seulement de me servir de son essence pour dire des choses que je croyais intelligentes mais de gagner ma vie avec elle, qui est restée dans son petit univers, alors que moi j'ai acquis, en partie sur son dos, ma réputation à travers la monde?" Les artistes ne devraient sans doutes pas se poser ces questions. N'ont-ils pas tous les droits? ... En écrivant *Le Vrai Monde?* je pensais que ça pourrait être intéressant pour le public de voir un écrivain transformer la réalité.   ("Par la porte," 70)

My aunt, the model for Albertine, is dead. From that moment, guilt – I really hate this word –, Judeo-Christian guilt appeared. "She's dead now. Did I have the right? Did I have the right, all that time, not only to use her character to say what I thought were clever things, but to make a living out of her, who was stuck in her little world, while, partly off her back, I was making my reputation all over the world?" Artists probably shouldn't be asking themselves these questions. Don't they have every right? In writing *Le Vrai Monde?* I thought maybe it would be interesting for the public to see a writer transforming reality.

Le Vrai Monde? is a kind of inversion of Molière's *L'Impromptu de Versailles*: the playwright places a version of himself on the stage, not so that he can *respond* to his detractors but so that he can allow himself to be *attacked* properly. In essence, Tremblay places that internal debate, which is quoted above, in the mouths of the prototypes of his characters.

Predictably, those family members who have read his play are less than thrilled about the liberties Claude has taken in representing their lives. And he has, unquestionably, skewed the portrait. He has portrayed his mother as suffering under the heel of a vulgar oppressor (his father), and has attempted to ennoble her by having her character listen to the third movement of Mendelsohn's fifth symphony – the quintessence of tragic romanticism. Madeleine angrily confronts her son with this evidence of his unconstrained bias:

Tu nous as enlaidis, nous autres, mais tu nous fais écouter d'la musique que toi tu trouves plus belle, plus savante que celle qu'on écoute! Tu ris de nous autres, là-dedans, Claude, sais-tu?   (24)

You make us ugly, all of us, but you've made us listen to the music that you find more beautiful, more high-brow than what we listen to! You ridicule us in that, Claude, do you realize that?

In trying to make his observations about the family into a work of art, then, Claude has transformed the very essence of his family, has subjugated it to his own aesthetic sensibility. (We may recall Tremblay's ascription to Armand in *Bonjour, là, bonjour* of a naïve, though profound and touching enthusiasm upon hearing classical music.) Moreover, the effect of this endeavour is itself worked into the complex equation of the family as a whole, for Claude and his observations have themselves become determinants of the nature of this family. Tremblay illustrates the point through the use of double identities for all the members of the family but Claude. One set of family members corresponds to Claude's imagination; the other is, nominally, Claude's "real" family. All the characterizations of, and relations between, the imagined family members serve, in the end, to focus Claude's contempt for his father. "Dans ma pièce, j'ai mis tout ce mépris-là dans le personnage de maman [...] parce que c'est elle qui a probablement le plus souffert de ce que t'étais" (In my play I put all this contempt into Mom's character [...] because she's probably suffered the most from what you've been – 104–5), Claude tells Alex. Claude's plot ends with a defeated Alex storming out of the house after upturning all the furniture (94). However, in the world of the "real" characters, the lion's share of contempt is directed at Claude for presuming to meddle with the family, and it is Claude who leaves the house.

From this point of view, *Le Vrai Monde?* is analogous to an experiment in a theatrical version of the Heisenberg uncertainty principle, the scientific theory that declares that any attempt to fix the location of a particle will, in itself, alter the particle's location. In other words, the act of observation always alters the observed. Moreover, having chosen to observe one aspect of the particle's behaviour, other aspects are rendered unpredictable: if one measures for velocity, position is indeterminable; if one measures for position, velocity is indeterminable. One must either choose between realities or think of reality as a construct of a number of probabilities without any fixed outcome.[20] Without putting too fine a point on it, it is possible to see this same pattern in Tremblay's play. Claude's observations of his family have rendered any certainty about the nature of this family impossible. His play has clearly concentrated on one aspect of their characters, but that means other aspects of their characters have become unpredictable. The question asked by the play's title is unanswerable because not only is Claude's play subjective but the behaviour of the "real" family consists of subjective responses to his observations.

Yet the play is even more problematic than this, for taking a further step backward, one realizes that in using the theatre to represent the futility of any endeavour to capture "le vrai monde" on stage, Tremblay has attempted to do just that. In this sense, as Michael Sidnell has pointed out, *Le Vrai Monde?* is one enormous ironic trope; a theatrical version of preterition, the rhetorical figure through which, as Bernard Dupriez puts it, "a declaration of omission is in fact a way of emphasizing the allegedly omitted material" ("Realities," 5–16).[21] The irony becomes most trenchant when Claude says, after his remark about putting his own contempt for his father into his mother's mouth:

> [*Ironique.*] J'ai fait ce qu'on appelle ... un transfert. C'est ça mon rôle ... j'pense. De faire dire aux autres c'qu'y sont pas capables de dire pis ce que chus pas capable de dire moi non plus. Mais chus pus sûr. Après ce soir chus pus sûr. Chus pus sûr d'avoir le droit de devenir écrivain. Maintenant, j'ai peur de devenir aussi manipulateur que toi [...] Déchire-là, ma pièce, si tu veux, papa, mets le feu dedans, c'est plein de ... [*Silence.*] Mensonges. J'ai essayé, à travers des mensonges, de dire ce qui était vrai. (105)

> [*Ironically.*] I've done what is called ... a transfer. That's my role ... I think. To make others say what they're incapable of saying, and what I'm incapable of saying as well. But I'm not sure. After tonight I'm not sure. I'm not sure I have the right to become a writer. Now, I'm afraid of becoming a manipulator like you [...] Tear it up, my play, if you like, Papa, set fire to it, it's full of ... [*Silence.*] Lies. I tried, by means of lies, to say what was true.

After Claude leaves, Alex indeed burns the play. For Tremblay's play, however, there can be no burning, although the work is figuratively immolated through the transparency of its preterition. John Van Burek's 1988 production for Théâtre Français underscored this built-in deconstruction with a false audience of white masks that was revealed by a curtain behind the stage at the play's end.

Following *La Vrai Monde?* Tremblay challenged his own work from another perspective in *La Maison suspendue* (1990). Not only does he therein juxtapose characters from various periods of his own work, but he looks back to his cultural heritage for inspiration as well. The image of the title arises in a story told by Josaphat-le-violon, who expands on a French-Canadian folk-tale, "La Chasse galerie" – about a group of lumberjacks who take a demonic canoe trip through the sky – to include the anchoring of a house to the canoe (see Aubry, "La Chasse-galerie"). Each character in *La Maison suspendue* appears in one of Tremblay's earlier works, though the play reaches further back in history than any previous work. The elderly Josaphat and Victoire of the Plateau Mont Royal novels are seen in *La Maison suspendue* as a young couple in 1910 with their eleven-year-old son, Gabriel. The next generation is represented by Victoire's children Albertine and Édouard (*alias* Duchesse de Langeais), with their sister-in-law, here called only La Grosse Femme (though elsewhere she is called Nana), and Albertine's son, Marcel, in 1950. Finally, in 1990, we see Jean-Marc (*Les Anciennes Odeurs*), the adult son of Nana, as well as Mathieu and his son, Sébastien (who appear with Jean-Marc in *Le Coeur decouvert*). All three generations are presented simultaneously on the veranda of the house at Duhamel (*Albertine en cinq temps*), confronting their identities and coming to terms with the past and future.

It is evident that Tremblay has pulled together threads from his various works to form a coherent mythopoeic saga, his own *comédie humaine*; here he places Josaphat and Victoire at the beginning of this saga as a kind of incestuous Adam and Eve, the figurative and, to some extent, literal progenitors of all the other characters in this huge family. We see how the personalities of these two (Josaphat the fanciful fiddler, Victoire the earthy pragmatist) have been passed on as dichotomous characteristics to their descendants. Albertine, for example, has taken Victoire's resolve against being carried away by dreams and turned it into a barely containable rage against the world's lack of neatness. Her rage is focused most intently on her brother Édouard, who takes after his uncle (father?) Josaphat, although again with an extra twist of his own. The allegiance to a fertile imagination has led Édouard into the life of elaborate disguise and affectation that we see so extravagantly in *La Duchesse de Langeais*. Marcel is another example of this kind of fanciful personality. Here he is seen as a rather peculiar but charming boy; the full-blown dementia of the adult Marcel has yet to emerge. As in her eponymous novel, La Grosse Femme is a stalwart maternal figure, good-humoured and generous, embodying a *joie de vivre* that tacitly corrects all the bitter misunderstandings and sour squabbles of the other family members.

Particularly appealing in this play is the harmony of the tones suggested by the three generations. The middle group, of 1950, comes closest to representing the characteristic ethos of Tremblay's earlier work. The characters are all grotesques of one sort or another; or, to put it another way, they are humours (in the Jonsonian sense) who seem to belong to the margins of an urban society, where they can most comfortably exercise their fanaticisms or eccentricities. This kind of character was essential to Tremblay's vision of the society riven by a garrison mentality; characters as extreme as these were necessary in order that his polemic should be embodied theatrically.

The characters of 1910 are Tremblay's newest addition to the saga. In them we find a serenity and moderation highly untypical of the work that introduced the 1950s characters. Tremblay has fleshed out his central myth with the youthful versions of these characters, who contribute a sort of genesis, a primordial phase in which the folk tradition out of which modern Québécois culture grew is alive and vivid. The contrast between the personalities of Victoire and Josaphat is stark, but the two are clearly deeply in love with one another; their differences seem to spring more from a sense of competing necessities than from mere personal predilection. Josaphat's unfettered mythopoeic fancy is essential to a culture that is still establishing its place in the natural environment, even as Victoire, who is driven by pragmatic concerns, stands at the threshold of the new life in the city into which she will take their son, Gabriel. There, she will be able to marry sensibly and establish the material security necessary to raise a family. Yet this extirpation of the family from the house at Duhamel will result in a complete schism between the two character traits and lead to the deranged urban versions of these traits seen in the grotesque humours of the next generation.

In 1990 Jean-Marc recognizes in himself a muted version of the characteristics stemming from his grandparents, which had driven his aunt and uncle to such behavioural extremes. But the strife these cause him is altogether internalized; he experiences the struggle in the isolation endemic to the individualistic modern age. Jean-Marc teaches French literature in Montreal, a job in which he has found himself growing stale and cynical with the years. His (Victoire-like) need for security has been at odds with his (Josaphat-like) craving for creative satisfaction. He explains to Mathieu that this debilitating internal battle has brought him back to the house at Duhamel for inspiration as he embarks on his true vocation as a writer:

> au lieu de m'en aller dans un coin perdu du monde d'où j'enverrais à mes amis des cartes postales idiotes, j'ai décidé de me réfugier dans un coin perdu de mon enfance ... pour essayer de ressusciter les colères de ma tante Albertine, les hésitations de ma grandmére, le désespoir de mon grand-père, l'intelligence de ma mère ... l'imagination de mon cousin, le pyjama rose de mon oncle Édouard.   (83–4)

> instead of taking myself off to some lost corner of the world from where I would send idiotic post cards to my friends, I decided to withdraw into this lost corner of my childhood ... to try to revive the rages of my aunt Albertine, the hesitations of my grandmother, the desperation of my grand-father, the intelligence of my mother ... the imagination of my cousin, the pink pyjamas of my uncle Édouard.

Here at the old family home the rivalry between the two competing elements of his character will be reset within its original and most meaningful context.

Once again Tremblay presents his drama in an often lyrical, quasi-oratorio arrangement of voices from diverse settings, seeking out, as it were, an instinctive harmony. However, the project is more ambitious than any of Tremblay's previous plays; for *La Maison suspendue* reworks all of the main dialectics of Tremblay's personal mythology as a series of often bitterly divisive character traits, the whole falling within the purview of Jean-Marc's self-examination. All the dualities – wilderness versus civilization, chthonian nature versus Apollonian order; marginalized versus authoritarian figures, La Main versus the Rue Fabre, imagination versus material security – all these collapse into the relatively simple and purer questions of Jean-Marc's own authenticity. Thus, the return to this house, to the original field of debate, signifies an internalization, or in political terms a repatriation, of the struggle. The whole battle for authenticity is brought beneath one roof and focused on one man; and in the presence of the original loving relationship of Josaphat and Victoire these divisions are finally revealed to be the components of an ultimately harmonious whole.

We saw earlier that Tremblay's central myth – most evident in his early fantastic works – involved the decision to invoke poetry from within his own society rather than accepting external control. The myth was shown to have a personal variation in the existentialist decision to vanquish the eyes of others as a defining force through an act of will and to assume responsibility for one's own character. With *La Maison suspendue* Tremblay completes a cycle and draws the social and personal myths together in the most coherent statement of his mythology to date. The image of a house full of characters drawn from every stage of Tremblay's career, suspended from a canoe drawn from traditional Québécois folklore is, in itself, as plain a statement of his mythopoeic purpose as we could want. The entire culture, with all its infighting among the dreamers and the pragmatists, the conservatives and the libertines, is anchored to the magical canoe in the sky; in the hands of the impetuous mythical lumberjacks lies a whole society's provenance.

Marcel poursuivi par les chiens (1992) is set not long after the middle of the three time-settings of *La Maison suspendue*, in 1953, just after the fifteen-year-old Marcel has witnessed the tavern-owner Maurice brutally murder Mercedes, a singer and prostitute on La Main who appears in several of the novels. Marcel imagines that he is being chased through the streets by dogs, whose howling he hears in the police sirens. The play, which is performed without intermission, is styled much in the manner of Greek tragedy, where conversations between two characters are punctuated at regular intervals by choral commentary. In *Marcel poursuivi par les chiens* there is only one long conversation between Marcel and Thérèse, his sister, which is watched and commented upon by a chorus of four ghosts, Florence and her daughters, Mauve, Violet, and Rose.

Marcel poursuivi par les chiens is best approached as a sequel to the novel *Le Premier Quartier de la lune* (1989). The novel describes the tragedy of Marcel's passage from childhood into adolescence, which entails the final decay of his magical relationship with the cat Duplessis and the four ghosts, Florence and her daughters, whom he meets in "la forêt enchantée" (the enchanted forest) – a thicket of trees in the yard of a vacant house (37ff). Throughout the sequence of novels, from *La Grosse Femme* on, Duplessis is Marcel's constant companion: first as a living creature, then as a ghost. With *Le Premier Quartier de la lune*, however, heartbreakingly, Duplessis has begun to disappear in patches, leaving to the last his whiskers, ears, eyes, and finally, like the Cheshire Cat, his grin. While Marcel grieves over his lost childhood and undergoes a decisive isolation from his society, his cousin, the Fat Woman's child (who goes nameless in the novels, though in *La Maison suspendue* he is revealed to be to be none other than Jean-Marc, Tremblay's autobiographical stand-in), makes a passage of his own out of childhood into a condition of objective observer, guiltily stealing elements from Marcel's imagination to establish a reputation for himself as a great creative mind.

Marcel poursuivi par les chiens, then, documents the final disappearance of Marcel's mind into the subjective world of madness behind his sunglasses, the state in which we first encountered him in *En pièces detachées*. At the same time, there is consolation for the extremely melancholy destiny to which Marcel seemed doomed at the end of *Le Premier Quartier de la lune*: Florence and her daughters exist in a kind of liminal state between the material and the more fantastic aspects of Tremblay's poetic cosmos, and are thus enabled to perform several important functions. On a formal level, because throughout most of the play Marcel and Thérèse are oblivious of their existence, the detachment of Florence and her daughters allows them to supply an objective perspective, thus abstracting the tragedy from the personal realm to the social, as Greek tragic choruses so often do. But their very detachment serves, at least for those who have read the novels, to underscore the threat of Marcel's awful, tragic isolation from a world of social meaning. Whereas most of those who find the rue Fabre unbearable have the option, upon reaching adulthood, of escaping to La Main, as Thérèse did, Marcel has encountered so awful an example of La Main's brutality that he must escape even beyond that refuge of misfits.

For Thérèse, the loss of a meaningful connection with Marcel and his gentle, charming imagination means that an essential magical ingredient has been permanently removed from La Main. For a time she hopes to use Marcel's witness of the murder to control that brutal aspect of La Main personified in Maurice. But when this prospect is denied her, it seems clear that she will simply seek refuge in her alcoholism. Leaving La Main, she explains, is not an option: "Chus faite pour vivre la nuit, Marcel, dans un monde qui respecte juste le jour" (I was made to live at night, Marcel, in a world that respects only the day – 22). For Marcel, however, there is another possible world, as the presence of the four ghosts indicates:

Qu'est-ce qu'on fait pour oublier les affaires qui font mal, Thérèse? Où c'est qu'on peut se sauver? Y'a-tu une place oùsqu'on peut se sauver, oùsque les affaires qui font mal peuvent pas nous rattraper? Avant, pendant longtemps, j'en avais une place ... Y'étaient quatre ... Quatre femmes ... Y prenaient soin de moé, y me montraient toute c'qu'y'avait à savoir, pis quand ça allait pas dans ma tête, y chantaient eux-autres aussi pour consoler. Pis ça me consolait pour vrai. Depuis que j'les vois pus, j'ai jamais eu de vraie consolation. (60).

How are you supposed to forget the things that go bad, Thérèse? Where are you supposed to run away to? Is there somewhere you can take off to where the bad things can't get you? Before, for a long time, I had this place. There were these four ... Four women ... They looked after me, they showed what there was to know, and when things didn't go right in my head, they'd sing to me, to console me. And it really did console me. Ever since I haven't see them, I've never had any real consolation.

At last Florence approaches him and promises that if he stays hidden behind the sunglasses, he can continue to share the rich world of her and her daughters. Thus, Marcel's final tragic isolation from society is, as in *Oedipus at Colonus*, also an apotheosis of sorts. By donning the sunglasses, he is made in his own mind into a kind of demi-god, who will hereafter live mostly in the enchanted forest of his imagination.

Encore une fois, si vouz permettez (1998), Tremblay's most recent play, and the first to première simultaneously in Montreal in French and English – as *For the Pleasure of Seeing Her Again* – might have almost been called *Nana, en cinq temps*, for Tremblay again shows a character at five times of her life and provides her with an interlocutor to act as a foil. However, in lieu of the atemporal premise of *Abertine, en cinq temps*, here we have only one Nana, in five different scenes, and her interlocutor is a thinly veiled representation of Tremblay himself. The English title clearly declares the thrust of the play: it is Tremblay's pretext for taking one more fond look at a favourite character, a sort of loving filial tribute. The French title gives a sense of just how intimate the play is: we are asked to permit the return of the character as if this were a personal indulgence. The play is Tremblay's simplest, in terms of both its uncomplicated attitude towards its subject and its dramaturgy.

Indeed, *Encore une fois* begins with the narrator citing a long list of famous dramatic moments that will *not* occur in the evening's performance.[22] In a sense, though, this is another example of Tremblay's using the trope of preterition. True enough, the listed dramatic moments are not in *Encore une fois*; but having been mentioned, having evoked memories of the thrill we feel when such moments arise in the theatre, and at the same time having made us smile at what, to an unheated imagination, seems the great improbability of such moments, they take up residence in the imaginative climate of the play. For these great dramatic moments, which we have at once honoured and humoured, become touchstones of Nana's impressive instinct for the theatrical. It is remarkable how many of the most famous dramatic characters – Oedipus, Clytemnestra, Hamlet, Cleopatra, Rosalind, Alceste, Cyrano, Faust, Hamm – are self-conscious performers, predisposed to consider their actions in terms of what is appropriate to their dramatic roles. Nana is a self-dramatizing character in their line, and though the narrator shares our amusement at this predilection for self-dramatization (as does Nana, on and off), Tremblay also wishes to honour it.

In this, Tremblay has captured a paradox lying at the very core of Quebec culture, and one that is well worth celebrating. Virtually any anglophone encountering Quebec culture for the first time will be struck by the intense degree of passion and poetry expended on what often seem to be trifling occasions. For instance, an advertising blurb for theatrical performances will often contain prose so extravagant that it seems almost hilarious when translated into English. Yet at the same time Quebec is, for the most part, a very practically minded society, and the mild rebuke "il ne faut pas exagérer!" (let's not exaggerate!) is far more commonly heard amongst French-speaking Canadians than its equivalent is in English-speaking Canada. Indeed, one could say that the whole rue Fabre–la Main schism in Tremblay's world is rooted in this paradox, a suggestion Tremblay made implicitly with the relationship between Victoire and Josaphat in *La Maison suspendue* and here restates as a pattern of the Narrator's alternating mutual delight in and ironic distance from his mother. Yet where this sense of division has been antagonistic in many of the earlier plays, here it is couched in such a profound and apparent love that the play remains fundamentally joyful throughout, even as it comprises feelings of scepticism, anger, and sorrow.

It is love, then, that gives this play its essential quality. *Encore une fois* is a gift from Tremblay to his mother, a gift of actual dramatization for a woman possessed of a *joie de vivre* that manifests itself chiefly as a *joie de la dramatique*. In terms of its contribution to dramatic literature, what Tremblay offers here is one of his simplest yet most accomplished exercises in transumption of Western dramatic idiom. The point is most obvious in the final scene, in which the Narrator presents Nana with a *trompe du théâtre* of the sort that might have been seen in the *salle des machines* used by the court of Louis XIV, but modified to embrace quintessentially Canadian content of the sort in which his mother would take pleasure: plains of golden wheat stretching out in a display of seemingly infinite bounty. For Nana, this gift of spectacle is as splendid and as direct a fulfilment of her theatrical fancy as there could be. For us in the audience, the gift is as great: this apotheosis of a native personality that Tremblay has devised may stand as an emblem or icon of the sublime enrichment the creations of our finest playwrights have conferred upon our imaginations.

5 George F. Walker: Postmodern City Comedy

Give me back the Berlin wall
give me Stalin and Saint Paul
Give me Christ or give me Hiroshima
Destroy another fetus now
We don't like children anyhow
Ive seen the future, brother:
It is murder.
... When they said REPENT
I wonder what they meant.

Leonard Cohen, "The Future"

THE DEATH OF BAZAROV AND
THE POSTMODERN INHERITANCE

In Ivan Turgenev's 1862 novel *Fathers and Sons*, Arkady Nikolayevich Kirsanov, having recently graduated from university in St Petersburg, returns home to the small country estate of his father, Nikolai, bringing with him a new friend, Yevgeny Vassilovich Bazarov. Arkady's eyes have been opened to a whole new aspect of the world while he has been away, and one of the chief instigators of these first steps from innocence to experience has been Bazarov, a nihilist who refuses to respect any established moral system or social station whatsoever. Turgenev's novel depicts the clash of the new ideas of these young men with the conventional values of their elders, with the Russian social structure, and, finally, with their own experiences of the world. For his part, Arkady is confused by his divided loyalties to, on the one hand, Bazarov and his new ideas, and, on the other, his simple, muddled, kindly father, and old-fashioned, pretentious, but basically decent uncle. Bazarov becomes equally perplexed when his supercilious dismissal of all tradition and sentiment begins to crumble as he falls hopelessly in love with a woman named Anna. Heartsick, Bazarov returns home to his own doting, simple parents. There the discovery he had made through love, of his own compassion, takes deeper hold as he cares for his parents and for their recently freed serfs. In the end, while caring for a sick serf, Bazarov cuts himself, is infected, and dies.

The description of Bazarov's death is surely among the great passages in modern fiction, evoking at once tragedy, absurdity, and beauty. It is also one of the most compelling indications of Turgenev's ambivalence about the confrontation of old and new his novel depicts. The difficulty of determining the final significance of Bazarov's death – whether it represents a devastating blow to great human promise, or a pointless and arbitrary accident in a meaningless world, or whether Bazarov, despite himself, dies for a fine ideal – stems from the difficulty of the social questions the novel poses as a whole.

There can be little doubt Turgenev believed that there was something profoundly wrong with Russia as it stood and that enormous changes were necessary to remedy the social malaise. His novel shows real sympathy for the impatient rebelliousness of Bazarov and his kind. But a strong scepticism towards nihilist thought is equally apparent; it would seem that Turgenev was reluctant to wield such a ruthless scalpel as the nihilists proffered, partly out of pity for those who would be left behind, bewildered by the quick march into the future, but partly too because he saw something callow and impractical in the nihilists' wholesale rejection of traditional values. Human nature, he demonstrates, is ruled more by affection than reason, and it is difficult to hate all human traditions without hating human beings themselves, a position that, presumably, any would-be social reformer would eventually find untenable. Thus, if in the end Turgenev's social analysis seems a little muddled, it is muddled above all by honesty, by his inability to shut his eyes to individual human beings in order to prescribe solutions for humanity in the abstract.

George F. Walker read Turgenev's *Fathers and Sons* with great enthusiasm when he was seventeen. At forty he was to turn the novel into his most commercially successful play, *Nothing Sacred*. To suggest that through all the intervening years Walker's own outlook was informed in some essential way by Turgenev's would be extravagant. Yet there can be little doubt that Turgenev's novel touches upon many of the central paradoxes of modern experience in ways that resonate extensively with Walker's work. This is perhaps less a matter of any direct influence than the effect of Walker's grappling with certain basic problems of living in the modern age, problems that troubled Turgenev in the mid-nineteenth-century Russia and remained essentially recognizable and pertinent in late twentieth-century Canada.

It is difficult to elucidate these problems or paradoxes without recourse to many specific examples. But generally speaking we are dealing with such issues as the anxious question of what should or should not be destroyed in the name of creative progress; the difficulty of reconciling our distrust of exploitative social institutions and authorities with our need for civic order; the prospects for forging an ethical society in a world seemingly governed by moral relativism; the tension between specific human affection and abstract social idealism; the difficulty of finding plausible new social ideals in a world that has demonstrated the folly of so very many former social ideals; the dangerous attractions inherent in either enjoying or destroying various popular aspects of a given culture; and so on. Of course, where the social context for these conundrums has so much changed, the entire texture of any artistic treatment of them must also change. Turgenev's ambivalence is pre-modern regarding elements of the incipient modern age. Walker stands at what is possibly the close of the modern age, and his ambivalence is of a sort that has come to typify "postmodernist" culture.

"Postmodernist" is admittedly an elusive term. But, however controversial the concept is in some applications, there is, as Terry Eagleton has suggested, "a degree of consensus that the typical postmodernist artefact is playful, self-ironizing and even schizoid; and that it reacts to the austere autonomy of high modernism by impudently embracing the language of commerce and the commodity. Its stance towards cultural tradition is one of irreverent pastiche, and its contrived depthlessness undermines all metaphysical solemnities, sometimes by a brutal aesthetics of squalor and shock" (cited in Harvey, 7–8). All of those elements are present to some extent in Walker's work. He also exhibits many of what Linda Hutcheon has described as the "common denominators" of the postmodernist literary style, such as the tendencies "to use but also abuse, install but also subvert, conventions," to "usually negotiate these contradictions through irony," and to "challenge the fixing of boundaries between genres, between art forms [...], between high art and mass-media culture" ("Postmodernism," 612). Indeed, Walker provides compelling evidence for Hutcheon's theory that Canada's cultural circumstances, especially vis-à-vis the United States, "make it ripe for the paradoxes of postmodernism" (Canadian Postmodern, 3), for the plays draw extensively on pop (i.e., American) culture in a quintessentially Canadian manner, simultaneously evincing the familiarity of the insider and the scepticism of the outsider.

Still, if attaching the postmodernist label to Walker is to be made at all useful, there is a further consideration. The one factor more important than all others in defining postmodernism is, as the name implies, its position with respect to the modern itself. The point has a particular relevance to Walker's work because his playwriting career began with two plays that were (in a loose sense) reworkings of two classics of modern drama.

SEARCHING FOR FORM: THE ABSURDIST TRAVESTIES

To be sure, there is no evidence that Walker explicitly set out to rework Eugene Ionesco's *The Lesson* and Samuel Beckett's *Waiting for Godot* in, respectively, *The Prince of Naples* (July 1971) and *Ambush at Tether's End* (December 1971). But the provenance of much of the dramatic form of these two plays is vivid enough to have been remarked upon by other critics. For example, Chris Johnson observes that *The Prince of Naples* "models itself after the Theatre of the Absurd in general and after Ionesco's *The Lesson* in particular" ("B-Movies," 90). Then, on *Ambush at Tether's End*, he cites Edward Mullaly, who asks, rather more harshly, "why Walker has spent his time on a script Beckett has already written with much greater discipline, intelligence, and skill" (91).[1] Johnson is mild in his defence of Walker, replying in part that "while Walker's early efforts are in many respects undergraduate exercises, few saw at the time that they are superior undergraduate exercises" (91).[2] True enough, Walker was only twenty-two or so when he wrote these plays, but there is still more to be said for them, especially when they are considered in the context of his work as a whole.

The Prince of Naples in particular remains an interesting play, in some respects specifically because of its resemblance to *The Lesson*. it. If, in one direction, *The Prince of Naples* looks back twenty years to *The Lesson*, in the other it looks forward twenty to David Mamet's *Oleanna*. As I have argued elsewhere ("Three"), these tutorial plays dramatize three moments of crisis in the transmission of cultural tradition in three different ways, each of which seems ultimately to have been informed by concerns related to Nietzsche's observations about the inseparability of knowledge and power.

In particular, *The Prince of Naples* evokes the Nietzschean assault on reason that found some highly articulate apologists during the 1960s. The roles of professor and student featured in *The Lesson* are here given a twist: the professor, Sayer, is a young radical in his twenties, while the student, Oak, is a more conservative man in his fifties. The course they are undertaking was initially to consist of an enormous reading list of the classics of Western literature. However, Sayer is more interested in dislodging Oak from his attachment to and veneration for the humanist tradition, attempting to lead him instead into a state of vague, anti-establishment radicalism. By the end of the play

Oak has just about embraced Sayer's view. He prepares to lecture to a group of students who are heard outside, converging by the thousands. Suddenly fearful of approaching the mob armed only with his new ecstatic radicalism, Oak recants, reaffirming his love for the humanist tradition. Sayer then appears with the tape-recorder that had been emitting the sound of the approaching crowd and prepares to begin the process once again. That was only the second time, he says to Oak; it may take as many as four times to achieve the full transformation.

Apart from sharing the basic premise of a tutorial that gets absurdly out of hand, the play bears a number of resemblances to *The Lesson*; the rhythmic use of language and the nonsensical reasoning are two obvious examples. We can also see a parallel between Sayer's relationship to Oak and Bazarov's to the Kirsanov family. In particular Oak resembles Arkady's father, Nicholai: a middle-aged man who has never questioned the values embedded in his culture. Hence, he is bewildered and intimidated by Sayer's destructive radicalism in much the same way that Bazarov's nihilism leaves Nikolai doubting himself.

Another connection to Turgenev is the ambivalence implicit in *The Prince of Naples*. The play dramatizes Walker's ambivalence towards his patrimony as a Canadian WASP male in a manner comparable to Turgenev's ambivalence towards his aristocratic Russian heritage. On the one hand, Walker's tone, here and elsewhere, suggests that he shares something of Sayer's bellicosity towards cultural tradition; on the other, he does not allow Sayer's rhetorical flood to uproot Oak's unprincipled but intuitive allegiance to humanism. (Having noticed the symbolism in the names, it becomes difficult to escape punning upon them.)

To be sure, in this battle of revolutionary versus traditional values Oak is, as the student, badly disadvantaged. But given that Walker's sympathies usually rest with the underdog, this indicates less about Walker's personal desires than his sense of the state of the world. And here, as in *The Lesson*, the terms of understanding are derived from Nietzsche. Indeed, the title of the play is itself a Nietzschean reference. In the third scene Sayer comes upon Oak reading *Thus Spoke Zarathustra*, the chapter on "Voluntary Death." Has Oak ever tried it, Sayer asks, consoling him on his evident failure. In any case, Sayer opines, "All of Nietzsche's works are worthless up until the time he started signing his correspondence – The King of Naples" (18). In other words, Nietzsche's thought became worthwhile only sometime after he had become insane. Lest we should dismiss this as mere rhetoric, Walker has Oak comment: "It's the word insane that troubles me. The word insane has always meant ... insane to me. But the way you use it, you seem to imply something else" (12). Sayer replies that "the word insane has been reapproached by the wide-eyed armies of time and given a new meaning. The word has been dragged out of the dampness of our mental basements and placed on the clouds of our consciousness" (12). This sends him into a rhapsodic ecstasy about "the great awakening which occurred in the sixth decade [he means the seventh – the sixties] of this century ... [W]hat had been coming about slowly until then suddenly burst upon the scene as fresh and honest as a hollering new-born baby. The madman became prophet!" (24) Finally he leads Oak in a chant of "Glory to the sixties!" (25) The title, then, suggests that Sayer is heir to the later, mad Nietzsche.

In attributing the "cults of Dionysus" that arose during the 1960s back to Nietzsche's influence, Sayer is on fairly solid ground. Indeed, his remarks about insanity seem to echo one of Nietzsche's most famous interpreters of the fifties and sixties, Georges Bataille. In his writings Bataille always seems happiest with the extremes of Niet-zsche's thought. Although a Marxist, Bataille was fascinated and even somewhat enthused by fascist violence because he believed that vio-lence, death, evil, insanity could erupt through social taboos to create the opportunity for totality or sovereignty in human beings. Hence, Nietzsche is praised as a "philosopher of evil" whose thought offers a "signal dissolution in totality ... an unmotivated feast; it celebrates in every sense of the word, a laughter, a dance, an orgy which knows of no subordination, a sacrifice heedless of purpose, material or moral" (Bataille, 51, 56). It appears that it is just such an unmoti-vated feast that Oak is supposed to be preparing for at the end of *The Prince of Naples* when he shrinks from the implications of the teach-ings he has embraced and reaffirms his faith in the humanist tradi-tion. Nevertheless, Sayer's suggestion that they will repeat the tutor-ial until Oak's transformation is successful implies that the overthrow of reason by chaos cannot be put off indefinitely, that, finally, Oak's humanism will prove eradicable.[3] Indeed, this threat hangs like a sword of Damocles throughout Walker's subsequent work as we see these two basic positions in various guises confronting one another over and over again.

The relation of *Ambush at Tether's End* to *Waiting for Godot* is not so close as that of *The Prince of Naples* to *The Lesson*, but at the same time its departures from its model also seem less confidently motivated. Hence, *Ambush at Tether's End* inevitably suffers in a comparison with its model in a way that *Prince of Naples* does not (though, to be sure, *Waiting for Godot* is a lofty object of comparison). At any rate, in *Ambush at Tether's End* the enigmatically powerful character to be reckoned with in place of the elusive Godot is Max. Max is, in fact, present throughout the play, but only as a dead body presenting

270 The Buried Astrolabe

intractable problems of disposal. In this the play may also owe something to Ionesco's *Amédée; or, How To Get Rid of It* (and so, remotely, to Sophocles' *Antigone*).

In place of Vladimir and Estragon we have Galt and Bush, two quintessentially ordinary, albeit very insecure businessmen who have been summoned by their friend Max to the site of his suicide. Concealed upon Max's hanging body are a series of hand-written notes that anticipate every question or decision Galt and Bush produce. Max taunts the men through his notes, accusing them of indecisiveness and a lack of existential authenticity, and laying the responsibility for disposing of his body squarely upon their shoulders. Galt and Bush are unsure of what to do, continually erupting into mutual recriminations. Eventually they are joined by Jobeo, a rival to Max in the field of existentially definitive acts, who is piqued by Max's having apparently ended the contest with an unsurpassably definitive act. He takes his frustration out on Galt and Bush, accusing them of existential insubstantiality. Max's parents arrive but shrewdly disavow any connection to Max, then leave. Jobeo now announces a plan to surpass Max's gesture; he will have Galt and Bush murder him cold-bloodedly, merely to make an existential point. However, the two men cannot bring themselves to murder in absolutely cold blood, so Jobeo insults them into a rage – at which point they are capable, but the whole idea of the act of pure rationality is lost, so Jobeo flees. Galt and Bush, in despair about their purposelessness, attempt suicide, using a double-noosed rope Max has left for the purpose, taunting one another to take action. Again they fail. As the play ends, they have retreated to separate corners, snarling at one another.

The Prince of Naples depicted what was to become a perennial theme of Walker's: the indoctrination of a recalcitrant humanist into an anarchic, anti-humanist position. *Ambush at Tether's End* depicts another such theme: the fragility of the average, common ego – and hence, its manipulability – when confronted with a ruthless, self-assured ego. Where Vladimir and Estragon attempt to cope with the nihilist idea that the universe is void of meaning, Galt and Bush seem rather to be coping with the presence of nihilists themselves. One doubts that these two superficial businessmen would have ever thought their world meaningless had they not been bullied by Max's suicide notes and Jobeo's taunts. Ultimately, it is the apparent indefatigability of Max's and Jobeo's nihilist interpretation of experience, not their own direct experience, that causes Galt and Bush to doubt themselves and "lose the name of action."

The intellectual postures of Max and Jobeo themselves are made to seem absurd not merely in an existential sense but in terms of sensible human behaviour. The idea of suicide or murder as "definitive acts," examined with great seriousness in mid-century works such as Albert Camus's essay *Le Mythe de Sysiphe* or his novel *L'Étranger*, is here made ridiculous. As Chris Johnson says, "Walker sees both the society he satirizes and the modish pseudo-romantic challenge to that society as inadequate, and in the play constructs a theatrical model of the intellectual quandary in which many of his generation found themselves" ("B-Movies," 90). In other words, the entire dilemma in which Galt and Bush find themselves is depicted as an absurd cliché of modernist construction; hence, Walker's playful reflections on their self-conscious predicament are, by definition, post-modernist.

The play is postmodernist in another respect, which invites comparisons to another play indebted to Beckett, Tom Stoppard's *Rosencrantz and Guildenstern Are Dead*. The actions of Galt and Bush are anticipated and driven by the notes found on Max's body; in essence, these supply a sort of script that, as in Stoppard's play, the pair are forced to perform without ever understanding it (the frequent references to an undisclosed "plot" underscore this notion). So while they are faced, on the one hand, with the "death of the author" (a popular post-Saussurian concept), on the other their experience appears to be entirely pre-inscribed. To wit: they embody an archetypal postmodern paradox.

Walker's first two plays are, then, absurdist travesties in more than one sense. But with hindsight it is evident that Walker's use of Ionesco and Beckett's absurdist models reaches far beyond mere derivative imitation. Rather, Walker used them as a provisional framework to work through his own attitude towards some of the conundrums he had indirectly inherited from Turgenev along with something of Turgenev's ambivalent response. What that ambivalence means in the absurdist travesties is that, if Walker cannot bring himself to celebrate absurdity as the immensely liberating, all-embracing condition that Ionesco found it, neither does he cling resolutely to Beckett's sense that there is a core within the human soul that endures as the one ineradicable fact of existence.

To elaborate: Ionesco's work shows a world in which there is no meaning; those who would *make* meaning are exposed as wilful monsters who ruthlessly impose their interpretations of "reality" upon others. Having lived under the Nazis in his youth, Ionesco feared totalitarian reason. Accordingly, his work demonstrates that reason is arbitrarily imposed upon an absurd world. Beckett's work, by contrast (I have in mind the novels and later plays as much as *Godot*), shows the firm centre of the self caught with nothing real to reflect its own truth back at it, possessing no faith in a larger world of meaning, but merely an ineluctable sense of a self, however ill-defined. Beckett observes the absurdity of the larger world, and retreats within to find what little seemingly absolute assurance of truth may be found there.

Walker stands in contrast to both authors, then; for he maintains a troubled bewilderment at the loss of humanist values even as he appears to accept many of the philosophical premises that make the very maintenance of humanist values an absurdity. His work often implies distaste for an absurd world; but it also conveys his antipathy to cutting the Gordian knot by simply devising more propitious fictional circumstances in which a liberal humanist outlook might thrive. Naturally, the dilemma does not invariably emerge with that kind of binary simplicity. Rather, Walker's sense of the world's various absurdities and horrors, together with his articulation of the philosophical premises by which such a world can be understood, are revealed in a gradual dialectic between form and content.

Now, all that sounds extremely ponderous, and we would be doing Walker a great disservice were we not to acknowledge that however serious such concerns may be, above all his plays are meant to be funny. As he often stresses in interviews, however, even his commitment to humour has a cognitive purpose. Laughter is his means of gaining ironic distance on a painful situation: "I try to put evil at arm's length, somehow," he declares (*Work*, 220),[4] thus affirming the Kierkegaardian idea of using irony as the means of shifting from one mode of perception to another. To be sure, the humour in Walker's work does not always obviously work in that way: sometimes he is just having fun, being silly. But at other places in his work – though it only becomes fully apparent when one keeps the progression of the work as a whole in mind, not just the individual plays – the humour definitely functions as a trope arguing for a certain kind of recognition.

A good example of humour's being used in this way is Walker's third play, *Sacktown Rag* (1972). Unusually for Walker, the play is vaguely autobiographical, revolving around twenty-five-year-old Maxet Barrett's memories of life at the age of twelve, during the late nineteen-fifties, in the east end of a large city like Toronto. Life as Max recalls it was comically distressing, beset as he was at home by his pathetically escapist, alcoholic father, and at school by a brutal and stupid principal, Mr P., and a sexually repressed and rapacious teacher, Miss Missus. The story centres on the budding sexuality of Max and his best friend and worst influence, Brick Spencer, and on their confrontation with authority (Mr P. and Miss Missus and, in one section, a Priest). Near the end it is suggested that Brick died of a brain tumour, which Miss Missus makes Max feel he caused by striking Brick on the head while playing. However, in the last scene of the play everything Max has remembered is thrown into question. His memories of the brutality he suffered prove ridiculously inaccurate, and Max's sober father insists that Brick is alive and teaching in their former school. The disjunct and absurd scenes from Max's childhood have all been projections from Max's fantasies and anxieties. He appears to suffer from paranoid delusions, a persecution complex, feelings of guilt, and rather Oedipal fantasies focusing upon his teacher, Miss Missus.

At one level *Sacktown Rag* satirizes a type of modernist memory play (cf Williams' *Glass Menagerie*, Miller's *After the Fall*, or Wilson's *Lemon Sky*), toying with the conventions and unravelling much of the sense of the form's reliability with the closing deliberately anticlimactic disclaimer. But at another level it implies a genuine self-examination, though one couched in a self-reflexive irony the effectiveness of which is dependent on our recognition of the pseudo-autobiographical conventions. Max's memories are unreliable in part because he sees his life in absurdly simplified figures. This aspect of the play emerges most vividly in one of several scenes in which the adult Max accosts a local man (much as Coleridge's Ancient Mariner waylays the wedding guest, although the immediate inspiration is probably the importunate title character of Henry Miller's 1938 novel *Max and the White Phagocytes*). Max offers the man a comic book for his children, then shouts:

> Tell them life is a comic book. Tell them the past is a cartoon you have to fill in yourself. Buy them some fat crayons and *see* if they don't have a helluva time staying inside the lines. That's a metaphor, you cretin!
> (I.31)

Lest we should be left feeling cretinous ourselves, the metaphor is worth analysing. Max implies that the events of the past appear to us in simplified, conventionalized, two-dimensional forms with hard outlines. In the process of bringing meaning and truth to these outlines, however, we find that our sense of what *should be* is not altogether congruous with what we discover *can be*, or what *is*. The observation is not in itself philosophically complex, to be sure, but the comic book indicates a context for the observation that proves richly significant for Walker's future work. Indeed, judged solely for its assurance of form and coherence, *Sacktown Rag* looks like a step backward in Walker's work. But in terms of texture, the many allusions to pop-culture – the comic book, for example, or the fantasy scenes drawn from the movie *High Noon*, or Miss Missus's appearance as a striptease dancer – signal an important development in Walker's work and inaugurate the next period: the Pop Art plays.

AESTHETICS OF HYPERBOLE: THE POP ART
PARABLES

At Factory Lab Theatre, where most of Walker's plays have pre-miered, one of the outstanding personalities in the 1970s was John Palmer, a playwright and director. As it happened, Palmer did not direct a Walker play until 1977 (and that was over at Toronto Free Theatre), but as a leading creative spirit Palmer exerted a strong general influence on the Factory Lab group (Johnston, *Up*, chaps. 3 and 6, esp. 178). Ken Gass, Factory's founding artistic director, argues that, in particular, Palmer's plays *Memories for My Brother, Part Two* (1971) and *A Touch of God in the Golden Age* (1971) "had a seminal influence" on Walker (Gass, 9). The aspects of Palmer's work that seem to have excited Walker's interest are, first, the highly personal, idiosyncratic nature of his writing, which is at times fairly realistic but at others approaches an impenetrable surrealism; second, his satiric use of pop-culture clichés for an effect comparable to that associated with Sam Shepard (then an obscure avant-garde writer); and third, his approach to theatrical meaning, which looks a bit like a throwback to Dadaism.

For example, in Palmer's *A Touch of God in the Golden Age* two men share a rambling discussion about personal and social obses-sions on Christmas Eve as they drink and drug themselves into a stupor and while slide projections and audio tapes comment upon, frequently undercutting, their conversation. Palmer explains in his preface that "the effect desired is a barrage of ideas, emotions, images and sounds for the purpose of wreaking such havoc on the logical impulse of the normal mind that one might begin to question one's approach to "truth" whatever that means. I know no truths any more. I certainly have nothing to tell you. Here is what is; any common denominator is in the dark. Perhaps we all breathe the same air" (v). While Palmer's refusal to recognize common denominators is by no means shared by Walker, his implicit repudiation of formal unity and definite meaning and his ambition to dislodge the logical mind from its habitual perceptions are easily traceable in Walker's work: "I like to let images collide and see what happens," Walker has said (Conlogue, "Walker," c1).

Sacktown Rag already exhibited certain features that may be par-tially attributable to Palmer's influence: for example, its often highly personal themes, its use of pop culture, and the muted impulse towards formal unity. But with *Bagdad Saloon: A Cartoon* (1973), Walker brought these elements to a new level of dramaturgical freedom and confidently struck a style of his own. As Stephen Haff puts it, the first two plays may have "demonstrated Walker's skill as a dramatist, but his insights were so deeply couched in the idiom of those European models as to relegate the plays to obscurity. Walker's own distinctive voice emerged when he turned to pop-culture, particularly the styles, structures and icons of B-movies and *film noir* as sources" (Haff, 59–60). The result was like nothing Canadian theatre had seen before, and predictably, some found the unfamiliar style bewildering.

Bagdad Saloon tells the story of Ahrun, a rich sheikh who lives with his thirteen-year-old daughter Sara and his assistant Aladdin in an unnamed desert, where he yearns to become a famous artist. To this end he attempts to found a cultural life in the desert by having Aladdin import some American cultural icons: Henry Miller, Gertrude Stein, Doc Halliday, and an obscure sex symbol named Dolly Stilletto, a former lover of Halliday who also knew Miller in Paris. Instead of establishing a new culture, however, the American expatriates simply degenerate into grotesque, bickering self-parodies. Although the characters are apparently immortal, they become increasingly moribund – albeit Sara, enchanted with Doc's fame, ends up being impregnated by him. In the chaotic penultimate scene there arrives Ivanhoe Jones: son of Doc and Dolly, a hideous, indestructible, world-conquering monster and golf-pro who is working on a night-club act. At the end Ahrun and Aladdin have disappeared and what is left is a sort of animate graveyard in which the decrepit and senile remains of the American icons (along with Sara, now Doc's mistress) endlessly repeat pointless gestures and phrases.

Much of the allegorical significance of the play falls into place as soon as we recognize that Ahrun's desert is not an actual desert location but a metaphor for a cultural and intellectual state. Walker may have been partly inspired by a historical fact: in the early seventies the shah of Iran had been spending a staggering amount of money and effort on acquiring Western artwork. However, in reading any of Walker's work, we do well to keep in mind his declaration that "everything I have written is about Toronto ... and no matter where I am, in some way everything I will write will also be about it" (Conlogue, "Walker," C4). Thus, whatever inspiration the Shah provided for the character of Ahrun, the desert of *Bagdad Saloon* chiefly stands for the condition of the Canadian cultural imagination as Walker saw it in Toronto in 1973.

Ahrun attempts to feed his hunger for artistic recognition by importing fragments of American popular culture into his world, apparently hoping these will foster the sense of folklore. However, all he manages to round up by way of "artifacts ... cultural tidbits" (44) is what we might call (a little unkindly) the detritus of American culture. Gertrude

Stein and Henry Miller were certainly gifted and important writers of the high modernist period, but they represent unique and inimitable cases: cultural dead-ends, as it were. Moreover, shoved into a group with Doc Halliday and a fading minor sex symbol, Dolly Stilletto, this unit can hardly be said to represent a cross-section of American culture at its finest. At any rate, having been removed to the desert, the American icons have no proper context in which to function, so they quickly meet the fate that so frequently befalls those elevated into the ether of pure celebrity, becoming grotesque parodies of themselves.

But there is another way to look at this play, which helps us to see the place of Walker's work within the broader field of cultural expression. Walker gave *Bagdad Saloon* a subtitle, *A Cartoon*, which Ken Gass argued "tends to belie its thematic density" (11), apparently feeling, not unreasonably, that there was something self-deprecating in Walker's use of the label. At the back of Gass's comment, however, there is implicit something of that old distinction between "high" and "low" art forms, which has become so thoroughly confused in the second half of the twentieth century. Where at one time thematic complexity was associated with high art intended for an elite group (such as easel paintings, classical music, and avant-garde drama) and simplicity with mass-produced works intended for broad general consumption (such as comic books, popular music, and movies), now the distinction has more or less collapsed under the pressure of the traffic crossing from one sector to the other.

One of the principal events in that collapse was the advent in the 1960s of the Pop Art movement – which, in retrospect, appears to have been less an autonomous movement than the vanguard of the post-modernist aesthetic. Undoubtedly one could find parallels between Walker and pop artists such as Andy Warhol or Claes Oldenburg, but probably most pertinent to Walker's work is the example of Roy Lichtenstein, whose paintings used comic books as subject matter. Initially, the most striking thing about Lichtenstein's work was the simple fact of what he had done; comic-book figures had been enlarged to assume the dimensions and, implicitly, the importance of framed gallery paintings – high art. To many this still seems an irritatingly pointless or fraudulent exercise. But leaving aside the question of whether we like Lichtenstein's art or not, there are a number of elements arising from his work that are worth considering in the present context.

Consider, for example, Lichtenstein's use of the Benday dots with which comics are often coloured. Reduced reproductions of Lichtenstein's paintings cannot fully disclose an interesting effect: once a cartoon is enlarged to fill a six-foot-square canvas or more, the Benday dots become no longer a simple medium of the cartoon but a motif of

Roy Lichtenstein, *Magnifying Glass*, 1963.
Oil on canvas, 16" × 16".
Collection Gianenzo Sperone; courtesy Leo Castelli Gallery.
Photograph by Rudolph Bruckhardt. © Roy Lichtenstein/VAGA New York
1988.

the painting. Lichtenstein makes the point most vividly, perhaps, in
"Magnifying Glass" (1963), which depicts a cartoon magnifying glass
examining a Benday dot pattern (see Figure). What are the implications, the painting asks, of an unthinking acceptance of a representation of the world that is no more substantial than a set of dots?

   Of course, a comparable convention in high art is the Impression-
ist Georges Seurat's use of pointillism. Yet the differences in intention
and effect are crucial. Pointillism was primarily intended to create a
startling imitation of the play of light that would demand an effort of
active synthesis from the normally passive viewer. The texture provided by the dots of paint themselves, however, was really a sec-

ondary element of Seurat's work, an accident of the technique he was using to achieve an impressionistic effect and so an afterthought, as it were, to the viewing experience. For Lichtenstein, however, the Benday dots are themselves part of the work's subject. What was, in comic books, a cheap, mechanically reproducible technique essentially analogous to Seurat's becomes, painted in large spots upon Lichtenstein's canvas, thematic. Here Marshall McLuhan's aphorism is most accurate, for the medium has indeed become the message. In making what had been invisible (or at least ignorable) so obvious, Lichtenstein's paintings make the gaps between the dots as important as the dots themselves. The gaps seem to represent what is absent or merely adumbrated in contemporary experience. They could symbolize those "aporias," or gaps in coherence, that, not long after Lichtenstein's emergence on the art scene, became a chief preoccupation of poststructuralist criticism.

As far as I know, no one has ever staged one of George F. Walker's early plays with the characters appearing in patterns of enlarged Benday dots, promising though the idea sounds. But in *Bagdad Saloon* and the other pop art plays – in other words, those plays that derive various motifs from comic books and B-movies – there is an analogy to Lichtenstein's work in the way that Walker takes a clearly outlined but sketchily filled personality, such as Doc Halliday or Rita from *Beyond Mozambique*, and by foregrounding the "flatness" of the character and the gaps in personality, manages to symbolize a cultural malaise and to provoke a sustained thematic examination of the issue of artistic representation of human identity.

Furthermore, the extremity of Walker's ironic treatment of his subject matter – embracing that postmodernist ambivalence about the artistic conventions that, in Hutcheon's phrase, it "uses and abuses, installs but subverts" – invites analogies to Roy Lichtenstein's own ambivalence towards his subject matter. It is widely presumed that Lichtenstein's paintings celebrate a sort of comic-book view of the world, but when asked once whether it was proper to find pop art despicable, Lichtenstein said this:

Well it *is* an involvement with what I think to be the most brazen and threatening characteristics of our culture, things we hate, but which are also powerful in their impingement on us. I think art since Cézanne has become extremely romantic and unrealistic ... Pop art looks out into the world; it appears to accept its environment, which is not good or bad, but different – another state of mind. ... I suppose I would still prefer to sit under a tree with a picnic basket rather than under a gas pump, but signs and comic strips are interesting as subject matter. There are certain things that are usable, forceful and vital about commercial art. We're using those things – but we're not really advocating stupidity, international teenagerism and terrorism.   (Swanson, 111–12).

In his own way Walker holds with a position about artistic representation closely akin to Lichtenstein's: "Like so many of my generation, my mind is a sort of media garbage bag sometimes. We're all so heavily influenced by television and movies and you don't have to be very perceptive to see it coming out in new plays. The dilemma for me was not to rebel against the problem – it is, after all, a fairly central reality – but to assimilate it and make something of it" (Fraser, 23). Five years later in a 1982 interview Walker expanded upon these remarks, explaining: "I'm not trying to reproduce those influences. I'm trying to fight my way through the chaos of what, in fact, has been garbage and what, in fact, has been worth saying about things that concern me, using those forms to write, say, a political play which is not obviously a political play but which makes people think about politics" (*Work*, 219). Hence there are, as Gass observed, "not many prairie landscapes in George Walker's plays" (9). In other words, rather than attempting to reach some sort of "pure Canadian" experience beyond the corruption of internationalized urban life, Walker, especially in his early work, acknowledges that the greater part of the aesthetic environment of contemporary Canada is provided by commercial culture, and so uses the popular "mediascape" to comment on Canadian experience.

As unexceptionable as that idea may seem today, during the seventies Walker was regularly criticized for this approach to Canadian drama, as he explains:

It would be very dishonest of me to attempt to write any sort of rural play. I had been surrounded by things like movies, television ... theatre and literature of all kinds all my life. What did I know about the farmer and his wife? And yet I was criticized. Everyone kept telling me I should go to the grass roots and that Canadian plays should be naturalistic or historical. Naturalism was very big in Toronto for a long time. I couldn't help thinking that was one kind of theatre, but there were other types of theatre as well.   (Galloway, 18; cited in Johnson, "B-Movies," 89).

So, like Lichtenstein and the other pop artists, Walker set out unapologetically and unsentimentally to reflect something of the world as it appeared before him, "garbage" and all, in his work. At the same time, his work remains decidedly unlike that of the pop artists in the very significant respect emphasized in that 1982 interview: he has never shared the commitment to conformity, the representation of images from mass culture in a virtually unaltered state, which is common to many pop artists. Rather, Walker has always been heavily committed to the principle of transformation, the alteration of his subject-matter to express something in his own personality.

That fact is obvious in Walker's treatment of B-movie conventions in *Beyond Mozambique* (1974). Rocco, a mad doctor and former Nazi (Joseph Mengele seems a likely model), lives deep in an unnamed, exotic jungle with his wife, Olga, who believes herself to be one of Chekhov's three sisters. Rocco conducts experiments on native cadavers, which are illegally exhumed by his brain-damaged assistant, Tomas. Lately, however, Tomas has taken to murdering the natives instead of merely robbing their graves. Also living in the jungle are Rita, a pornographic movie actress named after Rita Hayworth, who smuggles guns to raise money for a legitimate film debut, and Lance Corporal (or Corporal Lance: as with Joseph Heller's Major Major, there is a confusion about name and rank here), a deranged RCMP officer who has been exiled to the jungle for killing cows to end what he felt was their "evil whining misery." They are joined by Father LiDuc, a drug-addicted, paedophilic Catholic priest, born to Chinese and Jewish parents. The main thrust of the plot is the growing threat of violence from the natives as the characters drift into degeneracy and hallucination – apart from Tomas, who becomes ever richer and more powerful. The play ends as a violent apocalypse is closing in from all sides. Olga, who has killed herself, is used as a mannequin by her husband to speak her namesake's wistful speech from Chekhov's play; then the cast retreats into the house, staring at the audience "in confusion and growing anxiety."

It is not difficult to find overtones of such horror movies as (to name only the most famous) *The Island of Doctor Moreau* or *Frankenstein*.[5] The *Globe and Mail*'s Bryan Johnson went so far as to call the play a "fifties Tarzan epic gone mad," which seems more of a stretch, but still comprehensible (13). In any case, it is equally clear that, in making his priest a drug-addicted pederast, or his heroine a pornographic film star, or in drawing in the Chekhovian character and the Mountie, Walker departs considerably from his popular sources and, hence, from the pop art practice of conforming closely to the original subject-matter with a minimum of transformation.[6] Here the popular sources are removed to a degenerate colonial setting and integrated into a parable about the decline of the West and the uncontainable chaos caused by the confusion of civilized values.

In that respect the play also bears traces of an earlier source, Joseph Conrad's *Heart of Darkness* – arguably the most important literary prototype for portraying twentieth-century colonial experience. If Chinua Achebe's objection to *Heart of Darkness* – that it is not really about Africa at all, that it "eliminates the African as a human factor" – points to what is, in fact, a fundamental tenet of Conrad's novel, the point holds doubly true for Walker's play. Yet it is unlikely that anyone would find offence in so obviously fictional a location as Walker's. Where Conrad took a social and geographical reality and turned it into a figure for the moral condition of Western civilization, Walker takes that figure and advances it into a state of hyperbole. To wit: a location literally beyond Mozambique, which lies on the east coast of Africa, would be, from an occidental perspective, somewhere out in the Indian Ocean; but figuratively the place is located in an advanced state of the malaise Conrad adumbrated as a "heart of darkness."

What lies "beyond Mozambique," then, is a moral state in which "the horror, the horror" that Kurtz bore witness to with his last words has become an acceptable banality. Here, Kurtz's "intended," as she is called (i.e., his fiancée), is no longer an ignorant, pure idealist left at home whose frail innocence seems crucial to the preservation of the idea of civilized goodness. Now, she (Olga) has married her man (Rocco) and lives with him in the jungle, merely asking that the bodies be kept out of the house and off the picnic table during mealtimes. Olga's detachment from the bloody horror in which the other characters are drenched is not rooted in an innocence like that of Kurtz's intended but in a wilfully ignorant retreat into a passive, wistful irony like that of her namesake – what Chekhov saw in the waning aristocracy of pre-revolutionary Russia. As for Conrad's embodiment of objectivity and common decency, Marlow, a Canadian who expected the Mountie to fill this role would be sadly disappointed. As the putative emissary of peace, order, and good government in the jungle, Lance has only one strategy for dealing with evil: to kill the sufferers.

If indeed *Beyond Mozambique* allegorizes the moral collapse of Western civilization, it would perhaps be too much to look to Walker for not only an artistic rendering of the observation but an analysis of causes and a prescription of remedy too. Still, Walker's play at least delineates a number of what we might call the symptoms of the social malaise, and these hark back to the postmodernist representation of character associated with Lichtenstein's artwork. For example, an obvious moral problem in the world of *Beyond Mozambique* is the commodification of human life resulting from the remorseless pursuit of material self-interest. The most materially rapacious characters, Tomas and Rita, are capitalists without consciences. Tomas's problem is possibly that the ethically reflective part of his brain has been damaged or removed. But Rita is missing something fundamental in her psyche rather than her brain, a condition related to the general malaise. She first enters carrying a severed head in a shopping bag, her arms bloody; when Olga asks if it scares her, she responds: "Well, it doesn't seem real. I mean no more real than the movies. [*Looks at her arms*] Stage blood looks the same way" (92/*SA* 8).[7] The metatheatrical reference emphasizes the contingency of the world of the play itself; reality is doubtful and elusive.

Rita is by no means alone in her ontological confusion. Later, Rocco explains to LiDuc that Olga believes herself a character from *Three Sisters*:

LIDUC: How does she reconcile this belief with reality?
ROCCO: Which reality?
LIDUC: I understand.
ROCCO: Do you?
LIDUC: No.
ROCCO: No. The only way to understand it is to become a part of it.

(114/*SA* 29)

The notion of characters caught amidst discrete, competing, or overlapping ontologies is a prevalent conceit of postmodernist literature, closely connected to the radical subjectivity and depthlessness of experience so often delineated by postmodern thought. If, as post-Saussurian theories of language assert, words have no determinable external referent, there are no means of testing or mediating between two conflicting claims of truth; so choosing what is "true" is a matter of arbitrary aesthetic inclination. But where there is no context of meaning, it is impossible to exercise preference; consequently, personal agency cannot exist in any real sense.

Walker briefly dramatizes the conundrum in scene 5. Olga enters from her house armed with a parasol and a book, declaring:

I've decided to make a comeback. First things first. I'm going for a walk. [*Down the steps. Several confident steps straight ahead. Stops. Turns. A few paces to the left. Stops. Turns. Looks right.*] It's all the same. Foreign. Uninviting. Blandness in one direction. Danger in the other. Why bother choosing. [*Returns to her chair on the porch. To no one in particular.*] It's like this, I think. One cannot afford to be a romantic. In this time. At this place. It's just too dangerous. Emotion is apt to be mistaken for weakness and weakness as an invitation to manipulate. (118/*SA* 32)

From one perspective, Olga's closing analysis merely describes her reasons for eschewing sentiment under the circumstances. But with the postmodern problem of personal agency in mind, her words recall

Nietzsche's analysis of the social consequences of bringing meaning to a context in which there is no inherent or transcendent meaning; those who are willing to exercise power most ruthlessly are those who determine which "truth" prevails.

The phrase Nietzsche gave to the philosophical imperative of taking responsibility for the interpretation of truth in such circumstances is "will to power." Though the particular phrase is never spoken in *Beyond Mozambique*, "will to power" forms the chief attribute of Rocco's character; it is precisely what makes him at once so disturbing and so compelling. Conventional morality, argued Nietzsche, was based in a cowardly refusal to take responsibility for determining one's own values, the task being deferred instead to some fictitious transcendent system that had in fact been invented by some self-serving sector of society. No slave to convention himself, Rocco has his own self-determined, self-aggrandizing course of action. At first he is vague about his objective, though he says he is "searching for the cure to cancer [of all kinds]" (112/SA 27). Soon, however, this becomes "the cure to end all cures," because, he admits, "it's not glory I'm after. It's redemption" (126/SA 40).

But Rocco's "redemption" is defined in terms of the "will to power." Accordingly, the main part of his program is directed at embracing evil in its rawest form. "When I was of an age when men make those kinds of decisions," he says, "I decided to steep myself in corruption. Because corruption was the only powerful force around. And now because the age of passion is dead there is no energy to reverse the decision" (113/SA 28). Later he adds that "there's something about committing crimes against humanity that puts you in touch with the purpose of the universe" (126/SA 40). His chief obstacle appears to be civilization itself, the lingering evidence that humanity is capable of worthwhile accomplishment. "There is a tower growing in the jungle," he tells LiDuc. "It is the power of light and the shrewd mind of darkness. It is the culmination of all history and civilization. And it is turning my mind into soup" (113/SA 28). But eventually he is able to claim: "I have finally destroyed that fucking tower and now there are only three forces in the world. God. Ignorance. And me" (126–7/SA 40).

It is worthwhile to push these philosophical dimensions a little further. Notwithstanding the sense in which, as Chris Johnson suggests, Rocco is the most positive character in the play, there is something almost unbearably stark about the idea that Nietzsche's "will to power" is the only real solution to the chaos of the modern world, especially having seen the form it can take – in this play and in this century. Given too that Nietzsche is probably the single greatest influence on modern and postmodern existentialist philosophy, a real crisis in contemporary thought is indicated. To be sure, we may turn to the next most important influence, Kierkegaard. However, while Kierkegaard's framework can be applied to the ethical problems of *Beyond Mozambique*, it by no means offers an unproblematic solution. In *Either/Or* Kierkegaard argues that perception moves from an aesthetic mode (based in subjectivity, and in which identity is fluid, but which, in itself, ends in despair) on to a phase of objectivity and a self-assured sense of moral duty (which ends in crisis as it falls into conflict with the irrational). A third and transcendental phase is possible, however: the religious, achieved through a commitment to faith.

The condition of some of the characters in *Beyond Mozambique* seems to be described in Kierkegaard's aesthetic mode: Lance, Olga, and Rita, for example, cannot see beyond their subjective role-playing. If we think of the play as picking up morally where *Heart of Darkness* left off, it is evident that characters such as LiDuc or Rocco are stalled in the crisis met at the end of the second phase: the moral remains in conflict with the irrational. The problem is that the leap of faith necessary to enter Kierkegaard's third phase is unviable here. And where such a leap is impossible, the temptation is either to fall back in confusion to the subjective, aesthetic phase, or to take arms against a sea of troubles – as Rocco does.

Apparently, there was indeed a time when Rocco considered a religious solution – a leap of faith – to his sense of the chaos of modern life, though in the end he repudiated the idea. He is beyond psychiatry, he boasts to Father LiDuc, because he is now "the absence of God." When LiDuc demurs, Rocco replies:

> Ah, I'm not listening to you. Where was the Church when I needed her? I'll tell you. The world was being torn apart. Mothers walked around grinning foolishly at their children's graves. Compromise was ruining good men forever. Chronology and reason were being shot to hell. And the Church was locked up inside an old stone palace hiding under a gigantic mahogany desk with His Eminence. (113/*SA* 28)

The Church lacked the moral courage to confront chaos directly, according to Rocco, so he began to reinvent himself as a sort of alternative to God. Especially interesting is the suggestion not that "God is dead" (the assertion associated with Nietzsche) but that *the Church has in some way made God irrelevant and unknowable*. In fact, that assertion is much closer than is the popular notion of the "God is dead" phrase to what Nietzsche's Zarathustra actually argues. Expression of faith in God is a sham, Zarathustra says, because religion has

285 Walker: Postmodern City Comedy

become so profoundly hypocritical; God has been betrayed and effectively murdered by the very people who profess belief.

A similar murder story lies at the core of Walker's next play, the most claustrophobic, morbidly ironic, and perhaps least penetrable of his works to date, *Ramona and the White Slaves* (1976). The play opens in Hong Kong in 1919. Its complicated plot may be related to Ramona Maria da Costa's opium nightmare – mentioned at the outset of the play by a man named Cook, who is investigating a murder. He tells us that, in her nightmare, Ramona is about to be raped by a lizard. We hear her rambling, apparently calling the lizard "father," and imagining herself in a convent. Ramona, a former nun, runs (or was running at the time of the murder) what appears to be a brothel, though we never see any clients. As a young nun Ramona had run off with a priest named Miguel, who later died in cloudy circumstances. After a period of mourning Ramona ended up in Hong Kong.

In a series of flashbacks ("time is at play here," says the opening stage direction) we meet two young women who live with and work for Ramona: Leslie, a seventeen-year-old with a prosthetic hook on one arm, and her older sister, Gloria, an angry and demoralized woman. They call themselves not whores but slaves. Also living with them is their brother, Friedrich, a legless piano player. Ramona speaks of Friedrich as her son, but she never quite calls the girls her daughters. Sebastian, the man whose murder Cook is investigating, is called the Boss, or sometimes "the bald-headed man." He appears at first to be keeping the women prisoners. The girls are terrified of him, for Ramona describes him as tyrannical and violent. Yet doubts are gradually sown about this judgment. At one point Sebastian gives Friedrich new legs – "some kind of miracle or something," Gloria calls it (149). Friedrich practises walking, then disappears, only to re-emerge later as Mitch, a heroic aviator, in which guise he proceeds to seduce Leslie.

Under Cook's questioning and in the flashback scenes, the truth gradually emerges that Sebastian has very little real power anymore; he is timid, and cowed by Ramona. Moreover, it was Ramona herself who was responsible for severing Friedrich's legs and Leslie's hand, whereas it was Sebastian who had supplied not only Friedrich's new legs but Leslie's prosthetic hook. Ramona becomes more and more sinister, seducing Mitch to do her will, lying and bullying the girls into submission. In the penultimate scene Ramona and Sebastian are cross-dressed and appear to have switched identities. Sebastian (as Ramona) is gently maternal with the girls but Ramona (as Sebastian) enters, announcing that she has once again lopped off Mitch/Friedrich's legs. When Sebastian protests, she sticks a gun in his mouth. In the last scene Ramona speaks resentfully about being raped (if not literally, virtually) by the priest Miguel, explaining how this made her vengeful. Then she declares:

> Oh this nightmare is real. It tells the story of – *[Stops. Sniffs]* Christians? *[Sniffs again]* Cannibals? *[More quickly]* The story of a family and Miguel's deterioration and how small he became and how he changed disguises. Priest to poppa to pimp, not that it was his idea, by the time he'd sunk to poppa he had no ideas and his mind was – *[She observes herself in the suit for the first time]* Oh look at this then. *[A couple of steps]* Very smart. Very strong. Oh yes this will do. *[Stops suddenly. Sniffs]* The lizard again. *[Looks over her shoulder]* Where? (190)

Presumably, the return of the lizard mentioned at the outset of the play suggests that the story does not end with the final blackout; the nightmare will prove cyclical.

Ramona and the White Slaves is a difficult work in several respects, a point that Walker acknowledged in saying that, if his plays in general can be regarded as being "out of the mainstream, this one is way, way out of the mainstream" (*Work*, 215). Yet the element undoubtedly contributing most to the difficulty here is Walker's greatest accomplishment: the correspondence of the tone and structure of the play to the peculiar ordering of experience associated with dreams. It is not merely time at play in *Ramona* but reality, the identity of characters, the sense of place, and the meaning of the action. Having so many dramatic elements fluid at once demands much of an audience. But if *Ramona and the White Slaves* is approached with an open-minded suggestibility like that of a dreamer, the play becomes not opaque but disturbingly permeable, not incoherent and awkward but a cogent and intense rendering of a particular theme. To paraphrase an earlier dream play, taken altogether it grows to something of great constancy.

With regard to the meaning of Ramona's "opium nightmare," Ken Gass suggests that "the essential narrative is revealed unequivocally" (14) in Ramona's last speech, quoted above. "Unequivocally" may overstate the case a little, but Gass's point is well taken, so long as we keep in mind the loosely allegorical approach demanded by the previous two plays. The story is about "Christians" or "cannibals," the uncertainty about the subject expressing the profoundly ambivalent treatment of the religion. The fusion of religion and opium recalls Marx's famous condemnation of religion as "the opiate of the masses." Extending this metaphor to the setting, we should consider that, in 1919, Hong Kong was arguably the opium-consuming capital of the world, so the setting may be seen as an intensified embodiment of religion as a social condition. This experience of religion, in which Christians and cannibals are interchangeable, forms the heart of the opium nightmare from which, implicitly, we in the audience are struggling to awake.

The enigmatic relationships among the characters are also clarified by this approach. Behind the action lies the deterioration of the character alleged to be the boss: "the bald-headed man" also known as Sebastian and Miguel. Through most of the play he is offstage: a terrifying rumour, a former authority, and, as we discover in the matter of Friedrich's legs, possibly a worker of miracles. In the symbolic pattern of the nightmare he represents God, and his degradation from "priest to poppa to pimp" is a deterioration in the way Ramona chooses to regard him. As Ramona's relationship to him changes, so does his identity and his strength.

One of the most expansive metaphors in the Judaeo-Christian tradition is the Church as the bride of God, part of a complex of symbols extending from the Song of Solomon, with its associations of insemination and inspiration, to the heavy identification of the Virgin Mary (who bears the earthly incarnation of God) with the Catholic Church. If we think of Ramona, bride and intermediary to Miguel/Sebastian, in this light, we see how she is like the Church, which interprets the will of God. Once Ramona was (like the Church at its inception) a devoted follower and loving bride to her father/lover/God, but the relationship changed with time. She discovered that an enormous scope of power was hers for the taking, though she continued to let on that the "boss" was standing behind whatever action she took.

Of course, all this implies a terrible indictment of institutional religion, but one that is consistent with Walker's incidental treatments of the theme of religion in *Sacktown Rag* and *Beyond Mozambique*. Not least damning are the implications of Friedrich/Mitch's role. As Ramona's son, begotten upon her by Miguel, he must be seen as a Christ figure. Hence, Ramona's chopping off his legs suggests the Church's undermining of the authority and power of Christ, to instead do its own will; and her intervention to prevent Mitch from establishing an independent relationship with Leslie could be seen in the same vein. We are looking at an example of the Church "invented as a homeopathic cure for the teachings of Jesus," in Northrop Frye's memorable phrase (*Fearful*, 61).

In this reading, then, Leslie and Gloria are the people themselves, their private-school uniforms marking them as members of this church of Ramona. Leslie follows Ramona's leadership innocently and unquestioningly, whereas Gloria is wavering on the verge of apostasy, little knowing that it is not the "boss" who is responsible for her misery but her stepmother, as we might call her. But eventually Gloria is browbeaten into submission by allegations of her own sinfulness; Ramona declares that Gloria herself was responsible for the amputation of her sister's hand, at which she becomes docile and subservient. That victory leaves Ramona ready for the final scene; the reversal of roles and costumes is merely the logical extension of the grotesque masquerade that has unfolded throughout the play.

Naturally, such a reading will please neither those offended by scurrilous critiques of religion nor those resistant to the idea of joining together patterns of symbol and theme to the point of allegory. Whether Walker ever intended his figurative treatment of the religious theme to be extended quite so far would be difficult to say, given his reluctance to interpret his own work.

At any rate, an important indicator of Walker's intentions is Cook, the detective. As detectives in mystery stories often do, Cook serves as what Peter Szondi calls an "Epic-I," a surrogate for the audience, an agent who focuses the narrative and marshals it into a plot. Significantly, Walker stipulates that Cook should be played by the actor playing Sebastian. The godlike character is thereby identified with the objective investigator, the very character with whom the audience is most likely to identify. I am not suggesting merely that Walker's meaning here could be summed up by saying that "God is made in man's image," though that idea is perhaps part of the picture. The main implication is that any possible source of providence, of moral authority – deteriorated and occluded by a corrupt world though it may be – is now most identifiable with the sceptical onlooker who asks questions. In short, barring miracles, if there is to be any moral recovery out of the world's chaos, the process would have to begin with an investigation of ourselves and our circumstances. Such a process of investigation provides the ethical centre of Walker's next series of plays. Whoever else he may be, Cook is forerunner to one of Walker's most important characters, the reluctant detective, Tyrone M. Power.

INVESTIGATING ARMAGEDDON: POWER PLAYS AND MORE PARABLES

Walker's Tyrone Power is a human paradox. Balding, middle-aged, and overweight, sporting thick-rimmed glasses, a walrus moustache, and an old, poorly fitting suit, this unprepossessing figure has been saddled by his romantic mother with the name of one of Hollywood's most dashing and heroic stars. No wonder he is a sceptic. Indeed, Power's ironic detachment is his primary character trait and, in the world of the Power Plays, his chief virtue. It is also an attribute he shares with his prototype, Raymond Chandler's private eye, Philip Marlowe.

Chandler's selection of the name Marlowe suggested a link between the urban ethos explored by his private detective and the decay of Western civilization adumbrated by Conrad's narrator Marlow. Walker takes a similar attitude to the detective story. The cataclysmic rendering of culture found in his parables is scaled down to a contemporary urban setting, but the basic ethical problems remain. And while the man made to investigate such a world is very much a creation of Walker's imagination, he is not altogether unlike Chandler's hero.

Like Marlowe, Power is a man whose cynicism has crystallized around an all but forgotten, yet finally incorrigible kernel of idealism. His role as a perpetually wisecracking *eiron* to his society's follies demands that he maintain an aloof existential detachment. Accordingly, he lives alone and largely unloved in a big, dirty city, possessing almost no current friends and only a nostalgic attachment to a few cherished old ones. Even there, his existential autonomy demands, dramaturgically, that these be killed off in each play (like Captain Kirk's love interests in the old *Star Trek* series). Power's dramatic job is to interpose his ironic commentary into a melodramatic battle between corruption and innocence where the latter is really something of a bad joke. When we first meet him, however, in *Gossip* (May 1977), he is an investigative reporter: the perfect job for a cynic who can't help sticking his nose into trouble.

Besides being the first in the trilogy of Power Plays, *Gossip* is also one of Walker's lightest and most popular works. Perhaps because its targets have been hit more often than those of, say, the East End plays, the actual satiric content in *Gossip* seems mild, with the humour stemming chiefly from the farcical action and dialogue. The plot is a fairly close parody of the traditional Chandleresque detective mystery, though it drifts a little more into the British version of the genre for its denouement. *Gossip* begins with a brief prologue depicting the murder of a useless socialite, Jane "Bitch" Nelson, at the gala opening of a modern art show. Then we meet Power, who, despite his indignant protests that he is a political journalist, not a gossip columnist, is assigned by his young editor, Baxter, to investigate the murder. "Who killed Bitch Nelson," asks Power in his opening line – then adds, characteristically, "and who the hell cares?" (17)

In the course of his investigation, Power encounters a theatre director, Peter Bellum; two actors, Anna and Allan; two lawyer brothers, Sam and Norman Lewis; and Bitch Nelson's sister, Brigot. Through much of the play he is accompanied by Margaret, a former lover (by whom he was, naturally, jilted) now involved in an incestuous relationship with her brother, Paul, a notoriously corrupt federal Cabinet minister. Finally, in a parody of the typical British murder mystery,

Power sits the entire cast down to a swank dinner and reveals all, explaining the murders of a series of previously unmentioned characters and exposing a scam involving an Argentine copper mine and the enslavement of a lost race of natives. As in *Murder on the Orient Express*, every guest is implicated in the impossibly complicated plot. But the one point Power neglects (as had Chandler in his first Marlowe novel, *The Big Sleep*) is to solve the original murder. So, as an afterthought, he guesses that his editor, Baxter, committed the murder merely to set Power to work on an investigation that might lead to the Cabinet minister (a jibe at the post-Watergate ambitions of journalists). His guess having proved correct, the despondent Power invites Baxter to linger with him until he can recover from the death of his dog, which, he reveals, expired that morning.

To some extent Walker is just having fun, playing with conventions and exercising his gift for witty dialogue and eccentric characters. Yet the confrontation between the extremely cynical but basically decent Power on the one hand and an absurd world of immoral cultural types on the other constitutes a new way of exploring some themes that are basic to Walker's vision. In the first scene Baxter confronts Power about the tone of his recent columns:

> BAXTER: ... I want to give those poor suckers who read your little doom report a bit of a break. I mean what exactly is it that you think you write about?
> POWER: What's that supposed to mean?
> BAXTER: In the last two weeks you've used the word cataclysm eighteen times, anathema eleven times, and get this, Armageddon twenty-six times. In short you are writing about the end of the world.
> POWER: So what?
> BAXTER: Well it's depressing. (18–19)

Given the apocalyptic overtones of Walker's work – however comically, Armageddon, the final battle between good and evil, has been imminent (or immanent) in several of his plays – there is more than a hint of self-mockery in the passage. Yet even while Power's propensity for hyperbole is mocked, Walker is careful not to discredit the sensibility behind those words entirely. Notwithstanding Power's inclination to overwrought hysteria (unlike the consummate cool of his precursor, Marlowe), the absurdly immoral quagmire with which the play ends ultimately constitutes an endorsement of Power's view. Chandler's novels always ended with at least *some* suggestion that a morally balanced world was a tenable ideal, whereas by the end of *Gossip* any implicit notion of natural law would be flatly ridiculous.

The difference in question here has to do a distinction between the ethical perspectives implicit in the two writers' works. Chandler took a fundamentally melodramatic framework populated with a few innocents (such as the old man in *The Big Sleep* or the orphaned boy in *Farewell My Lovely*) and a great many corrupt predators, then set his hero to the job of protecting the former from the latter. The effort exhausts Marlowe's spirit and erodes his capacity for joy, but he soldiers on, solid in his knowledge that these distinctions do mean something – that, whatever else may be doubted, for him (and, implicitly, the reader) justice is sacrosanct. Power, by contrast, neither holds nor encourages any such certainties. As William Lane suggests in his introduction to the Power Plays, "he seems less motivated by an heroic devotion to justice, than by a simple hatred of sham and flim-flam. To be perfectly frank, he's a bit of a misanthrope" (10). Or in Baxter's description, which Power himself accepts, he is "a nihilist" (18).

Yet the world of *Gossip* is very different from that in which Turgenev set his nihilists, for Power's nihilism is finally justified by the total immorality of the other characters. As Denis Johnston says, "we come to realize that there are no innocent people in this intrigue; there are only those who create and control the evil, and those who accede to it" (198). The world of *Gossip* is a world of surfaces, of performed and disposable selves rather than real identities, and hence a world of emotional and moral incoherence. The ethos of melodrama, with its opposition of innocence and corruption and, invariably, its final endorsement of social norms, is out of place here. So, while elements of the melodramatic framework are retained, the basic moral assumptions needed to support that framework keep deteriorating. By the end of *Gossip* Power has exposed corruption and attacked wickedness, but we would be at a loss to identify any positive value he has protected within the world of the play. Positive values remain entirely external to the play, existing only as a part of the perspective implied by the corrective function of satiric laughter.

Gossip inaugurates a period that includes seven related works. Four detective mysteries are interspersed with three plays written in a broader style, each of which also treats the Armageddon theme: desperate resistance of a possibly final triumph of evil and chaos. Evidently, *Gossip* did not exhaust Walker's interest in exploring the Armageddon theme through a melodramatic framework. Before the year was out, he made his interest more explicit with *Zastrozzi: The Master of Discipline* (November 1977), which bore the label "A Melodrama." Walker's use of melodramatic conventions is unmistakable here, though so are his very significant departures from the genre.

The configuration of the dramatis personae of *Zastrozzi* comes very close to pure melodrama because Walker's original source was a gothic novel written by the sixteen-year-old Percy Bysshe Shelley in 1809.[8] Walker did not base his play on the novel itself, which he found unreadable, but on a short synopsis of the work.[9] Walker's many departures begin with the setting, which is advanced from the beginning to the end of the nineteenth century – the brink of the modern age. Zastrozzi, who describes himself – "this is not a boast ... it is information" – as "the master criminal of all Europe" (12), has, together with his brutish sidekick, Bernardo, devoted himself for the last three years to hunting down Verezzi, the embodiment of goodness and idiocy. Verezzi and his father had killed Zastrozzi's mother in revenge for the murder of Verezzi's sister. Verezzi has evaded Zastrozzi's clutches so far, but only because the pragmatic Victor, a former priest who is Verezzi's tutor, has managed to keep his ward one step ahead of Zastrozzi and Bernardo through one subterfuge after another.

David Bolt, who played Tyrone Power throughout the Power trilogy, was Victor in the original production of *Zastrozzi*, and his portrayal of both roles underscores the similarities of these characters.[10] As with Power, Victor's job (about which he feels similarly ambivalent) is to protect innocence from evil. However, the problem is a little different. Whereas in *Gossip* there seemed to be no characters finally identifiable as innocent, in *Zastrozzi* Verezzi fills that role, but only through being an utter fool. Victor's nagging doubt has to do with whether, as stupid as Verezzi is, he is in the least *worth* protecting. As the play begins, Victor is rapidly approaching the point at which he will have to make a decision, for Verezzi refuses to flee, declining even to believe in Zastrozzi's existence and maintaining that he has a messianic duty to await a horde of imaginary followers.

Rounding out the dramatis personae are two women, Mathilda, a dangerous, raven-haired beauty devoted to Zastrozzi, and Julia, a fair-haired virgin (or so everyone assumes) who is Verezzi's love interest. In the hope of sending Verezzi to hell, Zastrozzi tries at first to lure him to commit suicide by having Mathilda seduce Verezzi and then reject him. That plan is foiled because Verezzi is too mindless to form any deep attachments, but in the end Verezzi and Victor fall into Zastrozzi's clutches anyway. In the meantime, Julia has killed Mathilda in self-defence; Bernardo has killed Julia in reprisal; and Zastrozzi has killed Bernardo for failing to kill Victor as instructed. Victor and Zastrozzi have a final duel in which Victor nearly prevails but is at last killed too. Zastrozzi then has Verezzi at his mercy, but instead of killing him offers a day's head start before resuming pursuit, "because it will keep me preoccupied" (69).

The starkness of the confrontation between good and evil is emphasized by the symmetry of the dramatis personae: the villain, Zastrozzi,
his sidekick, and a wicked woman are pitted against the nominal hero,
Verezzi, his assistant (Victor, the *real* hero), and an innocent woman.
Even the two main antagonists' names are similar. This melodramatic
framework licenses the kind of characterization normally considered a
fault in a contemporary play: evil characters can be very evil indeed
and the innocent as innocent as imaginable. In other words, the characters embody abstract moral conditions, thus enabling Walker to
explore the essential nature of the conflict between evil and goodness.

However, in melodrama proper, once the delineation between good
and evil characters is established, there is not only little attempt to
account for the characters' motivations but seldom any reflection on
the cultural significance of the presence of evil and good among
humanity. *Zastrozzi*, by contrast, although it does not round out psychological motivations (the back-plot of the murder of Verezzi's sister
and Zastrozzi's mother is dealt with summarily), is heavily preoccupied
with the meaning of the existence of evil within society. In a sense it
picks up where Jacobean tragedy leaves off. With a fascinated blend of
sadism and science, like that of ghoulish boys who drop a black ant
into a red ant colony, the authors of such plays as *The Duchess of
Malfi* or *'Tis Pity She's a Whore* seem to have been morbidly intrigued
by the idea that, without an immediate fear of God, nothing moderates
evil except the frail and dubious notion of pity for the innocent. That
removed from the antagonists, the (usually) sole wholly innocent character is destroyed while a vaguely (psychopathically?) detached villain
such as Bosola reflects philosophically upon the implications.

In *Zastrozzi* the reflections on the nature of evil come mostly from
Zastrozzi himself, who espouses a Zarathustran enthusiasm for evil as
the chief means of purging the world of its weaknesses. Zastrozzi's
account of his role in this process is at least as self-aggrandizing as
Rocco's was in *Beyond Mozambique*. He proudly claims to be:

> The force of darkness. The clear sane voice of negative spirituality. Making
> everyone answerable to the only constant truth I understand. Mankind is
> weak. The world is ugly. The only way to save them from each other is to
> destroy them both. (12)

His creed is based in a philosophical observation like that which
prompted Rocco's Nietzschean will to power. He explains to his
cohorts: "there are only two things worth knowing. The first is too
complex for you to understand. The second is that life is a series of
totally arbitrary and often meaningless events and the only way to

make sense of life is to forget you know that" (55). The thing they do not understand, and what sets Zastrozzi apart from such lesser villains, may be what Victor alludes to when he taunts Bernardo from a similarly Nietzschean perspective: "You are going to spend the rest of your life fulfilling someone else's wishes that you do not understand. That, sir, is a state of mental chaos usually associated with purgatory" (49).

Faced with a meaningless world, Zastrozzi is determined to spin a web of meaning from within himself rather than accept any inherited system of meaning. This is creativity of a sort, notwithstanding the diabolism of his proclamation that revenge against Verezzi is merely the centrepiece of a general project of annihilating civilization. But there is something further that irks him about Verezzi "which must be destroyed. He gives people gifts and tells them they are from God" (23). In other words, despite his apparent stupidity, Verezzi tends to inculcate optimism and faith in others, directly challenging Zastrozzi's ambition to eradicate such faith from the earth.

Zastrozzi's philosophy of evil appears to be so powerful as to make him virtually invulnerable. Yet an enormous amount of willpower is necessary to sustain his position, for, as Bernardo puts it, "the insulation of evil is the only thing that makes you survive" (42). Zastrozzi divulges two secret nightmares, neither of which he fully understands. The first has to do with an anonymous vanquished innocent who tells Zastrozzi that he has discovered his weakness: "Misery loves chaos. And chaos loves company" (13). In the second nightmare he is leading the forces of good, and he is captured and executed by – Zastrozzi. He dies with the thought that he will be made a martyr. Both nightmares may be related to Victor's theory about Zastrozzi, that "he is to blame for his own mother's death in a crime of passion but hounds a poor lunatic because he cannot accept the blame himself" (59). In short, Zastrozzi is at bottom no superman but a mere man driven by human-all-too-human fears and cravings: fear of the chaos his mind apprehends, a related need for antagonists against whom he can assert himself (hence his sudden extension of clemency to Verezzi), a craving for redemption, and (if Victor is right) a fear that he is inadequate to such redemption if any system but his own prevails.

The one part of Zastrozzi's philosophy never quite resisted by the play that bears his name is his assertion of the inherent meaninglessness of life. On the contrary, it is precisely Victor's shared existential conviction that we each make our own meaning that makes him Zastrozzi's most formidable opponent. In his first encounter with Zastrozzi, Victor is asked if he left the priesthood "just to protect Verezzi." His evasive reply implies that a loss of faith may be involved (40). The possibility is raised again by Victor himself in a soliloquy, when he remarks on the absurdity that

> Zastrozzi steals, violates and murders on a regular basis. And remains perfectly sane. Verezzi commits one crime of passion then goes on a binge of mindless religious love and becomes moronic. Something is wrong. Something is unbalanced. I abhor violence. But I also abhor a lack of balance. It shows the truth is missing somewhere. And it makes me feel very, very uneasy. Uneasy in a way I have not felt since I was ... (59)

"... a priest wrestling with my faith," was he going to say? In any case, the only faith that sustains Victor in any certain way – until his last scene – is a faith in himself. The point is figuratively rendered in the climactic sword-fight. Against all odds, Victor's eccentric technique appears to be handily keeping Zastrozzi at bay: "Eventually I will find a way to penetrate your unorthodox style," says Zastrozzi. "That might be difficult," replies Victor, "since I am making it up as I go along" (65). As he approaches the duel, so Victor approaches life: shrewdly, pragmatically, self-sufficiently, but improvisatorially. Indeed, it looks possible that Victor might actually win the battle of swords and wits with Zastrozzi right up to the moment he declares: "I am the emissary of goodness in the battle between good and evil. I have found God again" (67). Zastrozzi kills him immediately. Victor's Achilles heel is his tendency to fall prey to what he has rationally decided is self-delusion. He can resist evil so long as he relies only on himself; but once he surrenders his moral autonomy by thinking himself an agent of God, he is doomed.

The point is connected to an earlier discussion of art between Victor and Verezzi. Victor maintains that the artist has a responsibility to convey truth, no matter how unattractive; Verezzi believes that it is more important that his "heart is in the right place" (16). Any such retreat into the glow of good feeling is dangerous, as Victor tries to convince Verezzi when the latter denies the existence of Zastrozzi: "You're getting worse daily. You're almost insensate. The danger is here and you can't appreciate it" (28). If there is no provident deity controlling the world – if, indeed, the world is meaningless – then for those like Verezzi it may be true that, as T.S. Eliot liked to say, "human kind cannot bear very much reality."[11] But in that case, it will be only resolutely inhuman monsters like Zastrozzi who face reality and hence control the world. The need revealed in *Zastrozzi* (a need that Victor almost, though not quite, fulfils) is to face up bravely to the prospect that humans are alone in the world without retreating into either self-delusion or self-aggrandizement. That, as the play implies, is an

296 The Buried Astrolabe

onerous task, all the more so in that, having seen the world in such a light, the conflict between evil and goodness does not become any more tractable. Hence neither Zastrozzi nor Verezzi is destroyed at the end of the play; their battle must remain open because the question remains open: given a realistic picture of the world and human nature, how may one navigate a passage between the Scylla and Charybdis of egoistic evil and self-deluded goodness?

Having probed the question of the battle between evil and goodness more deeply, if perhaps a little despairingly, Walker was ready to send Tyrone Power into the fray once again. Yet if Power was to see the dilemma in the terms described above, it would make little sense to assume that he would cheerfully shuck off his jaded state of mind to investigate Armageddon – hence the advanced state of cynical paralysis with which Power begins *Filthy Rich* (1979). Power has left the newspaper business and is holed up in his apartment, futilely attempting to write a novel while supporting himself with vapid articles for a travel magazine. In the first scene Jamie, a "smart-ass punk" delivery boy, brings Power a telegram announcing a relative's death. Apparently Power's relatives have been dropping like flies, which only serves to fuel his morose, drunken cynicism. Then he is visited by first one, then the second of two high-society sisters, Anne and Susan Scott, who try to coax him back to detective work to solve the disappearance of mayoral candidate Michael Harrison. A Detective Stackhouse shows, reiterating the Scott sisters' request.

The motives of the two sisters are unclear, as are their connections to a thug named Henry "the Pig" Duvall. The story they tell Power is that Michael Harrison had been given evidence of political corruption that compromised his millionaire father, James. Michael had been threatening to blow the whistle on his father in order to propel himself into office when his source, a political journalist and old friend of Power's named Whittacker, in turn suddenly began a blackmail scheme directed at the corrupt past of Michael Harrison himself.

Much prodding is necessary to get Power involved in the investigation: he resists like a mollusc being forced from its shell. When Whittacker is killed just as he enters Power's apartment bearing half a million dollars, Power's cynicism is merely exacerbated: he is sorely tempted to take the money and leave matters to the corrupt rich. However, it turns out that Whittacker intended to pass Harrison's money along to worthier mayoral candidates. So Power is pushed back into action by Jamie, the sardonic delivery boy, and together they work their way through a labyrinthine underplot and discover that Susan Scott and Pig Duvall murdered Whittacker. Stackhouse tries to persuade Power to remain quiet about the whole scandal in order to preserve Michael Harrison's candidacy, but in the end Power throws the half-million dollars out the window as he shouts to the people below: "Don't vote for Michael Harrison!"

Such is the plot of *Filthy Rich*; but the underlying ethos of the play is effectively summed up in a long speech by Stackhouse:

> It's a story about a bad smell. About a bunch of rich powerful people pushing and screwing each other and everyone else to get a whole lot more money that they don't really need in the first place. It's about the way the cities in this country were first formed. Through pay-offs and favours and double-plays and connections between a select handful who never let go and who can't be gotten rid of because they were in there from day one. So even when you get an honest man like my employer is, the best he can do is hold the compromise as close to the level of decency as possible. It's a matter of history. And there's no sense trying to be specific about what crimes we're talking about. Go backward. Go forward. Turn around. It's everywhere. In every department of the city's government. In every deal every contract every decision that's ever made. The same names always appear. The Harrisons. The Scotts. A few others. And now we have the Duvalls. Organized crime's gone respectable and we have dirty old money mixing in with the dirty new. So the only thing a man like the mayor can do is try to make sure that when something like this Harrison nonsense goes too far it doesn't ruin the city. That's all. We can't do more. We can't understand it because we can't talk details because we can't see the whole goddamn picture. It stinks. You're a citizen, it stinks for you. I'm a working cop and it stinks for me too.   (103)

The peculiar thing about Stackhouse's speech is that it gives a credible, serious rendering of a situation that is repeatedly made comic through the play. The speech so nearly approximates the Chandlerian style that it can hardly even be called parody. It is more like pastiche: the Chandlerian style seems to be embraced rather than mocked.

Any ironic humour in this scene has more to do with our sense of Stackhouse's listener, Power, than with anything said. We can hardly doubt that the city is every bit as corrupt as Stackhouse suggests; the play confirms this much. Moreover, Stackhouse is already speaking in a mode of dark irony, so it is not as though he embodies some preposterous type of moral earnestness easily susceptible to mockery. But because Power is even more cynical than Stackhouse, there is an additional ironic context that shows up the speech as a cliché: Stackhouse's cynicism is made ironic by Power's even worse cynicism. We are not quite at the level of irony we would be brought to if the listener were, say, Groucho Marx, but there is nevertheless an unmistakable ironic relativism framing the scene. The ironic outstripping of Stackhouse's cynicism lies in Power's nihilism, which the events of the play only prompt him to reaffirm:

> Nothing makes sense. Just like I always knew it wouldn't. Innocent people are getting killed because of other innocent people. Politicians are being assassinated by their fathers. Policemen are trying to prevent crimes only because they don't want to prosecute the people who commit them. And beautiful, intelligent young women are falling in love with the scum of the earth. (119)

Clearly, the difference between Power's speech and Stackhouse's is merely one of degree. Where Stackhouse evinces disgust at the sordid inadequacy of the city as measured against his implicit moral expectations, Power evinces helpless dismay that the sordidness has fully met all his worst expectations.

To put the point another way, the difference lies in the scope of action these two characters implicitly claim for themselves. Stackhouse's hope is a modest one: to "sort of balance the books in a way" (104). He is in this sense a little like Victor in *Zastrozzi*, who confesses that he "abhor[s] a lack of balance" and hopes "to restore truth to [the] lunatic world" (59). But it seems as though Power has – as David Bolt, the actor playing him, had indeed – already been through Victor's modest ambitions and been disillusioned. At the outset he declares that for him, "cases like this are always loaded with metaphysical angst. Or even worse. Existential nausea. Face to face with your own terrible limitations. Your own stupidity. Or loss of faith" (98). The events of the play bear him out. In only a narrow sense does Power solve the crime, for his solution demonstrates the moral insolubility of societal corruption.

So, if Power is so beset with cynical misgivings, why exactly does he overcome these to engage once again in the struggle against evil? That is one of the chief dramatic pleasures we find in *Filthy Rich*: watching Power's Faustian struggle with his better and worse selves, unsure of which is which. Before the possibility of a new case even arises, we see Power in a quarrel with himself:

> What's wrong with my mind. It's drunk. Shut up, Power. Well it is drunk. Shut up, Power. You're self destructing. [...] Ignore him Power. Self-destruction is good for you. It makes your usual state of obscene neutrality seem almost euphoric. Oh please do shut up Power. (76–7)

Jamie speculates that Power's condition is endemic to his reluctant vocation:

JAMIE: All good private eyes are disgusting drunks. It has something to do with self-hatred conflicting with high moral standards of a rigid upbringing or something. They all suffer from it.
ANNE: Perhaps they're all Presbyterians.   (88)

We know nothing, alas, of Mrs Power's religious persuasion, but it does appear, according to the telegrams from home intercepted by Jamie, that Power's mother continues to exert some sort of moral influence on her son. Not only has she stuck him with his romantic name, Tyrone; she apparently makes her expectations of him regularly felt. One of the points of leverage Jamie uses is Power's lie to his mother that he is a private eye (83), enabling Jamie to say, in persuading Power to take the case, "it's your chance, besides making a lot of money, to make your mother very proud of you" (94). Evidently, the side of Power that remains something of a soft-boiled mama's boy is sufficient to pull him back to an almost Stackhousian level of vague optimism and moral earnestness – at least, for long enough to solve the case.

The significance of Power's conflicted character extends well beyond the scope of a mere personal struggle with a superego. In *Postmodernism; or, The Cultural Logic of Late Capitalism* (1991) Frederic Jameson argues that the schizoid personality offers the best figurative characterization of the state of contemporary culture (25ff). Now, in the present context, even if it is understood that in speaking of virtual schizophrenia we do not use the term in a proper clinical sense, we should still avoid the popular misconception of identifying schizophrenia with the phenomenon of the "split personality." Rather, the central characteristic of schizophrenia *per se* is the loss of the ability to order past and future, signifier and signified, into coherent experience.

In a way, that inability characterizes the underlying problem Power faces: not merely the fact of political corruption but, again, the apparent depthlessness of the personalities he encounters. Just as there is no reliable correlation between a social position (e.g., politician) and behaviour, so there is no necessary connection between the apparent character of someone like Susan and her subsequent actions, or between a stereotypical thug like Pig Duvall and the social role he plays. To be sure, these sorts of discontinuities were explored by Chandler, but to a different degree. Power's own personality is disintegrating as he operates in a society where discontinuities of identity, meaning, and morality have reached such a degree of chaos that assuming a balanced and coherent attitude towards it – such as that represented by Stackhouse – is nearly impossible. His anxious, slightly hysterical personality springs from the conflict between, on the one hand, his residual impulse to insist that such coherence must be achievable and, on the other, his despairing conviction that it is impossible.

Walker's next play, *Rumours of Our Death* (1980), examines some of the factors that cause the kind of helpless, cynical paralysis with which Power began *Filthy Rich*, though the focus has shifted from the crisis and response of one individual to the malaise affecting an entire society. The original production was a rock musical, though the songs were inessential to the play's basic form, which is described by the subtitle, *A Parable in 25 Scenes*. Certainly, the style suggests a partial return to earlier "parables" like *Bagdad Saloon* and *Beyond Mozambique*; but it is also comparable to Edward Bond's quasi-Brechtian "parables," such as *Early Morning*.

The referents of this parable are the circumstances of the Cold War. A nameless country is threatened with imminent war – according to the irrational though good-humoured King. The King is suspected of being a machine rather than a human being. He constantly declares arbitrary laws and depends heavily on the visions of his wife, the Queen, Maria I. Meanwhile, the people – represented by Raymond, a novelist, and Maria III, who runs a café, as well as a Farmer and his Son – subsist on rumours about what is in store for the country. Many of the rumours concern the different sorts of bombs threatening them: a bomb that "only kills machines" (110), one that kills only children under the age of twelve (113), one that evaporates water (119), and one that causes people to disappear into another dimension (124). A revolution is rumoured to be occurring, although it is in the hands of foreigners. Irresistible foreigners are also rumoured to be buying up most of the country. Meanwhile, the Princess, Maria II, is kidnapped by terrorists who demand an exorbitant ransom, which the King expects the people to pay. As it turns out, however, Maria II joins the terrorists herself, like Patty Hearst, so her ransom fund is turned into an arts endowment fund, to which the terrorists apply for grants to fund the revolution. The Farmer suddenly dies, though he continues to walk about aimlessly, becoming a folk hero whom the people look to for leadership. Raymond, having briefly led a monarchist counter-revolution, returns with an arm and an eye missing. Later he gives up his personal struggle and decides to live vicariously, attaching himself (literally) to the Farmer's Son. The two of them henceforth act as a single entity. Raymond/Son then joins all the other aimless people, including the recently dead but still mobile Maria III, who are waiting in the countryside for some direction. Eventually, the King hands over his throne to the foreigner and, having died during his search for his father, joins his people in the café, where together they all wait, enervated, for something to happen. The rumour is that it will be a new bomb. What that bomb does, "no one wants to know."

The humorous, fantastic overlay cannot obscure the inherent grimness of this work. Walker is exploring the demoralizing, creeping apathy that is the consequence of a perpetual threat of imminent annihilation from a source of which one has little certain knowledge and over which no real control. As in Orwell's *1984*, public complacency is secured in part through dictatorship, in part by maintaining a constant threat of war, and in part by tossing out bones of illusory social reforms to maintain the appearance of social progress (e.g., 109). The people submissively accept the revocation of all civil liberties (54) with only the slightest of grumbles, their collective will sapped by constant anxiety about the bomb and by their resigned inability to see the truth behind all the official propaganda.

In a way, the problem is even worse than the conspiratorial bureaucracy imagined by Orwell. O'Brien, the executive party member in *1984*, could still explain the basic nature of Oceania to Winston; but in *Rumours of Our Death* the disjunction between propaganda, rumour, and truth has grown so absolute that no one, not even the King, knows what is going on. However insidious and illusory it may have been, the image of *1984*'s Big Brother at least reassured those who craved security at any cost: Big Brother was an apparent still point of authority in a world threatened with dissolution on all sides. The world imagined by Walker, however, just whirls helplessly into a state of chaos:

> MARIA III: A rumour has it that a space ship came for [the King]. Took him away. Things were getting out of hand so they removed him.
> RAYMOND: In the most ridiculous rumours often lie[s] a grain of truth. He does seem to have vanished.
> MARIA III: Then who is in charge? Who has the power?
> RAYMOND: The foreign revolutionaries I suppose.
> MARIA III: Where are they?
> RAYMOND: I don't know.
> MARIA III: What do they look like?
> RAYMOND: I don't know. This is intolerable. Why doesn't someone do something?
> MARIA III: This is frightening.
> RAYMOND: Someone must do something. (115)

Clearly these anxieties have to do with more than a mere lack of leadership. There is a general sense of helplessness in which rumours about their leader's absence, fear of the bomb, and the absurd alien threat of the foreign revolutionaries have all combined to suggest a set of powers not only godlike in their ubiquity and omnipotence but hopelessly unpropitiable, because they are inaccessible and finally unverifiable.

Neither can there be any deliverance from the sense of helplessness in the simple stratagem of ignoring the rumours. Raymond's philosophy, "to disregard all rumours except those which can be used for a good laugh" (62), might be fine for the short run, but the release of ironic laughter is only effective when one is being released back to a comfortable sense of reality. In this world any such context has dissolved, as each of the characters in turn eventually recognizes. Personal agency is nullified because there can be no coherent course of action where there is no apprehensible context to give meaning to any particular act. Consequently, the dissociation of act and context, of word and meaning has created a condition of mass virtual schizophrenia. As Jean Baudrillard argues, where capitalism and mass communications have created a world in which property and information are seen as simulations without any material referents, the real nuclear event may have already taken place.

Such a disturbing and serious problem might seem to demand a commensurate seriousness in the artistic treatment. But Walker is by no means alone in addressing such a subject by means of grotesque comedy. A seminal discussion of the concept is Friedrich Dürrenmatt's 1955 essay "Anmerkung zur Komödie" (Notes on Comedy), where he suggests that, to come to terms with a world overshadowed by the horror of atomic weaponry, tragedy is a wholly inappropriate genre. The only suitable artistic response is to embrace the grotesque, which, Dürrenmatt argues, is not the work of nihilists but of moralists (25). Dürrenmatt's essay could easily serve as a manifesto for many of the post–Second World War playwrights: indeed, it would seem to describe the "theatre of the absurd" that provided Walker's earliest inspiration. With his next play, *Theatre of the Film Noir*, Walker returned to the setting from which that movement sprang: Paris, at the end of the Second World War.

Denis Johnston's suggestion that "*Theatre of the Film Noir* is almost a rewrite of *Ramona and the White Slaves*" ("George," 197) may overstate the case somewhat, but it is true enough that there are a number of resemblances. As with *Ramona*, the play has a post-war setting – this time in the liberated Paris of 1944 – and once again the figurative use of an exotic location allows Walker to explore extreme social and moral degeneracy.

Inspector Clair is investigating the murder of a handsome young man, Jean, whose political background was dubious: he is said to have fought with the Resistance, but the Communists are suspected in his murder. When Clair questions Jean's sister, Lilliane, she is evasive. We find out why through Bernard, Jean's former lover, who now skulks in the graveyard, doting necrophilially over Jean's disinterred body: Lilliane has been hiding a German lover, Eric, in her apartment. Jean knew of the relationship; hence both Eric and Lilliane are suspects in Jean's murder. Bernard threatens to expose them unless Lilliane marries him so that he can conceal his homosexuality. Meanwhile, Lilliane acquires a new lover, Hank, an American soldier, who offers better security than Eric now that the tide of the war has turned. In the denouement Eric discloses that he was also Jean's lover, and in a sadistic-sexual moment, while Eric points his gun at the head of Bernard, who is fellating him, Bernard nudges the gun aside and Eric fatally shoots himself. Lilliane arrives with Hank, who tries to murder Bernard, but Bernard kills Hank instead. When Lilliane leaves, Inspector Clair arrives and kills Bernard. He then tells Lilliane that Bernard murdered her brother, although in soliloquy he confesses to have no basis for that conclusion. Nevertheless, Clair says:

> Bernard had to die. He was just a part of what we have become. But it was the saddest and most unpredictable part. Where would he go. How would he live. How could the rest of us survive and prosper with him out on the streets making other people sad and unpredictable too. (48/*SA* 159)

When the play ends, then, the only survivors are Inspector Clair and Lilliane, whom Clair sets up with a film company, telling her to "just be yourself" (47/*SA* 158). In his epilogue he tells us that "Lilliane will go on to become one of this country's most successful film actresses," whereas he will be stuck with a perpetual film of Bernard running inside his head (48/*SA* 159).

Because *Theatre of the Film Noir* is, like the Power plays, a black comic detective mystery, it might seem natural to look for comparisons between Inspector Clair and Tyrone Power. But Clair's description of the immoral quagmire he must investigate marks him as a very different man:

> Behaviour has no recognizable pattern. Morality is a question of circumstance. And guilt a matter of degree. For a police detective like myself this is not an easy time. I am used to a precise definition of my job. I am used to a pattern of behaviour, a clear consensus of morality and a belief in absolute guilt. (1/*SA* 115)

Obviously, Clair bears a much closer resemblance to Stackhouse than Power; though, by the time we come to Clair's rationale for murdering

Bernard, his ruthless reaction to the sense of ethical vertigo recalls a more sinister precursor: Lance, the mountie in *Beyond Mozambique*. Herein lies one of the main differences between *Theatre of the Film Noir* and the Power plays. Where the keynote for the latter was set by the attitude of the chief investigator – that is, by Tyrone Power's heavily ironic perspective on the situation – the centre of gravity in *Theatre of the Film Noir* falls to the similarly ironic Bernard (played, again, by David Bolt), notwithstanding his merely contingent power to control events and his only marginal sanity. As Bernard himself declares, having been told that he is disgusting, "I am the moral conscience of the day" (14/*SA* 127). Bernard's character is analogous to the ethos of post-Vichy Paris. Walker's choice of this period as a dramatic setting is clearly based in the moral uncertainty and compromise endemic to any society as it switches allegiances between warring powers. As Michael Cook intimates in *Colour the Flesh the Colour of Dust*, the desperation to maintain survival or achieve comfort in such circumstances begets so much vicious opportunism and panicked scrambling for footholds amidst the shifting power structures that almost everyone living in such a community is morally compromised to some degree.

However, Bernard has not relinquished his moral sense altogether. He is, rather, a moral relativist:

> LILLIANE: You're vermin. The biggest coward in Europe. Pissing in a private hole since the war began. Protecting your own skin and nothing more. Save your disgust for yourself. You have no right to judge me.
> BERNARD: Certainly true. However it's the ideal that's important. Realistically I'm a self-serving mouse but ideally I am an enemy of fascism and a supporter of freedom. We are in a temporary state of peace. In times of peace self-serving idealists surface and do well. (12/*SA* 125)

Moreover, Bernard continues to honour an ideal that transcends mere self-interest. His obsession with the death of Jean is based in his distress at the destruction of an aesthetic ideal. For Bernard, Jean's physical beauty and sexuality – indeed, Jean's very perversity – achieved a perfect purity of the sort celebrated by Jean Genet in *Funeral Rites* – a clear source for this play. In this, Bernard complements Inspector Clair. While Clair, as his name emphasizes, is attempting to re-establish moral clarity, regardless of the cost, Bernard is preoccupied with avenging the murder of the aesthetic perfection that Jean represented. When moral clarity becomes an end sought through indiscriminate means, it is effectively an aesthetic rather than an ethical preference; thus, Bernard's sybaritism and Clair's fastidiousness are two sides of the same coin.

Taken as a whole, however, the play suggests that it is Bernard who is on surer ground, simply because sustaining Clair's hope for an earthly order corresponding to a transcendent moral idealism requires a program of deliberate deception (of oneself and others). Clair suggests that "what you cannot make clear, you should at least make complete" (48/*SA* 159), thus declaring a puritanical preference for the illusion of justice even at the cost of committing deliberate injustice. Bernard, however, is by philosophic descent another of Walker's Nietzschean existentialists (by way of Genet). He uses his two-headed coin to buttress his own wishes, because in his view providence is a void into which one projects one's own will. There being no power greater than personal will, and self-interest being the only real motive for action, the good and the beautiful are self-defined in terms of one's own desires. It is for Jean's sublime self-interest as much as his physical beauty that Bernard promotes him into a kind of religious ideal.

Bernard's perspicacity about the devotion to self-interest prevalent in this world is inseparable from his strong sense of irony; but (ironically) it seems that his own selfishness is somewhat blunted by his self-consciousness, his ability to see ironically how his own behaviour relates to the interests of others. It proves to be Lilliane, the character with the most heightened instinct for self-interest and the least sense of irony, who emerges most successfully in the end. She is very much her brother's sister, magnetically attracting devotion and using anyone whose path she crosses for whatever she can get. That she goes on to become an immensely successful film star implies that what Lilliane represents to the others is ultimately extended, via popular culture, to envelop Western culture. The worship of Lilliane's enigmatic, self-interested beauty (attributes of the classic *femme fatale*), along with the ethical vortex that surrounds her, is expanded via mass media to exert a pull on all of us.

The references to Hollywood films underscore how, with its post-Vichy Paris setting, *Theatre of the Film Noir* looks back to a historical provenance of the *noir* ethos underlying the first two Power plays, for Hollywood noir films owed something of their sophisticated veneer to war-weary cynicism. In his next play, *Science and Madness* (September 1982), Walker looked back to the beginning of the modern age to explore the origins of "rational madness" – the fetishization of instrumental reason and scientific progress that led to the nuclear-weapon-haunted context behind *Rumours of Our Death* and the next Power play, *The Art of War*. For *Science and Madness* Walker chose the same turn-of-the-century, gothic, Scottish setting that Ann-Marie MacDonald would later use for her clever critique of Darwinist thought in *The*

Arab's Mouth (1991). The appeal of this setting for both playwrights evidently has something to do with its gothic fecundity: inherent in turn-of-the-century Scotland is the notion of a residual, slightly barbaric pre-modern culture being invested with a current of dangerous modern thought.

Science and Madness begins with a nightmare in which Doctor Benjamin Heywood confronts a shrouded patient whom he has been unable to cure. Indeed, his operations have been disastrous, but, at the patient's insistence, he continues working, now outside the realm of established scientific knowledge. By the end of the play, Heywood recognizes that he himself is this bandaged patient he speaks to in his dreams. Meanwhile, in reality, Heywood is visited by his sister Lillianne, who balances his scientism by being herself a poet.[12] She discovers that, together with his technician, the mysterious Medeiros, her brother is performing a kind of vivisectionist experiment on the brain of a local idiot, Freddy, which increases his intelligence while making him homicidal. She also discovers that Medeiros has mesmerizing powers with which he is controlling Freddy and heavily influencing Heywood. In her confusion over how to combat the kind of rational evil in which her brother is engaged, Lillianne slips into a kind of religious fanaticism. She enlists the aid of a local girl, Mary, to try to seduce her brother back to innocence. She herself sets out to seduce Medeiros, but succeeds only in turning herself into a whore. Mary, revealing that Freddy is her missing brother, determines to avenge herself on Medeiros, whom she believes is the Devil. But before Mary can confront Medeiros, Lillianne, having slept with Freddy, talks him into killing her. At this, Heywood, seemingly more in compassion than in revenge, kills Freddy, then destroys his laboratory and sets himself and it on fire. Mary confronts Medeiros, trying to terrify him with a supernaturally invoked apocalyptic fire, but he merely laughs. As the play ends, the hideously burned Heywood comes to Medeiros in the guise of the patient, begging for help. "Sure," replies Medeiros.

Science and Madness invites comparison with two of Walker's previous plays. Most immediately apparent are the similarities between *Science and Madness* and *Beyond Mozambique*: Heywood, like Rocco, is a scientist in a remote place, experimenting upon human beings; Freddy is, like Tomas, a violent, animalistic servant who has undergone brain operations; and Lilliane, like LiDuc, serves as a weak representative of religious authority. Less obvious, perhaps, is the play's relation to *Zastrozzi*, where the relevant aspects are the time-setting (the threshold of the twentieth century) and the similar characters of Zastrozzi and Medeiros, each of whom embodies a kind of superhuman demonic energy.

To an extent, the reuse of those elements in *Science and Madness* indicates a melding of the themes of the earlier plays into a new dramatic form. In *Beyond Mozambique* Rocco's experimentation was a last-ditch attempt to assert a personally willed order (it hardly mattered what kind) in the face of imminent apocalypse. In *Zastrozzi* Victor's intervention in the struggle between the wilful innocence of Verezzi and the wilful rational evil of Zastrozzi probed the question of what the viable nature of modern man would be. *Science and Madness* asks what the nature of humanity will be as an old world order collapses and the pre-eminent force determining ethics in the emergent new order is increasingly based in the scientific rationality Medeiros represents. As Heywood says just prior to immolating himself (anticipating the epigraph to this chapter): "I don't like the future! I've seen it. It's him. He's the new man. Intrepid. And cruel. And seductive. No I don't like the future at all!" (51) Meanwhile, Freddy shows what the human product of this trend could be: man made vicious and unconscionable as the aggression begotten by instrumental reason takes hold.

Heywood resembles Faust in his overreaching scientific aspirations and troublesome conscience. Compassion and humility forgotten, his humanity (and, by implication, humanity itself) is endangered. Medeiros plays Mephistopheles, and as he points out, it is not he who brings about the chaos; the others, especially Heywood, are responsible. All Medeiros really does is draw out the scientist's latent hubris, urging him to join

the world of godless imagination. Where the scientist is the real poet. The pragmatic visionary, who discovers the function of things and then makes them function. You can come into this world and still have your intuition, your emotions, all your senses. But they will be better. They won't be tugging at you from the past. They will be drawing you into the future. They will be godless. And they will have real power.   (32)

In this lies the chief difference between Zastrozzi and Medeiros. Whereas Zastrozzi found the end for his evil actions in himself, in the satisfaction of pursuing revenge, Medeiros is devoted to evil for its own sake, believing that "revenge is for people with plenty of spare time" (27). So, while the chief trait of Medeiros is a monumental assertion of will and personality akin to Zastrozzi's, his ultimate ambition is of much greater scope: to remake the future world in the image of himself. Zastrozzi, being merely human, found that he needed an adversary to continue enjoying the assertion of his will. Medeiros, being inhuman, a veritable personification of abstract evil, finds contentment only in the notion that everything that is not him should be eliminated, a goal he has pretty much achieved by the end:

> All gone. The weak. The self-doubting. The possessed. The frightened.
> The superstitious. The sentimental. All dead and gone. Except me ...
> Because I am the reasonable man. (53)

On that cue, the disfigured Heywood stumbles in, begging for help, which Medeiros grants. Of course, the only help Medeiros could offer would be to assist Heywood in extirpating the last vestiges of his conscience, so that he might be a "reasonable man" in the new uncompassionate, self-assured, and unflinching rational order. Thus the victory of Medeiros is related to the rational, scientific madness overshadowing *Rumours of Our Death*.

As for the various alternatives to rational evil shown in the play, Walker, however regretfully, unsentimentally sends them to their defeat. Lilliane's embrace of religious fanaticism is an act of reckless irrationality that merely leaves her more susceptible to the evil represented by Medeiros. And while at first the hope is raised that Mary's powerful, romantic humanism will be commensurate to Medeiros's powers, in the end she too is defeated – more, it would seem, through her own efforts than by the power she is resisting:

> MEDEIROS: This is your storm isn't it girl. You brought it on. Slowly.
> Deliberately.
> MARY: Full of purpose. Gathering strength.
> MEDEIROS: Purpose? Revenge. All this crackling energy. Just for revenge.
> MARY: And because you're evil. You destroy things.
> MEDEIROS: You're responsible for the destruction here. Your storm scared
> these people into senselessness. But of course senselessness is your entire
> world, isn't it. (52)

Medeiros is hardly what we would think of as trustworthy, yet it is true that Mary seems to have done far more to bring about this Armageddon than he. Rational madness may threaten massive destruction, but embracing pre-enlightenment irrationality makes a poor alternative. The real solution probably lay with Heywood, back when he might have resisted his own scientific hubris. The idea that a solution might have been contrived through a later act of violence is untenable. As in *Zastrozzi*, where Victor could not bring himself to kill Zastrozzi when first given the chance, Heywood, having repudiated ruthless scientism, finds that his liberal humanism leaves him morally incapable of killing Medeiros when urged to by Mary. Instead he destroys himself.

A similar problem of confrontation is explored by Walker in the last of the Power plays, *The Art of War*. Here the scale of the evil Power confronts has been promoted to its logical extremity: a fascistic, militaristic plot to control the world – the contemporary, worldly counterpart to the demonic ambitions of Medeiros. As if he were impatient to get the question of Power's motivation (so gradually and reluctantly established in *Filthy Rich*) out of the way as soon as possible, Walker simply reprises the earlier play's motivation by beginning *The Art of War* with the murder of another old journalist friend, Paul Reinhardt. Even the element of mystery has lost its appeal for Walker; the murderers are identified right away. They are Hackman, a "retired" general who is now adviser to the Minister of Culture, and his loyal goon, Brownie Brown, an ex-commando with a troublesome head injury and a propensity for violence.

Hackman and Brown, along with Karla Mendez, the daughter of a fascist leader imprisoned in South America, are engaged in a vague international conspiracy involving illegal arms trading. Power is again teamed up with Jamie, who is working undercover as Hackman's gardener. They are joined by Heather Masterson (another daughter of a rich man), a mutual friend of Power and the late Reinhardt. Heather's character contributes little to the plot; she is present, it would seem, chiefly for reasons of maintaining the moral symmetry of the play: villain, henchman, and femme fatale versus hero, helper, and innocent heroine – a reprise of the melodramatic framework of *Zastrozzi*. Power and Jamie attempt the improbable task of thwarting Hackman and bringing him to justice, but their efforts are farcically inept. The play moves inevitably towards a confrontation between Power and Hackman, but when Power ends up with Hackman at his mercy, he finds himself incapable of killing. As the play closes, Power has been shot in the shoulder and Jamie badly beaten, while the three villains, having escaped scot-free, stand at the top of a cliff, waving down gleefully at our outmanoeuvred heroes.

The Art of War was commissioned to serve as the keynote address to a conference on Art and Reality at Simon Fraser University in August 1982. The play bears marks of its origins, though predictably, Walker's chief interest has little to do with any mimetic aspects of the conference's theme. Instead he focuses on the questions of what art's relation to a *realistic attitude* towards the world might be, and indeed, of what ideas a "realistic attitude" would comprise. Walker's touchstone for these issues is the idea of war, not only because it represents the most brutal of all the realities art might be expected to accommodate but also because it has historically provided the central test of how prepared one is to sacrifice ideals and morals to a "realistic attitude" towards the problems of civilization.

The probing begins with the punning title, *The Art of War*. Whether or not the title is taken, as Denis Johnston suggests, from Brecht's *The Messingkauf Dialogues* (204), it implies several meanings. The phrase can be construed, in the tradition of the works of that title by Sun Tzu or Machiavelli, as a meditation on the craft of waging politically expedient and materially effective warfare. Alternatively, the phrase can be read as alluding to the sort of creative art appropriate to an environment overshadowed by war, or the threat of war. A third possibility lies somewhere between the first two: the phrase could describe art that itself makes a kind of war, in the sense of "guerrilla theatre".

There is a depressing air of futility inherent in these ideas as a group; war as art may be answered by war art, or perhaps art as war, but always there is that initial obscenity waiting: war considered an art. Walker refuses any façile release from this vicious circle. For example, in having a warmonger like Hackman made deputy minister of culture, there is enough improbability to make the notion humorous; but it is not so far out of line with the familiar vein of political philistinism that the satiric edge does not bite. Moreover, the conceit keeps the ideas of art and war in close proximity and the stakes invested in their relation apprehensible throughout the play. Accordingly, a comment like Hackman's telling Brown that his killing has "an artistic touch" (137), or his sharing of ruminations on the nature of art with Brown and Karla, returns us to the uneasy notions raised by the title. As a dramatic trope, Hackman's new job is a synecdoche for a larger problem; one approach to civilization, warmongering, is hidden behind another, culture. The underlying question, then, is whether we finally accept that artistic culture is only a veneer disguising the real destiny of humankind: to obliterate ourselves with our power struggles.

The question is put into related terms in a debate that takes place early in the play, when Power challenges the truth of Hackman's putative new "passion" for culture:

POWER: ... Men like you have room for only one passion in their lives. And yours is not art and culture.
HACKMAN: What is it then.
POWER: Oh God. Well let's simplify it. Let's call it the communist menace.
HACKMAN: [*groans*] And you don't believe in the communist menace.
POWER: Actually I do. The communist menace. And the fascist menace. The menace of the church. The menace of channelled information. The menace of ignorance. The menace of indifference. The menace of war. I'm a sort of menace specialist.
HACKMAN: No. You're just a liberal.
POWER: What's that supposed to mean.

HACKMAN: You think the human race is going on a journey. To peace and enlightenment. And that it's a journey everyone has the ability and the right to make.

POWER: And you don't.

HACKMAN: Let's just say that I don't insist upon it. And another thing. You probably have an unholy fear of something which I take more or less for granted.

POWER: What.

HACKMAN: The vast darkness. [...]

POWER: The vast darkness. The existential version?

HACKMAN: No, let's simplify it. Let's call it war. The new war. The inevitable destruction of everything. Life-ending war. But even without war, it ends. Everything we build now will be ruins in, what, a thousand years, anyway. [...] War is a way of taking temporary control, that's all. Try thinking about war that way and it won't scare you so much.   (148)

In this confrontation lies Walker's most troubling meditation on the theme of art and reality. Any number of dramatic approaches to these ideas might have been taken, but Walker chose the vehicle of Tyrone Power. Evidently he intended to confront the vestiges of optimism inherent in the detective-story genre with the cold, penetrating light of harsh reality. The play moves relentlessly towards its final anticlimax. It is difficult to escape the feeling that Walker was determined from the outset that this time out his erstwhile hero would suffer not merely a hollow victory but a real failure.

Denis Johnston implies that Walker had become disenchanted with the attitude Power represents, observing that "the audience is not invited to identify with Power in *The Art of War* as they were in the previous two plays" (202) and that the Power trilogy shows "the progressive seediness of the fruits of liberal idealism" (201). Certainly, Power is in a situation where the enormity of the threat to him will inevitably expose the inherent inadequacy of his approach. Part of the inadequacy has to do with what Johnston calls "the intrinsic weakness of the liberal position," that Power and Jamie "are honour-bound (instinctively) to play by humanitarian rules which the other side despises" (203). This difficulty is responsible for the paralysed stalemate in which the play ends. As Power stands pointing a gun at Hackman and Karla, catastrophically hesitating, Hackman surmises what Power is thinking about:

HACKMAN: The sanctity of life, probably. The moral implications of taking action. The pros. The cons. The pros. The cons. Ad infinitum ... Perhaps you should try getting mad, Mr. Power.

POWER: I am.

HACKMAN: No. You're indignant. You're outraged. You just don't understand, do you. Anger is a weapon. Allowing you to be brutal. Brutality is
another weapon. Allowing you to take action. In this way, you build your
arsenal. Until you have the ultimate weapon. Immorality. Which allows
you to take any action in any way at any time. Immorality is a great
weapon. And you don't have it.   (182)

All Power really has by way of weaponry is his armoured sense of
cynical, ironic detachment; but cynical sneering finally looks puerile as
a response to evil. However much we agree with the substance of what
Power says, we wince a little to hear him snarl at Hackman, "any
asshole can get the trains running on time!! Any asshole can do that,
but it takes something more to get the people on the trains for any
reason other than the fact that they're scared shitless of the asshole"
(171). The irony may be true enough: cynically forcing a society to
move in preordained directions generally paralyses any real growth of
civilization. All the same, as we saw in *Filthy Rich*, Power's own cynicism is such that he has difficulty coming up with reasons to leave his
apartment, let alone reasons for humanity to board trains and keep civilization (figuratively) moving. A disorganized soul cannot be expected
to impose any coherent, lasting order on the world, and by itself irony
finally leads only to inaction.

The question that naturally follows is: what would a more constructive response to such circumstances look like? This is an immensely complicated issue, because it draws on the whole scope of ethical and cosmological issues touched on by Walker's plays to this point.
Approaching any sort of answer involves passing through a series of
further philosophical questions, questions that Walker considers
obliquely in his subsequent plays. But in the meantime we can at least
answer the question on a literal level. Had Power been able to provide a
truly constructive solution to the problems raised in the play, *The Art of
War* would have looked more like comedy than irony.[13] One of the con-
stitutive features that differentiates comedy from irony is that comedy
usually ends with the foundation of a new society. This "new" society is
generally a redeemed version of an older society; it forms around the
hero and heroine of comedy once they have prevailed over the "alazon,"
the character who blocks the flow of vitality a healthy society requires.
Now, the prospect of a new society forming around an *eiron* such as
Walker's Tyrone Power is slim, to say the least. Power's cynicism can
only frustrate the progress of evil: it is not, in itself, a creative force.

Why this should be so and why Walker should be so preoccupied
with this problem are questions that can be answered, in part, by Peter

Sloterdijk's monumental 1980 study, *Critique of Cynical Reason*. Sloterdijk defines cynicism, in the widespread social form in which we experience it today, as "enlightened false consciousness." The term "false consciousness" is associated with Marxism. It refers to people's belief that their actions are freely chosen when all the while their environments are so totally pervaded by cultural, racial, or economic forces that they are as incapable of seeing how their behaviour is predetermined as a fish would be of describing water. With no opportunity to stand apart from one's environment, there is no possibility of objectively analysing it. Hence, any sense of consciousness about social issues in these circumstances is false. Now Marxism, among other ideologies (Marxism is more exemplary than critical to the argument), purports to provide an objectivity that enlightens such consciousness, which would seem to entail a negation of the "false" part of the phrase. However, Sloterdijk contends that such enlightenment normally removes the individual mind far enough from its habitual environment for the problem to be recognized, and no further. At this point, cynicism of the kind we see in Tyrone Power sets in.

Sloterdijk discusses many difficulties with moving beyond this state into something more productive, but for our purposes – contextualizing the difficulty Walker had in creating a more positive character than Power – a simplified version will do. Individual enlightenment does not in itself change the nature of civilization or, indeed, any of those determinants that seem to have the force of destiny. Hence, many would-be enlighteners have little faith that they can alter the conditions of their own lives through reason, let alone prevail against the overwhelming intransigence of a whole society dominated by false consciousness. Moreover, while ideologies such as Marxism (or indeed any other "ism") may purport to recognize the problem, the programs of reform they propound have proved disappointingly ineffective in practice – even disastrous. So would-be enlighteners tend to slip into a state of paralysis like Power's, adopting a mode of cynicism that, at its crudest level, merely sneers at authority and scoffs at the naïveté of those who prescribe social remedies. A higher level of this syndrome is the attitude exemplified by Michel Foucault, who argues that personal identity is merely a tissue of determinants and codes; the best efforts can do no more than recognize and label those determinants and codes, perhaps rearranging but never actually transcending them.

Thus what lay for Walker beyond the Power plays was an idea he first raised in *The Prince of Naples*: the Nietzschean observation that there is no truth outside of a given structure of power. Yet so long as observing truth's subordination to power entails only recognition of humanity's flaws, and no hope of reform, only ironic endings like those of the Power plays are possible. For the notion that "knowledge is power" is shared by Walker's smiling villains and his fumbling heroes, and while it is only the ruthlessly immoral who exploit the insight, it begets a cynicism that sets the Hackmans and Powers, the Zastrozzis and Victors, apart from others. In *The Art of War* Walker demonstrates this shared cynicism through the artistic theories propounded by the two adversaries. Hackman declares that "art is the leisurely reflection of an elite society" (162) and that "the best art is the art of superficial spectacle which demonstrates the beauty of art for art's sake" (177). Power might spit on the latter part of Hackman's philosophy, but at bottom he is not so far off in his beliefs. According to Jamie:

> Power hates art. He thinks it's "the leisurely reflection of a dying society." Those are his words, not mine. It just twists and turns, this thing between him and Hackman. And it's growing. I'm beginning to feel it myself. It would be funny if Hackman really did care about culture, you know, the fascist who cares about culture. And Power wants to destroy him.   (159)

As Jamie sees, although Hackman is a bad man and Power is not, there is not much to choose between their respective cynicisms, the one opportunistic ("the leisurely reflection of an elite society"), the other nihilistic ("the leisurely reflection of a dying society"). In a field so entirely defined by cynicism, the only possible ending is ironic. Walker's earlier plays had already demonstrated this, so it may be that with *The Art of War* he set out to have Power fail and to show the inadequacy of his hero's attitude. In any case, the last words of the play, spoken by Power, might be Walker's own *cri de coeur*: "I'm tired of losing. It's so ... depressing" (184). In his next plays Walker began to investigate the possibility of a program for winning.

CLOSER TO THE BONE: THE POSTMODERN CITY COMEDIES

In 1959, a few years after making his remarks about the suitability of the comic grotesque for the atomic age, Friedrich Dürrenmatt was awarded the Schiller Prize. In his acceptance speech he returned to the question of what sort of dramaturgy suited the contemporary political world. Looking to the shift in Schiller's own work, from early angry rebelliousness to later abstract classicism, Dürrenmatt asks:

Doesn't the realization that the world is in bad shape presuppose an insight into the way the world ought to be, and doesn't it also morally require some indication as to the way in which the world can be set aright again, and doesn't such an indication necessarily involve the demand that one take these steps? Now, if this question is answered in the affirmative, it is not sufficient to describe the world as unjust. It must be described as a world that can be changed, that can be set aright again and in which man need no longer be a victim. But if this is the case, the writer turns from a rebel into a revolutionary. ("Friedrich," 241–2).

Certainly, Dürrenmatt remarks, that is the path Brecht followed, not stopping at mere protest and satire but going on to promote communism. But then Brecht's work arose from his direct confrontation of a "homogenous, centralized, dictatorial empire" (that is, the Third Reich), whereas Schiller, writing after the collapse of the Holy Roman Empire, confronted a disorganized world that is in some respects (here Dürrenmatt lays out a few caveats) comparable to ours. Emerging from the upheaval of communist revolutions, two world wars, and the detonation of the atomic bomb, the political shape of the postmodern age can be seen, suggests Dürrenmatt, as a larger-scale version of Schiller's own post-revolutionary age:

The old maxim of the revolutionaries, that man can and must change the world, has become unrealizable for the individual, out of date; this sentence is now applicable only to the crowd, as a slogan, as political dynamite, as an incentive for the masses, as a hope for the grey armies of the hungry. The part is no longer absorbed in the whole, nor the individual in collectivity, nor man in humanity. The individual is left with a feeling of impotence, of being left out, of no longer being able to step in and influence things, of having to lie low in order not to go under, but also there is the presentiment of a great liberation, of new possibilities, of the time having come bravely, decisively to do one's part. (245)

On this occasion Dürrenmatt is silent about his own dramatic solutions to the problem, though it is clear enough that Brecht's solution would not suit him. As he put it in an earlier essay,

I refuse to find the universal in a doctrine. The universal for me is chaos. The world (hence the stage which represents this world) is for me something monstrous, a riddle of misfortunes which must be accepted but before which one must not capitulate. ("Problems," 857)

But, of course, neither is Schiller's solution – a quest for some kind of transcendent ideal through the medium of poetic drama – at all typical of Dürrenmatt's work. Rather, his plays are characterized by a caustic cynicism attacking the complacency of a society that assumes itself to have already transcended its immoral excesses. But the transition from there to more positive solutions – the shift from "rebel" to "revolutionary," as he put it – seems to have remained elusive.

In other words, although his tone is admittedly more savage, the essential ethical attitude of Dürrenmatt's work is comparable to the outlook of the Power plays – the very outlook that, I have suggested, Walker was determined to transcend. Now, on the face of it, writing a non-cynical play may not look like such a difficult matter. But the problem is connected at a deeper level to the integrity and essential character of the playwright's vision. The difficulty is that, having written one's way into a truthful, albeit cynical rendering of the failure of liberal humanist enlightenment to make a better world, it becomes extremely difficult to write a plot that traces a path back out again. The task entails not only a remodelling of one's habitual view of the world but an attempt to answer some of the thorniest philosophical problems of our age. Nevertheless, with *Criminals in Love*, Walker began to dramatize the possibility of transcending cynical critique to emerge with positive values.

In a 1988 interview Walker spoke about this change in his writing over the preceding few years, which had seen the production of the first three East End plays and *Nothing Sacred*:

For me it was a matter of letting more light into my plays; just naturally, I felt I had to do that, see what sort of hope – that's not a good word; "possibility" might be better – I could find. More than anything, that's the major change I think: I'm getting more possibility, more future into the work. The early plays don't have much hope for the future; their essential concern is "what is the world?" – what is the nature of the chaos there? Now it's more a question of how to deal with it, how to fight through it.   (Wallace, "Looking," 22)

Of course, where the scale of the chaos in question assumes the proportions of an imminent Armageddon, as it had in some of the preceding plays, with their international, gothic settings, the prospect of coherently and persuasively dramatizing the "fight through it" looks dismal. But if the question of the future and possible redemption of civilization ultimately rests in issues about basic human nature, there is no reason that the reappraisal of human relationships cannot begin in one's own neighbourhood. Accordingly, Walker returned to a setting like that of his coming-of-age play, *Sacktown Rag*: the East End of an unnamed city resembling Toronto. As he put it in the 1988 interview: "I believe that the East End plays allowed me to get closer to the bone. I started them because I thought I was avoiding stuff in the writing – where I was brought up, notions of class ... I wanted to address these things with my own voice" (28). Apparently he had decided to set his own house in order before extending his solutions, to recover a sense of positive values he could then take out in into the wider world.

At the centre of *Criminals in Love* (1984) are two young lovers, Gail Quinn and Junior Dawson, who are manipulated into joining the criminal world. Junior comes from a family of criminals who are spectacularly unsuccessful in their vocation. Possibly the most inept of them is Henry, Junior's father, who at the beginning of the play is, as usual, in prison. Junior has deeply ambivalent feelings about his father. He wants to repudiate the family legacy of crime, but his father declares that if Junior does not join forces with his Uncle Ritchie and Ritchie's common-law wife, Wineva, he, Henry, will be killed by Ritchie. Unable to turn his back on his father, Junior accedes; loyally, Gail accompanies him. Uncle Ritchie never does appear, but they soon meet Wineva, a domineering, maniacal woman who insists on kissing to establish "family loyalties." Gail's friend Sandy, a waitress who is experimenting with prostitution as a possible career to fall back on, also joins them, hoping to pick up some criminal skills as further financial security.

More importantly, Junior and Gail are joined by a self-appointed protector, William, a derelict former revolutionary who fell into skid row, he says, out of sympathy for the downtrodden. From the beginning the effectiveness of William's protection looks dubious, and it proves all but wholly inadequate when Wineva reveals her true colours. She is a crazed revolutionary armed with a cache of explosives with which she hopes to "destroy the world." Luckily, her plans are as impractical as they are dangerous, and things go no further than blowing up a warehouse. By the end of the play Junior's house is surrounded by the police (tipped off by Henry as a ploy to reduce his sentence). It looks inevitable that they will all end up in jail, but William goes out to face to the police, carrying the semi-conscious Wineva and accompanied by Sandy. He stalls the police long enough to give Gail and Junior a few moments alone, in which they renew their optimism and begin to make love once more.

The most important word in *Criminals in Love* is "destiny." A vague but abiding presentiment of destiny is the main problem of Junior Dawson, whose very name seems to insist on his regrettable "legacy" as a Dawson. When he suggests to his father that they should end their "relationship," Henry replies: "What are you talking about, you dumb fuck. We're father and son. That's not a relationship. It's destiny" (33). Much as Junior objects to his father's use of the word (35), privately he concurs: "If you put all the things of life along a ruler," he says to Gail, "legacy is at one end and destiny is at the other" (21). The rigidity of the ruler image shows how much he believes that connection to be predetermined. Nevertheless, he resists his "true destiny" – the idea, as he puts it, that he is doomed to "fuck all" – by clinging to Gail, who is, he insists, his salvation (17). And yet Junior's attachment to Gail, while endearing and sympathetic, finally represents another sort of helpless infantilism, as is indicated by his more than merely adolescent fixation on her breasts.

Junior's conception of destiny is complicated by William, who declares himself "the inventor of the modern connotation" of the word. Where Junior is afraid of "destiny as a concept of mind and soul," William's own understanding of the concept is based in "pure economics, politics, social patterns" (28). He argues for a "historical perspective": for example, the menacing Wineva is part of a "class" that has been "bent from years of repression" (59). In other words, William uses the word "destiny" in a quasi-Marxist sense that assumes the possibility of becoming enlightened about the various material and psychological forces one experiences as "destiny" and thus of beginning to overcome feelings of helplessness. He attempts to enlighten Junior and Gail on this point:

> This I stress ... To understand the possibility of progress you must first identify the force which keeps you static. Is it external. Does it lie within. To find the answers you require self-awareness. (64)

Or, as Stevie Wonder succinctly says in the song from which the epigraph to *Criminals in Love* is drawn, "When you believe in things you don't understand, you suffer. Superstition ain't the way." William is determined to demonstrate to Junior that the worst obstacles to his happiness are based in a superstition that is finally educable, and that the ability to choose a better life is chiefly contingent upon an informed will.

Yet there is a paradox here; if William is capable of the kind of enlightenment that not only recognizes adverse social forces but is able to suggest ways of transcending them, why is he in such a wretched condition himself? We are told that William "used to be something big," that "he's been in four revolutions" (82), and, despite appearances, he evidently still has enough money in the bank to consider himself middle class. William's own account of the matter is this:

> I have great sympathy for the truly sad cases of our world. The victims. I have felt so badly that I fell amongst them. This is the truth. This is not melodrama. Their misery made me useless. I fell. (77)

William's condition is a version of the malaise described by Sloterdijk, the cynical paralysis that arises from "enlightened false consciousness." The difficulties he had with helping "victims" through enlightenment may be surmised by considering the (at best) equivocal social justice produced by *any* four revolutions he conceivably might have taken part in – and, of course, by observing the action of the play.

Walker brings home the demoralizing sense of futility that has undone William by making his arch villain, Wineva, a self-proclaimed revolutionary. In a way, Wineva is heir to Sayer, from *The Prince of Naples*: an enthusiast of the violent overthrow of established order who holds no conviction whatsoever that a more humane and equitable world will follow – although, in contrast to Sayer, Wineva is actually equipped with grenades. Superficially, her plans for a violent insurrection present a sort of reckless alternative to the passive acceptance of "destiny," however defined. But, sensibly speaking, this is no alternative at all: not for Junior, trying to escape a criminal "destiny," nor for any philosophical attempt to grapple with the large-scale problems implicit in this play. Indeed, this is approximately the philosophical stalemate described in *Critique of Cynical Reason*: "In a system that feels like a cross between prison and chaos, there is no standpoint for a description, no central perspective for a compelling critique" (xxxiii). With minor adjustments, that sentence could describe the situation of Junior and Gail as the play ends.

Perhaps this sounds distressingly like a step backwards into the existential paralysis that beleaguered the protagonists in Walker's previous plays. But against such an impression we should consider, first, that while the negative forces are by no means wholly vanquished at the end of *Criminals in Love*, they are at least neutralized. Moreover, this play inaugurates a decisive shift in the tone of Walker's work. The most obvious change is spelled out in the title of the play. Junior and Gail are in love – real, vital, earnest love – a concept unheard of in the earlier plays. Furthermore, they are still in love when the curtain falls; indeed, their love has been fortified by their ordeal. As Walker declared in his 1988 interview: "Their love is so strong and clean and clear-headed, especially hers, that it might be able to meet the challenge. As long as she keeps her head and he keeps his heart, they have a fighting chance. I thought the ending was pretty desperate but that there was some kind of hope or, if not hope (I really don't like that word), then possibility for the future" (26). So, while it may be true that, as regards social thought, Gail and Junior are trapped in the sort of paralysis Sloterdijk describes, they also possess a faith in one another that promises some means of transcending their problems.

This does not represent a momentary romantic lapse for Walker; it is a key element of all his subsequent work. In *Criminals in Love* itself the theme of love is extended in two important ways. First, there is the character of William. Like Power, he attempts to intervene to foil the plans of social predators, and like Power his cynicism is based in a disaffected humanism. But in his optimism and genuine affection for Junior and Gail he represents a major departure from Power, providing more emotional uplift than acidic commentary. Downtrodden and almost incapacitated by physical decay though he is, William's handicaps only underscore his resilient spirit, as if he were a sort of Fisher King in whom the hope of social reform resides.[14]

To be sure, William does not represent a repudiation of the cynicism associated with the earlier work so much as a slight reform of its essential character. He belongs to the type Sloterdijk calls by the older Greek word, the "kynic," of whom Diogenes the Cynic is Sloterdijk's *exemple par excellence*. Diogenes, probably the funniest of all Greek philosophers, is the eccentric tramp who claimed to be "looking for an honest man" and who chose to live in a tub rather than a home and indigent rather than wealthy – the better, it seems, to maintain a marginal position from which to criticize the mainstream. According to Sloterdijk, the outlook of Diogenes is one of the few ways of avoiding the more destructive kind of cynicism arising from the limitations and misuses of enlightenment. His is what Sloterdijk calls an "uncivil enlightenment," a subversive provocation from the margins of society that sets in motion a "dialectic of disinhibition," a satirical loosening of hardened critical positions (101–3). William shares some of this Diogenic function with earlier Walker characters like Power or Bernard, but in both his more extreme disaffection and his terrific buoyancy, he is a purer example of the type.

Another aspect of the theme of love in *Criminals in Love* is manifest in the tensions attached to the idea of family. Three concepts of family are juxtaposed. First there is Junior's actual family: his father, Henry, and his Uncle Ritchie, both of whom see familial relations solely in terms of the opportunities they present for exploitation. Similar is the idea of family promoted by Wineva: "We're doing it together. Like a family. It's a family business" (53). Comical though she is, this is the idea of family by which the Mafia sets such store: loyalties made absolute through a ritual show of affection, creating impenetrably powerful allegiances. These notions of family are a kind of demonic parody of the sort promised by Gail and Junior's union. Even their alliance with William is closer to a morally true image of what a family might be: a group of human beings who are related to one another not by some pattern of exploitation but by, foremost, an abiding sense of mutual love and respect.

In part because of its functions as the intermediary of the individual and community, family has always provided one of the richest grounds for drama. It is a natural context in which personal and social values meet and conflict, in which individual aspirations are frustrated or supported, and in which human relations must more often be negotiated than avoided. Walker evidently became extremely interested in further exploring his themes in this framework. In his next play, *Better Living* (1986), called a "prequel to *Criminals in Love*," we meet Gail Quinn's family: her distracted and eccentric mother, Nora, her older sisters, Elizabeth, a tough lawyer, and Mary Ann, a nervous wreck, and her Uncle Jack, a jaded and disaffected priest. As the play opens, Nora is digging a new underground room. Mary Ann has returned home from a failed marriage, and Junior, Gail's boyfriend, is spending most of his time in the house.

Into this environment returns the father, Tom, a former policeman who left the family ten years earlier after a succession of violent, lunatic outbursts. Like Odysseus on his return to Ithaca, Tom wants to reassert order in the household. He warns of an imminent apocalypse in which the have-nots of the world will attack and loot the Quinn home. Shortly after he arrives, Gail moves out, breaking off all contact with the family. Meanwhile, despite Elizabeth's plans to assassinate him, Tom establishes his hegemony over the family, turning Nora's underground room into a bomb shelter, surrounding the property with barbed wire, and building up huge stockpiles of canned food in preparation for the expected siege. Nora and Elizabeth become meekly subordinate; Junior is Tom's mindless helper; and Mary Ann is increasingly frustrated. When Gail returns, confident and happy, she announces that she now remembers that Tom beat her: "That was the crime, eh. The secret all these years" (211). She threatens Tom with a gun, but Jack takes the gun himself and drives Tom from the house. In the last scene Jack reveals that he has hired Henry Dawson, Junior's father, to finish off Tom, and that he intends to retire from the priesthood. The rest of the family are bewildered by their ambivalence about Tom. Though frightened of him, they realize that, as Elizabeth put it, "certain things" that Tom brought into the family "are worth retaining" (190): a sense of order and security that, at some level, they cherish. Tom's tyranny is perhaps too high a price for these things, but they are valued none the less. The family begin to regroup: Mary Ann announces that she and her baby will return to the house, and Nora resumes plans for their "new world down below." But in the final moment of the play Tom reappears at the screen door, holding a large old portable television.

The ambiguity inherent in the final image of Tom standing at the door could serve as a synecdoche for the play as a whole. There is at once both penitence and menace here. The television set is a fascinatingly ambiguous symbol because, for most middle-class North Americans, it arouses profoundly ambivalent personal feelings and memories. Depending on how one interprets it, the television in Tom's arms can represent either a threatening external intrusion into the privacy and delicate ecology of family life or a symbol of family togetherness. It could be a sort of Trojan horse for the inimical forces Tom represents (e.g., patriarchal aggression), or it could be a genuinely good-willed and humble peace offering.

To attach a single conclusive meaning to Tom's gesture would be to ignore the essential ideas of the play. "Has everyone forgotten," asks Elizabeth late in the play, "there are things that go on in this world that aren't easy to understand, aren't easy to take a position on" (214). Chief, perhaps, among things difficult to take a position on is the question of the best response to a threatening sense of social disintegration. The concern causes all the characters some degree of anxiety. Indeed, it pervades their world with the kind of vague yet omnipresent menace we associated earlier with the threat of nuclear annihilation; for some, it results in a similar kind of hopelessness. Mary Ann, for example, ascribes the sense of doom to a malevolent deity, thus burdening herself with a fatalism not essentially different from that from which, in *Criminals in Love*, William was trying to free Junior and Gail.

Even where the characters refuse to be defeated by their premonition of apocalypse, it is a terrifically destructive force. By far the most fanatic in this respect is Tom, who, upon his first entrance, nearly quotes Yeats: "Things just fall apart," he says, adding portentously, "Be careful, the worst is yet to come" (147). While Nora is not possessed of so certain a foreboding, she has already been vaguely resisting the threat of the outside world, trying to extend the protected enclave of her home by means of her subterranean room. In a way, Tom simply brings more force and aggression to the deployment of such measures. Nora's room naturally lends itself to becoming a bomb shelter, and her notion of organizing the family into a unit that will resist external threats slips all too easily into Tom's declaration of martial law within the household. The motives of Tom and Nora are finally quite similar (as is the tenuousness of their sanity); it is their methods that differ – with such drastic, even frightening consequences.

But the play is about more than the struggle between two crazed parents for control of a household. The underlying issue has to do with who can provide "better living" for the family, and what that would mean. To set the idea in perspective, consider Arthur Miller's argument:

all plays we call great, let alone those we call serious, are ultimately involved with some aspect of a single problem. It is this: How may a man make of the outside world a home? How and in what ways must he struggle, what must he strive to change and overcome within himself and outside himself if he is to find the safety, the surroundings of love, the ease of soul, the sense of identity and honour which, evidently, all men have connected in their memories with the idea of family? (73)

In the East End plays Walker focuses on the most basic version of the problem, asking: How does one make of a *house* a home? How can one provide one's family with the sort of security and assurance that ultimately one would like to extend into the world at large? Yet one eye is still on the larger questions of social reform – so much so, indeed, that the relation of the domestic concerns to the broader social sphere has a consistency verging on allegory or parable.

Tom's Odyssean efforts to re-establish domestic order after his ten-year absence are identifiable with attempts to reassert an older patri-archal governing structure based in a stick-and-carrot combination of demagogic fomentation of fears and paternalistic assurances of protec-tion. Here, as so often in literature, a father represents the authority of the past over the present; more specifically, Tom's re-emergence in the family home suggests the neo-conservative resurgence of the mid-1980s. The popularity of Ronald Reagan and Margaret Thatcher at that time was largely attributable to their promises to re-establish, amidst widespread social anxiety, the security and confidence of an earlier age by taking aggressive measures to defend national interests against putative military and economic threats. In Canada the mandate attached to the Mulroney years was not so definite, but there was abundant evidence of the climate of opinion associated with Thatcher and Reagan. This is not to say that *Better Living* satirizes specific polit-ical events; rather, Walker uses parable form to explore the psycholog-ical concerns and anxieties that engender the sense of social despera-tion from which such political events arise.

Among the responses of the others to the anxieties about social dis-solution, those of Jack, the disaffected priest, are particularly revealing. Jack is one of the most sympathetic characters in the play; yet, in terms of contributing a positive solution to the underlying social problems, Jack (like Walker's earlier disaffected priest, Father LiDuc of *Beyond Mozambique*) has little to offer, a deficiency of which he is well aware. Tom suggests that Jack is jaded because he "has spent too many years living in the shadow of God. It sucks the will right out of a man." Moreover, he argues, priests can no longer be effective, "and do you know why?" "Yes," replies Jack, "because they're perceived as being outside society in the first place and all their actions, even the sacrificial ones, are perceived as actions, once removed, of personally motivated, non-political symbols" (171). In so far as he is "perceived as being outside society," Jack fulfils a role in *Better Living* comparable to William's Diogenic function in *Criminals in Love*, and to the ethical functions of Power or Victor. Indeed, in Jack we may see something like the last gasp of the "liberal idealism" that Denis Johnston suggests was Power's downfall. Jack finally turns his back on the moral restrictions contingent upon being a man of the cloth and forsakes pacifist persuasion for, as Mao put it, the power that comes from the barrel of a gun.

As it happens, Jack is the single character who does not go on from *Better Living* to *Escape from Happiness*. This probably has to do with what was, for Walker, the ultimate untenability of Jack's position. Maintaining any loyalty to a transcendent moral code of the kind Jack represents demands a modicum of detachment from the world. Where this consists in cynical disaffection yet not quite wholehearted disavowal, the sense of detachment results simply in moral paralysis. True, Jack ends that paralysis by taking action near the end of the play, getting his hands dirty with the real world, so to speak, even if that means embracing Henry Dawson's way of getting things done. Yet doing so not only prompts Jack's resignation from the priesthood but apparently causes the disintegration of his dramaturgical function in Walker's work.

Elizabeth points to the crux of the problem: "Political involvement often causes moral confusion. I mean, unless you're mentally rigid" (189). Her point applies to more than the compromise of Jack's pacifist convictions. In a different way Tom's pursuit of personal security and order for his family represents a kind of mental rigidity that finally must be confounded. Nevertheless, the family's contact with Tom proves that the notion of his being purely and utterly villainous is mental rigidity of another kind. Confusion in such matters may feel demoralizing, but is less dangerous than moral certainty.

Ruthless certainty appears in different guise in *Beautiful City* (1987). While Walker retains the East End setting, he sets the Quinn family aside to focus on the architect Paul Gallagher and his relations with three other families: the wealthy, corrupt Rafts; the stupid, criminal Moores; and the charming, eccentric Sabbatinis. The play opens with Paul in a state of crisis as Tony Raft involves him in plans for a monstrous Harbourfront mall linked by tunnels to other major commercial buildings. Paul collapses in pain, fearing, by turns, appendicitis, heart failure, or an anxiety attack. In hospital Paul meets Jane Sabbatini, a young volunteer who introduces him to her mother, Gina Mae, a benevolent witch who works at Bargain Harold's discount store and heals people by forcing them to face "the simple ugly truth."

Meanwhile, Tony and his intimidating mother, Mary, bribe Paul's brother, Michael, to persuade Paul to return to work for them. For insurance Mary Raft hires Stevie Moore, a moronic small-time crook whose father, Rolly (an only slightly less moronic small-time crook), has been embezzling from the Rafts' pornography business. The Moores, though close spiritual cousins to the criminal Dawsons, are actually distantly related to the Sabbatinis, so Gina Mae undertakes Rolly's reformation to prevent his disgracing the family name. When the incorrigible Stevie, accompanied by Michael and Tony, detonates a bomb under the Sabbatini house, Paul and the Sabbatinis escape, taking Tony hostage. There is an armed showdown between the two matriarchs, Gina Mae (representing the forces of good) and Mary (representing the forces of evil), but before anyone is seriously injured, a *deus ex machina*, Dian Black, an unorthodox police officer, arrives. Illegally, she negotiates a settlement in which the Rafts will fund the rejuvenation of poor sections of the East End in a socially responsible and financially unprofitable manner. In a coda Paul shows up at Bargain Harold's and humbly proposes marriage to Gina Mae. Eventually she accepts, though both are left shrugging awkwardly at the final blackout.

If architecture is, as Mies van der Rohe suggested, "the will of the age conceived in spatial terms" (Harvey, 21), then it provides a uniquely rich figurative battleground for ideas of social reform. Architectural planning is a form of social engineering; thus she who controls the architects is she who directs "the will of the age" (and in the matriarchal world that, in *Beautiful City*, has succeeded the dissipated patriarchy of Walker's earlier plays, it is definitely a "she" who ultimately calls the shots). Hence, the contest to determine whose influence over Paul will prevail, Mary's or Gina Mae's, is symbolically crucial. The connection between the Rafts' moral outlook and the architectural vision they are hiring Paul to realize is spelled out by Tony:

> My mother was born in a police state. Eventually she escaped. [...] But when she lived in a police state, she had values. I got my dream for this city from the part of my mother that's still under siege. It's based on family. Family and safety. Everything indoors. My motto is "No more strangers in your life." (234)

The kernel of this vision – "family and safety ... everything indoors" – is related to Nora's "new world down below." And just as Tom's "consumer socialism" amplified the acute paranoia latent in Nora's domestic vision, so are Tony's xenophobic urban plans a grotesque extension of the protective values forged in his mother's youth. In either case, once an ordered defence against a sense of external threat is extended beyond a certain point, it becomes a species of fascism. Construed as a pointed sociological critique, this is fairly solid; National Socialism, in the first instance, established its roots in the besieged psyche of a people who had been badly battered and humiliated by war and economic hardship. Germans tried to exorcise their fear and resentment by protecting themselves from the so-called alien element in their society, and ended up creating the Third Reich.

However, set against the Rafts' etiolate urban vision, as Saint Augustine set the City of God against the city of Rome, is the vision of Gina Mae:

> I want a community centre. I want two new parks. I want low cost housing. I want a shelter for the homeless and the mistreated. I want big bright wonderful stores where people get useful products at reasonable prices. I want halfway houses for people who are trying to re-enter the world from the unfortunate darkness of their circumstances. I want a throbbing, connecting, living, creative neighbourhood. (314)

What she wants, in short, is the socialist vision: accessible, publicly owned space that would provide whole communities with the comfortable sanctuary that, under laissez-faire capitalism, remains the exclusive preserve of the wealthy. In Canada, with its long-standing liberal-socialist traditions, one would be hard pressed to find someone who would not pay at least some lip-service to such ideas; as Dian says of Gina Mae's vision, "it seems deeply connected to a kind of popular fantasy" (315). But few are willing to dislodge their first priority of undaunted pursuit of self-interest in favour of such communal values. So Gina Mae provides not only the moral centre around which this play revolves (charitable, quirky, self-righteous, angry, ironic, afraid of sentiment, utopian but a little embarrassed by this, and accordingly, defensive); she also serves as a moral conscience for the others.

The paradox of characters like Gina Mae is that, central as their moral function of critique may be, they are usually depicted as being outside the social order. William's place on the social margins was guaranteed by his homelessness; Gina Mae's is guaranteed by her status as a witch. As Jane comments, "The power is awesome, but it kinda removes you from the rest of the world. Puts you in opposition" (236). Inherently, most moral touchstone characters are self-righteous like Gina Mae, though seldom do they emit the whiff of sanctimony; their ironic detachment means that their more usual contribution is, again

like Gina Mae's, humorous. Depending on whether the play ends with
a successful achievement of social integration or a failure, the alienation of the moral touchstone may be (a) finally fatal and therefore
tragic, as with the Fool in *Lear*; (b) perpetually frozen and therefore
ironic, as with the savage moralist Thersites in *Troilus and Cressida*; or
(c) temporary and therefore comic, as in the case of Feste – whose
nature is, as his name suggests, to bring about the festivities with which
Twelfth Night ends. Prototypes for this character may be found in two
holy fools: Prometheus, who is forcibly exiled and tortured for his
moral role, though with the hope of eventual emancipation and integration; and Jesus, whose martyrdom is meant, ideally, to prompt a
massive penitence leading to the absorption of his moral view into an
integrated, redeemed society.

The scope of redemption assumed by Gina Mae is far more modest,
though none the less decisive. To be sure, she undertakes the conversion of one of two thieves (Rolly) while damning the other (Stevie), but
we should not make too much of that. Though Gina Mae claims that
her message, "the simple ugly truth," is "metaphysical" (267), the
redemption she purveys is ultimately humanist. The principal beneficiary of her efforts, dramatically speaking, is Paul, whose sickness is
diagnosed as follows:

> You've been living like a a fool ... You've lost touch with the genuinely
> complex nature of reality. All your friends think alike, talk alike, want the
> same things. [...] You're dying from a kind of simplicity .. It's like you've
> taken the huge throbbing life force and turned it into a piece of
> thread...and it's not enough to hold you together (266).

In short, Gina Mae declares: "the simple ugly truth" Paul is missing is
that "there's life right here on earth and you're not a part of it" (267).
Accordingly, Paul's impending marriage to Gina Mae represents not
only personal rejuvenation but the invigorating promise of social integration. The implicit possibility is that through marriage to Gina Mae,
Paul may become the architect of a better society. Naturally, the sentimental optimism inherent in such an idea is enormous, so much so that
the characters themselves retain their scepticism, shrugging awkwardly
even as they decide to hope.

Walker's own optimism returned undaunted in *Nothing Sacred*
(1988), his adaptation of Turgenev's *Fathers and Sons*. This play,
notwithstanding any purist objections Turgenev's admirers might raise,
is a beautiful piece of work, perhaps Walker's finest. Here the suggestion of faith in charitable socialist humanism that had been creeping
into Walker's work emerges in full flower. Where the intentions of Tur-

genev's Bazarov had been dubious even to him upon his deathbed, Walker's Bazarov is able to articulate a much more coherent view, and his legacy is less ambiguous. In the course of reworking Turgenev's novel for the stage, Walker pushed Bazarov's awakening further and bestowed some of his own new convictions on the character.

In the preface to *Nothing Sacred* (excerpted from his 1988 interview), Walker discusses Bazarov's awakening, saying:

during the play he somehow comes to understand that [...] the roots of his nihilism are a profound concern. Unless you reconcile the roots of nihilism with the ways in which your actions affect people, you really are a person out of your time, perhaps out of your planet. [Cf Gina Mae's comment about "life on earth."] If you forget that your work, and all your indignation and your anger, comes from the way people are being treated – the so-called victims – then you can't talk to the victims, and your feeling for them is useless. I watched Bazarov make that journey, took it with him; and I tried to lay in that understanding so that he would undergo more than a mental exercise. (7)

As his interviewer, Robert Wallace, observes, Bazarov's journey is "very similar to the overall journey charted by [Walker's] plays," moving from "nihilism to a type of social commitment, even action, in the face of social problems" (26–7). In effect, Walker changes Bazarov from a nihilist into a proto-socialist.

Therein lies Walker's main departure from his source. Turgenev's Bazarov, however strong his dislike of the aristocracy and real his human sympathy, is no socialist. Indeed, Isaiah Berlin suggests that in Turgenev's view socialism was "a fantasy" (44). If all people have the same worth in the eyes of the Bazarov of *Fathers and Sons*, it is only in so far as they are all more or less worthless. Turgenev's Bazarov is a man who believes at first that his ideas are ahead of his time and, hence, that he stands apart from his countrymen; but he finds out gradually that he has not transcended love and, finally, that (to be brief, at the risk of making a profound discovery sound trite) no man is an island. Whereas in *Fathers and Sons* Bazarov is torn between his urge for disaffiliation from other human beings and his desire to reform, in *Nothing Sacred* he is much more consistent in his inclinations. Walker achieves this by muting the first part of the dilemma, the urge for disaffiliation, and giving it a more rationally consistent basis in an antipathy for society's injustices. Though Walker's Bazarov is at first unable to speak directly to a peasant, he is committed to an abstract love of humanity from the beginning. He frequently uses the word "love," by which he means, of course, not *eros*, but *caritas* – charity.

Naturally, the change makes Bazarov into a much stronger (not to mention more likable) character in *Nothing Sacred* than he is in Turgenev's novel. Indeed, Bazarov is probably the strongest and most independently willed character Walker has written since Zastrozzi or Medeiros. Arkady is being hyperbolic, but only a little, when he says of Bazarov: "He's not a man. He's a primal force" (49). We see Bazarov's physical strength as well as his strength of character in the first scene when he handily overwhelms the Bailiff (19), a feat he repeats more spectacularly when the Bailiff attempts to clobber him with a board (37–8). He is similarly able to overcome the much larger Sergei through his wits (49); and his self-confidence in intellectual matters is justified by his persuasive analysis of Pavel's weakly self-delusory obsessiveness (67–8).

Even Bazarov's greatest weakness in *Fathers and Sons*, his relationship with Anna, is turned into another kind of strength. Where Turgenev suddenly undermines Bazarov's posture of rational indifference by having him fall in love with Anna Odintsov, a friend of Kirsanov's, Walker gives the prior friendship with Anna to Bazarov. This he reveals with a device familiar from the movie *Butch Cassidy and the Sundance Kid*: Bazarov appears to be taking impertinent liberties with Anna when, with a familiar embrace, they reveal their long intimacy. Accordingly, Bazarov seems more suave and self-assured in his relationship with Anna and far less vulnerable than he had been in Turgenev's hands.[15]

Yet by far the most prepossessing feature of Walker's Bazarov is his robust espousal of charity. Turgenev had created in Bazarov a character who denied the existence and necessity of all moral frameworks whatsoever. Walker, however, in having Bazarov affirm ecumenical love, has created a character who rejects all pre-existing frameworks in favour of one central principle: universal suffrage. One might easily argue that by changing Bazarov's character in this way, Walker has derailed much of Turgenev's story. In *Fathers and Sons* Bazarov considers himself a kind of scientist, ruthlessly regarding all situations with sceptical, rational utilitarianism and therefore free of any transcendent scheme of values; then, having fallen in love, his compassion and instinctive humanitarianism spring forth unbidden. In the novel it is while helping his father – who himself acts with a sense of *noblesse oblige* towards the tenants who were formerly his serfs – that Bazarov receives his mortal infection. In short, Turgenev suggests that Bazarov is infected by caring for others; this is what destroys Bazarov – and, by implication, the nihilist ideas he represents. In *Nothing Sacred* Walker has Bazarov infected by caring for others much earlier in the story. Bazarov dies absurdly in the course of his kindly, albeit reluctant efforts to accommodate the honour ethic of Pavel Kirsanov.

All this makes Bazarov into much more of a linchpin to social history than Turgenev could ever have imagined him to be. For example, in having Pavel and Bazarov duel inconclusively over Fenichka's honour, Turgenev evidently has a vague parable in mind. Russia's future is like Fenichka's child, the offspring of peasants and aristocrats, whose future, depending on whether the parents can bring themselves to marry, will either be legitimate (i.e., a part of civilized progress) or illegitimate (i.e., a rejection of civilization). Walker displaces the question on to the hunt for the elderly brothers, Kirsanov and Pavel, in the woods. "All Russia," says Pavel, "is searching for her wayward son. I am moved by her concern. Worried a bit about her competence" (84). The question has shifted to one about finding a way forward for Russia (and, by extension, for civilization at large) through the cataclysmic onset of modernity, while preserving what is worthwhile in her past. But where Turgenev had left the question open, in Walker's hands the answers are very nearly embodied in Bazarov.

Accordingly, though Bazarov himself dies, what he represents in *Nothing Sacred* is passed on. At the end he sends from his deathbed for the servants; it is to them that he chooses to speak his final words. For Gregor, at least, Bazarov was a kind of messiah. And, as people do after the demise of an alleged martyr, once Bazarov dies, the arguments begin about what he wanted to say, what he represented. Then, in the deeply moving final moments, Gregor begins to teach Sergei the principles of socialism he learned from Bazarov. The Christ-like overtones of Bazarov's virtually superhuman status are affirmed, for his legacy is to be passed on through his disciples.

Love and Anger (1989) returns to the idea of a martyr who attempts to pilot the way through the injustices and confusions of the modern world. But it does so by integrating themes from some of Walker's earlier plays. Where *Beautiful City* ended – with the impending marriage of a penitent former adherent of patriarchal corporatism and an eccentric, unprosperous, marginal social reformer – *Love and Anger* begins: with a protagonist in whom all those features are already married. Peter ("call me Petie") Maxwell was one of the city's toughest corporate lawyers until he suffered a stroke, which precipitated a spiritual reformation. Maxwell gave away his money; he now keeps a basement office "on the fringe of the downtown," where, with his strait-laced assistant Eleanor, he serves a marginalized and indigent clientele. His latest client is Gail Jones, a young black woman whose husband has been jailed for his part in a break-in at a newspaper office. It emerges that the break-in was sponsored by Babe Conner, multimillionaire newspaper publisher, who, coincidentally, has retained Maxwell's former partner, Sean Harris, as his attorney.

Because the odds against liberating Gail's husband by legal means are overwhelming, Maxwell decides to proceed outside the law. With the help of Gail and Sarah, Eleanor's schizophrenic sister, he drugs and kidnaps Conner in order to put him on trial, securing the co-operation of Harris with some phoney photos that link Harris and Conner to the small-time crooks (Dawson and Moore, though they never actually appear) who were responsible for the break-in. With Sarah serving as judge, Maxwell as prosecutor, and Harris as the attorney for the defence, Conner is charged with "being consciously evil" (69) and with knowingly pursuing "a career injurious to the public well-being" (73). But before he can complete his case, Maxwell, upset by the people outside who are rummaging through the garbage for food, suffers another stroke and concedes victory. Gail is not willing to let things ride so easily. She pulls out a handgun, warning Conner that she will murder him if he ever crosses her family again. Conner and Harris leave, and then Maxwell dies, wishing with his last words that he had begun his reformation earlier. As the play ends, the three women concentrate on reviving Maxwell through their combined wills.

The stroke Petie Maxwell has suffered prior to the play's action functions dramatically within the story in several different ways. In the first place, the injury is implicitly a consequence of his previous behaviour: just as indulging in the luxury of eating fatty, high-cholesterol foods leads to cardiac arrest, so does indulgently profiting from a legal system that neglects the miseries of the underclass lead to collapse. The enemy here is the voracious appetite of instrumental reason unchecked by humanitarian considerations, and Maxwell's stroke brings that syndrome to a halt.[16]

Maxwell's stroke also represents the handicap under which his side of the conflict must labour. But here we see an example of the phenomenon discussed by Edmund Wilson in his famous essay "The Wound and the Bow" (1941): the sense of mutilation seems an inextricable feature of any virtues and strengths Maxwell and his allies may claim, because that mutilation is integral to their full humanity (223–42). The idea is related to the fusion of emotions set out in the title, *Love and Anger*. Gail, the purest embodiment of love in this play (in this, as her name suggests, she is the doppelgänger of Gail Quinn), also turns out to be the most focused embodiment of anger when she threatens Conner. Love and anger are also fully embodied in Maxwell himself. There, however, the two emotions are in constant turmoil: a consequence and a symbol of his broken rationality. In other words, there may be some truth to Eleanor's suspicion that Maxwell is inclined to express irrational, hyperbolic ideas because his formerly rational mind has been injured. More significant is the idea that Maxwell's broken rationality symbolizes a breaking of the covenant with reason formed in the Enlightenment.

There are intimations that this is what is at stake in Maxwell's speeches in the opening scene. He begins with a critique of one of the pillars of enlightenment reason, the law, which, he tells Gail, "is vulgar in its rigidity. Insensitive to the nuance of human existence. Derived and constructed from knowledge within a narrow historical corridor. In short, it's in love with itself" (13). This attack on the law, Maxwell admits, is part of his plan "to undermine the entire institutional basis of our culture" (14). And he begins to sound a little like one of the most formidable critics of the Enlightenment, Michel Foucault, when he declares medicine to be "number four on my hit list. Right after law, religion, government" (17).

Gail's case, then, is merely one specific opportunity for action within Maxwell's overall scheme. Similarly, he tells Gail that "the love you have for your husband is just one arm of a many-armed beast. Full of compassion for everything in the world that needs love" (15). This, of course, is very like the sort of love Bazarov espoused, just as Maxwell's anger at social injustice resembles Bazarov's indignation. In a way, then, *Love and Anger* shows an attempt to realize a part of the socialist hope that Bazarov had introduced in *Nothing Sacred*. Maxwell, Gail, Sarah, and Eleanor form an alliance of seekers after justice, a confederacy of the marginalized who are united in both love and anger. Arrayed against them are the forces of the establishment: law, politics, capitalism, and the media, all incarnate in Babe Conner and Sean Harris. The attempt to bring these forces to a reckoning by staging the trial of Conner reveals a yearning for some kind of higher, more conclusive moral judgment of the injustices of the world. If in earlier plays Walker explored the ultimate confrontation between good and evil, Armageddon, then the mock trial at the centre of *Love and Anger* is a sort of parody of the Day of Judgment following Armageddon. The scene is humorous, but the accusations of evil levelled at Conner and his kind are unmistakably real. Thus, though the trial disintegrates, the indictment remains.

Walker contrives to place the apparent perpetrators of evil under the thumbs of his protagonists again in *Escape from Happiness* (1991), the third play to feature members of the Quinn family. Ostensibly a sequel to *Better Living*, *Escape From Happiness* is in many respects a reworking and expansion of the earlier play rather than a foray into wholly new territory. At the literal level, the setting of the two plays is identical: the Quinn family kitchen. Moreover, the women of the Quinn family are still coming to terms with the return of Tom and, at the same time, are wrestling with the question of how to cope with the violence threatening their family from beyond their walls.

However, where in *Better Living* it was the difficulty in accommodating Tom that presented the primary problem, with external violence a secondary, related issue, in *Escape from Happiness* the ratio of emphasis is reversed, the issue of external violence now predominant. In part, this is because Tom is reputedly dying of some vague sickness that leaves him docile and unaware, so he poses little threat – though he is still shunned by his two older daughters. The play begins when Gail and Nora arrive home from shopping to find Junior lying on the floor, having been badly beaten. Right away the reliability of any external authorities to cope with the family's problems is questioned. Gail calls 911, but the women are doubtful of a prompt response; Nora insists that what is needed is for Junior to get himself on his own feet. In the event, the police and ambulance do arrive. Two officers begin an investigation, Dian Black, from *Beautiful City*, and her partner, the plodding, apparently rather backward Mike Dixon.

Unfortunately, Dian and Mike are more interested in investigating the Quinns than in probing the assault on Junior, and they discover large bags of drugs in the basement. Elizabeth tries to take things in hand by kidnapping one of Junior's assailants, Rolly Moore, the pathetic small-time crook from *Beautiful City*, who, despite his terror, can tell them nothing about the drugs. Junior and Tom assume that the drugs have been planted in reprisal for their vigilantism. Tom has been feigning illness to avoid being driven from the house, meanwhile operating a scheme with Junior that involves setting all the local criminals on a path of mutual destruction. As it turns out, Rolly and Stevie were only indirectly connected with the drugs. The real culprit was Dian Black, who is here revealed as not merely unorthodox but dangerously fanatic in her devotion to the police. She has planted the drugs in order to thwart Elizabeth's plans to attack the police with a series of charges of police brutality. Mike, for all his reactionary defence of police methods, insists that they must fight Elizabeth by the book.

Once the police have left, the question of Tom's presence in the house is raised once more, for he and Nora have begun to talk honestly to one another again. Bashfully, Tom declares that all he wants is to express his love for his family in whatever way he can, admitting that he needs the strength their love provides. Elizabeth seems almost ready to relent, demanding that Tom's love should include respect for them all, but in the end she remains implacable, leaving the house without having accepted Tom. Mary Ann is prepared to accept Tom, so long as he follows a list of demands. Gail, however, forgives Tom outright. It appears that, despite the incompleteness of his daughters' blessings,

Tom will stay living with his family, trying, as Nora puts it, "to make something positive out of the experience."

Whereas in *Better Living* Tom's return home was Odyssean in terms of his attempt to re-establish order, in *Escape from Happiness* the pathos of Tom's diminished stature before his three daughters is redolent of *King Lear*. The connection intensifies when it is Tom's youngest daughter, Gail, who most readily forgives him, despite having suffered most from his history of tyrannical domestic violence. In so far as his mental collapse and sickness is feigned, Tom perhaps recalls his namesake, Poor Tom, the character affected by Edgar to deflect danger. But the more important comparison is undoubtedly between Tom and Lear, both erstwhile, seemingly omnipotent patriarchs. Tom's fatherhood, symbolic of the authority of the past over the present, is now much diminished, with nothing imperious left in it. The Tom of *Escape from Happiness* shows virtually no signs of the coarsely arrogant and foolish ranter he was in *Better Living*, or that Lear is in the first two acts of his play. Rather, he is like Lear in his last three acts, by then shut out of his daughters' houses and left in the storm; he has been forced to change his self-image, and our sympathies have slipped towards him. Tom is fully penitent and eager to atone for his past. Junior, a younger, humbler man, loyally accompanies and protects Tom, like Kent or the Fool does Lear, helping to guide him through to some kind of redemption.

As we find so often with literary treatments of the theme, the only real path for the redemption of male violence lies through women – or, more exactly, through the humble recognition and honouring of those virtues most often associated with women. There remains some question, however, of what, precisely, atoning for male guilt through women might consist in doing ("when they said repent, [we] wonder what they meant"). Dian's summary of the tensions involved has much validity: "It's big this thing we're engaged in! Big and contradictory. It's new and old. Woman and man. Daughter and father. Smart and dumb. Really, really smart! And really, really dumb!!" (119) And yet, thinking of the problem in terms of polarities like that is of limited usefulness, as the play reveals. Even while evidently accepting the premise of a kind of collective male guilt in need of expiation, Walker seems determined that no purely simplistic, politically correct interpretation of the idea should be allowed to prevail unchallenged.

Thus, as in *Beautiful City*, and to a lesser degree *Criminals in Love* and *Better Living*, a kind of matriarchal power structure has arisen to fill the space left by the played-out patriarchy; but that in itself does not provide a solution. On the one hand there are recurring examples in the play of an immensely positive, virtually mystic power associated with females, particularly in their maternal aspect. The threatening visit of Rolly and Stevie Moore, for instance, is foiled when they see Gail nursing her baby (41–2); the Moores become frantic as their brutality is overwhelmed by innate reverence. Similarly, when Gail goes off to secure Junior's job, she is armed with her baby, confident that it will command the foreman's sympathy (63). Nora uses another kind of maternal power when she defuses Elizabeth's savage temper tantrum by blowing a raspberry on her stomach (89). All these examples are essentially pacific, but in themselves they are enough to intimidate men like the Moores.

On the other hand there are situations in which some of the women reveal a wolfishness as ugly as the patriarchal excesses. Undoubtedly the most disturbing examples of this aspect of matriarchal power come from Elizabeth and Dian Black. As a lawyer, Elizabeth is at least as insanely aggressive in her work ethic as Sean Harris or, prior to his stroke, Maxwell, in *Love and Anger* (81–2). With her family, too, Elizabeth teeters on the brink of a lunatic violence much like Tom's (87–8). She also drifts into her brutalism for virtually the same reasons her father did: a conflicted mixture of familial protectiveness and personal pride. Furthermore, clear parallels are laid between Elizabeth's protection of her family and Dian's protection of the police. For Dian, loyalty to her fellow officers (despite her personal scorn for Mike) is a paramount value overriding any other humanist imperatives; similarly, for Elizabeth, the bond of family (despite her open scorn for some, like her sister Mary Ann) justifies any measures she takes.

Even the police brutality that Elizabeth has determined to wipe out is sarcastically put into perspective by Mike: "I mean, who the hell are [the police] to get brutal. All the nice people they get to deal with. All that love and affection they get from that wonderful scum out there" (119). Walker's point is hardly to excuse police brutality by pointing to provocation, but rather to show that the situation is too complex to justify any simplistic, self-righteous moralizing. Earlier, Elizabeth refused to accept that Tom's love for his family could in any way exculpate him for acts of vigilantism that, in the end, endangered the family. "He loves us," she exclaims: "Amazing. Can you imagine what he'd do to this family if he hated us. The mind boggles. I don't know, could be anything ... little nuclear devices shoved up all our assholes!" (101) The reference to "nuclear devices" returns us to the larger social dimensions of this issue of protectiveness raised in *Better Living*. The mind-set perpetrating the small-scale vigilantism seen in this play is continuous with that which uses the threat of nuclear holocaust to extort peace and security for a nation. So Elizabeth may well be right in saying that having a pure motive for aggressive actions doesn't change the fact that they are more likely to escalate violence than to decrease it. However, she hypocritically fails to acknowledge how deeply implicated her own behaviour is in this syndrome.

Repentance for male violence, then, is rather more complicated than it first appears to be. Perhaps the most promising line of thought about the problem emerges when Nora at last admits that she has known that Tom is her ex-husband all along, but has been withholding recognition to maintain a modest balance of power (93). She suggests that the time has now come to acknowledge who Tom is and, by implication, how his actions have been an integral part of their family, for better or worse. Such an acknowledgment is essential to make any positive progress. "What this family needs now," argues Nora, "is something more clear. Clearer roles. Lighter burdens for ... some of us" (94). The need for repentance, she submits, is far more general than the focus on Tom would suggest:

> I think we believe that we don't deserve to be happy. I know Mary Ann believes it's just fate. But Mary Ann is too distressed to think clearly about these things. My theory is better. We're running away from happiness. We think we need to struggle, and suffer, and work really hard before we can just stay still, and let happiness catch up and surround us. (94)

In the end, then, the difficulties devolve upon the question of how to move from a state of penitence to a state of happiness. Naturally, this involves extending some kind of absolution, and it is with this possibility that the play ends. Elizabeth still refuses to absolve Tom, though Nora's theory suggests this may have to do with an inability to forgive herself. Mary Ann, still too fearful even to trust herself, yearns for the assurance of rules and guidelines. Of the daughters, only Gail is able, from within a realm of love, to extend forgiveness and trust. In her easygoing nature resides the sense of hopefulness – or, as Walker prefers it, possibility – with which the play ends.

The intriguing effect that the accommodation of this kind of optimism has had upon the dramatic form of Walker's work becomes evident when we compare the East End plays to the conventions of Jacobean city comedy. Most obvious of the definitive features shared are that Walker's plays are comedies that also use a city setting, the unnamed Toronto standing in for Jacobean London; and that both depict a variety of social backgrounds that are similarly used to bring class tensions into open dramatic conflict.

Perhaps more significant, however, is the similar sense of the social ethos into which these plays enter. What gives Jacobean comedies an aesthetic distinct from that of their more romantic Elizabethan predecessors is the overtone of cynicism and banal immorality pervading the work. These overtones are related to what Una Ellis-Fermor has pointed to as the predominant metaphysical concern of Jacobean tragedy as well as comedy: "the loss of spiritual significance from within the revealed world of fact and event" (18). We have repeatedly noted the similar overtones of cynicism and banal immorality present in Walker's plays. One symptom is the postmodern "flatness" of many of his characters. To ascribe purely cynical motives to characters results in a cartoonlike delimitation of their psychological conception. This is true whether their nature is accounted for in terms of a Jonsonian theory of "humours" based in Renaissance science or Walker's ideas about obsession, which have their basis in a wide-reaching cultural and philosophical analysis.

On those grounds we could consider Walker's City Comedies close relatives of their Jacobean forebears, albeit written for the postmodern age. Yet this is too simple. For the shift that took place in Walker's work with the East End plays makes Walker's postmodern city comedy quite distinct from its Jacobean precursor. The basic difference lies in the degree to which the plays themselves partake of the cynicism of the world therein depicted. However much the East End plays embrace complexity and depict ambiguity, they all finally evince some kind of attempt to move dramatically towards a less morally ambiguous outlook. What should we do about our flawed society? What *can* we do? Of what values can we be certain? These are the questions that haunt the East End plays, and the characters grope their way towards a point at which answers will at least seem possible. Similar questions form a subtext to plays like *As You Like It*, *Measure for Measure* or *The Tempest*. In Jacobean city comedy, however, such questions are left to the side. They can be ignored with impunity as part of a metaphysical mode of inquiry belonging to an earlier age and dealt with by an earlier, more romantic kind of play.

As for the element of trickery endemic to Jacobean comedy, which is focused almost exclusively upon the acquisition of wealth, in Walker's postmodern city comedy a comparable trickery is practised by the protagonists, but it is focused upon tricking goodness out of a cynical world. In the case of Gina Mae in *Beautiful City* this trickery required a kind of magic; and in *Love and Anger* the effects of Maxwell's stroke were a sort of pseudo-miracle, almost a divine intervention. However, with *Escape from Happiness* Walker declines any sort of supernatural element, including any particular extraordinary trickster character. Whatever magic there is must be found among the flawed and suffering collective protagonists.

What Walker has moved towards, then, is a form of comedy in which characters are habitually defined by their obsessive relations to their culture and have accordingly become "flat" and cartoonlike. But these characters are now struggling to develop more complex relations to their society, and accordingly must reacquaint themselves with the sources of depth. By pressing the moral concerns of his characters, Walker's dramaturgy erupts through the very aesthetic conventions he had previously established. To return to the comparison with Roy Lichtenstein's work, it is as if a cartoon figure began to force three-dimensional flesh through the gaps among the Benday dots.

After *Escape from Happiness*, it was quite some time before Walker wrote another full-length stage play. Perhaps he felt he had taken the concerns that preoccupied him over the previous decade as far as dramaturgy and social realities would allow and he needed to retrench. He did, however, write some shorter works in the interim, including *Tough!* (1993), a short play primarily for young audiences, and the radio play *How To Make Love to an Actor* (1995) (his only radio play published thus far).

Tough! is the shortest and simplest of Walker's stage plays to date, and also one of his saddest works. There are only three characters: Tina, her boyfriend, Bobby, and her girlfriend, Jill, all of them nineteen years old. Jill has caught Bobby fondling another girl at a party, and told Tina. The play begins with Tina confronting Bobby about his betrayal, which he cannot defend or explain. Matters are complicated when Tina reveals she is pregnant by Bobby. Bobby, stunned, is unsure what to do; he cannot transcend his selfishness, but neither does he want to be altogether irresponsible or to feel he has wronged Tina. His immaturity and limited intellect make him slow to absorb his responsibilities or to articulate his intentions. This exasperates both Tina and Jill, whom Tina insists must remain party to the discussion for reasons of moral support.

Unfortunately, this further complicates the situation, for Jill has always hated Bobby – in fact, she claims to hate all men, though when pressed she admits to having known two who were tolerable – and she torments him mercilessly with the evidence of his weakness, humiliating him both mentally and physically. For her part, Tina is still in love with Bobby but reluctant to admit it or be gentle with him; she pushes him relentlessly to make a decision, to abandon his vague desire to preserve a future of indefinite possibility, but succeeds only in aggravating his feelings of self-contempt. By the end of the play the argument is exhausted and Bobby has left in confusion. Jill suggests that, despite her wholehearted contempt for Bobby, he might be reformable, that males may "just need more time and instruction." However, Tina has now lost interest, so when Bobby returns, announcing that he has "been thinking," the girls just leave, telling him to keep it up.

How To Make Love to an Actor features a similar triangle. Jess and Sandy, two female acting students, are taking a workshop with a more experienced actor, Willie. While Jess is highly sceptical of Willie's ideas, Sandy appears ready to accept them on faith. It turns out that Sandy is sexually involved with Willie, and she suggests that Willie's struggle with Jess, a lesbian, is based in some kind of power game. The sense of power struggle is then raised in a different context when the two women meet at an audition for an appalling exploitation film about a serial killer who murders prostitutes. Coincidentally, Willie is being read for the role of killer. Following a quarrel with Willie, the two women sleep together; then, in the climactic scene, Willie returns home, followed shortly afterwards by Ross, the writer-producer-director of the slasher film. They read from the script, but Jess refuses to play her murdered prostitute role as written. Ross is reduced to pathological whimperings of a sadistic and edipal nature and threatens that the women will never work in film again. After he leaves, Willie and Jess resume bickering, each accusing the other of being unsympathetic to the difficulty of trying to earn a dignified living as actors. They ignore Sandy, who complains that her sexual liaisons were merely an attempt to make some kind of meaningful friendly contact in an alienating world. The play ends with all three talking at one another simultaneously, each ignoring the others.

The two plays share a basic configuration of characters: a hapless male caught between two females, one strong-minded, impervious to the male's attractions and extremely aggressive, the other more vulnerable, with an emotional investment in the male. Essentially, this framework takes the situation of the Quinn family – Tom and Junior among the four emotionally divided women; ineffectual males among vulnerable and tough females – and confines it to three characters (Ross being a secondary figure, personifying a social force with which the other three must reckon). Though less complex than Walker's more ambitious full-length works, these plays offer new perspectives on familiar themes – most importantly, the redemption of man from violence and callousness by means of woman. It need hardly be said that, even while acknowledging the positive effects of such a syndrome, there is something irritating in this traditional theme from a feminist perspective. For one thing, the idea is finally male-centred. For another, it implicitly lays a burden upon women that most would undoubtedly prefer to evade. But as *Escape from Happiness* shows, Walker does not see the problem as being as simple as "responsible females versus irresponsible males."

Tough! portrays an early version of the confused relations between the sexes that too often result in a human mess in need of redemption. The play is hard on Bobby, but, as the title implies, there is no easy erasure of the responsibility of having conceived a child – not for the mother-to-be, at any rate. Furthermore, if the exposure and mockery of Bobby's weaknesses are humiliating for the adolescent boys in the audience, so are the harshly uncomprehending attitudes of Jill and Tina objectified for the girls. Here, the tough fact for both boys and girls to consider is that, whether because of different rates of biological development or for other reasons, boys do not always know how to behave in the ways that girls would like them to behave, nor to navigate the path to becoming admirable men. This has something to do with self-ishness, but Walker shows it to be a selfishness motivated by animal (or perhaps acculturated) fears, such as Bobby's ever-looming fear of failure and inadequacy (485).

How To Make Love to an Actor looks at this problem of warring, selfish, frightened egos from another perspective, where the characters are much more self-conscious about the nature of the difficulties they face. The idea of social role-playing settles very easily on to a group of actors trying to make their livings by playing roles in scripts founded in conventions that they all find contemptible. The characters waste the opportunity to explore that ground of agreement. All three are reluctant (to varying degrees) to take on the imprisonment of the two-dimensional role laid out for them, but their apprehensive egoism makes it impossible to establish the context of trust necessary to com-prehend each other's perspectives.

The phenomenon of "disposable selves" – the pre-conceived car-toonlike model of personality Walker used to explore the relation between the well-springs of our personal identities and our culture – has undergone a transformation. Where Walker's fascination with the flatness of identity was once perhaps somewhat morbid in its pes-simism, in these latter plays he chooses to expose the problems to examination. The characters themselves see the threat and more often than not resist becoming disposable selves.

SEEKING NEW EASTS: *SUBURBAN MOTEL*

Indeed, Walker's largest and most formidable work, the *Suburban Motel* cycle (1997–98), which he premiered after a four-year sabbati-cal from the stage (six years after his last full-length play for adults), plays a fascinating set of variations upon precisely that theme: how to understand the threat to humanity in the postmodern world, and thence to combat the phenomenon of disposable identity. All six *Sub-*

urban Motel plays – *Problem Child, Adult Entertainment, Criminal Genius, Featuring Loretta, The End of Civilization,* and *Risk Everything* – take place in the same rundown motel room, which provides not only the setting but an overriding metaphor for the cycle. This is life on the margins, geographically just beyond the East End of the earlier series (the real counterpart to this motel could be any of a dozen sad places on Kingston Road, in the far east end of Toronto) and figuratively just beyond the reach of any provisional claim to belong to the mainstream, a claim that, however tentatively, most of the characters in the East End plays could still make. Almost all the characters who find themselves living in this motel room have become social outlanders in some way, through indigence, exhaustion, desperation, outlawry, or simple disaffection.

Thus, the shift further east signifies a complementary shift in the ethos of Walker's writing. Whereas the East End series saw Walker moving into more positive realms, embracing love, redemption, and the prospect of social reform, these far–East End plays (as they might be called) show a gloomier prospect. Yet to call this shift a lapse into cynicism is simplistic. Walker never liked the idea of calling his East End plays "hopeful," yet the caustic passion evident in the new work certainly suggests nothing as passive as "hopelessness." Indeed, it would seem that, like Diogenes (or William in *Criminals in Love*), Walker ventured further into the social margins – drove for the ditch, so to speak – the better to criticize the mainstream.

The nuances of this new ethos are delineated clearly in the first play of the cycle, *Problem Child*. Denise and R.J., a young couple, are waiting in a motel room to hear whether a social agency will allow them to recover custody of their daughter, who was taken away while R.J. was in prison and Denise was caught using drugs and prostituting herself. Recently, they have been desperately trying to prove themselves model citizens, worthy of the custody of their own daughter; but Helen, the social worker assigned to their case, makes it clear that the cruelly vague demands of the agency's representative (i.e., herself) have not yet been satisfied, indeed, are not likely ever to be so. Denise particularly feels desperately bereft, and ends up in an angry confrontation with Helen, during which Helen cuts herself, then slips and hits her head, apparently killing herself. At this point there is a turn toward black farce. Denise, terrified, thinking only of her custody plea, enlists the help of Phillie, the drunken motel manager, to bury Helen's body out back, then persuades Phillie to kidnap her daughter from the foster home. Then, in a stunning theatrical coup, a new scene begins with Helen emerging from the shower – having been buried alive in a rather shallow grave, as it turns out. She is, naturally, enraged, but continues to dangle the hope of her finally relenting in the matter of custody. Meanwhile, Phillie proves incapable of carrying out the abduction, afraid of upsetting the little girl.

Thus matters are left at the end of *Problem Child*, little changed from the outset. Indeed, they would seem if anything even bleaker, except that Walker tosses a long-shot hope into the cauldron of despair. In a subplot, R.J., who became addicted to daytime talk shows of the Jerry Springer variety while in prison, has been repeatedly calling the producers of one such show to protest their inhumane treatment of certain guests. Notwithstanding the improbability, by the end of the play the producers become interested in hearing R.J.'s advice. So, implicitly, the possibility lingers that humanity might defy all expectations and redeem itself, a possibility symbolized in the return of Helen from the grave. But if we compare this return to another such symbol of redemption, Hermione's resurrection from apparent death in *The Winter's Tale*, it is easy to see the great difference in the degree of faith thereby expressed. Helen's resurrection is by no means certainly a good thing; it merely suggests that chance is not yet quite exhausted. There is no intimation that the future will hold anything better than the past.

Nor does the rest of the cycle provide any easy comfort in this regard. The next two plays, *Adult Entertainment* and *Criminal Genius*, offer us, respectively, cops and robbers. All the characters, whether they have set themselves to upholding or to breaking the law, have little regard for it as anything more than an instrument to be cynically exploited. Both groups are effectively outside the polity because they lack enough sense of common humanity to make the concept meaningful. *Adult Entertainment* begins with Max, a married police detective, and Jayne, a lawyer, having sex in the motel bed. They are here, they say, because they've "given up." As Jayne puts it, overriding Max's objections, they are "both finished. Two people of a certain age both done like dinner. Done being useful citizens and lawyers and cops and husbands" (55). Indeed, they no longer evince any real faith in the concept of civilized order.

Still, they both continue to harbour desires to get certain things done. Jayne wants Max to get one of her clients, a young woman for whom she feels sorry, off the hook by framing the woman's husband – whom they know as "scum" – with a crime. Max wants Jayne to have her client locate a suspect. Meanwhile, Donny, Max's partner, waits outside in the car, drunk. Donny has problems besides alcoholism: a sadistic streak and a failed marriage. His estranged wife, Pam, is living with Jayne and growing ever more horrified at what she sees in Donny.

Donny picks up the young man they intend to pressure and stupidly brings him to the motel; Max beats Donny up, then takes the young man out to a secluded spot they use to extract "confessions" from suspects. The young man stabs him; Max shoots, kills, and buries the young man. Bleeding, Max returns to the motel room, explains what happened, and why he feels little remorse.

Given that synopsis, it may be difficult to believe that *Adult Entertainment* is a comedy, but the play is often very funny indeed, a sort of black farce. Farce is predicated on a situation where normal codes of rational conduct and morality are apparently suspended, creating an environment as strange as if the laws of physics had been temporarily subverted; the chaotic series of events that follow usually seems to be manipulated by some perverse external clockwork mechanism, until the mechanism seems to break or exhaust itself. In *Adult Entertainment* the suspension of ordinary codes of conduct has occurred sometime before the lights first come up. Max, Jayne, and Donny have become utterly detached from any deeper moral convictions or any notions of duty beyond simple expedience; Jayne's description of Max as "a hollow man with a badge" (55) could easily be modified to include her and Donny. The action turns to farce when their efficient plans explode with inconvenient ramifications (though the stakes run considerably higher than those of most farces).

Sayer's program of uprooting Oak from his humanism in *The Prince of Naples* might have eventually resulted in a nihilism like that we see here. There is a kind of difference between Max and Donny: Max is still able to enter into some discussion of this state of mind with Jayne, whereas Donny has become totally blind to any value but loyalty to Max and his own drunken will. Donny is simply not strong enough to become a moral code unto himself; he has passed a breaking point and become, as Pam sees it, a "monster." We see something of what he must once have been through the bewildered comments of Pam, who ingenuously looks to Jayne for clarification: "So feeling someone is scum doesn't ... kinda make you feel like you're scum too." No, responds Jayne: "Scum doesn't have conversations like this with people like you. Scum grabs people like you by the throat, drags you into an alley then rapes and kills you" (96). It is rather difficult to argue with Jayne's nomenclature in this particular instance, but when we see what Donny and Max routinely do, it is clear that we are only looking at differences of degree. Indeed, Jayne has a nightmare about Donny entering the motel room with Pam dressed as a prostitute, which, like a Jacobean subplot, provides a more grotesque but parallel image of the central dilemma. The nightmare is not far from reality; Donny and Pam occupy an ethical space a short distance from that of Max and Jayne; and we have little reason to believe that Jayne's client and her so-called "scum" husband are much further off.

Criminal Genius brings two of Walker's funniest characters, the father-and-son duo Rolly and Stevie Moore (*Beautiful City, Escape from Happiness*), back to the stage. They are hiding out in the motel room; we are not sure why at first. The play begins with a Marx Brothers–style exchange (over forty dollars, a watch, and a pair of shoes) among the Moores and Phillie, the drunken motel manager from *Problem Child*. When Phillie leaves we discover that the Moores have been hired through a woman named Shirley by gangster-restaurateur Mike Castle to set fire to a restaurant across the street from one of Castle's. Afraid that they might hurt someone in the act, the Moores decided instead to kidnap the cook, who, Shirley informs them, happens to be Amanda Castle, Mike's daughter. Her defiant decision to work for his rivals was Mike's motive for destroying the restaurant in the first place. Rolly, attempting to redeem matters, goes back and burns down the rival restaurant, but at the same time Amanda burns down her father's. Amanda takes over the group, which now includes Phillie; she declares that the five of them will kill her father before he kills them. When they regroup afterwards, we discover that, predictably, Rolly and Stevie have botched the plans. Then, in an astonishing finale, all five characters are shot and killed while they stand in the motel room.

The chief issue arising throughout *Criminal Genius* is blame, or responsibility. On the first page of the script, in response to Rolly's worries about being blamed for the botched job, Stevie suggests that Rolly "kinda outsmarted" himself. Rolly responds:

> Sure you can look at it that way. I prefer to think of myself as a victim. Everything I do almost I get punished for it ... When was the last time I did something and got away with it. There's always some kind of punishment. I always gotta take a knock. Why is that.   (103)

Well, because whatever Rolly does is usually not only wrong but also stupid. The satire certainly strikes at a syndrome that has become prevalent in the late twentieth century: righteously claiming victimhood in sometimes preposterous circumstances (a claim often attached to exorbitant litigation settlements). But considered within the entire *Suburban Motel* cycle, this theme of the repudiation of blame is a vital part of Walker's portrait of a disintegrating civilization.

In *Featuring Loretta* the title character, known as Lorrie, is a young, recently widowed woman (her husband was eaten by a bear) who has decided – quite deliberately and rationally – to perform in pornographic films in order to make money. As she explains it:

> Money is the only thing that expands your options. No matter what anybody says, it's money. Only money. It's not love and respect and intelligence and hard work. The world doesn't give a shit about any of those things if they're not also connected to money. (180)

But Sophie, the daughter of the Russian emigré owner of the motel (who has, she says, yelled her mother to death and is continually yelling at her), insists that Lorrie wants the money for the baby she is expecting, which was conceived in a regrettable liaison with her dead husband's best friend. Lorrie insists she is only interested in the money, though she refuses Sophie's offer to buy the baby. Meanwhile, Lorrie's former in-laws and her sister are pressuring her over the phone, while she is trying to close the deal with the would-be film producer, Michael, who continually assures Lorrie of the wealth that awaits her. As it happens, Michael has more chutzpah than experience, and his interest in Lorrie is chiefly based on his ill-disguised lust for her. Also lusting after Lorrie is Dave, a casual date who has become desperately proprietorial towards Lorrie. Dave anxiously volunteers to be Lorrie's partner in the sex video, but is not up to the job. As Michael sees it, Dave's problem is that he can't "bring the business thing into the front [of his brain] and put the love thing in the back" (183). When the failure of the project becomes manifest, Lorrie calls it off. As the play ends, the two men are scuffling competitively outside Lorrie's room.

So the chief issue haunting *Featuring Loretta* is control, particularly the question of personal agency for Lorrie. Each of the other characters – including those only contacted over the phone, and even the otherwise sympathetic Sophie – tries to coerce Lorrie into accepting his or her priorities for her own life. The pornographic film project, then, constitutes Lorrie's attempt to wrest her fate back. If she is to be exploited, she reasons, then she might as well exploit herself and draw a reasonable profit. Naturally, the more desirable thing would be not to feel exploited at all, by anyone; but, as so often, Walker shuns any easy solution to his character's difficulties, offering only kinds and degrees of exploitation. At the very least, in her struggle to free herself from the control of others Lorrie must enslave herself to the making of money. She is imprisoned in a paradox: "I have to make a lot of money," she says, "because I want to make sure that money is not a factor in my decisions" (189). In short, Walker shows that, as Bob Dylan put it, "you gotta serve somebody."

The subplot involving Sophie and her father, a former KGB agent who eventually yells himself to death, offers an expanded view of the central theme. Where Lorrie must be in thrall to the capitalist system if she wishes to exert any control over her own life, Sophie's father depended upon its opposite for his power to control others and, with the erosion of the communist power bloc, now suffers the frustrations of his relative impotence. There is also an implicit parallel with Dave and Michael. The Cold War was essentially a face-off between attempts to assert control belligerently through threats on a colossal scale, an attitude that, even from our relatively close vantage point, looks excessively primitive and futile – not unlike the battle of Michael and Dave outside the motel room. Now that the Cold War is over, it would seem a fine opportunity to relinquish that sort of infantile controlling instinct, but this may pose an insurmountable challenge to human nature.

Perhaps the darkest and most compelling play in the *Suburban Motel* cycle is *The End of Civilization*. When we look at its place in the cycle, there is little wonder. When *The End of Civilization* begins, the preceding plays set in this motel room have established the premises that justice is a mockery, that law enforcers routinely lie and are unsure of their own motives, that the dissociation of act and consequences is a prevalent social malaise, and that the palette of options for human dignity is circumscribed by the priorities of capitalism. In this setting we discover an unemployed middle-class man, Henry, being examined by the police – Max and Donny. Someone has placed a bomb in a dumpster at a local plant, and suspicion has fallen on Henry, who had been there applying for work and punched a grossly insolent plant supervisor. Henry is not the only one being investigated, but as Lily, Henry's wife, establishes, only the many unemployed, rejected job applicants who were at the plant are under suspicion. There is evidently a ready acknowledgment that the business policies currently pursued are causing widespread misery and profound social disaffection. As Henry's analysis of the social problem has it:

> It's because a bunch of greedy pricks can't put any fucking limits on themselves. It's because every asshole who runs one of these fucking enormous companies can smell these fucking enormous profits, and he knows the only thing between him and these profits is a little human misery. [...] A prudent reduction in the labour force. And no one's trying to stop any of this because no one cares. (221)

Indeed, the only commitment that appears to have been made is to persecute anyone who tries to revolt against the injustice.

The story-line of *The End of Civilization* is relatively straightforward. Henry and Lily have arrived in the city and are staying in the motel while Henry looks for a job. Henry was laid off after years of service with one company, and while both were at first confident that he would soon be re-employed, as time has passed with no real encouragement, their confidence has slowly ebbed, along with the standards of his job expectations. After the bomb threat Max and Donny begin their investigation. It turns out that Lily knew Donny in high school and he is still fond of her, so he hangs around the motel room on slim pretexts. His presence complicates matters, for in the meantime Lily has met Sandy, the waitress-experimenting-with-prostitution from *Criminals in Love*, now a full-time prostitute who offers to help Lily break into the business so that she can solve her desperate financial problems. When Henry discovers what has happened, he is naturally appalled: "You can't do just anything for money, Lil," he says. "There are limits. Definite limits to what a person can do. There's a certain point at which you have to stop or everything becomes meaningless" (237). But then as Henry described in the speech quoted earlier, we are already faced with a social environment in which people are doing "just anything" for money, and thus making lives meaningless. Lily's choice might be a desperate one in her own life, but it surely is not anomalous in the context of the prevailing social ethic.

The police investigation turns ugly: a number of unemployed men who had been applying for work at the same businesses Henry visited have been murdered. Henry confesses himself guilty, but then we discover that Donny has planted evidence to frame another man, giving Henry money to buy a bus ticket out of town. But Henry has not left town. He returns to the motel room to confront Donny with a gun, insisting that Donny has been plotting to have Lily for himself. Henry threatens Donny with the gun, demanding that Donny acknowledge the impressive man he was before he lost his job. Donny shoots him dead.

Despite the simplicity of the story-line, Walker's plotting is powerfully affecting because he has reordered the time sequence with a series of flashbacks to maximize the dramatic impact. In a manner similar to the plotting of a number of detective stories – and, most famously, Sophocles' construction of *Oedipus Rex* – we are taken through the events of the play backwards and forwards, so that we gradually piece together the story. The play takes place over a month-long period, with the eleven scenes unfolding in the order H, B, I, C, D, F, E, G, J, K, A. Thus, the scene set earliest, depicting Henry and Lily arriving at the motel on a Tuesday, comes last; the second scene we see actually takes place three weeks to the day after their arrival, when things have already become desperate; the first scene, in which we see Henry being interrogated by Max and Donny, takes place sometime in the week after the second scene. Besides enabling Walker to control information in order to create a sense of mystery and anticipation, this structure creates a powerful instrument for self-investigation. When Henry and Lily are first seen by the audience, they are sympathetic characters, but probably in a rather more desperate state than most people in a middle-class audience have ever found themselves. We then follow them into a terrifying, vertiginous loss of identity and faith in the social order. Then, once we have reached the furthest extremity of this night-mare, Walker turns the story back to show us this couple as they were upon their arrival. They are a little overstressed and a little quarrel-some, but they would be instantaneously identifiable with just about any ordinary middle-class couple in the audience. When, at the very end of the play, Walker offers one last piece of information, that Henry is taking unfamiliar new prescription drugs to alleviate his stress and depression, the identification of the characters with the audience is complete. Henry's loss of job and, consequently, identity could happen to any of us; his frustration and rage are wholly understandable; and, given a certain medication and enough provocation, any one of us might lose the bonds of civil restraint.

Given what has passed in the cycle up to this point, the title of the last play, *Risk Everything*, sounds like a clarion call to battle. Denise and R.J., from *Problem Child*, return, along with Michael, from *Featuring Loretta*. Also appearing is Denise's mother, Carol, who is known to us by reputation from the earlier play: "My mother ...," Denise had explained to Helen, "you know we were fighting and to get back at me she made it look like I was neglecting the baby and called you people" (24). So it would be easy for us to hate Carol; indeed, it appears that she is habitually traitorous. Now we hear that she and her friend Murray Lawson have taken sixty-eight thousand dollars from a thug named Steamboat Jeffries, who has had Carol beaten because of her refusal to repay him – though she has told the police and Denise that she was beaten by her boyfriend. When Denise is out buying groceries, Carol advises R.J. that, in turning from his criminal past to television-watching (lately he has switched from dysfunctional talk shows to wildlife shows, having found the former too depressing), he is becom-ing boring, and that Denise will lose interest in him unless he takes risks – such as going to Steamboat Jeffries to negotiate on Carol's behalf. R.J. returns wired with explosives. When Michael, who has become infatuated with Carol, also tries to help, he too is wired with explosives. Murray Lawson is, we are told, brutally killed by Steam-boat.

Meanwhile, Carol insists upon calculating the odds of whether the explosives are real. "Well, it's better to be dead than have that big piece of shit dictate the terms," she argues (296). However, Carol's obstinacy is not solely based in avarice. While it is doubtful that she sincerely believes in the advice she gives R.J., she does genuinely find the taking of risks, such as gambling on long shots or negotiating with murderous thugs, vitalizing. "Life only pays off when you bet to win," she declares (297). But in her terms Denise and R.J. are playing the short odds, concerned only with not losing too badly. "What is the purpose of life," she asks Denise:

> I know that you and R.J. are trying to be useful careful citizens. Hold down jobs. Put all your sins behind you. But what's in that for you really. You'll never get your kid back from social services. Never. I'm sorry, Denise. But it's not going to happen. You can go to that stupid clothing store where you work for the next five years, without missing a single day, and it still won't make those social workers trust you enough to give you back your daughter. Because to them you're a bad girl who's just pretending to be a good girl [...] This is your chance. We could turn this thing back on Steamboat and make a lot of money. You could take a chunk of that money. And you and R.J. could just grab your kid from that foster home, and the three of you could take off and start a new life together.
> (299)

It is a measure of how grim the realistic possibilities have come to seem that Carol's argument, in the context of the play, sounds not wholly absurd but fairly positive and even rather compellingly clear-sighted.

In the end it turns out that Murray has been dead for weeks and Carol has had the money all along. She also knew that the explosives were real, but was trying to play out the odds, to "risk everything." Denise finally pries the money out of her mother's possession simply by being more obstinate, demanding relentlessly: "Give me the money." Meanwhile, Carol and Michael had been preparing to have sex. Grasping at "a victory over all the negative mingy shit that goes on in this world," Carol suggests to Michael: "When you and I crawl into bed and begin to have free wild uninhibited sexual intercourse while we both face imminent destruction it will be a blow for our side" (313). Delighted with her inadvertent pun, she is on her knees in front of Michael, unzipping his pants, when Denise comes back in to demand the money. So the money is handed over, and R.J. and Michael go outside to be unwired by Steamboat. In the final moment, Michael returns to the motel room; he is still erect.

Perhaps, as more than one reviewer complained, ending the play and the cycle in this way seems "anti-climactic." But the implications of that pun and Carol's are worth examining. At its basic level, comedy ultimately celebrates the vital over the moribund, life over death. The reason so many classic comedies end with a marriage, or the promise of a marriage, is not, as some argue, merely due to bland, conservative, heterosexual bias but is because marriage inherently represents a commitment to procreation (as the traditional "Solemnization of Matrimony" emphasizes) and is thus implicitly a symbol of a renewed commitment to life. Thus, the most archetypal of romantic comedies, such as *The Winter's Tale* or *Much Ado about Nothing,* end not only with incipient marriages but with hints of miraculous resurrections. Nowadays, of course – and this would have to be especially true of the worldly-wise characters of Walker's plays – the connection between marriage and procreation seems rather less essential; but the connection between sex, procreation, and renewed life continues to assert itself afresh.

Certainly, *Suburban Motel* ventures much further into death than most comedy does. *Problem Child* poses a version of the harrowing, unnatural beginning common to so many comedies: a young couple has been deprived of the child, the new life they have made. It also contains a death that turns out to be false. Every succeeding play contains an actual death as part of the action: in *Adult Entertainment* it is the young man Donny kills; in *Criminal Genius* it is the whole cast; in *Featuring Loretta* it is Sophie's father; in *The End of Civilization* it is the unemployed men. So when we come to the other bookend, it is appropriate that we have another death that, in a sense, turns out to be phoney: Murray Lawson is not brutally killed during the course of the play; he had died a relatively good death at the race track some weeks earlier; Carol's scheme was partially a tribute to the memory of Murray's spirit. This may be a way of saying that death is not what is most real, and not the final statement, about life. And Michael's erection may be a way of saying that what *is* most important is embracing life in the face of death, and that the life-instinct has the power to transcend, however perversely, the death-instinct. Thus, an erect penis is perhaps the most appropriate image with which to end this cycle. Perhaps, as the Greeks believed when they made the *phalloi* an essential part of the celebrations at the City Dionysia, it is one of the most honest, simple, and unambiguous symbols of vital uplift there is.

Walker's *Heaven* (2000) features another character who, like Tyrone Power, embodies the failure of liberal idealism. Jimmy – James Joyce Milliken – is a human-rights lawyer who appears to be something of a bigot until we realize that he does not discriminate; he has lost his faith in humanity altogether. Essentially, Jimmy's disillusion-ment is a version of the general spiritual crisis adumbrated through-out *Suburban Motel*.

Now, where such a crisis is so acute as to be apparently insoluble, and the means of relief are not readily apprehensible on earth, the tra-ditional recourse is to look to the hope of transcendent relief – in other words, to heaven. But given Walker's previous treatments of the theme of religion, it is not likely that he would be sanguine about the promise of justice in the afterlife. Neither is Jimmy. Like his namesake, James Joyce Milliken is an Irish Catholic who is disgusted with the hypocrisy of his church and, indeed, with the hypocrisy and intolerance of all creeds. Once regarded by the downtrodden he defended as "the one true light of moral indignation" (139), Jimmy has now undertaken instead (as his wife Judy puts it) "an unofficial campaign to eradicate all the bullshit from the world" (54).

Judy is Jewish, and whereas it had originally been a point of pride for her and Jimmy that their families were hostile towards their exogamous marriage, there has gradually emerged a rift between the couple them-selves that is now, as Judy seeks solace in her faith (and more intimate comfort in her rabbi, David), compounded by their religious differ-ences. Meanwhile, Jimmy has become the nemesis of Karl, his former childhood friend, now an undercover policeman who has turned to out-lawry, having lost faith in the justice system. Karl blames Jimmy for instigating the suicide of his partner, whom Jimmy had prosecuted for shooting a black youth. Karl kills Judy in revenge; then he kills Derek, a young black petty criminal and drug addict, whom Karl has been exploiting; finally, he kills Jimmy. Derek's friend Sissy, a sixteen-year-old drug addict and would-be juggler-acrobat, stabs Karl to death with a knife, which puts all the characters except David and herself in heaven. Here we encounter the chief target of Walker's satire, and perhaps another reason that he named his protagonist after James Joyce.

In *A Portrait of the Artist as a Young Man* Joyce attacks Catholicism by describing hell as imagined by a fanatical priest: a place one suffers eternal torture for succumbing to one's human nature (117–35). Walker accomplishes something similar by depicting heaven as implied by the popular imagination. The premise for these conceits is that heaven and hell stand at the apex and the nadir of particular moral conceptions of the universe: if these transcendent extremes of justice are skewed, the whole will be likewise unjust. Thus, heaven being the tip of a conceptual pyramid that has its base here on earth, by taking aim at the popular concept of heaven Walker indirectly attacks a broad complex of syndromes related to the predominant moral outlook of our society. Systematically, he raises the common ideas about heaven

– a place of wish-fulfilment, a promise of redemption for sinners, an incentive to goodness, a state of oblivion – and demonstrates their insidiousness.

When Judy dies, she becomes first "a member of some kind of killer elite" (86), taking advantage of the opportunity to beat up Jimmy; later, fulfilling a childhood dream, she plays at being a surgeon, operating on other souls who, naturally, do not require her attentions. These are sordid, puerile fantasies. For his part, Derek becomes a racing car driver, but after the brief satisfaction of crashing and burning spectacularly, he complains: "This is fucked [...] I mean I think I saw a Formula One race on TV once. Once. I remember thinking that looks cool. So what's this. Is that the closest I got to having a fucking dream. Is that the only thing I ever wanted to be besides what I was. Which was some white cop's bum boy" (112). As a place of wish-fulfilment, heaven is circumscribed by the limits of our imaginations, and inasmuch as a limited scope of life tends to limit the reach of imagination, heaven can provide no satisfactory compensation for a life of frustrated possibility and oppression. The insidiousness of the notion that heaven promises redemption for sinners is shown when Karl, having shouted "Jesus Christ" in pain when he was stabbed, is admitted to heaven, where as a happy, redeemed soul he taunts Derek.

Probably most prevalent among the various conceptions of heaven, however, are those holding that heaven is a reward and an incentive for goodness, or a state of oblivion that releases us from the pain of the world. These ideas are implicitly criticized throughout the play, but Walker reserves his most direct attack for Jimmy's powerful final monologue at the play's end. Part of the power of this ending stems from the element of surprise, for the penultimate scene in *Heaven* would make a plausible closing for the play. David is sitting in the park, tormenting himself with jealous imaginings about Judy and Jimmy having sex in heaven, when Sissy enters on her stilts. She dismisses his guilt about the unworthiness of such thoughts for a rabbi by observing that he is only human. Moreover, she points out the absurdity of his believing in heaven when he has confessed to no longer believing in God. She then performs a trick on the stilts. Evidently, despite the improbability, Sissy has successfully managed to transform herself into a juggler-acrobat. We may be reminded a little of the ending of *Problem Child* and the unlikely success of RJ's persistent phone-calls to the talk-show producers. The interpretation of this delightful trope of Sissy's juggling is crucial. David's idea is that there is a reason she is good at these things, some unrevealed purpose. Were this true, Sissy's juggling would be an affirmation of providence similar to the obsessive practice of a bizarre basketball move by the boys in John Irving's *A Prayer for Owen Meaney,* which prepares them for the destiny revealed at the end of the novel. Sissy rejects David's interpretation, but as the scene ends and she is walking on the stilts and juggling at the same time, she says: "I don't know why this feels so good" (134). Undoubtedly part of the reason it feels good is that she has achieved an improbable state of equilibrium and co-ordination through self-reliance. She embodies a compelling symbol for the difficult challenge of bringing the moral chaos of this world into balance.

Then suddenly, after this false ending, Jimmy appears in a spotlight with a microphone to deliver a stand-up comedy routine in "the Celestial Improv": a monologue on the theme of "unbearable soul sucking pain. And what we do to escape it" (135). Naturally, the idea Jimmy returns to is heaven. He demonstrates the vulgarity of the notion of heaven as an incentive God uses to encourage goodness with a parable: a candidate for hosting a "be-a-better person" television talk show agrees to improve his character in exchange for the right salary offer. He summarily discards the conception of heaven as a state of oblivion: "I mean okay I'm … here in heaven but am I just supposed to forget that happened … I mean talk about insensitive … I guess we'll take just about any fucking excuse to feel good" (141). As he sees it, feeling good has more to do with the illusion of having achieved justice than with any actuality. Hence, Jimmy opts to feel pain rather than pleasure.

That seems to imply a grim conclusion, but there are several elements working against such negativity. First, there is the image Sissy left us with in the previous scene: her joy at her own ability to balance. Then, there is the undeniable fact that Jimmy's monologue is often very funny. And finally, we are struck by the feat of dramaturgical balance Walker has managed to achieve with this scene. To have dared to have his dead protagonist address the audience with a stand-up comedy routine at the end of his play, and to make this conceit work, is a feat of virtuosity that parallels Sissy's. So the peculiar sensation of buoyancy that Sissy inculcates in the audience is carried through to the end of the play. In creating this effect, Walker has made dramaturgical form play a crucial role in conveying his underlying philosophical themes.

Considered as a genre of discourse, most stand-up comedy is essentially a species of rhetorical argument: the comic provides a series of observations that, in sum, argue the absurdity of human behaviour. Rarely does the monologue urge the audience towards any specific action, for its point is less exhortation than provocation. Accordingly,

Jimmy's final monologue presents no solutions, no advice, only an ironic perspective that signifies his transformation from cynic, a man who despises all humanity, into kynic, philosophical joker. Thus we see him as standing in a line of similar embattled defendants of liberal humanism: Tyrone Power, Victor in *Zastrozzi*, William in *Criminals in Love*, Jack the priest in *Better Living*, Petie Maxwell in *Love and Anger*, and so on. Yet it is impossible not to feel that in Jimmy these figures have been supplanted by a more determined, more competent character. Where, for example, the death of a kynic like Petie seemed equivalent to the failure of social idealism, Jimmy, though dead, has been given an eternal platform from which to vent his discontent. The point may not seem to make much practical difference, but in drama emotional effect supercedes logical conclusions, and by giving Jimmy a permanent role as a subversive voice in heaven, Walker evidently has drawn a line from which he is unwilling to retreat.

Indeed, in suggesting that Jimmy's voice and ideas outlive his death, Walker invites a comparison to his most heroic kynic, Bazarov. The differences between the characters have to do with the different ages in which they live. In Walker's hands Bazarov's nihilism is a mask worn by a passionate social liberal who tempers his early-modern idealism about human potential with a stern and ruthless cynicism about humans as they are. Jimmy's cynicism is not a principled policy choice in the same way; it actually stems from his misery at finding his modern liberal principles untenable in a postmodern world that pays hypocritical lip-service to those principles. So where the discussion of Bazarov's ideas after his death seemed to herald the possibility of a new, socially progressive society, Jimmy's after-death contribution can offer only an ironic commentary upon the inadequacy of the current society. But in the postmodern world Walker shows us it is in such voices as Jimmy's, the voice of an untiring kynic, that the true possibilities of human improvement lie. Here, as throughout Walker's work, humour provides the vital corrective force that the pragmatic moralist requires to maintain a balanced perspective in an absurd world.

6 Judith Thompson: Social Psychomachia

> Theatre is not realistic in a vulgar, wide-awake fashion: it is realistic as dreams are realistic; it deals in hidden dreads, and it satisfies hidden, primal wishes.
>
> Robertson Davies, A Voice from the Attic

LEAKING THE REPRESSED

When, in 1990, Judith Thompson described herself as "a devoted Freudian in some ways" (*Fair*, 99) some of her admirers may have been disconcerted. By then the great man's reputation was already manifestly in decline. A series of increasingly biting attacks were being made by writers such as Adolf Grünbaum, Jeffrey Masson, Frederick Crews, and even Gloria Steinem, that represented the father of psychoanalysis as patriarchal, sexist, unscientific, capricious, irrational, egotistical, deluded, paranoid, dishonest, sexually perverted, and just plain wrong. Many people apparently felt that the time had come simply to junk Freud and his ideas altogether.

To be sure, there has been a predictable rallying of the defence among psychoanalysts with a vested professional interest in Freudian theories, though inevitably responses from this quarter are regarded with some cynicism, as ultimately self-serving. More persuasive have been those commentators not themselves engaged in psychological practice who argue that, in spite of his errors and missteps, Freud's contribution to Western thought remains valuable for its general insights into the human condition. An early example of such a defence is Lionel Trilling's 1955 address to the New York Psychoanalytical Society. He maintains that Freud permanently altered our world-view by articulating a vision of the relation between the self and culture that emphasized the irreducible biological core of the person, an aspect of humanity not easily susceptible to social determinants. In Trilling's view this central Freudian idea is indispensable to achieving a mature, coherent, and liberal understanding of human possibility. He implies that the sort of understanding Freud provides is crucial at a time when the old intermediaries between mass culture and the individual – such as the family or religion – have weakened and there is a corresponding growth in the effects of mass cultural determinants.

Most of the more persuasive recent defences of Freud (by such writers as Jean Bethke Elshtain, Thomas Nagel, Camille Paglia, Paul Robinson, and Richard Wollheim) have been mounted along similar lines, with no intention to absolve Freud entirely of his faults. On the contrary, the persuasiveness of these writers has to do, in part, with their leavening of arguments for Freud's continuing relevance with a ready acknowledgement of his shortcomings. Similarly, Judith Thompson, despite her admiration for Freud, acknowledges his "fairy-tale desire to make everything fit into his scheme. It doesn't" (*Fair*, 99).

By the same token, there is little doubt that part of the antipathy towards Freud is rooted in the obstacle his view of human nature presents to various ideological schemes.[1] For example, in *Civilization and Its Discontents* Freud dampens the glow of social optimism with a dousing of biological fatalism:

We may expect gradually to carry through such alterations in our civilization as will better satisfy our needs and will escape our criticisms. But perhaps we may also familiarize ourselves with the idea that there are difficulties attaching to the nature of civilization which will not yield to any attempt at reform.   (306)

The expectations inherent in social idealism are related to what Freud calls the "cultural super-ego." Just as the moral demands of the personal super-ego can be unrealistically severe,

Exactly the same objections can be made against the ethical demands of the cultural super-ego. It, too, does not trouble itself enough about the facts of the mental constitution of human beings. It issues a command and does not ask whether it is possible for people to obey it. On the contrary, it assumes that a man's ego is psychologically capable of anything that is required of it, that his ego has unlimited mastery over his id. This is a mistake; and even in what are known as normal people the id cannot be controlled beyond certain limits.   (337)

Had Freud included only the various manifestations of Eros, or the life instinct, among these insubordinate aspects of the id, that would be inconvenient enough; but in *Civilization and Its Discontents* he explicitly includes the urges associated with the death instinct, or Thanatos. And whereas earlier, in *Beyond the Pleasure Principle*, he had meant by this an urge "to return to the quiescence of the inorganic world" (86), he now had in mind as well the human impulses towards aggression, violence, and destruction (*Civilization*, 310–11). In short, where they are given any kind of credence, Freud's ideas about the difficulties human nature represents for programs of social reform cause extensive complications for any ideological modelling of reality.

Part of what I want to argue in this chapter, then, is that Judith Thompson's work introduces repressed or denied evidence into our perception of human interaction, and this evidence complicates our social ideas in ways that are analogous (and in some cases closely related) to Freud's theories. We see, for example, Thompson's quasi-Freudian determination to utter the repressed, and the similar natural terms in which she regards the sources of what is repressed, in a comments such as those she made in a panel discussion on women's theatre in 1995:

Theatre has to be embarrassing, and theatre has to be slovenly ... When I have young babies I like to let my breast milk leak through my blouse in public at nice restaurants. I will not wear those breast pads! And the looks of disgust on people's faces are the same looks on people that walk out of my plays. I've let something leak that's not supposed to be leaking.   ("Look," 23)

In the same discussion she speaks about how, having grown up as a Catholic girl with a "psyche bound like the feet of women in ancient China," she asserted her inner self against the sense of repression through an "unlady-like" clumsiness, "because it illustrated the schism between my private and public self, and then in [the] Grand Mal seizures" of her epilepsy (23). She goes on to suggest that her first play, *The Crackwalker*, might be seen as a sort of figurative seizure, a different way of defiantly uttering what is socially repressed.

At the same time Thompson is determined to resist any program of transgression that would in itself result in a new, equally false kind of mask. For instance, for the anthology *Language in Her Eye* she was asked to describe the relationship of feminism to writing; in her reply she notes:

none of my characters defines herself as a feminist, *or* as someone opposed to feminism. Most of them have been successfully brainwashed by the patriarchal society in which they live, and the others are in a fight to the death with themselves because of it. But there is one I have overlooked, I think.   ("One")

She then proceeds to sketch this character, who she suggests is "one-twelfth" of Judith. The woman she describes is disturbingly complex:

rebellious but timid; politically astute and assertive of feminist rights, but only where convenient; both proud and self-hating; sympathetic and ethically aware, but also selfish and dishonest. The portrait refuses any sentimental ideas about the basic goodness of the oppressed, even as it makes clear that this character is indeed to some a degree a product of sexist oppression – mixed with feminist awareness, her own personal urges, and other factors. The inner truths she utters here (or leaks) are just as "embarrassing" to any tidy, sunny image that a façile, sentimental conception of feminist emancipation might cherish as they would be for any blinkered insistence on modest decency associated with a patriarchal outlook. Thompson sums the idea up neatly when she says: "That's why I'm a playwright – to explore the huge chasm between the social persona and the inner life, to find out who people really are" (Steed, E5).

To this point then, despite the differences that (leaving aside considerations of gender) we would expect their different societies to effect in their separate outlooks, some of the affinities Thompson has with Freud's general program of transgressing social norms and exposing the repressed are clear enough. But I want to go further than that, to demonstrate over the course of this discussion a possibly more controversial point. For while at one level Thompson's work seems to support the validity of certain basic Freudian insights by disclosing and dramatizing repressed elements of the social psyche, at another she achieves a vision of humanity that stands well beyond the reach of any purely psychoanalytic outlook. In so doing, she incidentally offers a solution to what is perhaps the single greatest problem facing psychoanalytic theory, a problem that remains notwithstanding any of those spirited defences of Freud's relevance, and that is potentially much more serious than the faults of any particular aspect of clinical analysis.

The seriousness of the problem is underscored by its being raised by one of Freud's greatest apologists, Norman O. Brown. In *Life against Death* (1959) Brown writes that, if psychoanalysis is right, the whole of culture consists of sublimations, and the history of civilization is therefore the history of neurosis. Moreover, psychoanalysis being inside history, Freud could find "no way of avoiding the internalization of aggression, the accumulation of guilt," and hence could offer no means of escaping the dismal closed circle his own theory described (152–3). Brown feels that the solution lies in an eschatology drawing on both psychoanalysis and Christian theology; but the closer he comes to articulating this vision, the more woolly his argument becomes.

By comparison, Judith Thompson's work holds out a sense of promise analogous to Brown's, but it reaches further in its realization of this promise. Her plays employ aspects of psychoanalytic theory as a conceptual framework, or a sort of grammar of the private and social imagination. This framework facilitates her exploration of that place in the collective imagination where class tensions and personal anxieties meet and social malaise roots itself in the neurotic configurations of the private mind. Through her dramatization of these forces she also seeks a means of transcending psychological determinism, and to this end her work posits a counterpart to Brown's Christian eschatology: a sort of existential Grace.

Thompson's first encounter with psychological theory likely came through her father, the late William Robert Thompson, a professor of psychology and for many years head of the department at Queen's University. She consolidated her understanding of psychology more formally in the early 1980s when she used a Canada Council grant to study Freud and autism at the University of Toronto, reading all of Freud's work "in about a year and a half" (*Fair*, 99). Thompson says that she has "never used those subjects directly, but the plays were infused with what I had learned" ("Happy," 134) – a subtle distinction that may guide us towards balanced critical interpretation. Thus, while George Toles's 1988 psychoanalytic essay is certainly one of the most penetrating commentaries published on Thompson's work, it should be emphasized that her plays tend to accommodate rather than insist on such a psychoanalytic reading.

OUBLIETTE OF THE SOCIAL PSYCHE

The earliest critics of Thompson's work seldom took anything like a psychoanalytic approach. In reviews of her first play, *The Crackwalker* (1980) – which, in the opinion of Toles, "from the time of its first production has been wrongly identified as a naturalistic play" (122) – the aspect of her work eliciting the most comment was her gift for representing the lives and voices of a particular milieu never represented on stage before, the lower-class residents of Kingston, Ontario. John Astington, for example, in his review of the published script, declared that "Judith Thompson is most impressive in recreating the language of the people of this insecure, poor society," and suggested that *The Crackwalker* marked "an important stage in the development of Canadian dramatic writing in English, since for the first time a playwright has felt confident enough to write a major play in a convincingly real dialect of the poor, the petty criminals, and the marginally employed, and by doing so has made directly accessible to an audience a whole world of experience which otherwise would remain merely sociological statistics" ("Drama" 1982, 382–3). Undoubtedly Astington's assessment extends to the setting and the action of the play as well. *The Crackwalker* tells the story of Therese, a mildly mentally handicapped, part-Native woman who has a child by Alan, an emotionally disturbed young man who is incapable of holding down any kind of job for long. For most of the play these two are living with friends, Sandy and Joe, who are themselves little better off, spending most of their time getting drunk and quarrelling. There is a fifth character, a drunken Native man who wanders about the town, mumbling and shouting incoherent obscenities. The plot reaches its climax when Alan, after losing his job as a dishwasher, strangles his and Therese's baby to death.

In focusing on the representation of the underclass, as Astington and other reviewers did, the predominant emphasis was laid on the mimetic aspect of the play. So considered, *The Crackwalker* has a clear lineage, belonging to a series of works embracing successively greater degrees of reality by moving down through the social classes to focus on previously ignored groups. The tradition may be traced as far back as Diderot's bourgeois drama of the eighteenth century. As the middle class grew, Diderot's innovation was carried through various stages of realism, moving from plays that merely portrayed the middle class to plays that took a critical stance against it and exposed the seamy underside of apparently respectable middle-class life. The trend reached its furthest extreme in the nineteenth century with the shocking "comédies rosses," the most notorious of which was August Linert's *Christmas Story*, which bears a superficial resemblance to *The Crackwalker* in that at one point a child is murdered and thrown into a pigpen.

In the twentieth century we see realism shift its focus still further down the social hierarchy: what is deemed most "real" is often that previously deemed most squalid. Drama continues to be written for the consumption of mainly middle-class audiences, but plays that, like *The Crackwalker*, focus on the lower classes, particularly the more sordid aspects of the urban sub-proletariat, have practically become a genre of their own: Edward Bond's *Saved* (1965), Xaver Kroetz's *Staller's Farm* (1971) and *Michi's Blood*, David Mamet's *American Buffalo* (1977), and, in Canada, Marcel Dubé's *Zone* (1953) and John Herbert's *Fortune and Men's Eyes* (1967). Like *Crackwalker*, these plays dramatize unhappy and often quite dreadful lives at the lower margins of the social system, the "derelicts" who, to one degree or another, have been abandoned by their societies. Invariably poor, frequently illiterate, sometimes criminal: these characters are not the kind of people a playwright would normally expect to turn out to see the play. It is reasonable to suppose, then, as Astington does, that part of the value of these plays is instructive: they expose middle-class audiences to an underworld they would not ordinarily come into contact with or think much about. Furthermore, such plays expand the mimetic scope of the theatre by bringing previously excluded aspects of society on to the stage, and at the same time extend the range of dramatic language by moving outside previous conventions to retrieve new elements of language from the streets. That idea is obvious enough: the playwright tries to recreate the argot heard in a certain environment and, in doing so, broadens the varieties of diction and syntax heard in the theatre.

But the point goes deeper, because in expanding the scope of an art to represent more kinds of human beings, the artist inevitably represents more of human nature itself – of humanity *qua generis*, so to speak. In other words, in seeing more of humanity, the range of our understanding of what constitutes any given individual of the human species is extended. This perspective is useful in approaching Judith Thompson's plays, for all her best work manages to explore the levels of both social class and psychic consciousness at once.

Now, to an eighteenth-century European like Diderot, it would no doubt seem strange that an anxious preoccupation with class would continue in the twentieth century, particularly in a putatively classless society like Canada. But, as Alexis de Tocqueville pointed out in *Democracy in America*, the anxieties of social class may be even more pronounced in a democracy because there is a greater threat of having nothing significant to mark one apart from one's fellow citizens, and this anxiety begets a more strenuous search for marks of distinction. Furthermore, because these anxieties of class consciousness work both upwards and downwards, virtually any question of class barriers will inevitably invoke levels of psychic anxiety.

Consider, for example, this passage from *The Crackwalker*, which at a deceptive first glance may look a little banal:

ALAN: ... d'ju hear about Boyd's GTO?

JOE: What the one that used to be parked on Johnson below Division?

ALAN: Yeah, you know, green with chrome mags and chrome cut outs.

JOE: Yeah. What a fuckin beast. What about it?

ALAN: He totalled it.

JOE: Hah. Well it was a shitty lookin car anyways.

ALAN: Yeah but fuck it had – it had them high lift cam solid lifters, and, and high compression kit and –

JOE: You name it.

ALAN: He had it. Yup. Hey – did you know it had four fuckin carbs?

JOE: Eat shit.

ALAN: No kiddin, four! But you know how come he kept it looking so shitty?

JOE: Beats me.

ALAN: So the cops wouldn't notice. They all knew, though eh, they knew what he had. Fuck that thing was fast he used to shoot the main drag doin one-fifty.

JOE: Yeah? That's fast.

ALAN: Fuckin fast. You know how he totalled it?

JOE: No.

ALAN: Fuck it was funny. We were gettin polluted up at the Manor, eh, and Alfie decides he's gonna go up to Gan. He was about half-pissed I guess. So parently he tries to pass three or four cars same time except one of em happens to be a truck goin left. So I guess he almost makes it but the truck catches him by his back right fender and spins him. Huh. Flipped the car six fuckin times.

JOE: Jeez. How is he?

ALAN: Alfie? He's okay now but he got stabbed in the heart with the rearview mirror. Had an operation. [...] What's that a present for the wife?

JOE: Yeah. That Charlie perfume shit.

ALAN: Hardly nice. Yeah, that's nice stuff. Women – they like that kinda stuff.

JOE: I know. Smells shitty to me.

ALAN: Yeah.

JOE: Well I gotta move buddy catch you later.

ALAN: Hey! Hey! [*From his pocket,* ALAN *takes an ornamental iron monk with a hard on. It is wrapped in newspaper*] Here.

JOE: What's this?

ALAN: Just somethin.

JOE: Oh yeah. I seen one of these. Well I'm gone.

ALAN: See ya... Bye Joe!   (65–7)

There are three elements to notice here that are typical of *The Crack-walker* and connected with three ways of approaching the play. First is the observation made by the early critics: the convincing representation of the vernacular of a particular social sector.[2]

Second is the imagery and symbolism of the passage. The GTO that looks like a wreck but has a powerful engine and many accessories under the hood; the colloquialisms and brand names that pepper the conversation; the little iron monk: all these, together with the profanity, suggest the thought-patterns of people whose lives are bereft of meaning, for whom the trivial has come to symbolize the significant. The souped-up car gives rise to a local legend about an outlaw's elusion of the authorities; the profanities, colloquialisms, and brand names in the play are shibboleths – they establish membership and hence status in the tribe; and the little monk, a gag ornament, becomes a kind of talisman that Alan gives to Joe to symbolize a bond of friendship. Of course, all those elements are indigenous to the milieu of the play and could easily be accommodated within a naturalistic reading. But they also point to something outside the naturalistic realm, supporting a poetic interpretation that becomes more obviously valuable as we go on to consider the third approach, which has to do with the theme of Alan's story.

Alan is fascinated by the notion that beneath the surface of the GTO is an almost legendary formidable power that, unleashed, has a terrifying capacity for destructiveness. We should not be fooled by the false bravado of "Fuck it was funny." Alan is transfixed by the horrific, and is tormented with nightmarish visions at all hours of the day. We get a fuller sense of this ghoulish element of Alan's mind in his soliloquy (over the course of the play, each of the four main characters has a major soliloquy), when Alan asks the audience:

> Did ya ever start thinkin somethin, and it's like ugly ...? And ya can't beat it out of your head? I wouldn't be scared of it if it was sittin in front of me, I'd beat it to shit – nothin wouldn't stop me – but I can't beat it cause it's in my head fuck. It's not like bein crazy, it's just like thinkin one thing over and over and it kinda make ya sick. Like when I was a kid and I used to have these earaches all the time, you know? And I would keep thinkin it was like a couple of garter snakes with big ugly teeth all yellow, like an *old* guy's teeth and there were the two of them suckin and bitin on my eardrum with these yellow teeth. Makin noises like a cat eatin cat food, I could even hear the fuckin noises. [*makes the noise*] Like that. Just make me wanta puke thinkin that – made the pain worse I'd think of their eyes, too, that made me sick, black eyes lookin sideways all the time while they keep suckin and chewin on my eardrum. Fuck. Do youse know what I mean? No offense or nothin I don't mean no offense I wish youse all good luck in your lives I was just – like I just wanted to know if any of youse like knew of a medicine or somethin ya might take for this ...   (55)

The desperate impotence of Alan's consciousness, his inability to keep unconscious horrors from intruding into his thoughts, or to keep his primal urges from becoming actions, is one of the chief themes of *The Crackwalker*. This free flowing of the unconscious is a feature of almost all Thompson's work. She has described herself as being "in contact with the dark," a state she likens to a "screen door swinging between the unconscious and conscious mind" (quoted in Hunt, 12). In *The Crackwalker* Alan's suffering from this flow of the productions of his unconscious is central not only to the plot (Alan kills his son chiefly because he is overcome with psychological stress) but to the ethos of the whole play. For the configuration of Alan's troubled mind invites comparisons with the imaginative structure of the larger world as conceived by Thompson for this play.

The analogy I am pressing here is not rooted simply in the famous Freudian notion about ontogeny recapitulating phylogeny – that is, that the psychic development of the individual is a shortened repetition of the development of the race. Rather, it belongs to a conception that may be inherent to social thought. The earliest well-known version of this conception is Plato's parallel between the structure of the individual mind, which he saw as consisting of Reason, Will, and Desire, and his ideal political structure, which he imagined would consist of a Philosopher King, the Military, and the People. The medieval world assumed a religionated form of this same analogy; and, with modifications, its legacy is evident in literature right through to the eighteenth century. But a turnabout occurred during the Romantic period, the effects of which we are still feeling today. There, the most interesting analogies between larger social structures and the organization of the individual mind are those found in the Romantic poets' treatment of the French Revolution and its aftermath. The pattern is neatly displayed in Shelley's *Prometheus Unbound* or in William Blake's "prophecies," which argue a correspondence between the overthrow of the aristocracy by the proletariat and the revolt of imagination against empirical reason within the individual mind. Blake's whole poetic grammar is founded on a schematic picture of a moribund social hierarchy transformed by powerful humanistic energies from the lower depths, the revolution in social classes occurring at the same time as, within the individual mind, the establishment-mindedness on the conventional surface of the psyche is transformed by creative energy bubbling up from a deep primal level.

The legacy of such Romantic thought is evident in the closely related symbolic structure of Marx's conception of the levels of social hierarchy and his ideas about the potential for emancipation latent in the suppressed proletariat. Marx shares the Romantics' essentially optimistic Rousseauvian view, wherein revolution in society and its complement in the individual mind is regarded as purely and simply a liberation of humanity from tyranny. This common philosophy was the basis of André Breton's notion that Surrealism was the most appropriate art for Marxists: in both cases, what surges up from the suppressed sublevel of the structure, the level of the unconscious or the proletariat, is conceived of as having a salutary and liberating effect on the whole.

The example of the Surrealists begins to lead us back to Thompson, for we notice that there exists in much Surrealist art a fascination with grotesque bodily imagery that is comparable to some of the imagery found in Thompson's work. Indeed, that coincidence, together with the similar interest in the tensions of social class, may encourage us to feel that we have discovered here a congruity of poetics; but there are some crucial distinctions to take into account. First, we should acknowledge that this addition of bodily imagery to the structural conceptions of psyche and social class confirms the observations of Stallybrass and White, who, in *The Politics and Poetics of Transgression*, suggest that the three conceptual realms go hand in hand with a fourth: geographical space. The authors assert:

The high/low opposition in each of our four symbolic domains – psychic forms, the human body, geographical space and the social order – is a fundamental basis to mechanisms of ordering and sense-making in European cultures. Divisions and discriminations in one domain are continually structured, legitimated and dissolved by reference to the vertical symbolic hierarchy which operates in the other three domains. Cultures "think themselves" in the most immediate and affective ways through the combined symbolisms of these four hierarchies. (3)

One of the chief paradoxes Stallybrass and White address is that the cultural determination of what is ennobling and exalted depends in no small part on its relation to what is despised and debased. Moreover, this interdependent relation becomes a vital field against which a variety of crucial transgressions take place – as we see, for example, in the process whereby what is consigned to the realm of the low and disgusting is inevitably transformed into an object of illicit desire.

In the historical pattern of transgression we encounter a much darker and more unsettling version of the congruent imaginative structures we have been discussing, and hence a perspective apprehending more of the complexity inherent in the poetics of Judith Thompson's work. In contrast with but parallel to the Rousseauvian idealism described above is a literary tradition that begins with those who found the French Revolution as much a liberation of indiscriminate butchery as egalitarian democracy, and who asserted a correspondingly dark view of the human mind in their work. This is the tradition examined by Mario Praz in *The Romantic Agony*, an exploration of the connections between desire, cruelty, and religion and the confounding of the beautiful and the ugly, pleasure and pain, the sacred and the profane in literature from the Marquis de Sade through to Byron and Baudelaire. These authors all embrace an aesthetic of transgression, but they imply that the energies seething up from the lower sectors to transform society and the individual mind might as easily be destructive as salutary.

While it would be misleading, perhaps, to suggest that Judith Thompson properly belongs to this latter tradition any more than she does the former, it is none the less true that her work does not repudiate the outlook on human nature such writings embrace. In this we see another of Thompson's affinities with Freud, for while Freud was in accord with the Rousseauvian optimists in so far as he spoke of the dangers inherent in the repression of natural instincts, he was by no means of the opinion that the simple release of repressed elements would be all to the good, as his theory of the related Life and Death instincts suggests. Transgression of the various conceptual hierarchies may be in some circumstances a creative act, but there are also frightening implications involved.

Returning now to *The Crackwalker*, we are in a better position to understand the ambivalent poetics of the play. The horrifying images that erupt on to the surface of Alan's mind are associated with the play's social imagery, the patterns of spatial metaphor, and the treatment of the body. We see Alan's aghast fascination with the "lower" parts of the body, for example, in the latter part of the monologue quoted earlier, when he morbidly relates the story of an impoverished farm-wife afflicted with a cauliflower-like growth in her vagina (OSD 51). But the four different symbolic structures – psychic, social, bodily, and spatial – are most clearly unified in the central metaphor of the play: "the Crackwalker" himself. This character, who never appears on stage but is ominously alluded to several times, was based on a man widely familiar in Kingston at one time, known as the Crackwalker because he would walk along the downtown sidewalks obsessively avoiding the cracks. For Alan the Crackwalker, along with the Man, a drunken Indian character (whom Alan eventually joins), represents a frightening extreme of physical decrepitude, one with which by successive degrees he is gradually brought into all too intimate contact.

Near the end of the first act Alan comes upon the drunken Man bleeding from his slashed wrists, so he binds them, only to have the Man make a sexual pass, which Alan furiously rebuffs. In the second act, having been fired from his job, Alan shares a bottle with the Man; and then, once he has strangled his son, they share a hot-air vent, where, to Alan's helpless distress, the Man vomits upon him. In the intimacy of sharing bodily fluids, a physical identity between Alan and his *bêtes noires* has been asserted. And, of course, on the social level the Crackwalker and the Man clearly represent for Alan the sub-proletariat class he has struggled to keep himself and Therese from slipping into, just as he tries to avoid the cracks in his own psyche, the fissures through which all his nightmare visions seep into his consciousness.

As Robert Nunn has pointed out, in the 1982 production of *The Crackwalker* this implied spatial metaphor was extended to the design; the acting space was separated into different levels, and a huge sewer pipe emitted a trickle of sludge into the centre of the stage, suggesting, perhaps, that these characters had been drained out of the mainstream of society ("Spatial"). Effective as that design choice was in one way, however, it was problematic in that the implied comment was liable to misinterpretation, as Thompson remarked in an interview several years later: "The big drainpipe in *The Crackwalker*. I don't know if I'd like that again. I loved it then. In a way I don't like it because I hate the notion that *The Crackwalker* is about the underbelly of society. They're not that horrible. They're not that different from anybody [...] But that's how people make themselves comfortable, by saying, "Oh that play is not about me, it's about the underbelly" (*Fair*, 101). In other words, the risk of using an image like that drainpipe was that, in a play dealing frankly with aspects of social class and anxieties about human degradation, some kind of dismissive disgust for the characters might be misconstrued. In no way would this accurately reflect Thompson's own attitude, or the position of her play. On the contrary, as her discussion of the point above indicates, her work intensely embraces Terence's maxim "Nothing human is alien to me." Indeed, that principle is the very source of Alan's anxiety; he cannot detach himself from his identification with the Man. Alan's experience is related to what audiences at *The Crackwalker* should experience; as he reluctantly recognizes himself in the Man, so, ideally, is the audience forced to recognize themselves in Alan and his friends.

The effect achieved by this sympathetic identification is an unusually trenchant and honest rendering of what is too often a mere platitude: "there but for the grace of God go I." To secure pious but trite agreement with the sentiment, acknowledgment by rote, is one thing; but it is quite another to cause an audience to feel the truth of the observation profoundly. Yet that is just what a first-rate production of *The Crackwalker*, or indeed any of Thompson's plays does. Forced to confront what we find at the end of the drainpipe, we see it not merely as the detritus of our society but as an aspect of our own consciousness that we have conveniently siphoned away into a place of ignorance. Before it was razed during the French Revolution, the Bastille was rumoured to contain a certain kind of dungeon, a secret pit accessible only through a trapdoor at the top, into which prisoners could be consigned in perpetuity; it was called an oubliette – from *oublier*, to forget. At the end of the drain in *The Crackwalker* lies the oubliette of social consciousness.

Now, the play would be almost perversely disturbing were our only model for sympathetic identification the desperate and defeated Alan. But each of Thompson's characters invites a different sort of identification. Superficially it might seem that Joe, the one character who manages to extricate himself from the desperate world of the play, would be the strongest and most admirable character. But Joe is only able to achieve that detachment from a bleak destiny by closing himself off from his identification with the others. In this he represents a pole of experience that finds its opposite in the indefatigably innocent Therese. As a sort of fool saint, Therese attains a state of grace through a purity of spirit that allows her to transcend the fears, anxieties and rage gnawing at Alan.

Sandy is quite another matter. In her final monologue we encounter a sense of spiritual reckoning and uplift, for she becomes the chief beneficiary of the insight or *anagnoresis* in this tragedy, attaining a maturity of understanding in which she is able to look upon the others without judgment. It is a remarkable (and typical) achievement of Thompson's writing that this development seems an utterly natural and unforced change in Sandy's character; her speech and behaviour retain their authenticity even as she embodies a degree of humane honesty few of us can boast of possessing. At the end of Sandy's speech is a trope summing up the total effect of the play. Speaking of the baby's funeral she says:

> They had them flowers round Danny's neck so's to hide the strangle but I seen it. The flowers never hid it they just made you look harder, ya know? They just made you look harder.   (71)

The Crackwalker is a play about "looking harder," in the sense implied here. The underworld exposed in Thompson's work, like that of David Lynch's *Blue Velvet*, suggests that the comparative tidiness of middle-class life is a deceptively pleasant veneer that covers much messier truths. Bourgeois civility is a ring of flowers or a concrete sidewalk laid imperfectly over the frightening complexity of human nature, a nature that will not be denied indefinitely but will eventually pull our attention down through the cracks into the oubliette to compel acknowledgment.

A DREAM OF PASSION

The extent to which Thompson deliberately crafts her work to dramatize the elements of social consciousness is evident in her response to the suggestion that her plays are purely a reflection of her personal concerns: "I never think [my plays] are a map of my unconscious. I really do believe they are a map of the collective unconscious" (*Fair*, 100). Thompson's next play, *White Biting Dog* (1984), was an even more direct attempt to map the collective unconscious than was *The Crackwalker*. It was in preparation for *White Biting Dog* that Thompson undertook the studies in Freud and autism that infused her subsequent work; and the more deliberate use of the unconscious showed itself in what Carole Corbeil called the "orgiastic and poetic" language of the play (E4).[3]

Thompson's increased focus on the unconscious may have been responsible for much of the critical confusion that met *White Biting Dog*. For example, John Astington, who had warmly praised *The Crackwalker* for its bracing realism, complained about the dramatic cliché of the "eccentric family," saying: "one greets yet another household on the psychic rocks with a yawn of recognition" ("Drama," 1985, 380). He felt that the intense poetic rendering of the unconscious had overwhelmed the family drama and suggested: "The connection between the two plays is to be found in the concern with the fantasies and imaginings in them, but whereas, in *The Crackwalker*, those inner lives were rooted in a gritty, brutal, real world, in *White Biting Dog*, they are allowed to float free, taking over the play entirely. The difference is one measure of the relative inferiority of the second play, in that the dramatic texture has been dangerously thinned out: if we dismiss the characters, we dismiss everything" (380). Astington's comments are typical of much of the critical response to the play. Generally speaking, the skill and imagination of the play have been praised while reservations are expressed about its final effect. Richard Plant probably speaks for many when, on one the hand, he praises it as "an exuberantly metaphorical play whose emotional impact is strong" ("Drama," 168), while on the other he regretfully suggests that it is "so overburdened with imagery that it is finally inaccessible" ("Opening," 23–4).

There is little doubt that, approached primarily as a family drama, *White Biting Dog* both overwhelms reasonable expectations of coherent behaviour and seems in its characterizations to drift into a style one writer likened to cartoons (Cooper, 61). Critics used a remarkable variety of language and analogues to explain their impressions of the play when it first appeared. For example, in the eyes of a less friendly critic, Mark Czarnecki, the play was a "disorienting example of theatre of the absurd" that attempted "to yoke pungent realism with airy fantasy," resulting in what he deemed a "hostile and often tedious enigma." Yet even while calling parts of the play "boring gibberish," Czarnecki felt compelled to admit the power of Thompson's "disturbingly inventive imagination" (51). More kindly, though evidently bewildered, Paul Walsh felt the play was "deep down" most like "a nineteenth century melodrama [that] brood[ed] with predictability on a bed of old answers," though it ultimately failed by being "unaware of its own ideological commitments" (145). Ray Conlogue, by contrast, found the play funny enough that he felt that he was seeing "a comic romance" with "a lot of dirty talk and emotional violence à la kitchen-sink realism [and] more than a touch of desperate absurdity" ("Funny," E10). Richard Paul Knowles, perhaps hedging a little against premature pronouncements, called it "poetic drama of a very different kind" – a tantalizing phrase he explained only by suggesting that the difference had to do with Thompsons being a "street poet" ("Dramatic," 85–6). Family drama, cartoons, absurdism, fantasy, melodrama, comic romance, kitchen-sink realism, and poetic drama: taken as a whole, the critics' comments suggest the play was both like everything and unlike anything seen in the theatre before: a dramaturgical chimera.

Generally speaking, *White Biting Dog* enjoys considerably more success with audiences in the theatre than when read. The immediate emotional impact of the play seems to overwhelm any attempts at rational justification (in perhaps all but those who must meet a deadline with an articulate analysis). The rapidity with which the play jolts audiences from one kind of emotional extreme to another (a range that, in itself, fully justifies the bewildering array of analogues quoted above) is startling and a little ineffable. Even in a summary of the action, something of the bewilderment and the excitement of the play comes through.

The play begins with Cape playing his drums. He suddenly stops and tells us that he was about to throw himself off the Bloor Street viaduct when a white dog spoke to him, giving him a mission to save the life of his father, who is dying of a strange disease contracted from gardening. Glidden, the father, enters raving, peat moss falling out of his pyjamas; Cape sends him back to bed. The dog's owner, a young woman named Pony, shows up, tells Cape that the dog, Queenie, is now dead, then promptly falls in love him. Cape entertains the idea that if his mother, Lomia, returned to his father, his father might survive; lo and behold, Lomia shows up with her lover, Pascal, in tow.

From this point there follows a series of horrifying and rationally inscrutable incidents and revelations about the various characters. (A few of these are of dubious authenticity, though the whole issue of authenticity is probably rooted in a misconceived approach to the play anyway.) For example, Lomia used to make Cape keep his own nose-bleeds in preservation jars and drink them (21); Pony's childhood in Kirkland Lake included vile anti-Semitic acts (60); Lomia's erotic conversation with Pascal includes her request that he "take a spoon and and pop out my eyeballs, shave off my nipples" (87); Cape separates Pascal from his mother, humiliates, then sodomizes him (80–83); three dead dachshunds, former family pets, are stored in the downstairs freezer, and Pony claims at one point (though she later recants) to have eaten them, then vomited into the coffee cups she is at that moment offering Cape and his father (92–4). Finally, at the end of the play, Glidden dies after all; Pony kills herself, a decision she explains in an afterlife monologue to her father in Kirkland Lake; and Pascal simply disappears, leaving Cape and Lomia alone to come to terms with their lives.

In fairness to those who first struggled to make sense of the play, it must be admitted that this is undoubtedly all a little bewildering. And, of course, it would be doubly so to anyone who primarily thought of *The Crackwalker* as a naturalistic work and hence was expecting more of the same. The heart of the difficulty is that the play's structure corresponds not to any linear pattern of causation or ordinary expectations of realism but to the paralogic of the unconscious. Accordingly, it would be quixotic to attempt to make perfect sense of everything in the play, but by the same token the relationships and incidents of *White Biting Dog* assume a more meaningful coherence if the play is approached as if it were a dream vision. The proximity of event to thought, as we see in Lomia's arrival immediately after Cape hopes she stays away; the surrealistic elements, such as Queenie, the talking dog, or Cape's summoning of Pony by playing his drums; the breathtakingly uninhibited divulgence of inner thoughts; and even the uncertain geography of the set, which alternately demands walls and doors or proceeds as if there were no spatial boundaries whatsoever: all these peculiarities assume a natural status within the context of a dream.

To be sure, there is no specific declaration that *White Biting Dog* is a dream play, and the dream framework is not necessary for us to approach the play through the paralogic of the unconscious. But imagining *White Biting Dog* as a dream is probably the easiest way of invoking the mental attitude Thompson used to order the events and characters. At any rate, the suggestion is not really very radical, for Thompson pointedly uses this analogy in describing how she wants her plays to be received. She says that dreams, with their combination of implication and helplessness ("they're your dreams, but it seems as if they're just happening to you") constitute for her "the ideal theatrical experience," adding that: "we all dream, we all have an unconscious life. And I hope I have stumbled upon a kind of collective unconscious so that it's like a dream happening" (Tomc, 19).

In one sense, any argument for a "dream" reading is merely an argument for an especially liberal tolerance of poetic tropes. This line of thought was opened by Jacques Lacan (see Lemaire, 43–9), though the idea is more clearly articulated by Bert O. States in *The Rhetoric of Dreams*. While discarding as untenable the early Freudian idea that every dream is the disguised fulfilment of an unconscious wish, States follows Lacan in picking up on other parts of Freudian dream theory. He suggests that what Freud called the "dream-work" may be understood in terms of the four master tropes: metonymy and synecdoche correspond to Freud's concept of "condensation," metaphor to "displacement," and irony to "contradiction." Accordingly, States argues that a dream "manifests strategies of thought that if traced upward into language would eventuate in the master tropes." In short, a dream constitutes a kind of internal poetic drama, perhaps related to that "very different kind" of poetic drama Ric Knowles had in mind in his review of *White Biting Dog*.

The poetic fluidity extends even to the characters. As in a dream, when one's own identity is sometimes rather fluid, while at first we seem to be experiencing the story chiefly through Cape's eyes, the play then seems to foreground the perspectives of Cape, Pascal, and Pony alternately, as if they were all aspects of a single mind, or as if the anxieties driving this play reach beyond the particular concerns or ego of any one character and stem rather from something of more collective concern. In short, considered as a sort of poetic dream play, *White Biting Dog* effectively resembles a modern version of the medieval genre of "psychomachia" – a "war within the soul," of which *Everyman* is the best-known example – a story in which the characters correspond to aspects of a single universal consciousness.

Reading *White Biting Dog* in this way alters the significance of what was complained of as its clichéd representation of family life. The difference between a cliché and an archetype lies entirely in the perspective from which they are regarded. The word "cliché" implies mindless stumbling into hackneyed ideas, whereas "archetype" suggests the deliberate choice of a well-established pattern for reworking. One might, for example, see a cliché in the Oedipal pattern of Cape's complicated love-hate relationship with his mother, his ambivalence about his father's imminent death, and his certainty that his mother doesn't love his father. But this is the central source of anxiety in the play, and, given Thompson's preparatory study of Freud for the year-and-a-half prior to writing it, she is unlikely to have just negligently fallen into the pattern.

Similarly, the correspondence between *White Biting Dog* and *Hamlet* is presumably no mere accident. Aside from *Oedipus Rex*, *Hamlet* was the play in which Freud saw the Oedipus complex working most powerfully; indeed, he treats the two plays equally in his famous discussion of the topic, "On Oedipus and Hamlet." In Freud's reading, Hamlet's difficulty in avenging his father's death arises because Claudius, in killing

Hamlet's father and marrying Gertrude, has realized Hamlet's own repressed desires. Now, whether or not one likes Freud's psychoanalytic reading, it is interesting to look at *White Biting Dog* as a reworking of the complex Mother-Son-Father-Stepfather relationship Freud saw as the main theme of *Hamlet*. A neat series of parallels can be drawn between the two casts: Cape is in the Hamlet role; Lomia stands in for Gertrude; the dual role of Old Hamlet and his Ghost is split between Cape's father, Glidden, and the dog Queenie, who prompts Cape to take action for his father's sake; standing in for Claudius is Lomia's crass young lover, Pascal; and for Ophelia, the suicidal Pony.

In effect the ambivalent, only barely ethical context of Hamlet's dilemmas has been displaced on to something more nakedly primal: a version of the psychological and class anxieties explored in *The Crack-walker*. For instance, Hamlet assumes a moralistic tone when rebuking his mother, but his ranting about "the rank sweat of an enseamed bed" reveals a rather unsettling focus on the corporeal. Cape is more overt, discarding any pretence of moral outrage and openly expressing the visceral nature of his disgust for his mother: "she *farts* like no person should" (21); "You're old. Your arms are like bat's wings" (56). Similarly, there may be an implicit ethical ground for Hamlet's "Hyperion to a satyr" comparison, although Hamlet can't quite decide whether it is Claudius's lesser person ("the bloat King") or his immorality that is most abhorrent; the underlying point seems to be that Claudius doesn't cut it as a father-figure, unlike the tough and imposing Old Hamlet. In *White Biting Dog* this cryptic disdain shifts openly to a more modern and familiar psychopathology when Cape, immediately after being struck by his father, mocks Pascal's incompetence at sports, calling him "Daddy's little girl" (80). And, instead of the vaguely moralistic tone laid across Hamlet's sneering "nunnery" speech and the coarse allusions to "country matters" he makes to Ophelia, Cape simply abuses Pony by saying: "YOU BORE ME. You're from the lower class "*eh*," "eh" – you're wearing fake fur and desert boots for fuck sake you're laughable!!" (49) In short, the royal garment of the setting at Elsinore has been stripped from the drama and stands naked, having barely the demotic trappings of middle-class Canada in which to dress itself.

Emphatically, my point here is not that Judith Thompson set out to rework *Hamlet* directly. If she had, the play would look quite different. Rather, I want to suggest that in *White Biting Dog* she set out to treat a primal psychological archetype, the same one Freud had found articulated so well in *Hamlet* and *Oedipus Rex*. Certainly, the conclusion of the play, in which Lomia and Cape are left to work out their relationship, is appropriate if the Mother-Son relationship is seen as the centre around which the play's various themes revolve.

Yet in this context we need to remember that in Freud's view the final significance of this archetype does not rest in its comment on family relations. Rather, it has foremost to do with the drama of the self, the characters in the psychological drama standing as figures within the *mise en scène* of a single psyche, as it were, as aspects of the self in conflict. Hence, those who indignantly suppose Freud to have been possessed by some dirty-minded obsession with maternal incest miss the point. Freud was much less interested in incest *per se* than in viewing the incestuous impulse as the expression of a primal psychic urge for completion. In Freud's theory, the sexual yearning for one's mother is a kind of sensual articulation of a deeper desire for transcendence, for a correction of the state of nonfulfilment into which we were plunged at birth. Much of the rest of the controversial apparatus of the theory – the anger and envy fastened upon the father as rival, the often misrepresented hypothesis about penis envy, and so on – has to do with the inevitable frustration of this desire, which, of its nature, could never be satisfied. (Though, by way of realizing the latent impulses of the complex, probably the next best thing to impregnating your mother, as Oedipus does, would be to sodomize your mother's lover, as Cape does.)[4]

Having now pressed the point about the Oedipal complex so far, it will be wise to stand back a little and acknowledge that many of the elements in the play do not fall within its scope of explanation. What, for example, could it have to say about Glidden's obsession with the peat moss responsible for his disease? Or the tale about the jars of nosebleeds kept in the cellar? Or Pony's posthumous visit to her father, the film projectionist, in Kirkland Lake? Well, these incidents may still connect to the archetype as we have been discussing it, in so far as they also draw on that aspect that lies beyond any quasi-sexual manifestation: the larger imaginative scheme in which the aspiration for transcendence and its material frustrations are profoundly affiliated with death and life.

As Urjo Kareda has remarked, Thompson is: "overwhelmingly aware of the physical side of our biology. Her characters are not spared revelation of the intimate details of their bodies. Piss, shit, sweat, blood, saliva, vomit, tears, mucous, semen, amniotic fluid – these are as central and as inescapable a part of our beings as our heart, our mind, our soul" ("Introduction," 10). These material aspects of human identity cause difficulty for abstract or immaterialist ideals, the notions aimed at a transcendence of the natural condition of human imperfection. Fantasy may provide temporary escape, but eventually the material conditions of human nature will expose self-delusions. So it follows, given that the chief obstacles to transcendence are attached to organic, biological existence, that death constitutes perhaps the only decisive means of escape.

In that light Glidden's peat moss, with its simultaneous associations of putrefaction and vitality, is a suggestive symbol for his efforts to transcend the circumstances of his life and imminent death, and the impossibility of doing so. A related organic symbol is the basement stocked with jars of nosebleeds, one of several images of bodily functions in the play that evoke disgust and horror. Ultimately, the disgust evoked probably has to do with the evidence of our inevitable failure to transcend our earthly condition and achieve perfection of any kind. Pony's evanescent posthumous appearance in the light of her father's projector is contrasted with the physicality of her experience with Cape. She tells her father that she was

> *filled* by the worst evil – I guess it happened when I fell in love, on account of I had to open my mouth so wide to let the love in that the evil came in, too ... and living with it was just like being skinned alive; worse pain even than your kidney stones.   (107)

The impossibility of being transformed into, or by, what one desires without also accommodating that which is vile was, in Freud's view, an inherent paradox of life; Eros and the death instinct are inextricably intertwined.

All that is to suggest, in effect, that we should look for the unity of *White Biting Dog* in its exploration of the psychic warfare and subliminal connections among the desires and taboos of the unconscious. But we should be cautious with this kind of analysis because, having accepted the premise of the unconscious as a theme, it becomes difficult ever confidently to declare it absent thereafter. Its presence becomes a sort of article of faith. Thus, it would easily be possible to extend such a reading to apply to the whole of Thompson's work to date, but we must beware of dwelling on a psychoanalytical approach at the expense of more immediately crucial aspects of the work.[5]

THE BEAST BEHIND THE WALL

In *I Am Yours* (1987) the theme of parent-child relations is again central. The play also touches upon certain familial archetypes, but to different effect than had *White Biting Dog*, *I Am Yours* striking a much more realistic impression in terms of dialogue and the motivation of characters' actions. So, while *I Am Yours* makes extensive use of characters' dreams, and George Toles has even spoken of what he sees as "the collective dream quality of the play's entire action" (124), it would be misleading to think of the play as a dream vision in quite the same mode as *White Biting Dog*. The difference is that *I Am Yours* has an apprehensible social context within which the unconscious elements flow. As in *The Crackwalker*, Thompson depicts a familiar hierarchy of social classes that becomes a sort of semantic framework for the exploration of psyche.

At the centre of the play is Dee, a middle-class woman undergoing a psychological crisis. She finds herself by turns unrestrainedly desirous and breathtakingly vicious towards her husband Mack. They separate, and she has a one-night stand with her building superintendent, a lower-class ex-convict named Toilane, by whom she becomes pregnant. Dee's predicament is exacerbated by the arrival of her pathetically neurotic sister, Mercy, who has been pursuing a life of emotional recklessness in an effort to overcome a sense of inadequacy that is rooted in Dee's closer relationship with their father. Worse things await Dee when Toilane's formidable mother, Pegs, joins Toilane in a battle against Dee for custody of the baby.

The tone for much of the play is set by the anxiety dream with which it opens:

> *The stage is dark.* TOILANE *walks slowly toward the audience, on a ramp that juts out into the audience. He is his six-year-old self, in a dream he is having as an adult. He is walking up to what he sees as a giant door, the door of his own home.*
> TOILANE: Mum! Muum, I'm home!
> Hey, Mum, I'm home!
> Where's my mummy?
> But this is my house! I live here. [*pause*]
> I do so! I do so live here! I do so live here! [*pause*] I do so! My parents are in there! I do so live here, they're in there! I do live here, I do live here! I do live here! I do live here!
> [*The "door" slams. The audience should serve as the door. Do not bring in a real one.*]   (119)

A stage direction declares that Toilane's dream is shared by Dee and Mercy, establishing that, despite the differences among these characters, something fundamental is shared in their inner lives.

In an early draft of the play, called *The Daredevils' Club*, Dee, Mercy, and Toilane were actually given shared memories and a childhood connection. Dee and Mercy had formed the Daredevils' Club of the title, and one of their dares was to kiss Toilane Crease (whose putative repellence makes the idea of kissing him outrageous), then to run when he attempted to pursue them. In the final version of *I Am Yours*, however, the identification among the characters is of a more primordial psychological nature. The anxiety dream of being shut out of the home, which all three characters share, is apparently among the most common such dreams among children. According to Bruno Bettelheim in *The Uses of Enchantment*, this anxiety, which has to do with the difficulties of growing up and leaving security behind, is the cryptic subject of many of the best-known fairy tales.

As she had with Freud, Thompson herself invokes fairy tales as a context for her work. She has said of the Grimms' *Tales*: 'They influenced me greatly. Anyone who looks closely at my work can see that. But again, we're talking about tapping into a collective unconscious. They do, and I hope that when my plays are working they do the same kind of thing' (*Fair*, 99). *I Am Yours* contains a number of elements corresponding to fairy tales. For example, Dee and Mercy resemble the two antithetical siblings found in many of these tales. Bettelheim argues that the device suggests conflicting aspects of a single personality in need of resolution. He also points out that such stories often contain some kind of central object, or two identical objects, and that the reconciliation of the two siblings is focused on this talisman. In *I Am Yours* we see such a talisman in the locket that Dee was given by her father, inscribed with the words "Ich bin dein." It may also be that Mercy was given an identical locket by her older lover, Raymond, although this could be purely her own fantasy; typically, Thompson does not settle the point unequivocally for us, because in the uncertainty and doubt lies part of the play's meaning.

Another fairy-tale aspect to the play is evident in the main plot: Dee's use of Toilane for emotional consolation, and her consequent pregnancy. She immediately regrets having had anything to do with Toilane, but finds that in his eyes she has made a kind of bond with him, one that subsequently becomes terrifying when he and his mother demand possession of the baby. The story shares resonances with "Rumpelstiltskin," the Grimms' tale in which a young woman makes a deal for her preservation with a despised little man in a moment of desperation, and later regrets her promise when he returns to take away her baby.

Rumpelstiltskin himself is physically loathsome, but the repulsiveness of Toilane in Dee's eyes has, it would appear, more to do with differences of class and refinement – the same displacement (unrefined manners for hideous appearance) Thompson uses for the ogrelike villain in her adaptation of a Sri Lankan tale, "Mouthful of Pearls." As in *The Crackwalker*, the social class beneath the main character's is associated with repressed anxieties in the psyche, yet with an additional complicating element: Dee finds that what she has despised is erotic. The syndrome is described by Stallybrass and White, wherein "the 'top' attempts to reject and eliminate the 'bottom' for reasons of prestige and status, only to discover, not only that it is in some way frequently dependent on that low-Other [...], but also that the top *includes* that low symbolically, as a primary eroticised constituent of its own fantasy life (5). Dee not only depends upon Toilane in the way that all middle-class people depend upon the working class (that he is her landlord is significant); he has an intuitive sense of her fantasy life. Herein lies the special knowledge possessed by Toilane that is equivalent to Rumpelstiltskin's knowledge of how to spin straw into gold. As Toilane puts it to Dee: "you got ... somepin ... like ME, somepin YOU know, you KNOW ... I SEEN IT, ohhh you DO" (132). Dee tacitly acknowledges the truth of what he says when she engages in a sexual act later described by Toilane as "You showin me your ... your animal" (136). So while Dee's revelation of the hidden and terrifying elements of her own nature to Toilane fulfils her momentary desperate need, it also joins the two of them in a sort of conspiracy against the daylight world of rational order, and thus gives him a kind of perpetual hold over her.

The animal Dee shows Toilane is an element of her character that she attempts to deny from the beginning of the play, when we hear her repeating a mantra: "There is nothing behind the wall. There is nothing behind the wall" (119). Mack provides a metaphor for the kind of threat that might lurk behind his wife's wall:

> First just one, buzzing around, then two, three we barely notice, then wham! someone gets stung, something's going on – what, what is it? Call in the pest people, "gotta be a nest" they say, "behind the wall, a nest"! Shit! We call in the contractors, gotta do something, somebody could have an allergy, DIE; they knock down the wall, just BASH the thing down; all this dust, white dust, plaster everywhere, and there, standing there, six feet high, *there*, this ... honeycomb, dripping, drenched, pouring out ... honey into the store, this ... structure ... thousands of bees, *fifty thousand* BEES, living there all the time, serving the queen, all the time, while we, on the other side – doing cash, taking inventory – these bees were building, building, *making*. The pest people, they get this SPRAY, this green shit and they carve these HOLES in it
> They CARVE
> Her fear about things ... behind walls?
> Her ... eyes?   (142)

Despite experience the habit persists in most of us of expecting tidy and familiar appearances to indicate tidy and familiar realities. To be unpleasantly surprised by deceptive appearances in general, or even hidden, inimical aspects of life (Thompson truly observes that unfamiliar animate and organic things always frighten more than anything inorganic), is not in itself so very disturbing, provided that these elements appear to be random, rare exceptions to the familiar rule. But Mack's anecdote is horrifying because of the enormity and complexity of the hidden life he describes. An ordered, alien life-form has infiltrated the subcutaneous level of a familiar environment to such an extent that there can be no trust in ordinary appearances. The effect on rational thought is vertiginous. As Mack implies in his juxtaposition of the holes in the wall with Dee's eyes, the wall barely separating Dee from the fearful hidden things is finally as much an internal barrier as an external one. The threat Toilane and his mother present to Dee is equalled by the threat of the animal he has seen within her.

The use of this strikingly vivid image of the bees behind the wall as a means of representing a fear of her unconscious is one that might invite any number of artistic associations. Placed in the framework of a refined, middle-class young woman's struggle with her own demons, and juxtaposed with other elements in the play, a particular literary analogue begins to force itself on our attention. Consider, for example, the passage in which Mercy speaks about her teenaged encounter with an older man, Raymond:

He actually ... believed me to be ... lovely. Lovely. Not like you you FUCKER DADDY. I HEARD you, I SAW you giving her that locket "for my favourite daughter, *Deirdre*" – that heart with the ICH BIN DEIN engraved. What does that mean, anyway, eh? What the hell does that mean? (133)

What it means, literally, is "I am yours." Thematically it alludes to the inescapable assertion of identity and possession that is central to the play. But another field of meaning is invoked when we consider the question of possible literary antecedents. In so far as it appears in a story that features no other German references, the German phrase is slightly peculiar; but, appearing as it does in context of cursing "Daddy," and further considered alongside the imagery of the bees, it brings to mind Sylvia Plath's *Ariel* poems. Whether Thompson actually drew (consciously or unconsciously) on Plath as a source for describing the inner lives of her characters or the similarities are merely a coincidence, Plath's poems offer a rich and suggestive literary analogue.

One of the most famous poems in *Ariel* is "Daddy," in which, as Mercy does in the passage quoted above, Plath vents all her hurt and anger towards her dead father in an attempt, it seems, to come to terms with her sense of abandonment.[6] The poem contains lines like:

I never could talk to you.
The tongue stuck in my jaw.
It stuck in a barb wire snare.
Ich, Ich, Ich, Ich,
I could hardly speak.   (Plath, 54)

Plath gradually turns her German father, Otto, into a Nazi in her imagination, coming to think of herself as a Jew. The poem ends with the line: "Daddy, Daddy, you bastard, I'm through."[7]

Ariel includes, furthermore, a series of four poems using bee imagery (Otto Plath was an amateur bee-keeper), the bees usually representing the fearsome power of the poet's inner life. For example, in "The Arrival of the Bee Box" Plath writes:

The box is locked, it is dangerous.
I have to live with it overnight
And I can't keep away from it.
There are no windows, so I can't see what is in there.
There is only a little grid, no exit.

... How can I let them out?
It is the noise that appals me most of all,
The unintelligible syllables.
It is like a Roman mob,
Small, taken one by one, but my god, together!

She ends the poem by trying to reassure herself:

... I am no source of honey
So why should they turn on me?
Tomorrow I will be sweet God, I will set them free.
The box is only temporary.   (63–4)

In "Wintering" she writes of the exposed apiary of hibernating bees, which seem to say to her, in effect, "I am yours":

This is the room I have never been in.
This is the room I could never breathe in.
The black bunched in there like a bat,
No light
But the torch and its faint

Chinese yellow on appalling objects –
Black asininity. Decay.
Possession.
It is they who own me.
Neither cruel not indifferent,

Only ignorant. (68)

On their own any one of these references would not signify much, but considered as a pattern, they provide a suggestive context in which to think about *I Am Yours*.

To an extent, Plath's work as a whole provokes comparison with Thompson's, in that the subject of most of Plath's poetry is the turmoil and vitality produced by a socially inaccessible and not always wholly conscious aspect of her person. Her poems divulge the chaos of a richly creative but sometimes frightening inner self that seethes beneath the veneer of her civilized persona. Regrettably, according to her biographer Anne Stevenson, the effect of this divided self upon Plath's outer life was that she sometimes seemed to "swing from violent vampire to virtuous nun" (78) – a condition all too similar to the agonized eraticism suffered by Dee (and hence Mack) in *I Am Yours*. Stevenson might as easily have been speaking about Dee as Plath when she suggests that lines in "Spinster" reveal the poet's "profound terror of an inner chaos she constantly suppressed":

And round her house she set
Such a barricade of barb and check
Against mutinous weather
As no mere insurgent man could hope to break
With curse, fist, threat
Or love, either. (Stevenson, 101)

Perhaps it is only part of the resonance that Plath's work and life have found with so many contemporary women, but one may find further analogues in certain other characters in Thompson's work who are, like Dee, socially secure middle-class women driven to a compelling but sometimes frightening degree by an immensely powerful inner self.[8] As in Plath, this inner self can be the source of both positive and destructive behaviour, and whether it is released or repressed, it sets a barrier between themselves and the rest of the world. It is little wonder Thompson chose to adapt Ibsen's *Hedda Gabler* for the Shaw Festival in 1991.

This inner self (or at least an aspect of the inner self) constitutes the animal Dee discovers within, which seems to be saying to her, despite her strenuous denials, "I am yours." Like Plath, Thompson is not moved by this notion of personal possession to sentimentalize the animal aspect of the inner self. Hence, where an Apollonian playwright (say, Bernard Shaw) might be content to call these forces that underlie the civilized surface of our lives a "life force," Thompson's more ambivalent view is closer to the Freudian idea of a struggle between the life and death instincts. Norman Brown, emphasizing the connection between Freud and Nietzsche, calls this struggle "Dionysian" – which happily directs us to a theatrical context. Indeed, in terms of dramatic history we might say that Thompson follows Euripides in showing the Dionysian forces in human experience to possess both joyful and terrifyingly destructive aspects. In *The Bacchae* as in *I Am Yours*, ecstasy and terror intermingle; sexual and psychic release leads to orgasm but also to violence. Indeed, it may be, as Camille Paglia argues, that the word "Dionysian" has become too "contaminated with vulgar pleasantries" to express the darker side of these instincts, and that it is better to use the word "chthonian" (*Sexual*, 5).

Standing as an alternative exploration of some of the themes of *I Am Yours* (loss of control, betrayal, envy, childbirth, kidnapping, social-class anxieties, and exogamous sexual relations) is *Tornado*, the play that may also be Thompson's most direct attempt to represent the chthonian dramatically. *Tornado* exists in two quite different versions: a 1987 version for radio and a 1992 version for the stage. Although there are reasons to delay the main discussion of *Tornado* until we come chronologically to the stage version, there is one aspect I want to raise here. Despite the substantial differences between the two scripts, they have in common the character of Rose, a impoverished young mother who suffers from epilepsy. Thompson has spoken in public on more than one occasion about her own epilepsy. Although she seldom has seizures now, the impact they made on her in childhood has been substantial. In a speech given at the Stratford Festival in 1996, she explained:

The seizure is a form of death. One has no choice but to surrender to the darkness and the chaos, and hope one will come out alive at the other end. But there is no guarantee of that. The electrical impulses in the brain are storming, in a state of chaos. The inhibitors, those chemicals that keep things orderly and relatively calm, are not working. When all is restored it is a kind of miracle. ("Epilepsy," 4–7)

Then, having described a particularly frightening *grand mal* seizure that she suffered at the age of fifteen, Thompson adds:

I am sure that I almost died. And there was no white light. No kindly figures. Just horror. And chaos [...] But I have learned a great deal from these encounters with death. I have learned why we fear disorder and chaos. I have learned that one must be brave or foolish to enter chaos. But that somewhere in chaos is art. The white light I didn't see. Chaos is sabotage. Chaos is not feminine. But for me, it is the only place from which to create.   (6)

Elsewhere she has speculated that her epilepsy may have given her a stronger sense of the powers of the unconscious than she would otherwise have known, saying that it kept her "in contact with the dark" as if she had "a screen door swinging between the conscious and unconscious mind" (Hunt, 11–12). Indeed, one wonders whether it can be merely coincidence that two of the few writers who have possessed a facility for representing the inner lives of characters comparable to Thompson's, Dostoevsky and Flaubert, also suffered from epilepsy, and a third, Plath, underwent an analogous experience (in electroconvulsive shock therapy) when she was twenty.[9]

The image of being "in contact with the dark" during a seizure suggests a confrontation of sorts with what we have called the chthonian – the profoundly irrational, chaotic, and frighteningly powerful force found deep within the self. One of Thompson's best representations of the experience occurs in the monologue in *Tornado* that was the source for the title of an anthology of her plays – *The Other Side of the Dark*. Jake, Rose's son, is talking her through her epileptic seizure:

JAKE: ... you think you're on the other side of the dark but I'm holding onto ya I'll bring ya back, I know I know, I can see what it's like, I can see it ma, I can see you're turning upside down and around a million million times and as fast as inside a dryer and falling and faster and faster and ice picks and scissors and snakes and every sick sound like throwin up and crushin eggs and mean laughin and everybody's laughin and you're fallin, I know, fallin fallin so fast so fast and you're at the bottom you're at the bottom now covered with mud and if you don't breathe if you don't breathe the light will be covered with mud, black, covered with mud if you don't breathe you'll be dead underground, COME ON, COME ON, YOU CAN SEE IT, you can see it at the top, TRY I'm here, your Jakey's here, so just scream, just scream mummy, scream your scream out and you'll fly to the top burst through the air let the scream take ya let it carry ya up bang! through the air
ROSE: [*screams a blood-curdling scream*]
JAKE: It's okay everybody, she's screamin up! She's screamin up!
(*Other*, 98)

There is something shamanistic about Jake's psychic accompaniment of his mother through her seizure, an aspect of the scene that is perhaps as crucial as its more obvious function of indirectly representing what Rose is going through. The idea of a character empathetically assuming an experience known only deep within another person, one normally incommunicable, assumes an important place not only in this play but in much of Thompson's subsequent work.

Significantly, Rose's seizures are loosely associated, especially in the radio version of *Tornado*, with her childhood experience of a kind of profound evil, the sexual abuse she suffered as a child at the hands of her father. Her account of these experiences is told in a similarly dithyrambic manner, suggesting a confrontation with the evil side of chthonian nature. Yet Rose explicitly characterizes her desire to procreate as a reaction to the sexual abuse; giving life and nurturing to her children is her compensatory, loving, creative response to the experience of chaos and evil. The parallel this strikes with Thompson's statement of how she discovered the possibility of responding creatively to the horror she confronted in her *grand mal* seizures is self-evident. What is perhaps less immediately evident is how this concept is assimilated into the larger world of Thompson's dramatic imagination

IN PURSUIT OF THE CHTHONIAN

Thompson's next full-length play for the stage, *Lion in the Streets* (1990), again explores the violent eruption of elements of the unconscious, but with perhaps even more intensity than any of her previous work. The play is structured in what has been called a "relay" or "daisy chain" pattern; in other words, rather than pursuing one scene causally to the next in a single linear plot-line, Thompson links scenes by means of the reappearance of a character from a previous scene. The pattern is similar to that of Schnitzler's *La Ronde*, although in other ways the two plays are quite unalike. One might characterize the difference by saying sexuality links the scenes in Schnitzler's play, and so, in Freudian terms, the life instinct is pursued as it moves through a series of encounters. By contrast, in Thompson's play it is something like the death instinct, the darker, evil side of the chthonian, that is pursued from one scene to the next.

The other link between the episodes of *Lion in the Streets* is Isobel, a nine-year-old Portuguese girl who, the opening stage direction informs us, is actually the ghost of a little girl murdered in the neighbourhood seventeen years before. Isobel may seem an unlikely surrogate for the audience (few of whom are likely to be little Portuguese girls), yet when we examine her function closely, she is ideal. Her naïve and initially uncomprehending odyssey through the neighbourhood at first appears to be merely a random exposure to the series of horrifying events that constitute the play. But her journey turns by slow degrees into a terribly earnest crusade, a quest to locate the "lion in the streets": in effect, to seek out the agony, violence, and despair that lie at the core of these characters. In earlier chapters I have made use of Peter Szondi's theory of the "epic-I" in modern drama, and it may seem that Isobel's character would be another likely embodiment of the concept. Yet ordinarily the phrase suggests a purposeful mind linking and directing the dramatic episodes, the kind of deliberation that is inappropriate in the case of Isobel. In fact her function is something closer to an "epic-Eye," by which I mean that her (for the most part) passive voyeurism strikes closer to the inductive exploration that structures this play than the suggestion of directed narrative implied by an "epic-I." Isobel, then, serves as the counterpart for the audience: a terrified and at first passive observer fumblingly attempting to grasp the meaning of the sequence of horrifying events, thence to determine a course of action for the self. The effect is again related to Thompson's description of the dreamer's experience: "They're your dreams, but it seems as if they're just happening to you." Over the course of *Lion in the Streets* the dreamer Isobel gradually assumes more control, and the audience's passage through this painful grasping after reason would end ideally where Isobel does, with renewed compassionate insight into humanity.

The relevance of an at first passive, then active observer to the themes of the play emerges with special clarity when we consider the original source of Thompson's title, Proverbs 26:13 (RSV): "The sluggard says, 'There is a lion in the road! There is a lion in the streets!'" The implication is not merely that we indolently decry external evils without taking action but also that we use external evil as an excuse for inaction rather than making the effort of looking for the evil within. Or, as Thompson once said, "We're living in a pathological state of denial, as a society, as a culture, and we have to stop it right now" (Wachtel, 38).

Now, Thompson needn't have been thinking specifically of Proverbs when she chose her title. The image has been often used to convey a sense of the danger lurking within civilization, from Shakespeare's *Julius Caesar* – in which Casca, on the eve of Caesar's assassination, describes a lion in the streets as a sign of chaos unleashed, of wild nature overwhelming human order – to the 1953 movie "A Lion Is in the Streets," in which James Cagney plays a man who struggles against political rapaciousness but eventually succumbs to his own urges. Among the most interesting such uses of the lion as a symbol of the ferality within human nature is in Wallace Stevens's "The Man with the Blue Guitar" (Stanza XIX), where this hope is expressed:

That I may reduce the monster to
Myself and then may be myself

In the face of the monster, be more than part
Of it, more than the monstrous player of

One of its monstrous lutes, not be
Alone, but reduce the monster and be,

Two things, the two of us together as one,
And play of the monster and myself,

Or better not of myself at all,
But of that as its intelligence,

Being the lion in the lute
Before the lion locked in stone.   (*Palm*, 142)

Explaining that stanza in a letter, Stevens said:

Monster = nature, which I desire to reduce: master, subjugate, acquire complete control over and use freely for my own purpose, as a poet. I want, as a poet, to be that in nature which constitutes nature's very self. I want to be nature in the form of a man, with all the resources of nature = I want to be the lion in the lute; and then, when I am, I want to face my parent and be his true part. I want to face nature the way two lions face one another – the lion in the lute facing the lion locked in stone. I want, as a man of imagination, to write poetry with all the power of a monster equal in strength to the monster about whom I write. I want man's imagination to be completely adequate in the face of reality. (*Letters*, 790)

It is not likely that Stevens's poem was actually a source for Thompson; in terms of style, Stevens's calculated cerebrations do not strike nearly so apt a comparison for Thompson's work as do Plath's passionately visceral and psychic outpourings. Still, the poem and remarks provide an analogue that can help us to understand what Thompson is doing in her play. Stevens's sense of nature's ferocity as both a threatening force and, properly harnessed, as abetting his creativity recalls Thompson's point about how her "contact with the dark" was transformed into art. Figuratively speaking, Thompson's work exists somewhere between Stevens's lute and the stone. There is a feral element in her writing that refuses to be tamed and subordinated to form, a chthonic turbulence that will not remain within doors but wanders the streets to spring randomly and wreak violence on the pacific surface of urbane complacency. The savagery and passion must be given life, not denied, if we are adequately to confront and understand the violence and cruelty inherent in human nature.

An essential difference between Thompson's lion image and Stevens's is the aspect of mobility. Thompson's lion is not hidden in one place but prowls through the streets, suggesting the fluidity of the chthonian force as she sees it. In *Lion in the Streets* there is a strong sense of the savage aspects of human nature being able to move from character to character, almost like a virus. To look at the problem in this way seems more threatening, yet it is precisely the possibility of identifying a similar inner nature in several characters that allows us to enter into the perspective of one character after another. Here the matter of Jake's uncanny identification with his mother during her *grand mal* seizure is again relevant.

Early in *Lion in the Streets* is a scene that dramatizes the concept of psychic identification with chilling effectiveness. Laura reminds her husband, George, of the nervous breakdown she suffered in sympathetic grief for her Portuguese friend, Maria, the mother of Isobel. George puts a tablecloth around his head and begins to imitate Maria mockingly. Then suddenly he seems actually to become (or be possessed by) Maria as she explains to Laura that she was folding laundry when she in turn felt herself enter Antony, her husband:

> I am foldin a light sheet of blue then and sudden, I can see through his eye, am at subway, in him, he stands on the platform, is empty empty and I am his head, circles and circles like red birds flying around and around I am his throat, tight, cannot breathe enough air in my body the floor the floor move, and sink in, rise up rise like a wall like a killin wave turn turn me in circles with teeth in circle and under and over I fall! [*ISOBEL falls on an imaginary track in front of her mother*] I fall on the silver track nobody move I hearing the sound. The sound of the rats in the tunnel their breath like a basement these dark rats running running towards me I am stone I am earth cannot scream cannot move the rats tramp ... trample my body flat-ten and every bone splinter like ... [*We hear the sound of a strong .27*).

Theatrically, the trope here is similar to what Brecht advocated for his epic theatre, citing the example of a man using a fluid combination of impersonation and narration to describe a traffic accident to bystanders (*Brecht*, 121–9). Yet while the theatrical technique is similar, the effect is rather different. Brecht argued that the switch from narration to impersonation and back would not confuse the spectator; rather, because the speaker-performer's purpose was transparent, it presented a point of view for spectators to judge independently. In the George-Maria-Antony scene, however, any moments of confusion the spectator experiences as the shift is made from one character to another, with no return, only serve to support the underlying theme. The effect of this uncanny transmigration of souls, as it seems, is further augmented when Isobel falls before "Maria" in impersonation of her father falling on the subway tracks.

Given the emotional force of the scene, it is senseless to ask whether we are meant to understand this as George imitating Maria or if it is "really" Maria we are hearing. In the first place, this is theatre, and so, as the epigraph to this chapter from Davies reminds us, nothing we see or hear is "real" in that literal-minded way. Accordingly, it is almost equally pointless to argue that the scene "problematizes" reality, for this assumes an inappropriate ontological context; we introduce the premise of a mimetically represented world only to remark the play's odd lack of conformity to those parameters. Moreover, such questions distract from the thematic point of the scene, which is conveyed more emotionally than any rationalistic discussion of ontology can comprehend. Thompson pointedly eschews consistently represented illusion here, instead aggressively deploying the theatre's proficiency in representing states of consciousness. Thus, what is most real here is the experience itself, regardless of what the ontological status of the moment would be were it to occur in the quotidian world outside the theatre.

A related development of this theme occurs in the scene between David and Father Hayes. At first we are led towards a confrontation regarding the old priest's sexual interest in David, who had been an altar-boy years before. But suddenly the scene veers off in a completely unforeseen direction as Father Hayes speaks of his guilt at having allowed David to drown during a picnic. He was, he confesses, vainly preoccupied with proving his manly competence to his parishioners by carving a chicken, all the while knowing at the back of his mind that he was sacrificing the boy's life to his own sense of pride. Naturally, David at first denies Father Hayes's claim, but gradually he begins to embrace the idea that he died on that summer day, his promise unfulfilled but pure.

Now it may be that the priest could not cope with his sexual interest in the boy and developed a death fantasy, upon which he subsequently transferred his sense of sinfulness. It may be that the priest is simply senile and David finds that he prefers his role in the more romantic scenario that the priest describes so vividly. Or it may be that the whole scene is a projection from the mind of either character. The question of which of these interpretations is the "correct" one, of how reality is "constructed," so to speak, is far less important than the sense of emotional (or, if you prefer, spiritual) truth this scene opens up within the audience – just as Father Hayes's "confession" opens up something within David. That emotional or spiritual truth lies beyond all possible literal realities, embracing instead a struggle deep within the soul between the sense of guilt and the longing for atonement and hope of redemption, or that "return of the quiescence of the inorganic world" that Freud saw as the seductive promise of death.

The premise advanced in those two episodes, that some kind of deeper human experience could find its way from one individual to another, is crucial to our understanding of the rest of the play. We might call it the trope of metempsychosis: that is, the transmigration of souls. The idea is found in *Tornado*, as I have suggested, but its roots go back even further in Thompson's work. Metempsychosis is really only an intensified version of what the earlier plays manifested as an often alarming psychic resonance between two characters: Alan and the Man, Cape and Pony, Dee and Toilane, and so on. Furthermore, the trope reveals a latent implication of the multiple role-playing common in the theatre: namely, that there is something continuous within human nature that lies behind the social roles we play.

Perhaps the most powerful version of the metempsychosis theme in *Lion in the Streets* occurs in the scene between Christine, a reporter, and the paraplegic Scarlett. Christine betrays Scarlett's confidence, declaring her intention to print details Scarlett has divulged about her sex life (the extent to which the account is real or fantasized is, again, irrelevant). Christine shrugs off Scarlett's pleas by accusing her of trying to "obstruct the freedom of the press." But as Christine is about to leave, Scarlett suddenly declares:

SCARLETT: ... you'll go right to hell for this!

CHRISTINE: I don't believe in hell.

SCARLETT: Joke's on you, girl, cause I'm in it, right now, live from hell, and if you do this, you're gonna be burning here with me, maybe not today, maybe not tomorrow but soon, soon, you'll be whizzing down the highway with a large group of handsome friends to some ski resort or other, and your male driver will decide to pass on the right, you will turn over and over, knocking into each other's skulls breaking each other's necks like eggs in a bag, falling through windshields it's gonna rain blood and I will open my big jaws and swallow youuuu! YOU will spend the rest of eternity inside me. Inside my ... body and ooooh time goes slowwwwwe ... [...]

CHRISTINE: STOP THAT. Stop that craziness NOW there is no such thing, there is no such thing as any of that ANY of it. You live and you die in your own body and you go up to heaven or just nowhere.

SCARLETT: Into the middle of Scarlett [...] Inside my big wet behind [...] In the bummy of a big dead fish... (48–9)

Christine, overcome by horror and losing her self control, kicks Scarlett to the point of death. "You shouldn't have made me kick you like that," says Christine when her rage is exhausted. "The way you, you, you talked to me like that. Like, like you belong. In the world. As if you belong. Where did you get that feeling? I want it. I need it" (49). Christine's sense of alienation probably has something to do with her incapacity to accept that the reality of the world includes Scarlett and all that she represents. Indeed, the reality of Christine's own self includes what Scarlett represents, and it is her refusal of ugliness and horror in both herself (e.g., her denial that her exploitation of Scarlett is immoral) and her world that leaves her susceptible to evil. Just before Scarlett dies, she invites Christine to bend down and kiss her, "like a lion." Christine does so, "swooping down like a condor" to give Scarlett "the kiss of death" (49–50). In that moment, the union of the two souls that Christine had so vehemently struggled against is fulfilled. The external horror represented by Scarlett is now Christine's internally, a notion Isobel underscores by declaring that Christine is now "a slave of the lion! You lie with him you laugh you let him bite your neck, you spread your legs. You will take me to him now" (50).

Isobel is taken through a few more episodes in her pursuit of the lion before she finally confronts the man who murdered her seventeen years ago. Between the premiere of *Lion in the Streets* at the World Stage Festival in Toronto and its regular run at the Tarragon Theatre five months later, the route to this climactic confrontation was changed, with one of the episodes substantially altered and another cut altogether. Though there were good reasons for reworking the scenes (liability to misinterpretation in one case and dramatic expediency in the other), I am not alone in regretting these changes to the script. Fortunately, the discarded scenes have been published separately (Knowles, "Great," 8–18), so readers can reconstruct the original shape of the play for comparison.

The scene between Sherry and Eddie originally focused mostly on Sherry alone. In the final version Eddie bullies his fiancée into admitting that she deliberately enticed the man who raped her some years earlier, into declaring it "the best fuck I ever had." To sit and watch this scene is unquestionably agonizing. But the original scene, in which

Sherry began by confronting a lesbian feminist at a bus stop and ended by savagely addressing the audience with a self-hating, anti-feminist diatribe, was possibly more difficult still. Consulting my own experience of the première, as well as that of acquaintances, it seems that what made the original so very difficult is that, in the context of a very harrowing play, one's initial discomfort with the wrong-headedness of Sherry's argument, mingled with pity for the evident destruction of her self-regard, quickly turned to anger and even hatred of the character for the trauma she was inflicting upon us in the audience. Sympathetic feelings were swept away by an urge to yell at the character: "Shut up!"

To have one's own rationally based pity so easily overwhelmed by a more violent emotion was, in effect, a shocking revelation of the lion within each of us. The central conflict of the play was thus internalized. In the revised scene one feels a similar mixture of agony and rage; but one's anger at Eddie is far more easily exculpated than one's unconscionable anger at Sherry. Still, it is perhaps not a majority of spectators who would cherish such a disturbing confusion within their own response, and undoubtedly even fewer are comfortably confident about the confused responses of others. In his commentary on the original scene, Richard Paul Knowles says some people objected that the monologue was itself anti-feminist and "could serve in support of the reactionary backlash against supposed feminist gains." Regretfully, he admits that "in the wrong actorly or directorly hands, or taken out of context [...] it could be devastating in unforeseen and unfortunate ways" ("Great," 17). The revised scene, though still immensely forceful and harrowing, is surely safer in that respect. But the question persists whether, in portraying a more admissible because more readily condemnable truth, however skilfully, some of the play's extraordinary power to compel self-examination has been sacrificed.

What originally followed the Sherry episode, but was cut until its restoration for the 1999 Theatre Kingston production, was a scene in a graveyard (following the funeral of Father Hayes) between Joan and her adopted son, Ben, a disagreeably crass and bitter man. Once they are alone at the gravesite, Ben gradually, painfully reveals the sources of his implacable anger towards the world: the sexual abuse he suffered at the hands of his adoptive father, Walter, and – almost equally – Joan's incorrigible, obdurate innocence about it. But something deeper is clearly driving this scene, and we begin to grow queasily more aware of this hidden truth with Joan's passing remark that "anybody who knows anything knows you did not kill that little girl." Finally we see it, hideously and unequivocally: Ben is Isobel's murderer. The path of evil, the spoor of the lion that Isobel has been following, leads here. In this moment there is a disconcerting sensation that Joan's innocence is in some sense our innocence: a culpable innocence. Perhaps it is partly a purity of heart; but at least equally it is a wilful ignorance and hence a half-witting connivance at evil. A variation of such innocence in Isobel, evident in her "unusually trusting, wide-apart" eyes, was what Ben felt compelled to snuff out. There are some who shrink fastidiously away from the horrors that appear in Judith Thompson's work. But it is all but impossible to imagine someone sitting through *Lion in the Streets* with anything like an open mind and coming out at the other end of this particular scene feeling righteous about his or her fastidiousness.

In the revised version of the play, Isobel simply goes directly from Sherry and Eddie to Ben in the graveyard. The horrified realization that Ben is Isobel's murderer is still there, of course, only very much telescoped to the point of epiphany that will follow. What is missing is the information about Ben's past and the insight into his character and the ambiguous concept of innocence embodied in Joan (and, less importantly, the information that Christine, who killed Scarlett, was Ben's adoptive sister). Instead we move immediately to the harrowing moment in which Ben speaks of the small mitigating act of mercy he was able to make within his violence. When Isobel pathetically begged not to be strangled, Ben explains that he

> stepped out of the twister cause that's what it's like, when you're doin something like that, you're inside a twister and to step out, is like ... liftin a dishwasher, eh, but I did. So I go to the back of the warehouse and I picked up a brick and I hit her – cause she touched me okay? She touched me, right? (62)

The "twister" of evil Ben was caught within is another version of the deathlike vortex of helplessness and chaos described by Thompson as the effect of a *grand mal* seizure. So, while it would be easy at one level to dismiss as absurd Ben's claim to have his humanity recognized because he was "touched" by Isobel's distress and moved to that tiny mercy, in the context of that overwhelming "twister" the sincerity and truth of his claim should not be façilely gainsaid.

Isobel at first wants to return Ben's violence, but changes her mind because of a comparable inner recognition. The stage direction says: "*she is about to kill him with the stick, the forces of vengeance and for-giveness warring inside her – forgiveness wins.*" Instead she tells Ben: "I love you" (63). That moment of epiphany enables Isobel to "take back" her life, and thus to end the play with her apotheosis as she "*ascends, in her mind, into heaven.*" Just before doing so, Isobel speaks to the audience once more, urging them to follow her example: "I want you all to have your life."

There can be little question of the ending's being ironic, though the manifestly Christian ethic was evidently difficult for some to accept. I suspect this is the case even for one of Thompson's most devoted admirers (and a participant in the workshop), Richard Paul Knowles, who declares:

If the ending is genuinely redemptive it is perversely so, in that its final lines, in the face of the horror and anguish cumulatively revealed and evoked by the play, are a call to the *audience*, beyond all causal logic, and beyond the frame of the play, to engage in a subjective act of faith, and to "*take* your life." ("Dramaturgy," 229)

Even taking into account that Knowles tends to use the word "perverse" as an honorific, it is difficult to understand how he comes to such a conclusion. I would say that, on the contrary, the dramaturgical structure, with its cumulative revelations and the use of Isobel as a guide for the audience, points very naturally beyond the frame of the play towards aspects of human nature in which the onlookers are implicated. If Isobel's direct address to the audience at the play's end is at all shocking, perhaps it is because of its very traditionalism. The gesture of speaking out "beyond the frame" of a play dealing with various evils in order to urge some kind of redemptive response and closure in the audience is made, for example, at the conclusion of *The Tempest*, *Doctor Faustus*, *The Castle of Perseverance*, *Everyman*, and the *Oresteia*.

To be sure, the device is seldom seen in modern drama, but its rare appearances help to show why this is so. With the advent of naturalism in the theatre, the theatre's propensity towards ironic detachment became accentuated and cherished. But in the last part of Eliot's *Murder in the Cathedral*, or Brecht's epilogue to *The Good Woman of Setzuan*, or the multilingual ending of René-Daniel Dubois's *Don't Blame the Bedouins*, we see attempts to transcend the usual ironic detachment of modern drama and instead prompt a new awareness – even a conversion – in the minds of the audience, to place the power of response delineated in the play into their hands. Naturally, in an ironic and often cynical age, to tell an audience baldly that you would like them to join in some sort of conviction risks derision and accusations of didacticism, but it is difficult to imagine any of the above-mentioned playwrights being very worried by the point.

In fact most plays that use such a device articulate a kind of religious sensibility (and I use that phrase loosely enough to include Marxism, existentialism, humanism, and so on – i.e., any overarching outlook on life that depends partly upon articles of faith). Thompson herself, when questioned directly on the point, readily agreed that her plays, *Lion in the Streets* especially, "express a religious sensibility" (Zimmerman, "Conversation," 185). Isobel's forgiveness of Ben suggests that sensibility is essentially Christian. But it is important to notice that Thompson does not present this moment as a response to a moral imperative – i.e., the Christian command to love one's enemies, which Freud argued would inevitably prove an unrealistic demand of human nature – but as a natural outcome of the recognition of one's self in others, the existential insight that is one of the chief themes of *Lion in the Streets*.

A similarly non-dogmatic use of Christian sensibility appears in the stage version of *Tornado* (1992). As I mentioned earlier, there are substantial differences between the two versions of *Tornado*; in the stage version Thompson has not merely changed names and details but added a new subplot, additional characters, and made a significant shift in tone. For example, though both versions begin, as so many of the Grimms' *Tales* do, with a couple who as yet have no children, the relation to fairy tales only really becomes evident in the more pronounced "magic realism" of the stage version.

In the radio script of *Tornado* the central female character is Mandy, a social worker. Mandy's husband, Bill, is having an affair with one of their middle-class friends, Jane, and is trying to work up the courage to tell Mandy he wants to end their marriage. Among the reasons Bill is attracted to Jane is her readiness to conceive a child, a prospect Mandy openly disdains. Once Mandy discovers the affair, however, she is determined to have a child herself in order to keep Bill. On Mandy's caseload is Rose, an impoverished young mother of four who is expecting a fifth and who suffers occasional epileptic seizures. When Mandy proves to be sterile, she devises a plan to confiscate Rose's baby at birth, convincing her that fourth and fifth children of epileptic mothers often die in their mothers' homes because of a mysterious virus. Mandy tells Bill she has paid a surrogate mother, but her ruse is exposed, and the play ends on the Scarborough bluffs, with Mandy deliriously insisting that she is the real mother of the baby and finally suffering an epileptic fit herself.

In the stage version of *Tornado* Mandy has become Viola, who is not a social worker; Bill has become Dexter, who is even more pathetically ineffectual than Bill was. More extreme is the transformation of Jane into Velveteen, a nineteen-year-old lower-class stripper who is pregnant by Dexter. Shirley, Jane's confidante, re-emerges in a much larger role as Red, a lesbian colleague of Velveteen's who is in love with her. The chief changes in the plot have to do with Viola's attempts to take legal custody of Velveteen's baby, a fate Velveteen avoids by leaping into Niagara Falls; only subsequently does Viola plan to take Rose's baby. Rather than playing on Rose's simple gullibility, as in the radio play, Viola makes a bargain with Rose. Rose has custody of only one of her children, Jake, the eldest (here a boy of fourteen, whereas he seems about ten in the radio play). Viola offers to pay for home care for Rose and thus allow her to recover custody of her other children, provided she hands over her newborn baby. In agony, Rose agrees, though when Jake discovers the plot, he is enraged and vows revenge. In the climactic scene on the cliff's edge he first attempts to cut off Viola's hands ("red" on stage, "big" on the radio) before being persuaded to show mercy. Then, as in the earlier version, he helps Viola through an epileptic seizure; but, rather than ending here, the stage *Tornado* ends with Viola surrounded by the comforting attentions of Rose and the ghost of Velveteen.

Significant as the changes to the characters and the plot are, most striking is the overall shift in tone. Whereas the radio play *Tornado* was, albeit unusual and slightly stylized, a fundamentally realistic portrait of a woman driven to madness in her desperation to keep her husband by becoming a mother, the stage version assumes a more poetic overtone, employing more surrealistic imagery and a more explicit symbolic framework. The stage *Tornado* begins just outside a church, and the entire subsequent action of the play is haunted by religious perceptions of one kind or another. It is specifically revealed that each of the main characters is a Catholic, though their diverse interpretations of their religion ensure this does not imply any one stable ethical context for their behaviours. To take the most obvious example, Viola insists that her marriage cannot be allowed to end because, she tells Dexter, "We're Catholics, remember?" (50) – although that has not prevented her from having three abortions (54). Clearly, in so far as the characters themselves invoke their Catholicism, it represents for them religious authority of a kind that has more to do with their personal desires than with any official teachings.

By no means, however, should we assume that Thompson's invocation of Catholicism is intended to be simply ironic. She has a manifestly serious interest in the more profound aspects of Catholicism lying beyond moral dogma. One may identify in Thompson's work variations on all the main theological apparatus by which Catholicism aspires to bring meaning to human life: the notions of evil and goodness, of sin and purity, of confession, atonement, and forgiveness, of redemption, transcendence, and grace, of epiphany, and, not least, of teleological mystery: the final unknowability, despite moments of apparent revelation, of the mind of God. These concepts do not emerge in anything like an orthodox shape under Thompson's hand. But their presence in other forms is persistent enough that a recognition of them is fundamental to understanding Thompson's poetics.

One of the most compelling and uncanny religious themes in *Tornado* is the occasional bald identification of characters as God or the Devil. Thompson takes a metaphor that is often used casually and facetiously, but then pushes it, so that real meaning is wrung from what might otherwise be discarded as stale hyperbole. For example, Dexter and Velveteen are "making out" at one point, when the conversation turns from the familiar and foolish and escalates into something disturbingly portentous:

> DEXTER: Oh God I sometimes think you must be a witch ... you ... have you put a spell on me? I think of you and it rips through my body, this desire, it is stronger than than, my marriage, than my beliefs, than ... than
> VELVETEEN: Than God.
> DEXTER: Oh no.
> VELVETEEN: Yes it is.
> DEXTER: Vel, there is nothing stronger than God.
> VELVETEEN: Then it must be Her will.
> DEXTER: God is a Father, Vel, you don't call God HER.
> VELVETEEN: God is my mother.
> DEXTER: You're taunting me with this God thing, aren't you? Playing with me?
> VELVETEEN: Is that what you think?
> DEXTER: Like a cat, and and you know what a cat makes me think of?
> VELVETEEN: What, Dex?
> DEXTER: The devil. You tempt me, and play with me, and try to keep my child from me and call God a mother, I sometimes I really think you're from the other side. [...] I'm beginning to think you're not human.

Then, a few lines later, the tables are turned:

> DEXTER: The judge has ruled in my wife's favour, Velveteen. Yesterday. [...] Shall I tell you what he said?
> VELVETEEN: Why? Are you the devil?   (56)

The conversation externalizes what Thompson has described as the "constant struggle inside – a sort of St. George and the Dragon [...] Was this an evil thought? Was this a good thought?" She adds that "certainly in the Catholic religion the struggle between Satan and God is a constant thing" (Zimmerman, "Conversation," 185, 186). In having the characters project the elements of this internal struggle upon one another, Thompson has created something like religious expressionism: the inward psychic battle between spiritual forces is imposed in broad symbolic figures upon the social world.

All the same, were the externalization of the spiritual struggle to go no further than the name-calling seen above, there would be nothing very remarkable about it. We might consider it an unusually intense rendering of common hyperbole, but little more. However, that there is something far more important at stake in these religious references becomes evident when they are considered within the thematic pattern of the play as a whole. In an earlier scene Velveteen and Dexter discuss her pregnancy:

> VELVETEEN: The quickening has started. The kicking. THE BABY IS KICKING.
> DEXTER: Oh! Oh my God in heaven is it? Is it?
> VELVETEEN: It's not an it, it's a she. SHE.
> DEXTER: Oh a she? A she? How do you know, Vel?
> VELVETEEN: I'm going to call her Jesus.
> DEXTER: Vel. Please. This isn't funny.
> VELVETEEN: Actually, I'm going to call her god.
> DEXTER: Vel, isn't that kind of sacrilegious?
> VELVETEEN: No. No it's not, Dex. My baby is going to be god [...] I'm not joking.
> DEXTER: Our baby is going to be god. Yeah. I can see it. Cause she's from you and me, she's from love.   (54)

Dexter has found a comfortable platitude with which to apprehend Velveteen's extravagant claim. But it is evident that Velveteen – and Thompson – mean something more.

One of the chief departures the stage *Tornado* makes from its predecessor is in a stronger parallel between Rose and Velveteen than had been possible between Rose and Jane. The new parallel amplifies the symbolic significance of the two expectant mothers. Asked once about the numerous mother and son relationships in her work, Thompson answered (perhaps a little jocularly) that "the obvious answer as to why I write about mothers and sons is that I was brought up a Catholic and there's one big mother-son relationship!" (*Fair*, 99) As I suggested earlier, another explanation that applies in certain cases (e.g., Lomia and Cape in *White Biting Dog* or, less surely, Pegs and Toilane in *I Am Yours*) would be the importance of the Oedipal complex to Freudian thought. Yet in *The Crackwalker*, and certainly here in *Tornado*, the Madonna-Christ archetype is clearly much more relevant. It would be misleading, however, to expect any close adherence to religious allegory. For any allusions to the Madonna-Christ relation have more to do with a conception of spirituality than with the outlines of the myth (i.e., the nativity story).

In the same interview quoted above, Thompson says:

> God is a newborn baby. Truly. You can really see God in a newborn baby. And it stays with them for a long time. God is in every person – that's really hard to remember sometimes. I do believe that God is in every one of my characters showing me herself. At little moments. That's as scary as it is beautiful. God is the innocence of a newborn baby; when people show that part of themselves, that eternal flame that's guarded; when they show that that's a moment of pure beauty, when they let you see it. Some people's flame seems to have gone right out ... Spontaneity – that's what we look for on stage. Bring on a dog or a baby and everyone's blown away. The search for that spontaneity is religious. (*Fair*, 96).

Thus, Velveteen's declaration that her "baby is going to be god" is more than mere whimsy. Indeed, the concept Thompson is delineating has an important place in Catholic mysticism. The most important of all the medieval mystics, Meister Eckhardt, spoke of giving birth to God's Son within the soul, thus making explicit a chief symbolic undercurrent of Judaeo-Christian mythology: the idea that spiritual redemption begins with a figurative conception of the Godhead within the human soul much like the literal conception of new life within a womb. (Indeed, almost all the sexist residuum in the Christian church is rooted in a regrettably literal-minded interpretation of the symbolism of spiritual conception.)

In this light the significance of the yearnings of several of the characters in *Tornado* may be reinterpreted. To give birth to God is, in Eckhardt's conception, to experience grace and attain redemption. The idea attaches to the pregnant Velveteen, although for her the notion of redemption is cast partly in terms of a retrieval of inherent social dignity. She claims that her Polish ancestors were aristocrats, and she feels that she is living in a kind of spiritual exile from her rightful ancestral destiny. Where the Judaic conception of spiritual exile from ancestral destiny is apprehended as a geographic and political displacement from an idealized Jerusalem, Velveteen's sense of alienation springs from having been exiled to the other side of a class barrier. As she explains to Red, the prospect of having a child with Dexter promises a means of transcending the class barrier and recovering a sense of spiritual home:

> I always thought that since my family crossed over worlds we could never get back ... to that, right? Never get back through the glass, but with

Dexter, I'm back, I feel back. And I think he's my only chance. He talks gentle. (50)

Dexter in turn finds with Velveteen refuge from his life, but while his passion for having a child looks genuine enough, any spiritual element in his yearning seems to have been displaced on to sexual fantasy. His lust for Velveteen is an example of the eroticization of transgression documented by Stallybrass and White, in which the "lower" elements of a cultural and psychological hierarchy are fetishized. (Another such example of the eroticization of transgression is Red's use of a maid's outfit for her striptease routine.)

Yet, by the same token, Velveteen's own routine demonstrates that transgression of a different kind is possible by confounding the spiritual and the erotic. In a scene Thompson would reuse in *Sled*, Velveteen performs a striptease while costumed as a Mother Superior. When she ends up with her "black torn filmy slip, she "shows off her five month pregnant belly," while Dexter and the other men watch "entranced" (49). The image could be said, from one perspective, merely to trade upon the cliché of the Madonna-whore oxymoron as the quintessential object of male sexual desire. But in the context of the other religious allusions in *Tornado*, more significant is the idea that Velveteen evokes and embraces both spiritual aspiration and sexual desire through her dance. Moreover, it is appropriate to consider this combination of spirituality and sexuality as not merely an affective evocation – i.e., an experience produced in the minds of the onlookers – but as an expression of Velveteen's own uplifted state of eroticism and faith.

While the redemptive aspect of childbirth as it applied to Rose was made more explicit in the radio version of *Tornado*, in the stage version it remains apparent that in some way Rose's motherhood is a deliverance from the evil and a transcendence of the chaos into which she is regularly plunged by her seizures. Something very similar goes on in Viola's mind. What begins as a desperate attempt to hold on to her husband's love through the conception of children soon reaches well beyond the simple wish to hold on to Dexter. Viola's progressively more irrational actions evince the desperation of a woman who feels herself becoming a spiritual outcast: her lack of children has become for her a denial of grace. Hence, while Viola's kidnapping of Rose's baby, however impractical, has a modicum of rational motivation, the deeper significance of her actions becomes manifest in her totally irrational attempt to identify herself with Rose as mother, maker of life.

Significantly, Viola's identification extends not only to Rose's motherhood but to her sufferings as well. As innumerable cultural references attest, there is a natural imaginative connection between the notion of martyrdom, which involves suffering through to a triumphant state of purity, and the experience of childbirth, in which the mother's suffering begets and thus renews human innocence. Thompson further connects this pattern with the idea of the achievement of grace, a theme that as Richard Paul Knowles has remarked, "consistently" appears in her work ("Plays," 36). In *Crackwalker*, for example, the theme is hinted at in subtle ways, as when Alan and Therese talk about getting married at the Church of the Good Thief (a real church just down the street from the Kingston Federal Penitentiary and the Prison for Women). The church name invokes the resilient possibility of salvation held out in Luke 23:43, where Jesus saves one of the two thieves crucified along-side him – clearly a notion pertinent to the vaguely criminal underworld of *The Crackwalker*. More obviously, there are the several occasions Therese is identified with the Madonna. That association also hints at a potentially redemptive way of regarding the death of her child (as occurs in the development of Sandy's humanitarian compassion).

A similar possibility of retrieving grace from morbidity inheres in *White Biting Dog*. At the end of the play Glidden & Pony are dead; Pascal has perhaps suffered a spiritual death; and, if we count Queenie and the Dachshunds as well, we have here a slaughter approaching *Hamlet* proportions. But Thompson has specifically argued that Pony's suicide, at any rate, signifies not a defeat but an achievement of grace:

Pony achieves Grace because she understands when she falls in "love" that something has possessed her, taken her over, and that that something can wipe out all her moral character [...] Anyhow, Pony had the strength to conquer that radical evil [...] The old man [i.e., Glidden] in *White Biting Dog* also achieves Grace, also at the expense of his own happiness. Lomia and Cape, on the other hand, are amoral human beings who didn't even take the first step. You have to work and work and pray.   (*Fair*, 103)

The kind of work Thompson has in mind involves not merely humility but an endurance of suffering until self-awareness is attained and a childlike innocence becomes retrievable: hence the connection with childbirth, an idea dramatized in the penultimate scene of *I Am Yours*. Dee moves into the nursery at the hospital, where she believes her child is sleeping, and the stage directions tell us that "She feels purified – through birth – and also through understanding her self-hatred, her guilt about her mother – she is now able to love after having grappled with her 'shadow' or 'animal'" (176).

At any rate, the notion of "suffering through" to a state of grace is cer-tainly the relevant spiritual model at the end of *Tornado*. As the police and the other characters close in upon Viola at the edge of the Scarborough bluffs, the scene takes on a magic-realist tone that foregrounds the religious themes. Jake (who, despite being older than in the radio version, retains something of his status as an "angel," as Rose called him) foregoes retribution for mercy as his mother reminds him of the principle of Christian forbearance. Viola's red-handedness is an emblem of her guilt; thus, to cut off her hands would be appropriate and even just, not only in terms of what is loosely referred to as "Old Testament justice" but in the gruesome, fantastic manner of some of the Grimms' *Tales* (see the red-hot iron slippers used to punish the wicked Queen at the end of "Snow White" – though not in the expurgated Disney version). Instead, the Christian notion of suffering through to grace is embraced, so all the terror and rage within Viola erupt in a "sympathetic" epileptic seizure, a journey through the chthonian, which, once she has emerged, may enable her to retrieve control of her soul.

UNHEIMLICH MANOEUVRES

Apart from reworking *Tornado* for the theatre, Judith Thompson did not produce a new full-length stage play in the almost seven years from *Lion in the Streets*, in May 1990, until January 1997, when *Sled* had its première. In the interim she wrote several scripts for film (most of which were commissioned but are as yet unproduced projects), a number of radio plays, one adaptation (*Hedda Gabler*, for the Shaw Festival in 1991), and some shorter original works for the theatre. Among the works from these years that have been published are two radio plays and two very short stage plays.

Thompson's interest in reaching past the conscious defences of her audiences to create a dreamlike state in the theatre is also served by radio drama, which she treats as if it were an inner voice for the listener:

I like this idea of voices in the dark, whispering; schizophrenics hear voices in the dark, it affects them deeply. The voice and you – I just love that, no distractions. It's a pure experience [...] I think radio is about poetry, because poetry is about rhythm, word choice. It's something that actually *carves* into you, the poetry and the word choice. That's what radio should do, carve into you, make those big holes like in the wheat, the circles.   (*White Sand*, 5)

That concept of being helplessly, profoundly penetrated by a mesmerizing voice is bound up with the themes of the two published radio plays, both of which deal with a foreboding sense of destiny.

The radio play *White Sand* (1991) carefully orchestrates the alternating voices of Velma, a Caribbean immigrant to Canada; Eleanor, her young white ward; Carl, a white supremacist skinhead; and Kimberly, Carl's girlfriend, at age eighteen – when the main events are occurring – and at thirty-one, when she is in prison. The play moves towards the murder of Velma with a dreadful inevitability, the audience knowing that all these separate sectors of voices must inevitably collide. What is surprising, however, is that it is the relatively benign Kimberly who commits the decisive violent act, for no better reason than her anxiety to make herself "worthy" of Carl's love. But, having murdered Velma, Kimberly feels the expression in Velma's eyes wearing her down like water wears rock down to white sand (27). The hard, solid rock of a soul wedded to white supremacism is, through conscience, becoming something pure and malleable, related to the Caribbean beaches Velma came from. The sense of destiny leading to Velma's murder, then, is juxtaposed with another destiny that will eventually bring Kimberly to humanism through the workings of her conscience.

In *Stop Talking Like That* (1995) the sense of destiny is given a more supernatural resonance. Joanne, an anorexic Canadian teenager, goes on a trip to Australia to visit her paternal grandfather, Fergus, with her family.[10] She feels there is something supernatural in Australia, lying beyond the material landscape and calling to her, a feeling she shares with her grandfather, Fergus. The dreadful foreboding haunting the play is offset by the implication that Joanne and Fergus are in some way yearning for death's oblivion. It would release them from their sense of not fully belonging on earth, where they feel life to be in some way *unheimlich* – a German word translating literally as "unhomelike," used to describe an uncanny or eerily alien experience. Joanne's anorexia thus suggests something symbolic, for while in some ways she remains a relatively ordinary teenager, Joanne is so preoccupied with the afterlife and the noumenal world that her insistence on annihilating her material self through starvation evokes the asceticism of the medieval mystics, those who practised self-abnegation to extremity because they believed that the soul's passage to its true and eternal home was obstructed by any fleshly indulgences whatsoever.

In such a spirit, then, she ventures with Fergus into the outback on a walkabout, a sort of quest for her own Dreaming-track – the path that the Australian aboriginals believe was laid out by their spiritual ancestors, and which are ideationally related to the migratory paths of birds, fish, and animals (see Chatwin). Fergus eventually leaves Joanne behind to pursue death and his afterlife as a bird, his totemic creature. Joanne chooses instead to return to life, but as she leaves the Rock she is picked up by a stranger in a car, who rapes and kills her, telling her: "I'm ice and I'm snow, snow inside your sweetness you ripened for me all your life little passionfruit" (165). A further way of reading Joanne's anorexia is thereby introduced: an unconscious attempt to keep herself from ripening into readiness for this brutal destiny. As the surviving members of Joanne's family search for her, only Lily, Joanne's sister, stricken with profound remorse for her betrayal of her Joanne, hears amidst the birds the strains of a church choir.

The themes of a young woman who feels she doesn't belong in her world and the haunted conscience of a woman who betrays her appear in a very different way in one of the most impressive, though certainly the shortest, of Thompson's published works from this period, the monologue *Perfect Pie* (1993). Patsy, a woman in her late thirties, living in Marmora, a small town north of Belleville in southeastern Ontario, is tape-recording a message for an old friend she has seen on television, while at the same time she makes a meat pie from scratch for a local pie-baking competition. Gradually, however, we discover that Marie died many years ago, when she and Patsy were still teenagers. In a reversal of the Father Hayes and David scene in *Lion in the Streets* Patsy has imagined a continued parallel life for the long-dead Marie.

The play is supported by a subtle repetition of imagery associated with bodily organs. These references, metaphoric and literal, to the internal secrets and the vaguely threatening (to Patsy) mysteries of life and death, would remain discrete images, perhaps, were it not that Patsy is all the while occupied with tucking animal organs into her meat pie, enfolding the "secrets" neatly within the smooth white dough before sealing and baking the result into a "perfect pie." The meat pie, in turn, is linked with the central incident around which the monologue revolves. Marie had persuaded Patsy to commit suicide with her on the railway tracks. Patsy accompanied Marie until the consuming thought of her mother's meat pie burning in the oven, the pie she had promised to look after, tore her away from Marie's side, and she abandoned her friend to a solitary death. Thus, Patsy's pie-making is a sort of cross between a therapeutic activity and a hellish punishment similar to that inflicted on Tantalus; she speaks of being blanketed beneath falling snow as she makes her pies – like the characters in James Joyce's "The Dead." Condemned to remember, Patsy compulsively, figuratively, puts the contents of a recollected inner life into her pies, never quite able to achieve perfection using the messy ingredients of the past.

Several years later Thompson expanded the *Perfect Pie* monologue into a full-length play for four characters (Patsy and Marie as adults and as children), directing it herself for the Tarragon in early 2000. The full-length version begins as did the monologue, with Patsy recording a message to her long-lost friend as she prepares a pie, though here the filling is a rather more innocuous rhubarb. The more striking difference is that as Patsy continues to speak, the adult Marie, who has changed her name to Francesca, begins to answer and moves to join Patsy in her kitchen.

The dramatic construction of the scene is echoed by that of the play as a whole. The conversation of the adult women is interspersed with scenes of them as children, and both plots, past and present, lead inexorably to the same point: the moment in which the two stood together on the tracks before the oncoming train (represented in Sue LePage's design for the première production by the foreboding presence of a distorted railway track). The poetic effect of this construction demands figurative comprehension of some sort. For example, one might feel that the psyches of the two women, and of their younger and older selves, were sliding towards one another like binocular lenses coming into joint focus on one subject; or that interleafed stories were combining to form a single tale. However, the most compelling metaphor by which to comprehend the structure is provided by Thompson in the stage directions. The theatrical device by which Francesca appears before Patsy at the play's opening could be a figurative rendering of a real visit, but because Patsy continues to make her pie throughout this section, a feeling persists that Patsy has invoked Francesca's presence as she kneads and rolls and cuts the pastry dough. The entities in the play divide, fold, conjoin, and interpenetrate in a dramatic process that parallels Patsy's preparation of her pie.

The scenes depicting the development of Patsy and Marie's friendship as children recall Rodney's description of his boyhood friendship with Michael in Lion in the Streets. Again an peculiar child, a despised social outcast, is desperately grateful for the friendship of a "normal "child." Again too there is a public betrayal of the outsider's trust by someone who is horrified to have befriended a "loser," though in Perfect Pie the betrayal comes not from Marie's best friend but from her date for a school dance; Patsy (to that point at any rate) remains faithful. In the case of Rodney and Michael the recapitulation of the relationship and its betrayal emanated from the mind of Rodney, the outcast, the loser. In the case of Patsy and Marie the recollection is initiated by Patsy, and the scenes from the past adumbrate the nature of Patsy's fascination with Marie, a fascination that she is unable to explain when asked (52–3). The source seems to be the exotic and vulnerable qualities, the unheimlich or chthonic features of Marie Begg's character that, for Patsy, speak compellingly of "a world out there, an unimaginable world" (82). However, to the boys who assault her after the dance, they are chiefly threatening, however sexually arousing –

another example of the eroticization of transgression. The boys try to prove to themselves that the force Marie represents is not indomitable by raping and then urinating on her. Patsy, by contrast, decides to embrace all that Marie represents by accompanying her to the tracks to await the oncoming train.

That the chthonic forces the others see in Marie, however terrifying, may be an omnipresent element of life is suggested by several allusions. Patsy's father, who is described by Francesca as a lovely man, is also remembered as slicing open the stomachs of cows that are bloated with gas – an act that is none the less horrific for Patsy's insistence that it is necessary (12–13). Worse still is Patsy's defensive account of her father shooting the family dog, Belle, then leaving its corpse tied to a tree to rot (62). So we see at least that the sort of brutality Marie experiences at the hands of the boys after the dance is endemic to this farming community. But in Marie there are glimpses of something more primal than mere human brutality, something uncanny that is related to the phobia that Patsy's mother has about lightning. Here, as in *Tornado*, this terrifying power is encountered most intensely through the *grand mal* seizures of epilepsy, which Thompson represents vividly with the image of a menacing stalker "with his knife and his dirty long fingernails," the spectre of death (50–1).

In childhood it is Marie who is epileptic; in adulthood it is Patsy. The transference of the disease from one to the other is given a material (if implausible) explanation: Patsy injured her head in the incident at the train tracks; Marie's father stopped striking her on the head when she left Marmora. The deeper truth, however, has to do with the intensity of Patsy's identification with Marie. From the time of the incident at the train tracks, Patsy has suffered from epilepsy because she made a profound identification with Marie and in doing so acquired her friend's access to that chthonic power, a power represented on that occasion by the instrument of their impending deaths, the oncoming train (see 61).

Now, the account we are given of the train incident in this full-length version of the play has it that Patsy, though she was tempted to flee as the smell of her mother's burning pies beckoned her back to home and safety, changed her mind and decided to remain on the tracks to be killed; apparently – and here is where the account becomes suggestively vague – Marie pulled Patsy from the tracks at the last moment. "Are you saying that I ... saved *your* life?" asks Francesca. "You saved my life ... but you always had ... saved my life," responds Patsy (85). Shortly afterwards Francesca leaves to attend a gala that may or may not be real, and Patsy is left alone to remark: "We aren't going to see each other ever again. It's going to be like you were never here. Like you were a dream" (87). So, if we have not been inclined to ask them before, a series of questions are suddenly forced upon us at the play's end: Has the visit of Francesca been a dream conjured up by Patsy as she made her pies? Is Patsy's relationship to Marie more than a memory; is it a dark place of awful power hidden within herself that she revisits privately to reacquaint herself with the thrilling, terrifying experience of being open to the "unimaginable world"? It is not merely our knowledge of the original monologue that might lead us to believe that Patsy actually abandoned her friend to die alone on the train tracks, that she chose instead a parochial life of safety, familiarity, and perfect pies, using denial and self-deception to buttress her outer self against the threat of self-doubt, but haunted within by that recurring image of the stalker.

Off the 401 (1995), a short play first produced as part of a larger multi-author work called *Stolen Lands*, takes place not very far from Marmora geographically, at and near a roadside restaurant somewhere east of Kingston along the 401 (the largest multilane highway in Canada). The setting also has a similar figurative significance, functioning as a metaphor for the characters' forcible confrontation of horrific aspects of life existing just outside their mainstream, fast-paced lives. The play chiefly depicts an ethical chasm opening up between Val and John, a middle-class couple, in a manner reminiscent of Raymond Carver's "So Much Water So Far from Home." The two see a man and an Amerindian boy sitting together in the restaurant. Val suspects – correctly, as it turns out – that the man is exploiting the boy sexually. Val insistently demands that they take action, but John refuses, and when he offers her the option of walking back along the highway the "half a mile or so" (68) to the restaurant by herself, she says that she is "too tired. It's too cold, and I've got the wrong shoes" (69). The core of selfishness, complacency, and classism hinted at in their earlier conversation and persisting immovably beneath their ethical postures has been exposed. Disillusioned and demoralized, but otherwise unchanged, they move on down the highway.

Life in bewilderingly rapid motion also provides the eponymous image of Thompson's largest play to date, *Sled* (1997). Whereas all her previous work had been under two hours' duration, Thompson remarked that seeing Robert Lepage and Ex Machina's *Seven Streams of the River Ota*, a seven-hour production, prompted her decision that her new play should be "as long as it needs to be, not as long as it conventionally should be" (Duschene, 34). The larger scale allowed Thompson to revisit a number of the themes of her earlier work and draw them into a unifying pattern. Unfortunately, some critics complained that the effect of combining all the different strands in one play was unwieldy and incoherent. Be that as it may, it is impossible not to admire Thompson's magnificent ambitions, and while there is no telling what the ultimate fate of *Sled* will be, the play contains so many deeply fascinating and troubling elements that it would be a grave error to dismiss it lightly.

Sled depends upon the inevitable collision of action arising from two antithetical locations, the wilderness of northern Ontario and a residential neighbourhood in downtown Toronto. At a lodge in northern Ontario, Annie, an unusual lounge singer, is insulted by Kevin and Mike. Annie's husband, Jack, a policeman known for his violent temper, forces the two to apologize. That night Kevin kills Annie in reprisal when, encountering her in the woods, he pretends to mistake her for a moose. When Mike wants to inform the police, Kevin kills him as well, then steals Annie's red dress. Meanwhile, on Jack and Annie's street in Toronto we meet Joe, who carries all the history of his multi cultural neighbourhood in his memory. One neighbour, Evangeline, desperately longs for the return of her little brother, who was kidnapped from the house many years before. The brother is Kevin; and when he returns to his childhood home on the run from the police, he bullies Evangeline into incest and into a job as a stripper. Though Annie's ghost continues to haunt him, Jack becomes romantically involved with Evangeline, not recognizing Kevin from the lodge. When he sees Annie's dress in Kevin's room, however, the two begin a fight, which Evangeline ends by killing Jack. Kevin then kills Joe for his money and urges Evangeline to escape with him. Instructed by Annie's ghost, Evangeline takes Kevin back into the northern wilderness, where, after having a baby she names Annie, she ends by indefatigably carrying the exhausted and dying Kevin while singing a Cree hymn and awaiting acceptance into the spirit world.

The sense of inevitable doom arising from the alternation between the two main settings of *Sled* is closely related to the effect of *White Sand*, where the fatal collision proceeds from the alternating sectors in a similarly ineluctable dialectic. The original concept governing the dialectic of *Sled* seems to have been the idea of Canada itself. That fact may not be so readily apparent from the script as it now exists. But, because of the publicly and academically supported workshops that eventually produced *Sled*, the genesis and development of the play is well documented; and records of the earlier drafts helpfully deepen our understanding of the final script.

During the workshop process, the scene in the original script to which Thompson is said to have given more attention than any other, and that which she most often offered for public consumption – choosing it to be recorded for radio, for example – was what she called "the

Barbecue Dream scene." The scene was finally cut from play late in the workshop process and so does not appear in the published version of *Sled*, for two reasons that Thompson explained in a post-workshop interview: "First, it is better to show rather than to tell; and second, there is so much vulnerability to failure [i.e., on the part of directors and actors] in that scene" (Fletcher, 39). Yet Thompson continued to emphasize the importance of the scene. In the interview she asserted that "the Barbecue Dream scene *is* the politics of the play. In a sense it is the springboard of the play for me intellectually" (39). Even after cutting the scene, Thompson continued to append it to the copies of *Sled* she sent out because, she explained, "it's my way of summarizing what the play is about" (40). Fortunately, the scene has been published in its original form in CTR, so the intellectual "springboard" remains available for consultation (Knowles, "Great," 12–16).

In the scene, Jack, after Annie's murder, is asleep on his couch in front of the television. He dreams of a barbecue at which Annie and other characters in the play appear, greeted by a home-made sign: "Welcome Neighbours." The conversation turns towards the multicultural nature of Canadian society, and the characters, of various ethnic backgrounds – Cree, Irish, Austrian Jewish, French Canadian, Portuguese, Italian, Norwegian – discuss the "balkanization" of Canada and the threat of separatism. They all begin to revert to their ancestral languages, yearning for a sense of home, angrily laying blame for the unfortunate aspects of their histories. Meanwhile, amidst the discussion, Kevin, masked in a black balaclava, interjects allusions to his violent murder of Annie. Though he is not at first acknowledged, we feel him poisoning the atmosphere of the party – a catalyst of discord and disaster like the mythical Ate, whose uninvited appearance at a wedding set off the Trojan War, or the wicked thirteenth Wise Woman of "Sleeping Beauty" who curses the heroine at her christening. At last the anxiety and hostility reach a crescendo. Jack tries to remove Kevin's mask, but he is easily overcome, and awakes screaming Annie's name.

Taking Thompson at her word about the scene representing "the politics of the play," we may say that *Sled* uses the Canadian political context to explore the disintegration of social goodwill into the kinds of xenophobic hostility and violent self-protectiveness that destroy the possibilities of peaceful civilization. The topic is clearly enormous in its complexity and scope of possible reference. Accounts of the workshop indicate that much time was spent whittling down a vast range of allusions and plot elements into an efficient dramatic shape. The explicit references to any particular Canadian political dilemma, for example, are gone entirely from the final script. Instead, the field of concern has moved to something more internal, more to do with essential human nature.

The notion of heritage as an aspect of identity is present in *Sled*, but the chief emphasis is on its spiritual aspect. Annie's deep feeling of affinity towards her Irish heritage, or Evangeline's discovery that her previously unknown Cree heritage resonates within her own soul, recall the treatment of the theme in *Tornado*, where for Velveteen, her Polish-Catholic ancestry represents her authentic place in the world of human spirit, a sort of personal Jerusalem. Thompson even dispensed with some of the rudimentary elements of realism that would root the theme of heritage in a material setting. In an earlier draft, for example, Evangeline learned Cree in prison, from a fellow Cree prisoner. In the final version of *Sled* she adopts the Cree language and culture almost as instantly and fluently as the characters in Jack's dream had done.

What remains very strongly of the Canadian cultural theme is in the shape of a path traced from the savage and mystical Canadian wilderness to the confusing multicultural reality of Canadian urban life. The record of violence that lingers in the memories and consciences of the city-dwellers (for instance, Joe's memory of the death of his father, Jack's shame about the youth he terrorized as "Diablo" while on police duty, or Evangeline's memory of her brother's kidnapping) lurks just outside normal civilized life, as the indomitably lawless wilderness awaits just beyond the boundaries of civilization. At the same time an identification is made between the vaguely atavistic aspirations of the characters and the mystic, primordial power inherent in the wilderness. In other words, the wilderness is a figure in which both the violence and the spiritualism of the inner life finds a counterpart in the horrors and serenity beyond civilization – truly a desperate wilderness.

Robert Nunn has argued that much of the complex symbolism of *Sled* may be understood in terms of Freud's theory of the uncanny, or *unheimlich* ("Strangers"). While many of the specific references he cites (such as the parade in honour of Saint Catherine, torn apart by wild beasts, or the recurrent fox and wolf imagery) have been excised from the final version of the play, the principal tenet of his argument remains applicable. He suggests that the symbolism draws on two opposing realms of meaning, which he calls the "demonic" and the "totemic," identifying them respectively with Catholic and native spirituality. The appropriateness of the terms of opposition is arguable, given that within native spirituality there can still be a kind of demonic significance attached to some animals' behaviour, and within Catholicism animals are often represented benevolently, as in the imagery of the dove, the lamb, and so on. Still, there is no doubt that the pattern of imagery in *Sled* does evince such a double feeling towards the wilderness, taking the ambivalent totemic symbolism of *Stop Talking Like That* several steps further.

It would be possible to treat the ambivalence as a version of the "garrison mentality" described by Frye – the split personality of the depiction of the Canadian wilderness as both a threat against which civilized communities provide protection and a source of mystic identification for the repressed elements of the inner self. Yet Nunn's use of Freud's theory of the uncanny is perhaps a more promising interpretive model, given the affinities between Thompson's work and Freud's theories already delineated. Freud's discussion of the uncanny centres on the idea that what is deeply rooted in the self can be hidden, only to appear suddenly as something dangerous and threatening. The uncanny is therefore attached to a sense of the familiar and unfamiliar at the same time, and arises where the incommensurable perspectives of the conscious and the unconscious are suddenly made to focus upon the same object. One place we experience the uncanny, then, is where an external act of violence corresponds to an inner suppressed thought, or when those whom we thought of as close neighbours reveal a side corresponding to our deepest fears.

Thus we might say that in *Sled* Thompson offers another variation on the Freudian theme of how the repressed continues to leak out on to the tidy surface of civilized life. Moreover, as Nunn points out, Freud argues that the uncanny is especially wont to appear "in relation to death and dead bodies, to the return of the dead, and to spirits and ghosts" (Freud, "Uncanny," 241, cited in Nunn, "Strangers," 39). because the older superstitions about death persist beneath the surface of modern rationality. This takes us much further into the heart of the discussion, for as Nunn says, *Sled* is above all "a play about the interpenetration of the worlds of the living and the dead, [a] motif that can be traced through Judith Thompson's work" (31).

With *Sled*, however, Thompson had set out to address this theme more directly than in any previous work. Her original title for the play was *The Last Things*, a reference to the four last things comprised by eschatological thought: death, judgment, heaven, and hell. Thompson moves the eschatological theme away from a purely biblical context, using elements of indigenous myth. In a note placed in the program for the Tarragon première (reproduced in the published play) she quotes *Aurora* by Candace Savage:

The Iroquois people ... imagined the aurora as the entry point into the Land of Souls, where the sky rose and fell to let spirits into the world beyond ... The lights were seen as the actual spirits of dead ancestors. Sometimes their progress across the sky was interpreted as a torchlight procession or a joyful dance. According to the circumpolar tradition, the northern lights are the souls of those who have died through loss of blood, whether in childbirth, by suicide or through murder. Inuit shamans have been visiting the moon for millennia. Often the journey began at night, under a full moon, when the shaman was standing at a blowhole, staring into the black, swirling water and waiting for a seal to rise. Suddenly, he would notice a sled descending out of the sky. It would land nearby, and the shaman would climb on board. Once he reached the land of the moon, he might meet dead relatives or watch spirits playing ball in the northern lights.

The *Sled* image, then, suggests a headlong plunge into the life to come, including the promised four last things. At the same time Thompson shows that a powerful element of human aspiration reaches back, not forward, attempting to retrieve memory and ancestral heritage to complete personal identity. The sense of destiny thrusts us forward blindly, even while we struggle to make sense first of where we have already been and who we are.

In short, the tremendous task to which *Sled* is addressed is the articulation of that eschatology that Norman O. Brown argued was the only hope of escaping the vicious, neurotic circle that psychoanalysis had revealed within the history of civilization. Thompson provides a glimpse of how the difficult project of maintaining social kinship with other human beings, represented here through the model multicultural neighbourhood over which Joe watchfully presides, is related to how we face the four last things awaiting the individual soul. If, as Freud suggests, all images of the hereafter are intimately related to our unconscious lives, then death, judgement, heaven, and hell do not necessarily await us only at the end of the sled ride. The confrontation of these last things occurs within each of us as we go, through an encounter with the inner life. And to transcend the barrier between our conscious selves and these four last things hidden deep within marks the first step towards transcending the barriers between us and our fellow human beings.

Notes

PROLOGUE

1 An intriguing development of this metaphor can be traced from John Donne's "Elegie XIX: Going to Bed" ("Licence my roaving hands, and let them go, / Before, behind, between, above, below. / O my America! my new-found-land, / My kingdome, safliest when with one man man'd"), where the speaker contemplates the question of possession, through LePan's "Astrolabe," where the speaker chooses to surrender to the land explored, and Neil Young's "Cortez the Killer," where remorse for the devastating effects of the imperialist instinct become a part of an extended, and partially disguised, lover-as-explorer metaphor.

2 "It seems to me that Canadian sensibility has been profoundly disturbed, not so much by our famous problem of identity, important as that is, as by a series of paradoxes in what confronts that identity. It is less perplexed by the question 'Who am I?' than by some such riddle as 'Where is here?'" Frye, *The Bush Garden*, 220.

3 I use the term "trope" throughout this book as a general name for the poetic unit (i.e., a figure that refers to or sensually evokes an isotopy). Verbal tropes may be called metaphor, metonym, synecdoche, or irony. While it is often possible to specify the kind of theatrical device in these terms, it is not always easy or helpful to do so, in part because a given figurative unit may involve several elements. In a sense, such a unit may be closer to what used to be called a "scheme," but using that term in such an obsolete sense would only further confuse the matter – especially

given that a particularly complex trope might comprise many figures in itself, while functioning as a unit within the overall poetic "scheme" of a play.

4 Lescarbot's production is the earliest recorded performance, though there is a mention of some mummers being on board a vessel that visited Newfoundland in 1583 (see Gardner, *passim*). The earliest recorded theatrical performance in North America is the 1567 performance of two comedias at the Spanish mission in Tequesta, Florida.

5 MacLennan drew his title from an explicitly positive image in a Rilke poem in which the poet says: "Love consists in this, that two solitudes meet and touch and protect one another."

6 See Bloom, *The Anxiety of Influence* and *A Map of Misreading*.

CHAPTER ONE: JAMES REANEY

1 Stated so baldly, Douglas's thesis is discomfiting in that it suggests a sort of anti-feminist bias. Nothing is further from the truth. She expresses misgivings about such an interpretation in her introduction (10-13), but explains: "Nineteenth-century American women were oppressed and damaged; inevitably, the influence they exerted on their society in turn was not altogether beneficial. The cruelest aspect of the process of oppression is the logic by which it forces its objects to be oppressive in turn, to do the dirty work of their society in several senses. Melville put the matter well: 'weakness, or even depravity in the oppressed is no apology for the oppressor; but rather an additional stigma to him, as being, in a large degree, the effect and not the cause of oppression.' To view the victims of oppression simply as martyrs and heroes, however, undeniably heroic and martyred as they often were, is only to perpetuate the sentimental heresy I am attempting to study here" (11).

2 In "The Second Coming":
Things fall apart; the centre cannot hold;
Mere anarchy is loosed upon the world,
The blood-dimmed tide is loosed, and everywhere
The ceremony of innocence is drowned. *(Yeats's Poems, 294)*

3 Indeed, it would not be going too far to say that a full critical understanding of Reaney's work without recourse to Frye's would be extremely difficult, if not impossible. The first full-length study of Reaney — Alvin A. Lee's *James Reaney* — remains in many ways one of the best statements on Reaney for the very reason that it was so thoroughly marinated in Frye. Frye's theories helped Reaney to identify and articulate his own central myth, and thereafter their relationship remained one of mutual inspiration. The influence of the older man upon the younger is naturally more obvious: e.g., Frye supervised

Reaney's doctoral thesis, "The Influence of Spenser on Yeats,"; Reaney calls *Anatomy of Criticism* "a poet's handbook" ("The Canadian Imagination," 188); he acknowledges that *One-Man Masque* is structured according to "Frye's mandala" (letter to John Ayre, 21 July 1987, cited by Ayre in *Northrop Frye,* 276). But the inspiration seems to have moved in the other direction at times: e.g., Frye cites Reaney's "Klaxon" as evidence that "the imaginative energy of an expanding economy is likely to be mainly technological" in "Preface to an Uncollected Anthology" *(The Bush Garden,* 166); and he uses Reaney's "Rachel" to support a lecture: "in effect a very beautiful and very eloquent paraphrase of this chapter in Ezekiel" *(The Bible and Literature,* 5).

4 Compare Samuel Taylor Coleridge's "Dejection: An Ode": "O Lady! we receive but what we give, And in our life alone does Nature live."

5 This brief summary is perforce something of a distortion in that, according to Berkeley, God's activity is not best characterized by the word "perception" (see J.D. Mabbott, "The Place of God in Berkeley's Philosophy," in Berkeley's *A Treatise Concerning the Principles of Human Knowledge,* 201–19); it is nevertheless a close enough approximation for the purposes at hand. See also Berkeley's *Three Dialogues between Hylas and Philonous.*

6 The lantern image is used by Jesus again when he speaks of the five wise and five foolish virgins who went to meet the bridegroom, only the former of whom have oil in their lamps: Matt. 25.

7 The scheme outlined in *A Vision* is considerably more complex than this: for example, there are twenty-two phases of personality that move between these states and among Four Faculties: Will, Mask, Creative Mind, and Body of Fate. Nevertheless, the simple dialectic of the two conditions leading to one forms the basis of Yeats's argument, and this Reaney picks up on fairly consistently in his thesis. See Yeats, *A Vision,* 71ff.

8 Edward Conze, *Buddhism* (1951), 127–8; cited in James Reaney, "The Influence of Spenser on Yeats," 212–13.

9 Reaney makes this distinction in *The Real Foundation for the Spree* (5) as well as in *Fourteen Barrels from Sea to Sea,* 130.

10 Admittedly, Prometheus is cursed in *Colours in the Dark* (Vancouver: Talonbooks 1969), 115. However, Prometheus is cursed in his "progenitor of technology" aspect. Here Reaney is being identified with Prometheus in his Shelleyean, imaginative aspect.

11 Respectively, the settings of the principal works of Thomas Hardy, William Faulkner, Margaret Laurence, and Claude Monet. The last worked at his country estate in Giverny.

12 Reaney's story anticipates a similar idea in the René Clement film *Les Jeux interdits* (1951).

13 Most of the stories have been republished in *The Box Social and Other Stories*.

14 "The Dead Rainbow" is in *Selected Longer Poems*; the others are in *Selected Shorter Poems*.

15 These points do not require much demonstration, particularly in light of some of the excellent critical attention this book has received already. See Northrop Frye's review for UTQ, reprinted in *The Bush Garden* (87–91); Germaine Warkentin's introductions to the 1975 edition of *A Suit of Nettles* and to the collected *Poems*; and Alvin Lee's and Ross Woodman's comments in their respective full-length studies.

16 "Necessary angel" is Wallace Stevens' figure to describe the function of metaphor in his book of that title.

17 The reference to Cohen probably alludes to his review of *The Killdeer*, which Cohen scathingly and characteristically called "a desperately bad play which only someone of talent could write" (35).

18 Centenarial: once every hundred years. To discuss the music of John Beckwith and Harry Somers, the composers Reaney collaborated with on his operas, is outside the scope of this book. But the continuity between Reaney's librettos and his plays is so apparent that it seemed arbitrary to exclude the operas from mention altogether.

19 *The Killdeer* was revised in 1970 (published in *Masks of Childhood*) and again in 1991 (unpublished).

20 The college may be based on United College – now the University of Winnipeg – where Reaney taught in the 1950s.

21 Barr's critical study of good and evil in *The Killdeer* and *The Easter Egg* seems to have interpreted Ross Woodman's comment about Reaney, that "Poetic drama [...] bring[s] into play forces above or below consciousness to guide and determine action," as referring to a rigid moral geography. Her commentary therefore becomes limited to remarks such as: "Both George and Bethel are evil characters. Both have perverted and sick minds. Bethel has purposely stripped Kenneth of all that was familiar to him, all he could connect with feelings of love" (88). Another essay in that issue of *Canadian Drama* is in the same vein: Schneider, "Negative and Positive Elements in James Reaney's Plays."

22 My metaphorical use of the word "entropy" draws analogy to both its classical and quantum physical applications in that (a) the energies expended on performing certain aspects of some romances seem to become easily lost from the effort of creating a cogent overall effect; and (b) there is a consequent danger that the aggregate of those lost energies – squandered dramatic tensions – will outweigh what is left for the performers and their audience to shape into an effective resolution. That this is a problem endemic to romance in the theatre I hope may be persuasively demonstrated through reference to the difficulties encountered in

perhaps the best romances ever written – Shakespeare's. (My comments are, of course, meant to describe the challenges to a production rather than to dismiss the plays critically.) Aside from the unusual stylistic unevenness of *Pericles* – only the latter three acts having certainly been written by Shakespeare – its diffuseness of setting is only somewhat tempered by the strength of the central character (at least in the last three acts) and by the use of Gower as narrator. *Cymbeline* lays itself out over such a broad scope of plots and themes that, in its effort to comprise all the various resolutions, the last act offers a spectacle something like that of a snake attempting to swallow a bullfrog. *Henry VIII* is nominally a historical-tragicomedy, but it is more the history of Henry, the tragedy of Buckingham, and the comedy of Cranmer, all bunched together with Wolsey playing a protean role that varies according to each plot. *The Winter's Tale* comprises two plots that are nearly completely separate, demanding different settings, characters, and tone. The notable exception to the entropy of the last plays is, of course, *The Tempest*.

23 Dudek also cites Brian Parker's faintly damning remark that "Act I of *The Killdeer* [is] still Reaney's most successful drama" *(Masks, 289)*.

24 Respectively: repetition of a word or phrase at the beginning of successive lines; repetition of a word or phrase from the end of one line at the beginning of the next; and repetition of a word or phrase throughout a passage.

25 Cocteau makes the point in his preface to *The Newlyweds on the Eiffel Tower*: "L'action de ma pièce est imagée tandis que le texte ne l'est pas. J'essaie donc de substituer une 'poésie de théâtre' à la 'poésie au théâtre.' La poésie au théâtre est une dentelle délicate impossible à voir de loin. La poésie de théâtre serait une grosse dentelle; une dentelle en cordages, un navire sur la mer. *Les Mariés* peuvent avoir l'aspect terrible d'une goutte de poésie au microscope. Les scènes s'emboitent comme les mots d'un poéme. ("The action of my piece is full of imagery, whereas the text is not. I am trying to substitute a 'poetry of the theatre' for 'poetry in the theatre.' Poetry in the theatre is a delicate lace, impossible to see at any distance. Poetry of the theatre should be a coarse lace, a lace of rigging, a ship upon the sea. *The Newlyweds* could be as terrifying as a drop of poetry under the microscope. The scenes interlock like the words of a poem.") Cocteau, *Oeuvres Complètes* 7:14.

26 I am drawing on my own professional acquaintance with Hirsch here, but there is ample material evidence to support these remarks, such as the record of Hirsch's early work in children's theatre in Winnipeg in the fifties (and still earlier, as a boy in Hungary); his notes for the 1982 production of *The Tempest* at Stratford; his children's play *The Box of Smiles*; and his many public remarks about the importance of training young actors.

27 Robert Wallace remarks, "Today, most Québécois playwrights have direct, on-going experience in the theatre as directors, actors or scenographers – which influences not only how but what they write. Until recently, this has been the exception rather than the rule in English-Canadian theatre, where playwrights usually create in isolation from other theatre artists and, in many cases, with little direct experience of theatrical work" (*Producing Marginality*, 180). To whatever degree this generalization is supportable, Reaney stands as a very significant exception, for his collaboration with Hirsch dates back to a time when most important Québécois playwrights (e.g., Marcel Dubé) were still writing in solitude, and even those who worked in the theatre, like Gratien Gélinas, created autonomously. More-over, Reaney's work, with Hirsch and subsequently, anticipated by two decades the collective creation of imagistic theatre that Wallace sees as the most significant avant garde work in the country and treats as almost solely a French-Canadian phenomenon (Theatre REPERE, Carbone 14, etc.).

28 For further discussion of the concept of the *poeta-magus*, which origi-nates with Novalis and Goethe, see Kurt Weinberg, "Romanticism: First Period," in Preminger, *Princeton Encyclopedia of Poetry and Poetics*, 718–19; and Silz, *Early German Romanticism*.

29 The two sides of this question echo the dispute between Sir James Frazer and Lord Raglan.

30 I am thinking, for example, of the particular accounts of the workshop process in *Wacousta!*, "The Story Behind King Whistle," and "Cycle;" as well as remarks in "Ten Years at Play;" *Performance Poems*, and *The Real Foundation*.

31 *Ignoramus* was first performed in February 1967, *Geography Match* in May (*Geography Match*, 7).

32 For example, see the mystical paintings of Lawren Harris or E.J. Pratt's *Moby Dick*-like iceberg in *The Titanic*. Also see the discussion of Michael Cook's use of iceberg imagery in the next chapter. Note that Reaney has made the iceberg a *lady*. Margaret Atwood points out that the personifi-cation of a hostile North is most often female, alluring, and devouring. Writing of Pratt's description of the iceberg that sank the Titanic, Atwood seems to speak directly to Reaney when she says: "Those who have followed the Nature-as-metaphor battle that raged throughout the 19th century – in which Wordsworthian good-mother imagery wrestled with Darwinian bad-mother imagery, and, by and large, lost – and espe-cially those steeped in, say, Rider Haggard's *She* and Bram Stoker's account of Lucy's metamorphosis from bride to vampire in *Dracula*, will know better than to trust anything wrapped in white [...] Pratt doesn't say what gender it is, but we get a hint [... The] phrase 'ringed by its icy broods,' so closely associated with hens and chicks, pushes the berg in the direction of the female" (Atwood, 23).

33 Ricoeur's concept is extremely valuable to any theory of poetic meaning, and so is worth some special attention here. He argues that the process of poetic meaning should not be understood as a simple recognition of "substitution," whereby a deviant denomination is substituted for the ordinary name. Deviance is indeed involved, but "this deviance concerns the predicative structure itself [...] While it is true that the effect of sense is focused on the word, the production of sense is borne by the whole utterance" (143–4). In this model there is a "collapse of literal meaning," out of which a "new predicative meaning" emerges. Ricoeur goes on to model the process of imagination in three stages: schematization, picturing, and *epoché* or suspension. The first stage involves a "predicative assimilation," or "synthetic insight," which refers to a process by which similarity is created between entities "not above the differences [...] but in spite of and through the differences" (146). The picturing stage, also referred to as "iconic presentation," evokes an "imaging" faculty, "the concrete milieu in which and through which we see similarities." Here Ricoeur stresses that to imagine "is not to have a mental picture of something but to display relations in a depicting mode" (148). In other words, while any mental picture is itself external to the process, the arousal of such sensorial experience is a necessary activity in order to create a meaningful context. Finally, there is a suspension or *epoché* of ordinary descriptive reference that allows "the projection of new possibilities of redescribing the world" (152). This last stage involves a use of the "split reference," but Ricoeur argues that "the structure of the fiction not only reflects but completes the logical structure of the split reference" by creating "positive insight into the potentialities of our being in the world" (153). He goes on to show how feeling may be integrated into this three-stage

34 Reaney keeps the main structure of Haggard's novel, but adds some incidents and changes facts and names. The script includes a chart of the relationship between the dramatis personae of the frame story and "The Saga of Caresfoot Court." To supplement that chart, here are the corresponding characters in Haggard's novel:

Saga of Caresfoot Court	*Dawn*
Devil Caresfoot	Devil Caresfoot
Douglas (a foundling)	George (D.C.'s bastard nephew)
Piers	Philip
Angela	Angela
Arthur Brenzaida (Maria's son)	Arthur Heigham (Philip's cousin)
Maria Lawry	Maria Lee
Lady Geraldine Eldred	Lady Ann Bellamy

Sir John Eldred	Sir John Bellamy
Claudia Van Yorick (Danish)	Hilda Von Holtzburg (German)
Reverend Gleneden	Reverend Fraser
Martha	Piggot
Julia Elbe	Mildred Carr
Keeper	Aleck
Rogue	[no such character]

35 In this context one keenly feels the pathos of J. Stewart Reaney's confession that *Dawn* "does not have the same strength of meaning for me that it holds for my father" (75). The ambiguous double ending made possible by contrasting a frame-tale with an inner tale was also used later by Harold Pinter in his ingenious screen adaptation of John Fowles's *The French Lieutenant's Woman*; see Pinter, 98–104.

36 Compare Reaney's explication of Jay Macpherson's poem "Anagogic Man": "the very process of being interested in metaphor evidently must lead to an interest in giant and mythical figures. Once you start saying 'my love is like a red, red rose,' you might as well start saying that she is like a great many other beautiful things as well, and then of course if she really is a goddess she is like everything, because a goddess isn't just a goddess unless she can control both beautiful and ugly things, even things indifferent. So she *is* everything and contains all the things she is like. If anything is like anything (metaphor) it eventually is everything (myth) and is an anagogic figure similar to Miss Macpherson's" ("The Third Eye," 26–7).

37 A useful analogy is the breakdown of symbols for each chapter of James Joyce's *Ulysses*.

38 The remark echoes an idea that Eliot argues at length in "Dante" (1929): that poetry begins to communicate long before it is fully understood, so that one need not fully understand poetic structure for a poem to have an effect (*Selected Essays*, 237–77).

39 NDWT was a Toronto-based company run by Keith Turnbull that operated from 1975 to 1982. Its members always insisted publicly that the name was not an acronym, though some divulged privately that it stood for "ne'er-do-well thespians."

40 Incidentally, the antlers were supplied by Tomson Highway (Reaney, *Wacousta!* 115), who has become one of Canada's most celebrated playwrights and has often acknowledged the influence this production had on his own creative development.

41 Apparently the scene has a basis in fact. The incident was described to Reaney by none other than Tom Patterson, the founder of the Stratford Festival ("The Story Behind," 58).

42 Reaney took the character's surname from the actress Anita La Selva, who, as a high school student, participated in the *King Whistle!* workshops.

43 A donnish joke: Una and Britomart are the names of incorruptible virgins in Spenser's *The Fairy Queen.*

CHAPTER TWO: MICHAEL COOK

1 Indeed, if Ludwig Feuerbach is right in suggesting that religious belief is the result of a universal human urge to attach the individual imagination to a larger concept, it may well be that a more remote society would be likely to lay greater stress on spiritual matters. For where life is not attached to the simple (and undoubtedly deluded) assurance of a concept of massive social progress, it must anchor itself to some kind of ideal. In other words, a culture must derive its sense of animating power from somewhere, and where this power is clearly not material in nature, it may be inevitable that the sense of power devolves upon a notion of noumenal forces.

2 The phrase is Brian Parker's (28), and the condemnation he is citing came from Urjo Kareda, *Toronto Star,* 17 Oct. 1972.

3 Brian Parker stops just short of the mythological reading that I am arguing when he remarks that the "specifically sexual nature – impalement through the groin with a hook – seems intended to reflect relationships between potency and survival, imperialism and sexual exploitation that Cook has not really managed to make clear" (26).

4 It may be too that any attempt truly to comprehend a historical event in all its complexity must beget such a heterogenous dramaturgy. At any rate, there is a similar bricolage of dramaturgical styles in Cook's last history play, *The Great Harvest Excursion,* which was commissioned by the Stratford Festival in 1987 but left unproduced, and evidently not fully revised, at the time of Cook's death.

5 For a summary of the archeological and anthropological evidence that survived the Beothuks, as well as transcripts of the first-hand eye-witness accounts of the incidents that are Cook's original sources, see Speck, *Beothuk and Micmac.*

6 Cf Bob Dylan's "Blind Willie McTell," with its litany of pain capped with the refrain "and no one can sing the blues like Blind Willie McTell" (CD3, tr18).

7 The phrase "perspective of perspectives" is used by Kenneth Burke to describe irony in *A Grammar of Motives,* 512.

8 The Ringmaster (or equivalent) device is by no means new (cf Wedekind/ Barnes, *Lulu;* Kander, *Cabaret;* Luckham, *Trafford Tanzi;* even the travelling Showman in the *The Donnellys*). Its effectiveness as a means of contrasting native and European cultures is suggested by its reappearance in a more recent play in only slightly altered form, namely the Interlocutor in Daniel David Moses' *Almighty Voice and His Wife* (1991).

9 I have been unable to determine whether this story has a specific historical basis or not. In his piece for Geraldine Anthony's *Stage Voices* Cook
seems to suggest that it does: "Currently, I am going to have another
crack at what is laughingly called historical drama, which means that I
have a diary-to-hand, written by the last person to be hanged in St.
John's after being whipped through the fleet. I'm not going to give away
any more than that" (228). It may be that Cook was speaking figuratively; if he was not, such taciturnity seems to have followed William
Gayden and his putative diary into all corners of the globe, for having
researched extensively, I have not located a single independent reference
to either.

10 Whether the name Douell is meant to be significant (i.e., "do-well") is
difficult to tell because of the difficulty in determining whether Gayden's
story has a historical source or not.

11 Cf Charles Ryder's idea of Brideshead as the embodiment of gradually
ripening spirituality "until, in sudden frost, came the age of Hooper" –
his soulless subordinate (Waugh, 331).

12 See, for example, Kubler-Ross, chap. 9, or Lewis. Perhaps the most suc-
cinct point about the link between the literary treatment of the personal
experience of death (i.e., elegy) and the treatment of the social experience
of the death of all worldly experience (i.e., eschatology) is made by Frank
Kermode, who says of poets treating apocalypse: "The End is a figure for
their own deaths" (*Sense*, 7).

13 "Vomedic irony, as it may be called with pardonable ugliness, retains
enough buoyancy to function as comedy. But its spirit of the absurd is so
thoroughly amalgamated with bleakness, torment, and dread (Kafka's
narratives of clownish-torturous bafflement come to mind) that it may
seem to betoken the death of comedy. Yet Vomedic irony remains affiliated with certain ancient ironic insights that were intended to furnish a
stimulus and a salve" (Gurewitch, 55). Another variation of vomedic
irony is explored by Sartre in *La Nausée*.

14 "Apocalypses, by their very nature, were designed both to reveal (to
believers) and to conceal (from the unworthy)" (McGinn, 526). Of
course, even for believers the message is not by any means crystal clear,
as evidenced by the chequered history of interpretation accorded the
book of Revelation (see McGinn).

15 The idea was based on a folk story of allegedly true origin, "Pickled
Charlie," about a lighthouse keeper whose partner, having died at the
beginning of winter, was kept in a pickle-barrel, the keeper making conversation with the corpse until he was relieved in the spring (Cook, "On
Tiln," 245).

16 Bernard Dupriez defines prosopopoeia as "The presentation of absent,
dead, or supernatural beings, or even inanimate objects, with the ability

to act, speak, and respond [... It] is a figure of elevated or 'sublime' style." Dupriez goes on to compare the figure to the use of special effects in cinema to "make the fantastic seem true" (357–9).

17 E.g., Pratt is described as "the Newfoundland realist" by Kate Taylor (c1).

18 Vladimir Nabokov, "Signs and Symbols," in *Nabokov's Dozen* (52–8). In this story an old couple return from an unsuccessful visit to their hospitalized son, who suffers from "referential mania." "In these very rare cases the patient imagines that everything happening around him is a veiled reference to his personality and existence" (54). The story is full of inscrutable symbols that arouse a foreboding in the reader similar to the son's derangement.

19 *Jacob's Ladder* is particularly interesting in this context, for in his account of the screenplay's development, Rubin says: "In the early drafts of *Jacob* I had attempted to introduce a third layer [that is, beyond "reality" and "illusion"] to the script, the idea that Jacob's confrontations with demons might actually be connected to a larger world event, the Biblical Apocalypse. I wanted to portray the dissolution of an individual mind in the larger context of a dissolution of the entire world. For Jacob it would be impossible to distinguish between his own death and the catastrophic end of everything around him. In his internal landscape, the world would die with him" (Rubin, 175).

20 The disciples actually named in these passages are Peter and "that disciple whom Jesus loved," a phrase used in the Fourth Gospel only, and traditionally identified as referring to John.

21 E.g., "of a badness that must be called indescribable," *The Times*; "He never surfaced into comprehensibility for one single moment," T.C. Worsley, *New Statesman*; "I did not understand a word of the plot ... [it was] too startling to be tedious, too scatter-brained to be a bore," Alan Dent, *News Chronicle*; all cited by Eric Salmon, 128–9.

22 His name could be intended to recall Churchill's position in the darkest days of the Second World War (forced to stand alone and take responsibility), though this seems a little far-fetched.

23 Beckett's *Endgame* also contains an implicit allusion to this biblical passage in Hamm's repeated sending of Clov to check out the window with the telescope.

CHAPTER THREE: SHARON POLLOCK

1 It may seem pedantic to comment on what may be just a casual rhetorical gambit resting on the one form of class prejudice still permissible in polite society. Still, setting aside humanist ethics, the suggestion that this particular kind of egocentrism is a peculiarly white male trait is spurious.

White males have no monopoly on the literary convention of the omniscient narrator. Moreover, the deliberate exploration of authorial subjectivity is essentially a legacy of Romanticism and Modernism, movements largely driven by white males.

2 Playwrights Union of Canada will provide photocopies of *A Compulsory Option. And Out Goes You* exists only in the original typescript version, available in the Sharon Pollock papers in the Special Collections of the University of Calgary Library.

3 In his director's notes in the program for the Vancouver Playhouse production, Christopher Newton hints at the targets of these two caricatures; Malcolm Page identifies them more explicitly ("Sharon," 106).

4 "Sir John McDonald: I do not see how a Sitting Bull can cross the frontier. Mr. MacKenzie: Not unless he rises. Sir John: Then he is not a Sitting Bull" (House of Commons *Debates*, 1878; cited in Dee Brown, 394).

5 Although, for the sake of dramatic economy, Pollock's play has Sitting Bull murdered immediately upon his return to the United States, the assassination actually occurred on 15 December 1890 (Brown, 410–12).

6 Will Kane, played by Gary Cooper, is an ex-sheriff who decides to remain in the town alone to face three murderers though he has been abandoned by all the townspeople and his new wife has threatened to desert him.

7 E.g., *Fort Apache, The Searchers, The Man Who Shot Liberty Valance.* The pattern is also evident in Howard Hawks' *Red River.*

8 Other uses of such a device include the Ringmaster in Wedekind's *Lulu,* the M.C. in Kander's *Cabaret,* the Travelling Medicine Show Man in Reaney's *The Donnellys,* and the Interlocutor in Daniel David Moses' *Almighty Voice and His Wife.*

9 The point at issue here is succinctly addressed by Chekhov in a letter to Suvorin: "When I describe horse thieves, you want me to say stealing horses is evil. But surely that's been known for a long time now without my having to say it. Let the members of the jury judge them, but my business is only to show what kind of people they are" (914). To be sure, Chekhov was one kind of playwright and Pollock is quite another, but the question of whether the artist should reiterate familiar moral principles or pass on to the more difficult task of comprehending human nature remains relevant to the critical discussion of any art.

10 In fact, Pollock appears to have been working on at least *Blood Relations* and *One Tiger to a Hill* simultaneously, for Diane Bessai reports in her introduction to *Blood Relations and Other Plays* that work on *One Tiger* was started within a year of the 1975 incident on which it was based (8).

11 Compare, for example, Brecht's *Mother Courage* to Schiller's *Wallenstein,* or Shaw's *Saint Joan* to Shakespeare's *Henry VI, Part One* or Sally Clark's *Jehanne of the Witches.*

12 In this context it is significant that, having been playing the role of "nice girl," Lizzie feels unable to trust even her own perception of the temperature (56).

13 She was then married to actor Michael Ball, and altogether they had six children, five from Pollock's previous marriage and one from her marriage to Ball (see Hofsess, "Families," 41–60).

14 The "whiskey six" of the title is, according to Mr Big, "a six cylinder MacLaughlin, fastest car on the road. A most seductive vehicle" (193).

15 To be sure, Mr Big is not literally an aristocrat, as my reference to Foghorn Leghorn (the cartoon rooster) suggests, but he deploys his prairie dialect with a confident eloquence and an articulate vocabulary that seem patrician in self-possession. Furthermore, having the formidable actor Robert Benson in the première performance of the role would have guaranteed Mr Big a physically imposing but dignified and genteel presence.

16 A similar character, though portrayed with perhaps more pity, appears in Mordecai Richler's *Solomon Gursky Was Here*. The character seems to be a peculiarly Canadian type of alazon (though there are undoubtedly parallels in other post-colonial literatures): an insecure colonial prig who quixotically looks for self-respect by harking back to an absurd pride in Empire and paternalistic rule of law.

17 Pollock's father himself praised the play, admiring its understanding of how everyone in such a family suffers (Brennan), so any notion that *Doc* is a portrait of villainy is a canard.

18 It should go without saying that my intention is not to suggest any direct historical relationship between Heidegger's work and Pollock's, merely to point to a philosophical framework that suggests useful analogies to some of the ideas implicit in these plays.

19 Pollock was also writer-in-residence at the Regina Public Library in 1986.

CHAPTER FOUR: MICHEL TREMBLAY

1 The translations appearing in this chapter, unless otherwise specified, are my own. I have done this not out of any dissatisfaction with the published translations but because I assume many readers will use the English as a crib for reading the French rather than wanting versions that can stand on their own merits, as those of Glassco, Van Burek, and Fischman do.

2 For a dissenting view, see William James (11–12), whose fascination with many other psychological origins of religious experience would appear to give special force to his truculent dismissal of the role of sexuality, though his notorious squeamishness about any vaguely sexual matters – for example, he abandoned medical practice because midwifery "gave me

some embarrassment" (*Varieties*, xiv) – raises doubt about whether James is capable of disinterested analysis on this point.

3 The Chroniques du plateau Mont-Royal series is set in the neighbourhood and years of Tremblay's childhood, and includes five novels: *La Grosse Femme d'à côté est enceinte* (published in English as *The Fat Woman Next Door is Pregnant*); *Thérèse et Pierette à l'école des Saints-Anges* (published in English as *Thérèse and Pierette and the Little Hanging Angel*); *La Duchesse et le roturier* [The Duchess and the Commoner]; *Des nouvelles d'Edouard* [The News about Edouard]; and *Le Premier Quartier de la lune* (published in English as *The First Quarter of the Moon*). A number of other novels, such as *La Coeur Découvert* (1986), which has a contemporary setting, were technically not published as part of the series, although such discriminations become moot when, as in *La Maison suspendue*, previously unconnected characters from separate generations are suddenly brought together and revealed to be related.

4 Borduas was actually one of five contributors to a collection of essays bearing the title *Refus global*, but it was his own title piece that set the tone and made the collection's main points most trenchantly and most enduringly.

5 Sartre acknowledges his debt to Eliade on page 13.

6 See, for example: Dassylva; Gauvin, 85; Gelinas; Germain; Gingras; Major, "Michel" and "Un Exorcisme"; Thério; Usmiani, 3–4; and Warwick.

7 See Klein, *Hebrew*. Klein believes this is a universal principle: "Language is a mirror in which the whole spiritual development of mankind reflects itself. Therefore, in tracing words to their origin, we are tracing simultaneously civilization and culture to their real roots" (*English*, x).

8 To be sure, English profanity was once more blasphemous in character; consider "God's bodykins," "s'blood" or "s'wounds."

9 Rue Fabre is the residential street on which Tremblay grew up, located in northeast Montreal; "La Main" (as in "the main street," not "the hand") is a stretch of boulevard Saint Laurent where a number of nightclubs are located.

10 Cf the rebuke to modern society implicit in Eliot's classical allusions in, for example, *The Wasteland* or "The Lovesong of J. Alfred Prufrock."

11 Though first produced in English with its French title, *En pièces détachées* was more recently produced as *Counter Service*. The French title means literally "in separate parts." Parts of *En pièces détachées* were produced as early as 1966, but it was first produced as a full play in 1969 and revised for a 1971 television production. It is this latter production from which the published text is derived. See Usmiani, 169–70.

12 Cf the various cast lists in the 1975 English translation of *En pièces détachées* (5–6).

13 Jean-Paul Sartre once called John Dos Passos "the greatest living American writer," founding his judgment chiefly on Dos Passos' use of such a mirror symbol in one of his novels.

14 If La Femme's disclosure of her idea now seems rather anticlimactic, we should remember that the idea is more metaphorical than real, and, of course, the play was written in 1969. One can only suppose that the suggestion would have been more sensational before the advent of male strippers, a common phenomenon today and one that has as yet had little apparent impact on the public sexual consciousness. Few men seem to mind the idea and, to judge by its modest commercial success, few women are more than mildly interested. Nevertheless, Tremblay may not be so far from the mark, for like La Femme, those who do attend male strip shows are said to do so with an air of vengeful hilarity.

15 While Maurice Charney points out that these terms have historically been ill defined, he helps to clarify matters when, discussing the "pornokitsch" of pictures "in which very real, strikingly uncomfortable and gauche naked women are frozen in idealized settings," he then remarks: "The mood of slightly soiled innocence and factory seconds of real experience permeates the concept of kitsch and camp, which offers a tawdry comic escape to overly sophisticated persons" (16–18).

16 In the original version of the play the father was named Gabriel and one of the aunts was named Albertine. However, for a 1986 production Tremblay changed these names to Armand and Gilberte, in order to avoid confusion with the characters named Gabriel and Albertine in the Chroniques du plateau Mont-Royal novels and plays. Accordingly, I incorporate that alteration here.

17 Hence, Ray Conlogue's understandable error of assuming that the trilogy was named after André Brassard ("Upping," C2), director of the premières of all three plays and Tremblay's collaborator since 1964.

18 For a dissenting view see Micheline Cambron, who argues that the absence of this central trope is a fault in the play's construction (198).

19 The high mimetic mode is that in which the hero is "superior in degree to other men but not to his environment" (Frye, Anatomy, 33–4). As used here, "Dionysiac" refers to a tragedy about the death of a god.

20 A good straightforward explanation of this paradox and its importance to quantum physics may be found in Hawking, chap. 4.

21 While Sidnell does not actually use the term "preterition," his description and examples (i.e., Yeats's "No Second Troy" and Magritte's "Ceci n'est pas une pipe") make it clear that the figure he calls "negative affirmation" is a version of Dupriez's "preterition" (cf Dupriez, 353–5).

22 In For the Pleasure of Seeing Her Again some of the original French allusions have been altered to evoke equivalently famous plays from the English repertoire, although English-speaking audiences are still likely to

have difficulty recognizing plays such as Marcel Dubé's *Un Simple Soldat;* and the joke about Giraudoux's *The Trojan War Will Not Take Place* would be lost in English because the play is best known in Christopher Fry's translation, *Tiger at the Gates.*

CHAPTER FIVE: GEORGE F. WALKER

1 Herbert Whittaker, however, noticed a difference in tone, and suggested that *Ambush at Tether's End* "sits more comfortably in the Ionesco tradition than that of Beckett" (15).

2 Johnson goes on to argue, intriguingly if obscurely, that "in turning the form against its content, Walker avoided slavish imitation." I am not entirely sure what he means by this unless he has in mind something like the postmodernist reassessment of modernist form I discuss below. At any rate, his related point is well made: that the European-based theatre of the absurd seems out of step with North American culture, except where it appears in the versions of van Itallie or, especially, Shepard.

3 The suggestion of repetition with which *The Prince of Naples* ends is certainly related to the ending of *The Lesson,* in which we are informed that the student whom the Professor has killed is the forty-first victim on that day alone. Both endings may be more obscurely related to Nietzsche's nebulous "doctrine of eternal recurrence," which supposes that events would be repeated endlessly in time and connects this concept in various ways to the inherent weaknesses in human nature as it stands.

4 The specific remark is drawn from *The Work,* but this is a recurrent theme in interviews (e.g., Fraser, 23; Kirchoff, D2).

5 The films made of these stories seem more relevant to Walkers play than the original literary versions.

6 Two examples of pop art theatre that, by contrast with Walker, eschew transformation as far as possible are *The Brady Bunch Play* and *Schoolhouse Rock: The Musical.*

7 For the reader's convenience, references to plays republished in *Shared Anxiety* will be cited for the original publication and for that book, preceded by an SA.

8 The actual date of composition is uncertain, but this is the speculation of Shelley's biographer, Cameron, 45.

9 That the play is based on a synopsis rather than the novel itself is explained in a prefatory note to the play. Walker's claim never to have been able to read the novel was made during an informal talk at Massey College, Toronto, in winter 1992.

10 Indeed, Bolt had also played Cook in *Ramona and the White Slaves,* so he had enacted a analogous role in that play as well.

11 The line obviously pleased Eliot; he used it in both "Burnt Norton" of *Four Quartets* and in *Murder in the Cathedral*.

12 I can detect no reason why Walker chose to reuse this name from *Theatre of the Film Noir* (with the difference of one "n").

13 I use the terms in reference to the kinds of "mythos" Northrop Frye defines in *Anatomy of Criticism*.

14 Indeed, he anticipates the title character in the 1991 Terry Gilliam movie, *The Fisher King*, who is, like William, an infusively optimistic vagrant.

15 Incidentally, in making "Princess R.," the woman Pavel had been obsessed with in his younger days, into Anna's mother, Walker has picked up on a connection that is apparently latent in the novel. According to Rosemary Edmonds, translator of *Fathers and Sons,* both these characters and their effects on Pavel and Bazarov have their origin in Turgenev's lifelong obsession with the singer-composer Paulina Garcia-Viardot, a married woman (65).

16 Evidently, Walker's conceit of precipitating a lawyer's spiritual rebirth by temporarily destroying a part of his brain had a broad popular appeal; a few years later the idea was also used as the premise of one of the most popular movies of 1991, *Regarding Henry,* in which Harrison Ford plays a lawyer who becomes more humane after being shot in the head.

CHAPTER SIX: JUDITH THOMPSON

1 Let there be no mistake: the obstacles I am concerned with here are of the nature of logical antinomies. The strategy of disparaging opponents of psychoanalytic theory by suggesting that they harbour unconscious resentment of its unpleasant implications is finally rather dishonest.

2 Inevitably, some are shocked by the profanity in Thompson's work, a response that, aside from being overdecorous, ignores the essential role played by diction in forming the identity of any character. At some level, decrying the use of such language is equivalent to claiming that such people as use this language should not exist, a sentiment that is part of the very neuroses Thompson's work explores. The summer before *The Crackwalker* was written Thompson had performed in a production of David Mamet's *Sexual Perversity in Chicago:* "I think his freedom with four-letter words freed me" (Zimmerman, "Conversation," 188).

3 The precise influence Thompson's study of autism had upon her work cannot be certainly determined, but given the space I have given here to Thompson's connection with Freud, some sort of speculative discussion on the other subject of which she has made a special study seems in order. Certainly it is likely that, if Thompson much studied the ideas of Leo Kanner and Bruno Bettelheim on autism, these might influence her dramatization of family conflicts at some level. Leo Kanner was the early

pioneer in identifying autism as a particular syndrome, working in the early 1940s (see, e.g., chapter on autism in his *Child Psychiatry*). He was followed by Bruno Bettelheim, who, building on Kanner's observation that few of the parents of autistic children were "warm-hearted" but rather tended to be coldly intellectual, developed the psychogenic hypothesis that autism was caused by deprivation of affection (*Empty Fortress*). Kanner was himself persuaded by Bettelheim's further studies in autism, and thereafter adopted the psychogenic explanation. Consequently, through much of the sixties and seventies the psychogenic theory was prevalent, along with cruelly evocative references to "refrigerator" parenting. This mode of explanation for autism came at a time when prevailing fashions in general psychology were especially receptive. Then greatly in vogue were B.F. Skinner's theories of behaviourism and the role of parenting in producing personality; R.D. Laing's theories that madness was a pararational means of adapting to a dysfunctional family; and *Soul Murder*, Morton Schatzman's dubious though very popular reassessment of the most influential schizophrenic case in history, Daniel Paul Schreber's, to show that his condition had been caused by his father's experiments in child-rearing. By the mid-eighties the intellectual climate had changed, and the weight of subsequent studies on autism tended rather to confirm Kanner's earlier supposition: that where signs of parental detachment were found, these were not themselves the cause of autism but were probably evidence that a common genetic source induced both the parent's detachment and the child's autism. In the early eighties, however, when Thompson was studying autism, the psychogenic, "refrigerator"-parenting explanation still had currency alongside the emerging trend towards genetic theory (though possibly Thompson's father's specialization in behavioural genetics would predispose Thompson to respect the possibility of a genetic origin even in a time when this was not the most popular theory). In any case, Bettelheim's work would be a provocative source for someone with Thompson's creative imagination, particularly in the context of some of the more grotesque imagery of *White Biting Dog*. Consider Bettelheim's Joey, who imagined and drew a complicated machine that ran his mind and bodily functions by remote control (*The Empty Fortress*, 305). An early version of *White Biting Dog*, called "Dustbeam" (in the archives at the University of Guelph), has Cape, at the beginning of the play, rather than playing the drums, deploying a mechanical extension of the psyche similar to Joey's: a giant "wave machine" that captures spiritual waves.

4 The paradox that the Oedipal complex, though conceived as being universal, is associated with "sexual perversion" (implying whatever we mean by "normal" is neither usual nor natural) may bear on another sort of "perversion" that has been linked to Thompson's work. Richard Paul

Knowles has argued that Thompson's plays constitute a "perversion" of conventional dramaturgical form ("Dramaturgy of the Perverse"). Taking as his normative standard the Aristotelean anatomy of drama, Knowles argues that "reversal and recognition, like conversion, revolution, enlightenment, and salvation, are linear and dialectical concepts that invoke social containment and dramatic closure" (227). He shows that *White Biting Dog* and *Lion in the Streets* evince a "perversion" of this linear Aristotelean form. This is a provocative theory, but one of which I remain sceptical. Knowles is an insightful critic and a strong and loyal admirer of Thompson's. But, perhaps because perversion, disruption, subversion, alterity, contingency, and heterogeneity are all honorifics in the postmodernist vocabulary he favours, he seems to want to valorize Thompson by showing that her work embraces all these. I suspect these tropes could be descried in any given work of real complexity, simply because they describe effects that are practically synonymous with irony. As for the normative model that Thompson "perverts" according to Knowles, the question is begged of whether such linear dramaturgy has in actuality *been* the norm or we have often merely been fobbed off with linear *descriptions* of complex dramaturgy. *Hamlet* is as close to standing at the centre of a traditional canon as we are likely to get. Yet we may recall that in T.S. Eliot's view *Hamlet* itself constitutes a kind of perversion of tragic form. Eliot argued that the play lacked a sufficient "objective correlative," that the plot and action were inadequate to bear the emotional complexity of the poetry (i.e., it failed to achieve containment and closure) – an observation certainly related to the idea that *White Biting Dog* is "overburdened with imagery." At the same time, Knowles's notion that Thompson's work constitutes (creative) perversion of a norm is certainly applicable to her reformation of the soft-porn genre in her co-authored screenplay *Anne and Joey*. Conceived by the producers as an "erotic thriller," the work stands apart from the genre's usual scripts because of the unsettling revelations about the underlying psychological dynamics of the action. Inevitably, scenes that could have been made erotic in a façile way are vaguely disturbing. Paradoxically, these scenes are too mentally vivid and compelling – too psychologically graphic – to accommodate the average viewer's erotic fantasies comfortably.

5 A good example of a place where a psychoanalytic approach is less appropriate is Thompson's realistic script for *Turning to Stone* (1986), a CBC television movie about a naïve young middle-class woman incarcerated in the unnamed but unmistakable Kingston Prison for Women. The dynamics of psychological terror are acutely observed in a documentary manner, which in one respect constitutes a sort of rehabilitation of the discredited "women's prison movie" genre parallelling the relation of *Anne and Joey* to the soft-porn movie genre (see n4).

6 That interpretation may run against first assumptions, but as it turns out, there is no evidence whatsoever that Plath's father ever mistreated her. Rather, hers seems to have been a post-hoc situation, in which she had always felt abandoned by her father's death when she was eight and therefore finally decided to release the resentment by thinking of him as a bastard. In fact she dearly loved him: "I'll never speak to God again," she had declared when Otto died. If the poem "Daddy" seems inappropriate under these circumstances, Anne Stevenson explains, saying: "only a desperate bid for life and psychic health can even begin to excuse this and several other of the *Ariel* poems" (10, 265).

7 Granted, Plath's "bastard" is not Thompson's word, "fucker," but then Plath hadn't been liberated by David Mamet's use of four-letter words, as Thompson declares herself to have been.

8 Compare Viola/Mandy in *Tornado* or Annie in the unpublished screenplay *Annie and Joey*.

9 I am reluctant to make too much of this idea for a number of reasons, not least of which is my lack of expertise in either the pathology of epilepsy or in the effects of electroconvulsive therapy (ECT). Nevertheless, here is Anne Stevenson, Plath's biographer, on this point: "Attributable to her ECT is the unseen menace that haunts nearly everything she wrote, her conviction that the world, however benign in appearance, conceals dangerous animosity, directed particularly towards herself. Sylvia's psychotherapy also certainly opened up the dimensions of her Freudian psychodrama, revealing the figure of her lost, 'drowned' father, master of the bees, whose death she could neither forgive nor allow herself to forget" (47). Incidentally, Plath's honours thesis, which she was writing at the time of her therapy, was on "the double" in Dostoevsky's work.

10 Thompson's maternal grandfather, William Ford, was at one time prime minister of Australia.

Bibliography

PRIMARY WORKS CITED

Cook, Michael. *Maurice O'Leary: A Document*. Typescript in Special Collections, University of Calgary Library.

– *Colour the Flesh the Colour of Dust*. Toronto: Simon and Pierre 1974.

– Introduction to *Head, Guts and Soundbone Dance*. *Canadian Theatre Review* 1 (1974): 74–6.

– "St. John's Newfoundland." *Canadian Theatre Review* 2 (1974): 125–7.

– "Trapped in Space." *Canadian Theatre Review* 6 (1975): 117–20.

– "Under Assault." *Canadian Theatre Review* 7 (1975): 136–8.

– "Ignored Again." *Canadian Theatre Review* 10 (1976): 87–91.

– "The Painful Struggle for the Creation of a Canadian Repertory." *Performing Arts in Canada* 13, no. 4 (1976): 26–9.

– *Quiller* and *Tiln* in *Tiln and Other Plays*. Vancouver: Talonbooks 1976.

– "Christopher Pratt: A Personal Memoir." *Vie des arts* 23, no. 87 (Summer 1977): 42–4, 89–90.

– *On the Rim of the Curve* and *Therese's Creed*. In *Three Plays*. Portugal Cove, Nfld.: Breakwater Books 1977.

– "On Tiln." *Transitions I: Short Plays*. Vancouver: Commcept 1978.

– *The Gayden Chronicles*. Toronto: Playwrights Canada, 1979.

– "Island of Fire." In *Aurora: New Canadian Writing*, ed. Morris Wolfe. Toronto: Doubleday 1980.

– "The Last Refuge of the Spoken Word." *Canadian Theatre Review* 36 (Fall 1982): 49–51.

- "The Terrible Journey of Frederick Dunglass." *Canadian Theatre Review* 36 (Fall 1982): 85–101.
- Interview in Wallace and Zimmerman, eds., *The Work: Conversations with English-Canadian Playwrights*.
- *Jacob's Wake*. Vancouver: Talonbooks 1983.
- "Culture as Caricature." *Canadian Literature* 100 (1984): 72–8.
- *The Fisherman's Revenge*. Toronto: Playwrights Canada 1984.
- *The Head, Guts and Soundbone Dance* (corrected version). In *Major Plays of the Canadian Theatre: 1934–1984*, ed. Richard Perkyns. Toronto: Irwin 1984.
- "The End of the Road: Act I." In *Dramatic Voices from England, Canada and New Zealand: Festschrift für Albert-Reiner Glaap*, ed. Peter Mueller. Berlin: Cornelson 1989.
- "The Great Harvest Excursion." In *Inter-Plays: Works and Words of Writers and Critics: A Festschrift Published in Honour of Albert-Reiner Glaap*, ed. Rolf Althof, Rurik von Antropoff, and Klaus Peter Müller. St John's: Breakwater Press 1994.

Pollock, Sharon. *A Compulsory Option*. Toronto: Playwrights Union of Canada, n.d.
- *And Out Goes You*. 1975. Typescript in University of Calgary Special Collections.
- *Walsh*. Vancouver: Talonbooks 1976.
- *The Komagata Maru Incident*. Toronto: Playwrights Canada 1978.
- *The Wreck of the National Line*. Toronto: Playwrights Union of Canada, n.d.
- *Blood Relations, Generations*, and *One Tiger to a Hill*. In *Blood Relations and Other Plays*. Edmonton: NeWest Press 1981.
- Interview in Wallace and Zimmerman, eds., *The Work: Conversations with English-Canadian Playwrights*.
- *Doc*. Toronto: Playwrights Canada 1986.
- *Whiskey Six Cadenza*. In *NeWest Plays by Women*, ed. Joyce Doolittle. Edmonton: NeWest Press 1987.
- *Egg*. Typescript in University of Guelph Archives.
- *The Making of Warriors*. In *Airborne: Radio Plays by Women*, ed. Ann Jansen. Winnipeg: Blizzard Publishing 1991.
- "Towards a Better, Fairer World." Interview wih Cynthia Zimmerman. *Canadian Theatre Review* 69 (Winter 1991): 35–8.
- *Getting It Straight*. In *Heroines: Three Plays*, ed. Joyce Doolittle. Red Deer, Alta.: Red Deer College Press 1992.
- "Reflections of a Female Artistic Director." In *Women on the Canadian Stage: The Legacy of Hrotsvit*, ed. Rita Much. Winnipeg: Blizzard Publishing 1992: 109–14.
- *"It's all make believe, isn't it?" – Marilyn Monroe*. In *Instant Applause: 26 Very Short Complete Plays*. Winnipeg: Blizzard Publishing 1994.

– *Saucy Jack*. Winnipeg: Blizzard Publishing 1994.

– *Fair Liberty's Call*. Toronto: Coach House Press 1995.

Reaney, James. "Clay Hole." *The Undergrad* 1 (1946): 15–18.

– "Elevator." *The Undergrad* 1 (1946–47): 25–6.

– "The Box Social." *The Undergrad* (1947): 30–1.

– "Mr Whur: A Metamorphosis." *Here and Now* 1, no. 1 (Dec. 1947): 14–15.

– "The Book in the Tree." *The Undergrad* (Dec. 1947): 12–13.

– "Edith Sitwell's Early Poetry; or Miss Sitwell's Early Poetry." *The Undergrad* (Mar. 1948): 28–35.

– "Afternoon Moon." *Here and Now* 1, no. 2 (May 1948): 38–46.

– "The Young Necrophiles." *Canadian Forum* 28, no. 332 (Sept. 1948): 136–7.

– "The Bully." In *Canadian Short Stories*, ed. Robert Weaver and Helen James. Toronto: Oxford University Press 1952.

– "Dear Metronome." *Canadian Forum* 32 (Sept. 1952): 134–7.

– "To the Secret City: From a Winnipeg Sketch-book." *Queen's Quarterly* 61, no. 2 (Summer 1954): 167–8.

– "Another View of the Writers' Conference." *Canadian Forum* 35, no. 417 (Oct. 1955): 158.

– "Winnipeg Sketches." *Canadian Forum* 35, no. 418 (Nov. 1955): 175–6.

– "The Canadian Poet's Predicament." *University of Toronto Quarterly* 26, no. 3 (Apr. 1957): 284–95.

– "The Influence of Spenser on Yeats." PhD. University of Toronto, 1958.

– *Suit of Nettles*. 1958. Erin, Ont.: Press Porcepic 1975.

– "The Canadian Imagination." *Poetry* (Chicago) 94 (Apr.–Sept. 1959): 186–9.

– "The Third Eye: Jay Macpherson's *The Boatman*." *Canadian Literature* 3 (Winter 1960): 26–7.

– "Writing." In *The Mid-Continent Mosaic: Arts and Letters in Winnipeg,*. ed. John A. Russell. *Royal Architectural Institute of Canada Journal*, ser. 416, vol. 37, no. 4 (Apr. 1960): 136.

– "An Evening with Babble and Doodle: Presentations of Poetry." *Canadian Literature* 12 (Spring 1962): 37–43.

– *The Killdeer, Night-Blooming Cereus, One-Man Masque*, and *The Sun and the Moon*. In *The Killdeer and Other Plays*. Toronto: Macmillan 1962.

– "Search for an Undiscovered Alphabet." *Canadian Art* 98, vol. 22, no. 4 (Sept./Oct. 1965): 38–41.

– *Colours in the Dark*. Vancouver: Talonbooks 1969.

– "My Canada." *Maclean's* 84, no. 12 (Dec. 1971): 18–51.

– *Poems*. Ed. Germaine Warkentin. Erin, Ont.: Press Porcepic 1972.

– *The Easter Egg, The Killdeer* (rev.), and *Three Desks*. In *Masks of Childhood*. New Drama 2. Toronto: New Press 1972.

- *Listen to the Wind.* Vancouver: Talonbooks 1972.
- "Ten Years at Play." In New, ed., *Dramatists in Canada.*
- "Myths in Some Nineteenth-Century Ontario Newspapers." In *Aspects of Nineteenth-Century Ontario*, ed. F.H. Armstrong. Toronto: University of Toronto Press 1974.
- *Selected Shorter Poems.* Erin, Ont.: Press Porcepic 1975.
- *Selected Longer Poems.* Erin, Ont.: Press Porcepic 1976.
- *All the Bees and All the Keys.* Erin, Ont.: Press Porcepic 1976.
- "Cycle." *Canadian Drama* 2, no. 1 (Spring 1976): 73–7.
- "David Willson." *Dictionary of Canadian Biography.* Vol. 9. Toronto: University of Toronto Press 1976: 841–3.
- "Halloween 1: A Letter from James Reaney." *Black Moss*, ser. 2, no. 1 (Spring 1976): 2–10.
- "Kids and Crossovers." *Canadian Theatre Review* 10 (Spring 1976): 28–31.
- *Fourteen Barrels from Sea to Sea.* Erin, Ont.: Press Porcepic 1977.
- *Apple Butter.* Vancouver: Talonbooks 1978.
- *The Dismissal; or, Twisted Beards and Tangled Whiskers.* Erin, Ont.: Press Porcepic 1978.
- *Geography Match.* Vancouver: Talonbooks 1978.
- *Ignoramus.* Vancouver: Talonbooks 1978.
- *Names and Nicknames.* Vancouver: Talonbooks 1978.
- *The Real Foundation for the Spree: The Working Poet in the Contemporary World of Poetry and Criticism – The 1977 Pratt Lecture.* St John's, Nfld.: Memorial University 1978.
- *The Shivaree.* Libretto. Performing Rights Organization of Canada 1978.
- *Wacousta!: A Melodrama in Three Acts with a Description of Its Development in Workshop.* Toronto: Press Porcepic 1979.
- "Your Plays Are Like Movies – Cinemascope Ones." *Canadian Drama* 5, no. 1 (Spring 1979): 32–40.
- *King Whistle! Brick* 8 (Winter 1980): 5–48.
- "The Story Behind *King Whistle!*" *Brick* 8 (Winter 1980): 49–85.
- "Shepard: A Dialogue." *Brick* 11 (Winter 1981): 19.
- *The Donnellys: A Trilogy.* Victoria: Press Porcepic 1983.
- *Gyroscope.* Toronto: Playwrights Canada 1983.
- "Some Critics Are Music Teachers." In *Centre and Labyrinth: Essays in Honour of Northrop Frye*, ed. Eleanor Cook et al. Toronto: University of Toronto Press 1983.
- *The Canadian Brothers.* In *Major Plays of the Canadian Theatre: 1934–1984*, ed. Richard Perkyns. Toronto: Irwin 1984.
- Letters to John Astington. 22 Jan. 1986, 23 Oct. 1987.
- "The House by the Churchyard: A Play with Music – Work in Progress." *Books in Canada* 17, no. 2 (Mar. 1988): 14–16.
- *The Perfect Essay: A Farce. Quarry* 37, no. 2 (June 1988): 96–112.

- *Crazy to Kill: A Detective Opera.* Guelph, Ont.: Guelph Spring Festival 1989.
- *Stereoscope.* In *Dramatic Voices from England, Canada and New Zealand: Festschrift für Albert-Reiner Glaap.* Berlin: Cornelsen 1989.
- *Performance Poems.* Goderich, Ont.: Moonstone Press 1990.
- *Serinette: A Libretto for a Two-Act Opera.* Toronto: Cultural Support Services 1990.
- "Northrop Frye: He Educated Our Imagination." *Toronto Star,* 24 Jan. 1991, A22.
- OISE Seminar. Public seminar delivered at Ontario Institute for Studies in Education, 6 Apr. 1992.
- *Alice through the Looking Glass.* Erin, Ont.: Porcupine's Quill 1994.
- *The Box Social and Other Stories.* Erin, Ont.: Porcupine's Quill 1996.
- ed. *Alphabet* 1–19 (1960–70).
- and John Beckwith. *"In the Middle of Ordinary Noise…": An Auditory Masque.* In *The Legacy of Northrop Frye,* ed. Alvin A. Lee and Robert D. Denham. Toronto: University of Toronto Press 1993.
- and C.H. Gervais. *Baldoon.* Erin, Ont.: Porcupine's Quill 1976.
Thompson, Judith. *The Crackwalker.* Toronto: Playwrights Canada 1981.
- "Dustbeam." Typescript in University of Guelph Archives [1983].
- *White Biting Dog.* Toronto: Playwrights Canada 1984.
- *Turning to Stone.* Screenplay, dir. John Kastner. CBC television 1986.
- "The Happy Vessel," In *Still Running … : Personal Stories by Queen's Women Celebrating the Fiftieth Anniversary of the Marty Scholarship,* ed. Joy Parr. Kingston: Queen's University Alumnae Association 1987.
- *The Crackwalker* (rev.), *I Am Yours, Pink,* and *Tornado* (radio). In *The Other Side of the Dark.* Toronto: Coach House Press 1989.
- Interview in Rudakoff and Much, eds., *Fair Play: 12 Women Playwrights Speak.*
- *White Sand.* In *Airborne: Radio Plays By Women,* ed. Ann Jansen. Winnipeg: Blizzard Publishing 1991.
- "Six Scenes From *I Am Yours.*" *Exile* 16, no. 4 (1992): 251–63.
- *Lion in the Streets.* Toronto: Coach House Press 1992.
- "One Twelfth." In *Language in Her Eye: Visions on Writing Gender by Canadian Women Writing in English,* ed. Libby Scheier, Sarah Sheard, and Eleanor Wachtel. Toronto: Coach House Press 1992.
- "Revisions: Offending Your Audience." Panel Discussion. *Theatrum* 29 (June/July/Aug. 1992): 33–4.
- "Why Should a Playwright Direct Her Own Plays?" In *Women on the Canadian Stage: The Legacy of Hrotsvit,* ed. Rita Much. Winnipeg: Blizzard 1992: 104–8.
- "No Soy Culpable." In *Writing Away: The PEN Canada Travel Anthology,* ed. Constance Rooke. Toronto: McClelland & Stewart 1994. 307–16.

- *Perfect Pie*, In *Solo*, ed. Jason Sherman. Toronto: Coach House Press 1994. 161–71.
- "Second Thoughts (What I'd Be If I Were Not a Playwright)." *Brick* 51 (Winter 1995): 26–9.
- "Look to the Lady: Re-examining Women's Theatre." Panel discussion, ed. Soraya Peerbaye. *Canadian Theatre Review* 84 (Fall 1995): 23.
- "Mouthful of Pearls." In *The Monkey King and Other Stories*, ed. Griffin Ondaatje. Toronto: Harper Collins 1995. 209–217.
- "Epilepsy and the Snake: Fear in the Creative Process." *Canadian Theatre review* 89 (Winter 1996): 4–7.
- *Tornado* (stage). CTR 89 (Winter 1996): 46-64.
- *Off the 401* (from *Stolen Lands*). *Canadian Theatre Review* 89 (Winter 1996): 65–9.
- *Stop Talking Like That*. In *Airplay: An Anthology of CBC Radio Drama*, ed. Dave Carley. Scirocco Drama 1996.
- *Sled*. Toronto: Playwrights Canada 1997.
- *Perfect Pie*. Toronto: Playwrights Canada 2000.
- and Leonard-John Gates. *Anne and Joey*. Screenplay. 1981. Typescript in Queen's University Archives, Canadian Development Corporation Collection.
Tremblay, Michel. "loups se mangent entre eux, Les." 1959. Repr. in *Les Vues animées*. Montréal: Leméac 1990.
- *Le Train*. Montréal: Leméac 1990.
- *Les Socles*. *Canadian Theatre Review* 24 (Fall 1979): 52–77.
- *Contes pour buveurs attardés*. Montreal: Editions du Jour 1966.
- *Les Belles-Soeurs*. Ottawa: Editions Leméa 1972.
- *La Cité dans l'oeuf*. Montreal: Editions du Jour 1969.
- *En pièces détachées*. Ottawa: Editions Leméac, 1982.
- *Berthe, Gloria Star*, and *Johnny Mangano and His Astonishing Dogs*. In *Trois Petits Tours*. Ottawa: Éditions Leméac, 1986.
- *A toi, pour toujours, ta Marie-Lou*. Ottawa: Editions Leméac 1971.
- *Demain matin Montréal m'attend*. Ottawa: Editions Leméac 1972.
- *Hosanna* et *La Duchesse de Langeais*. Ottawa: Editions Leméac 1984.
- *Bonjour, là, bonjour*. Montreal: Editions Leméac 1974.
- *En pièces détachées*. Trans. Allan Van Meer. Vancouver: Talonbooks 1975.
- *Sainte Carmen de la Main*. Ottawa: Editions Leméac 1976.
- *Les Héros de mon enfance*. Ottawa: Editions Leméac 1976.
- *Damnée Manon, Sacrée Sandra*. Ottawa: Editions Leméac 1977.
- *La Grosse Femme d'à côté est enceinte*. Ottawa: Editions Leméac 1978.
- "Where To Begin the Accusation." *Canadian Theatre Review* 24 (Fall 1979): 26–37.
- *L'Impromptu d'Outremont*. Ottawa: Editions Leméac 1980.

- *Thérèse et Pierette à l'école des Saints-Anges*. Ottawa: Editions Leméac 1980.
- *La Duchesse et le Roturier*. Ottawa: Editions Leméac 1982.
- *Albertine en cinq temps*. Ottawa: Editions Leméac 1984.
- *Des nouvelles d'Edouard*. Montréal: Leméac Éditeur 1984.
- *Le Coeur decouvert*. Ottawa: Editions Leméac 1986.
- *Le Vrai Monde?* Ottawa: Editions Leméac 1987.
- "'Par la porte d'en avant ...': entretien avec Michel Tremblay." *Jeu* 47 (1988).
- *Le Premier Quartier de la lune*. Montréal: Leméac Éditeur 1989.
- *La Maison suspendue*. Ottawa: Editions Leméac 1990.
- *Marcel poursivi par les chiens*. Montréal: Leméac 1992.
- *Encore une fois, si vous permettez*. Montreal: Leméac 1998.
Walker, George F. *The Prince of Naples*. Toronto: Playwrights Co-op 1972.
- *Ambush at Tether's End*. 1972. Repr. in *Factory Lab Anthology*, ed. Connie Brissenden. Vancouver: Talonbooks 1974.
- *Sacktown Rag*. Toronto: Playwrights Union of Canada 1972.
- *Beyond Mozambique*, *Bagdad Saloon*, and *Ramona and the White Slaves*. In *Three Plays*. Toronto: Coach House Press 1978.
- *Zastrozzi*. Toronto: Playwrights Co-op 1977.
- *Science and Madness*. Toronto: Playwrights Canada 1982.
- *Rumours of Our Death*. 1980. Repr. in *The CTR Anthology*, ed. Alan Filewod. Toronto: University of Toronto Press 1993.
- *Theatre of the Film Noir*. 1981. Toronto: Factory Theatre Books in association with Shared Anxiety Press 1994.
- Interview in Wallace and Zimmerman, eds., *The Work: Conversations with English-Canadian Playwrights*.
- *Gossip*, *Filthy Rich*, and *The Art of War*. In *The Power Plays*. Toronto: Coach House Press 1984.
- *Criminals in Love*, *Beautiful City*, and *Better Living*. In *The East End Plays*. Toronto: Playwrights Canada 1988
- *Nothing Sacred*. Coach House Press: Toronto 1988.
- *Love and Anger*. Toronto: Coach House Press 1990.
- *Escape from Happiness*. Toronto: Coach House Press 1992.
- *Better Living* (rev.), *criminals in love* (rev.), *Escape from Happiness* (rev.), *Theatre of the Film Noir*, and *Tough!* In *Shared Anxiety: Selected Plays of George F. Walker*. Toronto: Coach House Press 1994.
- *How to Make Love to an Actor*. In *Airplay: An Anthology of CBC Radio Drama*, ed. Dave Carley. Scirocco Drama 1996.
- *Suburban Motel*. Includes *Adult Entertainment*, *Criminal Genius*, *The End of Civilization*, *Featuring Loretta*, *Problem Child*, and *Risk Everything*. Rev. ed. Burnaby: Talonbooks 1999.
- *Heaven*. Burnaby: Talonbooks 2000.

SECONDARY SOURCES

Abel, Lionel. *Metatheatre*. New York: Hill and Wang 1963.

Achebe, Chinua. "An Image of Africa: Racism in Conrad's *Heart of Darkness*." *Massachusetts Review* 18 (1977): 782–94. Repr. in Joseph Conrad, *Heart of Darkness*, Norton Critical Edition, 3rd ed., ed. Robert Kimborough. New York: W.W. Norton and Co. 1988.

Adam, Julie. "The Implicated Audience: Judith Thompson's Anti-Naturalism in *The Crackwalker, White Biting Dog, I Am Yours* and *Lion in the Streets*." In *Women on the Canadian Stage*, ed. Rita Much. Winnipeg: Blizzard, 1992. 21–9.

Anthony, Geraldine, ed. *Stage Voices: Twelve Canadian Playwrights Talk about Their Lives and Work*. Toronto: Doubleday 1978.

Aristotle. *Poetics*. Trans. George M. Grube. *Sources of Dramatic Theory* Vol. 1. Ed. M.J. Sidnell. Cambridge: University Press, 1991.

Artaud, Antonin. *The Theater and Its Double*. Trans. Mary Caroline Richards. New York: Grove Press 1958.

Astington, John H. "Drama." Review of *The Crackwalker*. *University of Toronto Quarterly* 51, no. 4 (Summer 1982): 382–3.

– "Drama." Review of *White Biting Dog*. *University of Toronto Quarterly* 54, no. 4 (Aug. 1985): 380.

Atwood, Margaret. "Concerning Franklin and His Gallant Crew." *Books in Canada* 20, no. 4 (May 1991): 20–6.

Aubry, Claude. *Le Violon magique et autre légendes du Canada français*. Ottawa: Editions des Deux Rives 1968.

Auerbach, Erich. *Mimesis: The Representation of Reality in Western Literature*. Trans. Willard Trask. Princeton: Princeton University Press 1953.

Ayre, John. *Northrop Frye: A Biography*. Toronto: Random House 1989.

Balzac, Honoré de. *Histoire de les Treize*. 1841; Paris: Editions Garnier Frères 1956.

Barfield, Owen. *Saving the Appearances: A Study in Idolatry*. New York: Harcourt Brace Jovanovich 1965.

Barr, Mary. "James Reaney and the Tradition of Poetic Drama." *Canadian Drama* 2, no. 1 (Spring 1976): 78–89.

Barthes, Roland. *Mythologies*. Paris: Editions du Seuil 1957.

Bartlett, Donald R. "Notes towards Putting Cook into Context." *Newfoundland Quarterly* 78, no. 3 (1983): 12–15.

Bataille, Georges. "On Nietzsche: The Will to Chance." *October* 36 (Spring 1986).

Baudrillard, Jean. *Simulacres et Simulations*. Paris: Galilee 1981.

Beauvoir, Simone de. *Le Deuxième Sexe*. Vol. 1, *Les Faits et Les Mythes*. Paris: Librairie Gallimard 1949.

Beckett, Samuel. *Watt*. 1953; New York: Grove Press 1959.

– *The Complete Dramatic Works*. London: Faber and Faber 1986.

Benson, Eugene, and L.W. Connolly, eds. *The Oxford Companion to Canadian Theatre*. Toronto: Oxford University Press 1989.

Berger, John. *Ways of Seeing*. London: BBC/Penguin 1972.

Berkeley, George. *Three Dialogues between Hylas and Philonous*. Ed. Colin M. Turbayne. New York: Bobbs Merrill 1954.

– *A Treatise Concerning the Principles of Human Knowledge*. Ed. Colin Murray Turbayne. New York: Bobbs-Merrill 1970.

Berlin, Isaiah. "Fathers and Children." 1970. Repr. as forward to Ivan Turgenev, *Fathers and Sons*, trans. Rosemary Edmonds. Markham, Ont.: Penguin 1975.

Bessai, Diane. "Sharon Pollock's Women: A Study in Dramatic Process." In *A Mazing Space: Writing Canadian Women Writing*, ed. Shirley Neuman and Smaro Kamboureli. Edmonton: Longspoon/NeWest 1986.

Bettelheim, Bruno. *The Empty Fortress: Infantile Autism and the Birth of the Self*. New York: Free Press 1967.

– *The Uses of Enchantment: The Meaning and Importance of Fairy Tales*. 1976; New York: Vintage Books 1989.

Bierce, Ambrose. "An Occurrence at Owl Creek Bridge." In *The Norton Anthology of Short Fiction*, 2nd ed., ed. R.V. Cassill. New York: W.W. Norton 1981: 92–100.

Bloom, Harold. *Shelley's Mythmaking*. 1959; Ithaca: Cornell University Press 1969.

– *The Visionary Company: A Reading of English Romantic Poetry*. Rev. ed. Ithaca: Cornell University Press 1971.

– *The Anxiety of Influence*. London: Oxford University Press 1973.

– *A Map of Misreading*. Toronto: Oxford University Press 1975.

Borduas, Paul-Emile. *Ecrits/Writings 1942–1958*. Ed. Francois-Marc Gagnon. Halifax: Press of the Nova Scotia College of Art and Design 1978.

Bowering, George. "Reaney's Region." In Dragland, ed., *Approaches to the Work of James Reaney*.

Brecht, Bertolt. *Brecht on Theatre*. Ed. and trans. John Willett. New York: Hill and Wang 1964.

Brennan, Brian. "Playwright's Father Gives *Doc* the Nod." *Calgary Herald*, 29 Nov. 1984.

Brown, Dee. *Bury My Heart at Wounded Knee: An Indian History of the American West*. 1971; Toronto: Bantam Books 1972.

Brown, Norman O. *Life against Death: The Psychoanalytic Meaning of History*. 1959. 2nd ed. Middletown, Conn.: Wesleyan University Press 1985.

Bruffee, Kenneth A. *Elegiac Romance: Cultural Change and the Loss of the Hero in Modern Fiction*. Ithaca, NY: Cornell University Press 1983.

Buber, Martin. *The Writings of Martin Buber*. Ed. Will Herberg. Cleveland: Meridian 1956.

Burke, Kenneth. *A Grammar of Motives*. 1945; Berkeley: University of California Press 1969.

Cambron, Micheline. "Michel Tremblay: Sainte Carmen de la Main." In *Livres et auteurs québécois*. Montreal: Editions Jumonville 1976.

Cameron, Kenneth Neill. *The Young Shelley: Genesis of a Radical*. New York: Collier Books 1962.

Campbell, Joseph. *Hero with a Thousand Faces*. 2nd ed. Princeton: Princeton University Press 1968.

– with Bill Moyers. *The Power of Myth*. Toronto: Doubleday 1988.

Cardwell, Ann. *Crazy to Kill*. 1941; London, Ont.: Nightwood Editions 1989.

Castelvetro, Ludovico. *Castelvetro on the Art of Poetry*. Trans. Andrew Borgiorno. Binghamton, NY: Medieval & Rennaissance Texts & Studies 1984.

Charney, Maurice. *Comedy High and Low*. New York: Oxford University Press 1978.

Chatwin, Bruce. *The Songlines*. Markham, Ont.: Penguin 1987.

Chaucer, Geoffrey. *The Works of Geoffrey Chaucer*. 2nd. ed., ed. F.N. Robinson. Cambridge, Mass.: Riverside 1957.

Chekhov, Anton. "Letter to A.S. Suvorin, 1 April 1890." In *Dramatic Theory and Criticism*, ed. Bernard Dukore. Toronto: Holt Rinehart and Winston 1974. 914.

Cocteau, Jean. *Oeuvres complètes*. Geneva: Editions Marguerat 1948.

Cohen, Nathan. "Mr. Reaney Writes a Play." *Toronto Daily Star*, 14 Jan. 1960, 35.

Conlogue, Ray. "Funny, Exuberant Spirit Fills *White Biting Dog*." *Globe and Mail*, 13 Jan. 1984, E10.

– "A Chilling Dance of Death." *Globe and Mail*, 11 Dec. 1986, C1.

– "Walker Has Left the City but the City Hasn't Left Him." *Globe and Mail*, 19 Sept. 1987, C4.

– "Upping the Intensity in Tremblay." *Globe and Mail*, 10 Oct. 1991, C2.

– "Lives of Moral Intensity and Danger." *Globe and Mail*, 8 June 1992, C1.

Conolly, L.W. "Dramatic Trilogies." *Canadian Literature* 112 (Spring 1987): 110–12.

– ed. *Canadian Drama and the Critics*. Vancouver: Talonbooks 1987.

Cooper, Douglas. "The Soul in the Cartoon." *The Idler* 24 (July/Aug. 1989): 61.

Corbeil, Carole. "The Observer: Plays in Which a Family Is Trapped in Its Own Creation: Variations on a Cliché." *Globe and Mail*, 23 February 1984, E4.

Crews, Frederick. "The Unknown Freud." *New York Review of Books* 40. (18 Nov. 1993).

– J. Schimek et al. "The Unknown Freud: An Exchange." *New York Review of Books* (3 Feb. 1994): 34–43.

Czarnecki, Mark. "A Drama of Weird Skills." *Maclean's*, 30 Jan. 1984, 51.

Dassylva, Martial. "Le Nouveau Realisme (?) des 'Belles Soeurs' et le joual." *La Presse*, 14 Sept. 1968, 28.

Doucette, Leonard E. *Theatre in French Canada: Laying the Foundations 1606–1867*. Toronto: University of Toronto Press 1984.

Douglas, Ann. *The Feminization of American Culture*. New York: Alfred A. Knopf 1977.

Dragland, Stan, ed. *Approaches to the Work of James Reaney*. Downsview, Ont.: ECW Press 1983.

Dryden, John. Preface to *Don Sebastian*. In *Four Great Tragedies*, ed. L.A. Beaurline and Fredson T. Bowers. Chicago: University of Chicago Press 1967.

Dudek, Louis. "A Problem of Meaning." *Canadian Literature* 59 (Winter 1974): 16–29.

Dunn, Margo. "Sharon Pollock: In the Centre Ring." *Makara* 1 (Aug.–Sept. 1976): 2–6.

Dupriez, Bernard. *A Dictionary of Literary Devices: Gradus, A-Z*. Trans. and ad. Albert W. Halsall. Toronto: University of Toronto Press, 1991.

Dürrenmatt, Friedrich. "Problems of the Theatre." 1954. In *Dramatic Theory and Criticism: Greeks to Grotowski*, ed. Bernard F. Dukore. Toronto: Holt, Rinehart & Winston 1974.

– "Anmerkung zur Komödie." 1955. *Theater: Essays, Gedichte und Reden*. Zurich: Verlag der Arche 1980.

– "Friedrich Schiller" (1959) in *Essays on German Theater*, ed. Margaret Herzfeld-Sander, vol. 83 of *The German Library*. New York: Continuum 1985: 241–2.

Duschene, Scott, and Jennifer Fletcher. "*Sled*: A Workshop Diary." *Canadian Theatre Review* 89 (Winter 1996): 33–8.

Dylan, Bob. *The Bootleg Series: Volumes 1–3 (rare and unreleased)*. CD set. Columbia Records 1991.

Eagleton, Terry. "Awakening from modernity." *Times Literary Supplement*, 20 Feb. 1987.

Edwards, Murray D. *A Stage in Our Past: English-Language Theatre in Eastern Canada from the 1790s to 1914*. Toronto: University of Toronto Press 1968.

Eliade, Mircea. *Le Myth de l'éternel retour: archétypes et répétition*. Paris: Librairie Gallimard 1949.

Eliot, T.S. *Selected Essays*. 3rd ed. London: Faber and Faber 1951.

– *The Complete Poems and Plays*. London: Faber and Faber 1969.

Ellis-Fermor, Una. *The Jacobean Drama*. 1938; London: Methuen 1965.

Elshtain, Jean Bethke. "Sic Transit Gloria." *New Republic*, 11 July 1994, 33.

Filewod, Alan. "Charles Mair." In *The Oxford Companion to Canadian Theatre*, ed. Eugene Benson and L.W. Conolly. Toronto: Oxford University Press 1989.

Fletcher, Jennifer. "The Last Things in *Sled*: An Interview with Judith Thompson." *Canadian Theatre Review* 89 (Winter 1996): 39–41.

Forster, E.M. *Aspects of the Novel.* 1927. Markham, Ont.: Penguin, 1976.

Foucault, Michel. *Histoire de la sexualité.* Vol. 1. Paris: Gallimard 1976.

– *Discipline and Punish.* Trans. Alan Sheridan. New York: Vintage Books 1979.

– *Power/Knowledge.* Ed. Colin Gordon. New York: Pantheon Books 1980.

– *Politics, Philosophy, Culture: Interviews and Other Writings 1977–84.* Ed. Lawrence D. Kritzman. New York: Routledge 1988.

Fox, Terry Curtis. "Unexaggerated Rumours." *Village Voice,* Apr. 1979, 90–1.

Fraser, John. "Walker Turns to Murder with Comedy." *Globe and Mail,* 19 Apr. 1977, 23.

Frazer, James. *The Golden Bough.* Abr. ed. 1922; New York: Macmillan 1958.

Freeman, Brian. "The Komagata Maru Incident." *Scene Changes* 5 (Dec. 1977): 20–1.

Freud, Sigmund. *Beyond the Pleasure Principle.* New York: Liveright Publishing 1950.

– "On Oedipus and Hamlet." 1900. In *Dramatic Theory and Criticism: Greeks to Grotowski,* ed. Bernard F. Dukore. Toronto: Holt, Rinehart and Winston 1974.

– "The 'Uncanny.'" In *The Standard Edition of the Complete Psychological Works of Sigmund Freud,* vol. 17, ed. James Strachey. London: Hogarth 1955.

– "Civilization and Its Discontents." 1930. In *Civilization, Society and Religion,* Penguin Freud Library 12. Markham, Ont.: Penguin Books 1991.

Fromm, Erich. *The Sane Society.* New York: Fawcett Premier Books 1955.

Frye, Northrop. *Fearful Symmetry: A Study of William Blake.* 1947; Princeton: Princeton University Press 1969.

– *Anatomy of Criticism: Four Essays.* Princeton: Princeton University Press 1957.

– *The Bush Garden.* Toronto: Anansi 1971.

– *The Bible and Literature: A Personal View From Northrop Frye.* Lecture Transcript 5. Toronto: University of Toronto Media Centre 1981.

– *The Great Code.* Toronto: Academic Press 1982.

– *The Double Vision: Language and Meaning in Religion.* Toronto: University of Toronto Press 1991.

– et al., eds. *The Harper's Handbook to Literature.* New York: Harper & Row 1985.

Galloway, Myron. "George Walker – Resolving the World's Chaos." *Montreal Star,* 2 Mar. 1979, 18.

Gardner, David. "Forum: David Gardner Argues the Case for 1583." *Theatre History in Canada / Histoire du théâtre au Canada* 14, no. 2 (Fall 1983): 226–37.

Gass, Ken. Introduction to *Three Plays* by George F. Walker. Toronto: Coach House Press 1978.

Gauvin, Lise. "Littérature et langue parlée au Quebec." *Etudes françaises* 10, no. 1 (Feb. 1974): 85.

Gelinas, Marc F. "Je pense en joual." *Magazine Maclean* (Sept. 1970): 46.

Germain, Jean-Claude. "Michel Tremblay, le plus joual des auteurs ou vice-versa." *Digeste-Eclair* (Oct. 1968): 15.

Gingras, Claude. "Mon Dieu que je les aime ces gens-là!" *La Presse*, 16 Aug. 1969, 26.

Glaspell, Susan. *Trifles*. 1920. In *Twenty Four Favorite One Act Plays*, ed. Bennett Cerf and Van H. Cartmell. Toronto: Doubleday 1963.

Golding, William. *Pincher Martin*. Harmondsworth: Penguin 1956.

Gombrich, E.H. *Art and Illusion: A Study in the Psychology of Pictorial Representation*. 1960; Princeton: Bollingen 1969.

Graves, Robert. *The Greek Myths*. 2 Vols. Rev. ed. Markham, Ont.: Penguin Books 1960.

– *The White Goddess*. Rev. ed. London: Faber and Faber 1961.

Grünbaum, Adolf. *The Foundations of Psychoanalysis*. Berkeley: University of California Press 1984.

– *Validation in the Clinical Theory of Psychoanalysis*. Madison, Conn.: International Universities Press 1993.

– Nagel et al. "Freud's Permanent Revolution: An Exchange." *New York Review of Books* 41, no. 14 (11 Aug. 1994): 54–6.

Gurewitch, Morton. "From Pyrrhonic to Vomedic Irony." In *Comedy: New Perspectives*, ed. Maurice Charney. *New York Literary Forum* 1 (Spring 1978): 45–57.

Haber, Ralph N. "Eidetic Images." *Scientific American* 220 (Apr. 1969): 36–44.

Haff, Stephen. "Slashing the Pleasantly Vague: George F. Walker and the Word." *Essays in Theatre* 10, no. 1 (1992): 59–69.

Haggard, Henry Rider. *Dawn*. 1884; London: George G. Harrap and Company 1924.

Harvey, David. *The Condition of Postmodernity*. Oxford: Blackwell 1990.

Harvie, Jennifer. "Constructing Fictions of an Essential Reality or 'This Picksur is Niiiice': Judith Thompson's *Lion in the Streets*." *Theatre Research in Canada / Recherches Theatrales au Canada* 13, nos. 1–2 (Spring/Fall 1992): 81–93.

– "(Im)Possibility: Fantasy and Judith Thompson's Drama." In *On-Stage and Off-Stage: English Canadian Drama in Discourse*, ed. Albert-Reiner Glaap and Rolf Althof. St John's: Breakwater 1998.

Hawking, Stephen W. *A Brief History of Time*. Toronto: Bantam Books 1988.

Hayes, Christopher. "Miss Pollock downs her axe. She settles out of court: the Borden film goes on." *Alberta Report*, 20 June 1983, 45.

Heidegger, Martin. *Being and Time.* Trans. John Macquarrie and Edward Robinson. 1927; New York: Harper and Row 1962.
Heys, Sandra. *Contemporary Stage Roles for Women: A Descriptive Catalogue.* Westport, Conn.: Greenwood Press 1985.
Highway, Tomson. *The Rez Sisters.* Saskatoon: Fifth House Publishers 1988.
– *Dry Lips Oughta Move to Kapuskasing.* Saskatoon: Fifth House Publishers 1989.
Hofsess, John. "Pollock Is an Exception to Rule." *Albertan's Sunday Tab,* 7 Jan. 1979, T03.
– "Families." *Homemakers,* Mar. 1980, 41–60.
– "Sharon Pollock Off-Broadway: Success as a Subtle Form of Failure." *Books in Canada* 12 (Apr. 1983): 3–4.
Hofstadter, Douglas R. *Gödel, Escher, Bach: An Eternal Golden Braid.* 1979; New York: Vintage Books 1989.
Honderich, Ted, ed. *The Oxford Companion to Philosophy.* New York: Oxford University Press 1995.
Huebert, Ronald. "James Reaney: Poet and Dramatist." *Canadian Theatre Review* 13 (Winter 1977): 125–8.
Hunt, Nigel. "Profile: In Contact with the Dark." *Books in Canada* 17, no. 2 (Mar. 1988): 12.
Husserl, Edmund. *Ideas Pertaining to a Pure Phenomenology and to a Phenomenological Philosophy.* Trans. F. Kersten. The Hague: Martinus Nijhoff 1982.
Hustak, Alan. "Sharon Pollock's Triumph: A Hit for Theatre Calgary's New Boss." *Alberta Report,* 30 Apr. 1984, 54–5.
Hutcheon, Linda. *The Canadian Postmodern: A Study of Contemporary English-Canadian Fiction.* Toronto: Oxford University Press 1988.
– "Postmodernism." In *Encyclopedia of Contemporary Literary Theory,* ed. Irena R. Makaryk. Toronto: University of Toronto Press 1993.
James, William. *The Varieties of Religious Experience: A Study in Human Nature.* 1902; Markham: Penguin Books 1985.
Jameson, Frederic. *Postmodernism; or, The Cultural Logic of Late Capitalism.* Durham: Duke University Press 1991.
Jansen, Ann, ed. *Airborne: Radio Plays By Women.* Winnipeg: Blizzard 1991.
Johnson, Bryan. "A Fifties Tarzan Epic Gone Mad." *Globe and Mail,* 10 Jan. 1978, 13.
Johnson, Chris. "George F. Walker: B-Movies beyond the Absurd." *Canadian Literature* 85 (Summer 1980): 87–103.
– "George F. Walker Directs George F. Walker." *Theatre History in Canada* 9 (1988).
– "George F. Walker." In *Post-Colonial English Drama,* ed. Bruce King. New York: St Martin's 1992. 82–96.

Johnston, Denis W. "George F. Walker: Liberal Idealism and the 'Power Plays.'" *Canadian Drama* 10, no. 2 (1984): 195–206.

– *Up the Mainstream: The Rise of Toronto's Alternative Theatres.* Toronto: University of Toronto Press 1991.

Kanner, Leo. *Child Psychiatry*. Springfield: C.C. Thomas, 1948.

Kareda, Urjo. "The Donnelly Trilogy Comes to a Rousing Close." *Toronto Star*, 31 Mar. 1975. Repr. in Conolly, ed., *Canadian Drama and the Critics*, 181–2.

– Introduction to *The Other Side of the Dark* by Judith Thompson. Toronto: Coach House Press 1989.

Keniston, Kenneth. *The Uncommitted: Alienated Youth in American Society*. New York: Harcourt, Brace & World 1965.

Kermode, Frank. *Romantic Image*. 1957; London: Routledge & Kegan Paul 1986.

– *The Sense of an Ending: Studies in the Theory of Fiction*. London: Oxford University Press 1968.

King, Deirdre. "L'Impromptu d'Outremont." *Canadian Forum* 63 (Dec./Jan. 1981–82): 45–6.

Kirchoff, H.J. "Money Helps after '20 years of freelance terror.'" *Globe and Mail*, 3 Mar. 1992, D2.

Klein, Ernest. *A Comprehensive Etymological Dictionary of the English Language*. New York: Elsevier Publishing 1966.

– *A Comprehensive Etymological Dictionary of the Hebrew Language for Readers of English*. New York: Macmillan 1987.

Klinck, Carl. Introduction to *Wacousta* by John Richardson. Toronto: McClelland & Stewart 1967.

Knelman, Martin. "Daddy Dearest." *Saturday Night*, Oct. 1984, 73–4.

Knowles, Richard Paul. "Dramatic Work: Retrospectives and New Directions." *Fiddlehead* 143 (Spring 1985): 85–6.

– "The Plays of Judith Thompson: The Achievement of Grace." *Brick* 41 (Summer 1991): 33–6.

– "The Dramaturgy of the Perverse." *Theatre Research International* 17, no. 3 (Fall 1992): 226–35.

– "Computers Keep Your Office Tidier: Interview with Judith Thompson." *Canadian Theatre Review* 81 (Winter 1994): 29–31.

– "Great Lines Are a Dime a Dozen: Judith Thompson's Greatest Cuts." *Canadian Theatre Review* 89 (Winter 1996): 8–18.

Kubler-Ross, Elisabeth. *On Death and Dying*. New York: Macmillan 1970.

Laing, R.D. *The Divided Self*. 1960. London: Penguin Books 1965.

– and A. Esterson. *Sanity, Madness and the Family*. 2nd ed. Markham: Penguin Books 1978.

Lane, Harry. "Redefining the Comfort Zone: Interview with Nancy Palk." *Canadian Theatre Review* 89 (Winter 1996): 19–21.

Langer, Susanne K. *Feeling and Form*. New York: Scribners 1953.

Lawrence, D.H. *The Complete Poems of D.H. Lawrence*. Ed. Vivian de Sola Pinto and Warren Roberts. New York: Viking 1964.

Leclaire, S. "Les Éléments en jeu dans une psychanalyse." *Cahiers pour l'Analyse* 5 (1966).

Lee, Alvin A. *James Reaney*. New York: Twayne Publishers 1969.

Lemaire, Anika. *Jacques Lacan*. London: Routledge and Kegan Paul 1977

LePan, Douglas. *Weathering It: Collected Poems 1948–1987*. Toronto: McClelland and Stewart 1987.

Lescarbot, Marc. *The Theatre of Neptune in New France*. Trans. Eugene Benson and Renate Benson. In *Canada's Lost Plays*, vol. 4, ed. Anton Wagner. Toronto: Canadian Theatre Review Publications 1982.

Lévi-Strauss, Claude. *The Savage Mind*. London: Weidenfeld and Nicolson 1966.

Lewis, C.S. *A Grief Observed*. 1961; London: Faber and Faber 1966.

Lindenberger, Herbert. *Historical Drama*. Chicago: University of Chicago Press 1975.

Lister, Rota. "Interview with Michael Cook." *Canadian Drama* 2, no. 2 (Fall 1976): 176–80.

Loucks, Randee. "Whiskey Six: Observations of a First Performance." ACTH *Newsletter* 7 (Fall 1983): 17–18.

Ludwick, Patricia. "Souvenirs of a Northern Ontario Tour." *Northward Journal* 13 (1979): 83–5.

MacDonald, Ann-Marie. *Goodnight Desdemona (Good Morning Juliet)*. Toronto: Coach House Press 1990.

– *The Arab's Mouth*. Winnipeg: Blizzard Publishing 1996.

McGinn, Bernard. "Revelation." In *The Literary Guide to the Bible*, ed. Robert Alter and Frank Kermode. Cambridge, Mass.: Harvard University Press 1987.

McKay, Jean. "Interview with James Reaney." In Dragland, ed., *Approaches to the Work of James Reaney*.

Macnamara, Charles. "Champlain's Astrolabe." *Canadian Field-Naturalist* 33, no. 6 (Dec. 1919): 103–9.

MacPherson, Jay. "Educated Doodle: Some Notes on *One-Man Masque*." *Essays on Canadian Writing* 24–25 (Winter 1982–83): 65-99. Repr. in *Approaches to the Work of James Reaney*, ed. Stan Dragland. Downsview, Ont.: ECW Press 1983

Mahsun, Carol Anne, ed. *Pop Art: The Critical Dialogue*. Ann Arbor: UMI Research Press 1989.

Maillet, Antonine. *La Sagouine*. Trans. Luis de Céspedes. Vancouver: Talon-books 1979.

Mair, Charles. *Dreamland and Other Poems and Tecumseh: A Drama*. 1886; Toronto: University of Toronto Press 1974.

Major, André. "Un exorcisme par le joual." *Le Devoir* (21 Sept. 1968): 14.
- "Michel Tremblay entre le joual et le rêve." *Le Devoir* (15 Feb. 1969): 17.
Masson, Jeffrey. *The Assault on Truth: Freud's Suppression of the Seduction Theory.* New York: Farrar, Straus and Giroux 1984.
Miller, Arthur. *The Theatre Essays of Arthur Miller.* Ed. Robert A. Martin. Markham, Ont.: Penguin Books, 1978.
Miller, J. Hillis. *The Linguistic Moment.* Princeton: Princeton University Press 1985.
- *Tropes, Parables, Performances.* Durham: Duke University Press 1991.
Milliken, Paul. "In Review: *Generations.*" *Scene Changes* 9, no. 4 (June 1981): 39–40.
Mitchell, Joni. "Lesson in Survival." *For the Roses.* LP. Asylum Records 1972.
Mullaly, Edward. "Waiting for Lefty, Godot, and Canadian Theatre." *Fiddlehead* 104 (1975).
Nabokov, Vladimir. *Nabokov's Dozen.* 1958. New York: Avon Books 1973.
Nagel, Thomas. "Freud's Permanent Revolution." *New York Review of Books* 41, no. 9 (12 May 1994): 34–8.
New, William H., ed. *Dramatists in Canada: Selected Essays.* Vancouver: University of British Columbia Press 1972.
Njal's Saga. Trans. Magnus Magnusson and Hermann Palsson. Markham, Ont.: Penguin Books 1960.
Nunn, Robert. "Sharon Pollock's Plays: A Review Article." *Theatre History in Canada / Histoire du Théâtre au Canada* 5, no. 1 (Spring 1984).
- "Spatial Metaphor in the Plays of Judith Thompson." *Theatre History in Canada / Histoire du théâtre au Canada* 10, no. 1 (Spring 1989): 3–29.
- "Marginality and English-Canadian Theatre." *Theatre Research International* 17 (Autumn 1992): 217–25.
- "Strangers to Ourselves: Judith Thompson's *Sled.*" *Canadian Theatre Review* 89 (Winter 1996): 29–32.
O'Driscoll, Robert. "Continuity in Loss: The Irish and Anglo- Irish Traditions." In *Anglo-Irish and Irish Literature: Aspects of Language and Culture*, vol. 1, ed. Birgit Bramsbaeck and Martin Croghan. Uppsala: Acta Universitatis Upsaliensis 1988.
O'Neill, Eugene. *Long Day's Journey into Night.* New Haven: Yale University Press 1956.
Page, Malcolm. "Sharon Pollock: Committed Playwright." *Canadian Drama* 5, no. 2 (Fall 1979): 104–11.
Paglia, Camille. *Sexual Personae: Art and Decadence from Nefertiti to Emily Dickinson.* New Haven: Yale University Press 1990.
- *Sex, Art and American Culture.* New York: Vintage 1992.
Palmer, John. *A Touch of God in the Golden Age.* Toronto: Playwrights Co-op 1973.

Parker, Brian. "Reaney and the Mask of Childhood." In *Masks of Childhood* by James Reaney, ed. Brian Parker. Toronto: New Press 1972.
– "On the Edge: Michael Cook's Newfoundland Trilogy." *Canadian Literature* 85 (1980): 22–41.
– "The Power Plays." *CTR* 43 (Summer 1985): 190–2.
Parker, Gerald. *How To Play: The Theatre of James Reaney.* Toronto: ECW Press 1991.
Perkins, David, ed. *English Romantic Writers.* Toronto: Harcourt Brace Jovanovich 1967.
Perkyns, Richard. "*Generations*: An Introduction." in Perkyns, ed., *Major Plays of the Canadian Theatre, 1934–1984* (Toronto: Irwin 1984.) 605–8.
Pinter, Harold. *The French Lieutenant's Woman and Other Screenplays.* London: Methuen 1981.
Plant, Richard. "Precious Blood." *Books in Canada* 11 (Apr. 1982): 8–12.
– "Opening Lines" (Review of White Biting Dog). *Books in Canada* 14, no. 3 (Apr. 1985): 23–4.
– "Drama in English 4." In Benson and Conolly, eds., *Oxford Companion to Canadian Theatre.*
Plath, Sylvia. *Ariel.* London: Faber and Faber 1965.
"Playwright Pollock's a Hit in San Diego." *Alberta Report*, 23 Nov. 1979, 46.
Praz, Mario. *The Romantic Agony.* 2nd ed. 1950. New York: Meridian 1956.
Preminger, Alex, ed. *Princeton Encyclopedia of Poetry and Poetics.* Enlarged ed. Princeton: Princeton University 1974.
Pressley, Nelson. "Defeating the Floor." *American Theatre* 10, no. 4 (Apr. 1993): 8–9.
Priestley, J.B. *An Inspector Calls.* New York: Dramatists Play Service 1945.
Reaney, James Stewart. *James Reaney.* Profiles in Canadian Drama. Toronto: Gage Educational Publishing 1977.
Richardson, John. *Wacousta; or The Prophecy: A Tale of the Canadas.* 1832. Ed. Douglas Cronk. Ottawa: Carleton University Press 1987.
– *The Canadian Brothers; or A Prophecy Fulfilled: A Tale of the Late American War.* 1840; Toronto: University of Toronto 1976.
Richler, Mordecai. *Solomon Gursky Was Here.* Markham, Ont.: Penguin 1989.
Ricoeur, Paul. "The Metaphorical Process as Cognition, Imagination and Feeling." In *On Metaphor*, ed. Sheldon Sacks. Chicago: University of Chicago Press 1979.
Robinson, Paul. *Freud and His Critics.* Berkeley: University of California Press 1993.
Ross, Malcolm. *The Impossible Sum of Our Traditions.* Toronto: McClelland & Stewart 1986.
Rubin, Bruce Joel. *Jacob's Ladder.* New York: Applause Theatre Books 1990.
Rubin, Don. "At Large." *Canadian Theatre Review* 3 (1974): 117–20.

Rudakoff, Judith "Under the Goddess's Cloak: reCalling the Wild, enGendering the Power." In *Women on the Canadian Stage: The Legacy of Hrotsvit*, ed. Rita Much. Winnipeg: Blizzard 1992. 115–30.

– and Rita Much, eds. *Fair Play: 12 Women Playwrights Speak*. Toronto: Simon & Pierre 1990.

Sacks, Peter. *The English Elegy: Studies in the Genre from Spenser to Yeats*. Baltimore: Johns Hopkins University Press 1985.

Salmon, Eric. *The Dark Journey: John Whiting as Dramatist*. London: Barrie and Jenkins 1979.

Salter, Denis. "(Im)possible Worlds: The Plays of Sharon Pollock." In Steele and Tener, eds., *The Sharon Pollock Papers: First Accession*.

Sartre, Jean-Paul. *Chemins de la liberté*. Paris: Gallimard 1945–9.

– *Saint Genet: Comédien et Martyr*. Paris: Gallimard 1952.

Schacht, Richard. *Alienation*. New York: Doubleday 1970.

Schatzman, Morton. *Soul Murder: Persecution in the Family*. Scarborough, Ont.: Signet 1974.

Schneider, Julia. "Negative and Positive Elements in James Reaney's Plays." *Canadian Drama* 2, no. 1 (Spring 1976): 98–114.

Shaw, George Bernard. *Heartbreak House*. 1919; Harmondsworth: Penguin 1964.

– *Pen Portraits and Reviews*. London: Constable and Company 1932.

Sidnell, Michael. *Dances of Death: The Group Theatre of London in the Thirties*. London: Faber and Faber 1984.

– "Realities of Representation in Michel Tremblay's *Le vrai monde?*" *Essays in Theatre* 9, no. 1 (Nov. 1990): 5–16.

Silz, Walter. *Early German Romanticism*. Cambridge: Harvard University Press 1929.

Sloterdijk, Peter. *Critique of Cynical Reason*. Trans. Michael Eldred. University of Minnesota Press: Minneapolis 1987.

Sontag, Susan. "Notes on Camp." *Against Interpretation and Other Essays*. 1966; Toronto: Doubleday 1990.

Speck, Frank G. *Beothuk and Micmac*. New York: Museum of the American Indian, Heye Foundation 1922.

Stallybrass, Peter, and Allon White. *The Politics and Poetics of Transgression*. London: Methuen 1986.

States, Bert O. *The Rhetoric of Dreams*. Ithaca, NY: Cornell University Press 1988.

Steed, Judy. "Thompson Different from her Characters." *Globe and Mail*, 11 Feb. 1982, E5.

Steele, Apollonia, and Jean F. Tener, eds. *The Sharon Pollock Papers: First Accession*. Calgary: University of Calgary Press 1989.

Steinem, Gloria. "What If Freud Were Phyllis?" In *Moving Beyond Words*. New York: Simon & Schuster 1994.

Stevens, Wallace. *The Necessary Angel*. New York: Vintage 1951.

– *The Letters of Wallace Stevens*. New York: Alfred A. Knopf 1966.

– *The Palm at the End of the Mind*. Ed. Holly Stevens. New York: Vintage 1972.

Stevenson, Anne. *Bitter Fame: A Life of Sylvia Plath*. Boston: Houghton Mifflin 1989.

Strindberg, August. *A Dream Play and Four Chamber Plays*. Trans. Walter Johnson. New York: W.W. Norton 1975.

Swanson, Gene. "What Is Pop Art?" In *Pop Art: The Critical Dialogue*, ed. Carol Anne Mahsun. Ann Arbor: UMI Research Press 1989.

Synge, John Millington Synge. *The Aran Islands*. Ed. Robin Skelton. Oxford: Oxford University Press 1979.

Szondi, Peter. *Theory of the Modern Drama*. Trans. Michael Hays. Minneapolis: University of Minnesota Press 1987.

Tait, Michael. "The Limits of Innocence." In New, ed., *Dramatists in Canada*.

Taylor, Charles. *Sources of the Self: The Making of the Modern Identity*. Cambridge, Mass.: Harvard University Press 1989.

Taylor, Kate. "Dealing with Mira: Mira Godard Marks 30 Years in the Art Business." *Globe and Mail*, 7 Mar. 1992, C1.

Thério, Adrien. "Un joual fringant à la scène en 1968." *Livres et auteurs canadiens* (1968): 78.

Tocqueville, Alexis de. *Democracy in America*. 1835–40. Ed. and abr. Richard D. Heffner. New York: Mentor 1956.

Toles, George. "Cause You're the Only One I Want: The Anatomy of Love in the Plays of Judith Thompson." *Canadian Literature* 118 (Autumn 1988): 116–35.

Tomc, Sandra. "Revisions of Probability: An Interview with Judith Thompson." *Canadian Theatre Review* 59 (Summer 1989): 18–23.

Toye, William, ed. *Oxford Companion to Canadian Literature*. Toronto: Oxford University Press 1983.

Trilling, Lionel. *Beyond Culture*. New York: Harcourt Brace Jovanovich 1965.

Trudeau, Pierre Elliott. "The Ascetic in a Canoe" (1944). In *Against the Current: Selected Writings 1939–1996*. Ed. Gérard Pelletier. Toronto: McClelland & Stewart, 1996.

Turgenev, Ivan. *Fathers and Sons*. Trans. Rosemary Edmonds. Markham, Ont.: Penguin 1975.

Tylor, Edward Burnett. *Primitive Culture: Researches into the Development of Mythology, Philosophy, Religion, Language, Art and Custom*. London: Murray 1871.

Usmiani, Renate. "The Tremblay Opus: Unity in Diversity." *Canadian Theatre Review* 24 (Fall 1979): 12–25.

– *Michel Tremblay*. Vancouver: Douglas and McIntyre 1982.

Vico, Giambattista. *The New Science of Giambattista Vico*. Trans. Thomas Goddard Bergin & Max Harold Fisch. Rev. ed. Ithaca: Cornell University Press 1961.

Wachtel, Eleanor. "An Interview with Judith Thompson." *Brick* 41 (Summer 1991): 37–41.

Wagner, Anton. "Herman Voaden's 'New Religion.'" *Theatre History in Canada / Histoire du théâtre au Canada* 6, no. 2 (Fall 1985): 187–201.

Walker, Craig Stewart. "Three Tutorial Plays: *The Lesson, The Prince of Naples* and *Oleanna*." *Modern Drama* 40, no. 1 (Spring 1997): 149–62.

Wallace, Robert. "Looking for the Light: A Conversation with George F. Walker." *Canadian Drama* 14, no. 1 (1988).

– *Producing Marginality: Theatre and Criticism in Canada*. Saskatoon: Fifth House 1990.

– and Cynthia Zimmerman, eds. *The Work: Conversations with English-Canadian Playwrights*. Toronto: Coach House Press 1982.

Walsh, Paul. Review of *White Biting Dog Canadian Theatre Review* 45 (Winter 1985): 145.

Warwick, Jack. "Joual." In Toye, ed., *Oxford Companion to Canadian Literature*. 401–2.

Wassermann, Earl. *The Subtler Language*. Baltimore: Johns Hopkins Press 1959.

Wasserman, Jerry. "Making Things Clear: The Film Noir Plays of George F. Walker." *Canadian Drama* 8, no. 1 (1982): 99–101.

Waugh, Evelyn. *Brideshead Revisited*. Rev. ed. 1960; London: Penguin 1962

Weiskel, Thomas. *The Romantic Sublime: Studies in the Structure and Psychology of Transcendence*. 1976; Baltimore: Johns Hopkins Press 1986.

White, Hayden. *Tropics of Discourse: Essays in Cultural Criticism*. 1978; Baltimore: Johns Hopkins University Press 1985.

Whitehead, Alfred North. *Science and the Modern World*. 1925; New York: Macmillan 1948.

Whiting, John. *The Collected Plays of John Whiting*. Ed. Ronald Hayman. London: Heinemann Educational 1969.

Whitman, Walt. *Leaves of Grass*. 1855. Scarborough, Ont.: Signet 1980.

Whittaker, Herbert. "One-Liners Play's Main Ploy." *Globe and Mail*, 9 Dec. 1971, 15.

Williams, Raymond. *The City and the Country*. London: Chatto & Windus 1973.

Wilson, Edmund. *The Triple Thinkers & The Wound and the Bow: A Combined Volume*. Boston: Northeastern University Press 1984.

Wollheim, Richard. *The Mind and Its Depths*. Cambridge, Mass.: Harvard University Press 1993.

Wonder, Stevie. *Talking Book* LP. Motown Records 1972.

Woodman, Ross. *James Reaney.* Canadian Writers 12. Toronto: McClelland and Stewart 1971.

Wordsworth, William. *The Prelude: 1799, 1805, 1850.* Ed. Jonathan Wordsworth et al. New York: W.W. Norton 1979.

Yeats, William Butler. *A Vision.* Rev. ed. 1937. London: Macmillan 1962.

– *Autobiographies.* London: Macmillan 1955.

– *Essays and Introductions.* Toronto: Macmillan 1961.

– *Yeats's Poems.* Ed. A. Norman Jeffares. London: Macmillan 1989.

Zimmerman, Cynthia. "A Conversation with Judith Thompson." *Canadian Drama / L'Art dramatique canadien* 16, no. 2 (1990): 184–94.

– *Playwriting Women: Female Voices in English Canada.* Vol. 3 of *The Canadian Dramatist.* Toronto: Simon & Pierre 1994.

Index

Manitoba Theatre Centre, 40
Marlowe, Christopher: *Doctor Faustus*, 393
Martyr play, 102, 104
Marx, Groucho, 297
Marx, Karl, 245, 286, 364
Marxism, 67, 68, 69–70, 269, 313, 318, 393
Massey College, 428n9
Masson, Jeffrey, 355
Matriarchal vs patriarchal power, 334–6, 339–40
Melodrama, 7, 45–6, 291–2
Melville, Herman, 414n1; *Moby Dick*, 175, 176, 418n32
Memory plays, 168
Mendelsohn, Felix, 254
Menendez, Erik and Lyle, 161
Menotti, Gian Carlo: *The Medium*, 33
Metamorphosis, 58, 73
Metatheatre, 155
Metempsychosis, 389
Miller, Arthur, 322–3; *After the Fall*, 273; *Death of a Salesman*, 104
Miller, Henry, 275–6; *Max and the White Phagocytes*, 273
Miller, J. Hillis, 108, 113, 120
Miracle plays, 45
Mitchell, Joni, "Lesson in Survival," 201
Modernism, problems of, 265–6
Molière: *L'Impromptu de Versailles*, 247–8, 254; *Le Misanthrope*, 262
Monet, Claude, 27, 415n11
Montreal, 204, 209
Moses, Daniel David: *Almighty Voice and His Wife*, 421n8
Mullaly, Edward, 267
Mulroney, Brian, 323
Munro, Neil, 127–8
Mythopoeic creation, 7, 8, 10, 11, 14, 202–3; *see also* Reaney, Cook, Tremblay

NDWT, 53, 59, 61, 67, 72, 420n39
Nabokov, Vladimir: "Signs and Symbols," 116, 423n18
Nagasaki, 188
Nagel, Thomas, 356
Nanabozho, 43
National Arts Centre, 127–8
National drama, vii
Natives: *see* Aboriginal characters

Nazis, 280, 326
Neatby, Hilda, 42
"Negative capability," 117
Newfoundland: *see* Michael Cook
Newton, Christopher, 424n3
New Westminster, British Columbia, 151
Nietzsche, Friedrich, 268–9, 283–4, 293–4, 313, 382; "doctrine of eternal recurrence," 428n3; existentialist disciples, 305; on knowledge and power, 267; *Thus Spoke Zarathustra*, 268, 284, 293
Nihilism, 91–2, 264–5, 270–1, 298, 354
Njal's Saga, 54
"Noble savage," 100–1, 103, 106
Noh theatre, 85
North West Mounted Police, 140; *see also* Royal Canadian Mounted Police
Noumenal, 12, 17, 19, 107; vs quotidian, 115–17
Nuclear warfare, 109, 188–9, 300–2, 335
Nunn, Robert, 137, 149, 367, 409–10

O'Brien, Flann, 85
October Crisis, 250
O'Driscoll, Robert, 84
Oldenburg, Claes, 276
O'Neill, Eugene, 22; *The Emperor Jones*, 142; *Long Day's Journey into Night*, 91
Orpheus and Eurydice, 73, 77, 238
Orwell, George: *Nineteen Eighty-four*, 301
Ottawa Citizen, 126
Oubliette, 367
Ovid: *Metamorphoses*, 73

Page, Malcolm, 145
Paglia, Camille, 212, 356, 382
Paine, Tom, 101, 106
Palmer, John, 274; *Memories for My Brother, Part Two*, 274; *A Touch of God in the Golden Age*, 274
Parables, 107–9, 113, 119, 300
Paris, 229–31
Parker, Brian, 25, 31, 86, 87, 112–13, 129, 417n23, 421n2, 421n3
Parker, Gerald, 21
Pastiche, 99–100
Pastoral elegy, 84
Patterson, Tom, 67, 420n41
Peking Opera, 48